ENGLISH PLACE-NAME SOCIETY

The English Place-Name Society was founded in 1924 to carry out the survey of English place-names and to issue annual volumes to members who subscribe to the work of the Society. The Society has issued the following volumes:

I. (Part 1) *Introduction to the Survey of English Place-Names.*
(Part 2) *The Chief Elements used in English Place-Names.*
(Reprinted as one volume.)

II. *The Place-Names of Buckinghamshire.*

III. *The Place-Names of Bedfordshire and Huntingdonshire.*

IV. *The Place-Names of Worcestershire.*

V. *The Place-Names of the North Riding of Yorkshire.*

VI, VII. *The Place-Names of Sussex*, Parts 1 and 2.

VIII, IX. *The Place-Names of Devonshire*, Parts 1 and 2.

X. *The Place-Names of Northamptonshire.*

XI. *The Place-Names of Surrey.*

XII. *The Place-Names of Essex.*

XIII. *The Place-Names of Warwickshire.*

XIV. *The Place-Names of the East Riding of Yorkshire and York.*

XV. *The Place-Names of Hertfordshire.*

XVI. *The Place-Names of Wiltshire.*

XVII. *The Place-Names of Nottinghamshire.*

XVIII. *The Place-Names of Middlesex (apart from the City of London).*

XIX. *The Place-Names of Cambridgeshire and the Isle of Ely.*

XX, XXI, XXII. *The Place-Names of Cumberland*, Parts 1, 2 and 3.

XXIII, XXIV. *The Place-Names of Oxfordshire*, Parts 1 and 2.

XXV, XXVI. *English Place-Name Elements*, Parts 1 and 2.

XXVII, XXVIII, XXIX. *The Place-Names of Derbyshire*, Parts 1, 2 and 3.

XXX, XXXI, XXXII, XXXIII, XXXIV, XXXV, XXXVI, XXXVII. *The Place-Names of the West Riding of Yorkshire*, Parts 1–8.

XXXVIII, XXXIX, XL, XLI. *The Place-Names of Gloucestershire*, Parts 1–4.

XLII, XLIII. *The Place-Names of Westmorland*, Parts 1 and 2.

XLIV, XLV. *The Place-Names of Cheshire*, Parts 1 and 2.

The volumes for the following counties are in preparation: *Berkshire, Cheshire* (Parts 3–), *Dorset, Kent, Leicestershire & Rutland, Lincolnshire, the City of London, Shropshire, Staffordshire.*

All communications with regard to the Society and membership should be addressed to:

The Hon. Secretary, English Place-Name Society, University College, Gower Street, London W.C. 1.

ENGLISH PLACE-NAME SOCIETY. VOLUME XLV
FOR 1967–8

GENERAL EDITOR
K. CAMERON

THE PLACE-NAMES OF CHESHIRE

PART II

ENGLISH PLACE-NAME SOCIETY.   VOLUME XLV

THE PLACE-NAMES OF CHESHIRE

By

J. McN. DODGSON

PART II

THE PLACE-NAMES OF BUCKLOW HUNDRED AND NORTHWICH HUNDRED

CAMBRIDGE
AT THE UNIVERSITY PRESS
1970

Published by the Syndics of the Cambridge University Press
Bentley House, 200 Euston Road, London N.W.1
American Branch: 32 East 57th Street, New York, N.Y. 10022

© English Place-Name Society 1970

Library of Congress Catalogue Card Number: 77–96805

Standard Book Number: 521 07914 4

Printed in Great Britain
at the University Printing House, Cambridge
(Brooke Crutchley, University Printer)

The collection from unpublished documents of material for the Cheshire volumes has been greatly assisted by grants received from the British Academy

CONTENTS

Addenda & Corrigenda to The Place-Names of Cheshire,
Parts I and II   *page* vii

The Place-Names of Bucklow Hundred   1

The Place-Names of Northwich Hundred   184

Index of cross-references to subsequent Parts   325

Index of parish- and township-names in Part II   328

ADDENDA AND CORRIGENDA

VOL. XLIV

THE PLACE-NAMES OF CHESHIRE PART I

p. 3, l. 7. Before 'Newcastle' add 'Swettenham **2** 283,'. Last line, before '1419' add '1335 (Swettenham Ch),'. After last line, add a new line '-*subtus Linee* 1335 (Swettenham Ch)'.

p. 13, l. 6 from foot. For BREEK read BROOK.

p. 22, s.n. DIPPING BROOK. Add "Perhaps 'brook at a deep hollow', from dēoping, but the allusion may be to sheep-dipping or the like, cf. Cann Lane **2** 98.".

p. 28, l. 15. For 'Keckwich' read 'Keckwick'. For '*infra*' read '**2** 152'.

p. 65, l. 26, and p. 332, col. 2, l. 6 from foot. For 'Lynney' read '*Lynney*'.

p. 113, s.n. MACCLESFIELD. For [mækəls-] read [makəls-].

Add the following notes on the pronunciation of Ch p.ns., deduced in part from observation and in part from R. Holland, *Glossary of Words used in the County of Chester*, Part III, English Dialect Society Vol. 51 (1886), 427–42. In these notes the p.n. is followed by an approximate phonetic transcript of the 19th-century dial. pronunciation, and where different the current modern pronunciation is added for comparison: p. 7, WIRRAL, [ˈwurəl] now [ˈwirəl]; p. 54, BOSLEY, [ˈbɔːzli]; p. 66, GAWSWORTH, [ˈgɔːzuþ] now [ˈgɔːzwərþ]; p. 75, CHELFORD, [ˈtʃelfərt] now [ˈtʃelfərd]; p. 76, ASTLE, [asḷ] now [ˈastəl]; p. 84, SIDDINGTON, [ˈsiðitṇ] now [ˈsidiŋtən]; pp. 88, 92, WITHINGTON, [ˈwiþitṇ] now [ˈwiðiŋtən]; pp. 94, 99, ALDERLEY, [ˈɔːðərli, ˈɔːdərli] now [ald-, ɔːldərli]; pp. 105, 226, LINDOW END, [ˈlində ˈɛːnd] now [ˈlindou ˈend]; p. 106, HURDSFIELD, [ˈuːtsfilt] now [ˈhərdz-, ˈhərtsfiːld]; p. 110, KETTLES-HULME, [ˈkjetḷsum] now [ˈketəlzjuːm]; p. 113, MACCLESFIELD, [ˈmaksfilt, ˈmaksilt] now [ˈmakəlsfiːld]; p. 130, POTT SHRIGLEY, [ˈpɔt ˈsigli] now [ˈpɔt ˈʃrigli]; p. 137, RAINOW, [ˈreinə, ˈreinər] now [ˈreinə, ˈreinou]; p. 159, WILDBOARCLOUGH, [ˈwilbərt-luf, ˈwilbərklʌf] now [ˈwaildbəːrˈkluf, ˈwilbərklʌf, ˈwil(d)bər ˈkluf]; p. 164, WINCLE, [ˈwinkə] now [ˈwinkəl]; p. 172, TAXAL, [ˈtaxə] now [ˈtaxəl]; p. 176, YEARDSLEY, [ˈjəːrdzli, ˈjurdzli] now [ˈjəːrdzli, ˈjurdzli]; p. 181, ADLINGTON, [ˈadlitṇ] now [ˈadliŋtən]; p. 187, BOLLING-TON, [ˈbɔlitṇ] now [ˈbɔlintən, ˈbɔliŋtən]; p. 199, CHARLES HEAD, [ˈtʃulz jed] now [ˈtʃaːrlz ed, -jed]; p. 207, POYNTON, [ˈpɛːəntṇ, ˈpɛintṇ] now [ˈpɔintən]; WORTH, [wuþ] now [wərþ]; p. 212, PRESTBURY, [ˈpresbəri, -buri, -beri] now [ˈpres(t)-]; p. 214, TYTHERINGTON, [ˈtiþitṇ] now [ˈtiðrin-, ˈtiðriŋtən]; p. 217, WOODFORD, [ˈwitfərt] now [ˈwudfərd]; p. 219, WILMSLOW, [ˈwimzlə] now [ˈwilmzlou, ˈwimzlou]; p. 221, HOUGH [þˈluf]; DEAN ROW, [ˈdein ˈrɔː] now [ˈdiːn ˈrou]; p. 225, ALDERLEY EDGE, [ˈɔːðərli-, ɔːdli ˈedʒ] (the latter archaic by 1886) now as for Alderley *supra* s.v. pp. 94, 99; p. 229, STYAL, [staiə] now [staiəl]; p. 230, LINDOW, [ˈlində] now [ˈlindou]; OVERSLEY, [ˈɔːərzli, ˈuːəzli] now [ˈou(v)ərzli]; p. 239, ETCHELLS, [ˈettʃəz] now [ˈettʃəlz]; p. 241, POUNDSWICK, [ˈpɛːinz-, ˈpaiənzwik] now [paunz-, ˈpaiənz-]; p. 247, CHEADLE HULME, [ˈtʃedl ˈuːəm] now [ˈtʃiːidl ˈjuːm]; p. 254, HANDFORTH, [ˈhɔnfəːrt] now [ˈhandfərþ]; p. 256, HAZEL GROVE, [ˈazḷ ˈgrɔːv] now [ˈheizəl ˈgrɔːv]; p. 258, BRAMHALL, [ˈbramə] now [ˈbramɔːl]; p. 269, DISLEY, [ˈdisli] now [ˈdizli, ˈdisli]; p. 276, DUKINFIELD, [ˈdukṇfilt] now [ˈdukinfiːld]; p. 279, HYDE, [ˈɛiːd] now [ˈhaid]; p. 281, MARPLE, [ˈmarpə] now [ˈmɑːrpəl]; p. 294, STOCKPORT, [ˈstɔppərt] now [ˈstɔkport]; p. 299, TORKINGTON, [ˈtɔrkitṇ] now [ˈtɔrkin-, ˈtɔrkiŋtən]; p. 303, COMPSTALL, [ˈkɔmstɔː] now [ˈkɔmpstɔː(l)]; p. 304, WERNETH LOW, [ˈwerni ˈlou] now [ˈwernəþ-]; p. 309, HOLLINGWORTH, [ˈɔlinwuþ] now [ˈ(h)ɔliŋwərþ]; p. 319,

HEY HEADS, now ['eijedz] but Holland reports the form *Hayhead* 1886 ['ei 'jed]; p. 322, WOODHEAD, ['wudjed] now ['wuded].

VOL. XLV

THE PLACE-NAMES OF CHESHIRE PART II

p. 41, s.n. Hob Hey; p. 67, s.n. HOBCROFT; p. 293, s.n. Hob Croft. Professor Bruce Dickins observes that in the numerous examples of this type of name it is impossible to say whether the etymon is **hob** 'a hobgoblin' or **hobb(e)** 'a tussock', except where there is a local tradition of a goblin, as in Hobcroft 67. Hob Croft 293, in Buglawton, may well contain **hob**, in association with the prefix in Buglawton 290.

p. 62, l. 8 from foot, s.n. le Brodeford; l. 2 from foot, s.n. Coithurst Meadows. These entries should be transferred to (*b*) on p. 63.

p. 73, s.n. *Luggebrigge*; p. 124, s.n. *Luggefote* (and cf. Hug Bridge Ch **1** 55). Professor Dickins hazards a lost r.n. of the type *Lugg*, as in R. Lugg, Lugwardine He (DEPN s.nn.). *Lugg* is related to Welsh *llug* 'bright' and means 'bright stream'.

p. 81, s.n. HEESOMGREEN; p. 170, s.n. Heesoms Fd. Professor Dickins draws attention to the surname *Heesom*.

p. 87, l. 5. The surname is pronounced ['fɔːdən].

p. 98, s.n. DIPPING BROOK. Add a reference to the addendum *supra* for Ch **1** 22.

p. 102, s.n. HIELD. Presumably there was a local dial. pronunciation ['jeld] or ['jiːld], cf. Yield Fd 105.

p. 104, s.n. Goodmanshey; p. 121, s.n. Goodmans Fd. Professor Dickins observes that 'good-man' might be an euphemism for the Devil, *v.* Ch **1** xxi s.v. 243. This is true, but some instances are contrasted with 'good-wife' and in others there may be the surname *Goodman*.

p. 104, l. 14 from foot. Before *le Culnegrene* insert 'cf.'.

p. 109, s.n. Pell Brook. The first el. may be **pill** 'a willow'.

p. 119, s.n. WHALEBONE FM. Professor Dickins suggests that there may have been some remarkable exhibit of whalebone here. No evidence has been noted.

p. 127, s.n. *Cranell*. Professor Dickins suggests this may represent a pronunciation of *Cranwell*, 'crane spring', *v.* **cran**, **wella**.

p. 181, s.n. MURDISHAW. Professor Dickins notes the ModE surname *Mottershaw*, which may be related to this p.n.

p. 188, s.n. EARNSHAW. The mod. pronunciation is ['ɛrnʃɔː], but ['jɛrnʃɔː] must have been current l19.

p. 205, s.n. Nestases. This may contain the term *net-stall*, for a place where birds or other game were netted.

p. 217, s.n. HULME. The local pronunciation is ['huːm, 'hjuːm].

p. 218, s.n. AXON'S SMITHY. Professor Dickins adduces the surname *Axon*.

pp. 223, 231, s.nn. JODRELL BANK, JODRELL HALL. The pronunciation is ['dʒɔdril, -əl]. Older local dial. pronunciations would follow those of the surname, reported by Holland in 1886 as ['dʒɔːdril, 'dʒɔːðril, 'dʒɔðril].

p. 224–5, s.n. RUDHEATH LODGE. Professor Dickins suggests the mining of bog-iron, which might account for the red (i.e. rust) colour in *Redlache* 225.

p. 255, s.n. STUBLACH. Add '[-latʃ]'.

p. 260, l. 3 from foot. Add 'Cf. Ettiley, Warmingham 270, 262 *infra*.'.

p. 263, s.n. STOCIA. Add '[stouʃə]'.

p. 264, l. 7, s.n. Slum. Add '(cf. Slum Wood 321 *infra*)'.

p. 277, s.n. Grammarian's Fd. Professor Dickins draws attention to Grammery Bank We **2** 25 and xi, from ME *gramarye* 'magic'. If Grammarian's Fd is not part of some scholastic endowment, then it might be 'wizard's field'.

p. 291, s.n. THE CLOUD. Professor K. H. Jackson defines the meaning of *Penket* as either 'Wooded hill (i.e. the hill of the wood)' or 'Place at the end of the wood'.

p. 292, s.n. HARDINGS BANK. At end of entry add 'However, cf. Hardings Wood 321 *infra*.'.

p. 313, s.n. Lunts Field Mdw. Professor Dickins points out the not uncommon La surname *Lunt* (cf. Bardsley, s.n.).

p. 313, l. 11 from foot, s.n. Moslin. Add a reference to another instance, 'Moslin Wood 285 *supra*'.

p. 321, s.n. HARDINGS WOOD. Add 'Cf. Hardings Bank 292 *supra*.'.

Add notes on the local dial. pronunciations reported by Holland in 1886 (cf. addendum to Ch 1, supra): p. 7, ALTRINCHAM, [ˈɔːtridʒəm, ˈɔːtədʒəm]; p. 12, BAGULEY, [ˈbagili, ˈbeigli]; p. 17, CARRINGTON, [ˈk(j)aritn̩] now [ˈkariŋtən]; p. 27, PARTINGTON, [ˈpartitn̩] now [ˈpartiŋtən]; p. 28, RINGWAY, [ˈrundʒə, ˈrundʒi] now [ˈriŋwei]; p. 34, WARBURTON, [ˈwɑːrbətn̩]; p. 43, BOLLINGTON, [ˈbɔlitn̩] now [ˈbɔliŋtən]; p. 51, BUCKLOW HILL, [ˈbukli] now [ˈbuklou]; p. 54, MILLINGTON, [ˈmilitn̩] now [ˈmiliŋtən]; p. 56, ROSTHERNE, [ˈrɔstərn]; p. 58, YARWOODHEATH, [ˈjarəd ˈiːəþ]; p. 73, KNUTSFORD, [ˈnutsfərt]; p. 79, OLLERTON, [ˈuːlər-, ˈoulərtn̩, -tən] now [ˈɔlərtən]; p. 82, MARTHALL, [ˈmarþə]; pp. 85, 90, 220, PEOVER, [ˈpiːvər]; p. 107, BUDWORTH, [ˈbuduþ]; p. 109, COGSHALL, [ˈkɔkʃl̩, kɔkʃəl]; p. 138, THELWALL, [ˈþelwəl] now [ˈþelwɔːl]; p. 140, GRAPPENHALL, [ˈgrɔpnəl, ˈgrɔpnə]; p. 146, ACTON BRIDGE, [ˈakn̩]; p. 148, DARESBURY, [ˈdɑːrzbri] now [ˈdɛːrzbəri]; p. 151, KECKWICK, [ˈk(j)egwidʒ] archaic by 1886, now [ˈkekwik]; p. 166, HALTON, [ˈhɔːttn̩] now [ˈhɔltən, ˈhɔːltən]; p. 182, WESTON, [ˈwesn̩] now [ˈwestən, ˈwessn̩]; p. 192, NORTH-WICH, [-witʃ, -wɛitʃ, -waitʃ]; p. 203, DAVENHAM, [ˈdeinəm]; p. 210, SHURLACH, [ˈsurlaʃ]; p. 216, ALLOSTOCK, [ɔːˈllostək]; p. 226, GOOSTREY, [ˈguːstri, ˈguːəstri]; p. 240, MIDDLEWICH, [-witʃ, -wɛitʃ, -waitʃ]; p. 247, EARDSWICK, [ˈjɑrzik] archaic by 1886; p. 253, RAVENSCROFT, [ˈriːnskrɔft] now [ˈreivəns-, [ˈrəiəns-]; p. 254, SPROSTON, [ˈsproussn̩]; p. 269, SANDBACH, [ˈsanbitʃ]; p. 273, WHEELOCK, [ˈwilək]; p. 278, HOLMES CHAPEL, [ˈouəmz]; p. 281, KERMINCHAM, [ˈk(j)ermidʒəm]; p. 283, SWETTENHAM, [ˈswetnəm]; p. 286, ASTBURY, [ˈasbəri]; p. 294, CONGLETON, [ˈkɔŋərtn̩]; p. 301, DAVENPORT, [ˈdeinpərt] now [ˈdavənpɔːrt, ˈdavn̩pɔːrt, ˈdavm̩-pɔːrt].

II. BUCKLOW HUNDRED

Bochelau Hd' 1086 DB, *hundred' de Bokelawe* 1287 Court, *-low(e)*
1398, 1399 ChRR, *Bokkelowe* 1354 BPR

(*Hundred' de*) *Boclawe* 1260 Court, *Plea, Boklowe Hundred* c.1310
Chest

Buche-, (*Buc*)*kelawe* 1260 Court, *-lowe* 1318 *Eyre, Bukkelowe* 1354
BPR

Bucklowe 1350 Chamb, *-low* 1402 ChRR, *Buclow(e)* 1392, 1397
Pat, *-lawe* 1423 ib, *Buklowe* 1445 *Eyre*

Bulk(e)lowe 1488 *MinAcct,* 1554 Sheaf

Buckley 1564 Sheaf

Bulkley Hundred 1656 Orm[2] 1 141

The hundred is named from the meeting-place at Bucklow Hill in
Mere 51 *infra*. The DB hundred of *Bochelau* included Northenden,
Snelson and Great Warford now in Macclesfield hundred 1 234,
93, 104, but not that part of the modern Bucklow hundred west of
Lymm, High Legh, Mere, Tabley Superior, Pickmere and Wincham.
This area was *Tunendun(e) Hd'* 1086 DB, 'Tuna's hill', from the OE
pers.n. *Tuna* and *dūn*, the meeting-place of which is unidentified,
cf. *Halton Hundred infra*. Since *Tunendune* is not recorded after DB,
the two hundreds must have been merged soon after, perhaps in the
twelfth century. Bucklow Hundred, the northern part of the county,
is bounded by Macclesfield Hundred to the east, R. Mersey and
Lancashire to the north, R. Weaver and Eddisbury Hundred, and
Peover Eye and Northwich Hundred, to the south-west and south.
The area is an undulating plateau of boulder-clay, with pockets of
glacial sand and gravel, overlying keuper marl and sandstones which
form elevations of 250 ft. near Halton, Hull-Appleton and High Legh.
These elevations are more abrupt to the west of the hundred, in the
peninsula between Mersey and Weaver. The northern edge of the
plateau overlooks the alluvial plain of the Mersey, formerly liable
to flooding, which broadens above the confluence with R. Bollin
which crosses the north-east corner of the Hundred. The south-
western edge descends steeply to the R. Weaver. The tributary
streams of the boundary rivers flow generally north and south, those
in the middle part being associated with extensive natural lakes at

Pickmere, Mere and Rostherne, which may have been formed by subsidence of the underlying rock-salt stratum as is the case at Witton.

HALTON HUNDRED (lost)

> *hundred court of Hethelton* 1174 Orm[2] I 605
> *hundredum (de) Halt(h)on(e)* c.1185 Facs, c.1200 Whall *et freq* with spellings as for Halton 166 *infra*
> *Hal(e)tonsir* e13 Whall, -*shir* 1286 ib, *Haltonesire* 1277 AD, -*schyre* 1305 Lacy, -*schiria* c.1310 Chest, *Halton'schyr'* 1307 *MinAcct*, *Halytonsire* c.1277 AD
> *baronia de Hauleton(e)* 1252 RBE, 1338 Pat
> *liberty of Haghton* 1287 Court
> *honor de Halton* 1332 Ipm
> *dominium de Halton* 1351 Whall, 1399 Pat
> *serjeanty of Halton* 1354 BPR

The area under the jurisdiction of the barony of Halton, the fee of the Constable of Cheshire, and of the Duchy of Lancaster, cf. Orm[2] I 703n., *v.* hundred, scīr[1]. The Honour of Halton became widespread in Ch, but its original extent, as appears from descriptions c.1300 and c.1320 in Tab 1063, and *Chol* E/93, comprised the territory of the old Hundred of *Tunendune supra*, except Antrobus, Marston and Anderton 127, 118, 95 *infra*, which belonged to different fees, cf. Sheaf[3] 3 (482). Gt. Budworth 107 *infra* was *Budworth in Halton* 1500 Tab. It may well be that this approximate coincidence of territories led to the disuse of the title *Tunendune*. There is no evidence for a coincidence between the meeting-place of the lost hundred and the centre of jurisdiction of the Norman barony formed from it at Halton, e.g. at Halton Hill, the site of Halton Castle, but this would not be improbable. Cf. Nantwich Hundred, *Caldy Hundred* 326, 325 *infra*, and Sagabook XIV 311.

LOST OR UNIDENTIFIED PLACE-NAMES IN BUCKLOW HUNDRED: *Arton* 1556 (1585) ChRR (DKR XXXIX 175, probably an error for Aston by Budworth 101 *infra*); *Chart. Well* 1551 Sheaf[3] 20 (4765) (near Nether Whitley, Little Leigh, or Dutton); *Neucroft* 1397 ChRR (*v.* nīwe, croft; the home of Robert son of William de *Warberton*, perhaps near Warburton 34 *infra*); *the Pynche Wares Heys* 1539 Sheaf[3] 18 (probably from a surname *Pinchware* and (ge)hæg); *Rucheford* 1317 Chol (p) ('rush ford', *v.* risc, ford); *Scole* c.1270–1300 (18) Sheaf[3] 20 (4807) ('shieling', *v.* skáli); *Sodala* 13 (17) Tab (p) (NRA 3636 II 235, perhaps 'south valley', from sūð and dæl[1]); *Tonlowe* c.1280–1300 (18) Sheaf[3] 20 (4807) ('mound at a farmstead or enclosure', *v.* tūn, hlāw, cf. *Thunlowe* 202 *infra*); *Waidall* 1673 ChRR (DKR xxxix 282); *Withenhull* 13 (17) Tab (NRA 3636 II 235, 'hill growing with willows' or 'willow hill', *v.* wīðigen or wīðegn, hyll).

i. Ashton on Mersey & Bowdon

Ashton on Mersey parish, an independent rectory by 1350, supposed to have been originally part of Bowdon parish (Chet OS VIII 310), contained the townships of Sale and part of Ashton, which was partly in Bowdon parish. Ashton and Sale are now merged in Sale municipal borough c.p.

ASHTON ON MERSEY (101–7792)

Ayston 1260 Court (p), *Ays(s)ton* 1326 *Dow* (p), *Ayhston* 113 Orm[2]
Ashton c.1284 (1353) *ChFor*, 1336 Plea *et freq*, (*-super Merseybanke*) 1584 Earw, (*-super Mercy*) 1633 ib, *Asshton* 1295 Cl (p), 1321 Plea, (*-iuxta Carynton*) 1336 ib, (*-on the bank of Mercie*) 1508 Sheaf, *Aschton* 1326 *Dow* (p)
Asseton 1287 Court (p)
Asscheton (*iuxta Merse*) 1310 Plea, *As(s)cheton* 1357 *ChFor*, *Assheton* 1336 *AddCh et freq*, (*-iuxta Caryn(g)ton*) 1376 Plea, (*-super Mercy*) 1421 ib, (*-iuxta Sale*) 1425 ChRR, (*-super Mersebonk*) 1439 *Eyre*, (*-vel Merseebanke*) 1480 Adl, *Asheton* (*super flumen Mersey*) 1536 ChRR
Ahston' 1318 *Eyre*
Aston 1345 Pap, (*-super Marcum*) 1653 Sheaf

'Ash-tree farm', *v.* æsc, tūn. The suffixes *-iuxta Merse*, *-super Merseybanke* etc., describe the situation on the south bank of R. Mersey, and the latter suffix stands alone in (Richard Assheton of) *Mers(s)ebank(e)*, *Mersay Bonk* 1445, 1448, ChRR, AD, (parish of Assheton vel) *Merseebanke* 1480 Adl, as an alternative name for the place, *v.* banke, cf. R. Mersey 1 31. It adjoins Carrington and Sale 17, 5 *infra*.

ASHLANDS, 1847 *TA*.   ASHTON HALL FM, *Ashton ... a hall there* 1724 NotCestr, *Old Hall* 1831 Bry.   ASHTON LANE.   ASHTON NEW HALL, *New Hall* 1831 ib.   BARKERS LANE, 1842 OS, *v.* barkere.   BARRACKS FM, cf. *Barracks Field* 1838 *TA*, *v.* barrack.

BROOK WOOD, on the course of Button Brook 1 17, cf. Brooklands 5 *infra*, and *Brook Field* 1838 *TA*. CORN HEY, 1847 *ib*. CROSSFORD BRIDGE, 1656 Orm², *Crosford* 1295 Cl (p), *-Bridg(e) on Mersey* c.1536 Leland, 'ford marked by a cross', *v.* cros, ford, cf. foll. CROSS ST., 1724 NotCestr, *þe Crosse Streete* 1586 Earw, 'street at a cross', *v.* cros, stræt, cf. prec., and 'Watling Street' 1 40, which crosses Mersey at Crossford, from which Cross St. extends southward to Washway Rd *infra*. DUMBER LANE, *v.* dumbel 'a hollow, a wooded dell'. EES, 1842 OS, 'water-meadows', *v.* ēg. THE FIRS, *Ashton Firs* 1831 Bry, a plantation. GREEN LANE, cf. *Green Lane Field* 1838 *TA* 23. IVY COTTAGES, *Old Toll Bar House* 1831 Bry, a turnpike gate on Washway Rd *infra*. IVY FM, with Oaklee Fm *infra*, was *Fiddlers Green* 1831 ib. KNATHOLE FM, *Gnat Hall* 1831 ib, *v.* gnætt, hol¹ or hall. LYON'S FOLD, *v.* fald. MACUM FM, cf. *Macum Croft* 1847 *TA*. MARSH FM, cf. *Marsh* 1847 *ib*, and Carrington Lane 18 *infra* on which this farm stands, *v.* mersc. MERSEY FM, HO & RD, named from the river. MOSS COTTAGE(S), FM & LANE, *Moss Cottage & House* 1831 Bry, *Moss Lane* 1842 OS, cf. Carrington Moss 18 *infra*, which extended into this township. OAKFIELD, 1860 White, *Oak Ville* 1831 Bry, *v.* āc, feld. OAKLEE FM, *v.* Ivy Fm *supra*. PARK HO. SIDDALL'S BRIDGE, *v.* 32 *infra*. WASHWAY RD, cf. 32 *infra*, Cross St. *supra*, *v.* 'Watling Street' 1 40. WEATHERCOCK FM, *Weathercock Hall* 1831 Bry. WELLFIELD, cf. *Well Field* 1838 *TA*. WOODHEYS FM, GRANGE & HALL, *Wood Heys Hall, Woodheys Nook* 1831 Bry, 'the wood enclosures', *v.* wudu, (ge)hæg. WOODHOUSE LANE, WOODHOUSES, (*Ashton*) *Woodhouses* 1831 ib, *Asshton Wode* 1353 *Indict*, *Assheton' Wode* 1422 *AddCh*, 'houses at a wood', *v.* wudu, hūs.

FIELD-NAMES

The undated forms are 1838 *TA* 23 (Bowdon part) and 1847 *TA* 22 (Ashton on Mersey part).

(*a*) Acres; Brook & Near Acton (perhaps 'oak enclosure' *v.* āc, tūn); Ash Platt ('plot of ground at an ash-tree', *v.* æsc, plat²); Bass Fd; Beet; Blake Fd (*v.* blæc); Bottoms (*v.* botm); Brick Cop (*v.* bryke, copp); Brickiln Fd; Broad Acre; Brow Fd (*v.* brū); Burn Fd; Butts Hey (*v.* butte); Capshoe; Carr (*v.* kjarr); Chapel Fd (1831 Bry, a house); Cinders (*v.* sinder); Cobbs Hinds; Collyland(s); Cop (*v.* copp 'an embankment, a hill-top'); Copy (*v.* copis); Corner Hill & Roughs (*v.* rūh); Cow Lane Fd; Croft Head (*v.* hēafod); Dikes (*v.* dīc 'a ditch'); Dirtbroad Butt (*v.* butte); Dog Hole; Doles (*v.* dāl); Eddish Fd (*v.* edisc); Eves Hey; Five Butts (*v.* fif, butte); Flash Mdw (*v.* flasshe); Flax Croft; Foot a Bank; Funny Acre; Gadding Lake (*v.* lacu); Gally Wood Fd (*v.* gagel); Geld; Grismor Leach (*v.* læ(c)c); Grisno Bank (perhaps a name related to prec.); Hanging Cop (*v.* hangende, copp); Hardy; Heath Fd; Hemp Croft; Hey (Bottom) (*v.* (ge)hæg, botm); Higher Ridding (*v.* ryding); Hollin (Fd), Hollinhurst (*v.* holegn, hyrst); How Ridding, Hows Bottom (*v.* hol¹, ryding, botm); Intack (*v.* inntak); Far Islam (probably a nickname for a remote field); Keddy Acre; Two Knows (*v.* cnoll); Land Fd & Rough (*v.* land, rūh); Ley Fd (*v.* lǣge); Long Furlongs (*v.* furlang); Long Lane Fd (cf. *Long Lane End* 1831 Bry); Looms (*v.* loom); Loont (*v.* land); Mag Hole (1842 OS); March; Marl Fd; Marna; Middle Shut ('middle enclosure', *v.* scēat); Middup (*v.* mid, hop¹ cf. 1 238; Mill Ground & Hey (cf. *molendinum aquaticum in Assheton* 1367 AD); Mistress Acre; Far Moll Fd; Mons Acre (*v.* mann); Moor Fd (1860 White); Mount Poverty (a nickname for poor land); Oven Croft; Patch (*v.* pacche); Pinfold Fd (*v.* pynd-fald); Platt Acre (*v.* plat²); Poor Fd; Rake Mdw (*v.* rake); Reach; Ready Acre; Red Brook, Croft & Fd (*v.* rēad 'red', brōc); Ridding Dole (*v.* ryding, dāl); Rough (*freq, v.* rūh); Rough Heys; Row Mdw; Royle Acre (*v.* ryge, hyll); Rye Croft; Sack Croft; Sandy Cobbs; Sandy Mares; Scholes Dole, Fd & Patch, Little Scholes (*v.* skáli 'a shieling', dāl); Slack Fd (*v.* slakki); Soont (*v.* sand); Stagoe (5x), Stagoe Bottoms & Head; Stock(e)y Fd (*v.* stocc, (ge)hæg); Stromford (perhaps 'ford of a stream', *v.* straumr, ford, cf. *Stromby* 327 *infra*); Sunder; Long Tews; Top Shut (*v.* scēat); Towns Croft; Two Sheets; Water by Land; Windmill Cop (*v.* copp); Yarn Croft (*v.* gearn).

ii. Ashton on Mersey

Cf. 3 *supra*.

SALE (101–7991)

> *Sala* 1199–1216, 1305 Orm², *Sale* 1199–1216 Whall, 1260 Court
> (p) *et freq, passim,* (*la-*) 1285 Court (p), 1317 ChRR (p), (*-behind*
> *Alteringham*) c.1703 Chol

'At the willow', *v.* salh (dat.sg. sale).

BAGULEY RD, leading to Baguley 12 *infra*.   BEECH FM, *Salt Pye* 1831 Bry, *v.* salt-pie.   BROAD OAKS, 1860 White.   BROOKLANDS, named from Button Brook 1 17.   CARLOON HO, cf. *Killoon Meadow* 1844 *TA*, from dial. *loon* for land, with kjarr and cyln. CROSSFORD BRIDGE, CROSS ST., cf. Cross Greens, Street Fd *infra*, *v.* 4 *supra*.   DANE RD, DANEROAD FM.   FAIRY LANE, *Highfield Lane* 1831 Bry, *v.* hēah, feld, lane, cf. Fairy Yard *infra*.   GRATRIX LANE, probably from the surname *Greatorex* (Bardsley s.n.) and lane. HOLLYHEY, *v.* holegn, (ge)hæg.   JACKSON'S BRIDGE, crossing R.

Mersey, from the surname and **brycg**.   LIMETREE FM, *Lime Tree House* 1842 OS.   MARSLAND BRIDGE & RD, *Marsland Bridge* 1831 Bry, *Marsland Lane, Marsland's Farm* 1860 White, from the surname *Marsland*.   MOORLANDS, MOOR NOOK, MOORSIDE, *Sale Moor Nook* 1831 Bry, *Moor* (*Nook*) 1842 OS, from mōr[1] 'a moor', with nōk, land, sīde.   NEW CHESTER, 1831 Bry, a modern hamlet named after Chester 325 *infra*.   NEW HALL, 1842 OS, *New Sale Hall* 1831 Bry, *v.* nīwe, hall.   NORTHENDEN RD, leading towards Northenden 1 234.   PRIORY BANK, cf. foll.   PRIORY GATE, 1860 White, *Miry Gate* 1831 Bry, 'muddy gateway', *v.* mýrr, -ig[3], geat, cf. Barrow Mire *infra*; the new name is a euphemism adopted from the artificial modern series Sale Priory and Priory Bank (*Priory* 1842 OS, *Priory Bank & Cottage* 1860 White).   RIFLE RD.   RUTLAND COTTAGES & LANE, *Rutland* (*Croft*) 1844 *TA*.   SALEBANK, *Sale Bank* 1842 OS, *v.* banke.   SALE EES, *v.* ēg 'a water-meadow'.   SALE GREEN, *The Green* 1831 Bry.   SALE HALL, *Salehall* 1684 Orm[2], *Old Sale Hall* 1817 ib.   SALEHEYS, 1831 Bry.   SALE LODGE, 1842 OS.   SALE PRIORY, *v.* Priory Gate *supra*.   SIDDALL'S BRIDGE, *v.* 32 *infra*.   TEMPLE FM & RD, *Temple* 1831 Bry, origin unknown, perhaps a 'folly'.   WALLBANK FM, *Wall Bank* 1831 ib, 'spring bank', *v.* wælla, banke.   WASHWAY FM & RD, cf. 22, 32 *infra*, *v.* 'Watling Street' 1 40.   WATERSIDE FM, 1831 ib, cf. *Waterside* 1831 ib, a lost place on the bank of Mersey, and *Waterside Meadow* 1844 *TA*.   WHITEHALL (RD), *Whitehall Farm* 1860 White.   WOODHEYS, 1842 OS, *v.* wudu, (ge)hæg, cf. 4 *supra*.   WYTHENSHAWE RD, leading to Wythenshawe 1 236.

FIELD-NAMES

The undated forms are 1844 *TA* 346. Of the others 1705, 1883 are Sheaf, 1831 Bry, 1842 OS, 1860 White.

(a) Adlant Fd ('headland field', *v.* hēafod-land); Bark Fd (*v.* bark(e)); Barlow Mdw; Barrowdale, Barrow Mire (*v.* Barrow Brook 14 *supra*, Priory Gate *supra*); Bent Fd (*v.* beonet); Bettinshaw; Boat Fd, Boats Hey; Boggart Fd (*v.* boggard); Bowl Fd; Briery Acres; Broad Eye Dole ('(a share of) the broad water-meadow', *v.* brād, ēg, dāl, cf. Sale Ees *supra*); Broad Lane; Brook Hey; Brown Fd; Butty Acre (*v.* butty); The Chequer (*v.* cheker); Chorlton Nook; Clarke Hey (1831); Cliffe Brow (*v.* clif, brū); Cock Edge; Cow Carr Fd (*v.* cū, kjarr); Cowley Mdw (*v.* cū, lēah); Cross Greens (*the great & little Cross green* 1705, 'green at a cross' *v.* cros, grēne[2], cf. Cross St., Crossford Bridge *supra*); Dole Croft, Dole in the Hole (*v.* dāl, hol[1]); Eye Mdw (*v.* ēg); Fairy Yard (*v.* faierie, geard; perhaps haunted ground, cf.

Fairy Lane *supra*); Flash (*v.* flasshe); Flax o Loont (*v.* land); Flying Pit Fd; Forry Mdw; Furlong (*v.* furlang); Furry Fd; Gorry Fd (*v.* gor, -ig³); Gravel Hole Fd; Gutter Fd (*v.* goter); The Hale (*v.* halh); Hardhurst (*v.* heard, hyrst); Hamnett Green (*the Hamnet green* 1705, from the surname *Hamnett* and grēne²); Harper Hill; Hart Lane Fd; Hey Bottoms (*v.* (ge)hæg, botm); Hollin Croft (*v.* holegn); Intack (*v.* inntak); Jack Hey (*v.* jack); the Lady Hole 1705; Loont Mdw (*v.* land); Marl Fd; Middlehurst (*v.* hyrst); Mistress Acre & Loont (cf. 5 *supra*); Mosley Acre 1883; Moss Mdw; Nook Fd; Oven Hey; Ovenhouse Croft (*v.* ofen, hūs); Pepper Hill 1842 (1860, on the road from Priory Bank *supra* to Sale Green *supra*, cf. Pepper St. (Chester) 327 *infra*); Pin Croft; Pinfold 1842 (-*House* 1831, *v.* pynd-fald); Pingot (*v.* pingot); Pit Eye, Pits Brow, Pitstead (*v.* pytt, ēg, brū, stede); Preston Fd; Purse Mdw (*v.* purs); Renshaw Mdw (after the family *Wren-, Renshaw*, land-holders here); Sandy Bank; Shaw Fd (*v.* sceaga); Shoe Broad (either scofl-brǣdu 'a shovel's-breadth', or an analogous formation from OE scōh 'a shoe' and brǣdu. The type appears as Shoe Broad 1 243, Shew Bread 1 262; Shooting Butts; Long Shut Fd (*v.* scēat); Slack (*v.* slakki); Slates Fd (*v.* slæget); Spout Green Mdw (*v.* spoute, grēne²); Street Fd (*v.* strǣt, cf. Cross St. *supra*, 'Watling Street' 1 40); Stubb Mdw (*v.* stubb 'a tree-stump'); Vineyard (*v.* vinȝerd); Warmishaw Field; Wasp Fd; Water Hey (*v.* wæter, (ge)hæg); Whip Oat Hill; Wreck Fd.

(b) Peter de *Totehull* 1414 Orm² may belong to this township (*v.* tōt-hyll 'a look-out hill').

iii. Bowdon

The ecclesiastical parish of Bowdon consisted of 1. Altrincham (now a Municipal Borough and c.p., including Timperley *infra* and part of Dunham Massey), 2. Ashley, 3. Baguley (a few fields of which lay in Northenden parish; it is now included in Manchester County Borough La), 4. Bowdon, 5. Carrington, 6. Dunham Massey, 7. Hale (formerly including Ringway), 8. Partington, 9. Ringway, and 10. Timperley (now included in Altrincham c.p.), and parts of Agden 42 *infra*, Ashton on Mersey 3 *supra*, and Bol-lington 43 *infra*.

1. ALTRINCHAM (101–7687) ['ɔltriŋəm] older local ['ɔ:tridʒəm]

Aldringeham 1290 Ch, *Alt-* 1397 ChRR, *-ynge-* 1444 Pat

Altringham 1309 InqAqd *et freq*, *Ald-* 1318 Ch, 1550 *MinAcct*, *Altryngham* 1385 Pat *et freq*, *Alteryngham* (lit. *Altyngham*) 1549 Pat, *-ing-* c.1703 *Chol*

Altrincham, -yn- 1321, 1348 Plea, (*le-*) 1400 Pat, *Altyrncham* 1434 ChRR, *Altringcham* 1547 Pat

Altryncheham 1326 Cl (p)

Alterkham, Altrikham, Altricham 1353 *MinAcct, Indict, -trycham* 1435 AD, *Alterchame* 1559 Orm²

At(t)ringham 1549 Pat

This may be 'the village of Aldhere's people'. The first el. is the OE pers.n. *Aldhere*. The final el. is hām 'a homestead, a village'. The medial el. may be *-inga-*, gen. of *-ingas*, 'the people of—'. However, Altrincham and Kermincham, Tushingham, Warmingham and Wincham 281, 327, 262, 136 *infra*, with Iddinshall, *Codingeheye*, Dane-in-Shaw 326, 326, 296 *infra* and Benchill 1 240, all belong to a class of p.ns. discussed in PN-ing² 170–172 exhibiting the Birmingham-'Brummadgem' phenomenon, a palatalized and assibilated medial *-ing-* (cf. Wa 34–36), supposed to be variants of *-inga-* compounds with the alternative *-*ingia-* form discussed in PN-ing¹ 170 ff, PN-ing² 169 ff, EPN 1 298 s.v. *-ingas*. In BNF NF 2 221–45, 325–96, NF 3 141–189, it is pointed out that the origin of such name-forms could be the composition of an -ing² formation with a further el. Altrincham would then be OE *Aldheringe-hām, in which *Aldheringe means 'at the place (called) *Aldhering* (i.e. named after *Aldhere*)', in which the *-ing* contained palatalized OE ġ, later assibilated ǧ, from a PrOE, PrGerm loc.sg. **-ingi*. The effect of this, is to suggest that the assibilated *-inǧ-* in this kind of p.n. is a toponymic variant of the *-ing-*⁴ function of the OE *-ing* suffix. The interchange of (-iŋəm) and (-indʒəm) pronunciations and their spellings in p.ns. like Altrincham and Birmingham would represent, in some instances, analogical reformations to the pattern of the *-inga-* type of p.n., and in others, a reflection of the parallel alternation in many p.ns. in *-ing* where a folk-name in *-ingas* and a related p.n. in *-ing²* are evidenced in use side by side (cf. PN-ing² 213), e.g. Halling K (PN-ing² 12, K 116, KPN 75, DEPN), Badlingham C (PN-ing² 128, C 190, this having the gen.sg. *-inges* of *-ing²* in a genitival composition). Instances of parallel *-ingas*, *-inga-* and *-ing* forms represented by ME *-inges*, *-ing(e)*, and of the confusion, in compounds, of the *-inge* dat. (locative) form of *-ing²* with *-ing-*⁴ or the uninflected form of *-ing²*, appear in Mongeham K (PN-ing² 120, K 569, DEPN), Chyngton Sx (PN-ing² 32, Sx 364, EPNS XI addenda xli), Bengeworth Wo (Wo 95, PN-ing² 173, DEPN). Wincham 136 *infra* has alternative forms of p.n., one where hām is compounded with the gen.sg. of a pers.n., another where it is suffixed to an *-ing-* formation upon the pers.n. in which an *-ing²* form has the attributive or possessive value of the *-ing-*⁴ function.

STREET-NAMES. THE DOWNS, *Bowdon Downs* 1819 Orm², *v.* dūn 'a hill', cf. Bowdon 15 *infra*; GOOSE GREEN, *v.* gōs, grēne²; OLD MARKET PLACE, *Market Place* 1860 White, a free market was chartered c.1290, Orm² 1 536;

Moss Lane, 1860 White, v. mos, lane; The Mount, 1860 ib, *Mount Pleasant* 1831 Bry; Sandiway Place & Rd, *Sandaway Head* 1831 ib, *Sandyway Place* 1860 White, v. sandig, weg, hēafod.

Ashley Rd, 1860 White, leading to Ashley 10 *infra*. Barrington Rd, cf. *Barrington Field* 1838 *TA*, *Barrington Terrace* 1860 White. Broadheath, 1831 Bry. Dunham Rd, 1860 White, *Dunham Lane* 1838 *TA*, leading to Dunham Massey 19 *infra*. Lovers' Walk, a footpath courting-place. Manchester Rd, *Washway* 1831 Bry, cf. Washway 22 *infra*, v. 'Watling Street' 1 40. Oldfield Hall, 1669 Orm², cf. Oldfield 20 *infra*. Pool Cottages, cf. *Pool Bank* 1772 Sheaf. Smith's Bridge, v. 32 *infra*. Springbank, 1831 Bry. Stamford Park & Rd, probably named from the earls of Stamford & Warrington, landowners here. Stockport Rd, 1860 White, cf. Stockport 1 294. Timperley Bridge & Brook, on the boundary with Timperley. Townfield Ho & Rd, cf. *Town Field* 1838 *TA*, *Altryncham Fylde* 1516 Sheaf, v. toun, feld. Woollam Ho.

FIELD-NAMES

The undated forms are 1838 *TA* 12. Of the others 1381 is Earw, 1400, 1468, 1475 Sheaf, 1423 Orm², 1433, 1459 AD, 1503 Plea, 1562 ChRR.

(a) Ackerley Fd; Beancroft; Black Fd; Blakeley (v. blæc, lēah); Bowling Green Fds; Bradley (*Bradleyhey* 1433, v. brād, lēah, (ge)hæg); Brownells Croft; Burgess Mdw (Altrincham was an ancient borough, cf. Mayer Fds *infra*); Charlemoor, Shorley Moor (perhaps from an old p.n. *Chorley*, v. ceorl, lēah, mōr¹); Coe Mdw (cf. Cow Lane 10 *infra*, v. col¹); Common Field; Cookstool ('cucking-stool' v. cucke-stole); Cow Hey; Cresswell Mdw (v. cærse, wella); Cut Meadow (v. cut²); Dirty Mdw; Eighteen Pennyworth; Galley Fd; Hale Moss Croft & Fd (cf. Hale Moss 25 *infra*); Heaton Mdw; Hob Fds (v. hobbe); Hodge Fd (v. hocg); Lock Fd; Loont (v. land); (Further & Nearer Moss-, Seaman's Moss-) Mayer Fd ('the Mayor's land' 1860 White 898, alluding to the 'mayor' or provost of the guild merchants of the borough, cf. Orm² 1 536, whose office drew the rents from this land, cf. Seamon's Moss Bridge 21 *infra*); Money Ash ('many ash-trees', v. manig, cf. Monyash Db 148); Omelant Hey, Oonlant Hey (perhaps *Almondley Hey infra*); Orchard Fd; Parks; Perrin Fd; Reeding Pit Fd (v. hrēoden); Round Hey; Shoot Butts (v. butte); Shorley Moor (v. Charlemoor *supra*); Skim Pit Fd ('pit where skins are soaked for tanning', v. skinn); Smithy Fd; Three Nooks; Tinker Loonts (v. tink(l)ere, land); Utley Croft & Mdw; Wall Fd (v. wælla); Walton Pickoe (v. pichel); Watering Hole Mdw.

(b) *Aldecroft* 1381 (p), *Aldcroft* 1562 (p) (v. ald, croft); *Almondley Hey* 1475 (perhaps 'Ealhmund's clearing', from the OE pers.n. *Ealhmund* and lēah, with (ge)hæg); *Brondurthfyld juxta Altryncham* 1423 'burnt-earth field', v.

brende², eorðe, cf. Brundrett's Flatts 11 *infra*); *the Cage Acre* 1468 (*v.* cage, æcer); *Croshouses* 1459 ('houses at a cross', *v.* cros, hūs); *Flaxyorde* 1503 (*v.* fleax, geard); *Smethyburgage* 1400 ('the smithy property', *v.* smiððe, burgage); *Tayntre Crofts* 1503 ('tenter crofts', *v.* tentour, croft); *Whytemore juxta Altryncham* 1423, *Whitmore* 1475 (*v.* hwīt, mōr¹).

2. Ashley (101–7784)

> *Ascelie* 1086 DB
> *Esceleia* 1170 Facs (p) (lit. *Esteleia*)
> *Axele* 1210 *Mass*, *Ahselegth* 1289 Court (p)
> *Asselche* H3 Orm³, *Asselegh* 1300 ChF, *H-* 1331 Tab, *As(s)heleg(h)*
>   1280 P (p), 1289 Court (p), 1296 Orm², 1343 Plea, *-ley(e)* 1301
>   ChancW, 1346 Pat, *-leigh* 1349 Earw (lit. *Dssheleigh*), *-le(e)* 1355,
>   1357 BPR, Chamb (p), *-ly* 1394 ChRR (p) (lit. *-by*), *As(s)chelegh*
>   1316 ib (p), 1326 *Dow*, *-ley* c. 1536 Leland
> *Aseleg'* 1286 Court (p)
> *As(s)hley*, *-legh(e)* 1296, 1308 Plea, 1300 Cl
> *Ay(i)ss(he)legh* 1326 *Dow* (p)
> *Assley* 1547 Pat, *Asley* 1673 ChRR

'Ash glade', *v.* æsc, lēah. For *Esceleia* cf. esc (Merc). *Assebe* 1287 Court 74 may belong here, but cf. *Assheby* 127 *infra*.

Ryecroft Fm, *Ruicroft* 1282 Court (p), *Ruycroft* 1318 JRL (p), *Rycroft(e)* 1335 ChRR (p), 1516 Sheaf, *Ryecroft(e)* 1570 Chol, 1760 Sheaf, 'rye croft', *v.* ryge, croft.

Arden Ho, 1698 Sheaf, *Arden's House or the New house in Arden's* 1706 ib, and Arden Lodge, probably named from the Arderne family of Timperley.   Ashley Bridge, Hall, Lodge & Mill, *Ashley Hall & Mill* 1831 Bry, *Ashley Lodge* 1838 *TA*, *molendinum de Axele super Bolin* 1210 *Mass*, *v.* brycg, hall, loge, myln. The bridge crosses R. Bollin.   Back Lane, *Back Lane* 1831 Bry, *v.* back.   Barley-brow, Barley Well.   Birkin Fm, Birkin Ford Bridge, *Berkin bridge* 1618 Sheaf, *v.* Birkin Brook 1 15.   Blackshaw Heys, 1831 Bry, '(inclosures at) the black copse', *v.* blæc, sceaga, (ge)hæg.   Blundering Hall Fm (lost), 1831 ib.   Brickhill Lane & Wood, *Brick Kiln Cover* 1831 ib, *v.* bryke-kyl.   Castlehill Fm, *Bank or New House* 1831 ib, cf. The Bank *infra*, Castle Hill 29 *infra*.   Castle Mill Bridge, *v.* 29 *infra*.   Chapelhouse Fm.   Coppice Fm, 1848 *TA*, *Coppy Farm* 1831 Bry, *v.* copis.   Cow Lane, *Coal Lane* 1831 ib, cf. *Coe Bank & Holmes* 1838 *TA*, *v.* col¹, 'coal, char-

coal', holmr.   DAIRYHOUSE FM, *Dairy House* 1831 Bry.   ECCLES-
FIELD WOOD, *Eccles Field* 1838 *TA*.   FISH HOUSE PLANTATION.
HARDY'S COVERT.   HIGGINSONS GREEN (lost), 1831 Bry, cf.
Higginson's Three Aspincrofts 1706 Sheaf, named from the family of
Ellin *Higginson* e17 Orm² 1 556, John and William *Higginson* 1706
Sheaf, cf. Aspin Croft *infra*.   HIGHERHOUSE FM, *Higher House*
1831 Bry.   HOME ACRE.   HOUGHGREEN FM, *Hough Green* 1831
ib, *v*. hōh 'a spur of land'.   JACKSON'S BANK.   LAMB'S COVERT,
cf. *Lamb Lane* 1706 Sheaf, *Lamb's Croft* 1838 *TA*.   LOWERHOUSE
FM, *Lower House* 1831 Bry.   MIDDLE HO, 1831 ib.   MILL
WOOD, near Castle Mill Bridge *supra*, *v*. myln.   PARK END (lost,
101–762846), 1842 OS, 1831 Bry, *v*. park.   PIGLEY STAIR BRIDGE
& COTTAGES, cf. *Pygley* 1489 *JRC*, *Big* & *Little Pigley* 1838 *TA*,
'young pig's clearing', *v*. pigga, lēah, with stǣger 'a stair', from a
path leading down to R. Bollin.   THE ROOKERY, 1842 OS.
ROUND COVERT.   STOCK FM, *Stock House* 1842 ib.   SUGAR
BROOK BRIDGE & FM, *Waltons Bridge* 1831 Bry, *v*. Sugar Brook 1
35, cf. Sugar Hill *infra*.   TANYARD FM, *Tan Yard* 1831 ib, *v*.
tan-yard.   THORNSGREEN, 1831 ib, *v*. þorn, grēne².   TRAFFORD'S
BANK COVERT.

FIELD-NAMES

The undated forms are 1838 *TA* 20. Of the others 1314 is Plea, 1349 Earw,
1351 Chamb, 1390 Orm², 1537 (17) Tab, 1706, 1759 Sheaf, 1831 Bry, and
1842 OS.

(a) (Black-, Bludley's-, Bowl-, Gorsey-, Long-, Moss- & Sand-) Acre(s);
Alder Croft; Ashley (*v*. æsc, lēah); Astill Fd (either a surname or an old p.n.
'the east hill', *v*. ēast, hyll); Aspin Croft ((*Higginson's Three-*) *Aspincrofts*
1706, *v*. æspen, cf. *Higginsons Green supra*); The Bank, Great & Little Bank,
Bank Fd & Head (*v*. banke, hēafod, cf. Castlehill Fm *supra*); Barass (*v*.
barras 'a barrier, a lists', perhaps used of a cock-pit, *v*. barrace NED, *barras*¹
EDD); Bath Fd (*v*. bæð); Bentley (*v*. beonet, lēah); Black Lees (*v*. lēah);
Bollin Mdw, Bollin Side Fd (named from R. Bollin 1 15); Britch Fd (*v*.
brēc); Brookfield Cover 1831; Brundrett's Flatts (*v*. branderith, flat; but the
first el. may be a surname); Burned Heys (*v*. berned, (ge)hæg); Long, Short
& Wall Butts (*v*. wælla, butte); Carr (*v*. kjarr); Cesters Fd; Cherry Barrow
('cherry grove', *v*. chiri, bearu); Cherry Tree Pool; Clay Fd; Cote Fd (*v*.
cot); Cow Hay, Hey; Crab Tree Hurst (*v*. hyrst); Crane Fd; Cress (*v*. cærse);
Dam Head (*v*. damme, hēafod); (Bridge-, Broad-, Grantham-, & Little-) Eye
(*v*. ēg 'a water-meadow'); Fawn's Clough; Ferney Croft; Flatt Mdw (*v*. flat);
Flax Croft; Gig Hole Fd (*v*. gigge, hol¹); Gorsey Hey; Half Demath ('half a
day's mowing', *v*. day-math); Ham Lane (*v*. hamm); Heatley (probably
'heath clearing', *v*. hǣð, lēah); The Heath, Long Heath; Hemp Yard (*v*.

hænep, geard); Heron's Fd; Hey Hole (*v.* (ge)hæg, hol[1]); High Fd; Great &
Little Hill; Hog Shoots; Hollin Croft (*v.* holegn); Hollows; Holme (*v.* holmr);
Horse Grass; Kid Field (dial. *kid* 'a young calf', cf. kide); Knowl Fd; Ladies
Mdw (*v.* hlǣfdige); Light Hurst ('light wood', lēoht, hyrst); Lime Fd; Little
Shaw (*v.* sceaga); Long Gate Fd (*v.* gata); Loon'd Fd, Loonds (*v.* land);
Maddishley; Madge Pitts (*v.* madge, cf. foll.); Mag Hey (*v.* mag, cf. prec.);
Marl Fd & Heys; Marn Croft; The Meadew, Meadow; Mellins (cf. Maloons
19 *infra*, Croft Mellon 326 *infra*); The Moss, Moss Hill; Nadder Hey
('adder enclosure', *v.* nǣddre (dial. *nadder*), (ge)hæg); Narrow Lane 1831;
New Hay, Hey; New Work; Oat Shuts (*v.* āte, scēat); Ollery Croft (*v.* alor);
Oven Fd; Ox Hey; Pasture Fd; Pear Tree Fd; Pease Croft (*v.* pise); Pier's
Croft; Pinfallow Fd (dial. *pinfallow* 'winter fallow'); Pingot (*v.* pingot); Rank
Wood 1843; Riddings (*v.* ryding); Ross Flatts (probably 'horse flats', *v.* hors,
flat, cf. foll.); Ross Mill Mdw (*v.* Rossmill 25 *infra*); Row Fd (*v.* rūh);
Rush(e)y Hey (*Rushey Heyes* 1759, *v.* riscig, (ge)hæg); Sandy Lees (*v.* lēah);
Shippon Croft; Slutch Croft; Smithy Croft; Spring ('a young wood', *v.*
spring); Sugar Hill (*v.* sugre, cf. Sugar Brook 1 35, Sugar Lane 1 184);
Swan's Fd & Moss; Swine's Croft; Tom Yard (*v.* toun, geard); Vicars
Fd; Wall Fd (*v.* wælla); Wheat Fd; White Fd (cf. *Whitefield Lane* 1831);
Wood Land(s).

(b) *Aldelondes* 1314 (p), 1351 (p) ('old selions', *v.* ald, land); *le Barewe*
1349, *Barwe* 1390 (*v.* bearu 'a grove'); *Blak Fild* 1537 (17) (*v.* blæc, feld);
Busshehey 1537 (17) ('bushy enclosure', *v.* busc, (ge)hæg).

3. BAGULEY (101–8090) [ˈbagli]

> *Bagelei* 1086 DB, -*l*(*ee*), -*ley*, -*legh* 1210 *Mass* (p), n.d. AD (iv, 350),
> 1378 *Eyre* (p), 1561 ChRR, *Bagil*(*eth'*) l12, e13 Facs (p), -*leg*
> m13 Dav (p), *Bagylegh* 1326 Ipm (p), *Bageyley* 1346 BPR (p),
> *Baguley* 1398 ChRR *et freq*, -*legh* 1406 ib (p), -*leigh* 1699 Sheaf,
> *Bagalegh* 1570 Orm[2]
> *Bagguley* H2 (17) Orm[1], 1559 Pat, *Baggelegh*(*e*), -*leg*(*a*), -*le*(*e*),
> -*ley*(*e*) 1249 Earw, 1259 Plea, n.d. AD (iv, 18), 1288 *Eyre*, 1296
> Plea, 1306 ChF (p), 1312 Tab (p), 1329 *Mass* (p), -*leie* 1347 BPR
> (p), *Baggyleg*(*h*), -*i*- c.1320 *Dow* (p), 1327 AD (p), 1330 *Fitt* (p),
> 1404 ChRR, *Baggaley* 1356 Orm[2] (p)
> *Baghileg'* 13 Dav (p), -*ley* 1302 (17) Tab (p)
> *Baggkeleg'* c.1274 Tab (p), *Badkley* 1308 Adl (p), *Backeleye* c.1320
> *Dow* (p), *Bacleg'* 1323 Dav (p)
> *Baglegh* l13 Adl (p), -*le*(*e*) 1310 *Dav*, 1326 Pat (p), -*ley* 1318 JRL (p)
> *Baygulegh* 1500 Plea
> *Begele* 1516 Sheaf

'Badger clearing or wood', *v.* bagga, lēah.

FLOATS FM, HALL & RD, *Enesebrocflotis, -brok-* 1259 Plea, 1260
Court, *le Flotes* 113 (17) Tab, *Floats Hall* 1831 Bry, *v.* flot[1] 'deep
water, the sea', here in the sense 'flooded land', cf. dial. *float* 'to
irrigate land, to dam up water, a dam'. Such a meaning would suit
the OE context *Spēda unrihtwīsra eall swā flot bēoð ādrūgude* BTSuppl,
'the wealth of the unrighteous shall be dried up like a flood', which
makes the emendation *flōd* (for Lat *fluvius*) unnecessary. Float Fm
Sx 517 may be a parallel case. *Enesebroc* seems to be the name of Mill
Brook *infra*.

BAGULEY BOTTOMS, *v.* 1 242.   BAGULEY BROOK (> Sinderland
Brook 22 *infra*), 1831 Bry, *Saxbroke* 1494 Earw 1 269. The earlier
name is a back-formation from Saxfield 1 236.   BAGULEY HALL,
1582 Earw, *Old Hall* 1842 OS.   BAGULEY HO, 1831 Bry.   BAILEY
LANE, cf. *Bailey Field & Meadow* 1838 *TA, v.* baillie, cf. 1 242.
BECCLES FM & WOOD, *Beccles* 1842 OS, *Birtles* 1831 Bry, *Long
Birtles, Birtles Lane & Wood* 1838 *TA, v.* bircel, cf. Birtles 1 72.
BLACKCARR WOOD, 1838 *TA,* 'black marsh', *v.* blæc, kjarr.
BROOKLANDS RD, *v.* 5 *supra.*   THE BRUNDRIT, *Brundrett(e)* 1838
TA, probably connected with William *Brond(d)ret* 1282, *Brandrid*
1288 Court, *v.* branderith 'a grating, a grate'.   CLAY LANE.
CROSS GREEN (lost), 1842 OS.   DOBBINETS LANE, *v.* 32 *infra.*
DUN'S LANE.   FAIRYWELL WOOD, *Fairy Well* 1838 *TA, v.*
faierie, wella, cf. 32 *infra*, Fairywell Brook 1 23.   GREENBROW
LANE, *Green Lane* 1831 Bry.   GREEN LANE.   HALL LANE,
leading to Baguley Hall *supra.*   HATTON FOLD, *v.* fald.   KNOB-
HALL, 1842 OS.   MAPLE FM & RD.   MILL BROOK, named from
Baguley Mill, cf. Millhouse *infra.* This may be the *Enesebroc, -brok*
named in Floats *supra*, the first el. of which is not known. The stream
runs from near Oldwood *infra*, and if *Enese-* were taken to be a
misreading of *Euese-*, this would indicate efes 'the edge of the wood'.
MILLHOUSE, *Brook House* 1831 Bry, *Oaks* 1842 OS, cf. prec. and foll.
MILLHOUSE FM, cf. *Baguley Mill* 1831 Bry, 1842 OS, Mill Brook
supra.   MOOR FM, MOORLAND HO, cf. *Baguley Moor* 1831 Bry,
1842 OS.   MOSS HO, 1860 White, *Moss Folly* 1831 Bry.   MOUNT
PLEASANT.   NEWALL GREEN, *New Hall Green* 1831 ib, *Newal Green*
1842 OS, *v.* nīwe, hall.   NORMANHURST, cf. *Norman Field* 1838
TA.   OLDHOUSE FM, *Old House* 1831 Bry.   OLDWOOD (FM
& LANE), *Old Wood House & Lane* 1831 ib, *Old Wood* 1842 OS, cf.
Mill Brook *supra.*   PEARTREE FM, cf. *Pear Tree Field* 1838 *TA.*

PETERS SPINNEY. PRINCES SPINNEY. ROUNDTHORN FM, *Round Thorn* 1831 Bry. ROYAL OAK (p.h.), *þe Oke in Baguley* 1580, *the Royall Oak* 1674 Earw, *v. āc.* SHADY LANE. SYCAMORE FM. THORLEY LANE, cf. *Thawley Lane Field* 1838 *TA*, *v.* 29 *infra.* TRUCK LANE, 1842 OS. WHITEHOUSE FM. WYTHEN-SHAWE BRIDGE, named from Wythenshawe 1 236.

FIELD-NAMES

The undated forms are 1838 *TA* 34. Of the others, 1261, c.1300, e14, 1422 are (17) Tab, 1373, 1427, 1449 *Dav*, 1404 ChRR, 1419 *SocAnt*, 1578 Orm², 1842 OS. (N) denotes a field in Northenden parish according to *TA* 34.

(*a*) Alderley Fd; Backster Fd (N) (cf. Baxter Fd *infra*); Barley Brow; Baxter Fd (cf. Backster Field *supra*, from bæcestre 'a baker' or the derived surname); Boosing Fd (a field near a cow-house, used for winter feeding, *v.* boosing); Booth Croft (*v.* bōth); Brancha Fd (N) (*v.* Brinkshaws Field 1 245); Brick Kiln Fd (N); Brierley Fd (*v.* brēr, lēah); Brook Fd (cf. *Brook-field Wood* 1842); Brook Shut (*v.* scēat); Brow; Burnt Croft; Butt Ridding (*v.* butte, ryding); Cat Tail Fd (*v.* catt, tægl); Clover Fd (N); Coat Croft (*v.* cot); Common Fd & Lot (*v.* hlot); Coney Greaves (*v.* coninger); Coppice Wd; Crabtree Croft; Crash 'em down (*v.* 326 *infra*); Cynderhill, Cynderlies (*v.* sinder 'a cinder', hyll, lēah); Duty Lane; Gentleman's Croft; Gibbon Lane; Gilbert Wd (cf. Gib Lane 1 237); Grubs Acre; Hanging Fd ('field on a hill-side', *v.* hangende); Hazelhurst (*Haslehurst* 1578, *v.* hæsel, hyrst); Head Acre (*v.* hēafod, æcer); Hey (*v.* (ge)hæg); High Fd; Hollins (*v.* holegn); Holly Plain (*v.* holegn, plain); Holme Fd (*v.* holmr); Horse Fall (*v.* (ge)fall 'a felling of timber'); Hungerhill (*v.* hungor, hyll); Lady Leng-then; Lime Fd; Long Acre; Long Dam (*v.* damme); Long Sides (*v.* sīde); Mankin Croft; Marled Croft, Fd & Hey; Mawkin Chapel (probably a humorous name for a place where cats, hares or wenches congregated, or a scarecrow presided, *v.* malkin, chapel(e), cf. parlur); Mead (N); New Hey; Oven House Fd; The Park, Park Wd (*parcum de Baggylegh* 1404, *Baguley Parke* 1419, *v.* park; this extended into Northern Etchells, cf. Toad Holes *infra*); Patch; Pease Croft (*v.* pise); Picha, Picher Fd (*v.* pightel); Pinfold Croft & Fd (*v.* pynd-fald); Pingot (*v.* pingot); Pit(t) Fd (N), Pits Brow; Pool Bank; Poundsack, Pownsack Patch (*v.* pacche, Poundswick 1 241); Raw Pool; Roast (perhaps *Rhuehurst* c.1300, 'rough wood', *v.* rūh, hyrst); Royal Fd (cf. Royalthorn 1 241); Rudd Parks (*v.* (ge)ryd(d), park); Rush(e)y Mdw (N); Rye Croft (N); Saw Pit Fd; Shoots (*v.* scēat); Shop Fd; Short Butts; Span (*v.* spann¹); Spark (*v.* spearca); Spur; Stash; Lower Suit (N); Tan Yard Croft & Fd (*v.* tan-yard); Tarshur Fd; Three Cornered Fd; Three Nooked Field; Till Hey; Toad Holes (N) (cf. *Foxwyste iuxta Baguley parke* 1419, 'the fox-earth, fox-holes', *v.* tod-hole, fox, wist, cf. Fox(t)wist 326 *infra*, 1 194); Tydo Fd; Wall Ridding (N) (*v.* wælla, ryding); Water-course Mill; Westage (Croft); White Carr (*v.* hwīt, kjarr, cf. Black Carr Wood *supra*); Wishing Croft; Wood Fd; Yarn Croft (*v.* gearn).

(b) *Bouker place* 1449 (a messuage named from John son of William *le Bouker* 1427, v. place 'a residence', cf. Fransson 109 s.n. *Boukere* 'buck-washer, bleacher'); *del Brom* 1373 (p) (v. brōm 'broom'); *Goldecroft* e14 (probably 'marigold croft', v. golde, croft); *Habbirley hirst* 1422 (from an old p.n. in lēah, with hyrst 'a hill, a wood'; the first el. may be a pers.n. such as OE *Hēahburg* fem. or *Hēahbeorht*); *Helmenhurst* 1261, *Hol-* c.1300 (probably 'hill growing with elms', v. elmen, hyrst).

4. BOWDON (101–7586) [ˈboudən]

> *Bogedone* 1086 DB, *Bowedon* 1345 Plea, *-den* 1724 NotCestr
> *Boudun, -donia* 1189–99 Orm² II 374, 12 Sheaf, Tab, *Bou-*,
> *Bowdon* 1275 Pat, 1278 Dugd, *-den(e)* 1438 Sheaf, 1488 ChRR
> (p), 1535 VE
> *Bothedun* l12 Facs, *Bthedut'* 1210 *Mass*
> *Bued'* e13 MidCh
> *Bodon* H3 (17) Orm², 1617 Sheaf, *-den* 1695 ib, *Boodon* 1549 Pat
> *Boedene* 13 Orm² (p)
> *Baw(e)-, Baudon* 1455, 1456 ChRR (p), *-den(e)* 1537 Orm², 1546
> Dugd

'Curved hill', v. boga, dūn, named from the elevation known as Bowdon Downs (cf. Downs Rd *infra*) which curves sharply to enclose a depression opening towards the north-west, cf. Bowdenhill D 214, Bowden Hall Db 61. The same hill gives name to Dunham Massey 19 *infra*. The forms *B(o)the-* appear in contemporary charters, and are difficult to reconcile with the usual tradition of spellings, cf. the unusual *Sur-* spelling of Corbishley 1 95 and *Bul-* for *Hul-* in Ullerwood 29 *infra*, from the same collection of documents. It is possible for a scribe c.1200 to write þ for p by a slip of the pen, but he would hardly write *-th-* for þ unless he were reading a p as a þ. A similar process of bad copying might explain *Sur-* for *Cur-*, where *C-* has been read as long-*s* and *Bul-* for *Hul-* where *h-* has been read *b-*. These phenomena indicate that some of the extant documents of this date among the *Massey* and *Fitton* charters (LRO, de Trafford MSS.) are contemporary copies of original deeds or drafts, made by a scribe prone to error through his not being personally acquainted with the p.ns. mentioned.

STREET-NAMES. BRICKKILN ROW, cf. *Brickin Field* 1838 *TA*, v. bryke-kyl, rāw; E. & S. DOWNS RD, *East Downs Road* 1860 White, cf. *Bo(w)den Down(e)s* 1644, 1659 Earw, 1819 Orm², and The Downs 8 *supra*, v. dūn 'a hill', cf. Bowdon *supra*, Rosehill *infra*; GREEN WALK, 1842 OS, v. grēne¹, walk; HEALD RD, *Heald* 1842 ib, v. helde; SPRING RD, near a hydropathic establishment, *v.* spring 'a spring'; VALE RD, *Bowdon Vale* 1860 White, cf. *Robert de Valle de Bued'* e13 MidCh, *v.* vale 'a valley'; VICARAGE LANE, 1860 White, cf. The Priory *infra*.

BOWGREEN (FM & RD), BOW LANE, *Bow Green* 1831 Bry, (*Field*) 1838 *TA*, cf. *Bow Hey* 1838 *TA*. The material is too late to show whether this is a back-formation from Bowdon *supra*, or another instance of the element **boga**, cf. Bow Field 22 *infra*.   BRICKFIELD.   CASTLE HILL (101-747858), 1838 *TA*, *v.* castel(1), **hyll**. This is the supposed site of *castellum de Duneham* 1173, held by Hamo de Massey against Henry II, and mentioned in a tenure of Tatton 1322-3, *v.* Earw 1 330, Orm² 1 440, 553, III 586, Sheaf³ 18 (4291), cf. Dunham Massey 19 *infra*, Castle Hill 29 *infra*, Watch Hill *infra*. The site commands the ford at which 'Watling Street' 1 40 crosses R. Bollin, cf. New Bridge, Watlingford *infra*.   CULCETH HALL, probably named from Culcheth La 97.   THE GORSE, *Moss Bottom* 1831 Bry, *v.* **botm**, cf. Moss Fm *infra*.   THE HALL (lost), 1831 ib, 1842 OS. HANGING BANK COVERT, *Hankin Bank* 1838 *TA*.   JOHN O' JERU-SALEM'S PATCH, land belonging to the Knights Hospitallers, cf. Sheaf³ 18 (4291), *v.* **pacche**.   MOSS FM, *Moss Bank* 1831 Bry, *Moss* 1842 OS, *v.* **mos**, **banke**, cf. *a great deep bog* 1666 Orm² 1 512. MOTLEYBANK, 1831 Bry, cf. Motley Hall 25 *infra*.   NEW BRIDGE, 1838 *TA*, cf. *Newbridge Meadow* 1654 Sheaf, *v.* 43 *infra*.   PARK RD, leading to Dunham Park 21 *infra*.   POOLBANK FM, *Pool(e) Bank* 1831 Bry, 1842 OS.   THE PRIORY, *Vicarage* 1831 Bry, 1842 OS, cf. *Vicarage Meadow, Vicars Meadow* 1838 *TA* and Vicarage Gorse *infra*, Vicarage Lane *supra*. The modern name is a pretentious antiquarianism. It may allude to the connection of this township with Birkenhead Priory (Orm² 1 512), to the religiosity of an incumbent, or to the shape of the vicarage windows.   ROSEHILL, 1860 White, *Bowden Hill* 1831 Bry, cf. Bowdon, Downs Rd *supra*. STREETHEAD COTTAGES & FM, *The Street* 1831 Bry, *Street Houses* 1842 OS, cf. *Street Head* ib at Shepherd's Brow 21 *infra*, *v.* **strǣt**. The place is on 'Watling Street' 1 40.   VICARAGE GORSE, 1842 OS, cf. The Priory *supra*.   WATCH HILL, near Castle Hill *supra*, probably 'look-out hill', from *watch* (OE wæcce) 'a watch, a look-out, a vigil', cf. Tooth Hill *infra*.   WATLINGFORD, WATLING Ho, alluding to 'Watling Street' 1 40 where it crosses R. Bollin, cf. Castle Hill, New Bridge, Streethead Cottages *supra*.

FIELD-NAMES

The undated forms are 1838 *TA* 64. Of the others, 1284 (17), 1516, 1704, 1713, 1882 are Sheaf, 1404, 1559 ChRR, 1535 AD, 1550 Pat, 1831 Bry, 1842 OS.

(a) Band Fd; Batter Edge, Batterage Eye (*v.* ēg); Bent(y) Croft (*v.* beonet); Black Fd (*Blacke Fylde* 1535, *v.* blæc, feld); Blue Berry; Botty; Bowden Eye (*v.* ēg); Bowling Green Fd; Broadshow (*v.* brād, sceaga); Brook Fd & Mdw (cf. *The Brooke* 1704); Bruckin Fd; Bur Fd; Butty Croft & Mdw (*v.* butty); Cellar Fd; Church Croft; Clay Fds (*Cley Feeld* 1535, *v.* clǣg); Coe Acre & Fd (*v.* col¹); Cooks Cross (1831, *v.* cros 'a cross', the site was at 101–766867 in Langham Rd); Croft Moss ('bog near a croft', *v.* croft, mos); Croppocks Hill; Dig Butts (*v.* dic, butte); Eye Brook(s) (*v.* ēg, brōc); Flatt(s) (*v.* flat); Green Eye Mdw (*quadam insula vocata Greeneway* 1284 (17), *Le Grene Yee* 1559, 'green island' *v.* grēne¹, ēg); Half Moon (from its shape); Handy Brooks; Hardy Fd (1713, *v.* Niths *infra*); Hash Fd; Heathy (*v.* hǣðig); Hough Fd (*v.* hōh); The Huggle 1882; Hulme Hey (*v.* hulm, (ge)hæg); Intake (Moss) (*v.* inntak); Know (*v.* cnoll); Long Acre; Loont Fd & Mdw (*v.* land); Lowe (*v.* hlāw); The Marsh; Meretons; Monks Acre (perhaps alluding to Birkenhead Priory's interest, cf. The Priory *supra*, *v.* munuc); Neset Fd; Nethershaw (*Neydur Shae* 1535 (lit. -*shac*, 'the lower copse', *v.* neoðera, sc(e)aga); Niths or Hardy Fd 1713; Nukou Fd; Pease Croft & Fd (*v.* pise); Race Ground 1831 (since built over, at 101–763867); Rough Hey; Salt Acre (*v.* salt); Shays (*v.* sc(e)aga, cf. Nethershaw *supra*); Sparrow Greaves, Sparrow Lane Fd ('woods and lane infested with sparrows', *v.* spearwa, grǣfe, cf. Sparrowgrove 259 *infra*); Stair Mdw (*v.* stǣger); Tooth Hill ('look-out hill', *v.* tōt-hyll, cf. Watch Hill *supra*); Wagger; Wan Butt & Mdw (*v.* butte); Warfield or Near White Fd (perhaps from hār 'hoary', ModE *hoar*, *v.* hwīt 'white'); Well Croft Downs ('part of the Downs at well-croft', cf. Downs Road *supra*); White Leach ('white bog', *v.* hwīt, læc(c)); Yate Fd (*v.* geat 'a gate').

(b) *Blymeley* 1550 (appurtenant of a chantry at Bowdon church); *Heylynche Feeld* 1535 ('high ridge' or 'enclosure bank', from hēah 'high', or (ge)hæg 'an enclosure' and hlinc); *Moston Hey* 1550 (*v.* (ge)hæg); *Pygattes Fylde* 1516 ('Piggott's field', from the surname *Piggott* and feld); *Warley Hey* 1535 (*v.* (ge)hæg).

5. CARRINGTON (101–7492)

> *Carrintona* H2 (17) Orm² (p), e13 Orm¹ (p)
> *Carintun, K-, -ton(a)* 12 Orm² (p), 1191 Facs, 1210 *Mass*, H3 Orm², 1294 Earw (p), *K-, Carynton* 1325, 1326 Cl
> *Carringtona* e13 Orm¹ (p), -*ton* 1367 ChRR (p), -*yng-* 1500 Plea
> *Carington* 1293 Court (p), *K-* 1404 *LRO* Dx, *Caryng-* 1325 ChRR (p), *K-* 1380 Plea
> *Karenton* 1355 BPR

2

From tūn 'a farm(yard), an enclosure', with an -ing-[4] or -ing[1] formation upon an unidentified base, cf. DEPN. Dr Barnes suggests an anglicized form of the pers.n. ON *Kári*, ODan *Kari*, an OE pers.n. *Cāra, *Kāra (cf. Feilitzen 126), which would produce in ME the characteristic wk.masc.gen.sg. form *Karen-* (< **Caran-*), whence spellings *Karin-*, *-en-*, and by analogy *-ing-*. This explanation means that Carrington is not a genuine *-ing-* p.n. Dr von Feilitzen thinks it is a true *-ing-* name, and that the Scand pers.n. is not a likely basis. *Caryngfeld* 325 *infra* appears to be analogous.

ACKERS FM & LANE, *Acres* 1831 Bry, *Akers Farm, Acre Lane* 1842 OS, *v.* æcer 'an acre, cultivated land'.   ASH FM, *v.* æsc.   ASHPODEL FM, from the dial. form of the plant-name *asphodel*.   ASHTON RD, leading to Ashton on Mersey 3 *supra*.   BACK LANE.   BIRCH RD, cf. Birchmoss 21 *infra*.   BLAKESWELL MEADOW, *Blakewell* 1841 *TA*, 'black spring', *v.* blæc, wella.   BOOTHHEY FM, *le Bothe* 1422 *AddCh*, *Booth Hey* 1831 Bry, (*Green*), *Booth Hedge Green* 1841 *TA*, *v.* bōth 'a booth, a herdsman's hut', (ge)hæg, hecg, grēne[2].   BROADOAK FM & WOOD, *Broad Oak* 1831 Bry, (*Covert*) 1842 OS.   BROOKHEYS RD, *v.* Brookheys Fm 21 *infra*.   CARRINGTON BRIDGE, cf. *Wistanley Bridge* 1618 Sheaf (a horse-bridge over Mersey), probably containing a surname from Winstanley La 104.   CARRINGTON HALL FM, the site of *Carryngton Haull* 1555 Pat, *v.* hall.   CARRINGTON LANE, *Marsh Lane* 1831 Bry, *v.* mersc, cf. Marsh Lane 4 *supra*.   CARRINGTON MOSS, 1831 ib, cf. *Moss Side* 1831 ib.   COMMON LANE (FM), *Common Lane* 1831 ib, (*House*) 1842 OS.   CORPORATION COTTAGE.   COVERSHAW BRIDGE, *v.* 21 *infra*.   CRAMPTON LANE.   DAINEWELL FM, *Court House* 1831 Bry, *Daines at the Well* 1860 White ('an ancient farm residence . . . in the occupation of Mr Peter Daine, in whose family it has been for the last five hundred years'), cf. *Daines Moss* 1841 *TA*, *v.* wella, mos, court 'a court(yard)'.   DUNHAM RD, cf. Dunham Massey 19 *infra*.   MANCHESTER RD, leading to Manchester La.   MILLBANK FM, *Mill Dam* 1831 Bry, cf. *Carrington Mill, Dam Field* 1841 *TA*, *Dam Lane, Mill Stream* 1842 OS, *v.* myln, damme 'a dam'. The stream is Button Brook 1 17.   MOSS HALL FM, MOSS RD, named from Carrington Moss *supra*.   PEAKSNOOK FM, *Peak* 1831 Bry, *-s Nook* 1842 OS, *v.* nōk.   ST GEORGES CHURCH, *Carrington Chapel* 1831 Bry.   STAMFORD FM, after the earls of Stamford & Warrington, landowners here.   WINDMILL INN, *Windmill* 1860 White.   WOODCOTE RD, cf. 22 *infra*.

FIELD-NAMES

The principal forms are 1841 *TA* 94.

(*a*) Amsterdam (perhaps an allusion to the high dykes banked beside R. Mersey to control the flooding of the river-meadows here); Back o' th' Dam; Ballanger; Barrow Croft (*v.* bearg); Black Croft; Blake Acre (*v.* blæc); Bottoms (*v.* botm); Brick Kiln Fd; The Broome (*v.* brōm); Butty Hill (*v.* butty); Capshoe; Carpet; Carr (*v.* kjarr); Carrington Hey; Clappers (*v.* clapere); Coney Grave (*v.* coningre); Corn Hey; Crab Tree; Cross Brook; Deep Carrs (*v.* dēop, kjarr); Down(e)s (*v.* dūn 'a hill'); Elleren Score ('alder cliff', *v.* elren, scora); Foalt Lane & Mdw; Forsenger; Gossam Mdw, Pasture Gossam; Green Butts; Hackin Graves; Ham Fd (*v.* hamm); Hardy Mdw; Hash Acre; Hastey; Hea Hey (prob. 'high enclosure', *v.* hēah, (ge)hæg); Heatley ('heath clearing', *v.* hǣð, lēah); Hemp Croft; Hen Butts (*v.* henn, butte); Hilleys; Hillins Bank; Intake (*freq*, near Carrington Moss *supra*, *v.* inntak); Kiln Fd; Knowl Brow (*v.* cnoll); Long Shoot (*v.* scēat); Lount (*v.* land); Maloons (cf. Mellins 12 *supra*, Croft Mellon 326 *infra*); Many Butts (*v.* manig, butte); Mare Hey (*v.* mere², (ge)hæg); Marl Churls (*v.* marle, Blackeyer 1 265); May Acre; Mizzey (*v.* misy); Narrow Fd; Old Woman's Acre; Outings; Over Hill; Partington Moss (cf. Partington 27 *infra*); Pillow Croft (*v.* pil-āte); Pingot (*v.* pingot); Pit Hey & Ridding; Poor House Fd (*v.* poorhouse); Potatoe Hole Fd; Poverty (a nickname for poor land, *v.* 327 *infra*); Pye Shaw & Wood ('magpie wood', *v.* pīe², sceaga); Radcliffe (*v.* rēad, clif); Rans, Rans Moss; Ridditch Fd (*v.* hrēod, dīc); Rough ('a rough piece of ground', *v.* rūh); Roughing (*v.* rūh, -ing¹); Royle (probably 'rye-hill', *v.* ryge, hyll); Rundle Fd ('round field', *v.* roundele); Sawpit Fd (*v.* saw-pytt); School Moss Fd; Shaw End (*v.* sceaga); Shuts (*v.* scēat); Soont (*v.* sand); Stockey Loons (perhaps 'selions full of stocks', *v.* stocc, -ig³, land); Stone Ford (*v.* stān, ford); Three Nook Fd; Tithe Barn Croft; Tithe Fd (*v.* tēoða); Tong's Croft; Turn Rough (*v.* trun, rūh); Weather Mdw; Well Croft; Wheat Hey, Wheat(e)y Fd (*v.* hwǣte, (ge)hæg); White-head's Bottom Moss (cf. *White Head* 1831 Bry, an area on Carrington Moss near Dunham Massey, cf. also Moss Brow 35 *infra*, 'white headland', *v.* hwīt, hēafod, botm, mos); Winstanley (cf. Carrington Bridge *supra*); Wood Acres; Yarn Croft (*v.* gearn).

6. DUNHAM MASSEY, comprising the hamlets Dunhamtown, Sinderland, Oldfield, Woodhouses.

DUNHAM MASSEY, DUNHAMTOWN (101-7487) [ˈdnn-, ˈdunəm]

Doneham 1086 DB, 1173 (12) Orm², 1274 Cl, (-*Mascy*) 1434 ChRR, *Donaham* 13 Tab, *Donham* 1278 Dugd, (-*iuxta Boudon*) 1296 Plea, (-*Massy*, -*Mascy*) 1437 Pat, 1482 ChRR, *Donam* c.1280 (1580) Sheaf, (-*Mascy*) 1418 ChRR

Duneham 1173 (12) Earw, *Dunham* 1274 IpmR, (-*Mass(e)y, Massy-*, -*Massye, -Mascy, -Masci*) c.1280 Fine, 1359, 1386, 1477, 1584 ChRR, (-*iuxta Boudon*) 1296 Plea, *Dunham Town* 1841 *TA*

Dounham 1297 Plea, *Downham* 1309 InqAqd, *Downam* 1559 Orm²

'Village or homestead at a hill', *v.* dūn, hām, toun, cf. Bowdon 15 *supra*, which is adjacent. The manorial suffix is derived from Hamo de *Masci* the DB tenant, and distinguishes this place from Dunham on the Hill 326 *infra*.

STREET-NAMES. DAVENPORT LANE, cf. Washway Rd; DEVISDALE RD, cf. *Davi(e)s Dole* 1838 *TA*, *v.* dāl 'an allotment'; HIGHER DOWNS, cf. The Downs, Downs Rd 8, 15 *supra*; DUNHAM RD, cf. Washway Rd *infra*; HIGHGATE RD, possibly 'high road', *v.* hēah, gata, cf. Washway Rd *infra*.

SINDERLAND (GREEN) (101–7390)

    Sundreland 1086 DB, *Sunderlond, -land* 1287, 1288 Court,   (*clausturam de-*) c.1290 (1667) Orm², (-*within Dunham Massey*)   1699 Sheaf

    (*parcum de*) *Sonderland* 1353 *MinAcct*

    Synderlond 1477 ChRR, -*land* 1607 ib, *Sinder-* 1639 Cre, (*Green*)   1831 Bry

'Detached land', *v.* sundor-land, grēne². The name may have arisen from the peculiar manorial tenure of this estate TRE and DB, *v.* Tait 56–57, which emphasizes its distinction from the surrounding estates.

OLDFIELD (101–7588), *Aldefeld* c.1293 AD, *le Oldefeld* 1296 Orm² (p), -*e* 1550 ChRR, Pat, -*feelde* 1602 Orm², *Oldfeld* 1354 BPR (p), cf. *Ham Oldfield* 1838 *TA*, 'the old field', from ald and feld. The prefix *Ham* is also found in Christleton 325 *infra*, denoting the nucleus of the hamlet, *v.* hām.

DUNHAM WOODHOUSES, WOODHOUSE LANE (101–7287), (*Dunham*) *Wod(d)ehouse* 1522 *ChEx*, -*howse(s)*, -*Woodhouse(s)* 1535 Plea, 1547 Orm², 1559, 1601 ChRR, 'house(s) at a wood', *v.* wudu, hūs.

ALDCROFT (lost), 1665 Sheaf, *Aldecroft* 1260 Court (p) *et freq*, -*e* 1467 ChRR (p), 'the old croft', *v.* ald, croft. This place was near Bowdon and Dunham Massey; persons of the surname held land in the Dunham barony.   ASH FM.   ASH WALK, *The-* 1838 *TA*, an avenue in Dunham Park, *v.* æsc, walk.   BACK LANE.   BARNLANE FM, BARNS LANE, *Barons Lane Croft* 1838 *ib*, *Barns Lane* 1842 OS, on the boundary of Warburton, cf. Barns Lane 35 *infra*, and probably

alluding to the barony of Dunham Massey, *v.* **baron.** Birchhouse
Fm, Birchmoss Covert, *Birch House* 1831 Bry, (*Cover*) 1842 OS,
v. **birce, mos.** Blackbrow Fm. *Blackbrows* 1831 Bry, 'dark banks',
v. **blæc, brū.** Black Moss Covert, *Cockeridge Covert* 1831 Bry,
Little Cockridge 1838 *TA*, cf. foll., perhaps 'cock ridge', *v.* cocc[2] 'a
(wood)cock', **hrycg,** but cf. *Cokridmosse* 27 *infra.* Black Moss
Fm, 'dark bog', *v.* **blæc, mos.** Bollington Mill, 1831 Bry,
molendinum de Bolyn(*g*)*ton* 1354 BPR, ChRR, cf. Bollington 43 *infra.*
Boxtree Fm. Brick Field, Brickkiln Nursery Wood, cf. *Brick
Kiln Field, Brick Kiln Yard Nursery* 1838 *TA*. Broadheath Fm,
cf. (*Little*) *Broad Heath* 1831 Bry. Brookheys Fm & Rd, *Brook
Heys* 1831 ib, 'enclosures at a brook', *v.* (ge)hæg, named from
Sinderland Brook *infra*, cf. foll. Brookside Fm, *Brook Side* 1842
OS, *Brook Houses* 1831 Bry, cf. prec. Charcoal Rd. Covershaw Bridge, *Coversal Bridge* 1842 OS, crossing Sinderland Brook
into Carrington 17 *supra*, cf. *Cubbershaw* 1838 *TA*, perhaps 'dove
copse', *v.* **culfre, sceaga.** Dairyhouse Fm, *Dairy House* 1831 Bry,
a Dearye house 1580 Orm[2], *v.* **deierie.** Dark Lane, 1842 OS.
Dunham Fm, Hall & Mill, 1831 Bry. Dunham Park, *parcum
de Donham* 1353 *MinAcct*, 1362 BPR, cf. *le Hegh Parke alias vocat'
le Hegh Shawe* 1481 ChRR, *Highe Parke* 1585 Orm[2], *v.* **park, hēah,
sceaga.** Greenbank. Green Lane (Fm). Grovehouse Fm.
Headsman's Covert. Heath Fm, cf. *Heath Hey* 1838 *TA*, near
Carrington Moss 18 *supra*. Henshall Fm & Lane, *Henshaw
Lane* 1831 Bry, probably 'hen wood', *v.* **henn, sceaga.** Higher
Ho, 1831 ib, cf. Lower House(s) *infra*. Hogswood Fm, *Hogs i' th'
Wood* 1831 ib. Langham Grove, a wood in Dunham Park.
Limetree Ho. Lower House(s), 1842 OS, cf. Higher Ho *supra*.
Malljurs Covert, *Marle Geers* 1838 *TA*, *v.* **marlede** and Blackeyer
1 265. Manor Fm. New Bridge, *pons de Bolyn* 1353
MinAcct, *v.* 43 *infra*. New Park, 1831 Bry, cf. *Park House*
1842 OS, *v.* **nīwe, park,** cf. Dunham Park *supra*. Oldfield Brow,
1831 Bry, *v.* **brū.** Oldfield Ho, Lane & Rd. Orchard Ho.
Pike Lane. Pitstead Covert, *v.* **pytt, stede.** Redbeech Fm.
Red House Fm. Redmoor Covert, *Redmoor* (*Clough*) 1838 *TA*,
v. **rēad, mōr[1], clōh.** School Lane. Seamon's Moss Bridge,
a bridge over the Duke of Bridgewater's canal, apparently named
after a bog, cf. Mayer Field 9 *supra*. Shepherd's Brow, 1831
Bry, *Street Head* 1842 OS, *v.* **brū** 'a brow, a rise', **strǣt, hēafod** 'a
head; an eminence, the top of—'. This is part of 'Watling Street' 1

40, cf. Washway *infra*, Streethead 16 *supra*.   SIDDALL'S BRIDGE,
v. 32 *infra*.   SINDERLAND BROOK (> Red Brook[3] 1 34), 1842
OS.   SINDERLAND HO, LANE & RD.   SMITH'S BRIDGE, *v.* 32
infra.   SUNNYSIDE.   TIPPING'S BANK, cf. *Tipping Field* 1838 *TA*.
TOWNSEND FM, *v.* toun, ende[1].   TWO GATES, 1842 OS.   WASH-
WAY FM & RD, *Woods Farm* 1831 Bry, *Wood House* 1841 *TA*, from
the surname *Wood*. The modern name is from *Washway* 1831 Bry,
v. 'Watling Street' 1 40, cf. Washway 6 *supra*. The course of
the Roman road in Dunham Massey is from New Bridge northwards past Streethead 16 *supra*, Shepherd's Brow, Dunham Road,
Highgate Rd, thence by a footpath in a line to Davenport Lane, where
the modern road, Manchester Rd 9 *supra*, rejoins it.   WHITE-
HOUSE FM.   WHITEOAKS WOOD, *Whitewicks Nursery* 1831 Bry;
Bryant has misinterpreted a diphthongized and stress-shifted dial.
form of -*oaks*.   WOODCOTE FM & RD, *Wood Cote* 1831 ib, 'cote in
a wood', *v.* wudu, cot.

FIELD-NAMES

The principal forms are 1838 *TA* 152. Of the others e13 is MidCh, c.1278
(18), 1516, 1702 Sheaf, 1278 Dugd, 1353 *MinAcct*, 1376 *Eyre*, 1382 Plea,
1585 Orm[2], 1831 Bry, 1842 OS.

(*a*) Angle Fd & Piece (*v.* angle); Ardern Fd; Ashy Bottom(s) (*v.* botm);
August; Back Fd; Barrows Barn Croft; Bastard Fd (probably a nickname for
poor land, *v.* 325 *infra*); Beach Head (*v.* bece[1], hēafod); Bear Hey (*v.* bær[1]);
Bell Green; The Bent (*v.* beonet); Bill Style (*v.* stigel); Black Croft, Black
Gate Fd, Black Slack, Blake Ends (*v.* blæc, gata, slakki, ende[1]); Bollin Mdw
(cf. R. Bollin 1 15); Bottom Moss; The Bottoms (*v.* botm); Bow Fd &
Flatt (*v.* boga, cf. Bowgreen 16 *supra*); Brady; Breaketts Fd; Broad Eye
(*v.* ēg); Broome Croft (*v.* brōm); Brow Fd (*v.* brū); Brunt Heath ('burnt
heath' *v.* brende[2], hǣð); Burgess Mdw; Burnt Earth (*v.* brende[2], eorðe);
Busyman Fd; Butty Fd (*v.* butty); Cadmans Fd & Rough; Caldwell Fds (*v.*
Caldwell Brook 1 17); Calve(s) Croft; Care Fd; Great & Little Carr (*v.*
kjarr); Carrington Hey (*v.* (ge)hæg, cf. Carrington 17 *supra*); Cheetwood
Acre (perhaps 'escheated wood', cf. *cheet-land* WRY 7 169, but a surname
from Cheetwood La 33 is possible); Clough Wd (*v.* clōh); Coal Brow Bottom
(*v.* col[1], brū, botm); Cookstool Fd (*v.* cucke-stole); Corner Fd; Cow Head
(*v.* cū, hēafod); Cowherd Fd; Crabtree Hill; Croft Greaves (*v.* croft, grǣfe);
Cutting Loaf; Cutting Loont (*v.* land); Dangerous Acre; Deaneshuts 1702
(*v.* denu, scēat); Deansgate; Dreadful (no doubt poor land, cf. Terrible
infra); Epping Bank (perhaps a place where rose-hips grow, *v.* hēope, -ing[1]);
Feather Bed Fd (cf. Featherbed Moss 1 323); Finger Fd; Fitch Butts
(*v.* ficche, butte); Flake Fd (*v.* fleke); Flam Fd (*v.* flēama); Flash (*v.* flasshe);
Footway Fd; French Fd; Gale Fd, Geal(ley) Fd (*v.* gagel); Gore (*v.* gār);
Greenbury Hill (*v.* grēne[1], beorg); Handkerchief Nook (*v.* 326 *infra*);

Hardinge (perhaps a hard place, *v.* heard, -ing[2]); Hardy Fd; Hawthorn
Loont (*v.* land); Heath Fd (cf. *Little Heath* 1831); Heir Old Fd; Hemp Croft;
Hex Fd; The Heys; Hooly Edge, Hooley Hill (*Hooley Hill* 1842, probably
'clearing at a spur of land', *v.* hōh, lēah, ecg); Intack, Intake (*v.*
inntak); Kirgate (*v.* kirkja, gata); Knowle (*v.* cnoll); Ladyhey (*v.* hlǽfdige, (ge)hæg);
Langley Common (*v.* lang, lēah); Lapwing Hey; Long Acre; Longsides
(*v.* sīde); Mailed Fd; Great & Old Mant; Marl(e)d Earth, Fd, Hey &
Rough; Mean Mdw (*v.* (ge)mǽne); Mexon Fd (*v.* mixen 'a dung hill, a
midden'); Little Moor; Moss (cf. *Moss Ends* 1831, adjoining Carrington
Moss 18 *supra*); Newall Fd (*v.* nīwe, hall); Old House Croft; Old Lunts or
Heath (*v.* land); Old Woman's Crop; Ollery Fd (*v.* alor); The Ordern (*v.*
hord-ærn); Ouler Hey, Owler Hey (*v.* alor, (ge)hæg); Pack Fd; Padmore
('toad marsh', *v.* padde, mōr[1]); Partington Croft & Fd (cf. Partington 27
infra); Pinfold (*v.* pynd-fald); Pingot(t) (*v.* pingot); Plodding Fd; Poor House
Fd (after the *Poor House* 1831); Rats Fd; Ridding Hey (*v.* ryding); Riddish
Fd ('reed-ditch', *v.* hrēod, dīc); (The) Rough (*freq*); Round Hey; Rye Fd;
Shaw Intack (*v.* sceaga, inntak); Shee Platt ('plot of ground at a wood', *v.*
sc(e)aga, plat[2]); Sheep Hey; Shoot Butts Shotts (*v.* scēat); Sin Fd; Slack
Croft (*v.* slakki); Slip (*v.* slippe); Smithy Green; Soggs (*v.* sugga); Sour Fd;
Southern Heys; Squirely-, Squirrel Hill; Stake Fd (*v.* staca); Stocking Hey
(*v.* stoccing); Street Acre (*v.* strǽt, cf. 'Watling Street' 1 40); Swamp
Fd; Sweet Fd; Terrible (cf. Dreadful *supra*); Town Fd (cf. *Donnham Field*
1516, *v.* toun); (The) Trine; Wall Fd (*v.* wælla); Warburton Fd (cf. Warburton 34 *infra*); Ware Fd; Westells (*the Westelle* (*coppe*) 1516, perhaps
'west well' or 'west hill' from west and wella or hyll, with copp); Wheecock;
Whetstocks; White Ash Green; Wick Fd; Within Wall ('willow-tree spring',
v. wiðegn, wælla); Wood Fd; Yamshaw; Yarn Croft (*v.* gearn).

(b) *del Ackereʒ* 1376 (p) (*v.* æcer); *Aldelonde* e13 (17) (*v.* ald, land); *Calfe
Wood* 1585 (*v.* calf, wudu); *ad Cattelbectesstrenam* e13 (17) '(the course of)
the cattle stream', *v.* cat(t)el, bece[1], strēam); *the Clyffe hed* 1516 ('the head
of a cliff', *v.* clif, hēafod); *the olde Galowes* 1516 (*v.* ald, galga); *Goldcelo-
cheker* c.1278 (18) '(marsh at) the marigold valley', *v.* golde, clōh, kjarr); *le
Gosmede* 1353 (*v.* gōs, mǽd); *Kelsale in Dunham iuxta Boudon* 1382 (probably an error for Kelsall 326 *infra*); *Lacheker* 1278 ('marsh by a boggy stream',
v. lǽc(c), kjarr, cf. foll.); *Lasshleigh* 1353 (*v.* lǽc(c), lēah, cf. prec.); *Lynyerd*
1353 ('flax croft', *v.* līn, geard); *Lordesryddyng* 1353 ('lord's clearing', *v.*
hlāford, ryding); *parcum de Mareheye* 1353 ('mare's enclosure', *v.* mere[2],
(ge)hæg); *the Moreforlong* 1516 (*v.* mōr[1], furlang); *Moston Heys* 1585 (*v.*
(ge)hæg); *le Poolmulne* 1353 ('mill at a pool', *v.* pōl[1], myln); *Poolyerd* 1353
('yard or enclosure at or in a pool', *v.* pōl[1], geard); *Thornleigh* 1353 ('thorn
clearing', *v.* þorn, lēah).

7. HALE (101–7786), formerly including Ringway 28 *infra*.

The boundaries between the two for the purpose of this survey are those of
6″ OS (1910–11 ed.), which differ from Bry. The field-names for Ringway
are included here among those for Hale, since the *TA* does not distinguish
them.

HALE, 1086 DB *et passim*, (*-iuxta Tymperlegh*) 1350 Plea, *Hal'* 1260 Court (p), 'at the nook', *v.* halh (dat.sg. hale), from its situation in a hollow to the east of Bowdon 15 *supra*. A plural form *Hales* 1398 ChRR probably refers to this place and to *Eastoe Lane infra*, Easter-lane Fm 28 *infra*.

BANKHALL, *le Bonk* 1396 ChRR (p), *le Bank* 1398 ib (p), *le-*, *þe Banck* 1562 ib, 1640 NotCestr, *-Banke* 1683 Sheaf, *Bank Hill* 1724 NotCestr, *Bank Hall* 1831 Bry, 'the bank', from banke, with hyll, hall.

OLLERBARROW (lost, 101–773866), OLLERBARROW RD

> *Ollerbarwe* 1406 Plea, *-bar(r)ow(e)* 1443, 1599 Earw, 1637 *Chol*,
> *Oler-* 1576 ChRR, *Ollerbarrow* 1915 Sheaf
> *Ellerbarrowe* 1527 ChRR, *-borowe*, *-borough* 1580 Sheaf
> *Aldreburgh vulgo Ellerborough* 1580 Sheaf
> *Owlerbarrow(e)* 1613, 1683 Sheaf, *-Berry* 1831 Bry, *the Oulerbarrow*
> 1788 Cre

'Alder grove', *v.* alor, bearu. This may be the two acres covered with alders mentioned in 1350, Orm² 1 554n. The house was demo-lished early this century, Sheaf³ 32 (7179). It was in Ashley Rd between Cambridge Rd and Murieston Rd. Ollerbarrow Rd joins the other end of Cambridge Rd.

ASH LANE. ASHLEY HEATH, 1746 Cre, cf. Ashley 10 *supra*. ASHLEYMILL LANE, ASHLEY RD, leading to Ashley and Ashley Mill 10 *supra*. Part of Ashley Road was *Pale Causeway* 1831 Bry, *Peel Causeway* 1841 *TAMap*, 'causeway at, or to, a palisade', *v.* pēl, caucie. It gave name to a farmhouse on the site of Hale railway station (110–760869). BARROW LANE, cf. *Bar Hole* 1838 *TA* and The Clough *infra*; probably 'barrow-pig's lane', *v.* bearg, hol¹, cf. 29 *infra*. BENTLY BANK, cf. *Bentley Field* 1838 *ib*, 'bent-grass clearing', *v.* beonet, lēah. BROAD LANE (HEAD), 1831 Bry, *v.* hēafod. CHAPEL LANE, named from a Unitarian Chapel here. THE CLOUGH (FM), *Barrow House* 1831 ib, cf. Barrow Lane *supra*, and *The Clough* 1637 *Chol*, *Clough Field* 1838 *TA*, *v.* clōh 'a dell'. DELAHAYS RD, leading to Delahays Fm 32 *infra*. EASTOE LANE (lost), 1860 White, *v.* Easterlane Fm 28 *infra*. FIR TREE HO, 1831 Bry. FORDBANK, 1831 ib, on a bank overlooking Ashley Bridge, *v.* ford, banke. HALEBARNS, *-barnes* 1616 Cre, *Hale Barn* 1831 Bry, *Barns Green* 1842 OS, *Hale Barn(e)s Green* 1860 White, named from a tithe-barn here, demolished 1848, cf. *Tithe Barn Yard* 1838 *TA*. HALE CARR, *Carr* 1831 Bry, *Car Farm* 1842 OS, 'brush-wood, marsh', *v.* kjarr. HALECROFT, 1838 *TA*, *v.* croft. HALE FIELD (lost, near Cedar Rd and Stamford Park), 1860 White, *-feild* 1637 *Chol*, *v.* feld. HALE GREEN & LODGE, 1831 Bry. HALE LOW FM, *Halelowe* 1443 Earw, *Hale Low* 1831 Bry, *v.* hlāw 'a mound'. HALE MOSS, 1831 ib, *v.* mos. HALEMOUNT, *Hale Mount* 1841 *TAMap*, *v.* mont. HALE RD, *Long Lane (House)* 1841 *ib.* HALLIWELL CLOUGH, 1838 *TA*, *v.* clōh 'a dell'. *Halliwell* may be 'holy well', *v.* hālig, wella. HAWLEY LANE. HILLTOP, 1831 Bry. MOSS LANE, cf. Hale Moss *supra*. MOTLEY HALL (lost), 1831 ib, cf. Motleybank 16 *supra*. NEW FM. OAKLANDS FM. PARK FIELD & HILL. PARK RD, *Dob Lane* 1842 OS, 1860 White, cf. *Dob Field* 1838 *TA*, perhaps from daube 'clay'. PART-INGTON FM, *Partington's tenement* 1731 Cre, cf. *Partington Shutts* 1838 *TA*, from the surname from Partington 27 *infra*, *v.* tenement, scēat. PRESCOT RD, cf. *Prescot* 1838 *ib*, perhaps 'priest's cottage', *v.* prēost, cot. RAPPAX RD, cf. *Rappox* 1838 *ib*, *the (Further) Rawbuck(e)* 1637 *Chol*. *Rappox* is the plural of *Rawbuck*; *Rawbuck* is either the animal-name *roe-buck* or the surname *Roebuck*. ROSS-MILL, *Ross Mill House* 1831 Bry, *-Farm* 1842 OS, *Rass Mill* 1841 *TAMap*, cf. *Ross Mill Mdw* 12 *supra*, probably a horse-mill, *v.* horse-mylne, cf. Ross Flatts 12 *supra*. SHAY LANE, *Shaw Lane* 1842 OS, *Shea Lane* 1860 White, *v.* sc(e)aga. TOMFIELD BANK, *Gt. Tom Field, Tom Field Bank* 1838 *TA*, 'town-field', *v.* toun. WELL-FIELD LANE, running from Well Green *infra* to Newfoundwell 32 *infra*, cf. *Well Field* 1838 *ib*, *v.* wella 'a well, a spring'. WELL GREEN, 1841 *TAMap*, *Waugh Green* 1831 Bry, 'green at a well', *v.* wella, wælla. WICKER HO & LANE, cf. *Wicken Hey & Hill* 1838 *TA*, *v.* cwicen, dial. *wicken* 'mountain-ash'.

FIELD-NAMES

The undated forms are 1838 *TA* 183. Of the others 1260 is Court, c.1280 AD, 1349 Earw, 1353 *MinAcct*, 1585, 1712 Cre, 1586 *Dav*, 1594 JRL, 1637 *Chol*, 1841 *TAMap* 183, and 1842 OS.

(*a*) Acker (*acre* 1637, *v.* æcer); Adder Fd (*v.* næddre); Asp Acre; Aspen-, Aspin hurst ('wooded hill growing with aspens', *v.* æspen, hyrst); Astel Mdw ('east hill', *v.* ēast, hyll; or from the surname *Astle, Astell*); Bank Fd; Barn Fd (cf. *the barncroft* 1637, *v.* bere-ærn); Bent (*v.* beonet); Birch; Birchen Fd (*v.* bircen[1]); Bleak Mdw (*v.* blāc); Boat Oak (*v.* bōt, āc); Bollages;

Bollin Mdw (cf. foll. and R. Bollin 1 15); Bolling Bank 1841 (cf. prec.); Bonnet Mdw; Bow Croft (cf. *le Bawefeld* 1353, *v.* boga, feld); Bradshaw Fd; Brick Fd (*the-* 1637, 1842); Bridge Fd (cf. *Brydge Crofte* 1585, *Bridge Croft* 1712); Briery Croft & Fd; Brook Ridding (*v.* ryding); Brow (*v.* brū); Burn Fd; Butt Knowle (*v.* butte, cnoll); Butts Orchard (*v.* butte); Calverley Bent & Mdw ('calves' clearing', *v.* calf (gen.pl. calfra), lēah); Chapel Fd; Clay Croft & Fd (*the* (*higher*) *Clayfeild* 1637); Crutched Acre (*v.* crotched); Crying Fd; Dam Croft, Hey, Mdw (*v.* damme); Ding Well (1637); Dobbed Hedge (*v.* dubbed); Dobs Croft; Dry Hills; Eye (*v.* ēg); Eves Fd (*v.* efes); Flake Mdw (*v.* flak); Flash Pit (*v.* flasshe); Flatt (*v.* flat); Foot Way Mdw; Fox Fd; Frog Patch; Gawsey Heys (*v.* gorstig, (ge)hæg); Gibbon Mdw; Gill Croft; Glede Brow (*v.* gleoda, brū); Gorse Banks (*Gorsey Bank* 1842); Gueld Hey (three closes called *the geldheis* 1637, from ME, ModEdial. geld 'barren' (ON *geldr*)); Hale Greaves & Moor (*v.* grǣfe); Hand Ridding (*v.* ryding); Hanging Fd (*v.* hangende); Hemp Croft; Hennersley Bank; Hey; Hig Fd; Hill Field (*the Hill* 1637); Hitchum Pickum; Hob Fd (*v.* hobbe); Hole Wicken ('mountain-ash in a hollow', *v.* hol[1], cwicen); Hollit Fd; Hollow Flat (*Hollo flat* 1637, *v.* holh, flat); The Hollows; Hookers Fd; Horse Hey; Horselow (*v.* hors, hlāw); Hough (*v.* hōh); Hud Fd (perhaps from the ME nickname *Hudd*); Hungerley (cf. *hunger hey* 1637, *v.* hungor, (ge)hæg, lēah); The Knowles (*v.* cnoll); Lambs Mdw (cf. *lambscroft* 1637, *v.* lamb); Leach Butts (*v.* lǣc(c), butte); Ley Fd (*v.* lēah or lǣge); Little Hatch (*v.* hǣc(c)); Long Croft (*the-* 1637); Long Shutts (Clough) (*v.* scēat, clōh); Loon Fd (*v.* land); Lords Acre & Fd (*v.* hlāford); Lowk (*v.* lowk); Lucust; Madge Fd (*v.* madge); Marl Fd & Hey (*the* (*little*) *Marled feild, the marled hey* 1637, *v.* marlede, (ge)hæg); Marl'd Lont (*v.* marlede, land); Meade (*v.* mǣd); Mere Fd; Mill Hopp ('mill hollow', *v.* myln, hop[1]); Money Ash ('many ash-trees', *v.* manig, æsc, cf. 9 *supra*); Moor Heys; The Old Mother Croft; Nick Fd; Nickow Fd; Nine Guards; The Offshut; Ollerhey; Olliery Hey (cf. *the Oller croft* 1637, *v.* alor, (ge)hæg); Oven House Mdw (cf. *the oven Backe* 1637, *v.* ofen); Owler Bank (*v.* alor); Ox Hey (1637); Park Hey; Perries (*Peryes* 1585, *v.* pirige 'a pear-tree'); Pickers; Pinfold (*v.* pyndfald); Pingot (*v.* pingot); Pique Bottom; Ratcliffe Croft; Reddish Fd (*v.* hrēod, dīc); Ridding (*v.* ryding); Ripping Fd; Round Hey; Rush(e)y Fd & Hey; Rye Grass Fd (*v.* rye-grass); Salt Ridding (*v.* salt, ryding); Sand Fd; Savage Acre (1637, cf. *Savage butt* ib, both owned by John, viscount *Savage*); Shadow Moss (*v.* 1 242); Shairlock; Sharps Acre; Shaw Platts (*v.* sceaga, plat[2]); Shed Fd; Short Butts (*the-* 1637, *v.* sc(e)ort, butte); Shutts (*v.* scēat); Skin Croft (*v.* skinn); Sleghton; Slutch Fd & Patch; Small Greaves ('narrow groves', *v.* smæl, grǣfe); Soon Fd (*v.* sand); Soot Fd; Sound Fd & Hill (*v.* sand); Sparrow Hill; Square Croft; Stake Fd; Stile Fd (*v.* stigel); Stratton ('enclosure near a road', *v.* strǣt, tūn); Further & Nearer Stubble Ley (*Further-, Higher-* & *Nearer Stubby-, Stubbie Lee* 1637, 'stubby clearing', *v.* stubbig, lēah); Swang (*Swans* 1637, 'swamp', *v.* swang); Sweet Acre; Toad Hole (*v.* tāde); Tong Croft (*v.* tang); Toot Hill ('look-out hill', *v.* tōt-hyll); Utley Fd; Vaudrey Meadow (from the *Vawdrey* family, landowners here); Vine Yard (*v.* vinȝerd); Virjuice (a figurative name for sour land, *v.* verjuice NED, cf. 327 *infra*); Further-, Great- & Little Wall Fd (*further & nearer wal(l)feild* 1637, 'spring field', *v.* wælla); Waste Croft; Wat Fd; Wey Gates ('sour pastures', *v.* hwæg, gata); The Wheaty (*Wheathey* 1637, cf. *the Wheatefeild* ib, *v.* hwǣte 'wheat', (ge)hæg); White Flatt; White Leg Wd, Whitley Mdw (*v.* hwīt, lēah); Willey (*v.* wilig, lēah).

(b) *the Bradley* 1637 (*v.* brād, lēah); *le Cokridmosse* 1481 ('(moss at) the cock-clearing', *v.* cocc², ryde, mos, cf. Black Moss Covert 21 *supra*, which probably has the same origin); *the Corn field* 1637; *the Cowhey* 1637 (*v.* cū, (ge)hæg); *Croners feildes* 1637 ('coroner's fields', *v.* coroner, cf. Coroners Wood 27 *infra*); *Cuttinges* 1637 (pieces of land cut off, *v.* cutting); *Gretalre* 1260 (p) (lit. *Gretabre*), *-olre* c.1280 ('great alder', *v.* grēat, alor); *the green field* 1594; *the Hockle feild* (*medow*), *-Huckell-* 1637; *the Middlefeild* 1637; *Oustreys hill* 1637; *Pescod* 1637 ('peascod'); *the Roughfeild* 1637; *Shurley* 1637 ('bright glade', *v.* scīr², lēah); *Thenale* 1349; *three pence hey & wood* 1637; *Wheto(n)* 1637.

8. PARTINGTON (101–7191)

Partinton 1260 Court (p), *-yn-* 1321 Plea, *-ing-*, *-yng-* 1417, 1443 ChRR

Pertinton 1309 InqAqd, *-yng-* 1422 *AddCh*

'Farm associated with Pearta', from an OE pers.n. *Pearta* and *-ingtūn*. The pers.n. appears only in p.ns., cf. Partney L (DEPN), Pertenhall BdHu 17.

BAILEY LANE.   BRIDGE FM, near a railway bridge.   BROOK FM & HO, named from Red Brook³ 1 34.   CENTRAL FM. CHAPEL LANE, from a Presbyterian Chapel here.   CORONERS WOOD, 1831 Bry, *Corroners Wood* 1838 *TA*, either crown-land or the subject of an inquest, *v.* coroner.   CROSS LANE, *Pow Lane* 1831 Bry.   ERLAM FM, home of the *Erlam* family, cf. Irlam La 39. THE HALL, 1831 Bry, *Partington Hall* 1724 NotCestr.   LANDFIELD FM, 'field in selions', *v.* land.   LOCK LANE, 1842 OS, cf. *Lock Field* 1838 *TA*, probably named from a lock on R. Mersey before the Manchester Ship Canal was built.   MERSEY FM, named from R. Mersey 1 31.   MILLBANK COTTAGES & HALL, *New Houses*, *Millbank House* 1831 Bry, the site of a paper factory (*Paper Mills* 1831 ib), *v.* myln, banke.   MOSS VIEW, *Moss Lane* 1831 Bry, cf. *Moss Field* 1838 *TA*, *v.* mos.   ORFORD HO.   ORTON FM, cf. *Orton Field* 1838 ib.   RIVER LANE (FM), named from R. Mersey 1 31.   WARBURTON LANE, leading to Warburton 34 *infra*. The crossing of Red Brook may be the site of *Dean Bridge* 1618 Sheaf (a 'horse bridge'), *v.* denu 'a valley'.   WOOD LANE, leading to Coroners Wood *supra*.

FIELD-NAMES

The forms are from 1838 *TA* 314 and 1831 Bry.

(a) Alikar; Ash Mdw; Boans; Boar Car (*v.* kjarr); Broken Bank; Broom Hough (*v.* brōm, hōh); Carr (*v.* kjarr); Carrington Hey (*v.* (ge)hæg); Cliffe Bottom & Top (*v.* clif); Common Lane Fd; Cow Heys; Day-, Meadow-, Pool- & Welshman's Loont (from land 'a selion', with dey, mǣd, pōl[1] and Wels(c)h-man); Dobbin Croft ('old-horse croft', from dial. *dobbin* 'an old horse', a pet-form of the pers.n. *Robin*); Farthing Dole (*v.* fēorðung, dāl); Fitch Fd (*v.* ficche); Flash (*v.* flasshe); Gorsy Roughs; Green 1831 (*v.* grēne[2]); Green-, Kiln-, Many-, Marry-, Sandy- & Show Butts (from butte 'a head-land', with grēne[1], cyln, manig, sandig, sceaga, and the ME fem. pers.n. *Mary*); Har-Eye-Dole ('allotment in an old water-meadow', *v.* hār, ēg, dāl); Hemp Croft; Hoole (*v.* hulu); Hough Mere, -Mare (*v.* hōh, (ge)mǣre); Land Rough (*v.* land, rūh); Light Oaks ('light oaks', lēoht); Lords Moss (*v.* hlāford); Lowe (*v.* hlāw); Nethering (*v.* neoðera, -ing[1]); Od(d)croft Hey (*v.* odde, croft, (ge)hæg); Old Rough; Park Fd; Pig Hill; Pulchucks, Pulshacks; Red Leech ('red-' or 'reed-bog', from rēad or hrēod and lǣc(c)); Rock Brown (*v.* roke, brún[2]); Shoemaker Fd; Skier (apparently another instance of the el. OE *scȳr(e) 'a hut, a shelter', which appears in Skier's Hall WRY 1 xi, 112, Scarhouse WRY 2 xi, 292); Small Intake; Three Nook Croft; Three Quarters; Trap Hill; Upland Fd; Wheat Eye (*v.* hwǣte, ēg); Wheel; White Holland (*v.* hwīt, hol[2], land); Womans Croft (*v.* wifmann); Wood Bottoms (*v.* botm); Wych Croft (cf. Red Brook[3] 1 34).

9. RINGWAY (101–8184), formerly included in Hale 23 *supra*.

RINGWAY

> Ringheye 1260 Court, -hey (*Parke*) 1523 ChRR, *Ryng*- 1348 Plea, (*Parke*) c.1490 *Surv*, (*parcum de*) *Ryngehey(e)* 1353 *MinAcct*, 1482 ChRR, -haye 1354 BPR
>
> Ringeye 1260 Court, -ey 1402 (1666) Orm[2], 1584 Cre, -ei 1616 ib, *Ryngey* 1362 BPR, -ay (*Parke*) 1459 ChRR, -aie 1592 Sheaf
>
> Rungeay 1407 ChRR, -ea 1499 ib, -ey 1519 ib, -ei 1617 Cre, -ay 1752 Earw
>
> Rengesy 1407 Orm[2] II 846
>
> Ringwy 1665 Sheaf, -ue 1751 ib, -way 1838 *TA*

'Ring-hedged enclosure', *v.* hring, (ge)hæg or hege, park; presumably a circular, hedged, enclosure similar to Old- and New Pale in the Forest of Delamere, 326 *infra*.

EASTERLANE FM (101–797855), cf. *Eastoe Lane* 24 *supra* (1860 White), and the f.ns. in Hale and Ringway, *the Great, Little & Long Easto(e)*, *Mean & Perrin Eastoes* 1637 Chol, *Long Yeastow* 1838 *TA* 183. The

additions *mean* and *perrin* are (ge)mǣne 'common', and the surname
Perrin in *Perrin's Tenement* 1780 Cre. The series of f.ns. *Easto(e)* is
associated with that part of Ringway township which is adjacent to
Halebarns 24 *supra* and which Bry includes in the east end of Hale
township. It is, therefore, probably identical with *Easthal(e)* 1260
Court (p), Plea, *Estale* 1282 Court (p), 'the east part of Hale', or
'the eastern halh', *v.* ēast, halh, cf. Hale 24 *supra*.

LATHAMHALL, *Lathum* 1387 *Eyre* (p), *-e* 1440 (17) MidCh (p), *Latham*
1409 ChRR (p), perhaps an original name, 'at the barns', *v.* hlaða
(dat.pl. hlaðum), but probably called after a family from Lathom La
122, or some similarly named place.

THORLEY LANE, *Thorlegh* 113 Tab, 1394 *CoLegh*, *-ley* 1395 Orm[2],
(*-near Rungeay*) 1407 ChRR, (*-juxta Rengesy*) 1407 Orm[2] II 846, cf.
Thawley Lane Field 1838 *TA* 34 (14 *supra*), 'thorn-tree glade', *v.* þorn,
lēah. For loss of interconsonantal *-n-*, cf. Thorley Hrt 204, Wt 225.

ULLERWOOD (lost, 101–805838), 1842 OS, (*castellum de*) *Ullerwda*,
Ullerwell 1173 (l12) Earw, Orm[1], [2], *Ullerswode* c.1200 *Fitt*, *Hulreswud*
H2 (17) Orm[2], *Hulerswood* John (17) ib, *Bulriswode* c.1300 *Fitt*,
'Wulfrīc's wood', from the OE pers.n. *Wulfric* and wudu. This wood
formerly extended eastward to Shadow Moss 1 242 in Northern
Etchells and to Oversleyford in Styal 1 230, (*Vulverichelei* 12,
Ulresford 13), *v.* Orm[1] III 307–8. It gave its name to a castle held by
Hamo de Mascy against Henry II, probably sited at Castle Hill *infra*,
cf. another at Castle Hill in Bowdon 16 *supra*, *v.* Orm[1] *loc. cit.* and
1 405n, Orm[2] III 586, Earw I 55, 330, Sheaf[3] 18 (4291). Wulfrīc may
be one of the DB tenants of Butley 1 193, *v.* Tait 213n. The
spelling *Bul-* is discussed 15 *supra*.

ASH FM, *The Ash* 1831 Bry, *v.* æsc 'an ash-tree'. ASH LANE.
ASHLEY RD, *v.* 24 *supra*. BACK LANE. BARROW LANE, *v.* 24
supra. BROADOAK COTTAGES, *Broad Oak* 1831 Bry. BUCKHALL,
1831 ib. BUTTERYHOUSE FM, *Butterey House* 1841 *TAMap*.
BUTTSCLOUGH, *Butts Clough* 1842 OS, 'dell at the butts', *v.* butte,
clōh. CASTLE HILL (101–804837) & MILL (BRIDGE), *le Castell*
Milne 1481 ChRR, *Castill Hill* 1535 Sotheby, *Castell Hill* 1541 Orm[2]
II 775, *Castlehill* 1558 ib, *Castle Milne, Castle Hill* 1585 ib, *v.* castel(l),
hyll, myln, cf. *Ullerwood supra*. The bridge crosses R. Bollin.
CHAPEL LANE, *v.* 24 *supra*. CLAY COTTAGES, *Sinderland Green*
1831 Bry, cf. *Sinderlands Field & Meadow* 1838 *TA* 183, *v.* sundor-

land, grēne², cf. foll., Sinderland 20 *supra*, *Alretunstall* 31 *infra*.
CLAY HO, 1831 Bry, v. clǣg, cf. prec.   CLOUGHBANK FM, *Clews Bank* 1831 ib, v. clōh.   COTTERIL CLOUGH, *Cottrell Clough* 1838 *TA* 183, from the surname *Cottrell* and clōh 'a dell'.   DAVENPORT GREEN (FM), *Davenport Green & Hall* 1831 Bry, from the surname *Davenport* and grēne² 'a green'.   DOBBINETS LANE, v. 32 *infra*.
DOUBLE WOOD.   ETROP GREEN, *& Hollow* 1831 ib, *Athrop* 1535 *Sotheby*, *Athroppe* 1541 Orm² II 775, *Aplethropp* 1558 ib, perhaps from þrop 'outlying farm'.   FAIRYWELL BROOK, v. 1 23.
FIELDS FM.   FIRTREE FM, *Fir Tree* 1831 Bry.   FLAXHIGH COVERT, *Flax Eye* 1838 *TA* 183, 'flax meadow', v. fleax, ēg.   THE GRANGE, *Pinfold* 1831 Bry, -*Farm* 1842 OS, v. pynd-fald.   HALE-BANK, 1842 ib, *Tan Yard* 1831 Bry, v. tan-yard.   HALETOP, 1842 OS, v. topp, cf. Hale 24 *supra*.   HASTY LANE, 1842 ib.   LANE END COTTAGES.   HIGHER & LOWER MAINWOOD, *Mean(e)wood* 1535 *Sotheby*, 1541, 1558 Orm² II 775, *Main Wood* 1831 Bry, 'common wood', v. (ge)mǣne, wudu, cf. Ringway Woods, Outwood Lane *infra*.   MANOR FM, *Old Tan Yard* 1831 Bry, *Tanyard Farm* 1842 OS, cf. Halebank *supra*.   MILL LANE (lost), 1831 Bry, from Ring-way church to Castle Mill.   MOSS HOUSE FM.   OUTWOOD LANE, 1842 OS, *Ringway Outwood* 1831 Bry, 'outlying wood', v. ūt, wudu, cf. Mainwood *supra*, Woodhouse *infra*.   PINFOLD LANE, cf. The Grange *supra*.   PROSPECT HO, 1831 ib.   RINGWAY WOODS (lost), 1842 OS, *Wood House* 1831 Bry, v. wudu, hūs. The site is Ringway Airport.   ROARING GATE FM & LANE, *Roaring Gate* 1842 OS.
ST MARY & ALL SAINTS' CHURCH, *Ringey Chappel* 1666 Orm², *Ringway Chapel* 1838 *TA* 183.   SHAY LANE, v. 25 *supra*.   SUN-BANK WOOD, 1838 *TA* 183, *Dane Bank Wood* 1831 Bry, 'bank which catches the sun', v. sunne; the earlier form is 'bank near a valley', v. denu.   TANYARD FM, cf. Manor Fm, Halebank *supra*.   VICARAGE, *Glebe House* 1842 OS.   WARBURTON GREEN, 1831 Bry, from the surname from Warburton 34 *infra*.   WELLFIELD LANE, v. 25 *supra*.   WELL WOOD.   WHITECARR LANE, *White Carr* 1838 *TA* 183, v. kjarr.   WOODHOUSE FM, 'house at a wood', on Outwood Lane *supra*, v. wudu, hūs.   YEWTREE FM, 1831 Bry.

FIELD-NAMES

The field-names for this township are included in *TA* 183 with those of Hale 25 *supra*.

10. TIMPERLEY (101–7788)

Timperleie 1211–25 Facs (p), *Ti-*, *Tymperleg(h)*, *-legh(e)*, *-le(e)*, *-leg(e)*, *-leigh* c.1290 (17) Orm², 1293 Ch, 1294 CRC, 1296 Plea, 1300 Cl, 1304 Chamb, 1349 Earw, 1350 Chamb

Tympirleg' 1285 Court (p), *-pyr-* 1503 Plea

Tymporlegh, *-ley* 1367, 1389 ChRR, *Timporley* 1724 NotCestr

Tympurlegh 1371 AD, *-ley* 1419 JRL

Tympalegh 1375 Tab

Templey 1549 Pat

'Timber glade', *v.* timber, lēah.

ALRETUNSTALL (lost), John (17) Orm² 1 521, the name of an estate given with *Sunderland* by Hamo de Massey III to Cicely his daughter. *Sunderland* is Sinderland 20 *supra* in Dunham Massey. The lost place is probably the origin of the local surname *Artun-*, *Ardon-*, *Artonstal(l)*, *-e* 1354 BPR *et freq* to 1385 *Eyre*, of Timperley, cf. Bardsley s.nn. *Artin(g)stall*. The p.n. is formed from alor 'an alder-tree', tūn 'a farm, an enclosure' and stall 'a site'. It can be construed either as *Alre-tūnstall*, 'farm-site at an alder', or as *Alretūn-stall* 'site of *Alretūn* (farm at an alder)'. The latter construction involves the identification of *Alretone* DB f.266b with Ollerton 79 *infra*, *v.* Tait 183. The name is of a common type, and Ollerton need not be the only location, cf. Offerton 1 290, Oulton 326 *infra*. *Alretone* DB f.266b was held TRE by Ælward and in 1086 by Hamo de Mascy. So were Ashley, Hale (including Ringway, not named in DB), Bowdon, Dunham Massey (probably including Altrincham, not named in DB) and part of Sinderland in Dunham Massey, all contiguous and in the ancient parish of Bowdon. *Alretone* was probably hereabouts, and *Alretunstall* in Timperley probably represents it, for Timperley, also in Bowdon parish, adjoins Hale, Altrincham, and Sinderland. Cf. also Clay Cottages 29 *supra*.

BLOOMSBURY LANE, *Moss End* 1831 Bry, cf. *Bloomsbury Cottage* 1860 White, probably named after Bloomsbury Mx, cf. also Moss Lane *infra*.   BRANKSOME, cf. capital messuage called *Le Hal(l)e of Bromkes(s)haw(e)* 1562 ChRR, 1578 Orm², *v.* sc(e)aga 'a wood'. For the first el. Professor Löfvenberg suggests an OE *brōmuc* 'a clump of broom', (*v.* brōm, -uc), analogous with such els. as bēosuc 'a tuft of bent-grass', riscuc 'a tuft of rushes, a rush-bed'.   BROOK SIDE & LANE, *Brook Bank & Lane* 1860 White.   CHAPELHOUSES.

CLAY LANE, 1860 ib.   DEANSGATE LANE, 1860 ib, *Deansgate* 1842
OS.   DELAHAYS FM, *Delays* 1831 Bry, *Delay* 1842 OS, *The Delahays*
1838 *TAMap*; the surname form *Delahay* is substituted for a p.n.
perhaps 'dairy pasture(s)', from dey and læs or lēah.   DOBBINETS
LANE, leading to *Dobinets Hole* 1831 Bry, *Dobbins in the Hole* 1838
TAMap, Dobin-heads Hole 1842 OS, cf. *Dobbinet(s) Field* 1838 *TA*, a
place in a hollow near Fairywell Brook, presumably 'Dobbin's place
in a hollow', from the ME pers.n. *Dobbin*, diminutive of *Dobb*, a pet-
form of *Robert*, and hol[1].   FAIRYWELL WOOD, *v.* 13 *supra*.   FOUR
LANE ENDS (lost), 1831 Bry, 1838 *TAMap*, a hamlet in Stockport Rd.
FOX FM.   GRANGE FM.   GREENHEAD FM, *Green Head* 1831 Bry,
'the top end of a green', *v.* grēne[2], hēafod.   GREEN LANE, leading
to prec.   THE GROVE, GROVE COTTAGES & LANE.   HALE RD,
leading to Hale 24 *supra*.   FAR HEYES, HEYES LANE, *del Haghes*
1487 ChRR (p), *The Heys* 1831 Bry, 'the enclosures', *v.* (ge)hæg.
LANDFIELD FM, cf. *Land Field* 1838 *TA*, 'field in selions', *v.* land.
LARKHILL, cf. *Lark Hill Field* 1838 *ib*, *v.* lāwerce.   MANOR FM,
Manor House 1860 White.   MILL COTTAGE.   MOSS LANE, 1860
ib, cf. *Timperley Mosse* 1462 (17) Orm[2], 1842 OS, cf. Bloomsbury
Lane *supra*, *v.* mos, ende[1].   NEWFOUNDWELL, *Newfound Well* 1831
Bry, 'newly-found well', *v.* new-found, wella.   THE NOOK.   OAK
FM, *Mill Green* 1831 ib.   REDBROOK HO, near, and perhaps
named from Fairywell Brook 1 23, *v.* Red Brook[3] 1 34.   RID-
DINGS HALL (FM), 1831 Bry, *Riddyng* 1575 Sheaf, *Ryddinge* 1624
ChRR, *Ruddings* 1637 Sheaf, *Ryddinges* 1659 Earw, *Riddings* 1666
Orm[2], *the Reddings* 1683 Sheaf, 'the clearing(s)', *v.* ryding.   SID-
DALL'S BRIDGE, 1838 *TAMap*, carrying Washway Rd *infra*, over
Sinderland Brook; *Siddall* is a surname, cf. foll.   SMITH'S BRIDGE,
Washway Bridge 1838 *TAMap*, carrying Washway Rd *infra*, over
Timperley Brook; *Smith* is a surname, cf. prec.   STOCKPORT RD,
leading to Stockport 1 294.   SUGAR LANE, 1831 Bry, cf. Sugar
Lane 1 184.   THORLEY LANE, *Holly Lane* 1831 ib, *Horley Lane*
1860 White, unintelligible. The modern form may be due to a def.art.
and analogy with Thorley Lane 29 *supra*.   TIMPERLEY BRIDGE,
crossing Timperley Brook into Altrincham.   TIMPERLEY BROOK,
(Sinderland Brook 22 *supra*), 1842 OS.   TIMPERLEY HALL &
LODGE, 1831 Bry, *Timporley Hall* 1724 NotCestr.   VALE HO, *The
Vale* 1831 Bry, *v.* val 'a vale', cf. *Yhevale infra*.   WASH LANE,
(*Field*) 1838 *TA*, leading to Washway Rd *infra*, *v.* (ge)wæsc.
WASHWAY COTTAGES & RD, cf. prec. and Smith's Bridge *supra*, *v.*

'Watling Street' 1 40.   WATLING GATE, v. geat 'a gateway', cf.
'Watling Street' 1 40.   WOODLANDS PARK, & Bank 1860 White.
WOOD LANE, 1838 TAMap.

FIELD-NAMES

The undated forms are 1838 TA 396. The others are 1401 (17) Orm², 1502
Plea, 1831 Bry.

(a) Altrincham Mdw (cf. Altrincham 7 supra); Backside Fd; Bad Fd; Bank
Croft; Bare Hole; Bean Hey; Bentley (v. beonet, lēah); Black Acre; Black
Rooms (v. rūm¹ 'a space, an allotted plot', usually an apportionment of
moss or common); Bluck Fd; Bow Acre; Bradl(e)y (Fd) (v. brād, lēah);
Breach, Breeches Fd (v. brēc 'a breaking (of land for cultivation)'); Brick
Hill Fd; Brick Kiln Fd; Brook Fd; Broom Fd (v. brōm); Brow Fd; Burnt-
lands; Butty Patch, Butty Batch (v. butty, pacche); Cams Fd; Carr (v. kjarr);
Colley Croft (v. colig); Cow Hey; Crook (v. krókr); Dirty Spot (v. spot 'a
plot of land'); Dove House Fd; Dubbed Hedge Fd (v. dubbed); Dunham
Patch (cf. Dunham Massey 19 supra); Elder Fd; Enclosed Lands; Fall Fd
(v. (ge)fall 'a felling of timber'); Folds; Footway Croft; Granny Fd; Great
Eye Mdw (v. ēg 'an island, a water meadow'); Hams Fd (v. hamm); Hand
Acre; Handkerchief Fd (v. 326 infra); Harlequin Fd (perhaps a piece of land
cut in plots like a patchwork, or having patches of different soils of different
colours, v. harlequin NED); Hemp Pit Fd; Holland Mdw ('low lying land',
v. hol², land); Hollins (v. holegn); Hooley Acre; Hope Ridding Fd (v. hop¹,
ryding); Lady Fd (v. hlǣfdige); Lambs Fd; Leach (v. lǣc(c)); Long Flats;
Long Shutts (v. scēat); Marl(ed) Fd, Old Marl Fd (cf. croftum vocatum
Marled 1502, v. marlede, croft); Marsh Fd; Meer-, Mere Brooks Fd (probably 'boundary brook', v. (ge)mǣre, brōc); Millington Hey (cf. Millington
54 infra); Moat Mdw (v. mote 'a moat'; there is one at Timperley Hall
supra); Morley ('moor clearing', v. mōr¹, lēah); Nether Hag (v. hǫgg, dial.
hag 'a wood for felling'); New Ditch; North Fd (cf. Northhedis n.d. AD iv
320 (p), perhaps 'north enclosure', v. norð, edisc); Oak(s) Croft & Fd; Old
Land Fd (v. ald, land); Old Woman's Croft; Park Fd; Perrin Fd; Pingot (v.
pingot); Rough(s); Rye Fd (1831); Salters Acre (v. saltere 'a salter', æcer);
Saw Pit Fd; Smoothing Iron Fd (probably from its triangular shape); Sprint
Fd; Standy Lands; Stone Pit Fd; Tan Croft; Three Quarters Fd; Town Fd;
Truebys; Underhill (v. under, hyll); Vinegar Fd (no doubt a sour field);
Waugh Riddings (probably for Wall Riddings, cf. Waugh Green for Well
Green 25 supra, v. wælla 'a well, a spring', ryding); Way Fd; Well Croft &
Fd; Wheat Fd (cf. Wheitfild 1502, v. hwǣte, feld); White Gate Fd; Wick
Fd; Widow Croft; Windmill Fd (cf. Milnefild 1502, v. myln, feld); Withen-
shaw (Fd) ('willow copse', v. wiðegn, sceaga).

(b) Alton 1502; Chenall 1401 (17) (Orm² 1 546 describes this as a close in
Timperley, and it seems to be connected, manorially, with Yhevale n.d. AD
(C.5680), but neither form is intelligible. They may be forms for Vale Ho

supra 'the vale' from the def.art. and **val, vale,** but it is not evident that the name is old); *Kylnefild* 1502 (v. **cyln, feld**); *Medelwodfild* 1502 ('(field at) the middle wood' v. **middel, wudu, feld**); *Yhevale* (v. *Chenall supra*).

iv. Warburton

WARBURTON (101–6989) ['wɔːrbərtən]

> *War(e)burgetune, -tone* 1086 DB, *Warburg(h)ton(e)* e15 Orm[2], 1464 LRO Dx (p)
>
> *Wereburtuna* 1150 Chest, *Werburtona super Merse* 1190–1211 *Cott. Nero C III, Werbertune, -ton(a), -burton(a)* 12, l12, e13 (17) Orm[2], *-thon* l13 LRO Dx, *-tun* 1346 VR (p), *-birton* c.1275 *Chol, -breton* c.1536 Leland
>
> *Warburtona supra Merse* l12 Dugd, *-ton* l12 (17) Orm[2], 1340 MidCh (p), *-berton* 1349 (1576), 1404 ChRR, *-byrton* 1393 ib (p)
>
> *Weberton* 1304 Chamb, 1403 Pat (p), *-burton* 1415 ChRR (p)
>
> *Werburgtuna* c.1311 Chest, *-burghton* 1337 *Eyre* (p)
>
> *Werbeton* 1323 Plea
>
> *Werblyton* 1352 BPR (p), *Warbulton* 1439 Cl (p), 1447 Pat (p)

'Wǣrburg's farm', from the OE fem. pers.n. *Wǣrburg,* v. **tūn.** The p.n. appears to have prompted the dedication to St Werburgh (*Wǣrburg,* the Mercian saint and princess, d.700–707) of the chapel (now St Werburg's church) of a convent of Premonstratensian canons established here in the twelfth century, and later incorporated in Cockersands Abbey La, cf. *Sanctae Werburgae (Werberge) de Werburton (-bertun) et canonicis Premonstratensis ordinis ibidem (deo servientibus)* and *Sancte Werburge et capelle sue de Werburt'* R1 or John Orm[2], *capella de Werburton* 1271 Orm[2], cf. also Abbey Croft *infra.* It has also suggested a connection with the place *æt Weard byrig* 915 ASC(C) fortified, with Runcorn 176 *infra,* by Æþelflǣd, lady of the Mercians, v. Sheaf[3] 39 (8445). It might be convenient to find that place in this district, cf. F. T. Wainwright, 'North-West Mercia, 871–924', LCHS 94 3–55, and my remarks in Saga-Book XIV 313. Warburton is beside the Mersey, the old frontier between Mercia & Northumbria. Of course, the *tūn* might not have been near the *burh,* or alternatively the unattractive site might have been abandoned in favour of Thelwall 138 *infra* fortified in 919, and the disused works, which need not have been massive, may then have been regarded as a tūn 'enclosure', v. **burh-tūn.** Cf. Burford Lane 38 *infra.* However, there is no record of archæological evidence of a

fortification here, and the forms *Wareburge-*, *Werebur-* indicate the
pers.n. *Wǣrburg* rather than the p.n. *Weardburh*.

BACK LANE.   BARNS LANE, 1842 OS, *v.* 20 *supra*.   BENT FM
& LANE, *Bent House* 1831 Bry, *v.* beonet 'bent-grass'.   BIRCH FM,
cf. *Birch Croft* 1837 *TA*, *v.* birce.   OLD BOLLIN, a water-course,
formerly the course of R. Bollin 1 15 *v.* ald.   BOXEDGE FM,
'box hedge', *v.* box, hecg.   BRIDGE FM, not near a bridge.   BROOK
FM & HO, named from Red Brook³ 1 34.   CALDWELL BROOK,
v. 1 17.   CARRGREEN, *Car(r) Green* 1831 Bry, 1842 OS,
'marsh green', *v.* kjarr.   CHURCH HO.   GATEHOUSE FM.
HEATHLANDS FM.   HOLLINS FERRY, *Hollin-* 1831 Bry, named from
Hollins Green La 95.   HOLMES COTTAGE, *The Holmes* 1837 *TA*,
v. holmr 'a water-meadow'.   JACK HEY GATE FM, *Jack Hay* 1837
ib, *v.* jack.   LANDS END FM.   LANE-END.   LIGHT HO.
LONGRIDGE COTTAGE & FM, not near each other, *v.* lang, hrycg.
MATCHINGTON FM.   MIDLANDS FM.   MILL DAM.   MOSS
BROW (FM), LANE & WOOD, *Moss Brow & Bank* 1831 Bry, named
from *Whitehead or Warburton Moss* 1831 ib, cf. Whitehead's Bottom
Moss 19 *supra*.   ORCHARDHOUSE FM.   OVERTOWN FM.   PAD-
DOCKLAKE FM, probably 'frog stream', *v.* padduc, lacu.   PADDOCK
LANE, *v.* pearroc.   PARKGATE FM, cf. *Park Gate Meadow* 1837 *TA*,
cf. Warburton Park *infra*.   PETERSHOUSE FM, *Oughty Wells* 1831
Bry.   POOLHEAD FM, cf. *Pool Head* 1837 *TA*, 'the top end of a
pool', *v.* hēafod.   REED HO.   TOWNFIELD LANE, cf. *Town Field*
1837 *TA*.   WARBURTON BRIDGE, 1618 Sheaf, crossing R. Bollin.
WARBURTON LANE, *Common Lane* 1842 OS.   WARBURTON MILL,
1842 ib.   WARBURTON PARK, *-Parke* 1706 *Dep*.   WHITELAKE
FM, *White Lake* 1837 *TA*, *v.* hwīt, lacu.   WIGSEY FM & LANE,
Broad Eye Lane 1831 Bry, *Wigsey Farm, Broad Eye (Banks)* 1837
TA, 'broad island or water-meadow', *v.* brād, ēg. *Wigsey* may also
contain ēg.   WITTENSPITHALL, cf. *Wittins Field* 1837 *ib*, *v.* wiðegn,
pytt, hall.

FIELD-NAMES

The undated forms are 1837 *TA* 412. Of the others 13, 1465, 1819 are Orm²,
1831 Bry, 1833 *TAMap*.

(*a*) Abbey Croft (1819, *v.* abbaie, traditionally supposed to be the eight
bovates of land granted, t. John, by Adam de Dutton to the canons of St
Werburgh, which were relinquished, m13, by the abbot of Cockersand, *v.*
Orm² 1 567, 575–6, cf. Warburton *supra*); Ackers (*v.* æcer); Backside; The

Bank; Boat Fd (*v.* bāt); Bows Ridding (*v.* **ryding**); Brickiln Fd; Broad Acre; Broad Moss Fd; Byrons or Bryn Yard; Cat Tail Fd (*v.* **cat(t)**, tægl); The Clough, Clough Brow (*v.* clōh, brū); Coney Grave (*v.* coningre); The Coppy (*v.* copis); Corn Hill; Crooked Acre; Dam Fd; Depshaw or Deptear; Earlams (from a surname from Irlam La 39); Fickey Fd; Floodalls; The Folly (*v.* folie); Garland Brow 1831; Gold Croft & Fd; Guttershall; Hanging North Fd (*v.* hangende); The Hill; Hob Heath ('tufty heath', *v.* hobb(e), hǣð); Hodge Ridding (*v.* hocg, ryding, cf. *Hodg Croft* 1 58); Hop Pickow, Hoppikel Mdw ('hop croft', *v.* hoppe, pichel); Howe's Head; Irons Mdw (*v.* hyrne); Kiln Fd; Lascar Hill; Long Earth & Loont (*v.* erð, land); Lords Mdw (1833, *v.* hlāford); Marl(ed) Fd; Mather Croft ('madder croft', *v.* maðra); Megshut; Mill Fd & Hill (cf. Warburton Mill *supra*); The Moor(s), Moor Hill, Loont(s) & Mdw (*v.* mōr¹, land); Mount (*The-* 1831); New Hay, -Hey; Nick Acre; Odds Riding Mdw; Pale Fd (*v.* pale); Picton Fd; Pill Fd; Pingott (*v.* pingot); Pit Green & Pingle (*v.* pingel); Platt Fd (*v.* plat¹); Podmaster Mdw; Round Hey; Rushes; Sand Fd; Shippon Flatt; Smellers; Smiddleshaw; Spark Fd (*v.* spearca); Stock(ey) Fd (*v.* stocc, -ig³); Swine Hay (*v.* swīn¹, (ge)hæg); The Three Quarters; Twig Bank Cover 1831 (*v.* twigge, banke, cf. *Beuernes infra*); Ware Butty Mdw ('butty meadow near a weir', *v.* wer, butty); Wet Fd; White Acre, White Rushes; The Wild Acre (*v.* wilde); Yieldnow, Yield Rough (*v.* helde, cnoll, rūh).

(*b*) *Beuernes inter Limme et Werberton* 13, *Buernes* 1465 (perhaps 'beaver headland', *v.* beofor, ness, alluding to the spit of land between Mersey and Bollin at Twig Bank *supra*).

v. Lymm

The part lying between the Manchester Ship Canal and R. Mersey is now included in La.

LYMM (101–6887) [lim]

> *Lime* 1086 DB, 12 *Dow* (p), *Lyme* c.1200 Whall *et freq*, *Lyma* 12 (17) Sheaf, *Lima* 13 Orm²
>
> *Limme* 1194 Facs, *Lymme* e13 Whall (p) *et freq*, *Limma* l12 Orm², *Lymma* 13 Bark, *Lymm* 1635 ChRR, *Limm* 1724 NotCestr
>
> *Lymmya* 1270 Sheaf
>
> *Lym* 13 Whall (p), *Lim* 1680 Sheaf
>
> *Lynm* 1496 Sheaf
>
> *Lynne* 1549 Pat
>
> *Limb* 1673 AddCh

'The torrent', *v.* hlimme (cf. OE *hlimman* 'to resound'), from the noise of Slitten Brook 1 35 in its course in a ravine through the middle of the village, cf. The Dingle *infra*. *Limmya* probably represents 'the Lymm stream', with ēa suffixed to the p.n. Cf. DEPN s.n.

Street-Names. Pepper St., 1839 *TA*, 1842 OS, perhaps associated with William *Pepur'* 1356 *Indict* (p), cf. Pepper St. (Chester) 327 *infra*.

Booth's Hill & Lane formerly Lymm Booths (101–675870)
> *Lym(m)e Bothes* 1284–5 ChF, Orm², *Lym(m)bothes* 1377 *Eyre*,
> *-Bothez* 1538 Plea, *-Boothes* 1639 ChRR, *Lymm Booths* 1831
> Bry, 1860 White, *Lim(m)e-Bo(o)th(e)s* 1666 Orm², (*Over-*) 1666
> ib, (*Higher-*) 1700 Sheaf
> *le Bothes* 1347 Plea (p), *Booths Lane* 1831 Bry, *Booth's Hill* 1860
> White

'The booths', *v.* bōth, probably referring to herdsmen's huts at a pasturage, cf. Somerford Booths 1 63, Knutsford Booths 76 *infra*.

Broomedge, 1831 Bry, *Brown Egge* 1519 Plea, *-Edge* 1666 Orm², probably associated with *Bromhull* c.1220 Tab, *le Brom* 1289 Court (p), 1363 Plea, (*le*) *Brome* 1489, 1528 ChRR, *Broome* 1559 Orm², *Brom* 1639 ChRR, 'the broomy place', 'the hill growing with broom', *v.* brōm, hyll, ecg.

Cherry Hall & Lane, *Red House*, *Cherry Lane* 1831 Bry, *Cherry Lane Farm* 1842 OS, perhaps the location of *Cheretrehurst(e)* 1434, 1494 Orm², *Cheri-* 1452 *CoLegh* (p), *-y-* 1522 Orm², *Cheritrihurst* 1553 Pat, *Cheare-*, *Chearitre(e)hurst* 1626, 1639 ChRR, *Cherrytree-Hurst* 1666 Orm², *Cherytree* 1543 ib, 'wooded hill at a cherry-tree', or 'growing with cherry-trees', *v.* cheri(e), trēow, hyrst.

Foxley Hall, Ho & Lodge, *Foxleg(h)* 1272, 1302 Plea (p), *-leia*, *-ley* 13 Tab (p), 1489 ChRR (p), 'fox clearing', *v.* fox, lēah, cf. Higher Lane *infra*.

(Lt.) Heatley, 1842 OS, *Hey-*, *Hayteley* 1525, 1528 ChRR, 1559 Orm², *Hae-*, *Haitley* 1531 Plea, 1542 ChRR, *Heat(e)ley* 1666 Orm², *Heatley Heath*, *Little Heartley* 1831 Bry, 'heath clearing', *v.* hǣð, lēah.

Oughtrington (Hall) (101–695870) [ˈuːtriŋtən]
> *Hughtrington* John, 1345 Orm², *Uughtrynton* 1354 *Eyre*, *Ughtrin(g)-ton*, *-yn(g)-* 1354 Orm², 1357 ib, 1397 Plea, 1409 JRL, *Hughtrenton* 1629 Sheaf, *Uctrington* 13 Tab
> *Hutt(e)rin(g)ton(e)* 13 Orm², Tab, l13 AD, *Uttrington* 1296 Plea, *Uthrinton* 1353 *Eyre*

Hoctrington 13 Tab (p), *Oghtrynton* 1409 JRL, *Uoghtrynton* 1539
Plea, *Oughtreynton* 1544 ib, *Oughtrington* 1578 ChRR, *-Hall* 1831
Bry

Utrynton 1516 *ChEx*
Ughterton 1574 Sheaf
Outrington Hall 1842 OS

'Ūhtrǣd's farm', from the OE pers.n. *Ūhtrǣd* and *-ingtūn*.

REDDISH (LANE), 1831 Bry, *Ruedis* 13 *AddCh*, *Rediche* 1511 Plea,
Red(d)is(s)he, *-ysshe* 1532 Mere (p), 1533 *LRO* Dx (p), 1539, 1544
Plea, *Redysh* 1613 Sheaf, *Reddish* 1666 Orm², 'rough enclosure', *v.*
rūh, edisc. The later form of the name has been influenced by the
p.n. Reddish La 30 (*v.* hrēod, dīc), the surname of a family owning
land in Grappenhall and Lymm, cf. Reddishhall 141 *infra*, *v.* Orm² I
584n, 596, II 846.

STATHAM (LANE, LODGE & POOLS), *Stathum* (*in Lymme*) 1284–5 ChF
et freq, *-am* 1349 (1576) ChRR (p), (*-wthyn Lyme*) 1677 Sheaf, (*-Eye*,
-Lodge, *-Pool*) 1831 Bry, (*-Ees*, *Ees Lane*) 1842 OS, *-om(e)* 1486
MinAcct, 1551 Orm², (*-More*) 1540 *AddCh*, *-on* 1532 Plea, 'at the
river-banks; at the landing-places', *v.* stæð (dat.pl. staþum; cf. stǫð,
the cognate ON el. preferred by EPN). *Statham Eye*, *-Ees*, *Ees Lane*
were the marshes and water-meadows beside R. Mersey, and the lane
leading to them, *v.* ēg, mōr¹.

AGDENBRIDGE HO, AGDEN LANE (FM), AGDENBROW FM, cf. 42 *infra*.
BARSBANK FM & LANE, *Bass Bank* 1831 Bry, *Barrs Bank* 1839 *TA*,
Yeld Bank or Baras Bank 1839 *ib*, named from a turnpike toll-bar,
v. barre, barras, cf. Yellbrow *infra*.   BEECHWOOD HALL, 1860
White.   BIRCHBROOK LODGE.   BOARDED BARN FM, *Boarded
Barns* 1831 Bry, *v.* borded.   THE BONGS, *Bongs Wood* 1842 OS, *v.*
banke, cf. 46 *infra*.   BRADSHAW'S LANE, cf. *Far*, *Further & Near
Bradshaw(s)* 1839 *TA*, 'broad copses', *v.* brād, sceaga.   BURFORD
LANE (FM), 1831 Bry, cf. *Burfords*, *Burford Lane Croft* 1837 *TA*,
also Mill Lane *infra*. Burford Lane (6″) extends 101–705860 to
698875, but in 1842 OS from 705860 to 703885, that is, to Warburton
Bridge on R. Bollin. The evidence is not sufficient to prove a derivation 'ford at, or to, a stronghold', from burh and ford, which would
be relevant to the location of *Weardburh* at Warburton, *v.* 34 *supra*.
BUTCHERSFIELD BIGHT, *Butcherfield Bight* 1842 OS, a bend of R.

Mersey at Butchersfield in Rixton La, *v.* **byht.**   CAMSL(E)Y (FM
& LANE), *Kemsley Lane* 1831 Bry, *Kemsley, Cansley* 1839 *TA.*
CHURCH GREEN.   CROFT.   CROUCHLEY FM & LANE, *Crouchley
Lane* 1831 Bry, *-Farm* 1842 OS, perhaps 'clearing near a cross', *v.*
crūc[3], lēah.   BOTTOM & TOP DAM, *Higher & Lower Dam* 1839
TA, cf. *Dam Pool* 1831 Bry, the mill-dams of Lymm Corn Mill, *v.*
damme.   DAIRY FM, *Dairy House* 1831 Bry.   DANESBANK HO,
Dane Bank 17, 1718 Orm[2], 'hillside overlooking a valley', *v.* denu,
banke, cf. Slitten Brook 1 35.   DEANSGREEN, 1831 Bry, *Dean
Green* 1842 OS, 'green at a valley', *v.* denu, grēne[2], cf. 47 *infra.*
THE DINGLE, a deep, narrow valley, *v.* dingle, cf. Lymm *supra.*
DITCHFIELD'S BRIDGE, cf. Ditchfield's Covert 47 *infra.*   EAGLE
BROW, 1860 White, cf. *Eagle Croft* 1839 *TA.*   FIELDHOUSE.   FOX
HOW.   GAILEY WOOD, 1839 *ib,* *Gaily-* 1831 Bry, *Galee-* 1842 OS,
v. gagel, lēah.   GLEBE FM.   GRANTHAM'S BRIDGE & LODGE, cf.
Grantham Wood Field 1839 *TA.*   HELSDALE BROOK & WOOD,
Ellsdale (Wood) 1839 *ib, v.* dæl[1].   HIGHERHOUSE FM, *Higher House*
1831 Bry.   HIGHER LANE, 1666 Orm[2], *Foxley Lane* 1831 Bry, cf.
Foxley *supra.*   HILLTOP, 1831 ib.   HOWSHOOTS, *Houghshots or
Howshoots* 1831 ib, 'corners of land at a hill', *v.* hōh, scēat.   KAY
LANE (BROOK), *v.* 47 *infra.*   LONGBUTT LANE, 1831 ib, cf. *Long
& Short Butts* 1839 *TA, v.* butte.   LYMM EYES, *Eylond* 13 *AddCh,*
the lym heys 1637 *Chol, Lower Eye* 1731 White, *Lymm Eye* 1839 *TA,*
'water meadow(s)', *v.* ēg, ēg-land; beside R. Mersey.   LYMM HALL,
1831 Bry.   LYMMHAY LANE, *Lymm Hey* 1839 *TA, v.* (ge)hæg.
MASSEY BROOK FM & LANE, *Massey Brook House* 1831 Bry, *Massey
Brook* (a hamlet) 1860 White, *Tan Yard* 1839 *TA,* named from
Massey Brook 1 31.   MILL LANE (101–704874 to 703885),
Burford Lane 1842 OS; leading to Warburton Mill, cf. Burford Lane
supra.   MODEL FM.   MORLEY FM, cf. *Morley (Meadow)* 1839
TA, 'moor pasture', *v.* mōr[1], lēah.   NARROW LANE.   NEW FM.
NEWFIELD HO, 1831 Bry, cf. *(the) Newfeild* 1637 *Chol, v.* nīwe, feld.
NEWHEY'S PLANTATION, *New Hay(s), -Hey* 1839 *TA, the two new heis*
1637 *Chol, v.* nīwe, (ge)hæg.   THE NOOK.   OXHEYS, 1831 Bry,
v. oxa, (ge)hæg.   PENNYHILL.   PLATT FM, *Heatley Plat* 1831
ib, *v.* plat[2] 'a level spot', cf. Heatley *supra.*   POOL FM & LANE,
named from Statham Pools *supra.*   RAVEN BANK.   REDBANK
BRIDGE, 1831 ib, *v.* rēad, banke.   RUSHGREEN, 1831 ib, *v.* risc,
grēne[2].   RUSHGREEN FM, *Parkgate Ho* 1831 ib, cf. prec., *v.* park,
geat.   SANDY LANE, (-*Field*) 1839 *TA.*   SCHOLARS BRIDGE,

Scholar Bridge 1839 *ib*, perhaps from skáli 'a shieling', as Scholar Green 308 *infra*. SPRINGBANK, SPRING LANE, *v*. spring. SUTCH LANE, *The-* 1831 Bry, cf. *Such* 1839 *TA*, *v*. sīc 'marshland stream'. OLD TANNERY HO. WARRINGTON LANE, 1831 Bry. WETGATE, 1831 ib, 'damp pasture-allotment', *v*. wēt, gata. WHITBARROW HO & LANE, *Whydebarrowe* 1538 Plea, *Whitbarrow Lane* 1831 Bry, 'white grove', *v*. hwīt, bearu, cf. *Whitbarrows Field & Sparth* 1839 *TA*, *v*. sparð. WHITEFIELD, 1839 *TA*, *Whitfield Cottage* 1831 Bry, *v*. hwīt, feld. WILDERSMOOR (FM & HALL), *Wildsmoor Farm* 1831 ib, *Wilders Moor* 1842 OS, 'deer's moor', *v*. wilder (wīld-dēor), mōr[1], cf. Wilderspool 145 *infra*. YELLBROW, *Yield Brow* 1831 Bry, *Heald, Heald Browfield, Yeld Bank or Baras Bank* 1839 *TA*, *v*. helde 'a slope, a declivity', brū, banke, cf. Barsbank *supra*. YEWTREE FM, 1842 OS, *-House* 1831 Bry.

FIELD-NAMES

The undated forms are 1839 *TA* 245. Of the others c.1220 (17) is Tab, 1284[1] ChF, 1284[2] ChFine, 1287 Court, 1352 *Eyre*, 1356 *Indict*, 1474, 1536[2] Orm[2], 1524, 1578 ChRR, 1536 Dugd, 1538 Plea, 1538[2] *AOMB* 399, 1547 *MinAcct*, 1555 *CoLegh*, 1560, 1751 Sheaf, 1637, 1668 *Chol*, 1721 White, 1739 *LRMB* 264, 1831 Bry and 1842 OS.

(a) Acre; Alder Hey; Alley Brook Hey; Apple Fd; Ash Acre & Butts (*v*. æsc, butte); Backside; Ban Greaves (*v*. banke, græfe); Bank Fd; Barrister; Bay Fd; Bean Hay (*v*. bēan, (ge)hæg); Bent Hole (*v*. beonet, hol[1]); Birch Heys; Bollen-, Bollin Mdw (cf. R. Bollin 1 15); Booty-, Bouty-, Bouting Hough (*Bultynghalff* 1524, perhaps 'hough where boulting is done', from *boulting* 'a sifting of grain, flour, etc.' and halh 'a nook, a corner', cf. Grindleton *infra*); Boozey Croft (*v*. bōsig); Breech (*v*. brēc); Brick (Kiln) Fd; Bridge Foot (*v*. fōt); Brierly Loont (*v*. brēr, lēah, land); Britch Brow (*v*. brēc); Brook(e)field; Browfield (*v*. brū); Brutches (cf. Breech, Britch *supra*, *v*. bryce); Buck Foot; Bullar; Burnt-, Brunt Heath ('burnt heath', *v*. brende[2]); Butry Mdw (*v*. butere, -ig[3]); Butty Croft (*v*. butty); Bydells Mdw (from the family *Boydell*, landowners here); Far, Middle & Near Byfin (*Boyfennes* 1284, 'boy's or servant's marshes', *v*. boi(a), fenn); Capel Fd (*v*. kapall); Chaise (*v*. sc(e)aga); Chrimbers Mdw (cf. *le Crymbe* 171 *infra*); Clan-, Clunbrook (perhaps 'clean brook', *v*. clǣne); Clay Holt (*v*. holt); Collicks (cf. *the collocke acre* 1637); Cray Mdw; Cross Bank 1831 ('hillside at a cross' *v*. cros); Delf (*v*. (ge)delf); Dig Lake ('ditch stream', *v*. dīc, lacu); Dob Hey (*v*. daube); Door Tee (a T-shaped field in front of the door of a farm-house, *v*. duru, cf. Tee Fd 71 *infra*); Broad & Lower Eye (*v*. ēg 'an island, a water-meadow'); Farthings (*The-* 1637, *v*. fēorðung); Fetter Pasture; Fry Fd; Fid(d)le(r)s Croft (*The Fidlers Croft* 1637, 1668, from the occupational name *Fiddler* (ME *fithelare*) 'a fiddler'); Flax Mdw (*Flaskmedowe* 1524, *v*. flask 'a swamp'); Fool Such ('foul drain', *v.* fūl, sīc); Gap Fd (*v.* gap); Green Hey(s) (*Grene Heyie* 1555, 'green enclosure', *v.* grēne[1], (ge)hæg); Green Lane; Grindleton (perhaps 'mill-stone yard', from tūn with OE **grindel* 'a thing for grinding with', as in ME *grindel-stane* 'a grind-stone', cf. Grindleford Db 94; but Professor Löfvenburg suggests that the first el. may be OE *grindel* 'bar, bolt', in the plural 'grating, hurdle', and the p.n. might mean 'an enclosure made of hurdles', cf. Staverton Nth 28–9); Guild Heys (*v.* gildi, (ge)hæg); Gutters Brook (*v.* goter); Hatchell Fd; Hatchet Fd; Hatchwood Fd (*v.* hæc(c)); Hawker(s); Hayes Fd (*v.* (ge)hæg); Hemp Yard (cf. *Hempeyeard* c.1220 (17), 'hemp enclosure', *v.* hænep, geard); Henley Hill; Hob Hey (*v.* hobb(e)); Holes; Holloway Side (*v.* holh or hol[2], weg, sīde); Horns Moor; House of Office Fd (a field adjoining a lavatory, *v. house*[1] 14b, *office* 2c NED); Hullarts; Hulme (*v.* hulm); Hungry Croft (*v.* hungrig); Ingo; Intake; Kadles (cf. keddle-dock); Kiln Mdw; Kitchen Croft; Knowl Hatch & Rough (*v.* cnoll, hæc(c), rūh); Lady Acre (*v.* hlæfdige); Lapwing Fd; Lock Fd; Long Loons (*v.* land); Longshaw (*v.* sceaga); Loom (*v.* loom); Loont (*the lount* 1637, *v.* land); Madbrook (*v.* Mag Brook 1 30); Madge Hole (*v.* madge); Magistrate; Main Hay ('demesne enclosure', *v.* main); Manyways; Marklands (*v.* mearc, land); Marl(d) Earth (*v.* marle(de), eorðe); Masons Stones; May Lane Fd; Meadow Brow; Mere Mdw; Mickley Hill (1831, a tumulus at 101–679890 on the bank of R. Mersey; *Mickley* may be 'great water-meadow', *v.* micel, ēg, hyll); Middup(s) (*v.* mid, hop[1], cf. 1 238); Mizz(es), Mizzey (*the Mizeys* 1751, *v.* misy); Moor (cf. *Lymmore, Litelmore* 1524, *v.* lȳtel, mōr[1], cf. Lymm *supra*); Moss; Nameless Fd; Newarth, New Earths (*v.* eorðe or erð); Nickle Yard; Nimlow; North Carr (*v.* kjarr); Ocar, Okers (*v.* āc, kjarr); Oldgreave 1739 (*Oldegreve juxta Lymme* 1536, 1538, 1547, 1560, *Oldgreve-* 1536[2], 'the old wood', *v.* ald, græfe); Old Hough (*the* 1637, *v.* halh); Old Shoots (*v.* scēat); Ollers Hey (*v.* alor, (ge)hæg); Other Bit; Owls Croft; Parsons Yard (*v.* persone, geard); Pilley Fd (*v.* pīll, ēg); Pine Heys; Pinfold (*v.* pynd-fald); Pingot (*v.* pingot); Puddle Docks; Quaker Fd; Quillet (*v.* quillet(t)); Radley Hill (1831); Rags Loont; Ridding; Ridgeway (from the local landowning family *Ridgway,* Orm[2] 1580); Rough; Roundabout (*v.* 327 *infra*); Round Fd (cf. *Round Hey* 1721); Rush(e)y Fd; Sand(y) Fd; Shatelees Mdw ('meadow edged with copses', *v.* sceagiht, læs, cf. *Shaghteles* in Barrow 327 *infra*); Sheep Hey(s); Shoulder Mutton (shaped like a shoulder of mutton); Shut Fd (*v.* scēat); Slack (*v.* slakki); Snail Fd; Snape (*v.* snæp); Sour Moors (*v.* sūr, mōr[1]); Sparks (*v.* spearca); Sparth(s) (*v.* sparð); Spit Jack; Stanfield (*v.* stān); Stone Delf Fd (*v.* (ge)delf); Sun Croft (*v.* sunne); Sway Bridge Mdw; Tan Yard Fd (*v.* tanyard); Tarsey; Tenter Croft (*v.* tentour); Thrasher Fd; Timber Brow (*v.* timber, brū); Tom Hey (*v.* toun); Tongue Shaft (*v.* Tongue Sharp 1 162); Town Croft; Turner; Weir Ley & Yard; Whatcroft, Wheatcroft (*v.* hwæte); Whiteledge ('white bog', *v.* hwīt, læc(c)); Wickens Croft (*v.* cwicen); Windmill Fd (site of a windmill 1831 Bry, 1842 OS).

(b) *Balewestall* c.1220 (17) (*v.* stall); *Bokenhale* 1356 (p) ('nook growing with beech-trees', *v.* bōcen, halh); *Boro Croft* 1637 (*v.* burg, croft); *del Brokes* 1287 (p) (*v.* brōc); *Doo Parke* 1474, 1524, *le Doe Park* 1538 (*v.* dā, park); *the Ether loundes* 1637 (*v.* land); *Harpisforth* 1578 (*v.* ford 'a ford'); *Kerkheth* 1637 ('church heath', *v.* kirkja, hǣð); *Lumbo Lane* 1668 (*v.* lumber); *le Marchey* 1524 (*v.* mearc or mersc, ēg or (ge)hæg); *Meddebroc* c.1220 (17) ('middle brook', *v.* mid, brōc); *Oldfield* c.1220 (17) (*v.* ald, feld); *Ravenhurst* 1524 ('raven's wood', *v.* hræfn, hyrst); *Wilmundismor* 1284[2], *Wol-* 1284[1], *Wylmundesmor* 1352 ('Wilmund's moor', from the OE pers.n. *Wilmund* and mōr[1]); *Wyndhylle* 1434 (*v.* wind[1], hyll).

vi. Bowdon & Rostherne

The two townships Agden and Bollington were each in the two parishes of Bowdon and Rostherne. In terms of physical geography they belong with Rostherne parish, being south of R. Bollin.

1. AGDEN (101–7287)

Acton H3 (17) Orm[2], 1287 Court, (*-juxta Lyme*) 1527 ChRR
Aketon 1270 (17) Orm[2] (p), c.1300 *Dav* (p), 1328, 1330 *CoLegh*
Akedon' 1346 *CoLegh*, *-den* 1391 Orm[2] (p)
Aghton 1431 Pat (p), *Agton* 1448 ChRR
Agden 1434 Tab, 1519 ChRR, *-don* 1498 ib
Ageton 1448 ChRR

'Oak farm', *v.* āc, tūn. In this name *-t-* was voiced to *-d-*, perhaps through confusion with dūn 'a hill', and the preceding consonant (*-k-*) was voiced by assimilation, cf. Agden 325 *infra*, also Acton 146, 325 (2x) *infra*, Agden BdHu 268.

WOOLSTENCROFT, (mansio de) *W(o)lstan(e)scroft* 1330 *CoLegh*, 1335, 1376 *Eyre*, 1436 ChRR, *Wolstancroft, Wolston Croft(e)* 1527 ChRR, c.1602 *Chol, Woolston Croft* 1842 OS, *Woolstercrofte* 1549 Pat, *Ousingcroft farm* 1669 Orm[2], *Ouzencroft Farm* 1831 Bry, 'Wulfstān's croft', from the OE pers.n. *Wulfstān* and croft.

AGDEN BRIDGE, 1831 Bry.   AGDEN BROOK (R. Bollin), 1842 OS. AGDENBROOK FM, *Brook House* 1831 Bry, named from Agden Brook. AGDEN BROW, 1842 OS.   AGDEN HALL, 1831 Bry.   AGDEN LANE, *Woods Lane* 1842 OS, cf. 46 *infra*.   AGDEN PARK.   BOOTHBANK FM & LANE, *v.* Boothbank 55 *infra*.   NEWROAD COTTAGE.

FIELD-NAMES

The undated forms are 1839 *TA* 2 (Bowdon part), 1848 *TA* 6 (Rostherne part). The others are 13 *LRO* Dx, 1330 *CoLegh*, 1668 *Chol*, 1831 Bry.

(a) Alder Fd; Blazes Fd (*v.* blesi); Bollin Mdws (named from R. Bollin 1 15); Boozing Pasture (*v.* boosing); Lower & Upper Braddow (*the Higher & Lower Bradwalles* 1668, 'broad streams', *v.* brād, wælla); Brook Hey (cf. *Broche Hayes* 1668, 'brook enclosures', *v.* brōc, (ge)hæg); Cross Fd & Mdw (*v.* cros); Cut Fd (*v.* cut); Dirty Mdw; Eight Butts (*v.* eahta, butte); Footway Fd; Glaves Fd; Hasty; Hill Hay (*-e* 1668, 'hill enclosure', *v.* hyll, (ge)hæg); Hole Acre; Long Slip (*v.* lang, slipe); Marl Fd; Meadow Lane 1831; Mode Yard ('mould enclosures', *v.* molde, geard); The Mosses (cf. *bruer' que vocatur Aketonmosse* 1330, *v.* mos); Parlour Fd (*v.* parlur); Plumb Tree Croft; Push Ploughed Fd (*v.* push-plough); Robin Hood Hay; Roe Barn Fd; Sand (Hole) Fd; Smithy Fd; Stone Delph (*v.* stān, (ge)delf); Town Fd; Twenty Shilling Fd (presumably from the rent); Wood Fd.

(b) *Burnt Haye* 1668 ('burnt enclosure', *v.* brende[2], (ge)hæg); *the great & litle Eastof(f)e* 1668 (perhaps from eāst and hōh); *Lefsies Croft* 13 ('Lēofsige's croft', from the OE pers.n. *Lēofsige* and croft); *the Long & Short Lunts* 1668 (*v.* land); *New Haye* 1668 (*v.* nīwe, (ge)hæg); *Roweyes meadowe neere Agden Mill* 1668 ('rough islands or water-meadows', *v.* rūh, ēg); *the Russhe Acre* 1668 ('rush plot', *v.* risc, æcer).

2. BOLLINGTON (101–7286)

Bolintun 13 Tab, *-ton(a)* c.1222 (1580) Sheaf, c.1233 Dow, *-yn-* 1312 Plea *et freq*, (*-iuxta Dunham (Mascy)*) 1382 ib, 1408 ChRR, (*-iuxta Akedon'*) 1431 JRL, *Bollinton* 1320 Mere
Bolington (iuxta Dunham) 1287 Court, *-yng-* 1353 BPR, *Bollyngton* 1549 Pat, *-ing-* 1584 ChRR *et freq*

'Farm by R. Bollin', from the r.n. Bollin 1 15 *supra*, *v.* tūn. Cf. Bollington 1 187. Bollington adjoins Dunham Massey and Agden 19, 42 *supra*.

NEW BRIDGE, *-Bridg* 1618 Sheaf, cf. *pons de Bolyn* 1353 *MinAcct*; crossing R. Bollin on the boundary of Bollington, Rostherne, Bowdon and Dunham Massey. NEW FM. NEWFIELD COVERT, 1831 Bry. REDDY LANE, 1842 OS, *Ready Lane (Field)* 1848 *TA* 58, perhaps 'reedy lane', from hrēodig and lane. REID'S BANK, *Reeds Cover* 1831 Bry. SPODEGREEN, *Spodes Green* 1831 ib, *Spords Green* 1842 OS, from the surname *Spowde, Spoude* 1488, 1489 ChRR (p) and grēne[2] 'a green'. STAMFORD FM, after the earls of Stamford & Warrington, landowners here, cf. the Stamford Arms Inn so-named 1831 Bry. SUTT'S HOLLOW, *Scots Cover* 1831 Bry, *The Sutts* 1842 OS. This is the course of Stanney Brook 1 35. The name may be a corruption of *suche* for sīc 'a watercourse'. YEWTREE FM, *Yew Tree House* 1860 White.

FIELD-NAMES

The undated forms are 1839 *TA* 59 (Bowdon part), 1848 *TA* 58 (Rostherne part). The others are 13 Tab, 1285, 1286, 1287 Court, e14 *AddCh*, 1316, 1318, 1431, 1440 JRL, 1320 Mere, 1345 *Eyre*, 1402 *CoLegh*, 1666 Orm[2] 1842 OS.

(a) Acres; Bassendale (perhaps originally *Baxendale* 'valley where bake-stones were got', v. bæc-stān, dæl[1]); Beach Mdw; Black Earth, Blake Fd (v. blæc, eorðe); Blakeley ('black clearing', v. blæc, lēah); Bog; Bollin Mdw (cf. R. Bollin 1 15); Bollington Eye, -Hey (*insulas de Bolinton*' e14, *Bolinton Ees* 1666, from ēg 'an island, a water-meadow' confused with (ge)hæg 'an enclosure'); Bon(d) Croft (v. bóndi); Bottoms (v. botm); Brick Foot Eye (perhaps 'meadow at the foot of a hill', v. brekka, fōt, ēg); Broad Heath; Brund-, Brunt Heath (v. brende[2], hǣð); Butters Croft; Butty Moor (v. butty); Camp Hill (v. camp); Crook Fd (v. krókr); Crooked Loont (v. croked, land); Cross Moor (v. cros); Dumbe Hough; Fairy Brow 1842 (v. faierie); Flatt Steele (v. flat, stigel); Geale; Hand Fd; Heynorth Bottom; Hitchell; Hob Fd (v. hobbe); Holt Rough (v. holt); Great & Little Hough (*le Litulhoch* 1320, 'the little tongue of land' v. lȳtel, hōh); Humprey; Intack, Intake (v. inntak); Kiln Croft; Kitchen Croft; Latter Lake (v. lacu); Long Acre(s); Loont Adlands ('the selion headlands', v. land, hēafod-land); Marl'd Hey (v. marlede, (ge)hæg); Moor Acre & Clough (v. clōh); Moss-inders; Nag Fd (v. nagge); Old Hey Lount (v. land); Peak Butts, Pick Moor (cf. *le pekesmedusyde* 1318, 'the side of the hill-meadow', v. pēac, mǣd, sīde); Picon's Croft; Pigeon Mdw; Pooley Bank; Poor House Intack (v. poor-house, inntak); Quarter; Reddish Croft; Rothwell Clough 1842 (v. clōh); Rough; Round Heath; Rye Hey; Saint Mary's Headlands; Sloop (v. slope); Sound Fd & Heath (v. sand); Stoney Lake Mdw ('stony stream', v. stānig, lacu, cf. Stanney Brook 1 35); Street Hey (v. strǣt, cf. 'Watling Street' 1 40); Throstle Nest; Toll Bar Fd (named from *New Bridge Toll Bar* 1831 Bry, south of New Bridge *supra*); Town Fd; Two Penny Patch; Yarwood (v. Yarwoodheath 58 *infra*).

(b) *le Brodemedewe* e14 (v. brād, mǣd); *le Croppted holler* 1318 ('alder-tree with a cropped head', from alor, v. cropped, hēafod); *Ellotesmedu* 1318 ('Ellot's meadow', from the ME fem. pers.n. *Ellot*, diminutive of *Ellen*, and mǣd); *Heskith-acres* 1666 (perhaps 'horse-track', v. hestr, skeið, but *Hesketh* is a well-known surname); *le Hewode* 1318 ('high wood', v. hēah, wudu); *Hoggefeld* 1402 ('hog field', v. hogg); *Langley* 1440 (v. lang, lēah); *le leghmos* 1318 ('moss at a clearing', v. lēah, mos); *Longhey* 1316, *Longay* 1431 (v. lang, (ge)hæg); *Quike* 13 (p), 1287 (p), *la Qike* 13 (p), *del Quyk* 1285 (p), *Qwike* 1286 (p), *Whyk* 1345 (p) ('quickset-hedge', v. cwic); *le Were* 1318 ('the weir', v. wer; probably connected with Bollington Mill 21 *supra*).

vii. Rostherne

The ancient parish of Rostherne comprised 1. High Legh, 2. Mere, 3. Millington, 4. Rostherne, 5. Tabley Superior, 6. Tatton, and also parts of Agden
and Bollington 42, 43 *supra*, and the parochial chapelries of Knutsford and
Over Peover 72, 82 *infra*. DB mentions a church under High Legh, but
none at Rostherne. The parish church is located at Rostherne before 1188,
v. Orm² 1 429.

1. HIGH LEGH (101–7084) [li:]

Lege 1086 DB, *Lega* 12 (17) Sheaf (p), 1209 Tab, (*Alta-*) 1318 JRL
   Legh 1153–1181 (1285) Ch (p), Chest (p), 1260 Cl *et freq*, (*-iuxta
      Routhestorn*) 1295 ChF, (*-Uttrington*) 1296 Plea, (*-Lymme*) 1355
      Eyre, (*-Mulyngton*) 1464 CoLegh, (*la-*) 1325 Cl (p), (*High-*) 1488
      ChRR, (*H(i)egh-*) 1493, 1495 ib, (*Hye-*) 1522 Mere, *Leghe* 1293
      Ch, (*High-*) 1531 Orm², *Leh'* c.1230 *JRC* (p), *Leg'* 1245 Chest
      (p), *Legth'* c. 1300 CoLegh
   Leeye c.1220 Tab (p), *Ley(-e, -a)* 1230, 1245, 1250 CoLegh, *Lee*
      1384 ChRR (p), *Le* 1553 Pat, *Hyle* c.1536 Leland
   Leigh 1320 JRL (p), (*Heigh-*) 1602 ChRR, (*High-*) 1635 ib, *Liegh*,
      Lyegh, *Leygh* 1321 AD (p), *Leyg'* 1328 CoLegh, (*High*) *leighe*
      1584 ChRR, (*Highe-*) 1590 Orm², (*Heigh-*) 1660 Sheaf
   High Ligh 1515 ChEx, *-lye* 1554 Pat

'The glade', *v.* lēah (dat.sg. lēage). The affix 'high', (hēah),
distinguishes this place from Little Leigh 115 *infra*. High Legh lies
on the crest of a broad ridge at an altitude of 240 feet.

NORTHWOOD HALL, HO & LANE

Norwood 1278 IpmR, *-wute* 1304 Chamb (p) (?)
   Nortwode 1318 Eyre (p)
   Northwode 1332 Ipm, 1336 ChRR *et freq* to 1517 AddCh, *-wod* 1348
      CoLegh, 1529 Tab, *-wodd(e)* 1510 ChRR, 1512 ChEx, *-woode*
      1531 Plea, *-wood* 1590 Orm², *Northewode* 1365 ib, *-wod* 1430
      AddCh

'North wood', *v.* norð, wudu.

SINK MOSS, 1831 Bry, *Sy-*, *Sinkemosse* 1336, 1340 CoLegh, *Synkmosse*
1452 *ib*, *Sinks Moss* 1842 OS, from mos 'a moss', with ME sinke 'a
sink, a cesspool, a bog, a sump', first recorded 1440 NED, cf. WRY
7 243.

SWINEYARD HALL & LANE

Suinesheued 1184 P, *Swynesheved* 1331 Cl (p), *-heued* 1368 *Eyre* (p),
   -hed 1519 Plea, *Swyneshedde* 1543 Tab, *Swy-, Swineshead* 1619
   Orm², *Swins-* 1724 NotCestr

Swyneheueyt 13 Tab, *Swinehevet* 1278 Ipm, *Suyneheued* 1348 *Eyre*,
   Swynehed 1377 *ib*, *-e* 1484 CoLegh, *-head* 1555 Pat, *Swinehead*
   1590 Orm², *Swynhed* 1440 ib, *-hedde* 1525 *ChEx*

Swynyard 1603 Sheaf, *Swineyard* 1666 Orm², (*Hall & Lane*) 1831
   Bry, *Swineyherd* 17 Tab, *Swinyard* 1842 OS

'Swine's head', *v.* swīn¹, hēafod. Since there is no topography like
that of Swineshead WRY 3 178, this appears to be an animal-head
name of the type discussed at Sr 405. The form *-yard* (*v.* **geard**) is
probably due to stress-shifting in the dial. pronunciation [jed] for
head.

SWORTON HEATH

Suerton 12 (17) Sheaf, *Swerton* 113 CoLegh, *Scwerton'* 1320 *ib* (p)
Swirton, -y- 1216–72 Orm²

Sworton, Suor- 13 Orm², 1270 CoLegh et freq, *Sworton* (*-Heath*)
   1548 ChRR, *Sworeton* 1381 Earw (p)

Swarton 113 (17), 1619 Orm²

Soorton 113 CoLegh, *Sor(e)ton Heath* 1842 OS, 1849 *TA, Sowton
   Heath* 1831 Bry

Swordton 1307 *Eyre* (p)

'Farm at a neck of land', *v.* swēora, tūn. The place is on a ridge
running westwards from High Legh, cf. Street Fd *infra*.

ABBEY COTTAGES, cf. *Abbey Leys* 1849 *TA, v.* lēah.   AGDEN LANE,
v. 42 *supra*.   ARLEYVIEW FM, *Quebec* 1831 Bry.   BACK LANE.
BADGERSCROFT FM, cf. *Badger's Croft* 1849 *TA*.   BEARSPAW FM,
Bears Paw 1831 Bry.   BENNET'S COVERT, cf. *Bennetts Fd* 1849 *TA*.
BIG WOOD, *The Coppice* 1831 Bry, *-Wood* 1842 OS.   BIRCHELS
GORSE, *Birchall Fox Cover* 1831 Bry, *Birches Gorse* 1842 OS, *Birchalls
Park* 1849 *TA, v.* bircel.   BOLTS SPINNEY.   THE BONGS, *-Wood*
1842 OS, *v.* banke.   BOUNDARY FM, in the middle of the township,
probably between the East Hall and West Hall estates.   BROAD-
HEYS FM, cf. *Broad Hay, -Hey* 1849 *TA, v.* brād, (ge)hæg.   BROAD-
OAK FM & LANE, *Broad Oak* 1842 OS, *Big Oak* 1831 Bry.   BROOK
FM, named from Arley Brook 1 31.   BROOKHOUSE FM, named

from Bradley Brook 98 *infra*. BROOMEDGE COVERT, *Brown Edge*
1844 *TA*, cf. Broomedge 37 *supra*. COWAP'S COVERT. CRAB-
TREE FM & LILAC FM, on Crabtree Lane *infra*, were *Heywood Farms*
1831 Bry, *v*. Hey Wood *infra*. CRABTREE LANE, cf. prec. and
Crabtree Flatts & Hay 1849 *TA*. CROFT FM, cf. *Croft* 1849 *ib*
(*freq*), *the croft fild* 1574 CoLegh, *v*. croft. CROSSROAD FM, *v*.
cross-road. CROWLEY BROOK & LANE, cf. Crowley 131 *infra*.
CROWSNEST FM, *v*. crāwe, nest. DAIRY FM, *Le(i)gh Common* 1831
Bry, 1842 OS. DEANSGREEN HALL, *Dean Green* 1842 ib, *Dean's
Green* 1750 Sheaf, *v*. 39 *supra*. DITCHFIELD'S COVERT & LANE,
cf. Ditchfield's Bridge 39 *supra*, named from the *Ditchfield* family of
Swineyard *supra*, cf. John *Dychefeld* 1394 ChRR. DOBB LANE,
Dob Lane 1831 Bry, perhaps from daube 'clay'. ENDFIELD FM.
FANNER'S LANE. GANDERS BRIDGE (lost, 101–688814), GANDERS
BROOK FM (lost, 101–688816), 1831 Bry, cf. Arley Brook 1 13
THE GORSE, *Square Cover* 1842 OS. GOULBORN LANE (FM).
GRANTHAMS. GREATOAK FM. HALLIWELL'S BROW, *v*. brū.
HEATH LANE, named from Sworton Heath *supra*. HEY WOOD,
1842 OS, *Haywood* 1849 *TA*, cf. Crabtree Fm *supra*, 'fenced-in
wood', *v*. (ge)hæg, wudu. HIGHLEGH HALL, 1831 Bry, *East-High-
Legh* 1673 Sheaf, *Easthall* 1724 NotCestr, 'the east hall', *v*. ēast,
hall. There are two manor-houses here, cf. West Hall *infra*, Boundary Fm *supra*. HIGHLEGH PARK, cf. *le Park* (*Moor*) 113 (17) Orm[2],
v. park, mōr[1]. HOBSHILL FM & LANE, *Holes Hills* 1831 Bry,
Bobs Hillock 1842 OS, from *Hob*, *Bob*, pet-forms of *Robert*, and
hyll, hylloc. HOOGREEN LANE, *v*. 51 *infra*. THE HOWLERS,
Alder Wood 1842 ib, *v*. alor. INTACK FM, cf. *Intack* 1849 *TA*
(*freq*), *v*. inntak. KAY LANE (FM), KAYLANE BROOK, *Quay Lane*
1831 Bry, *Riddings Brook* 1842 OS, cf. *Key Hay, -Hey, Gutter Acre
or Key Lane Field, The Cages or Further Key Lane Field* 1849 *TA*.
This is probably 'cows' lane', from cū (pl. cȳ, ME and ModEdial.
kie, kye) and lane, with (ge)hæg, goter, cage. The stream is 'brook
at the cleared-lands', *v*. ryding, brōc, and joins Bradley Brook
infra. KIRKMANSGREEN COTTAGE, *Kirkman's Green* 1831 Bry, from
grēne[2] 'a green' and the surname *Kirkman*. LEGH'S FOLLY, *v*.
folie. *Legh* is the surname of the local magnates. LEIGH OAKS
FM. LITTLE OAKS. LONG SHOOTS, *Long Shoot Woods* 1842
OS, *v*. scēat. LOWER MOSS FM, named from Sink Moss *supra*.
MAG LANE, cf. Mag Brook 1 30. MANOR FM. MERE
HEYES FM, cf. *Mere Hay(es)* 1849 *TA*, 'enclosures belonging to

Mere', *v.* (ge)hæg, cf. Mere 51 *infra*, Mere Heyes 53 *infra*.
MILL FM. MOSS BROW & LANE, MOSSHALL FM, MOSS HOUSE
FM, *Moss Brow* 1831 Bry, *Legh Mosse Houses* 1557, 1558 Tab, (*the*)
Mosse House(*s*) 1666 Orm², named from Sink Moss *supra*, *v.* mos,
brū, hūs. MOSS FM & LANE, *Moss Lane, Legh Moss* 1831 Bry,
cf. *bruerium de Leyg' jacens inter Leyg' et Aketon* 1328 CoLegh, *le heth*
1333 *ib*, 'the moss, the heath', *v.* mos, hǣð, cf. Agden 42 *supra*.
MOSS OAKS (FM). MOSS'S STRIP, *v.* strip. MOWPEN BROW,
Mappins Brow 1842 OS, *Mowpin or Mowfield* 1849 *TA*, 'stack pen',
v. mūga, penn². OLD FM. PARK COTTAGE & FM, *Park Cottage*
& *House* 1831 Bry, named from High Legh Park *supra*. PARKGATE
FM. PEACOCK'S LANE, *Cross Lane* 1831 Bry, cf. *Peacock's Croft* &
Pingot 1849 *TA*, *v.* cros, pingot. *Peacock* is a surname. PEAR
TREE COTTAGE, cf. *Pear Tree Field* 1849 *TA*. REDBANK BRIDGE,
1831 Bry. REDOAK, *Millers or Mollarts Green* 1831 ib, from
grēne² and a surname. THE ROODE. ROWLEYBANK FM &
LANE. ROWLINSON'S GREEN, from grēne² and a surname.
SEBASTOPOL COVERT. STOCKS COTTAGES, named from the adjacent
stocks. STORES FM. THOWLER LANE, probably 'the alder lane',
from alor and lane, with a prefixed def.art. WALNUT FM. WEST
HALL, 1666 Orm², *West-High-Legh* 1673 Sheaf, *v.* west, hall, cf.
East Hall *supra*. WEST LANE (FM). WHITEFIELD COVERT, cf.
White Field 1849 *TA*. WHITLEY LANE, 1831 Bry, cf. *Whitley*,
Big Whitleys 1849 *TA*, 'white clearing', *v.* hwīt, lēah. WITHER'S
LANE, *Big & Little Wither* 1849 ib. WITHIN HALL (lost), 1842
OS, 'willow hall', *v.* wīðegn; near Sink Moss. WOODIERS FM.
WOODSIDE FM. WRENSHOT LANE, 1849 *TA*, *Rensherds Lane* 1831
Bry. YEWTREE FM, *Hedge Croft* 1831 ib.

FIELD-NAMES

The undated forms are 1849 *TA* 237. Of the others 12 (17)¹, 1617 are Sheaf,
12 (17)², e13 (17) Tab, H3, 13, E2, 1582 Orm², 1304 Chamb, 1356 *Indict*,
1421 ChRR, 1473 Plea, 1831 Bry, 1842 OS, and the rest *CoLegh*.

(*a*) Acre; Alcock's Lane (1831); Ashby Mdw; Backside; Bank Fd; Barn
Fd; Barrow Croft (*v.* bearg); Benn; Bent Yards (*v.* beonet, geard); Berrins
Md; Birchens Fd (*v.* bircen¹); Black Butts (*v.* blæc, butte); Blackhurst (*v.*
blæc, hyrst); Black Lane 1831; Blake Fd (*v.* blæc); Bloody Mdw; Bottoms
(*v.* botm); Braddow ('broad dole', *v.* brād, dāl); Braglus; Brickiln Fd; Brook
Hayes, -Heys (*le Brokeheye* 1464, 'enclosure at a brook', *v.* brōc, (ge)hæg);

Burnt Earth (*v.* brende², eorðe); Long & Short Butts (*v.* butte); The Cages (*v.* Kay Lane *supra*); Clay Fd; Clumley (cf. Clemley 326 *infra*); Cob Fd (*v.* cobb(e)); College Lane (the tithes were appropriated to Christ Church, Oxford); Coot Fd; Copthorne (*v.* copped, þorn); Corn Hay (*le Corn(e)heye* 1310, 1367, *v.* corn², (ge)hæg); Cow Hay, -Hey; Cromley (*v.* Ormley *infra*); Cross Croft & Fd (*v.* cros); Cuckolds Croft (*v.* cukewald); Cuttings; Dig Flatt (*v.* dīc, flat); Dirt Mdw (*v.* drit); Driving Lane Field; Dry Fd; Finch Fd (*Fyncheffeld* 15, *v.* finca 'a finch', feld); Fittlans; Flatt Fd (*v.* flat); Flowery Lynch (cf. *le her-, lagherflowry feld* 1464, *v.* floury, feld, hlinc); Fold Fd; Forest Brook Hey; Fox Acre; Fryary Hay (cf. Abbey Cottage *supra*); Fur Croft; Gib Hay; Green Hill; Grimsditch (at 101–705821 at a kink in the parish boundary, perhaps named from some old earthwork, *v.* Grīm, dīc, cf. Grimsditch 58, 66, 134 *infra*); Grisdale Croft (perhaps 'young pig's hollow, *v.* gríss, dæl¹); Gutter Acre (*v.* Kay Lane *supra*); Haddocks Flatt; Hales Fd; Halton Fd; Ham (*v.* hamm); Haulmes (cf. *Hulmes Moss* 1842, *v.* hulm, mos); Hazen Fd (perhaps the same as *le heth fyld qui vocatur Hastanusfeld* 1333, *Hastansfeld* 15, 'Hasten's field', from the ODan pers.n. *Hasten* and feld. For the pers.n. form see Fellows Jensen 135 and lxxix–lxxx, Feilitzen 66–8); Head Acres (*v.* hēafod); Hemp Yard (*v.* hænep, geard); Hill; Hob Fd (*v.* hobb(e)); Hodge Croft & Fd (cf. *Hoggefild, -flatte* 1452, 'hog field & plot', *v.* hocg, hogg, feld, flat, cf. *Hodg Croft* 1 158); Holsheads; Hollywell's Park; Hoofield ('field at a spur of land', *v.* hōh); Hooley (*Leuyngerys-, Leuyngishulleg'* 1286, *Hullegh* 1348, 'Lēofing's hill-clearing', from the OE pers.n. *Lēofing* with hyll, lēah); Hough (*v.* hōh); House Fd; Hyans (*v.* hyrne); Island (a narrow strip of land between two fields, not near water); Big, Middle & Little Jacksons Fd (*Jackson's Fildes or Jacksons grounde* 1574); Kershot (*v.* kjarr, scēat); Kiln Mdw; Kitchen Fd; Knowl (*v.* cnoll); Land Mdw (*v.* land 'a selion'); Little Croft (*le Litelcrofte* 1464, *v.* lȳtel, croft); Long Acre; Long Flatt (*le longeflatte* 1464, *v.* lang, flat); Loonds (*v.* land); Lymm Woods (cf. Lymm 36 *supra*); Main Hey ('demesne enclosure', *v.* main, (ge)hæg); Make Good Hey (*v.* 326 *infra*); Manthin; Marl Fd; Meg Hey; Middle Wd; Milking Brow (*v.* milking); Mill Fd (*le milne felde* 15, *v.* myln, feld); Mizey Mdw (*v.* misy, dial. *mizzy* 'a muddy place'); Moor Mdw; Mopings Croft; Moss Hay (*Mosshawe* E2, *le Mosseheye* 1464, 'moss enclosure', *v.* mos, haga, (ge)hæg); Moss Room ('moss allotment', *v.* rūm); Nantray; (Near) New Hay, -Hey (*the further & nearer newhaye* 1574, *v.* nīwe, (ge)hæg); Nickow; Oakenhead (*le Hokinhedsnabbe* 1336, *le Oken(e)hed* 1340, 1452, *-heued* 1347, *Hokenhed* 1543, 'headland growing with oaks' *v.* ācen, hēafod, snabbe 'a steep place, a projecting part of a hill'); Orchard Flatt (*le Orcherdeflatte* 1363, *v.* orceard, flat); Ormley or Cromley; Outshot (*v.* ūt, scēat); Oven House Fd; Ox Pasture; Paddock('s) Pool(e) (*Padog-, (Litell) Padok Pole* 1488, 15, 'frog pool', *v.* padduc, pōl¹); Paradise (*v.* paradis); Peck Fd; Penny Croft (*v.* pening); Pickow (*v.* pichel); Pingot (*v.* pingot); Pinny Plackfield; Platt(s) (*v.* platt²); Pocket Fd (*v.* poket); Poor Acre; Ranstave; Riddings (*v.* ryding); Ridocks Close; Rix Eye Mdw ('rush-island', *v.* risc, ēg); Rushy Hay; Salfords Fd ('willow ford', *v.* salh, ford); Sand Fd; Shark Fd; (Fur & Near) Sharps Fd & Mdw (cf. *le Sharpe Feelde* 15, *Litell Sharpe fildes* 1488, *v.* scearp); Soonds (*v.* sand); Spike Mdw;

Stack Acre (v. stakkr); Stiff Fd (v. stiff); Street Fd (v. strǣt; the name of
two fields beside the Warrington–Knutsford road at 101–695840. Cf. *antiqua
via* 13 Orm² 1 451 at Sworton Heath, and the surname *de Stanystrete* 1352,
1378 *Eyre* connected with Legh, which suggest that this road is ancient, v.
stānig, strǣt. Cf. 1 44 XI, *Strettle* 52 *infra*); Sweet Fd; Tanyard Mdw
(v. tan-yard); Toad Hole (v. tāde); Tofts Piece (probably from a surname
from Toft 81 *infra*, with pece); Tother House Fd ('field belonging to
the other house', there being two manor houses); Town Fd; Turnhurst
(cf. *Turnehursthed* 1331, '(the top end of) the round wood', v. trun, hyrst,
hēafod); Twiggery (an osier bed); Two Cross Fd; Upcast; Wall Croft (v.
wǣlla); Washing Croft (probably a sheep-dip); Welchman's Acre & Hay (v.
Wels(c)h-man, cf. *Owencrofte infra*); Wood Fd (cf. *boscum de Legh* 1304);
Worthington.

(b) *Aluandelegh'* 1340, *Alvenesley* 1464 (probably 'Ælfweald's clearing',
from the OE pers.n. *Ælfweald* and lēah, cf. Alvanley 325 *infra*); *Astwalld-
more* E2 (v. mōr¹ 'a moor'); *Birchenhewed* 12 (17)², *Le Byrcheneheued* H3,
le Birchyne- 1280, *le Birchenes-* c.1300, *Byrchenhey woodd alias Myllington
Wood juxta Myllington* 1582 ('headland at a birch copse', v. bircen¹, hēafod,
cf. Millington 54 *infra*); *aqua del Blakebroc* 1331, *le Blakelake* 1333 ('the
black stream', v. blæc, brōc, lacu); (*le*) *Bocas F(e)elde* 15 (from the family
de Bogas, fifteenth-century tenants in High Legh); *le bothemore* 1330 ('the
booth moor', v. bōth, mōr¹); (*le*) *Calirmo(u)r* 1331, 1336, *le Cal(l)ermor* 1340,
1347 ('the calves' moor', v. calf (gen.pl. calfra), mōr¹); *Colheye* 1488, *le
Collhey* 15 ('charcoal enclosure', v. col¹, (ge)hæg); *Coysfelde* 1488 ('cow's
field', v. cū, (gen.sg. cūs), feld); *Croketesfeld* 1402 (perhaps from the surname *Croket*, ModE *Crocket*, and feld); *le Erliswode*, *-es-* 1336, 1340 ('the
earl's wood', v. eorl, wudu); *Foxhoc* 13 (from fox 'a fox' and hōc 'a hook of
land'); *le Halch* c.1250, *le Halw* c.1286 ('the nook', v. halh); (*le*) *Harlae*
1336, 1340, *heya de Harlagh* 1347 ('the hoar clearing', v. hār², lēah, (Angl.
lǣh), near Sink Moss *supra*, on the south boundary of the township, v.
Arley 101 *infra*); *le hayheye* 1381, *-hay* 15 ('hay enclosure', v. hēg, (ge)hæg);
Hole-, *Howelegreve* c.1250 (p), *Holgreue* 15 ('wood at a hollow', v. holh (dat.
sg. hole, holwe), grǣfe); *the Holyns* 1445 (v. holegn); *Kyngesbrokmulne* 1356,
le Polestydde et le Milnestyd vocat' Kyngbroke mylne 15 ('the site of a pool
and a mill called King's-brook mill', from myln, pōl-stede, and the name of
an unidentified stream, v. cyning, brōc. This context reveals two common
nouns *pole-stede*, *mylne-stede* 'place where a pool, a mill, stands'. The former
is *freq* among f.ns. in Ch, v. pōl-stede); *Lilleghhurst* 1340 ('wood at a little-
clearing' or 'little wood-at-a-clearing' or 'wood at little Legh', v. lȳtel, lēah,
hyrst); *þe-*, *le long(e)hurst* 1330, 1340, (*-lode*) 1348 ('the long wood', v. lang,
hyrst, (ge)lād 'a water-course'); *le Mascymedowe* 1421, *Massey meadows* 1617
(from the surname *Massey* and mæd, cf. Dunham Massey 19 *supra*); *Lemy-
dilchahe* c.1250, *le Middilchawe* c.1286, *le Wylkynmydelshaw Feld* 15 ('the
middle copse', v. middel, sc(e)aga, with the ME pers.n. *Wilkin*, diminutive
of *Will*, a short form of *William*); *le My-*, *Mikelfeld* 1464 (v. micel, feld);
Owencrofte 15 ('Owen's croft', from the ME pers.n. *Owen* (OWelsh *Oue(i)n*)
and croft, cf. Welchman's Acre *supra*); *le Perkynfeld* 1464 (from the ME

pers.n. *Perkin*, diminutive of *Peres* (OFr *Piers*) 'Peter', and feld); *Suthebroc* 12 (17)[1], *Southbroc* e13 (17), *Sudthebroc*, *-brok* 1270, *Sothebroc* c.1290 (p), *-brok* 1330 ('south brook', v. sūð, brōc, perhaps Arley Brook 1 13, on the south boundary of the township); *Stubbil'g* E2 ('clearing full of stubs', v. stubbig, lēah); *parcum de Thistilstak* 1473 ('a stack of thistles', v. þistel, stakkr).

2. MERE (101–7281)

Mara 1086 DB, *la-* c.1176 (17) Orm[2] (p), *del Mare* 1294 Earw (p), *la Mar* c.1262 Dav (p)

Mera 1086 DB, *Mere* c.1230 *CoLegh et freq*, (*-iuxta Assheleye*) 1301 ChancW, (*-iuxta Rothesthorn*) 1372 Cuer, (*alias Mera*) 1581 ChRR, *le-*, *del-* c.1290 JRL (p), 1293 Plea (p) *et freq*, *la-* 1407 ChRR (p), *Mer* c.1300 JRL (p), *le-* 1411 AD (p)

de Lacu c.1230 *Fitt* (p)

Meyr 1331 Earw, *-e* 1545 Plea, *Meir* 1534 ib, *-e* 1584 ChRR, *the Meire Town* 1661 Dep, *Meyer* 1694 Mere

(*le-*, *del*) *Meer(e)* 1336 (p), 1503 Plea, 1365 Pat (p), 1415 Tab (p), *The Meer* 1509 Sheaf, *Meere iuxta Rowthorn alias Rosethorn* 1543 Cuer

Mear 1739 LRMB 264

'(At) the lake', v. mere[1], named from The Mere *infra*.

BUCKLOW HILL (101–732833), 1831 Bry, *Buckley-Hill* 1750 Sheaf, *Boclou'* 1240 CAS (p) (NS x 26, xix which dates it c.1256), *Buckelawe* 1260 Plea, *Bochelau* c.1290 CAS (p), *Buclowe* 1511 ChRR, 'Bucca's mound', from the OE pers.n. *Bucca* and hlāw, the meeting-place of the DB hundred of *Bochelau*, v. Bucklow Hundred 1 *supra*, at the meeting of Mere, Millington and Rostherne townships, on 'Watling Street' 1 40.

HOO GREEN (LANE), HOUGH HALL (lost) & HULSEHEATH (LANE)

Hoh' l12 Chest, *Hoch* l12 (17) Orm[2], c.1245 *CoLegh* (p), *Hoc* c.1250 LRO Dx (p), *le Hogh* 1370 Orm[2], *Hoghgrene* 1347 ChRR (p), *Hogh'heth in Mulynton* 1427 JRL, *Hough Hall* 1831 Bry, 1842 OS

(*le*) *How* c.1245 *CoLegh* (p), 13 Cuer, *Hoo Green* 1831 Bry

The Hole 1662 Orm[2], *Hole House* 1831 Bry

Howes-Heath 1666 Orm[2], *Huze Heath* 1831 Bry, *Hulse Heath* 1842 OS

'The prominence', v. hōh (dat.sg. hōe, gen.sg. hōs), with grēne[2] 'a green', hǣð 'a heath', hall. Cf. Hough 326 *infra*, 1 221. The *Hulse-* series represents a genitival composition upon the p.n. *Hoo*.

STRETTLE (lost)

> *Strethul(l)* 112 (17), c.1210 Orm[2], (lit. *Stethul*) c.1261, 1382 ib, (*mora de*) c.1245 *CoLegh*, (*-more*) 1315 *ib*, (*-Farm*) 1666 Orm[2], *Strete-* 1289 Court, *Strett-*, c.1310 *CoLegh*, *Strette-* 1395 *ib*, *Strethill(e)* 1325 *ib*, *-hall* 1673 ChRR
> *Strathull* 1289 Court (p)
> *Strettle Hall* 1544 Mere, 1677 *CoLegh*, *Strettle or Holmes Tenement* 1676 *ib*

'Street hill, hill on a main or Roman road', v. strǣt, hyll, mōr[1], hall. The location of this place is to be sought in Mere, cf. *terras et tenementas in villa et territorio del Mere iuxta Rouesthorn scilicet hameletton' dict' Strethull* 1392 *CoLegh* (Misc 523). It is associated with the Hulme family cf. *Alexander Hulme of Strethull* 1587 (17) MidCh, *Strettle or Holmes Tenement heretofore in the possession of George Holme* 1676 *CoLegh* (Misc 546). Hulmebarns *infra* is a possibility. This location (101–722827) on the Knutsford–Warrington road, a mile north-west of the crossroads at Mere, might reinforce the suggestion of antiquity made by Street Field in High Legh 50 *supra* as to that road, if the allusion is not to the Roman road, 'Watling Street', at Mere. Cf. *Strettelegh* 61 *infra*. *Streethill(s) Green* 55 *infra* in the adjoining township, Millington, could be considered, from its having the same name, were it demonstrable that this part of Millington had belonged to Mere, and if *in villa et territorio* comprehends outlying or detached parts of the township and manor of Mere.

BENTLEYHURST FM, *Bentley Hurst* 1831 Bry, 'grassy wood', v. beonet, lēah, hyrst.   BELT WOOD, *Oak Wood* 1842 OS.   BOWDEN VIEW FM, *Tan Yard* 1831 Bry, v. tan-yard.   BRICKSHILL PITS, cf. *Brick Kiln Croft & Field* 1847 *TA*, v. bryke-kyl, pytt.   BURNT-HOUSES, 1831 Bry, v. brende[2].   CLAMHUNGER WOOD, *Clamhanger Wood* 1831 ib, *Clamhunger* 1847 *TA*, *Clemhunger Wood* 1853 Sheaf. This p.n. is similar to the f.ns. Clemonga, Clamhanger, Clemhunger 70, 85, 326 *infra*. The final el. is hangra 'a wood on a hillside'. The first el, is either clām 'clay, mud', or a derivative *clǣme 'a clayey or a muddy place', cf. Clemley 326 *infra*, Clayhanger 326 *infra*. The form has been influenced by ModEdial. *clam, clem* 'to starve', and hungor. DOBB LANE, *Dob-* 1831 Bry. GLEAVESHOLE WOOD, *Gleaves Holls* 1831 ib, from the local surname *Gleave, v.* hol[1]. GOODIERSGREEN FM, *Goodiers Green* 1831 ib, from the surname *Goodier, Goodyer* and grēne[2]. HOME FM. HULMEBARNS (101–722827), 1831 ib, *v.* bere-ærn, cf. *Strettle supra.* The first el. is the surname *Hulm(e)* of a family living at *Strettle,* cf. the f.n. *Hulm-pool* 1736 Mere, *v.* pōl[1]. KILTON INN, 1831 Bry, traditionally associated with Dick Turpin (White 973). KNOWLESPIT FM, *Knowles Pit* 1831 Bry. MALTKIN COTTAGES, *Maltkin Farm* 1831 ib, *v.* maltekylne. MEADOWLANDS. THE MERE, LITTLE MERE, *The Meer* 1509 Sheaf, *-Mere* c.1536 Leland, *The Great & Little Mere* 1847 *TA,* two lakes which give name to the township, *v.* Mere *supra.* MERE END HO (lost), 1831 Bry, cf. prec. MERE FM, 1847 *TA, v,* mere[1]. MERE HALL, 1842 OS, *Mere New Hall* 1847 *TA,* built 1834, cf. Mere Old Hall *infra.* MEREHEATH LANE & PLANTATION, *Mere Heath* (*Plantation*) 1831 Bry, cf. *Mere Common* 1723 Mere. MERE HEYES, 1831 Bry, *-Heys* 1666 Orm[2], *v.* (ge)hæg, cf. 47 *supra.* MERE MILL, 1831 Bry. MEREMOSS BRIDGE & WOOD, *Mere Moss* 1831 ib, *v.* mos. MERE OLD HALL, 1842 OS, *del Halle* 1337 Orm[2], *Mere Hall* 1831 Bry, cf. Mere Hall *supra.* MEREPLATT FM, *v.* plat[1] 'a footbridge'. MERESIDE FM, *v.* mere[1], sīde. MOSS LANE & LODGE, cf. Meremoss *supra.* PARKSIDE FM, adjoining Mere and Tatton Parks. RASPBERRYLANE PLANTATION. SQUARE WOOD, *New Cover* 1831 Bry. TOLLBAR COTTAGE, TURNPIKE WOOD, *Old Toll House* 1847 *TA.* WINTERBOTTOM, 1860 White, *Winterbottoms Farms* 1831 Bry, probably from the surname *Winterbottom, -botham.* YEWTREE FM, *-House* 1831 Bry.

FIELD-NAMES

The undated forms are 1847 *TA* 263. Those dated l12 (17), 13[1], 13 (17)[2] 1286 (17), E2 are Orm[2], 13[2] *Cuer,* 13 (17)[1] Tab, 1427 JRL, 1680 Sheaf, 1831 Bry, 1842 OS, and the rest *CoLegh.*

(a) Aspin Acre (*v.* æspen); Backside; Barn Fd; Birchin Acre (*v.* bircen[2]); Black Fd; Black Lake Plantation (site of *Black Lake* 1831, 1842, a mere, *v.* lake); Boon(d)s Croft; Bottoms (*v.* botm); Bradley (*Bradeleg(h)* c.1300, 'broad clearing', *v.* brād, lēah); Bradshaw ('broad copse', *v.* brād, sceaga); Breach Croft (*v.* brēc); Briery Heys; Broad Fd (1676); Broom Fd; Burnt Fd (*v.* brende[2]); Butty Mdw (*v.* butty); Calf Croft (cf. *the Calvers Croft* 1676, *v.* calver, croft); Carr (*v.* kjarr); Causey Croft (*v.* caucie); Clare Fd; Coachman's Pit Fd; Coal Mining Yards; Cobfield (*v.* cobb(e)); Cock Fd; Cow

Heys; Cow Lane; Crabtree Croft; Crib (*v.* crib); Cross Fd; Dam Stead (*v.* damme, stede); Ditchfield (*v.* dīc, feld); Driving Lane; Flash Fd (*v.* flasshe); Foxley ('fox's glade', *v.* fox, lēah); Fun Fd; Gatley Fd; Gorsty Fd (*v.* gorstig); Green Leech(e) (*Grenelache* 13², 'green bog', *v.* grēne[1], læc(c)); Hand Fd; Harehead; Hasbury Lane End; Hob Iron (*v.* hobbe, hyrne); Hollin(s) Hey(s) (*v.* holegn, (ge)hæg); Ice House Plantation; Intack (*v.* inntak); Old Key, Keys Fd; Kiln Fd (cf. *le Kylnebuttes* c.1280, 'the kiln selions', *v.* cyln, butte); Knowl; Mickow; Moor; Motley Heys (perhaps '(enclosures at) the moot clearing', *v.* mōt, lēah, cf. Bucklow Hill *supra*); Much Fd; New Hey; New Lane 1831; Nick Fd; Old Mdw; Ouler (*v.* alor); Outlet (*v.* outlet); Oxheys; Park; Peaks Fd; Pingot (*v.* pingot); Plock Fd; Round Croft; Rush(e)y Hey(s) (*v.* riscig, (ge)hæg); Rye Fd; Sand Fd; Sawpit Croft (*v.* saw-pytt); Shaws (*v.* sceaga); The Shurleys (*Sirleg'* c.1245, *Schirlehey* 13 (17)², *Schirley Hey* 1286 (17), *parcum de Shirley* E2, 'bright glade', *v.* scīr², lēah, (ge)hæg); Siddall Fd (*v.* sīd, halh); Sludge Croft (*v.* sludge); Snape (*v.* snæp); Sower Fd (*v.* sūr); Spark (*v.* spearca); Stocking Heys (*v.* stoccing, (ge)hæg); Stoney Lake Mdw ('stony stream', *v.* stānig, lacu, cf. Stanney Brook 1 35); Stotherds Lane 1831 (probably from the surname *Stotherd* 'a keeper of oxen', *v.* stot, hirde); Street Fd (*v.* strǣt, cf. 'Watling Street' 1 40); Sweet Fd; Swine Hey (*v.* swīn[1], (ge)hæg); Tan Yard Mdw (*v.* tan-yard); Tench Fd; Three Quarters; Town Fd; Wet Fd; White Moor; Wicken Stall (*v.* cwicen, stall); Great Woolmer, Little Woolmers (*Woluemor* c.1245, *le Olde Woluesmore* 1392, *Wollemor* 13[1], c.1300, 1340, *Wolmor(e)* 1323, 1395, *Wulmor* 1329, *Vlmore* 1364, 'wolves' moor', *v.* wulf, mōr[1], ald); Woolwithin (*v.* wīðegn).

(*b*) *Amotesfeld* 1427 ('Amyot's field', from the ME pers.n. *Amiot*, diminutive of *Amis*, and feld, but Professor Löfvenberg observes that ON á-mót 'a confluence' is formally possible and cites for comparison Ameshaugh Cu 173); (*le*) *Bancroft* c.1261 ('the bean croft', *v.* bēan, croft); *Culnerowe* c.1245 ('row of houses at a kiln', *v.* cyln, rāw); *Ellotescroft* 1325 ('Ellot's croft', from the ME fem. pers.n. *Ellot*, diminutive of *Ellen*, and croft); *Finchrudyng* 1323, *Fyncheriddyng* 1337 ('cleared land frequented by finches', *v.* finca, ryding); *Hamlont* c.1261 ('home selion', or 'selion in a hamm', *v.* hām or hamm, land); *Harestanesfield* 1l2 (17), *Horestonesfield* 13 (17)², *-isfeld* 13 (17)[1], *le horston feld* 1325 ('field at a hoar stone', *v.* hār², stān); *Lamplache* 13² ('lamb's stream', *v.* lamb, læc(c)); *the Linneys field* 1676 (*v.* lín, (ge)hæg); *the Sprostorne field* 1676 (cf. the surname *de Sproudestoren* 14, 'Sprot's thorn', from the OE pers.n. *Sprot* (Feilitzen 370) and þorn, cf. *Sproscroft* 127 *infra*); *Wayte Rustlache* 13² (perhaps a field near *Rusclache* 'rushy rivulet', *v.* risc, læc(c) 'a boggy stream', in which wheat was grown, hence the prefixed *Wayte* from ON hveiti for OE hwǣte).

3. MILLINGTON (101–7284)

Mulintune 1086 DB, -*tun* John *AddCh*, -*ton* 12 *Dow* (p) *et freq* with variant spellings -*tun*, -*ton*(-*a*, -*e*), -*thon*, -*in*(*g*)-, -*yn*(*g*)-, *Mull-to Mullyngton* 1517 Orm², *molendinum de Mulintona* 1190–1211

Cott. Nero c III, *Mulenton* 13 *LRO* Dx (p), *Mulneton* 1299 Tab
(p), 1339 Pat

Melintona H2 Tab, *-ynton*, *-in-* 1l3, 1300 ib, *Mellynton* 1487
MinAcct, *-yngton*(a) 1325 *CoLegh* (p)

Miltona H2 Tab

Moli(n)tona 1178 Facs, *-ynton* 1353 BPR, *-ington* 1288 Court (p)

Milint(on) l12 Facs (p), c.1300 *LRO* Dx (p), *Millyngton*, *-ing-* 1278
Chest, l13 (17) Tab *et freq*, with variant spellings *Mil(l)-*, *Myl(l)-*,
-yn(g)-, *-in(g)-*, *Myllenton* 1434 Tab

'Mill-enclosure', or 'mill farm', *v.* mylen, tūn, cf. *Mulnecroft infra.*
The example *Mulneton* 1259 Court in DEPN belongs in Broxton
Hundred and not here.

STREETHILL(S) GREEN (lost), 1831 Bry, 1842 OS, a hamlet at 101–
730852, half a mile west of 'Watling Street' 1 40, '(green at) a hill
near a paved road', *v.* strǣt, hyll, grēne², cf. *Strettle* 52 *supra.*

ARTHILL (FM), *Harthill Heath, Burnt House* 1831 Bry, *Arthill-* 1842
OS, *Hartils Croft, Hartley Heath* 1847 *TA*, 'stag hill', *v.* heorot,
hyll, hǣð.   BOOTHBANK, *Booth Bank* 1831 Bry, *v.* bōth, banke.
BUCKLOW HILL, cf. *Bucklow Hill Field* 1847 *TA*, *v.* 51 *supra.*
GREY'S GORSE, 1842 OS, *Greys Covert* 1847 *TA*.   HOPE COTTAGE,
1831 Bry.   MERESIDE FM, *Mere End* 1831 ib, near the north end
of Rostherne Mere.   MILLINGTON CLOUGH & HALL, 1831 ib.
MOSSHOUSE FM, *v.* mos.   NEWHALL FM, *New Farm* 1831 Bry,
-Hall 1847 *TA*.   RANGEMORE.   REDDY LANE, *v.* 43 *supra.*
RUSHYPITS COVERT.   SANDHOLE FM.   STONEDELPH FM, cf. *Stone
Delph Field* 1847 *TA*, *v.* (ge)delf.   THOWLER LANE, *v.* 48 *supra.*

FIELD-NAMES

The undated forms are 1842 *TA* 266. Of the others, c.1154 (1329), c.1200 are
Dugd, 1190–1211 *Cott.* Nero c III, 1350 Tab, 1427 JRL, 1441 Mere, 1517
Sheaf, 1666 Orm², 1676 *CoLegh* and 1831 Bry.

(a) Acres; Aldcroft (*v.* ald, croft); Alderney Hey; Bill Hall Fd; Birch Hey
(*v.* birce, (ge)hæg); Bitter Nails (*v.* 325 *infra*); Bloomly Fd; Bottoms (*v.*
botm); Brickhill Mdw; Burgess's Fd (*Burges fylder* 1517); Burnt Hey (*v.*
brende²); Chamber Croft; Chapel Croft & Fd; Cockram's Brow; Cotown
Fd (perhaps from cotum, dat.pl. of cot); Cow Hey; Drumble ('a wooded dell
or ravine', *v.* dumbel); Dung Bank (*v.* dung); The Flatts (*v.* flat); Gauk;
Hog Hole (*v.* hogg); Holme Croft (*v.* hulm); Intake (*v.* inntak); Knoll;

Leasows (v. lǽs, dat.sg. lǽswe); Long Fd (the- 1676, *Langfeld* 1441, v. lang, feld); Long Shoot (v. scēat); Marl Fd; Mart; Newfield; New Lane 1831; Oven Croft; Ox Hey; Pingot (v. pingot); Shakeshafts; Sound Heath (v. sand); Sour Butts (v. sūr, butte); Tenter Croft (v. tentour); Turn Croft (v. trun); Windmill Acre.

(b) *Hogh' heth* 1427 (v. Hulseheath 51 *supra*); *Mulnecroft* c.1154 (1329), 1190–1211, *Mulincroft* c.1200, *Milne Croft* c.1350 ('the mill croft', v. myln, croft, cf. Millington *supra*); *the Shaw-house* 1666 (v. sceaga).

4. ROSTHERNE (101–7483) ['rɔstə:n]

> *Rodestorne* 1086 DB, *-t'-*, *-tor(n)* l12–e13 Chest, Facs, Orm², *AddCh*, Bark, Dieul, *-thorn(e)* c.1190 (17) Sheaf, 13 Tab, *-ton* c.1220 *Clif*, c.1229 Bark, *-tu* e13 Orm², *Roddest'* c.1226–8 Dieul
> *Rosthorne* H2 (17) Orm², 1188 (17), 1270 (17) ib, 1366, 1443 MidCh, 1581 ChRR, *-thorn* 1408 Orm², 1724 NotCestr, *-torn(e)* 1554, 1671 Sheaf, *-thern(e)* 1324 Mere, 1388 ChRR, 1677 Sheaf, (*-alias Rotherston*) 1696 *Dep*, *-thern* 1724 NotCestr, *-tern(e)* 1589 ChRR, 1660 Sheaf, *-ton* c.1536–9 Leland, 1691 Sheaf, *-tarn* 1558 Orm²
> *Rothesterne* c.1188 Tab, *-torn* 1346 (1471) ChRR and 17 times ib, *Cuer*, Plea, Adl, Sheaf, with variant spellings *Rothes-* (to 1503 Plea), *Roths-* (from 1530 Plea), *-torn(e)* (to 1606 ChRR), *-thorn* (1372 *Cuer* to 1503 Plea), *-terne* (1662, 1673, 1694 Sheaf), *-torm* (1467 Adl) to *Rothsterne* 1694 Sheaf
> *Raudestorn'* c.1190 AddCh, 1190–1211 (1353–7) *ChFor*, *-tor'* 1202–14 Facs (p), *-thoren* c.1280 *CoLegh*
> *Roullestorn'* 1189–99 AddCh, *Roulistoren* c.1245 *CoLegh*
> *Roudestorn(e)* c.1188–1209 MidCh (p), c.1210 Orm², e13 Whall (p), Dieul, 1226–8 Chest, *-thorn(e)* e13 Dieul, 13 (17) Sheaf, *-thoren* 13 Orm², *-tone* e13 Sheaf, *-tro* e13 Orm², *Roud'* e13 Dieul, *Roudistor'* c.1300 Tab
> *Reudestorn'* 1195–1205 Facs
> *Rudest'* e13 Orm², *Rudeston* (p), *Ruddest'* e13 Dieul
> *Radestr'* 1208–10 Orm²
> *Rouistr'* 1210 *Mass*, *Rouestorn* 1214–23 Chest, and 45 times, ib, Tab, JRL, Pat, ChRR, Plea, *Chol*, *ChCert*, Earw, *Dav*, *Eyre*, Orm², Mere, BM, *Dow*, with variant spellings *Roues-* (to 1428 Orm²), *Rous-* (e13 Tab, 1319 JRL to 1530 Plea), *Rowes-* (1417 ChRR to 1437 Pat), *Rows-* (1431 BM to 1528 *Dow*), *-tornia* (13 Tab), *-torn(e)* (to 1530 Plea), *-thorn(e)* (1319 JRL to 1505 ChRR),

-therne (e13 Tab), *-terne* (1413 Mere) to *Roustorne* 1530 Plea,
Rouston' c.1468 *Dav, Rowston* 1558 Orm², *Rosethorn* 1543 *Cuer*
Rotherston c.1220 (17) Orm², 1618 Sheaf
Routhist' c.1225 CAS NS X (p), *Routhestorn* 1226-8 Chest (p),
   c.1232 *Fitt,* and 97 times, JRL, Orm², *Eyre,* ChF, CRV, Plea,
   Chamb, BPR, ChRR, Tab, *Chol,* Pat, Ch, CRC, Cl, *Dav,* Mere,
   Cre, Tax, MidCh, Sheaf, VE, *ChCert,* Bark, *CoLegh,* with
   variant spellings *Routhes-* (to 1535 VE), *Routhis-* (to 1318 *Eyre*),
   Rowthes- (m13 Tab to 1417 ChRR), *Rowthis-* (c.1295 *CoLegh*),
   Rouths- (1511 (1571), 1526 (1581) ChRR), *Rowths-* (1584 ChRR),
   -torn(e) (to 1526 (1581) ChRR), *-torna* (c.1295 *CoLegh*), *-thor'*
   (a.1261 Orm²), *-thorn(e)* (1291 Tax to 1584 ChRR) to *Rowths-*
   thorne 1584 ChRR, *-ton* 1386 IpmR, *-torum* 1391 Bark, *-tron*
   1421 Sheaf, *Routhastorne* 1385 BW, *Routhosturen* 1528 *Dow*
Rondethoren 1263-7 Bark
Rousthestorne 1308 (17) Orm², *-thorn* 1316 JRL, 1535 VE (lit.
   Bonstheshorn), *-thern* 1318 Mere, *Rousteston* 1385 IpmR
Rowthorn' 1308 JRL, (*-alias Rosethorn*) 1543 *Cuer, -thorne* 1536
   Dugd, 1554 *MinAcct,* 1560 Sheaf
Ruthesthorn 1312 ChRR
Routhethorn' 1443 JRL
Raustorne 1452 Sheaf, 1464 JRL, 1476 *Chol,* l15 Orm², *-thorn* 1656
   Orm², *Rawsthorne* 1493 Sheaf, *-torne* 1500 *AddCh,* 1554 Pat,
   1626 ChRR
Rauthestorne 1506 JRL, *-torn* 1511 Plea
Rornston 1517 *AddCh*
Raston 1546 Dugd, 1554 Pat
Rorstorne 1549 Pat
Rowherstone 1739 *LRMB* 264

'Rauðr's thorn-tree', from the ON pers.n. *Rauðr* (ODan *Røth*)
and þorn, þyrne. Professor Sørenson observes that þorn may have a
collective meaning 'thorn-trees; a place growing with thorn-trees'.

DENFIELD HALL, (*le*) *Denefeld* 14 Rich, 1334 ChRR (p), *Denfeld* 1349
Orm¹, (*le Hall de-*), *-e* 1592 Orm², *-fylde* 1554 *Chol, -field* 1600 ChRR,
'valley field', *v.* denu, feld.

DITCH HOUSE (lost), *le Diche* 13 Orm², *del Dych* 1295 ChF (p), *le*
Dyche 1336 ChRR (p), *-Houses* 1421 ib, (*a toft called*) *the Ditche*
House 1592 Orm², *Dich-house* 17 ib, *Dyke Houses* 1446-7 ib, '(house(s)
at) the ditch', *v.* dīc, hūs, cf. Camp Green *infra.*

MARSH FM & LANE, *Mershe* 1335 ChRR (p), (*le-*) 1438 JRL, *maner de le Mersch* 1350 ib, *le Mersshehey* 1431 ib, *Mersshe* 1515 ChEx, *Mersh* 1527 (1581) ChRR, *Marshe* 1619 Orm², v. mersc 'a marsh' and (ge)hæg.

ROSTHERNE MERE, *Routh(e)st(h)orn(e) Me(y)re* 1316 Orm², 1440 JRL, 1592 Orm², *mara de Raustorne* 1452 Sheaf, *Roston Mere* c.1536 Leland, *Rowston Mayre* 1558 Orm², *Rausthorn-mere* 1656 ib, 'the lake', v. mere[1].

YARWOODHEATH COVERT & FM, 1831 Bry, *Yarwode* 1384 *AddRoll*, *-woode* 1443 JRL, *-wood* 1677 CoLegh, *Yarewode* 1438 JRL, *3arewode* 1440 ib, *3arwode* 1500 AddCh, *Yerwod* 1558 Orm², 'eagle wood', v. earn, wudu. The forms evolve from prosthetic *i̯* and loss of *n* in the consonant cluster *-rnw-*. Cf. Arley 101 *infra*.

ASHLEY RD (101–737815 to 763838), *Salters Lane* 1842 OS, cf. *le Salteresway infra*, 'road used by salt-dealers', v. saltere, lane. This was probably part of a salt-way from Northwich to Stockport, leading from 'Watling Street' 1 40 towards Birkin Ford Bridge *infra* and Ashley, so as to by-pass Altrincham, cf. Crump 98–101.   BIRKIN FORD BRIDGE (101–763838), BIRKINHEATH (LANE & COVERT), BIRKIN COTTAGES, *Birkin Heath* (*Farm & Cover*) 1831 Bry, 1842 OS, cf. 10 *supra*, probably the origin of the surname *de Berkyn* 1348 ChRR, *-Birkyn* 1395 ib, *-Byrkyn* 1438 MidCh; v. bircen[1] 'a place growing with birch-trees', hǣð, ford. The *-k-* is due to ON influence, cf. Birkenhead 325 *infra*. The district gives name to Birkin Brook 1 15, which the ford crosses, cf. Ashley Road *supra*.   BLACKBURN'S BROOK (Rostherne Mere to Birkin Brook), from the surname *Blackburn*.   BOWDON VIEW, *Dirty Lane Farm* 1831 Bry, v. Dirty Lane *infra*.   BRIDDONWEIR, 1842 OS, *Bridge End Weir Farms* 1831 Bry, '(weir at) the causeway end', v. brycg, ende[1], wer, the place being at the north end of a crossing of Blackburn's Brook *supra*.   BUCKLOW HILL, v. 51 *supra*.   CAMP GREEN (101–744827), 1831 ib, cf. *Camp Field* 1847 TA 'a small circular plot of ground' 1879 Sheaf[1] 1 340, v. grēne². There is no material from which to determine whether this is from ModE camp² 'a camp'. If it is, and alludes to formerly existing earthworks, the place might be *Grymmysdiche iuxta Routhesthorn'* 1345 Eyre, v. Grīm 'Woden', dīc 'a ditch, an earthwork', cf. Grimsditch 49 *supra*, 66, 134 *infra*.   CHERRYTREE FM.   CICELY

MILL FM. DIRTY LANE, 1831 Bry, cf. Bowdon View *supra*, *v.*
dyrty, lane. GALE BOG, 1842 OS, *Gaily Bog* 1831 Bry, 'bog where
bog-myrtle grows', *v.* gagel, bog. HANCOCK'S BANKS, *Harrisons
Cover* 1831 ib. HARPERS BANK WOOD, 1831 ib, cf. *Harpers Bank
Farm* 1831 ib. MERE COVERT, *New Covert* 1831 ib. NEW
BRIDGE, *v.* 43 *supra*. OLDMILL COTTAGES, *Rostherne Mill* 1831
Bry, *molendinum aquaticum* 1439 Orm[2]. RAMSHEAD COTTAGE,
-*Farm* 1831 Bry. ROSTHERNE BANKS, 1842 OS, *Mill Bank Wood*
1831 Bry, cf. Oldmill *supra*, *v.* banke. ROSTHERNE BROOK, cf.
The Mar 1 30. ROSTHERNE HALL (lost), 1831 Bry, 1860 White.
ROSTHERNE MANOR. SHAWGREEN FM & WOOD, *Shaw Green* 1842
OS, *v.* sceaga 'a copse', grēne[2]. TOM LANE, cf. *Tom field*, *Town
Field* 1847 *TA*, *v.* toun. TWISS'S WOOD, *Twiss Wood* 1831 Bry,
'wood at a fork', *v.* (ge)twis, cf. the surname *del Twys* 1316 Mere,
1328 Tab, and Twiss Brow 101 *infra*. WOOD BONGS, 1842 OS,
'wooded slopes', *v.* banke. YEW WOOD, cf. *Evwode Medowe* 1431
JRL, *v.* īw 'yew', wudu.

FIELD-NAMES

The undated forms are 1847 *TA* 340. The others are 1300, 1307, 1343 JRL,
1489 ChRR, 1696 *Dep*, 1713, 1747 Sheaf.

(a) Ash Hill; Aspin Acre (*v.* æspen); Bay Fd; Bleases Bank (probably
from the local surname *Blease* and banke); Blundretts Moor; Brick Kiln Fd;
Broom Fd (cf. *Bromcroft* 1300, *v.* brōm, croft); the Burned Fd 1747 (1713,
v. brende[2]); Butty Croft (*v.* butty); Car Mdw (*v.* kjarr); the Cornfield 1747
(1713); Cross Fd (1713, *v.* cros); Dale Mdw (*v.* dæl[1]); Fitch Fd; Fox Hole
Fd; French Wheat Fd (*v.* french-wheat); Gip Gap; Glade Bank (*v.* gleoda);
Hamlets Mdw; the Hempyard 1747 (1713, *v.* hemp-yard); Hey Stall (*v.*
stall); the Housefield 1747 (1713); Kiln Mdw; Loont (*v.* land); Main Fd
('demesne field', *v.* main); Marl Fd (cf. *the marled field* 1713, *Marlehes* 1489,
v. marle(de), (ge)hæg); Mean Fd (*v.* (ge)mǣne); Mizzey (*v.* misy); Moor
Fd (cf. *the further & middle Moor* 1713, 1747); Old Womans Mdw; Ox Hey
Bank; Pedlars Croft; Penny Croft (*v.* pening); Pingot (*v.* pingot); Sport Fd;
Spout Mdw (*v.* spoute); Stock Hoe; Style Fd (*v.* stigel); Sweet Acre; Turn
Acre (*v.* trun); White Hill (*quythul* 1307, cf. *Quiter-hall* 13 (17) Orm[2] I 431
probably corrupt, 'white hill', *v.* hwīt, hyll).

(b) *le Salteresway, -is-* 1307 (*v.* 'Watling Street' 1 40, Ashley Rd *supra*);
Sandlebridge 1696 ('(bridge at) sand-hill', *v.* sand, hyll, brycg, cf. Sandle
Bridge 84 *infra*); *le Wodehouses* 1343 ('houses at a wood', *v.* wudu, hūs).

5. TABLEY SUPERIOR (101–7279), OVER TABLEY

Stab(e)lei 1086 DB

Thabbelewe 12 Chest, *Tabelle, Tab(b)eley, Thabelee* l12–e13 Orm², Tab, Dugd, Chest, *Fitt* (p) *et freq* with variant spellings *-leg(-a, -e, -h), -leth', -le(ia), -lg', -lee, -ly, -leh, -leye*; *Tabbele Superior, Over-* 1289 Court, Plea, 1295 Tab

Thebel' 1191 Facs, *Tebbelee* e13 Orm²

Tablia e13 Orm² (p), *-ley* c.1270 (17) ib *et freq* with variant spellings *-leg(h), -le(ighe), -laye, -ly,* Tabb-; *Overtable* 1355 BPR

Tab(b)ill(egh(th)) c.1281, 1294 JRL (p), 1289 Court (p), *-Superior* l13 Tab

Talbillegh 1294 JRL (p), (*Over(e)-, Houere-) Talbel(l)eg(h), -lee* 1295, 1297, e14 Tab

'Tæbba's clearing', from the OE pers.n. *Tæbba* and lēah, with uferra 'higher', distinguishing this township from Tabley Inferior 122 *infra*. For the DB form *v.* ANInfl 68.

BRADLEY (lost), 1847 *TA, Bradelegh* 1295 Tab, (*-Ssawe*) 1297 ib, *-le (shawe)* 1295 ib, (*-Schahee*) e14 ib, *Mechilbradley* 1322 ib, 'broad clearing', *v.* brād, lēah, sc(e)aga 'a wood', micel 'big'.

BUDDELEY (lost), *Buddelegh Broke* 1295, 1297, *Budleghschagh* c.1300, *-ley-, -schawe, Buddyleye, Bodelegh, Bodelybrok* 1320, 1322, *Bodileghseche* 1344 all Tab, *Great Buddeley* 1847 *TA*, 'Budda's clearing', from the OE pers.n. *Bud(d)a* and lēah, with brōc 'a brook', sceaga 'a wood', sīc 'a water-course'. The pers.n. appears in Budworth 107, 325 *infra*.

FERNILLY (lost), 1847 *TA, Fernile, -leg(h), Fernele(gh),* (*-Mor(h), -Moor*) 1295, 1297, 1320 Tab, *le Fernylegh* 1341 ib, *Fernileys* 1657 ib, 'ferny clearing', *v.* fearnig, lēah, with mōr¹ 'a moor'.

OVER TABLEY HALL, 1831 Bry, *Superior Aula* 13, 1320 Tab, *Ouer(e)-halle* 1295, 1297 ib, 1300 Chol, *the Hall of Tabley in Over Tabley* 1626 ChRR, 'the higher hall', *v.* uferra, hall, cf. Tabley Hall in Tabley Inferior 123 *infra*.

SLATEHURST (lost), 1353 BPR, *Slad(e)hurst* 1286, 1288, 1289 Court (p), 1297 Tab (p), 1312 Plea (p), 1328, 1331 *Fitt* (p), *le Scladehurstebroc* 1290 Tab, (*le*) *S(c)ladehurst* c.1300, 1316, 1320 Tab, Chol, 1336 ChRR, 1340 *Eyre, Schladehurst'* 1316 Chol (p), *Sladhurstmosse iuxta*

Lynstrete 1339 Tab, 'wooded bank at a valley', *v.* slæd, hyrst, brōc, mos 'a moss'. *Lynstrete* is 'Watling Street' 1 40.

STRETTELEGH (lost), 1316 Tab, *-lee* (*pullis*), *Dowe Streettelee* e14 ib, cf. *Strethleye, Stretleh* l12 Chest, *Stretlethfern* 1300, 1316 Tab, *Stredle* l12 Facs (p), 'clearing, or wood, at a Roman road', *v.* strǣt, lēah, pull 'a pool', fearn 'fern, a ferny place', cf. St Paul's Church *infra*, 'Watling Street' 1 40. *Dowe* is a manorial affix, from the ME pers.n. *Dowe, Dawe*, a pet-form of *David*, cf. Richard son of *Doew de Sladehurst* 1316 Tab. Chest 310 and Facs 18 identify the twelfth-century forms with *Strettle* in Mere 52 *supra*, but that is not historically necessary.

SUDLOW FM & LANE (101–7378), *Sudlaue* 13 Tab (p), *-low* (*-a, -e*), *-lou* (*-a, -e*) c.1250, c.1300, 1307 ib, *Sudelowe* 1346 Sheaf, *Sudde-* 1507 Orm², *Sodlowe* c.1290 Chol (p), *Sodelo(u)we* 1340, 1346 Tab, 1350 *Eyre* (p), 'south hill', *v.* sūð, hlāw, cf. *Sudlowemosse* 1339 Tab, *Sudlow(e) F(i)eld* 1563 ib, *Sudlowtownefeild* 1684 JRL, *Sudlow Hey* 1847 *TA*, also Sudlow Lane, Wash Fm 123, 93 *infra, v.* mos, (ge)hæg. The 'town field' was one of the common fields of the township, *v.* toun, cf. Townfield *infra*.

BELT WOOD. BLUEBELL FM, 1831 Bry. BONGS ROUGH & WOOD, 1842 OS, *v.* banke, rūh, wudu. BURNTHOUSE FM, BURNT-HOUSES, *v.* brende². THE COPPICE, cf. *Coppice Meadow* 1847 *TA*. DAIRYHOUSE FM, 1860 White. GREEN LANE, 1831 Bry. GROVE FM, *Tabley Groves* 1831 ib, *v.* grāf. HEATHFIELD. HEYROSE FM, *The Heroes Farm* 1831 ib. HOLEHOUSE FM, HOLEHOUSES, *Hole House* 1831 ib, *-s* 1842 OS, cf. *Holcloyt* c.1300, *Holeclowe Siche* c.1306 both Tab, 'houses at a hollow' and '(watercourse in) a hollow dell', *v.* hol², clōh, sīc. HOLLOW-WOOD FM, 1842 OS, *Hollow Wood* 1831 Bry, *the hall of the Woodlands* 1556 (17) Orm², *-the Woodd, -Wodde* 1557 ib, *-Wood* 1666 ib, 'the hall in the wood', *v.* hall, wudu, cf. Orm² 1 471 where the house is reported from 1483. It may be the house alluded to in Latin as *aula sambucca* 1500 AddCh 37239 'elder-tree hall'. The modern form is a misinterpretation of *Hall o' Wood*. IVY COTTAGE, 1831 Bry. MEREHEATH LANE, *v.* 53 *supra*. MOSS FM & LANE, *Moss Lane* 1831 Bry, *Moss Farm* 1842 OS. POWNALL GREEN, 1831 Bry, from the surname from Pownall 1 228 ROEBUCK FM, 1831 ib. ST PAUL'S CHURCH, *the Newe Chapell in the Stretefrith* 1493 Sheaf, *an ancient Chappel, called Over Tabley*

*Chappel, or more generally known by the name Chappel in the Street;
for it is situate in the High Street* 1666 Orm[2], *v.* chapel(e) 'a chapel',
strǣt 'a paved road' (referring to 'Watling Street' 1 40, *Tabley Street
infra*), (ge)fyrhðe 'woodland', cf. *Strettelegh supra.*   SWAINS
WALK, cf. *The Walk* 1847 *TA, v.* walk.   TABLEY BROOK (BRIDGE
& FM), *le Brok* 1290–1300 Tab, *Brook House* 1831 Bry, *Tabley
Brook* 1860 White, *v.* brōc. The brook joins Arley Brook 1 13.
TABLEYHILL, 1538 Plea.   TABLEY LANE, cf. *terra in venellis, les
veneles* 1344 Tab, *v.* lane (Lat. *venella*), cf. *Villa Fm infra.*   TAB-
LEYMOSS WOOD, *Ouertabbeleghmosse* 1355 ib, *Tabley Mosse* 1548 ib,
v. mos.   TABLEYPIPE WOOD, *Old Paddock Wood* 1831 Bry, *v.*
pearroc, wudu. The later name contains ModEdial. pipe 'a decoy
channel'. There was a decoy here 119.   TABLEY STREET (lost),
1842 OS, *v.* 'Watling Street' 1 40.   TABLEYVALE FM. TABLEY
WOOD, 1842 OS.   VILLA FM, *Tabley Lane End* 1831 Bry, cf.
Tabley Lane *supra.*   WATERLESS BRIDGE (101–704788), *Hatterley
Bridge* 1831 ib. It has taken the name of the next bridge downstream, *Waterless Bridge* (101–708785), 1842 OS, (*-Horse-*) 1831 Bry,
Watterlesse Bridge 1618 Sheaf, cf. *ford' de Waterles* 1381 Tab,
Waterless Meadow 1847 *TA*, from Waterless Brook[1] 1 37. There
is no evidence of the origin of *Hatterley.*   WATERLESS COTTAGES,
cf. prec.   WINDMILL INN, 1831 Bry.   YEWTREE HO, 1860
White, *-Cottage* 1831 Bry.

FIELD-NAMES

The undated forms are 1847 *TA* 382. Of the others, e13 (17) is ChRR, 1289
Court, 1301, 1538 Plea, 1352 *Eyre*, 1363, 1647, 1691 JRL, 1666 Orm[2], 1831
Bry, 1842 OS and the rest Tab.

(a) Adams Garden; Alder Fd; Antrobus Fd (cf. Antrobus 127 *infra*);
Backside; Bears Fd; Beesoms Hill (*Besemehull* (lit. *De-*) 1339, *Beesome Hill*
1671, 'besom hill', perhaps a place where twigs were got for making besoms,
from OE *bes(e)ma* and hyll); Black Croft; Blake Fd (*v.* blæc); Bramelow
('bramble hill', *v.* bræmel, hlāw); The Breach (*v.* brēc); Briery Knowl (cf.
Bramelow *supra*); le Brodeford 1647 (1322, *-forthe* 1363 (p), *Brodforde
Ruding* 1289, *Brodford* c.1300, 'the broad ford', *v.* brād, ford, ryding 'a
clearing'); Browey Fd (*v.* brū); Bull Acre (cf. *Bulehalith* 113, 'bull's corner',
v. bula, halh); Butty Fd (*v.* butty); Cinder Hill (*le Sindurhul* c.1300, from
hyll 'hill', with either sinder 'cinder' or synder, sundor 'asunder, separate',
cf. Sinderland 20 *supra*); Cocker(s)ley (*v.* cocker, lēah, cf. *Kockersley* 1
159); Coithurst Meadows 1666 (*le Kutehurst* 1301, *Kytehurst* 1538, 'kite
hill', *v.* cȳta, hyrst); Colesellers; Cote Fd (*v.* cot); Big Dale, Dale Fd (*Dalefeld*

1341, *v.* dæl[1], feld); Dam Croft; Old Dungfield; Flatt (*v.* flat); Flax Coppice; Fountain Mdw; Glade Butts (*v.* butte); Goslings; Old Hack (*v.* haca); Halkers; Hazledines; Hemp Pits; Hilker; Intack (*the-* 1563, *v.* inntak); Irish Intake; Key Rowes ('cow roughs', rough pasture for cattle, *v.* cū (gen.sg., nom.pl. cȳ), rūh); Kiln Fd; Kingpool Fd; the Kittling fields 1691 (*Celtyngesfeld* 1352, *Kyltynge Feld* 1356, 'young cat's field', *v.* ketlingr, feld. The first el. may have been a nickname); Knowl; Long Shoot (*v.* scēat); Marl Fd; Meeres (*v.* (ge)mǣre); Naugerhill (cf. *auger* (NED) 'an auger'); Nurrey Bragg Mdw; Orchinta; Oven Fd; Ox Bottoms (*v.* botm); Fur & Near Park (cf. *parcum de Ouere Tabbelegh* c.1220, *v.* park); Pike (*v.* pīc[1] 'a hill'); Pinfold Fd (*v.* pynd-fald); Pingot (cf. 'a *pyngallt* of land on the north side of Waterless Brook' 1548 Tab, *v.* pingot); Rapes Wd; Riddings (*v.* ryding); Roundabout (*v.* 327 *infra*); Round Hey (cf. *Round Wood* 1831, 1842); Rundle Mdw (*v.* rynel, dial. *rundle* 'a small stream, a runnel'); Shaw Fd (*v.* sceaga); Short Butts (*v.* sc(e)ort, butte); Stoney Croft; Street Mdw (*v.* strǣt, cf. 'Watling Street' 1 40); Sun Fd (*v.* sunne); Tabley Hey (*v.* (ge)hæg); Tan Yard Croft (*v.* tan-yard); Town Field (*v.* toun, cf. Sudlow *supra*); Great Wilmer Fd; Winterbottom Mdw (*v.* winter[1], botm); Witheys (*v.* wīðig); Wood Edish (*v.* wudu, edisc).

(*b*) *Aldfildhulm* 113 ('(water-meadow at) the old field', *v.* ald, feld, hulm); *Astebrighaleth* c.1300 ('east bridge nook', *v.* ēast, brycg, halh); *Bernardescroft, -is-* 1335 ('Bernard's croft', from the ME pers.n. *Bernard* (OE *Beornheard* or OG *Ber(e)nard*) and croft); (*le*)*Blakebrok* 1290, 1330 (*v.*blæc, brōc); *Black Lake* 1634 (*v.* blæc, lacu); (*le*) *Brodefeld* 1442, 1466 (*v.* brād, feld); *Bromylee* ?14 ('broomy clearing', *v.* brōmig, lēah); *le Brunhurst* 1322 ('brown hill', *v.* brūn[1], hyrst); *Dychebruch(e)* c.1300, 1339 ('ditch clearing', *v.* dīc, bryce); *Elotescrosse* 1339 ('Ellot's cross', from the ME pers.n. *Ellot*, diminutive of *Ellen*, and cros); *Foxglove Haye* 1543 (*v.* (ge)hæg); *Foxlache* 1322, 1340, 1381 ('fox bog', *v.* fox, læc(c)); *Gorsticroft* 1341 (*v.* gorstig, croft); *Hewe(he)th, Heweheih* 1339 ('the domestic's heath', *v.* hīwan (ME *hewe*), hǣð); *the Highfyld* 1545, *-Feilde* 1568 (*v.* hēah); *Longelee* ?14, *Long(g)eleg(h)* 1306, 1316, 1318 ('long clearing', *v.* lang, lēah); *Low(e)feld* 1320, 1337 ('field at a hill or mound', near Sudlow *supra*, *v.* hlāw, feld); *Merehege* c.1250 ('boundary hedge' *v.* (ge)mǣre, hege); *le Middelfeld* 1341 (*v.* middel, feld); *Northcroft* c.1300, 1337, *North Crofte Feld* 1316, *-Fylde* 1543, *Northe Croft alias Hynghe Feld* 1563 (*v.* norð, croft, hencg); *Porchcroft* 1341 (perhaps land dedicated to the maintenance of a church porch, from ME *porche*, *v.* croft); *Qwytstobbrugge* c.1220 ('(bridge at) the white tree-stump', *v.* hwīt, stubb, brycg); *the Ryng(e) Fyld(e)* 1543, *Ringefields* 1559 (*v.* hring, feld, cf. Rinks 123 *infra*); *Salter(e)sway(e)* (*v.* saltere, weg, cf. 'Watling Street' 1 40); *Scharesmethysrydyng* 1330 (from ryding 'cleared land' and a ME occupational surname *Scharesmeth* '(plough-)share smith', from OE *scear* and smið, cf. Reaney s.n. *Shearsmith*, Fransson 154 s.n. *Forceter*, for analogies); *Shatre* e13 (17) (there is no more material for this lost place, cf. Orm[2] 1 618n, and the etymology is uncertain); *del Sidhalle* 1339 (p) ('the wide hall', *v.* sīd, hall, cf. Siddal Wood 71 *infra*); *Sichebrok* 1341 (p) ('watercourse brook', *v.* sīc, brōc); *Smerefeld* c.1300, *Smefield* 1563 ('butter field', a rich pasture, *v.*

smeoru, feld); *Smithefeld* c.1320, *Smethefeld* 1337, 1339, 1341 ('smiths' field', *v.* smið, feld); *Sondiford* c.1250 (*v.* sandig, ford); *Sparghe Moss* 1567 ('sparrows' moss', *v.* spearwa, mos); *Spendelowerudyng* 1320 (from ryding 'cleared land', and the surname *de Spendeloue* (1320 Tab) of a tenant of Tabley, which seems toponymic (*v.* spenne, hlāw), but of Richard *Spendeloue* of Macclesfield e13 (1290) Court 243, i.e. 'spend-love'); *le Stonflatt* 1341 ('stone plot', *v.* stān, flat); *le Steyresthurst* c.1300 (perhaps 'very steep-, steepest wooded-hill', from hyrst and the sup. of stǣger[2] 'steep'); *Thertouereflatt* (lit. *-onere-*) 1341 ('plot of land lying athwart', *v.* thwert-over, flat); *Thornland in Sudlowe* 1341 ('thorn selion', *v.* þorn, land, a strip in *Lowefeld supra*); *Tokbruggemosse* 1442 (perhaps '(moss at) the bridge built of stocks', *v.* stocc, brycg, mos. Initial *s-* lost before *-t-* is due to AN influence, cf. ANInfl 68); *Whytemosse* 1339 ('white moss', *v.* hwīt, mos); *Wythinforde* c.1300 ('willow ford', *v.* wiðegn (or wiðigen), ford).

6. TATTON (PARK) (101–7581)

> *Tatune* 1086 DB, *Tatun(ia)* 12, 13 Tab
> *Tattun(e)* e13 *Mass* (p), Facs (p), *Fitt*, Orm[2], *-ton(-a, -e)* e13 MidCh (p), Orm[2], 1287 Court, 1294 CRC *et freq*, (*Old-*) 1288 Pat, *Tatton parcus* 1290 IpmR, Pat, *-Parke* 1339 Tab, c.1536 Leland
> *Taitun* 1385 Cl

'Tāta's farm', from the OE pers.n. *Tāta* and tūn. The township is almost entirely included within Tatton Park, in which was *The Green* (lost, 101–760812) 1831 Bry, the original site, near Old Hall, of the hamlet removed to New Tatton *infra*, cf. Old Hall, Mill Pool Wood *infra*.

HASULHURST (lost), (*-more*) 1430 AddCh, *Hesel-, Haselhurstescloh(e)* e13 Orm[2], *Helhurst* c.1230 Tab, *Haselhurst* 13 ib, 1333 ChRR (p), (*le*) *Hasulhurst* 1393 ib (p), *-il-* 1404 Pat (p), 'the hazel-wood hill', *v.* hæsel, hyrst. This is located 'between the vill of Knutsford and the park of Tatton' (*AddCh* 37233). The moor is *mora* e13 Orm[2] I 424, *v.* mōr[1]. The valley (*v.* clōh) contains Tatton Mere, cf. Orm[2] I 423–4 (12, 16). Cf. Hazelhurst Fm 67 *infra*.

NORSHAW (lost), (*-in Tatton*) 1676 Sheaf, *Northsahe* 1233 Orm[2] I xxxvi, (1580) Sheaf, *-shawe* c.1275 (18) ib, *-shagh(e)* 1304 Chamb, 14 Tab, *-sc(h)awe* 1362 Cl, *Norsah* 13 Tab, *-shagh* 1327 (17) Orm[2], *Nordschawe* c.1307 JRL, 'north wood', *v.* norð, sc(e)aga.

BIRKIN LODGE, 1842 OS, BIRKIN FORD BRIDGE, cf. Birkin 58 *supra*. BOUNDARY WOOD.   BULL RING, a ring of trees in the park.

COTTON RELIEF WOOD, a wood or plantation from which the timber would be sold for the relief of distressed cottonmill-hands in La and Ch during the great Cotton Famine of 1862–65. CROFTS WOOD. CROW WOOD. DAIRY WOOD. FLAGBRIDGE WOOD. GOLDEN BROOK PITS. LONG WOOD. MEREHEATH LODGE, cf. Mereheath 53 *supra*. MILL POOL WOOD, cf. *Tatton Mill* (101–759819) 1831 Bry. MOBBERLEY BOTTOMS, *v.* **botm** 'a valley bottom', cf. Mobberley 65 *infra*. MOSS PLANTATION, 1842 OS. OLD HALL (101–756813), 1831 Bry, *Tatton Manor* c. 1536 Leland, *v.* ald, hall, cf. Tatton Hall *infra*, Tatton *supra*. NEW TATTON (101–743809), 1831 Bry, cf. Tatton *supra*. TATTONDALE, 1831 ib, *v.* dæl[1]. TATTON HALL (101–744815), 1831 ib, built c.1794, super-seding Old Hall *supra*. TATTON MERE, 1656 Orm[2], the larger of two lakes, *magna & parva mara* e13 Orm[2] 1 423–4; the smaller (drained in 1816 Orm[2] *loc. cit.*, flooded again 1″ OS 7th ed.) was *the water of Bulmer* and *the water of Shalmer* 1553 Sheaf[3] 17, 78, 'bull's mere' and 'shallow mere', *v.* bula, sc(e)ald, mere[1]. WALK MILL COVERT, cf. *The Walkmill* 1751 Sheaf, *v.* walke-mylne.

FIELD-NAMES

The e13 reference is to Orm[2] 1 423–4, charters of Mobberley priory.

(b) *Alfielde* 1553 Sheaf ('old field', *v.* ald, feld); *Bruchel* H3 (17) Orm[2] ('hill where land is newly broken in', *v.* bryce, hyll); *Chepfaldefurluc'* e13 ('sheep-fold furlong', *v.* scēp, fald, furlang, cf. *Sepefurlong infra*); *terra del Egge* e13 ('the edge', *v.* ecg, at the brink of *Haselhurstescloh*, *v. Hasulhurst supra*); *pons de Elleche* e13 ('(bridge over) the el-stream', *v.* ēl[2], lece); *Lume'cloh* e13 (perhaps for *Lummecloh* 'dell with a deep pool in it', *v.* lum(m), clōh); *Mercroft* e13 ('croft near a mere', *v.* mere[1], croft, by Tatton Mere *supra*); *the Parson's Hey* c.1550 Orm[2] (*v.* persone, (ge)hæg); *(le) Port(e)stret(e)* e13 ('the road to a (market-) town', *v.* port[2], strǣt, probably a way to Knutsford 73 *infra*); *Sepefurlong* e13 ('sheep furlong', *v.* scēp, furlang); *Steinulves-, Steynulfves-, Stainilliscroft* e13 ('Steinolf's croft', from the ON pers.n. *Steinolfr* (OSw *Stenulf*) and croft, cf. *crux Steynulfi* e13, *v.* cros 'a cross').

viii. Mobberley

MOBBERLEY (101–7979)

Motburlege 1086 DB, *-leh* e13 Orm[2], *Modburle, -berleg(a), -birleye* l12 AddCh (p), Tab, (1353) CAS NS XIII *et freq* with variant spellings *Modd(e)-, Mode-, Mud-, Mad-, -lea, -l(e)ia, -legh(e),*

-leg, -ley (-e, -a), -lehia, -leth, -ledhe, -le(y)gh, -lee, -lay, -bor-,
-bier-, -burg (-h, -e), -bour(g)- to *Modburlegh* 1514 Plea

Moberlehe c.1170 Sheaf, -leh(a), -leth, *Mobburley*, *Mobberleia* e13
Orm[2], Chest (p), (1580) Sheaf *et freq* with variant spellings
Mobur-, *Mobbir-*, *Mubber-*, *Moubur-*, -legh(e), -laie, -le(y), -leg',
-ly, -lee

Mordberleg 13 Orm[2]

Murberley 1391 ChRR, Pat

Malberleye 1550 *MinAcct*

'(Clearing at) the fortification where meetings are held', *v.* mōt,
burh, lēah, cf. Modbury D 91, 279, 281, Modbury Hundred Do
(EHN[2] 116) and Burleyhurst, *le Dichegreaves* and *Grimsditch infra*.

BURLEYHURST FM & WOOD, 1831 Bry, (a wood called) *Birlehurst* 1434
ChRR, *Burley-* 1693 Sheaf, 'wooded hill belonging to the *burh-lēah*
(i.e. Mobberley *supra*)', *v.* burh (gen.sg. byrh), lēah, hyrst.

GLEVEHOUSE FM, *Gleve House* 1842 OS, *Gleave House* 1831 Bry,
named from John *Gleave* of High Legh, owner of *Holden-Cliff house
in Mobberley* 1672 Orm[2], cf. (*haia de*) *Holdenclif* c.1306 (15) JRL,
-cliff(e) 1334 ib, *Holden Cliffe* (*Bottoms*) 1847 *TA* (Sheaf[1] 3 23 reads
Holding Cliff), '(slope at) the hollow valley', *v.* hol[2], denu, clif.

GRIMSDITCH FM (101–790794), *Grimsditch* 1847 *TA*, cf. Grimsditch
134 *infra*. The p.n. may be manorial. If not, an allusion to a lost
ancient earthwork, 'Woden's ditch', would be pertinent to the p.n.
Mobberley *supra*, *v.* Grīm, dīc, cf. *le Dichegreves infra*, and Camp
Green 58 *supra*.

ANTROBUS BRIDGE & HALL, *Antrobus Hall* 1831 Bry, cf. Antrobus 127
infra. This may be manorial. BAGULEY GREEN FM, *Baggiley-green*
1672 Orm[2], cf. John *Baggiley* 1672 ib, surnamed from Baguley 12
supra, *v.* grēne[2]. BARLOW FM & HO, *Barlow House* 1831 Bry, cf.
Thomas de *Berlawe* 1362 Cl, Randle & Robert *Barlow* 1672 Orm[2].
BARNES BROW, cf. William *Barnes* 1672 ib, *v.* brū 'a brow, a hill-side'.
BENKEYHURST FM, *Dickin Barn* 1831 Bry, cf. *Dicken House Meadow*
1847 *TA*, probably from the ME pers.n. *Dicon*. BIRTLES FM, 1842
OS, *Birtles House* 1839 *TA*. BLAKELEY FM & LANE, *Blakeley
Farm* 1831 Bry, *Blakeley Lane* 1839 *TA*, *v.* Orrelhouse *infra*.
BOLLINHOUSE FM, named from R. Bollin 1 15. BRADBURY'S, cf.
Charles & Peter *Bradbury*, *Bredbury* 1672 Orm[2], surnamed from
Bredbury 1 262. BREACH HOUSE FM, *Breach House* 1831 Bry,

cf. Richard *Bruch* 1672 Orm[2], *v.* brēc, bryce.   BROADOAK FM,
Broad Oak 1831 Bry, *the Broad-Oak* 1672 Orm[2].   BROWNEDGE
COTTAGES, *Brown Edge* 1672 ib, *v.* brūn[1], ecg.   BUNNELL'S CROFT.
CHERRY HO (lost, 101–794786), 1842 OS, on Dam Lane *infra*, or
another house of this name, 1831 Bry, at 101–797823 on Wood Lane
infra, was *Cherrys Tenement* 1819 Sheaf, cf. *Cherry Field* 1847 *TA*,
named from Humphrey *Cherry* 1672 Orm[2].   CINDER LANE FM.
CLAY LANE, cf. *Clay Field* 1847 *TA*.   COLDSTREAM COTTAGES.
COPPOCK FM & HO, respectively *Coppock House, Cockup House* 1831
Bry, cf. Coppuck House Field 1 105, named from William *Coppock*
1672 Orm[2].   CORNEYCROFT, 1847 *TA*.   DAIRYHOUSE FM, cf.
Dairy Field 1847 ib.   DAMHEAD (101–790795), DAM LANE (101–
790795 to 800780), *The Dam-head* 1617 Orm[2], *Dam Head* (*Lane*) 1842
OS, *Cherry Lane* 1831 Bry, cf. *Damstead* 1847 *TA*, *v.* damme 'a mill-
dam', hēafod, stede, cf. Mobberly Mill *infra*, Cherry Ho *supra*.
DAVENPORT LANE, *Hough Lane* (*House*) 1831 Bry, cf. John & Edward
Davenport, John *Hough* 1672 Orm[2].   DICKEN BRIDGE, *Dickin
Bridge* 1842 OS, cf. Benkeyhurst Fm *supra*.   DUBB'D EDGE (lost),
1860 White, *-hedge* 1760 Sheaf, *the Dub'd hedge* 1672 Orm[2], 'the
trimmed hedge', *v.* dubbed, hecg.   DUKENFIELD HALL, *Duck-* 1831
Bry, *-in-* 1839 *TA*, probably from the surname from Dukinfield 1
276.   FAULKNER'S LANE, cf. *Faulkner* 1847 ib, from the surname.
FOURLANE-ENDS, 1847 *ib*.   GAUSTY CROFT FM, *Gorsty Croft* 1831
Bry, *v.* gorstig.   GRAVEYARD FM & LANE, *Graveyard Farm, Field,
House, Knoll & Lane* 1847 *TA*, named from a disused Quakers'
burial-ground here, *Quakers Burying Ground* 1831 Bry, *Grave Yard*
1842 OS, *The Quakers' Graveyard* 1883 (local) Sheaf[1] 3, 31.
GREENBANK.   GROVE HO, 1831 Bry.   HALL BANK & LANE.
HANGING BANK, *v.* hangende.   HANSON HO, *Anson House* 1831 ib.
HARGRAVE'S BRIDGE, cf. *Hargrove* 1847 *TA*.   HAZELHURST FM,
Hazelhurst Above 1831 Bry, *Far & Near Haslehurst* 1847 *TA*, cf.
the surname *Hazlehurst* 1672 Orm[2], *Hasulhurst* 1498 *Dow* in this
township, probably from *Hasulhurst* 64 *supra*.   HEALDMILL,
Hield Mill 1672 Orm[2], *v.* helde 'a hill-side, a slope'.   HILLHOUSE,
1672 ib.   HOBCROFT HO & LANE, cf. *Hob Croft* (6x) 1847 *TA*.
Sheaf[1] 3 30 reports local tradition of a hobgoblin hereabouts, *v.*
hob.   HOLLINGEE (101–813803), 1831 Bry, (*Le*) *Holynche* 1413,
1462 ChRR, 'ridge, or ledge, on a hill', *v.* hōh, hlinc.   HOLT HO,
1839 *TA*, *Holt's House* 1810 Sheaf, from the surname *Holt*.   KELL-
HOUSE, 1842 OS, *Kiln House* 1839 *TA*, *v.* cyln, hūs.   KEYHOUSE

Fm, *Key House* 1831 Bry, cf. *Kay Field* 1847 *TA*, 'cows' house', *v* cū (pl. cȳ).   Knolls Green, 1842 OS, *Knowl Green* 1672 Orm², *v.* cnoll, grēne².   Lady Lane, 1831 Bry.   Leycester's Firs, 1842 OS, named from the Leicester family of Toft 81 *infra*, landowners here.   Lindow Moss & Fm, *Lower Moss, Lindow House* 1831 Bry, *Lindow Moss* 1839 *TA*, cf. Lindow Moss 1 230. Manor Ho, on the site of a priory of Augustinian Canons dedicated to St Wilfrid, founded c.1206, *v.* Orm² 1 411, 421.   Mere House Fm, *Mere-house* 1672 Orm², *Mayer House* 1831 Bry, probably from the surname from Mere 51 *supra*.   Mobberley Brook (Birkin Brook 1 15), *Mylbrook* 1369 Orm² 1 495, *Mobberley Mill Brook* 1839 *TA*, *v.* myln, brōc, cf. *Mobberley Mill infra*.   Mobberley Old Hall, *Hall Farm* 1831 Bry, *Mobberley Hall* 1842 OS.   Mobberley Mill (lost, 101–790796), 1831 Bry, 1672 Orm², *molendinum aquaticum super aquam vocatam Mylbrook* 1369 ib, cf. *le Mulnerudyng*(k) 1334 JRL, *Mill Field* 1847 *TA*, *v.* myln, ryding, cf. Damhead, Mobberley Brook *supra*.   Modes Cottage, cf. *Modus Croft* 1847 *TA*, probably land subject to a *modus* (NED), either as a condition of tenancy or as a cash consideration in lieu of a tithe. Moss Bank & Lane, *Moss Lane & Side* 1842 OS, *the Mosse-side* 1672 Orm², cf. Paddockhill Moss *infra*.   Mossway Cottage, *v.* weg, cf. Lindow Moss 1 230.   New Mills, *New (Corn) Mill* 1831 Bry, 1842 OS.   Newton Hall, 1831 Bry, cf. *Newton's Intake* 1847 *TA* (Sheaf¹ 3 11 reads *Intack*), cf. Francis *Newton*, of Knolls Green *supra*, 1672 Orm² 1 418.   Norbury's Bridge, cf. *Norbury Hey* 1847 *TA*, from the surname *Norbury* and (ge)hæg. Oakbank Fm.   Orrelhouse Fm, *Orrel House* 1831 Bry, *Orrell's* 1810 Sheaf, *Blakeley Hall* 1839 *TA*, 1842 OS, cf. *Orrell Wood, Far Bleakley* 1847 *TA*, and Blakeley Fm *supra*, 'black clearing', *v.* blæc, lēah; the home of the *Orrell* family.   Ostler's Lane.   Owenhouse, *Black Johns* 1831 Bry, *Jack at a Pinch* 1839 *TA*, obviously from a nickname, but the story is not recorded.   Paddockhill, 1643 Sheaf, probably 'frog hill' from its situation in old moss-land, *v.* padduc.   Park Fm, cf. foll.   Parkside, 1860 White, *Marvel Hall* 1839 *TAMap*, cf. foll.   Parkside Fm, *Park Farm* 1842 OS, cf. *Park Field, Piece & Room* 1847 *TA*, named from Tatton Park 64 *supra*, cf. prec.   Pauldonhouse, cf. *Paulden Meadow* 1847 *ib*. Pavement Lane (Fm) (101–779797 to 774786), *Pavement Lane* 1672 Orm², (*House*) 1831 Bry, 'the paved lane', *v.* pavement, lane. Pepper Street (101–778813), 1831 Bry, (*Hall*) 1839 *TA*, cf. Pepper

Street 327 *infra*. PODMORE HOLLOW, *Pedmore Hollow* 1842 OS, probably 'toad-moor', *v.* pode, mōr[1]. RALEIGH WOOD, 1842 OS, *Reyley Wood* 1672 Orm[2], *Railey Wood* 1831 Bry, perhaps 'roe glade', *v.* rǣge, lēah. SALTERSLEY FM, *Saltersley* 1581 Sheaf, (*-gate*) 1608 ib, (*-Moss*) 1632 ib, *Sawltersley Mosse* 1620 ib, *Salterley* 1672 Orm[2], 'salter's clearing', *v.* saltere, lēah, perhaps a resting-place for salt merchants, but cf. *Brine Pits* 1847 *TA* (*infra*). SHELMERDINE, *-s* 1763 White, from a surname. SLADE COTTAGE, cf. *The Slade* 1883 (local) Sheaf[1] 3 12, the name of the bank at Tipping Brow *infra*, *v.* slæd 'a valley'. SMALL LANE, 1831 Bry, 'narrow lane', *v.* smæl. SMITH LANE (FM), *Smith House* (*Lane*) 1831 ib, *v.* smið 'a smith'. SPRINGBANK, *-Bonk* 1847 *TA*, *v.* spring, banke. SQUARE WOOD, *Mobberley Wood* 1842 OS. STACKHOUSE, 1842 ib, *v.* stakkr. STOCKINGHEY FM, *Stocking Hey* 1831 Bry, 'enclosure cleared of tree-stumps', *v.* stoccing, (ge)hæg. STUBBS FM & LANE, cf. George *Stubs* 1672 Orm[2], and *le Stubbehallond* 1334 JRL, 'half-selion at a stub', *v.* stubb, half-land. SUMMERFIELD, cf. *Summer Heys* 1847 *TA*, *v.* sumor, (ge)hæg. SUNNY BANK, nearly the site of *White Gate* 1842 OS, *Hough Lane House* 1831 Bry, *v.* hōh. TIPPING BROW, cf. *Tipping Meadow* 1847 *TA*, probably connected with *widow Tipping* 1672 Orm[2] 1 418, *v.* brū, mǣd, cf. Slade Cottage *supra*. TITHEBARN FM. TOWN LANE (HALL), 1831 Bry, *The Town-lane* 1672 Orm[2], *v.* toun. VALEWOOD FM, *Vale Wood* 1842 OS. WALLBROW, 1831 Bry, 'well brow', *v.* wælla, brū. WITCHCOTE WOOD, *Whichcote Wood* 1831 ib, cf. Thomas *Witchcot* 1672 Orm[2]. WOODEND, (*the*) 1672 ib, a hamlet at the west end of Burleyhurst Wood *supra*, 'the quarter near the wood', *v.* wudu, ende[1]. WOOD LANE, (*the-*) 1639 Sheaf. YARWOODHOUSE, 1831 Bry, cf. the surname *Yarwood* 1672 Orm[2], *Yearewood* 1674 Mere, probably from Yarwoodheath 58 *supra*. YEWTREE FM.

FIELD-NAMES

The undated forms are 1839 *TAMap* 268, 1847 *TA* 268 (Tithe Redemption Commission's copy). 'Holl.' refers to a local copy described by R. Holland in Sheaf[1] 3 (1883), 7–30. Of the others c.1206 (1615), c.1250 are Dugd, 13, 1672 Orm[2], 1301, 1306 (15), 1333, 1334, 1440 JRL, E3 *Surv*, 1341, 1439 Tab, 14 *JRC* 861, 1348, 1349 *MinAcct*, 1351 *Chol*, 1395 ChRR, 1831 Bry, 1842 OS, and the rest Sheaf.

(a) Acre (*the* 1620); Alice Bower (*-Brown* Holl.); Ankers; Ash Trough; Ashen Beech 1831 (a wood, 'valley growing with ash-trees', *v.* æscen, bece[1]);

Back Stone Fd (cf. *Bakestaneshull* c.1206 (1615), 'hill where baking-stones are got', *v.* bæc-stān, hyll); Bale Close (*Ball-* Holl.); Balshaw Mdw (probably from the surname from Bolshaw 1 244); Bent Hough ('spur of land growing with bent-grass', *v.* beonet, hōh); Bentley's Stone (cf. the surname *de Benteley* 1351, *de Bentylegh* 1439, of Toft, Rostherne *&* Tatton, *v.* beonet, lēah, stān); Berchin Fd (*v.* Birchen *infra*); Beswick (*v.* bēos, wīc); Birchen, -in, Berchin Fd *&* Lands (*le Birchenfeld* 1334, 'field at a place growing with birch-trees', *v.* bircen[1], feld, land, cf. Birkinheath 58 *supra*); Black Acre, Croft *&* Fd (cf. *le Blakehurthe* 1334, 'black ground', *v.* blæc, eorðe); Blue Button Fd (dial. plant-name for *Scabiosa succisa* (Holl.)); Bonistre; Bonny Marsh (*v.* bonny); Boos-, Boozing Field (*v.* boosing); Booth Fd (cf. Thomas *Booth* 1672); Bottoms (*v.* botm); Bowers Wall (cf. Ralph *del Boure* of Mobberley 1395, *v.* būr[1] 'a chamber, a cottage', wælla); Brier Hough (*v.* brēr, hōh, cf. Bent Hough *supra*); Brine Pits (*v.* brīne, pytt, cf. Saltersley *supra*, which may be connected with this if there were salt-works here); Broad Lane Croft (cf. *Wide Lane* 1831, *v.* Broad Lane 80 *infra*); Brocola Fd (*Broccoli-* Holl.); Brown Hill; Brows; Burgess (cf. John *Burgess* of Wood End 1672); Burnt Croft *&* Fd (cf. *close called Burnd Earth* 1643, *v.* brende[2], eorðe); Butty Piece (*v.* butty, pece); Carr (*v.* kjarr); Cash Fd (Holl. adduces a surname *Cash*); Colix (Holl. proposes dial. *kellock* 'charlock'); Chesnut Hey(s) (probably the same as *lane called Chesworth Hey*, *Chesworth Hey Meadow* 1693, cf. the surname *de Chesworth* 1440, from cēse and worð, *v.* (ge)hæg); Church Fd (cf. *Chirchecroft* c.1206 (1615) *v.* cirice, croft); Clemonga (cf. Clamhunger 52 *supra*); Clough Close (*v.* clōh); Cluckham Park; Cock Shoot, Cockshot (*v.* cocc-scyte); Coppin Heath (*Copton Heath* 1540, 1883); Cow Hey; Cragg (cf. Richard *Cragg* of Baguley Green *supra*, 1672); Cranberry Croft; (Big, Little *&* Middle) Crook (*the two Crooks, the Crook Meadow* 1620, *v.* krókr); Crow Knoll (*v.* crāwe, cnoll); Curr Hey (*Curre-* Holl.); Cutts Mdw (Holl. notes, 'cuts are short furrows in the corners of fields', *v.* cutte, cf. Cuts Clough 1 291); Dean (*v.* denu); Dear Bought (*v.* 326 *infra*); Doe Croft (Holl. suggests dial. *doe* 'to fatten', but *v.* dāl); Little Evans, Evans Hurst; Field at Door (*Field at the Door* 1620; Holl. supposes a lost house, *v.* duru); Fern Hurst ('fern wood', *v.* fearn, hyrst); Finney (cf. Finney 326 *infra*); Fitch Piece (*v.* ficche); Flam Hurst; Flash (*v.* flasshe); Gales Moss (*v.* gagel, mos, cf. Gale Bog 59 *supra*); Gipsey Patch; Glead Croft (*v.* gleoda); Goose Hey; Gors(e)y-, Gorsty Brow, Fd *&* Knoll (*v.* gorstig, brū, cnoll); Greaves (*the Greaves Meadow* 1620, *v.* græfe); Green Lane; Hag Hey, Little Hagg (*v.* hogg); Hall Room (an allotment on Lindow Moss belonging to Mobberley Hall, *v.* rūm); Ham Field (Holl. adds *Ham Hurst, Ham Hill Field*, *v.* hamm, hyrst); Harbour Hill (*v.* here-beorg); Harrow Butts; Hassack Fd (Holl. reads *Hassock*, *v.* hassuc); Hastings; Hemp Acres; Heskey Mdw; Hewitts Croft (cf. John *Hewet* 1672); Hey (*v.* (ge)hæg); Higginson Croft, Fd *&* Mdw (*the Higgenson fields* 1643, from the surname); High Fd; Hollinshead; Hop Wood Croft; Horse Head; Horse Lace (*-leys* Holl., 'horse pastures', *v.* hors, lēah or læs); Hurle Butt Hey (probably from the old Ch surname *Hurlebutt* (*Hurlebot(e)*)) and (ge)hæg); Hurstead; Kadle dock fd (Holl. reads *Kettle-*, *v.* keddle-dock); Kench Fd *&* Hall (Holl. has *Hench Hall*); Kitchen Ho 1831; Lee Fd, Ho *&* Mdw (*Lea-House* 1672, *v.*

lēah); Lingham Croft; Long Acre; Long Lace (Holl. reads -*Leys*, *v.* lǣs, lēah); Longley (*v.* lang, lēah); Lost Fd; Lurie Pit Land; Mam Fd; March Hey; Marl Fd; Marsh Croft; Mere Croft, Flatt & Platts (there is no lake here, cf. Mere Ho *supra*, *v.* plat[1]); Missey Croft & Wd (*v.* misy); Mobberley Fd; Mosley (*v.* mos, lēah); Long Moss, Moss Croft, Fd, Mdw, Piece & Room (*v.* rūm, cf. Lindow Moss *supra*); Mount Skip; Nan(ney) Hey; Nothing; Old Fd (cf. *le Holdefeld* 1334, *v.* ald, feld); Ousal; Oven backed fd, Oven Fd (*v.* ofen); Paddock (*v.* pearroc); Pin Fold (*v.* pynd-fald); Pingot (cf. *the Pingle* 1620, *v.* pingot, pingel); Pitstead Knowle (*v.* pytt, stede); Plumb Tree Croft; Poor Pipes (*v.* pīpe 'a decoy channel'); Priest Fd; Prize Acre Mdw; Push Ploughed Fd (*v.* push-plough); Reddish Hill (probably 'rye enclosure', *v.* ryge, edisc, cf. Rye Hill *infra*); Rid Heath ('cleared heath', *v.* (ge)rydd, hǣð); Riding, Ryding (*v.* ryding); Riddling Heath; Rough; Round Acre; Roundabout Fd (*v.* 327 *infra*); Rowley ('rough clearing', *v.* rūh, lēah); Rundle Fd (*v.* rynel); Rye Hill; Scotack; Scutchen (*Scutcher* Holl., from dial. *scutch* 'couch grass, *Triticum repens*'); Shoots (*v.* scēat); Short Butts (*v.* sc(e)ort, butte); Shoulder of Mutton (*v.* 327 *infra*); Siddall Wd 1831 (cf. Richard *Seddall*, of Woodend *supra*, 1672; the surname appears in Over Tabley, *v. Sidhalle* 63 *supra*, cf. Sidow 73 *infra*); Sin Acre ('seven acres', the area is in Cheshire acres, *v.* seofon, æcer); Slack Fd (*v.* slakki); Slips (*v.* slipe); Snooks; Sount Acre (*Sound-* Holl., *v.* sand); Sour Acre & Butts; Spark (*v.* spearca); Long Spring ('long wood' *v.* spring); Square Fd; Stand Stile (*v.* stigel); Star Pitts ('sedge pits', *v.* stǫrr[2] (dial. *star(r)*), pytt); Stretch Mdw (from the surname *Stretche* 1672); Sunday Fd ('said to be so named as the best field in Mobberley, Sunday being the best day of the week' Holl., *v.* Sunnan-dæg. This should be compared with the f.n. *Friday* for a poor field, *v.* Frīgedæg); Swan Neck (from its sinuous shape); Sweet Acre & Fd; Swine Hey (*v.* swin[1], (ge)hæg); Tee Fd (from its shape, like a T); Three Nooks; Tom Fd ('town field', *v.* toun); Turn Acre (*v.* trun); Twyford Mdw ('double ford', *v.* twī-, ford); Walley Mdw; Web Fd; Wellings ('springs of water', *v.* wella, -ing[1], cf. foll.); Whelm Fd ('a welling up of water', *v.* welm, cf. prec.); Wimbersough; Wood Heys; Little Wooley (-*Wolley* Holl.); Worrall Hill (*Wyralehul* c.1306 (15), (*le Coppede*) *Wiralehull* 1334, '(hill at) the myrtle-nook', *v.* wīr, halh, hyll, coppede 'furnished with a copp', cf. Wirral 1 7); Worthington Fd (cf. Roger *Worthington* 1672); Yams; Yarrow.

(*b*) *le Barchersefflat* 1333 ('the barker's plot', *v.* barkere, flat); *Bothim* 13 ('at the booths', *v.* bōth (dat.pl. bōthum)); *Brook-bank* 1672; *le Dichegreves* 1333, *le Dichehallond* 1334, *le Dychelond* 1333 (*v.* dīc, grǣfe, half-land, land, cf. Grimsditch *supra*); *Duningcroftham* c.1206 (1615) ('(enclosure at) *Dunning's* croft', from the OE pers.n. *Dun(n)ing* and croft, hamm); *Edricheford* c.1306 (15) ('Ēadrīc's ford', from the OE pers.n. *Ēadrīc* and ford); *Farneleia* 1206 (1615), *Farleg* 13, -*ley* c.1250 ('fern clearing', *v.* fearn, lēah); *le Fogh-legh(e)* E3, 1349, *le Fouleghe* 1348 ('fowl clearing', *v.* fugol, lēah); *the Fox-house* 1672 (*v.* fox-hol); *Gangkemonisacre* 1334 ('scavenger's selion', *v.* gang-man 'a scavenger', æcer); *Haselshawe* c.1306 (15) ('hazel wood', *v.* hæsel, sceaga); *le Helerenlond* 1334 ('selion at the alders', *v.* elren, land); *Holy Well Riddings* 1620 ('(cleared lands at) the holy well', *v.* hālig, wella, ryding); *Huglond* 1334; *Lightwode* 1341 ('sparse wood', *v.* lēoht, wudu); *le Nethercroftlondes* 1334 ('(selions in) the lower croft', *v.* neoðera, croft, land); *le Pyelond* 1334 (from pīe[1] 'an insect' or pīe[2] 'a magpie' and land); *The Quare Bank* 1683 ('quarry bank', *v.* quarriere); *le Sperthe* 1333 (*v.* sparð); *le Sterth(e)* 1334, *le Sterteshaye* m14 ('the tail', *v.* steort, (ge)hæg); *Tattonstye* 1334 ('the path to Tatton', *v.* stīg, cf. Tatton 64 *supra*); *the Three Thorns* 1608 (*v.* þrēo, þorn).

ix. Knutsford

This parish was created by Act of Parliament 1741, when St Mary's Chapel in Nether Knutsford became the parish church. This had been a chapel of ease to Knutsford Chapel at St John's *infra* (*v.* NotCestr 343, 344 n3), a parochial chapel of Rostherne parish 45 *supra*. The chapelry contained 1. Bexton, 2 & 3. Nether and Over Knutsford (now both included in Knutsford c.p.), 4. Ollerton, 5. Toft.

1. BEXTON (101–7477) ['bekstən] locally ['bekssn̩]

> *Bexton* 1260 Court (p), 1271 *Chol et freq*, *Bexis-* 1306 Tab, *Bexx-* 1316 ib (p), *Bexston* 1522 Mere
> *Baxton* c.1260 (17) Rich (p)
> *Pexton* 1553 Pat
> *Bexon* 1724 NotCestr

'Bēac's farm', from an OE pers.n. *Bēac*, *v.* tūn. For the pers.n. cf. Beswick La 35, Bexwell Nf (DEPN).

BEGGARMAN'S LANE, 1831 Bry.   BEXTON HALL, 1831 ib.   BLACK-HILL, 1831 ib, 'dark hill', *v.* blæc, hyll.   OAKHURST.   ROWLEY BROW, *Rowley Hill* 1540 Chol, '(hill at) the rough clearing', *v.* rūh, lēah, brū, hyll.   WHITEHOUSE FM, *Bexton Green Farm* 1831 Bry, *v.* grēne[2].

FIELD-NAMES

The undated forms are 1847 *TA* 47. Of the others c.1280, 1330, 1333, 1638 are Chol, 1315, 1316, 1331, 1653 Tab, 1358 Vern, 1831 Bry, 1842 OS.

(a) Acre; Agarmans; Angle Fd; Ash Fd (*the Ashfield* (*land*) 1638, *v.* æsc, feld, land); Black Fd, Blake Fd (cf. *the black(e)land* 1638, *v.* blæc, land); Brickkiln Fd; Broad Hay (*v.* brād, (ge)hæg); Brow Fd; Butty Mdw (*v.* butty); Chattoms; Cinder Hill (*v.* sinder); Cob Fd (*v.* cobb(e)); Common Fd; Cow Hay; Cragg Fd; Dale Croft, Dale Lilly (*v.* dæl[1]); Fill(e)y; Geneses Mdw (*v.* 326 *infra*); Green; Hand Croft; Heath Hay (*the heath hay(e) meadows* 1638, *v.* hǣð, (ge)hæg); Horse Hay; Hulmes Hay; Lane Fd; Ley

Fd (*v.* lǣge); Lyme Fd; Moor Head 1842 (1831, cf. *the moore* 1638, *v.* mōr[1], hēafod, cf. Sanctuary Moor 74 *infra*); Great-, High- & Middle Moss, Moss Fd & Mdw (cf. *Moselache* 1330, 'a boggy stream at a moss', *v.* mos, lǣc(c)); New Hay; Outlet; Pike Croft; Pingot(t) (*v.* pingot, cf. *the little Picowes* 1638, *v.* pichel); Rakes (*v.* rake 'a narrow path'); Riddings (*Bexton Rudynges* 1358, cf. *the three Howriddinges* 1638, *v.* hōh, ryding); Rough Moss; Rushy Fd & Mdw; Rye Fd; Sidow (*Siddall* 1638, 'broad nook', *v.* sīd, halh, cf. Siddall Wood 71 *supra*); Smithy Fd; Spa Well Mdw (*v.* spa); Swine Park (*v.* swīn[1]); Town Fd (*the townefield land* 1638, *v.* toun); Triangle Croft; White Acre.

(b) *Haytelegh'* 1330 ('heath clearing', *v.* hǣð, lēah); *the Hempe Yord,* *- Yard* 1638 ('hemp enclosure', *v.* hænep, geard); *Hogge Brugge* (p), *Luggebrigge* (p) (*v.* ı 55 s.n. Hug Bridge, cf. *Luggefote* 124 *infra*).

2. (NETHER) KNUTSFORD (101–7578) [ˈnutsfərd]

Cunetesford 1086 DB, *Knut(e)sford(e)* 1294 JRL, 1332 ChRR *et freq*
   with variant spellings *Knutt(i)s-, -ys-, -es-, Nut(t)s-, (Nether-)*
   1476 Orm[2], (*Neither-*) 1617 Sheaf
Knot(t)esford(e), -is- 1281 Plea, 1282 Court, 1307, e14 JRL *et freq*
   with variant spellings *-ys-, -us-, Cnotes-, Knot(t)s-, Nots-,*
   -forth(e), -fort to *Nether Knotsford* 1672 Orm[2], (*inferior villa de-*)
   1415 MidCh, (*the Nether towne of-*) 1516 Sheaf, (*Nether-, -ir-*)
   1419 JRL, 1518 Plea, (*Lougher-*) 1534 *Chol*
Knottefford c.1292 Tab, *-ford* 1381 ib, *Knotford* 1486 *MinAcct*
Knodesford 1354 *Indict*
Knyzteford 1398 Orm[2]

'Knut's ford', from the ODan pers.n. *Knut* and ford. A local tradition reported in 1860, White 947, associates the name with King Canute, d.1035, and is alluded to by Webb (Orm[2] ı 409) in the seventeenth century—'the name coming from Canutus, upon what occasion I find not', cf. Canute Place *infra*. The location of the ford is not certain. The 'brook *Birken*' in White is the 'brook which they call *Birkin*' in Webb (Orm[2] ı 409), the stream running down between Nether and Over Knutsford into Tatton Mere, cf. Birkin Brook ı 15, and, for an older name, Sanctuary Moor *infra*. The ford may have been about Brook St. *infra*, or at the old ford at 101–756795 in 6″ OS. The modern town of Knutsford is *noua villa de Knottisford* 1355 *Indict*, 1361 *CoLegh*, 'the new town' (cf. Canute Place *infra*) as distinct from *le Oldton de Knotesford* 1350 JRL, *senior villa de-* 1382 Orm[2], *Oldeknotesford* 1350 JRL, *-knottes-* 1489 ChRR, 'the old town', *v.* ald, tūn (cf. toun), which was probably towards Cross Town *infra* and St John's 78 *infra*, half a mile to the east. Cf. Norbury Booths 77 *infra*. The old town was nearer to the present Birkin Brook and the old ford may have been about Booth Mill *infra*.

STREET-NAMES

BROOK ST., 1860 White, *v.* brōc, cf. Knutsford *supra*.

CANUTE PLACE, *Market Place* 1860 White, cf. *novum forum de Knotisford* e14 Tab, *nouo mercato de Knotesford* 1368 CoLegh, *le markethsted* 1377 *ib*, *v.* nīwe, market, stede; the modern name alludes to the legend of King Canute, *v. supra*.

CHURCH HILL, 1860 White, *v.* cirice, hyll.

CRANFORD AVE., & GASKELL AVE., alluding to Mrs Gaskell's novel *Cranford* (1858), supposedly set in Knutsford.

HOLLOW LANE, *v.* holh, lane.

KING STREET, cf. *strata regia de Knottesford* 1380 MidCh, *v.* cyning, strǣt.

LOVE LANE, 1860 White, *v.* lufu.

MINSHULL LANE, 1860 White, *le Mynscul lane* 1430 JRL, *Munshull lone* 1436 Tab, *Mynshullawne* 1472 JRL, *-lane* 1475 Tab, *le Minchill' Lawne* 1511 JRL, *-Munchill-* 1511 Orm², *Minshall Lane* 1691 JRL, 'Minshull's lane', from the surname of the Minshull family (cf. William *de Munschull* E3 JRL), burgesses of Knutsford (Orm² 1 492), *v.* lane, cf. Minshull 247 *infra*.

CROSS TOWN, 1831 Bry, *-e* 1712 JRL, *Crossetowne of Knottesford* 1598 AD, *the Crostowne of Nether Knotsford* 1683 *ib*, 'the village at the cross', named from an ancient stone cross which formerly stood here, perhaps the market cross of the old town, cf. Knutsford *supra*, Norbury Booths 77 *infra*, *v.* cros, toun.

SANCTUARY MOOR, also in Bexton 73 *supra*, cf. *Moor Head* 1831 Bry, 1842 OS, *Moors Head House* 1681 JRL, the probable location of *mora de Creswalleclef* c.1292 Orm², Tab, 'a common of pasture between Nether- and Over Knutsford' (Orm² 1 489), and *Walleclif* e14 JRL, *le-* 15 Dav, in Over Knutsford. The moor occupies the valley south of Knutsford, between the boundaries of Bexton and Over Knutsford. The brook *Birken supra*, runs down it, and the sides are steep in places, cf. The Cliff and Vale Bank *infra*. The older name 'steep hill-side at the cress-stream', *v.* cærse, wælla, clif (nom.pl. cleofu), may contain an older name of the brook. The later name is 'top end of the moor', *v.* mōr¹, hēafod. The modern name is not explained.

SHAWHEATH (FM), *Shaw(e) Heath* 1661, 1688 *Dep*, cf. *Shahe* e13 (1622) ChRR, *Shawe* e13 Tab, *le Shagh* 1398 ChRR (p), '(heath at) the grove', *v.* sc(e)aga, hǣð. The farm is *Park Gate* 1831 Bry, 1842 OS, cf. Tatton Park 64 *supra*.

AYLESBY, probably a modern name, transferred from Aylesby L. CHELFORD RD, leading to Chelford 1 75. THE CLIFF, on the steep bank of the valley between Bexton 72 *supra* and Over Knutsford 76 *infra*, *v.* Sanctuary Moor *supra*. DOG LODGE & WOOD, *Mere Covert* 1842 OS, cf. *Dog Field* 1848 *TA*, Tatton Mere 65 *supra*. GROVE HO, 1842 OS. THE HEATH, 1831 Bry, cf. *Heath Side* 1860 White, *v.* hǣð, sīde. HEATH LODGE, near Shawheath *supra*. MANCHESTER RD, 1860 ib, part of the Warrington to Knutsford road. MANOR PARK. MOBBERLEY RD, leading to Mobberley 65 *supra*. THE MOOR, 1842 OS, *v.* mōr[1]. PODMORE HOLLOW, *v.* 69 *supra*. PARADISE GREEN, 1842 OS, *v.* paradis 'an enclosed garden', grēne[2]. ROBIN HOOD'S COTTAGE. SANDILANDS. SPARROW LANE, (*Field*) 1848 *TA*. TABLEY RD, leading to Tabley Superior 60 *supra*. TOFT RD, *v.* Toft 81 *infra*. VALE BANK, cf. The Cliff and Sanctuary Moor *supra*.

FIELD-NAMES

The undated forms are 1848 *TA* 227. Of the others, c.1293, 1358[1], 1398, 1435, 1476, 1620 are Orm[2], l13, 1450 Tab, 1307, 1358[2] *Eyre*, 1315 *Chol*, 1371, 1372, 1374 *CoLegh*, 1430 *AddCh* 37233, c.1468 *Dav*, 1511, 1512[1] Plea, 1750 Sheaf, 1831 Bry, 1842 OS and the rest JRL.

(a) Ash; the Blackshaw's Croft 1750 (from the *Blackshaw* family, of Shawheath *supra*); Booths Slate Intake (*le Both(e)slade* 1440, 1450, 1512[2], *Boothslade* 1620, 'valley with a booth', *v.* bōth, slæd); Bottoms (*v.* botm); Brickiln Heath (*Brickkiln-* 1831, bryke-kyl, hǣð); Brow Fd (*v.* brū); Burnt Yard Fd (*le Branderth*' 1440, *Overbrandyorth* 1512[2], *the Blente Erthe* 1571, *the Brandearthes* 1629, *the Brundearthes* 1634, *Overbrendyearthes* 17, 'burnt ground', *v.* uferra, brende[2], eorðe); Buskin Croft; Chapel Fd (cf. *the Chapel Croft* 1750); Dam Fd (*le Domfyld* 1434, *le Overmast Dam feld* 1472, *Medelest Danefeld* 1476, 'the uppermost and middlemost dam field', *v.* damme, feld, midlest, overmast); Flash Fd (*v.* flasshe); Hollins (*v.* holegn); House Fd; Ketlock Fd (*v.* keddle-dock); Lovers Fd; Mill Fd (*the-* 1750, cf. *molendinum de Knotisford* c.1292, *molendinum aquaticum in Knotesford* 1307, *molendinum inter Knottesford Bothes et Nether Knuttesford* 1419, *v.* myln); Mitley (*Myt-* 1536); Moss; New Ford (cf. the 'Old Ford' mentioned under Knutsford *supra*); Rye Fd; Sand Fd (*le Sondefelde* 1392, *le Sontfyld* 1450, *v.* sand, feld); Shooting Butts; Sweet Fd (*v.* swēte); Tabley Hey Mdw; Tan Yard Fd (cf. *Tan Yard* 1831, 1842, *v.* tan-yard); Town Fd (*le Tounfyld* 1430, *v.* toun, feld); Walk Mill Fd (v. walke-milne); the White Bridge 1750 (le Quitebruche 1371, 1373, le Qwytebruch iuxta Knotesford 1374, le Whitebruch' 1448, 'the white assart', v. hwīt, bryce. The final el. is confused with -brugge from brycg 'a bridge').

(b) Appultreflatte 1450 (v. æppel-trēow, flat); Calverheye 113 ('calves' enclosure', v. calf (gen.pl. calfra), (ge)hæg); le Campfeld c.1468 (probably from ModE camp[2], 'a camp' and feld, cf. Camp Green 58 supra); Cundeclif c.1300 (p), 1315 (p), -cliue c.1330 (p), -clyf 1358[1] (p), Cunteclyf 1358[2] (a surname appearing in the Knutsford district, probably from Cunliffe La 73, but perhaps of local origin, v. c(o)unte, clif, cf. Swillinditch I 20); Habels hous 1440 (probably from the ME pers.n. Abel and hūs); Merrottsfelds 1511, 1512[1] ('Mariot's fields', from the ME pers.n. Mariot, diminutive of Mary, and feld); Oulegreve 1382 (p), 1414 (p), (a surname at Knutsford, 'owl grove', v. ūle, grǣfe, perhaps from Hoolgrave in Minshull Vernon 248 infra, cf. Minshull Lane supra); le Redepot 1372 ('the reed-hole', v. hrēod, potte); Rigwey-, Rygewaye Closse 1547 (perhaps 'ridge-way enclosure', v. hrycg, weg, clos, but the first el. may be a surname); le Rowlowfyld 1430 ('the rough-mound field', v. rūh, hlāw, feld); le Slaynemonsfyld 1434, Slaynmonfeld 1472 ('the slain man's field', from ME slayn (OE slægen) 'slain', mann, feld); le Spicers Croft 1430 (from the ME occupation-name Spicere 'a spicer' and croft); the Townes end 1688 (v. toun, ende[1]); Wollardesdene E2, le Wollardesden 1440 (from wulf-weard or the OE pers.n. Wulfweard and denu 'a valley'); Wolmore 1435 (p), Wolmer 1440 (p) (a surname, probably 'wolfmoor', v. wulf, mōr[1]).

3. OVER KNUTSFORD (formerly KNUTSFORD BOOTHS) (101–7677)

Bothes 1230 Adl (p), 1267 (1285) Ch (p), Chest (p), Bothys 1275 Cre (p), (le) Bothes 1278 Ipm, 1282 Court (p) et freq with variant spellings (le)- (to 1515 Plea), (the)- (from 1426 Sheaf), Boþs (c.1292 Orm[2] I 488, lit. Boys), Bothus (1336 (17) Orm[2] to 1403 Pat), Bothis (1474 Pat), to 1527 ChRR, Bothes iuxta Cnotesford 1327 AddCh

(le) Booths 1398, 1403 ChRR et freq with variant spellings (le)- (to 1455 MidCh), (the)- (from 1602 Dow), Boothes (1430 MidCh to 1581 ChRR)

Bothe 1421 Cl (p), 1518 AD (p), 1560 Sheaf

Bouth c. 1536 Leland

Boithes 1547 JRL

Knottesfordebothes 1282 Court et freq with variant spellings as for Knutsford 73 supra and -bothus (1300 JRL), -Bothys (e14 JRL, 15 Dav), -Bothez (1466 JRL), -Booth(e)s (1294 (1653) Tab, 1672, 1680 Orm[2]) to Knottesford Boothes alias Overknotesford 1680 ib

Over Knotesford 1382 JRL et freq with variant spellings as for

Knutsford 73 *supra*, (-*Knuts*- from 1626 ChRR), *Overknottes-forde alias Knotesforde Bothes* 1557 JRL, *Over Knutsford* or *Knutsford Booths* 1724 NotCestr, *Over Knutsford cum Norbury Booths* 1667 Orm², -*Knutsford*- 17 (1724) NotCestr

superior villa de Knottesford 1430 MidCh, 1435 Orm², *Knottisford Superior* 1504 JRL

'The booths, the herdsmen's shelters, the out-pastures', *v.* bōth. Booths was manorially divided into Knutsford Booths and Norbury Booths. Knutsford Booths is 'the part of *Booths* belonging to Knutsford; the higher town of Knutsford', *v.* bōth, uferra, cf. Knutsford 73 *supra*, Norbury Booths *infra*. The same type of p.n. is found in Lymm- and Somerford Booths 37 *supra*, 1 63. The original parochial chapel of Knutsford lay in Knutsford Booths, *v.* St John's *infra*.

NORBURY BOOTHS

> *Nordbury Both* 1281 Plea, 1282 Court, *Norbury Booth Hall* 1831 Bry
>
> *Northtburibothes* 1294 JRL *et freq* with variant spellings *Nort-*, *North(e)-* (to *Northebury Bothes* 1506 JRL), *Nor-* (from 1316 ib), -*bury(e)*-, -*bothus*, -*Booth(e)s*
>
> *manerium de Bothes* 1355 Orm², -*del-* 1392 JRL, -*de Boothes* 1369 Orm², *the hall of the Bothes* 1544 JRL, *Booths Hall* 1842 OS, cf. *the mease place* 1528 JRL

'Booths at the north borough', or 'the north manor-house of Booths'. The latter is less likely, for the house is south of St John's *infra*, and south-east of Cross Town 74 *supra*. If St John's were the site of the market borough in Booths created at the same time as that in Knutsford (probably at Cross Town), c.1292 (Orm² 1 488), then this would have been 'the north borough', and would give name to the part of Booths so occupied, *v.* norð, burh (dat.sg. byrig), bōth, hall. Cf. Knutsford 73 *supra*.

BOOTH MILL (BRIDGE), *molendinum de le Bothes* 1304, 1321 JRL, *le Bothe Milne* 1396 BW, -*Mylne* 1419 JRL, (*Heyes*) 1512 Plea, *Booth Mills* 1749 Sheaf, *v.* myln, (ge)hæg, cf. Over Knutsford *supra*. BOOTHS MERE, *v.* mere¹ 'a lake'. BRICKHILL WOOD, *Brick Kiln Plantation* 1831 Bry, cf. *the Brickhill Field & meadow* 1629 JRL, -*Brickiln*- 1707 ib, *v.* bryke-kyl. CHELFORD RD, leading to Chelford 1 75. OLD COURT HO, an old sessions-house superseded by a new one built in Nether Knutsford. THE CROFT. GOUGH'S

LANE.   HIGHER TOWN FM, cf. Over Knutsford *supra*.   MOB-
BERLEY RD, leading to Mobberley 65 *supra*.   OBELISK COTTAGE,
Obelisk 1831 Bry, named from a monument here.   OLLERTON
GRANGE, cf. Ollerton 79 *infra*.   PARK HOUSE FM, *Park House*
1831 ib, cf. *a park* c. 1536 Leland.   PODMORE HOLLOW, cf. 69 *supra*.
ST JOHN'S CHURCH (site of, 101–765787) & WOOD, *Knottesford
Chirche* 115 Orm², *site of old church* 1831 Bry, *Old Church Yard* 1842
OS, cf. *Dunns Church Yard* 1847 *TA*, (*Duns-* 1707 JRL), and *Church
Bank & Field, Church Wood* (*Plains*) 1847 *TA*, (*le kyrkefeld* 1440
JRL, *the Church*(*e*) *Wood*(*land*) 1571 ib, (*the little-, the great-*) *Church
Wood,* (*Plain*) 1715 ib), *v.* cirice, kirkja, feld, cf. Norbury Booths,
Over Knutsford *supra*, Knutsford 73 *supra*. Leland 5, 24 names the
site *Aspebyri*, which, if not an error, is 'at the aspen-grown fortifica-
tion', *v.* æspe, burh (dat.sg. byrig).   SPARROW LANE.   SPRING
WOOD, 1831 Bry, (*Plain*(*e*)) 1707 JRL, *v.* spring 'a young plantation'.

FIELD-NAMES

The undated forms are 1847 *TA* 228. Of the others, c.1292, 1322, 1382²,
1434 are Orm², 1331 Plea, 1341, 1369, 1372 *CoLegh*, 15 Dav, 1831 Bry, the
rest JRL.

(*a*) Backside Croft; Bottoms or Bongs (*v.* botm, banke); Broad Lane
(*Wide Lane* 1831, *v.* 80 *infra*); Clay Pit Fd (cf. *le Cleypittes* 1430, *v.* clæg,
pytt); Clemley Heys (cf. Clemley 326 *infra*); Cross Fd (*Crosse Feld* 1512,
Crose- 1571, *the Crosse-feild* 1634, *-Cross-* 1715, *v.* cros, feld); Heath Fd
(cf. *the hethe parke* 1571, *v.* hæð, park); House Fd; Intack (*v.* inntak);
Marled Fd (cf. *the merlet earth medowe* 1571, *v.* marlede, eorðe); Marsh Fd
(*the mershe feld* 1571, *v.* mersc); Mill Fd (*the Millcroft* 1571, *the milne yordes*
1634, *v.* myln, croft, geard); Mill Pool Banks (cf. *the Pole Flate* 1571, *the
poole flatt meadowe* 1629, *v.* pōl¹, flat); Moor; Ollerton Heys (*the greate
Olerton hey, the greate Ollerton* 1571, *v.* (ge)hæg and Ollerton 79 *infra*);
Over Knutsford Heath; Pack Fd; Park, -Fd & Wd (*the wood parke* 1629,
1634, *the old- & the hethe parke, the Parke feld* 1571, *Parkwood* 1707, *v.* park,
wudu, ald, hæð); Pease Feild 1715 (*v.* pise); Sand Fd 1715; Sheep Cote Fd
& Flatt (*the Shepcote Flatt* 1628, *v.* scēp, cot, flat); Square Croft; Steeple
Fd; Sweet Fd; Three Land Lower Lute; Three Nooked Fd; the Toad Hole
Mdw 1715 (*the Todhall medowe, the greate Todhall* 1511, 'the fox-hole', *v.*
tod-hole); Toft Wd (cf. Toft 81 *infra*); Far Town Fd (*Overtounfeld* 1512,
v. uferra, toun); Well Mdw; Windy Mill Fd; Yarwood Acre (from the surname *Yarwood*).

(*b*) *le Birchynfeld* 1516 ('field growing with birch-trees', *v.* bircen², feld);
nemus de Boþs c.1292, *le Bothewode* 1331 (*v.* wudu, cf. Over Knutsford *supra*);
Crothers Croft 1571 (from the ME occupational surname *Crother* 'a fiddler');

Deplitches House 1682; *the great meadowe* 1629, 1634; *Horsedale* 1372 ('horse valley', *v.* hors, dæl[1]); *le leperusouerfeld* 1402, *le leporosfyld* 1430, *lepros(s)efeld* 1472, 1478, 1512 ('(upper) field belonging to a leper-house', *v.* lepre-hus 'leper-house', uferra, feld); *lilycok hey* 1440, *the Lyllicote hey* 1571 (*v.* (ge)hæg 'an enclosure', cf. Thomas *Lilicoke* E1, E2, a tenant here); *le Oldefeld* e14, 1382[1, 2] (*v.* ald, feld); *Pykstele* 1466, 1478, *a certaine Steele called the Picksteele* 1633 ('the pick-stile', perhaps a kind of turn-pike, revolving upon a vertical pike, *v.* pīc[1], stigel); *Ponstonesmere* 1430 (*v.* mere[1] 'a lake'); *the rough orchard* 1571, 1629, 1634, *the orchard flate* 1571 (*v.* rūh, orceard, flat); *the Shippen Flate* 1571 (*v.* scypen, flat); *the Stanfeld* 1571 (*v.* stān, feld); *Walleclif* e14 (*v.* Sanctuary Moor 74 *supra*); *Wallefeld* 1322, *le-* 1341, 1369 ('the well field', *v.* wælla, feld).

4. OLLERTON (101–7776)

Alretune 1086 DB f.263b, 267b

Ol(l)reton(e), *Holre-* 113 JRL, Adl, 1293 Cl, c.1300, 1334 *Dav*

Ol(l)erton 1319 *AddCh*, 1339 ChRR (p) *et freq*, *-ur-* 1333 *Dav*, *-ar-* 1543 Plea

Owlarton e14 (19) MidCh, 1667 Orm[2], *-er-* 1595 JRL, *Ou-* 17 (1724) NotCestr

'Alder-tree farm', *v.* alor, tūn. The *Alretune* of DB f.267b has been identified with Ollerton, *v.* Tait 215n., cf. 1 290, but that entry in DB is under *Hamestan* (Maccesfield) Hundred. If this identification stands, part of Ollerton was in that Hundred. Ollerton adjoins Warford, part of which also was in *Hamestan* Hundred, *v.* Great-, Little- & *Old* Warford 82, 83 *infra*, 1 104. *Alretone* DB 266b has been taken for Ollerton but it is probably *Alretunstall* 31 *supra*.

BABRINCHULL (lost), 1423 Orm[2], *barberin(g)chal* c.1281–90 JRL, *molendinum de Babrinchall'* e14 ib, a difficult name, perhaps 'nook or valley at a place called *Boar's brink*', *v.* bār[2], brink, halh, in which the medial consonant-group *-inkh-* has been treated as the *-ingh-* > *-inch-* form in the type of p.n. represented by Altrincham 7 *supra*. The place was the location of 'a certain mill or mill-site' c.1300 *Dav*, '*molendinum de Olreton*' c.1281–90 JRL, in Ollerton, 'between the road from *le Bothes* to *Olreton* on one side, and the watercourse of *Marthal*' on the other', and it is 'on *Wylebrok* in *le Bothis*' e14 JRL 25, (i.e. Birkin Brook 1 15). This location must have been about 101–780775, hardly a 'brink'. Perhaps the name is really an *-ing*[2] formation upon an unidentified component. This does not resemble a pers.n., and it is unfortunate that ME *barberi* 'the barberry', is not recorded before the fifteenth century (NED).

ASHTREE FM.   BLEAZE FM.   BROOKHOUSE FM, *Brook House*
1842 OS, near an unnamed stream.   HORSE BRIDGE (lost, 101–
785772), 1831 Bry, probably *Wallbrooke Bridge* 1618 Sheaf (a horse
bridge), cf. Birkin and Marthall Brook 1 15, 30.   LOUAGE
COTTAGE, cf. *Coat-, Great-, Hill- & Pool Lowage* 1847 *TA*, perhaps
from the rare word *lowage* (1531 NED), probably meaning 'a hiring-
fee', i.e. land on which a hiring-fee was levied, or which carried some
privilege in respect of remitted rent for which 'allowance' was made.
MANOR FM.   MARTHALL LANE, 1847 *TA*, leading to Marthall 82
infra.   MARTHALL PLAT, *v*. 85 *infra*.   MOSS FM, LOWER MOSS,
Moss Lane & Plantation 1831 Bry, *v*. mos.   OAK FM & WOOD,
Oak House & Wood 1831 ib.   OLLERTON FM, LANE & LODGE, *Hall
& Lodge* 1842 OS.

FIELD-NAMES

The undated forms are 1847 *TA* 306. Those dated c.1281, 1440, 1541 are
JRL, c.1300 *Dav*, 1423, 1466, 1666 Orm², 1831 Bry, 1842 OS.

(a) Alder Wd 1831 (*v*. alor, cf. Ollerton *supra*); Bailey Bank (*v*. baillie);
Big Green; Birchill Fd ('birch hill'); Bird Acre; Black Croft; Bleak Acre
(*v*. blāc); Bobshaw Fd; Bone Fd; Bracelet Fd (cf. *Bristlet Lane* 1831, perhaps
'scorched land and field', from eModE and dial. *bristled*, from *bristle* 'to
scorch'); Breech (cf. *le bruches* c.1300, *v*. brēc, bryce); Briery Acre; Broad
Lane (*a lowne called Wade lowne* 1541, *Wide Lane* 1831, cf. Broad Lane
(Croft) 70, 78 *supra*; a road from Gleve Ho in Mobberley southwards
101–783788 to 775769 across Marthall cum Warford 82 *infra* and along
the boundary between Ollerton and Over Knutsford; the earlier name,
Wade Lane 'ford lane', from its crossing Marthall and Pedley Brooks 1
30, 32 (*v*. (ge)wæd), was corrupted to 'wide lane' (*v*. wīd, brād)); Broadith
Lane (*v*. brād, hǣð); Buckstone Wd ('buck's stone', *v*. bucc, stān); Top
Common (cf. *Ollerton Common* 1831, *-Heath* 1842); Cote Fd (*v*. cot); Cow
Hey; Derry Ley Fd; Digleak ('ditch stream', *v*. dīc, lacu); Dun Fd (*v*. dunn);
Farnish; Fox Hole (cf. *Foxholes* 1369, *v*. fox-hol); French Wheat Fd (*v*.
french-wheat); Good Fd; Hack Croft (*v*. haca); Hall Heys (*le Halheye* 1440,
'enclosure at a nook', *v*. halh, (ge)hæg); Ham Heath (*v*. hamm); Hembrey
Fd; Hitch Croft (*v*. hiche); Hole, -Croft & Fd; Intack (*v*. inntak); Land Fd
(*v*. land); Ley Fd (*v*. lǣge); Loont Fd (*v*. land); Main Fd (*v*. main); Manor
Slack (cf. *le slacke qui est divisa inter villam de Ollreton et Werford* c.1300, *v*.
slakki 'a hollow, a valley '); Marsh Mdw; Mere Heys (cf. *Great Mare Hay
Plantation* 1831, on the boundary with Marthall 82 *infra*, *v*. (ge)mǣre,
(ge)hæg); Millstone Fd (*v*. mylen-stān); Nowles (*v*. cnoll); Old Woman's
Croft; Little Oulton (*campus vocat' Olton* c.1300, 'old farm', *v*. ald, tūn);
Pingott (*v*. pingot); Plat Fd (*v*. plat¹ 'a footbridge', cf. Marthall Plat 85
infra); Poor Fd; Pump Fd; Rail Fd (*v*. reille); Rye Croft; Sea Croft; Shed
Fd; Shippon Fd (cf. *le Cheponflatte* 1466, *v*. scypen, flat); Smithy Croft;
Town Fd; Turf Moss ('peat bog', *v*. turf, mos); Water Hall (*v*. wæter, hol¹);

Waterley Fd (*v.* wæter, lēah); Well Mdw; Wincha Croft, Wink(h)ow Hill (*v.* hōh, hyll; these may contain wince or less probably wincel).

(*b*) *the Bothe Parke* 1541 (*v.* bōth, park, probably referring to the park of Norbury Booths 77 *supra*); *le Bronteles-place* 1423 ('burnt-clearing', *v.* brende², lēah or læs, place); *le holt* c.1281 (*v.* holt); *le Marlet Erthe* 1466 (*v.* marlede, eorðe); *Priestland* 1666 (*v.* prēost, land); *le Shaghgreve* 1466 ('the copse wood', *v.* sc(e)aga, græfe).

5. TOFT (HALL) (101–7576)

> *Tofte* 12 Tab, 1210 *Mass*, *Toft* c.1233 Sheaf, 1245 Chest (p) *et freq*,
> (*le-*) 1403 Pat (p), *Tofft(e)* 13 Dav (p), c.1270 *Chol* (p), *Thoft*
> c.1283 Chest (p), *Tofth* c.1300 Tab (p)
> *Thofete* c.1200 Sheaf (p), *Toffet(e)* e14, 1327 Tab (p)
> *Toftes* 1305 Lacy, *Toft(e)s* 1325, 1327 ChRR

'The curtilage', *v.* toft.

ASH WOOD, 1847 *TA*.   BEXTON WOOD, 1842 OS, *George's Wood* 1842 ib, on the boundary with Bexton 72 *supra*.   CLUMP O' TREES FM.   FINGERPOST FM, *Red Rundle* 1831 Bry, 'red stream', *v.* rēad, rynel, cf. *Redbrokescroft infra*.   GARLANDS HOLLOW, *Garland Hollow* 1831 ib, *v.* holh.   HEESOMGREEN FM, *Easam Green Farm* 1831 ib, *Heesam Green* 1842 OS, first el. unidentified, *v.* grēne².   MOSSBANK FM, MOSSNOOK WOOD, MOSS WOOD, cf. *Tofte mosse* 1571 Sheaf, *Adlington Plantation* 1831 Bry, *Old Moss* (*Wood*) 1842 OS, 1847 *TA*, *Moss Knook* 1847 *TA*, *v.* mos, nōk; *Adlington* is the surname from Adlington 1 181.   NEW FM (lost), 1831 Bry.   OAK WOOD, *Highfield Wood* 1831 ib.   OLLERTON LANE, *v.* Ollerton 79 *supra*.   PLUMLEYLANE FM, on a lane leading to Plumley 90 *infra*.   SANDFIELD WOOD, *Sand Field* 1847 *TA*.   SIDDER PLANTATION, *Little Sidders*, *Little-* & *Grassey Furry Siddall* 1847 *ib*, perhaps 'wide nook', *v.* sīd, halh.   ULLARDHALL FM, 1842 OS, *Lower Farm* 1831 Bry, 1847 *TAMap*, from dial. *ullard* 'an owlet'.   VICTORIA WOOD, -*Plantation* 1847 *TA*, doubtless named after the Queen.   WILMER WOOD, 1847 *ib*.   WINDMILL WOOD, 1847 *ib*, *The Bog* 1842 OS.

FIELD-NAMES

The undated forms are 1847 *TA* 401. Those dated 1369, 1667 are *Chol*, 14 Tab, 1430 JRL.

(*a*) Acres; Ash Lane (*v.* æsc); Ball Fd (*v.* ball 'a rounded hill'); Blake Fd (*v.* blæc); Bradley ('broad clearing', *v.* brād, lēah); Bread Mead ('meadow divided into breadths', *v.* brǣdu, mǣd); Brick Kiln Fd; Broad Mead; Brund

Yard (*v.* brende², geard); Campt Plantation; Coppice, -Bank; Cow Ley (*v.* lēah); Cross Fd (cf. *Toftcrosse* 1430, *v.* cros); Dam Fd; Driving Road; Fodens Mdw (from the surname Foden, cf. *Fodon* 86 *infra*); Fold Mead (*v.* fald, mǣd); Granberry Patch (a cranberry patch); Hawkshaw ('hawk wood', *v.* hafoc, sceaga); Hop Yard (*v.* hoppe, geard); Hoveley Fd; Big & Little Lake (*v.* lake 'a lake'); Leghs Lane Plantation; Marl Fd; Mill Fd; Mistress Mdw; Mob Fd; Mount Fd; Nook Fd; Old Heys; Ox Hay Mdw (*v.* oxa, (ge)hæg); Pinfold Fd (*v.* pynd-fald); Pit Stead (*v.* pytt, stede); Pod Castle Mdw; Pool Fd; Pulse Moor; Little & Wall Ridding (*v.* lȳtel, wælla, ryding); Round Fd & Hill; Roylance ('rye selions', *v.* ryge, land); Short Butts; Skerratts Mead (*v.* mǣd); Sour Fd; Great Span Fd; Walley Acre; Wood Fd (*le Woodfeild* 1607, *v.* wudu, feld); Yarwoods Croft & Fd (from the surname from Yarwoodheath 58 *supra*).

(*b*) *Redbrokescroft* 1369 ('croft at Red Brook', *v.* croft, Red Brook¹ 1 34); *Rusfield* 14 ('rush field', *v.* risc, feld).

x. Over Peover Chapelry

Over Peover was a parochial chapel of Rostherne parish 45 *supra*, and contained the townships of 1. Snelson 1 93 (now in Macclesfield Hundred, but in *Bochelau* (Bucklow) Hundred DB), 2. Marthall cum Warford (now distinct c.ps. in Bucklow Rural District), 3. Peover Superior.

1. Marthall cum Warford, *maner' de Wereford et Marthale* 1297 Orm², *Warfurthe et Marthall* 1554 *MinAcct*, *Marthall cum Little Werford* 1724 NotCestr, comprised of the hamlets of Marthall, Little Warford, and probably *Old Warford infra*.

Marthall (101–800757, but 791774 in 1831 Bry) ['martɔ:l]

> *Marthal(e)* 113 JRL, 1297, 1342, 1369 Orm², 1335, 1608 ChRR, 1353 *Eyre*, 1355 *JRC* 890, 1616 Cre, -*hall* 1342 *ArlB*, 1353 BPR *et freq*, -*ha* 1724 NotCestr
>
> *Marchall* 1489 Plea, 1494 ChRR, *Marshall* 1496 Plea, 1618 Sheaf
>
> *Merthall* 1554 *MinAcct*, 1555 Pat, 1557 ChRR

'Weasel's nook, *v.* mearð, halh. The O.S. 1″ maps put the p.n. at *Glovers Cross infra*, near All Saints' Church (built 1839), but in 1831 Bry it is shown at Brook Fm and Firtree Fm *infra*, in the north part of the township. The halh was probably the tongue of land between Pedley and Marthall Brooks 1 32, 30. Cf. *Old Warford infra*.

Little Warford (101–8176)

> *parva*-, *Little Warford* 112, 1500 MainwB, 1573 Orm², 1595 ChRR, -*furthe* 1554 *MinAcct*

Wer(e)ford(e) c.1272, c.1285 Orm², 1289 Cl, *Little-*, *-Parva* 1290
Ipm
Worfourth (lit. *-so-*) 1558 Plea
  'The little part of Warford', *v.* lȳtel, **parva**, cf. Great Warford 1
104, *Old Warford infra*.

OLD WARFORD (lost), *Vetus Wer(e)ford* c.1260 *JRC* 851, 1271–4
Chest, E1 Orm², *Old-* c.1272 ib, *Holde Werford* 1342 Orm², *Werford
iuxta Olreton* 1343 Plea, 'the original Warford', *v.* ald. Orm² III 584n
observes its proximity to Ollerton 79 *supra*. It probably lay west
of Little Warford *supra* in the south part of Marthall township (the
hamlet of which was formerly to the north, cf. Marthall *supra*). The
boundary of *Old Warford* met those of *Fodon* (in Peover Superior)
and Chelford at *Leylache* 1 77, named in a survey of the Snelson–
Chelford boundaries. The moat at Moat Hall *infra* (101–805755)
may be the site of a mediæval manor-house of *Old Warford*. Near
Glovers Cross, at Beech Fm *infra* (101–797761), is a detached portion
of Little Warford, with which manor that of *Old Warford* is much
confused in the records (*v.* Orm², *loc. cit.*). There is evidence that
the mill belonging to Great Warford was on a stream bounding upon
Ollerton, *v.* 1 104. It appears that the southern part of the modern
Marthall township formerly consisted of Warford territory, probably
the original seat of Warford.

ALDER WOOD, 1847 *TA*, *v.* alor.   BAGULEY FOLD, 1831 Bry, cf.
Bagley Meadow 1847 *TA*, probably from the surname from Baguley
12 *supra* with **fald**.   BEECH FM, a detached part of Little Warford,
v. Old Warford supra.   THE BELT, a wood.   BROOK FM, cf.
Marthall *supra*.   BROWN GREEN FM (lost), 1860 White, *Broom
Green* 1751 Sheaf, 1847 *TA*, 'green where broom grows', *v.* brōm,
grēne².   CARTER LANE (101–810753 to 823757), 1831 Bry, on the
Chelford boundary, a continuation of *Pepper Street infra*.   CHAPEL
WOOD, *The Moss* 1831 ib, 1847 *TA*, *Marthall Cover* 1842 OS, cf.
Chapel Field 1847 *TA*, Stockin Moss *infra*, *v.* **mos**.   CHURCH LANE
(lost), 1848 *TAMap*, 1831 Bry (101–799756 to 792750 to 110–782744)
running south-westwards from Glovers Cross *infra* to Colshaw in
Peover Superior 87 *infra*, past Bowdonbank 87 *infra*; presumably
a church-way to Over Peover chapel, for it is older than All Saints'
Church in Marthall.   COLTHURST MILL, *Colliers Mill* 1842 OS, cf.

Thomas *Colthurst* 1615, Millington *Coulthurst* 1666 Orm[2], cf. Great Warford 1 104. CRAGHOUSE FM, *Cragg House* 1842 OS. DOG HOLE (WOOD), *Dog Hole* 1831 Bry, cf. 1 97, perhaps 'dog's hollow', *v.* dogga, hol[1], cf. Corbishley 1 95. FALLOWSCROSS, 1831 ib, probably from the surname from Fallows Hall 1 96, with cros 'a cross'. There is a cross-roads here, cf. *Glovers Cross infra.* FIRTREE FM (2x), *Fir Tree House* 1831 ib, 1842 OS, one at Marthall and the other at Little Warford. GLOVERS CROSS (lost, 101–799756), 1860 White, 1831 Bry, at a cross-roads (of Church Lane *supra*) on *Glovers Lane* 1848 *TAMap* (101–795759 to 805754, the Macclesfield–Knutsford road); from either the ME occupational term *glovere* 'a glove-maker', or the derived surname, *v.* cros 'a cross', lane. HENSON HOUSE FM, *Anson House* 1831 Bry, from the surname *Hanson*. KELL GREEN FM & HALL, *Kell Green* 1831 Bry, (-*Hall*) 1860 White, 'kiln green', *v.* cyln. LOMAS'S BOTTOMS, *v.* botm 'a valley bottom'. MARTHALL BROOK, *v.* 1 30. MILL LANE, 1847 *TA*. MERE HILLS (lost, 101–807753), 1860 White, 1831 Bry, on the Chelford boundary, 'boundary hills', *v.* (ge)mǽre. MOAT HALL, 1842 OS, cf. *Marthall Hall* 1860 White, from a moat here, cf. *Old Warford supra*, *v.* mote. MOUNT PLEASANT FM. OWLET HOUSE (lost), 1842 OS, *Tollet House* 1831 Bry, *v.* ullet. PECKMILL BOTTOMS & FM, *Peck Mill Farm & Wood* ib, -*Bottom* 1842 OS, *v.* botm, cf. Peck Mill 203, 326 *infra.* The name may refer to a type of mill with a 'pecking' movement, *v. pecker-mill* NED, or to the capacity of the grind-stones, i.e. a peck measure. PEDLEY BRIDGE, crossing Pedley Brook 1 32. near Pedley Ho 1 105, cf. *Pedley Field* 1847 *TA*, *freq.* PEPPER STREET (lost, 101–810753 to 100–797745), 1842 OS, *King Street* 1831 Bry, cf. *Street Meadow* 1847 *TA*. This is a straight road forming the boundaries of Snelson, Chelford and Marthall cum Warford, *v.* 1 46, cf. Carter Lane *supra*, Snelson Lane 1 94. For the road-names, cf. Pepper St. (Chester) 327 *infra*, King Street 1 44. PINFOLD FM, 1842 OS, -*House* 1831 Bry, *v.* pynd-fald. SANDHOLE FM. SANDLE BRIDGE (FM), *Sandle Bridge* 1706 Sheaf, (*House*) 1831 Bry, perhaps the site of the ford from which the Warfords are named, cf. Great Warford 1 104. The name appears to be from sand 'sand', with either hyll 'a hill' or lēah 'a clearing', cf. *Sandle-bridge* 59 *supra*. STOCKIN MOSS, 1831 Bry, -*ing*- 1842 OS, 'moss full of tree-stocks', *v.* stocking, mos. With Chapel Wood *supra*, this represents *profunda mossa* 1271 Chest in the Chelford boundary survey, *v.* I 77. WOOD PLATT COTTAGE, at a bridge over Marthall Brook, either 'wooden bridge' or 'bridge at a wood', *v.* **wudu, plat**[1].

FIELD-NAMES

The undated forms are 1847 *TA* 256. Those dated l12 are MainwB (from Barnes[1] 546–7), c.1285, c.1316 Orm[2], c.1300 *Dav*, 1831 Bry, 1842 OS.

(*a*) The Acre; Adams Wall (*v.* **wælla**); Basin Acre; Bear Croft; Bent (*v.* **beonet**); Blake Acre & Fd (*v.* **blæc**); Bossey Fd (*v.* **bōs, (ge)hæg**); The Bottoms (*freq, v.* **botm**); Brick Kiln Fd; Brown Hey & Hole; Bunr(o)y; Burgess Heys; Burry Fd; Chading Croft (probably a 'shading'-place, from dial. *shade* 'to shelter'); Chelford Flat (cf. Chelford I 75, *v.* **flat**); Clamhanger (*v.* Clamhunger 52 *supra*); Clay Heys; Clemmerton Heys; Colley Fd; Cow Hey; Cranberry Fd; Cripple Gate (*v.* **crypel-geat**); Cross Butts (*v.* **cros, butte**); Curbishley, -Mdw (cf. Corbishley I 95); Dod Hole; Dogmore ('dog moor', *v.* **dogga, mōr**[1]); Drumble Croft (*v.* **dumbel**); Dry Knowle; Flash Mdw (*v.* **flasshe** 'a swamp'); Flatt (*v.* **flat**); Fox Harbour Fd, Fox Holes (*v.* **fox, here-beorg, hol**[1]); Friday Flatt (*v.* **Frīgedæg** 'Friday', **flat**); Hare Hill; Heath Croft (*Heath* 1842); Holland Fd; Hollinshead (*v.* **holegn, hēafod**); Horse Grass Fd; Horse Hey; House Slack ('hollow or valley at a house', cf. *le slacke qui est divisa inter villam de Ollreton et Werford* c.1300, *v.* **slakki**); Intake (*v.* **inntak**); Irish Fd; Knowl; Lim(e) Fd; Linch Croft (*v.* **hlinc**); Madjays (perhaps *Madge Hays, v.* **madge, (ge)hæg**); Maridean (*v.* Merrydale 88 *infra*); Marl Croft, Fd, Heath, Marl'd Earth; Marthall Heys & Moor; Marthall Plat (1831, a bridge at 101–794760, *v.* **plat**[1]); Marthall Wd (1831, at 101–785785); Meadow Holes; Milking Bank & Brow (*v.* **milking**); Mill Fd; Mill Stone Mdw (*v.* **mylen-stān**); Narrow Nook; Outlet (*v.* **outlet**); Over Barrow (*v.* **uferra, bearu**); Ox Hey; Park; Pig Nut, Pingott (*v.* **pingot**); Poor Fd; Push Ploughed Fd (*v.* **push-plough**); Rape Fd; Rough Hey; Rye Croft; Sand Fd; Shay Fd (cf. *Schahe* l12, *v.* **sc(e)aga**); Shooting Butts; Stepping Croft; Street Mdw (*v.* **strǣt**, cf. *Pepper Street supra*); Tom Yard Mdw (*v.* **toun, geard**); Town Fd; Underhouse (*v.* **under, hūs**); Wall Hill & Mdw (*v.* **wælla**); Way Fd; Wide Lane 1831 (*v.* Broad Lane 80 *supra*); Woodfin Croft (perhaps 'wood-pile', *v.* **wudu, fin**).

(*b*) *Maidenis Lone* l12 ('maiden's lane', *v.* **mægden, lane**); *Shewilford* l12 ('ford with a scarecrow', from ME *s(c)heules*, dial. *shewell* 'a scarecrow' (1250, NED) and *ford*); *Semalebroc in Wereforde* c.1285, *Smalbrok* c.1316, 'narrow brook', *v.* **smæl, brōc**); *Theirlford* or *Theurlford* l12 (from *ford* and *þyrel* 'a hole, an opening', probably a ford at a narrow passage).

2. PEOVER SUPERIOR (101–7773) ['piː vǝr]

Pevre 1086 DB, -(*e*)*re*, -*er*, *Peu-* c.1232–3 Dugd, Tab, Dieul, 1260 Court, 1278 Ipm *et freq*, *Over(e)-*, *Ovre-*, -*Superior* 1287 Court, l13 ChF, e14 MainwB, *Phefre* 1317 Tab, *Pevur* 1382 JRL, -*yr* 1460 Cl

Peyvre 1248 Cl (p), *Peyfer'* 1291 P, (*Superior*) *Pieuere* E1 *AddCh,*
  -v- 1397 ChRR (p), *Peeuer* E1 MidCh, *-v-* 1332 ib
Peverhe 1260 Court (p)
Peover 1414 ChRR, (*Over-*) 1559 Pat, (*Higher-*) 1724 NotCestr
Paver 1492 ChRR (p)
Pyver 1530 Plea, *Pi-* 1601 Sheaf

'The higher part of Peover', cf. Nether Peover, Peover Inferior
220, 90 *infra*, named from the river Peover Eye 1 33.

CHAPMONSWICHE (lost)

Cepmundewiche 1086 DB
Cepmondswich e13 (17) Orm[2], 1333 ib, *Chemondswys* c.1287 MidCh
Chapmoneswyk H3, *-wick* E1 MainwB, *-wych(e)*, *-wich(e)*, *-(i)s-*
  e14, E2 ib, Tab, *-us-* 1354 ib, *-mounswych* (for *-monns-*?) 1322
  MainwB (p), *Chapmonswiche* 1450 *Dav*
Cape-, *Chapmondsiche* 1334 MidCh
Schappe-, *Scapimonneswic(ho)* 1249–65 Chest
Chapmonwich 1371 *Eyre*

The final el. is wīc, 'a dairy-farm, an industrial- or trading-
settlement'. If it were not for the *-mund-*, *-mond-* forms, the first el.
could be taken as OE cēap-mann 'a trader'. These spellings indicate
that cēap-mann replaces a compound of cēap 'trade, merchandise, a
market' and mund 'security, protection' but also 'hedge, fence,
mound' (EPN s.v., Ess 220). OE *cēap-mund would be analogous
with such compounds as OE cēapsetl, cēapstōw or cēapstrǣt. The p.n.
would mean 'wīc at a mound or enclosure where trade was con-
ducted', altered to 'chapman's-, trader's wīc'. The location is not
known. In 1086 DB the place was a waste manor, in 1334 Tab it was
a *villata* 'a hamlet', in 1371 *Eyre* the home of William de *Whistanefeld*
(Whisterfield 1 85), and in 1450 *Dav* it consisted of 'a messuage,
eighteen acres of land and one acre of wood in four separate parts
in the vill of *Ouerpeuere*', by which time it was a rent rather than a
place.

FODON (lost)

Fahedayn H3 MainwB
Faudon H3 MainwB, 1271–4 Chest, E1 Tab, MidCh, 1280 P (p),
  1336 ChRR, 1664 Tab, (*–in Peever*) 17 MidCh
Fandon 1327 Plea, 1336 ChRR

Fodon Eɪ (17) Orm², 1333 ib, *-land* 1591 (17) Orm², *(-in Over-Peever)* 1663 ib

'Colourful valley and hill', *v.* fāh (wk. obl. fāgan), denu (alternating with dūn 'a hill'), cf. Foden ɪ 198. This was a hamlet (*v.* Orm² ɪ 478, Chet NS LXXXII 328) giving rise to a surname *Foden* (*v.* Orm² III 632, 584). In 1271–4 Chest, the boundary of *Fodon* met those of Chelford and *Old Warford, v.* 83 *supra,* ɪ 77, cf. *vetus sepes de Faudon* Eɪ MidCh. In 1591 Orm² ɪ 477, it was 'half a messuage called *Fodon-land'.* It was probably in the north-east part of the township, about 110–790745. Bowdonbank and Merrydale *infra* may contain allusions to the name and topography of *Fodon,* but evidence is lacking.

HETHALES (lost), 1391 MainwB, *Hethalis* 1216 ib, 1260 *Plea (Hechalie* or *Hethabie* Court 26), 1303–5 MainwB, *-ys* H3 ib, *-es* 1303–5 ib (p), 'heath-nooks', *v.* hǣð, halh. This was a hamlet of Over Peover, presumably near Peover Heath *infra, v.* Orm² ɪ 478.

HUNGERHILL FM, *-hul* H3 MainwB, *-hil* (lit. *Himger-*) H3 ib, *Hongrill* 13 (1666) Orm², *Hungerhill* 1635 Sheaf, 'hunger hill, hill with poor soil', *v.* hungor, hyll, described as a hamlet of Over Peover, Orm² ɪ 478.

REDBROOK FM, *Radbroc* (terra quæ vocatur), *-brok(e)* Eɪ (17) Orm², c.1286 ib (p), *-brook* (lands in) 1371 (17) ib, *(-House)* 1666 ib, *-brooke* 1672 ib, named from Red Brook[1] ɪ 34, cf. *Redbrokescroft* 82 *supra;* described as a hamlet of Over Peover, Orm² ɪ 477–8.

TWYFORD (lost), *(-in Over Peover)* 1442 MainwB, *Twi-, Twyford* 1280 ib, 13 (1666) Orm², *(-e)* 1322 AD (p), 1332, 1333, 1432 ChRR, 1362 MainwB, 'the double ford', *v.* twī-, ford; a hamlet of Over Peover, *v.* Orm² ɪ 478.

AMBROSE ACRE, 1842 OS.　AMSTERDAM COVERT, 1831 Bry, *v.* 325 *infra.*　BATE MILL (FM), *Bates Mill, Wrights Farm* 1831 Bry, *Bate Mill* 1842 OS, cf. *Bate Moss* 1842 OS, *Bates-* 1831 Bry, from the surnames *Bate* (of Peover, 1632 ChRR) and *Wright.*　BIRCH FM.　BOWDONBANK (101–791752), *v.* banke, cf. *Fodon supra.*　CHEERSGREEN, *Cheer Green Farm* 1831 Bry.　CHURCH LANE (lost), 1831 ib, *v.* 83 *supra.*　CINDER LANE, *Back Lane* 1831 ib.　COLSHAW HALL, *Colshaw (Green)* 1844 *TA,* probably 'charcoal wood', *v.* col¹, sceaga.　DAISY BANK, 1844 ib.　FOURLANE-ENDS, 1844 *ib.*　FOXFIELD WOOD, 1831 Bry, *Foxfild* 1400 MainwB, *v.* fox, feld.

FOXWOOD FM.   FREEGREEN (LANE) FM, *Fray Green* 1831 Bry, 1842 OS, *Free Green* 1844 *TA, Robinsons Farm* 1831 Bry, 'free (i.e. not owned) green', a patch of no-man's land, *v.* frēo, grēne². GREAT WOOD, 1842 OS, *Great Peover Wood* 1831 Bry.   GREEN LANE FM, *Green Lane* 1844 *TA.*   GROTTO FM, HO & WOOD, *Grotto Wood, New Farm* 1842 OS.   HEATH COTTAGE, cf. Peover Heath *infra.* HOME FM.   LONG BELT, a wood.   LONGLANE FM, *New House, Longy Lane* 1831 Bry, cf. 1 47 XIX.   MEADOWBANK FM, *Daniels Farm* 1831 ib.   MERRYDALE FM (110–789744), *Mary Dale Covert* 1842 OS, cf. *Meridian, -Nook* 1844 *TA,* Maridean 85 *supra,* 'pleasant valley', *v.* myrge, dæl¹, denu, cf. *Fodon supra.*   MILL-BANK FM, near Peover Mill *infra.*   MOSS COTTAGE.   MOUNT PLEASANT, 1842 OS.   NEWHALL FM, cf. *Noua Aula* c.1290 Tab (p), *Chol* (p), *Neuhalle* 1293 Tab (p), *le Newehalle* 1356 Indict, *v.* nīwe, hall.   NIXON'S COTTAGE, cf. *Nixons Field* 1844 *TA.*   PARADISE-HOUSE, *v.* paradis.   PARKGATE, 1831 Bry, named from the park at Peover Hall, cf. 1 47 XIX.   OVER PEOVER BRIDGE, crossing Peover Eye into Allostock 216 *infra.*   PEOVER COTTAGE, *The Cottage* 1842 OS.   PEOVER HALL, *aulla de Peever* 1278 (17) Tab, *the hall of Over-Pever* 1666 Orm², cf. 1 47 XIX.   PEOVER HEATH (110–7973), *Over-* 1831 Bry, cf. *Hethales supra.*   PEOVER MILL, 1831 ib, *Over-* 1842 OS, *molendinum de Peuere* 1297 Tab.   POOLFIELD WOOD, 1842 OS.   RIBBLE BRIDGE, *v.* 227 *infra.*   SANDYLANE FM, cf. *Sand Field* 1844 *TA, Sandiflatte* 1303–5 MainwB, *v.* sandig, flat, feld.   SCHOOL FM, 1831 Bry.   STOCKS LANE, 1831 ib, leading to the Whipping Stock(s) (1831 Bry, 1842 OS) near the Mainwaring Arms p.h.   TURNPIKESIDE FM, (*Old*) *Dairy House* 1831 Bry, 1842 OS, beside the turnpike road from Knutsford to Cranage.   WHEEL FM, 1831 Bry.   WHITEFIELD COVERT, *White Field* (*Plantation*) 1844 *TA.*   WHITEHOUSE FM, *White House* 1831 Bry.

FIELD-NAMES

The undated forms are 1844 *TA* 319. Of the others, H3, 1303–5, 1387, 1388, 1391, 1400, 1601 are MainwB, 13, l13, 1301, e14 Tab, 13 (1666), 1320 (17) Orm², 1356, 1357 *Chol,* 1635 Sheaf, 1831 Bry, 1842 OS.

(a) Alderney Croft; Asp Fd (*v.* æspe); Bank Fd; Black Mdw; Bleak Fd (*v.* blāc); Bottoms (*v.* botm); Brick-Kiln-Fd; Bridge Hey Bank; Broom Fd (*v.* brōm); Bull Flatt; Burgess Orchard; Burn Acre; Buttermilk Fd (*v.* 325 *infra*); Long Butts; Chip Croft (*v.* chippe); Clough Mdw (*v.* clōh); Coltley Croft (*v.* colt, lēah); Cooks Acre; Coppy (*v.* copis); Cote Fd (*v.* cot); Court

Fd; Cow Hey; Cranberry Patch; Crow Heald ('crow's hillside', *v.* **crāwe, helde**); Ditch Croft; Doctors Mdw; Dove House Mdw; Little Eye (*v.* **ēg**); Fazeley Wd; Finger Post Fd; Flash Mdw (*v.* **flasshe**); Gallopsdale; Gilt Hedge & Stick; Gog Croft; Gom Croft; Goodenough (cf. Db 759); Goose Hey; Gravelly Fd; Green Fd (cf. *Grenefeld* l13, *v.* **grēne**[1], **feld**); Hatch Croft (*v.* **hæc(c)**); Hawkshaw Mdw ('hawk wood', *v.* **hafoc, sceaga**); Hollin Hey (*v.* **holegn**); Horse Heys; Hovel Fd (*v.* **hovel**); Intack, -take (*v.* **inntak**); Kings Ley (*Kengysley* 1301, 'the king's wood or clearing', *v.* **cyning, lēah**); Kippocks; Knowl Hill, Knowle; Lady Fd (*v.* **hlǣfdige**); Lessor Croft; Leycesters Plantation (named after the *Leycester* family of Tabley); Maggots Flat; Marl Heaps & Yards, Marl Pit Fd & Yards (*v.* **marle, hēap, geard**); Moss Knowle, Mdw & Room (*v.* **rūm**[1]); New Hurst (*v.* **hyrst**); Noble Hey (perhaps named from a rent or purchase of one noble, 6s. 8d.); Outlet (*v.* **outlet**); Oven Fd (*v.* **ofen**); Overton Fd (*v.* **uferra, tūn**); Ox Croft; Patch; Pingot (*v.* **pingot**); Plain; Priest Lake Mdw (*Priest Lake Lane* 1831 (110–782735 to 790732), (*le*) *Pre*(*y*)*steslake* l13–e14, cf. *Prestesahe* H3, 'priest's stream and wood', *v.* **prēost, lacu, sc(e)aga**); Red Eye Mdw (*v.* **ēg** or **ēa**, cf. Red Brook[1] I 34); Ridding Mdw (cf. *Littelruding* e14, *le Menerudyng* 1357, 'little- & common cleared-land', *v.* **lȳtel, (ge)mǣne, ryding**); Rye Grass Fd (*v.* **rye-grass**); Shark Mdw; Shepherds Flat; Long- & Peas Shoot (*v.* **pise, scēat**); Sign Post Fd; Smithy Fd; Sour Fd; Spark Fd (*v.* **spearca**); Stock Croft; Vetch Fd; Walk o'th' Hill (*v.* **walk**); Water Lees (*v.* **wæter, lǣs**); Wey Fd (*v.* **weg**); Wheat Fd (cf. *Wyetecroft* 13, *Wete-* H3, *v.* **hwǣte, croft**); Winters Croft; Womstall (perhaps *Wormstall*, *v.* **wyrm-stall**, but the first el. could be dial. *wom* for *home*, cf. **hām-stall**); Woodcock Fd (cf. *Woodcock Pits & Wood* 1831, 1842).

(*b*) *Bliffeld* 1400 (probably 'pleasant field', *v.* **blīðe, feld**); *Bradfield* 1635 (*v.* **brād, feld**); *Brydenbrugge* 13 (1666), *Le-* 1387 ('bridge made of planks', *v.* **briden, brycg**; described Orm[2] I 478 as a hamlet of Over Peover); *Heycroft* l13 ('hay field', *v.* **hēg, croft**); *Horeisyhengs* H3 (perhaps '(pastures at) the filthy watercourse', *v.* **horig, sīc, eng**; the final el. is rare in Ch); *Horewythynis* H3 ('hoar willows', *v.* **hār**[2], **wiðegn**); *Hunerefeld* H3 (probably for *Huuere-* from **uferra** 'higher, upper' and **feld**); *le Lit(t)lecroft* l13 (*v.* **lȳtel, croft**); *Motalowfeld* 1400 ('assembly hill', *v.* **mōt, hlāw**); *del Myxne* l13 (p) (*v.* **mixen** 'a dung-hill'); *Olmeresdene* H3 ('Wulfmǣr's valley', from the OE pers.n. *Wulfmǣr* and **denu**); *the forthe of Osmans Dene* 1303–5 (cf. *le Forde* 1356 (on Red Brook), from **ford**, with the pers.n. OE *Ōsmund* or ON *Āsmundr* and **denu** 'a valley'); *Pykedelow* H3 ('pointed mount', *v.* **pīced, hlāw**); (*le*) *Russ(c)ilach(e)* l13 ('the rushy bog', *v.* **riscig, læc(c)**); *le Scharmonswich* 1388 (probably a bad form for *Chapmonswiche supra*, otherwise 'the shearman's buildings', from the ME occupational surname *Sherman, Scharman* (Fransson 103) and **wīc**); *Spring Lane* 1601 (*v.* **spring** 'a spring of water' or 'a young wood'); *Wylahe*(*s*)*clow* H3, *Wellardisclok* 1303–5, *Welardesclowe* 1391 (these may refer to one place, but there are two names, 'Wīglāc's dell', from an OE pers.n. *Wīglāc* (cf. ON *Vígleikr*), and 'Wilheard's dell', from the OE pers.n. *Wilheard*, *v.* **clōh**); *Uurthfeld* H3 ('field at, with, or belonging to an enclosure', *v.* **worð, feld**).

xi. Nether Peover

A parochial chapelry of Great Budworth parish 95 *infra*, part in this Hundred and part in Northwich Hundred, *v.* Nether Peover 216 *infra*.

1. PEOVER INFERIOR (101–7474), LOWER PEOVER [ˈplːvar]

Parua Pefria c.1200 Tab, -*Pev(e)re* 13 ib, *Little Pever* 1465 (17) Orm[2]
Litle Peeuer 1614 *Chol*, *Parva-* 1637 Tab
Little Peover 1715 Tab, *Lower-* 1724 NotCestr

'The smaller part of (Nether) Peover', *v.* lӯtel, parvus, lower, inferior, cf. Nether Peover 220 *infra*, with which this formed one township and from which it is only distinguished, as *Little-*, in a few references. Lower Peover is the principal hamlet, and lies in both divisions of the township. The parochial chapel is in Lower Peover, in the Nether Peover part.

BROOKFIELD HO, cf. *le Brocfeld* 113 Tab, 'field near the brook (Peover Eye)', *v.* brōc, feld.   PEOVER EYE BRIDGE, *Nether Peever Bridge* 1618 Sheaf, *Stone Bridge* 1831 Bry, cf. Trouthall Bridge 93 *infra*. LOWER PEOVER HALL, *Stretch House* 1831 ib, cf. *la motte du manoir de Netherpeuere* 1350 *Chol*, *v.* mote; *Stretch* is a Ch surname. SMITHY GREEN, 1842 OS.   WELL COTTAGE.   YEWTREE HO.

FIELD-NAMES

The undated forms are 1844 *TA* 317.

(*a*) Bain Fd; Barrow Fd (*v.* bearg); Black Fd; Brickiln Croft; Bridge Croft; Chissill Green (perhaps from cisel 'gravel, shingle'); Crabtree Fd; Grass Foot; Green; Great Hey; Hinsticks; Hoo Field Moor (*v.* hōh); Hunting Bush; Intake (*v.* inntak); Long Edge (*the Edge felde*, -*Filde* 1597 *Chol*, *v.* ecg); Mill Fd; Moor Fd; Outlett (*v.* outlet); Pease Fd (*v.* pise); Sand Fd; Saw Pit Fd (*v.* saw-pytt); Three Nooks; Town Fd; Well Mdw; Withy Moor (*v.* wīðig, mōr[1]); Yain Croft ('yeaning croft', *v.* ēan, (ge)ēan).

2. PLUMLEY (101–7175)

Plumleya, -*leia* 1119 (1150), (1280), 1150 Chest, 13 *AddCh*, -*leg(h)*, -*ley* 1259–60 Plea, Court, 113 *Chol*, MidCh *et freq* with variant spellings -*leyg'*, -*lay*, *Plum(m)e-*
Plumbeia 1119 (1285) Chest, Ch
Plumb(e)legh 1288–9 Court, *Plumbley* 1579 Dugd

Plomle c.1290 *Chol*, *-legh* 1323 Plea, *-ley* 1452 Tab, *-ly* 1546 Dugd,
   Plomeley 1446 Tab

'Plum-tree glade', *v.* plūme, lēah.

HOLFORD (HALL), HOLFORD BRIDGE

Holeforde c.1270 *Chol*, *-ford* 1307 Plea
Holleford c.1294 *Chol*, 1320, c.1330 JRL (p), 1489 Pat (p)
Howeford c.1300 *Chol* (a ford)
Holford c.1300 ArlB, 1307 Tab *et freq* with variant spellings *-forde*,
   -fort(h); *Holfordeforde* c.1300 *Chol, Holford Bridge* 1619 Sheaf,
   -Hall 1659 Mere, *Olford* 1328 Tab (p)
Holdeford E2 *Chol* (p), *Holdford* 1411 ChRR (p), *Oldford* c. 1536
   Leland
Hulford 1326, 1328 ChRR (p)

'Ford in a hollow', *v.* hol[2], ford, brycg, hall. The ford from which
the hamlet takes its name was at Holfoɪd Bridge (101–704755), where
'Watling Street' 1 40 crosses Peover Eye, cf. the explanation by
Sir Peter Leycester, 1666 (Orm[2] 1 669), 'This place, or hamlet . . .
hath its name from the ford which runneth under the manner-hall,
which, because it is situate in a Derne Hole, was therefore called
Holford, as if you should say, A ford in a hole . . .' (*v.* derne 'obscure').
The hollow was also known as *Helle Clow* c.1300 *Chol, Hell Hollow*
1831 Bry, 'hell ravine', *v.* hell, clōh, holh, a boundary of the estate
represented by Winnington Wood *infra*. Leycester's subsequent
derivation from 'the old word Hale, which we now call Hall, and so
denotes as much as a ford under the Hall', is probably a confusion
with *Haleford* 124 *infra*.

HOLFORD MOSS, 1621 Orm[2], *-e* 14 Tab *et freq*, cf. *le Muses* c.1290
Chol, le Mos(se)feld 1317, 1322 *ib, Moss Room* 1844 *TA*, *v.* mēos,
mos, feld, rūm[1], feld. Cf. *Sandlow Moss infra*.

PLUMLEY MOOR, 1737 Mere, *-e* 1666 Orm[2], *Plumleg(h)'mor(e)* c.1270,
c.1300, 1330 *Chol, vasta de Plumlegh'* 1345 *ib, Plumley Mosse* 1499
Tab, cf. *le Morruding* (lit. *-ig*) 13 ib, *v.* mōr[1] 'a moor', waste 'waste
land' (MedLat *vasta*), mos, ryding.

SANDLOW MOSS (lost)

Son(e)walde(s)leg(')mos, (le) Sondwallde(leg')mosse l13 (lit. *Mon-*),
   c.1300, 14 Tab

Son(e)ward(is)lewemos c.1300 *Chol*, *Son(d)wardelegh'mosse* 1345 *ib*
Sandell mosse 14 Tab
Sondelemosse 1415 Tab, 1430, 1465 ChRR, *Sondelmoss* 1547 Orm[2]
Sandhyll Mosse 1533 Tab
Sandwell Mosse alias Sanderley (*Mosse*) 1535, 1536 Tab
Sandley or Sondel Moss 1547 Orm[2]
Sandlow Moss (lit. *Land-*) 1695 Tab, cf. *Sondlouwe* n.d. ib 1010

The basis of this name is *Sonewardislewe-*, *Son(d)wardelegh'-*, both
from *Chol*. The *Tab* spellings are from seventeenth-century copies,
but the earliest agree with this except in *-wald-* for *-ward-*, which
could arise from assimilation of *r-l* to *l-l*. The derivation is uncertain.
It might be '(moss at) Suneweard's glade' from an OE pers.n.
Suneweard and lēah, with mos. *Common Moss* (lost, 110–717740) 1831
Bry, *the Common Moss of Lostockgralam, Plumley and Peever* 1695
Tab, (*v.* commun), where the boundaries of the three townships meet,
south-east of Holford Moss *supra*, is the most probable location, for
the records place *Sandlow Moss* variously in Plumley and Nether
Peover, and it was part of Holford Moss *supra* in 14 Tab 999, 1533
Tab 1002.

WINNINGTON WOOD (101–703755), 1831 Bry, named after the family
de Wynin(g)ton (from Winnington 327 *infra*) who had land from the
de Lostok and *de Toft* families (Lostock Gralam 189 *infra*, Toft 81
supra), between *Peuerhee* and *le Lynstrete* (Peover Eye, 'Watling
Street' 1 33, 40) c.1277 *Chol*, and between *Helle Clow* (*Hell
Hollow, v.* Holford *supra*) and *Hasschuluestre forde* (*infra*), and between
Le Lynstrete and *peuerehee* c.1300 *Chol*. The estate was partly in
Lostock Gralam, *v.* 191 *infra*.

ALLEN'S BRIDGE, *Smoker Bridge* 1831 Bry, cf. Smoker Inn *infra*.
BOOTHS BRIDGE.   BROOKHOUSE FM, *Brook Farm* 1860 White,
named from Peover Eye 1 33.   BUCKLOW FM.   FIELDS
FM.   THE GRANGE.   HENSHAW GREEN, 1831 Bry, *Henshagh*
1512 ChEx, the home of Raufe *Henshaw* 1666 Orm[2], 'hen wood', *v.*
henn, sceaga.   HOLFORD FM, 1860 White, *v.* Holford *supra*.
HOLFORD MILL, 1831 Bry, *l'molaine de Holford* 1373 Chol, cf.
molendinum in villa de Plumley' super Peuerhee 1324 *ib*, *un nouel molyn
super Peueree* 1340 *ib*, *v.* myln.   HOLFORD STREET, 1831 Bry, *v.*
strǣt, 'Watling Street' 1 40.   MALTKILN FM & Ho, *Malt
Kiln* 1831 *ib*, cf. *Malt Kiln Lane End Chapel* 1831 *ib*, a methodist

chapel. MERRY FM. MILL BOTTOMS & WOOD, *v.* botm, cf. Holford Mill *supra.* MILTON BANK. MOORFIELD, named from Plumley Moor *supra.* MOSS COTTAGE & FM, *Moss House* 1842 OS, named from Holford Moss and *Common Moss supra.* PEAS WOOD, 1844 *TA, v.* pise. SMOKER INN, 1842 OS, *The Smoker* 1831 Bry, giving name to Smoker Brook 1 35, Allen's Bridge *supra* and Smoker Wood 119 *infra*, explained by Barnes[1], xcviii and 20, 'a sixteenth-century inn, which was renamed 'The Smoker' in the eighteenth century by the first Lord de Tabley in memory of his favourite horse *Smoker'.* TROUTHALL BRIDGE & FM, *Trout Hall, Wooden Bridge* 1831 Bry, cf. Peover Eye Bridge 90 *supra.* WASH FM, cf. *Wash Field* 1844 *TA,* named from *Sudlow Wash* 1842 OS, a ford at 101–730762 over Benstall Brook 1 15 to Sudlow Lane 123 *infra, v.* (ge)wæsc 'a flooding place, a flooded road, a ford', cf. Sudlow 61 *supra.* WHITE HO, 1831 Bry. WOOD'S TENEMENT. YEWTREE COTTAGE & FM.

FIELD-NAMES

The undated forms are 1844 *TA* 322. Of the others, 13, 1305, 1314, 1316[2], 1341, 1433, 1444, 1469, 1742, 1783 are Tab, 1288 Court, 14 Sheaf, 1548 AD, 1625, 1636, 1639, 1657, 1720, 1727 Mere, 1831 Bry, 1842 OS and the rest *Chol.*

(*a*) Acre; Alderley Fd (*v.* alor, lēah); Ass Fd; Back Lane 1831 (*le Houtlone de Plumeg'* c.1300, 'the outlying lane', *v.* ūt, back, lane; it becomes Cheadle Lane 220 *infra*); Bell Fd (perhaps dedicated to the maintenance of a church bell); Black Mdw; Bleachry Fd; Bradley (*v.* brād, lēah); Breech (*v.* brēc); Briary Moss; Brickkiln Green (*v.* bryke-kyl, grēne[2]); Broad Fd; Cartledge Fd ('boggy stream through rough stony ground', cf. *Cartelache* 1 17); Chapel Mdw; Colly Croft (*v.* colig); Common Lot (*v.* hlot); Cow Fd; Crabtree Fd; Cracks; Crow Hill; Down Loons (*v.* dūn, land); Eyes (*v.* ēg); The Fall (*le Fal* 1345, *v.* (ge)fall); Feathers Greaves (*Fitherisgreue* c.1300, *the Great Feathergreaves* 1727, apparently from OE fiðere (gen.sg. -*es*) 'a wing', perhaps used as a pers. by-name, cf. ME *Fether* from feðer[1] 'a feather', *v.* grǣfe 'a wood'); Gate Fd; Genesis Wd 1831 (*v.* 326 *infra*); Glade Fd; Gorsey Fd, Gorsty Mdw (*v.* gorstig); Green Hay; Hall Hay (cf. *le Hallecroft* 1345, *le Hallestude* c.1300, *v.* hall, croft, styde); Hatch Fd (*v.* hæc(c)); Hill Fd; Hogs Mdw; Hought Croft (probably from hōh); Intake; Kid Acre & Butts (*Kydebuttes* 1345, *v.* kide, butte); Kiln Hay; Light Oak (cf. *le lycte-, lyttehokes* 1313–1316, *le lyght'-, light'okes* 1429, *v.* lēoht, āc); Lungs Fd; Main Yard ('demesne enclosure', *v.* main, geard); Malkins Croft (*v.* malkin); Marl(ed) Fd; Miers Wd (*Mizewood alias Barrow's Wood* 1720); Milking Bank (*v.* milking); Moat Piece (named from the moat at Holford Hall, *v.* mote); Nick Fd; Nook'd Fd; Nurse; Old Mary's Fd (perhaps called after the celebrated Dame Mary Cholmondeley, the seventeenth-century lady of the manor, James I's 'bold lady of Cheshire'); Outlet(t) Mdw (v. outlet); Pasture Lane 1831, 1842 (running into Lostock Gralam 189 infra); Pinfold Fd (v. pynd-fald); Pingot (v. pingot); Pod Flat; Pool Croft; Riddings (v. ryding); Rindle Fd (cf. Rundle infra, v. rynel); Rough Hay (the Rughe Hey 1548, v. rūh, (ge)hæg); Round Robin; Rundle (cf. Rindle Fd supra, v. rynel); Rye Fd; Sand Fd (cf. Soond Fd infra); Shippon Fd; Shoulder of Mutton (v. 327 infra); Soond Fd (Soundefeld 1433, cf. le Sond Lond 1300, 'sand field', cf. Sand Field supra, v. sand, feld, land); Sparkes (v. spearca 'brushwood'); Swine Cote Fd (v. swīn[1], cot); Tan Pit Fd; Three Nook'd Fd; Walkmill House 1727 (Walk Milne House 1657, v. walke-milne); Way Fd; Well Mdw; Wet Wd (le Wetwode 1386, v. wēt, wudu); Withy Fd (v. wiðig); Workhouse Fd.

(b) her bache del heyeʒ 1373 ('the higher valley at the enclosures', v. hērra, bece[1], (ge)hæg); Berne 1316 (p), Le Berne 1335 (p), cf. de Grangia c.1300 (p) (v. bere-ærn, grange); Benteleg'yate c.1300 ('(the gate of) the grassy clearing', v. beonet, lēah, geat); le Blakehurst c.1300 ('the black wood', v. blæc, hyrst); Briddes lone 1434 ('bird's lane', v. bridd, lane); Bullonstree Croft 1639 (probably 'bolace-tree', v. bolace 'an elder'); Carlingkeslowe c.1300 ('old woman's hill', v. ME kerling (ON kerling), hlāw. There may be some more special connotation to this name, for Professor Sørenson points out that in similar Danish p.ns. kerling is taken to mean 'a witch, a troll-woman' or 'a beggar woman'); le Chippilake 1316 (v. lacu 'a stream, a water-course'); Collandes 1345 (first el. obscure, v. land); le Culne Hallond c.1300, Culleyn 1342 (v. cyln, half-land, leyne); le Crekeshurst c.1300, le Crakesehurst 14 ('crow's or raven's wood', v. kráka, hyrst); Cres(se)wal(le)-sc(h)awe 1305, 1314, 1316[2] (p), Crescewalshagh 1372 (p), Cresswalscha 1392 (p) ('(wood at) the cress-spring', v. cærse, wælla, sc(e)aga); Dammelcroft 1345 ('selions near a dam', v. damme, land); Danecroft 1313 (p), 1316 (p) (v. croft); le demine londis c.1300 ('the demesne selions', v. demeyn, land); le Efeld 1386, Le Erudyng 1335 ('field and clearing at a stream', v. ēa, feld ryding, cf. Peover Eye 1 33)); Forstleg' haluh c.1300, Forstyle(y) 1429 ('frosty glade', v. forst, forstig, lēah, halh); Hants Croft 1625, 1636 (a messuage, v. croft); Hasschuluestre forde c.1300 ('(ford at) Æscwulf's tree', from the OE pers.n. Æscwulf and trēow, with ford. This may have been in Lostock Gralam 192 infra, cf. Winnington Wood supra); le Hewefeld 1360 ('the domestic's field', v. hīwan (ME hewe), feld); Lyttill Hegh Feld 1444, the Hieghe Feld 1548, cf. superior campus de Plumleg' c.1300 (v. hēah, feld); le hurst c.1300 ('the wooded hill', v. hyrst); Lytillegh 1341 ('the little clearing', v. lȳtel, lēah); Litler Croft 1639 (held by Ralph Littler, v. croft); le Longe-flatte 1345 ('the long plot of land', v. lang, flat); le Lynstrete (v. 'Watling Street' 1 40); the mershe 1555, the merche feldes 1559, the marshe 1560 (v. mersc); Oueneford c.1270 ('ford near a furnace', v. ofen, ford, a place on Peover Eye near Holford); Plumlegh' lone 1382 (v. lane); Plumlegh plankus 1335 ('Plumley planks', a boundary line along Plumley Moor, either a sleeper-track or a fence of planks, v. planke); le quytelonde c.1300 ('the white selion', v. hwīt, land); le Rakes c.1300 ('the paths', v. rake); Raueneshurst-

(*esyord*) c.1300, *Raueneshurst* 1345 ('raven's wood', from OE hræfn or ON hrafn 'a raven', perhaps used as a pers.n., *v*. hyrst, geard 'an enclosure'); *Ionesfeld Symson*' 1382 ('John Symson's field', *v*. feld); *porta de Tofte* c.1300 ('the gate of Toft', *v*. geat, cf. Toft 81 *supra*); (*le*) *Wallemor(e)* c.1300, 1360, 1433 ('moor by a spring', *v*. wælla, mōr[1]); *the Warehowse* (a close) 1555, *Warehowse or Warehowse* (*-house*) *Ground* 1559, 1560 (perhaps a figurative use of ME *ware-house* 'a warehouse', describing fertile land, *v*. grund); *Wodewallebrouk* c.1300 ('brook called "wood-stream"', from wudu and wælla, with brōc, cf. *boscus de Plumblegh* 1288, *-Plomle* c.1290).

xii. Great Budworth

The ancient parish of Great Budworth extended into Northwich and Eddisbury Hundreds. In Bucklow Hundred it comprised 1. Anderton, 2. Appleton (including Hull), 3. Aston by Budworth, 4. Barnton, 5. Bartington (*v*. Dutton *infra*), 6. Great Budworth, 7. Cogshall (*v*. Comberbach *infra*), 8. Comberbach (now a c.p. including Cogshall), 9. Dutton (which included Poosey, a detached part of Runcorn parish, and is now a c.p. including Bartington), 10. Little Leigh, 11. Marbury, 12, 12a. Marston (in two parts, one of them now included in Wincham c.p.), 13. Pickmere, 14. Stretton, 15. Tabley Inferior, 16. Higher Whitley Lordship (which included 17. Antrobus, 18. Crowley and 19. Seven Oaks, the first of which is now a c.p. including the other two, Higher Whitley being joined with Lower Whitley in Whitley c.p.), 20. Lower Whitley, 21. Wincham (now a c.p. including the detached part of Marston). To Great Budworth parish belonged the parochial chapelry of Nether Peover 90 *supra*, 216 *infra*, in Bucklow and Northwich Hundreds, and that of Witton 184, 327 *infra* in Northwich and Eddisbury Hundreds.

1. ANDERTON (101–6475)

    Andrelton' 1182 P

    Aldreton' 1183 P, *Alderton* 1317 Misc, *Aldreson*' 14 AD (p)

    Anderton' 1184 P, 1287 Court *et freq* with variant spellings *-ir-*, *-ur-*, *Andre-*

    (*H*)*Enderton*' 1185, 1186 P

    v. tūn. The first element may be the same as that in Anderton La 128, for which the OE pers.n. *Ēanrǣd* has been suggested, while OE *Ēanðrȳð* (fem.) is also possible. But consideration should be given to the ON pers.n. *Eindriði*, **Andriði*, or ODan *Endrithi*, **Andriði*, as in Enderby Lei, L, Ainderby YN, *v*. Lindkvist 39, NRY 223, Fellows Jensen 75–6. The element tūn is not particularly Scandinavian, but cf. Gayton, Claughton, Storeton, Larton 326, 325, 327, 326 *infra*, *v*. Saga Book XIV 307. The OScand pers.n. is likely, with buskr, in Antrobus 127 *infra*, four miles from Anderton.

CLAYCROFT FM, *Claycroft* 1288 Court (p), 1504 Orm[2], *Cleycroft* 1363 ChRR, *-crofte* 1558 Orm[2], 'clay croft', *v.* clæg, croft.   COGS-HALL LANE, *Anderton Lane* 1831 Bry, cf. Cogshall 109 *infra*. COMMON HO.   GUNNERS CLOUGH, 1842 OS, *v.* clōh. The first element may be the ON pers.n. *Gunnarr*, ODan *Gunnar*.   HOUGH LANE, 1831 Bry, *v.* hōh 'a spur of land, a hill'.   SOOT HILL, *v.* sōt.   UPLANDS FM.

FIELD-NAMES

The undated forms are 1844 *TA* 15.

(*a*) Atill (probably 'oats hill', *v.* āte, hyll); Black Hay, -Hey; Booty Croft & Mdw (probably from butty, but cf. botye); Bottoms (*v.* botm); Bretta, Big Bretty (perhaps from Bretar 'the Britons', cf. Comberbach 111 *infra* which adjoins Anderton); Brockley (*v.* brocc, lēah); Clough Lane 1831 Bry (named from Gunners Clough *supra*); Dollys Carr (*v.* kjarr); Dunstow (apparently 'meeting-place at a hill', from dūn and stōw, but possibly 'site of a farm-yard', from tūn-stall); Flea Flat (*v.* flat); Glade Fd; Hatch Fd (*v.* hæc(c)); Heath Croft Lane; Hemp Yard; Hungrill ('barren hill', *v.* hungor, hyll); Intack (*v.* inntak); Long Hey Acre; Marl Fd; Mill Bank, Fd & Heys; New Hay; Pingot (*v.* pingot); Ridding (*v.* ryding); Sand Fd, Sandley ('sandy field' and 'clearing', *v.* sand, lēah); Sour Mdw (*v.* sūr); Woodhalls.

2. APPLETON (formerly HULL APPLETON) (101–6383), *Appelton et Hulle* 1314 Plea, *Hull et Apulton* c.1320 Chol, *Hulle-Appleton* 1563 ChRR, *Hull Appleton* 1860 White, *v.* Appleton, *Hull*, Hill Cliffe *infra*.

APPLETON (101–6383)

> *Epletune* 1086 DB
>
> *Ap(p)elton(a)*, *-tun*, *Appleton* c.1154–60 (1329) Ch, 1190–99 Facs *et freq* with variant spellings *-il-*, *-ul-*, *-yl-*, *Aple-*; (*-iuxta Hulle*) 1287 Court

'Apple-tree farm' or 'orchard', *v.* æppel, (Merc eppel, cf. epli), tūn, æppel-tūn.

HULL (lost, 101–615850)

> *Hull(e)* c.1200 LRO Dx, Tab (p), c.1220 Orm[2] *et freq*, (*-iuxta Apelton*) 1288 Court, (*le-*) 1334 VR (p), (*-infra Appleton*) 1630 ChRR, *Hul* 1260 Court (p)
>
> *Hille* 113 LRO Dx (p), 1452 CoLegh, (*le-*) 1400 Pat (p), *Hyll(e)* 1414 Plea

'The hill', *v.* hyll. This was the name of a hamlet which included the eminence at Hill Cliff(e), Hill Firs, Hillfoot and Hillside *infra*.

BRADLEY HALL (101–657845)

> *Bradelee (in vill' de Apilton)* l1̄3 Tab, *-legh'* 1354 Orm², *-ley* 1506
> Plea, *(-in Apulton)* 1527 ChRR
> *Bradley (in Appulton)* 1354 Orm², 1428 ChRR, *(-Hall)* 1724
> NotCestr, *-legh* 1355 BPR
> *(crux de) Braddelegh* 1386 Sheaf

'At the broad clearing', *v.* brād, lēah. The cross is lost. It was mentioned in the deposition of John de Massey in the case of Scrope *versus* Grosvenor, 1386. It had borne the challenged arms of Grosvenor (azure, a bend or) for twenty-six years and stood beside the highway from Warrington La, to Knutsford, probably at 101–658847, where Grappenhall, Lymm and Appleton meet, and where the line of Cliff Lane meets an old line of paths 101–645843 to 665848, *v.* Sheaf¹ 3 156, cf. 1 44 XI, Cliff Lane 141 *infra*.

HILL CLIFF(E), (101–6184, 6185)

> *Hullehul* 1278 Misc, *þe Hill* 1705 Sheaf
> *Hulleclyf* 1354 Plea, *le Hillcliff* 1464 LRO Dx, *Hill Cliffe* 1643
> Sheaf, *-Clift* 1705 ib, *-Cliff* 1831 Bry
> *High clyffhill* 1577 Saxton, *Clift Hill* 1690 Sheaf

'The steep hill at Hull', *v.* hyll, clif, cf. Hull *supra*.

SOUTHENHED (lost)

> *Southdeneheued, -v-* 1328 LRO Dx (p)
> *Sow-, Souda(n)he(ve)d* 1349 ArlB, 1352 Eyre (p), *-den-* 1350
> Chamb (p), 1354 Eyre (p), 1362 LRO Dx (p)
> *Soudenhull* 1357 Eyre (p)
> *Southenhe(ue)d* 1383, 1402, 1433 ChRR (p)

'(The head of) the south valley', *v.* sūð, denu, hēafod.

WITHERWIN FM (101–854267), *Wyther Wyne* c.1250 LRO Dx,

Witherwing 1768 EnclA, 1842 OS, cf. *Withowing Lane* 1831 Bry (Lumbbrook Road *infra*). Perhaps this p.n. is like *Mondrem* 1 10, an abstract noun, i.e. OE wiðer-winn 'contest, strife, conflict', e.g. a place where this occurred. Alternatively, the final el. may be winn¹, wynn 'a pasture', cf. *Comberwheyn* 1 211, Atlow Winn, Hognaston Winn Db 522, 376, 700, and the first el. ON viðr (gen.sg. viðar) 'a wood', or OE wiðer¹ 'a ram, a wether'.

APPLETON CROSS & HALL, 1831 Bry, cf. *Appleton-house* 1627 (1724) NotCestr, *v.* cros, hall. APPLETON MOSS, 1768 *EnclA*, *v.* mos. (APPLETON) THORN, *Appleton Thorn, Thorn Green* 1768 *ib*, 1831 Bry, a hamlet and public-house (*The Saracen's Head* 1831 Bry) named from a thorn-tree here, cf. Thornbrow Fm *infra*, *v.* þorn. BARLEY CASTLE, 1831 ib. BEEHIVE FM. BELLFIELD FM, *Bellfields House* 1768 *EnclA*, *Bellefield* 1831 Bry, cf. High Warren *infra*. BIRCHDALE, 1831 ib, 'birch valley', *v.* birce, dæl[1]. BIRCHTREE FM, *Birch House* 1842 OS, *v.* birce. BOOTH'S FM. BRADLEY BROOK (> Slitten Brook 1 35), 1831 Bry, *v.* brōc. BRADLEY GORSE, *v.* gorst, cf. Bradley Hall *supra*. BRICK FIELD, 1844 *TA*, *v.* bryke, feld. BROOM COTTAGE, 1831 Bry, *v.* brōm. BROOMFIELD FM, *Broom Fields* 1768 *EnclA*, *Broomfield* 1741 Sheaf, *v.* brōm, feld. BROW'S FM, *The Brows* 1831 Bry, *Brows Farm* 1844 *TA*, *v.* brū. BURLEYHEYES FM, BURLEY LANE, (*Old*) *Burley Heys* 1831 Bry, *Burleys Heys* 1854 *EnclA*, cf. *Buralys* 1249–61, *Burweleghhey* 1343 ArlB, '(enclosure(s) at) the clearing at a tumulus', *v.* byrgels, lēah, (ge)hæg. CABBAGE HALL. CANN LANE, *Kann Lane* 1768 *EnclA*, *Can Lane* 1831 Bry, *v.* canne 'a can, a cup', perhaps in a topographical sense, 'a deep valley', since the lane runs to the valley of Dipping Brook 1 22, cf. Cann Lane 103 *infra*, but there may have been a well or watering place here with a ladling can. CHAPEL LANE. THE COBBS, COBBS QUARRY, *Rock House* 1831 ib, *Cobbs* 1842 OS, *v.* cobbe 'a round lump, a cob'. CROFTON FM, *Crofton House* 1844 *TA*. CROSS FM, named from Appleton Cross *supra*. DAINTITH'S FM, *Hole House* 1831 Bry, cf. William *Dentith* 1666 Orm[2], *v.* hol[2], hūs. DAIRY FM. DENNOW FM & WOOD, *Dennal House, Denna Bongs* 1768 *EnclA*, *Denna Hall* 1831 Bry, *Denna Wood, Dennow Field* 1844 *TA*, cf. William de *Denale* l13 LRO Dx, 'valley nook', *v.* denu, halh. THE DINGLE, DINGLE BRIDGE, BROOK, FM & LANE, *v.* dingle 'a deep hollow'. The brook becomes Lumb Brook[2] 1 30. DIPPING BROOK, *v.* 1 22. DOOD'S BRIDGE, BROOK & LANE, cf. *Doodwell* 1768 *EnclA*, *Dood Croft & Field* 1844 *TA*, probably from dial. *dowed, dow'd* (*dow* vb[3] NED) 'dull, lifeless, stale' and wælla. *Doodwell* presumably gave name to the rest. The brook becomes Dingle Brook *supra*. DUDLOW'S GREEN, 1842 OS, *Dudley Green* 1768 *EnclA*, cf. *widow Duddle* 1666 Orm[2], from the surname *Dudley*. FORD'S ROUGH, *v.* rūh. GRAPPENHALL LANE, leading to Grappenhall 140 *infra*. GREEN LANE (FM), 1842 OS. HATTON FM & LANE, *Hatton Lane* 1831

Bry, *Hatton's Hey* 1844 *TA*, cf. Thomas *Hatton* 1666 Orm². The surname is from Hatton 149 *infra*. HIGH WARREN, *Hillcliffe Common* 1768 *EnclA*, *Hill Cliff* 1831 Bry, *Bellefield Hill* 1842 OS, cf. Hill Cliff(e), Bellfield *supra*, *v.* wareine. HILLCLIFFE, *Prospect Hill* 1831 Bry, 1842 OS, re-named from Hill Cliffe *supra*. HILL-FOOT FM, *Broady's Farm* 1831 Bry, *Hill Foot* 1842 OS, *v.* hyll, fōt, cf. *Hull supra*. HILLSIDE FM, *Hill Side* 1831 Bry, cf. *Hull supra*. THE HURST, 1831 ib, *v.* hyrst. THE KNOLL, cf. *Le Knolles* 1354 Plea, *the Knowl Croftes* 1844 *TA*, 'the hill', *v.* cnoll. LONDON RD, the line of a Roman road, called *le Grenegate* l13 *LRO* Dx, 'green road', from grēne¹ and gata, *v.* 1 43 X, cf. *le Sale(lyde)yate infra*. LUMBROOK RD, *Withowing Lane* 1831 Bry, *v.* Witherwin *supra*, cf. Lumb Brook² 1 30. LYON'S LANE. NEW LANE, 1842 OS. NOOK FM, *v.* nōk. OLD FM, 1831 Bry. PEPPER STREET (101–632833 to 637833), 1842 OS, *v.* 327 *infra*. QUARRY HO & LANE, cf. *Quarry Lodge* 1831 Bry, named from Hillcliffe Quarry. RED LANE, *the Red lane* 1768 *EnclA*, *v.* rēad 'red' from the colour of the sandstones here. SCHOOL FM, cf. *School Common* 1768 *ib*. GT & LT SHEPCROFT, *Sheppecrofte* 1452 CoLegh, *Shepcroft(e)* 1509 Mere, 1519 *LRO* Dx, *Sheepcroft(e)* 1555, 1560 Sheaf, (*Great & Little*) 1831 Bry, 'sheep enclosure', *v.* scēp, croft. SPINHEATH FM, *Spenheth* c.1580 Mere, *Spen Heath* 1768 *EnclA*, *v.* spenne, hǣð. SPRINGSIDE FM. STONECROFT. STRETTON RD, cf. Stretton 121 *infra*. STUD FM, *Appleton Cottage* 1831 Bry, 1842 OS, *v.* stōd. TANYARD FM, *Tan Yard* 1831 Bry, cf. *Tan House Meadow* 1844 *TA*, *v.* tan-yard, tan-hous. THORNBROW FM, *Thorn Farm* 1831 Bry, named from Appleton Thorn *supra*, *v.* brū 'the brow of a hill'. WINDMILL COTTAGE & LANE, cf. *Shaws Lane leading to the Wind Mill* 1768 *EnclA*, *Wind Mill Bank & Field* 1844 *TA*, Gorsty Hey *infra*. WOOD FM. WOODSIDE FM. WRIGHT'S GREEN, *Wrights Green* 1768 *EnclA*, from the surname *Wright* and grēne². YEW TREE FM, 1831 Bry, cf. *Yew Tree Lanes* 1768 *EnclA*.

FIELD-NAMES

The undated forms are 1844 *TA* 17. Those dated l12–e13, 14, 1362² are ArlB, c.1200, l13, 1321, 1328, 1362¹, 1393, 1464 *LRO* Dx, c.1240, 1315², c.1350, 1452, 1666 Orm², 1308 Whall, 1315¹, 1336, 1354 Plea, 1327, 1334, 1397, 1438 ChRR, 1357¹ Eyre, 1357² BPR, e14, 14², 1338, 1509, 1580 Mere, 1751 Sheaf, 1768 *EnclA*, 1831 Bry.

(a) Ackers (v. æcer); Alcar; Backside; Bason Fd; Birch Ridding; Black Flatts; Blake Fd (v. blæc); Blackshaw (v. blæc, sceaga); Bongs Fd (cf. *Bongs Lane* 1768, v. banke); The Bottoms (cf. *Hullebothemes* 1393, 'the valley bottoms belonging to Hull', v. botm, cf. *Hull supra*); Bow Croft; Breach (v. brēc); Briery Fd (cf. *Brerecroft* l12–e13, *le Brericroft* 1362[1] (p), v. brēr, brērig, croft); Broad Bent (cf. *Brown Bent* 1768, v. brād, brūn[1], beonet); Broad Hey; Brook Shoot (v. scēat); Brown Cramma; Brundreth (v. branderith); Brundy; Buggely Well 1831 (a road-side well beside London Road *supra*, at 101–616837; perhaps '(well at) the haunted glade', v. bugge, lēah, wella); Burnt House Fd (v. brende[2], hūs); Butty Fd (v. butty); Caldwells Fd (cf. *Caldewalle* c.1240, 'cold spring', v. cald, wælla); Carrs Brook (perhaps from cærse 'cress', cf. Cress Brook *infra*); Castle Croft & Fd (v. castel(l)); there was no castle here); Clares Barn Fd; Coal House Fd; Crabtree Fd; Cress Brook (v. cærse, brōc, cf. Carrs Brook *supra*); Big Cribb, Cribb Fd (v. crib); Cross Butts & Fd (v. cros, butte, cf. Appleton Cross *supra*); Davis's Pitts 1768 (*Davies's of the Pitts* 1751, v. pytt; *Davi(e)s* is a surname); Dean Hey (v. denu); Deep Snow Lane (*Dep Snow Lane* 1768); Dobsey; Dog House Fd (v. dog-house); Dove House Fd; Edge Fd (v. ecg); Ellam Fd; Ellens Hay, -Hey(s) (*freq*, v. ellern); Fallow Fd; Farrow Fd (v. fearh); The Flatts (cf. *Great Flat* 1768, v. flat); Gib Ridding (v. gibbe, ryding); Gig Hole (v. gigge); Glead Fd (v. gleoda); Golden Fd (cf. *Goldens Inclosure* 1768); Good Wives Hey (*Godewif Heys* 1580, 'enclosures belonging to the Mistress', v. god-wif, cf. Goodmanshey 104 *infra*); Gorsty Hey, Gorsey-, Gorsty Knowl (*Windmill Field or Gorsty Heys* 1768, v. gorstig, cf. Windmill Lane *supra*); Green (v. grēne[2]); Grimsditch Wd (probably *Grymyswood* 1509, (lit. *Gyneswode*) 1580, a close belonging to the Grimsditch family, cf. William *Grymesdich* de *Appulton* 1452, 'Woden's wood', v. Grīm, wudu, cf. Grimsditch Hall 134 *infra*); Hales Moss (v. halh, mos); Hawkeshaw (v. hafoc, sceaga); Heath Fd (cf. *bruera de Hulle* l13, v. hǣð, cf. *Hull supra*); Heifer Door; Hemp Yard; Hermitage Fd; Hickapell (*Hiccopel* 1768 *EnclA*); the Hill Fd, the hill Fields Fm 1768; Hollin Croft (v. holegn); Horns Croft & Fd (cf. *Horne Lane* 1762); Horse Hay; Houghton Croft (*Houghton's Croft* 1764); Houshoot (v. hōh, scēat); Intack, -take (v. inntak); Iron Fd (v. hyrne); Jews Mdw; Kiln Croft & Mdw; Kings Fd; Landers Fd; Lapwing Fd; Little Reed (v. hrēod); Long Bank, Hay, Hey & Hoult (v. holt); Lumbrook Close (cf. *Lumb Brook*[2] 1 30); Mage Acre; Marl(ed) Fd, Heaps & Hey; Martin's Groat (probably a rent); Meg Fd (v. meg); Milking brows (v. milking); Mill Lane; Moat Mdw; Moor; Moss Wd; Mothers Fd; New Hay, -Hey; Nicks Fd; Old Woman's Fd; Oulery Croft (v. alor 'an alder'); Outlet (v. outlet); Ox Heys; Painters Brow 1768; Paradice-, Paradise Mdw (v. paradis); Big & Long Park; Percivals Fd (cf. *Percival's Side* 1768, v. sīde); Pewters Pear Fd; Pickers, Pickows (v. pichel); Pinfold Fd, (*the Pinfold Field & House* 1768 *EnclA*, v. pynd-fald); Pingot (v. pingot); Plungeon Fd (*Plungeon* 1768, perhaps named after a wild-fowl, v. *plungeon* NED); Pocket (v. poket); Purgatory (v. 327 *infra*); Push plow'd Fd (v. push-plough); Queens Fd; Red Booths; Ridge Fd; The Rough; Rough Hoult (v. holt); Rundles (dial. *rundle* 'a streamlet', v. rynel); Rye Bank; Sand Fd; Shaw Fd (cf. *Shaw Green, Shaws Lane* 1768, v. sceaga); Slutch Fd; Smithy Croft & Fd (cf. *Smithy*

Lane 1768); Spit Jack; Spring (*v.* spring); Square Root Fd; Stack Croft; Stockton Heath (*Great Stockton Heath* 1768, *v.* 145 *infra*); Stone Delf Fd ('stone-pit field', *v.* stān, (ge)delf); Stoney Acre *&* Fd; Straw-Grave; Sweet Fd; Top Roof Fd; Town Fd or Pump Fd; Twambrook Brow (*Twanbrookes Brow* 1768, cf. Edward *Twambrooke* 1666, *v.* brū); Twiggery; Twiss Brow 1768 ('brow at a fork', *v.* (ge)twis, brū, cf. the surname *de*(*l*) *Twis*(*se*), *-Twys*(*se*) e14, 14², 1308, 1321 *et freq* to 1438, *de Tuwys* 1328, also Twiss's Wood 59 *supra* and Twiss La 97); Warehouse Fd; Warren; White Fd (cf. *le Quitefield* l13, *v.* hwīt, feld); Winton Green 1768; Wood Bank.

(*b*) *Blakrydyng* 1464 ('black clearing', *v.* blæc, ryding); *Crawholt* 1464 ('crow wood', *v.* crāwe, holt); *Liveschke* l12–e13 (perhaps 'ash-tree affording shelter', from hlīf or ON hlíf 'protection' and esc, eski); *le Middilforlong* 1321 (*v.* middel, furlang); *Mollewod iuxta Spenheth* 1580 (perhaps 'mole wood', from molle and wudu, cf. Spinheath *supra*); *Muclebroc* c.1200 ('the great brook', *v.* mycel, brōc); *Raweruding* 14 ('cleared land at a row (of trees?), *v.* rāw, ryding); *le Sale*(*lyde*)*yate* 1354 (perhaps 'gate at a willow', *v.* salh (dat. sg. sale), hlid-geat; a place on London Rd *supra* near the Stretton boundary, cf. 1 43 X); *Sartandal* c.1200 ('black dale', *v.* sweart, dæl¹); *Strethbrok* 1315² (p), *Stuthbrok* 1315¹ (p) ('brook at a paved road', *v.* strǣt, brōc, probably alluding to London Rd *supra*); *Thoraldcroft* l12–e13, *Thoraldescroft* 1354 ('Thorald's croft', from the ON pers.n. Þóraldr and croft); *Twenodeheth* 1362² (perhaps 'two-woods heath', *v.* twēgen, wudu, hǣð); *W*(*h*)*yt-*, *Whithull* 1357¹, ² (p), *del Quytehurst* c.1350 (p) (surnames at Appleton, *v.* hwīt, hyll, hyrst).

3. Aston By Budworth (101–685802)

Estone 1086 DB, *-tona* (*-juxta Buddewrethe*, *-worth*) 1190–99 (1666) Orm², 1296 Plea (DKR xxvi 45, lit. *Estova*), l13 Tab, *-tonna* e13 (1295) Orm², *Heston*(*a*) 1190 ArlB (p), c.1200 Tab, *-tun* e13 Orm² (p), *-tan* 1320 Mere (p)
Aston H3 (1669) Orm², 1255 Tab *et freq*, (*-juxta Pykemer*) 1295 Orm², (*-juxta Budworth*) 1318 Eyre, (*-neere Budworth*) 1534 *Chol*, *Astone* 1574 Tab, *-tun* 1305 ib, *Haston* 1306 ib.
Ashton nigh Budworth 1673 ChRR
Alston 1673 ChRR

'East farm', *v.* ēast, tūn. The township is east and north-east of Great Budworth, which it adjoins. Cf. Pickmere 13 *infra*.

Arley Hall, Mill, Moss Fm, Park *&* Pool (101–675808)

(*parcum-*, *le park de-*) *Arlegh* 1340 *CoLegh*, *-ley* 1360 Orm² *et freq*, (*the hall of-*) 1666 Orm², *-Mill*, *-Moss*, *-Park* 1831 Bry, *-Pool* 1844 *TA*, *Arleye* 1599 AD
Areley 1573 Sheaf, 1651 *LRMB*, 1673 Sheaf
Ardley 1646 Sheaf

For *Arley* Ekwall (DEPN) suggests 'eagle wood', from earn and lēah, with loss of *-n-* in the cluster *-rnl-*, as in Arley Wa 123–24, Wo 30, cf. Yarwoodheath 58 *supra*. However, *(le) Harlae* 1336, 1340, *heya de Harlagh* 1347 CoLegh, 50 *supra*, from deeds relating to the southern parts of High Legh 45 *supra*, probably refer to Arley, in which case, unless these contain inorganic *H-*, the first el. would be hār[2] 'grey, hoary'. This would suit Arley's situation on the boundary between the DB hundreds of *Bochelau* and *Tunendune*, cf. 1 *supra*. Cf. Hollins 128 *infra*, Arley Green *infra*. Arley Pool, now drained, was an ornamental lake.

EAST & WEST FELDY, (LOWER) FELDY GREEN (101–6979), *Felday* 1327 Pat (p), *Feldy* 1666 Orm[2], *-Green & Lane* 1831 Bry, *Higher Green* 1842 OS, 'hedged-in enclosure in an open tract of land', *v.* feld, (ge)hæg, grēne[2].

HIELD BROW, HO & LANE (101–672775) ['hi:əld]

Helda (in Hestona) c.1200 Tab, e13 Orm[2], c.1247 Tab, (*-in Estona*) 1296 Plea, *Helde* c.1247 Tab *et freq* with variant spelling *Held*; *Helde (-in Estona)* l13 (1653) Tab, (*la-*) 1328 ib (p), (*le-*) 1348 MidCh (p), (*the-*) 1513 Tab, (*-iuxta Budworth*) 1490 ib, *le Heldpark* 1331 ib, *Held Wood* 1576 ib, *Heldbroke* 1581 (1666) Orm[2]

Hield H2 (1666) Orm[2], *the hall of the-* 1568 Tab, *Hield Farm & Lane* 1831 Bry, *-Brow* 1842 OS, *del Heild* 1355 (1666) Orm[2], *Heild* 1637 Tab, *Heyld* 1601 ib, *Healde* 1556 ChRR

'The hill-slope', *v.* helde, with park, wudu, brōc, hall, brū. *le Heldpark* was between *Curtisford infra* and Budworth and Aston. The brook was probably *Cuttesfordbroke infra*, connecting the meres of Pickmere and Great Budworth.

LITLEY FM (101–692807)

Ly-, Litel(l)egh 1307 Tab (p), 1308 Whall (p), *Litley* 1335 (1666) Orm[2] *et freq* with variant spellings *Li-, Lyt(tel(l))-, Litt(le)-, -ley(e), -le(e), -leghe*
'The little clearing', *v.* lȳtel, lēah.

WATHALL FM, KAYS FM (101–685783) ['watɔ:l]

Wethal' 1185–90 Facs (p), *-hale* H3 (1666) Orm[2], l13 (1653) Tab *et freq*, (*-in Aston*) 1637 ib, (*-Farm*) 1666 Orm[2], *Wetale* e13 (1295) ib, 1279 Tab

Wethalle 1194 Facs (p), *Wethall in Aston* 1668 Tab
Wetehale e13 (1295) Orm², l13 Tab, 1293, 1296 Plea
Quetale 1273 ArlB, 1297 Tab (lit. *Q'tale*), *Whetaleloue* 1323 ib,
    Whetale 1336 ib, (*-in Aston*) 1390 ib, *-hale* 1316 ib, *Whetal* 1361
    ib
Whethalle 1316 Tab
Whetehale 1377 Tab, 1415 ChRR
Wheteall 1422 Tab

'At the wet corner', *v.* wēt (wk.obl. wētan), halh (dat.sg. hale).
The spellings show confusion with hwǣte, hwǣten 'wheat, wheaten',
and hall 'a hall', cf. Wettenhall 327 *infra*. *Whetaleloue* is 'the hill,
or mound, at Wathall', *v.* hlāw, cf. *Aston lowe infra*. Wathall Fm
(*Bird House* 1842 OS) is *Wethall* 1831 Bry, Kays Fm is *Wethall
Manor Farm* ib.

ALDERHEDGE WOOD, *Alder Hedge* 1831 Bry, *Alder Edge Wood* 1842
OS, *v.* alor, hecg. ALLFOURS. ARLEY GREEN, 1860 White,
Cowhouse Farm 1842 OS, *Arley Cow Houses* 1844 *TA*, cf. Arley *supra*,
Green Covert *infra*. THE ASHES, 1842 Os. ASTON PARK, 1831
Bry, *-Parks* 1742 JRL, *-Parke* 1762 LCWills, *v.* park 'a park', but
the plural may be from pearroc 'a paddock'. BACK LANE.
BATE HEATH, 1831 Bry, cf. *Bate Field* 1844 *TA* (5x), *the Baytefield*
1559 Tab, *the great Batefields* 1579 ib, from beit 'pasture'. THE
BELTS, a plantation. BIG WOOD, 1844 *TA*, *Arley Wood* 1831 Bry,
Great Wood 1842 OS, cf. Arley *supra*. BIRCH BROOK HO (lost,
101–674801), 1842 ib, *-Farm* 1831 Bry, cf. Arley Brook 1 13
BONGS WOOD, 1842 OS, *v.* banke. CANN LANE, *Can Lane* 1831
Bry, *v.* canne 'a can, a cup', here alluding to the hollow at The
Howie *infra*, to which Cann Lane leads. Cf. Cann Lane 98 *supra*.
COLLIERS LANE, 1842 OS, *v.* colere 'a charcoal burner'. CROFTON
COTTAGE. CROSSFIELD. FACTORY COTTAGES. GEORGE'S LANE,
1860 White. GORE FM & WOOD, 1831 Bry, *le Goore* 1523 ChRR,
v. gāra 'a triangular piece of land, a gore'. GRAVESTONE FM,
Gravestones Farm 1831 Bry, the home of one Jonathan Vernon,
d.1692, buried here in his garden with his wife Sarah. GREEN
COVERT, *Cow House Coppice* 1844 *TA*, named from Arley Green
supra. GUIDEPOST FM, *Finger Post House* 1831 Bry. HILLTOP
FM, *Hill Top* 1831 ib. THE HOWIE, a wooded hollow beside Arley
Brook. KAYS FM, *v.* Wathall *supra*. LADY PARK, 1844 *TA*, *v.*
hlǣfdige, park. LANDSEND FM. MILL WOOD, cf. *Mulne Croft*

1313 Tab, *Mylneclouse* 1500 ib, *Mill Wood, Mill Dam Pool & Wood* 1844 *TA*, v. myln, croft, clos, named from Arley Mill *supra*. Moss End, 1842 OS, named from Arley Moss *supra*. Nettle Gate, v. netel(e), geat. New Fm, 1831 Bry. Park Lane, 1831 ib. Pickmere Rough, *The Rough* 1831 Bry, cf. *Pickmere Field, Meadow & Wood* 1844 *TA*, adjoining Pickmere 120 *infra*. Sack Lane. The Slacks, v. slakki 'a hollow'. Stockley Fm & Rough, perhaps 'tree-stock clearing', v. stocc, lēah, cf. 121 *infra*. Stonegate Cottages. Westage Lane, 1831 Bry, cf. *Great & Little Westage* 1844 *TA* and 109 *infra*, from ModEdial wastage 'a waste place, waste land'. Willowbed (Wood), *Willow Bed* 1831 Bry, (*Wood*) 1842 OS, v. wilig, bedd. Yewtree Fm, 1860 White.

FIELD-NAMES

The undated forms are 1844 *TA* 25. Of the others, 1357 is *Eyre*, 1579 ChRR, 1831 Bry, the rest Tab.

(a) Alderley Croft; Backside; Barley Croft (*le-* 1305 Tab, v. bærlic, croft); Batching Acre; Bent (v. beonet); Clay Flatt; Cockfield (cf. *le Cokerfeld* 1316, v. cocker, cocc[1], [2], feld); Couch Croft, Couchey Mdw (places where couch-grass grows, v. cwice); Cough Fd; Cow Hey; Dingle Acre (v. dingle 'a deep hollow'); Dove House Fd; Fallow Fd; Faulter (a group of ten fields); French Fd; Fur Wd ('further wood'); Ganders Bridge 1831 (cf. foll., v. 47 *supra*); Gandys Croft (probably from the surname *Gandy*, cf. prec); Garden Fd; Glade Fd; Goodmanshey ('the master's enclosure', v. gōd-man, cf. Good Wives Hey 100 *supra*); Gorsey-, Gorsty Fd, Gorsty Brow (v. gorstig); The Great Lawn (v. launde); Green Duck Fd (cf. *Grindeck Lane* 1831, probably 'green dike', v. grēne[1], dīc); Hatch Croft (v. hæc(c)); Heath Fd (*Hetfeld* 1314, v. hǣð, feld); Hemp Yard; Old Hey Rough & Wd; Hide Flatt; Hollin Hey (v. holegn, (ge)hæg); House Fd; Intake (v. inntak); Kennerley; Kiln Butts, Croft, Fd & Mdw (*le Culnegrene* 1313, 'the green where the kiln stands', v. cyln, grēne[2]); Knowl; Lane Fd (*the* 1785); Long Shute or -Soote (v. scēat); Marl (Pit) Fd; Mere Croft (cf. Pick Mere 120 *infra*); Milk Ley (v. meoluc, lēah); Milking Bank (v. milking); Mistresses Fd; Moor Moss (cf. *le Moer* 1357, *the More* 1513, *Astonmoor* 1579, v. mōr[1], mos); New Earth (v. eorðe or erð); Normans Land (probably 'no-man's land', a common, v. nān-mann, land); Oat Hey; Ox Hay, -Hey; The Patch; Pinfold Fd (v. pynd-fald); Pool Sted (v. pōl-stede); Ridding (v. ryding); Rye Park (cf. *Rye Feld* 1314, v. ryge, feld); Sand(hole) Fd; Shrogs (v. scrogge); Stocken Mdw (v. stoccen); Three Angles; Three Nooked Piece; Triangle; Urchin's Moor (v. urchon); Vicars Nook; Wall Hill Fd or Big Wall Fd, Little Wall Fd (v. wælla); Wash Croft & Fd (v. wæsce 'a place for washing'); Waterless Bridge 1831 (101–693808, crossing Arley Brook, either 'bridge at water-meadows' v. wæter, lǣs, or a back-formation from Waterless Brook[1]

1 37, -Bridge, 62 *supra*, cf. Arley Brook 1 13); White Fd & Moor; Widders Moss; Winfar Flatt; Wrench; Yield Fd (*v.* helde, cf. Hield *supra*).

(*b*) *Aston lowe* 1323 (*v.* hlāw 'a hill, a mound', cf. *Whetaleloue* (Wathall) *supra*); *Barndefeld* 1316 (*v.* brende[2], feld); *Busshe Croft* 1526 (*v.* busc, croft); *Caluerheye* 1314 ('calves' enclosure' *v.* calf (gen.pl. calfra), (ge)hæg); *Cottons Crofte* 1506 (from the surname *Cotton* and croft); *Curtisford* 1313, 1331, *Cuttesfordbroke* 1452 ('Curtis's ford', from the ME (OFr) pers.n. *Curteis* and ford, with brōc, at 101–672772, cf. Hield *supra*); *le Heye* 1314 (*v.* (ge)hæg); *Ridwalhurst* 1348, *Redwal(le)hurst* 1357 (p) ('(wooded-hill near) the reed-stream', *v.* hrēod, wælla, hyrst); *Sawtys Crofte* 1513; *le Sernour* 1313; (*the*) *Swyn(e)hey(e)* 1500, 1507, 1514 (*v.* swin[1], (ge)hæg); *Wyldemare-flatte* 1306 ('wild mare's plot', *v.* wilde, mere[2] (cf. wilde-mere), flat).

4. BARNTON (101–6375)

Berthinton 112 Facs (p), -*yn*- 13 Orm[2], -*ing*- 1289 Court (p), -*yng*-, (-*iuxta Anderton*) 1300 Plea, Orm[2], *Bertenton* 1282 Court
Bertherton 1313 Plea, -*ir*- 1329 ChRR (p), *Berterton* 1437 Plea
Berneton 1319 ChRR *et freq*, *Bernton* 1413 Pat, *Barneton* 1517 ChEx *et freq*, *Barnton* 1577 Orm[2]
Berynton 1326 Tab, 1520 Plea, -*yng*-, *Berrington* 1520 Orm[2]
Bereston 1512 Orm[2]

v. Bartington 106 *infra*.

BESTWAY WOOD. GIBBONS BIGHT (lost, 110–633739), 1842 OS, *Gibben's Bite* 1831 Bry, a bend of R. Weaver, *v.* byht. GUNNERS CLOUGH, *v.* 96 *supra*. HILLTOP. HOLLYBANK FM. LEIGH'S BROW, *v.* brū. LYDYETT LANE, cf. *Lydia*-, *Lidgate Loont* 1844 *TA*, 'the swing-gate', *v.* hlid-geat, land. MANOR HO, cf. *manor-place of Berneton* 1510 Orm[2], *Barneton Hall* 1547 ib. OAKWOOD LANE, *Sandy Lane* 1831 Bry, cf. *Oak Wood* 1831 ib. ROPERY FM, named from a rope-works, *Rope Walk* 1831 ib. RUNCORN RD, leading towards Runcorn 176 *infra*. SALTERSFORD LOCKS & TUNNEL (101–627753), 1831 ib, on R. Weaver and the Trent & Mersey Canal respectively, cf. *Saltersford* (101–629753) 1842 OS, a hamlet on the Runcorn road presumably named from a salter's ford over R. Weaver, *v.* saltere, ford. Whether this was part of a salt-way is not apparent, *v.* Crump 98n. There was a salt-house in Little Leigh 117 *infra*, as well as those at Northwich. STONEHEYS FM, *Stone Heys* 1831 Bry, *Stoney Heys* 1843 *TAMap*, *v.* stān, stānig, (ge)hæg. TOWN-FIELD FM & LANE, *Townfield Lane* 1831 Bry. YEWTREE FM.

FIELD-NAMES

The undated forms are 1844 *TA* 36. Of the others, 1383, 1464, 1517, 1666 are Orm², 1750 Sheaf, 1831 Bry.

(a) Alderley Bank (the Stanley family of Alderley 1 94 were freeholders in 1666); Backside Fd; Bank Croft; Barley Loont (*v.* land); Barnton Moor (*Barnton Common* 1831); Black Croft; Blackley ('black clearing', *v.* blæc, lēah); Bottoms (*v.* botm); Bramows, -Hill & Wood Brow; Breeches Mdw (*v.* brēc); Brooms; Brown Mares; By Pasture (*v.* byge[1] 'the bend of a river'); Cockshuts Fd (*v.* cocc-scyte 'a cock-shoot'); Crab Tree Croft; Crocus (cf. the modern Crocus St.); Fearney Croft; Hemp Yard; Hob Riddings (*v.* hobbe, ryding); House Loont ('selion near a house', *v.* hūs, land); Kiln Loont (*v.* cyln, land); Lady Hat; Leather Mdw; Leghough (*v.* hōh 'a heel, a spur of land', cf. Little Leigh 115 *infra*); Lock Brow & Mdw (named from Saltersford Locks *supra*); Long Hey; Loont (*v.* land); Many Fd; Marl(e)d Fd; Merrishaw Field (probably 'pleasant wood', *v.* myrge, sceaga); Mickley ('great clearing', *v.* micel, lēah); Milking Bank (*v.* milking); Moor Fd & Heys; Old Ellen's Hill 1750; Outlet (*v.* outlet); Ox House Loont (*v.* land); Pansey; Philence (*v.* field-land(s)); Pinfold (*v.* pynd-fald); Poll Fd; Pownall Mdw (cf. the family *Pownall* of Barnton 1666); Push'd Ploughed Mdw (*v.* push-plough); Riddings (*v.* ryding); Round Hill; Shoulder of Mutton (*v.* 327 *infra*); Shutes (*v.* scēat); Sour Fd; Spout Mdw (*v.* spoute 'a spout, a spring'); Swallow Croft; Swine Park; Tunnel Fd (named from a canal tunnel here); Wallascoat Mdw (belonging to Wallerscote 327 *infra*, across the R. Weaver); Well Croft; Wildgoose Mdw; Winnington Mdw (near Winningtōn 327 *infra*); Winstanley (perhaps 'Wynstān's glade', from the OE pers.n. *Wynstān, v.* lēah, cf. Winstanley La 104); Withins, -Wood (*v.* wīðegn); Yew Tree Croft.

(b) *Simondestone* 1464, *Simonstone* 1517 ('Simon's farm or stone', from the ME pers.n. *Simond* (< OE *Sigemund*) and either stān or tūn, cf. Simonstone La 79); *Wolvylegh* 1383 (p) ('wolves' clearing' *v.* wulf, lēah).

5. BARTINGTON (101–6076)

Bertintune 1086 DB (2x), *Berthenton* 1199–1216 Tab, -*in*- 1209 ib, -*yn*- 1302 ChF (p), (-*iuxta Duderton*) 1356 Plea, -*ing*- 13 (17) Sheaf, -*yng*- 1353 BPR, -*untun* 1324 Tab, *Barthington* 1537 Plea, -*yn*- 1551 Sheaf

Berdintona 1170 Facs (p), *Bardinton* 1284 (1662) VR

Berthreton 1180–1208 (1580) Sheaf, *Bertherton* 1180–1208 (1666) Orm², 1281 (1338) VR (p), 1358 BPR (p), -*ir*- 1329 ChRR (p), *Berterton* E1 (1666) Orm² *et freq* with variant spellings -*ir*-, -*ur*-, -*ar*-; (-*iuxta Doutton*) 1330 *Vern*, *Barterton* c.1440 *Surv*, 1534 *Chol et freq* to 1860 White

Bertrinton 1285 Tab
Berthiton 1317 City

This place and Barnton 105 *supra* are frequently mentioned in early records, and as the manorial interests mostly devolved upon the Dutton family of Dutton, they are not easy to separate. Leycester (Orm² 1 638) in 1666 took the two instances of *Bertintune* in DB as moieties of Barnton 'unless the one of these should be meant for Barterton' (i.e. Bartington), whereas Tait (ChetNS LXXV 211) takes them both as Bartington. The majority of the *Bertherton* spellings (often mistaken, in printed calendars, as also the *Berthyn(g)*-, -*in(g)*-spellings, for *Berch*-) refer to Bartington, and this place seems never to have been called *Bern(e)*-, *Barn(e)ton*. The two places are distinguished by different forms of one p.n., as if originally parts of one manor. The p.n. is probably 'Beornðrȳð's farm', from the OE fem. pers.n. *Beornðrȳð* and tūn, alternating with -ingtūn. The various forms of the p.n. are due to loss of interconsonantal -*n*- in -*rnð*-, dissimilatory loss of -*r*- in -*ðrȳð*-, and variations between the full pers.n. and a shortened form before -ingtūn. Cf. Batherton 325 *infra*.

ACTON QUAY, 1831 Bry, a wharf on the Trent and Mersey Canal, cf. Acton Grange 146 *infra*, v. kay. BARTINGTON FM, *Amerys Farm* 1831 ib. DEAN BROOK & FM, *Dutton Dean Farm* 1831 ib, v. Dutton Dean 113 *infra*, v. denu, brōc.

FIELD-NAMES

The undated forms are 1841 *TA* 40. Of the others, 13 is AD, 1313 Plea, 1831 Bry.

(a) Bartington Heath; The Bottom (v. botm); Near Brow; Calf Park; Cow Hey; Crabtree Fd; Crow (v. crew 'a hut, a cote'); Dones Moor 1831 (cf. Dones Green 113 *infra*); Dutton Lane (*Dutton Hall Lane* 1831, v. 114 *infra*); Gale Mdw (v. gagel); Hovel (cf. Crow *supra*, v. hovel); Loonts Mdw (v. land); Low Hill (v. hlāw); Marl Fd; The Moss; Pump Head 1831; Springs (v. spring); Long Tongue (v. tunge); Way Croft & Fd.

(b) *quadam insula vocat' Brunteseie in Bertherton* 1313 (cf. *insula de Berter-ton* 13; 'Brunt's island', from ēg with a ME pers.n. *Brunt*, perhaps an -*et*, -*ot* diminutive of OE *Brūn(a)* 'Brown').

6. GREAT BUDWORTH (101–6677) locally [ˈbudə:þ]

Budewrde 1086 DB, -*worth* 1394 ChRR, -*worthe* 1554 Pat, *Budde-wrtha* 1190–1211 *Cott*. Nero C III, -*wrethe* 1190–99 (1666) Orm², -*wrd* c.1247 Tab, -*worth* 13 Whall, 1290 IpmR, -*worthe* 1375 Tab

Budeswurda c.1115 Pal (Barnes[1] 458)
Buddesworda 1154–60 (1329) Ch
Boddeworthe 12 *Dow*, *-worth* 14 *ChFor*, *Bodeworth* 1291 Tax, *-worhe* 1295 Lacy, *-worht'* 1306 *MinAcct*
Buddwrthe c.1174 Orm[2], *Budworth* 1209 Tab (p) *et freq* with variant spellings *-wurth(e)*, *-worthe*, *-wordeth*; (*-iuxta Comber-bache*) 1357 *ChQW*, (*-iuxta Mersshton*) 1382 Plea, (*-in Halton'*) 1500 Tab, (*-iuxta Aston*) 1511 Plea, (*-iuxta Northwich*) 1517 ib, (*Magna-*, *Great-*) 1554 Sheaf, 1578 ChRR
Bodesworth, *-is-* 1307 Plea (p)
Bodworth 1423 *MinAcct*, 1473 Tab, 1485 Plea
Badworth 1546 Dugd
Boodworth 1547 *Chol*

'Budda's enclosure', from the OE pers.n. *Bud(d)a* and worð. Spellings like *Bud(d)es-*, *Bodes-* may indicate *Budd, a strong form of the pers.n. (cf. *Boddus*, Feilitzen 204), but are probably due to an analogical gen.sg. inflexion, *v*. -es[2]. The p.n. recurs in Little Budworth 325 *infra*. The suffix *-in Halton'* 1500 Tab represents *Halton-shire*, to which the manor belonged, *v. Halton Hundred* 2 *supra*.

BUDWORTH MERE, 1452 Tab, *lacus de Budworth* 1335 (1666) Orm[2], 1500 Plea, *mar(r)a de Budworth* 1398, 1423 *MinAcct*, *Budwurth meir* 1503 Plea, *-worth Meere* 1506 Orm[2], *-Meyre* 1553 Tab, *-Meire* 1620 Orm[2], *-Mear* 1656 ib, *aqua de Budworth* 1584 ChRR, *v.* mere[1] 'a lake, a pool', presumably the location of *piscaria de Bodeworhe* 1295 Lacy, 'the fishery of Budworth'. The lake lies in the townships of Great Budworth and Comberbach, Marbury and Marston 111, 117, 118 *infra*.

BELMONT (DAIRY FARM), *Belmont & New Farm* 1831 Bry.   BOX-HEDGE, *-Field* 1844 *TA*, *Box Edge* 1831 Bry, *v.* box, hecg.   BROWN-SLOW, *-Green* 1831 ib, *Browneslow* 1666 Orm[2], cf. *Browneslane* 1619 Orm[2] II 127, *Browns Lane* 1842 OS, 'Brown's lane and hill', from the surname *Brown* and lane, hlāw, with grēne[2].   BUDWORTH HEATH, 1831 Bry.   COCK LANE, 1844 *TA*, named from the Cock Inn (1831 Bry).   CROWNEST LANE, cf. *Crow Nest House* 1674 *Dep*, *v.* crāwe, nest.   DENE COTTAGES, Ho & PUMP, *v.* denu 'a valley'. FAIRFIELD COTTAGE.   HOME FM.   LADIES WOOD, *v.* hlǣfdige. MOAT COVERT.   PINFOLD COTTAGE, cf. *Pinfold* 1844 *TA*, *v.* pynd-fald.   QUEBEC (COTTAGE), a house and plantation, cf. Whitehouse

infra. SANDICROFT. SOUTHBANK COTTAGE. WESTAGE LANE,
1831 Bry, cf. *Higher & Lower Westage, Westage Croft & Pingot* 1844
TA, v. **wastage,** cf. 104 *supra.* WHITEHOUSE FM, *Quebec* 1831
Bry, cf. Quebec *supra.*

FIELD-NAMES

The undated forms are 1844 *TA* 79. Of the others 13, 1333 are Orm[2], c.1300,
1356, 1477 ArlB, 1322 Bark, 1411 ChRR, 1538[1], 1544, 1552 Tab, 1538[2]
AOMB, 1560 Sheaf.

(a) Abbey Fd (cf. *Abbote Medowe* 1538[1], *le abbates medowe* 1538[2], *v.*
abbaye, abbat, mǣd; land belonging to Norton Priory 173 *infra*); The Acre
(cf. *The Acar* 1552, *v.* æcer); Arden (*Erredon* 1322, 1356, *Herredun* 1333 (p)
Erdun 1411, *Erdon Hey* 1477, from the OE pers.n. *Erra* (PN-ing[2] 124,
Erringham Sx 246, Redin 96) or perhaps *Heara* (Redin 97), *v.* dūn 'a hill',
(ge)hæg); Bean Fd; Black Flat & Hey, Blake Hey (*v.* blǣc); Bottom Croft;
Broad Mdw; Brook Fd; Broom Fd; Butt Croft, The Butts (*v.* butte); The
Carr (*v.* kjarr); Dings (*v.* dynge); Farnley Fd (*v.* fearn, lēah); Farthing(s)
(*v.* fēorðung); Filance (*le Fylands* 1538[1], *le Filandes* 1538[2]. These f.ns.
represent *filands* (EDD from 1681 in E. Anglia) 'tracts of unenclosed arable
land', probably from (ge)filde or feld and land, cf. ModE field-land (NED)
'level, unenclosed land'); Graves (*v.* grǣfe); Hanging Hill (*v.* hangende);
Hare Stile (*v.* stigel, cf. dial. *hare-gate* 'an opening in a hedge through which
hares run'); Heath Yard (*v.* geard); The Intack (*v.* inntak); Knowl; Loont
(*v.* land); Lords (*v.* hlāford); Lymm Lane Croft; Malt Kiln; Marl Fd; Mere
Croft, Fd, Lane & Mdw (cf. Budworth Mere *supra*); Mill Fd; Moor Mdw;
Newstage; Orchard Head; Ox Pasture; Pell Brook; Pingot (*v.* pingot);
Ridding (*v.* ryding); Spar Croft; Sparth Top (*v.* sparð, topp); Spring Mdw
(*v.* spring); Town Fd; Under Hill Fd (*v.* under, hyll); Within(s) Mdw (*v.*
wiðegn).

(b) *le Byrches* 13 (*v.* birce 'a birch-tree'); *Blakeforde* c.1300 ('dark ford',
v. blæc, ford); *Cherch hous* 1538[2] (*v.* cirice, hūs); *Dunberbath* 1544 (Tab 771,
probably an error for Comberbach 111 *infra*); *Hamond's Woode* 1560 (from
the ME (OFr) pers.n. *Hamon(d),* probably here used as a surname, cf.
Hammond's Hey 111 *infra, v.* wudu); *Sydenalwro* c.1300 ('(corner at) the
broad nook', *v.* sīd (wk. obl. sīdan), halh (dat.sg. hale), vrá; the ODan vrá
duplicates the OE halh).

7. COGSHALL (101–6377) ['kɔgsɔːl]

Cocheshalle 1086 DB, Coggeshall E2 MainwB, 1521 Plea, 1639
    Sheaf, Cogshall 1383 ChRR, Cogeshall 1581 Sheaf
Cogushal 1275 ArlB, Cogeshale 1317 City
Cogshul(l) E1 Tab, 1666 Orm[2], Kogeshult 1287 Court, Cogishull,
    -es- 1289 ib (p), 1295 ChF, Cogges- c.1296 Orm[2], c.1320 Chol

et freq, -hulle E2 (1666) Orm², 1416 Cl, Coggishil(l) 1305 Lacy,
1307 MinAcct, Coggeshyll 1419 Bark
Coksell 1511 Chol

The first el. is either an OE *cogg (ME **cogge**) 'a cog, a cog-wheel',
or an OE pers.n. Cogg derived from it, cf. Cogshall DEPN. The
second el. is **hall²** 'a slope, a hill' (confused with **halh** (dat.sg. **hale**)
'a nook, a corner of land') and **hyll** 'a hill'. Spellings in -hull from
the latter preponderate but the -hall form persists throughout. If the
first el. is the pers.n., Cogshall is 'Cogg's hill'. If it is OE *cogg, the
name is 'hill at a cog', supposing a mill-wheel or some such feature,
cf. Cogges O 333, Coggeshall Ess 365. However, Ekwall takes OE
*cogg in a figurative sense as a hill-name, DEPN s.n. Cogges. The
material is against derivation from the OE pers.n. Cocc proposed
NRY 121.

BURGHESS HALL (lost)

> Burwis 1317 Chol (p), 1318 Eyre, -es 1353 BPR (p), 1430 ChRR,
> (le-) 1418 ib
> (le) Burghes 1344 ChRR (p), 1369 Chol (p) et freq to 1507 MinAcct,
> Burghess Hall 1701 Orm² I 655
> (le) Borghus 1400 Pat (p)
> Borowes 1429 Orm², 1481 ChRR
> Burrowes Hall 1586 Map (PRO, MPC 57)

'The burrows', v. **burg** (ME **borow**). Since Williamson, Villare
Cestrense (1701, noted Orm² loc. cit.), observes that this place was the
seat of the Burghess family 'from Henry 3rds time', there ought to be
earlier references.

BOGS WOOD, The Bogs or Little Sandy Lane 1844 TA.   COGSHALL
BROOK (> Marbury Brook 117 infra), Mill Brook 1831 Bry, cf.
Marbury Mill 117 infra.   THE BROOK, BROOK HO, Three Houses
1831 ib, 1842 OS, a hamlet consisting of these and another house,
v. **þrēo**, **hūs**, cf. prec.   COGSHALL HALL & MILL, 1831 Bry.
COGSHALL LANE.   HALL LANE, near Cogshall Hall.   HOUGH
LANE (FM), cf. Hough (Lane) Meadow 1844 TA, Pingot Wood infra,
v. **hōh** 'an eminence, a spur of land', alluding to the ridge south-west
of Cogshall Brook.   PINGOT WOOD, Hough Lane plantations 1831
Bry, cf. Pingot 1844 TA, Hough Lane supra, v. **pingot**.

FIELD-NAMES

The undated forms are 1842 (1844) *TA* 127. Of the others, 1353 is *MinAcct*, 1397, 1398, 1400 ChRR, 1399 Plea, 1483, 1556 Orm², 1581 Sheaf.

(*a*) Backside; Bank Fd; Black Hey; Cross Fd; Gig Hole Mdw (*v.* gigge); Ham Bridge (*v.* hamm); Hammonds Hey (cf. *Hamond's Woode* 109 *supra*); Hand Heath; Hemp Yard; Old House Mdw; Leigh Wd (named from Little Leigh 115 *infra*); Long Fd; Old Marled Fd or Sandy Fd; Mill Ridding Brow & Rough (*v.* myln, ryding, cf. Cogshall Mill *supra*); (The) Moor (cf. *le le Medew Moor* 1353, either 'the moor at lea-meadow', or 'the meadow moor' with duplication of the definite article due to its use as a particle introducing the vernacular in a Latin document, *v.* mǣd, mōr¹); New Hey; Oak Hey or Outlet (*v.* (ge)hæg, outlet); Ox pasture; Pitstead Plantation (*v.* pytt, stede); The Pool Stead (*v.* pōl-stede); Priors Croft; Riddings (*v.* ryding); Rushy Fd; Rye Croft; Sandy Land (cf. Bogs Wood *supra*); Scotch Heys; Stoney Heys; Wet Acre; The Wives Hey (*v.* wīf); Little Yard (*v.* geard).

(*b*) *Colswaynesoke* 1397 (p), 1398 (p) ('Kolsveinn's oak', from the ON pers.n. *Kol(l)sveinn* and āc, cf. *Colstonstoke* 127 *infra*); *Filcokesfeld* 1399, 1400 ('Filcok's field', from the ME pers.n. *Filcok(e)* (Reaney 119 s.n. *Filkin*), a pet form of *Fill*, short for *Philip, v.* feld); *the grene* 1581 (*v.* grēne²); *Haliwallemor'* 1353 ('(moor at) the holy well', *v.* hālig, wælla, mōr¹).

8. COMBERBACH (101–6477) [ˈkʌmbərbætʃ]

Cambrebech 1172–81 Facs, *-bek* 1178 Whall

Combrebeche 1190 ArlB (p), *-bache* 1357 BPR, *Comberbach(e)* c.1230 *JRC* 841 (p), 1257 CoLegh (p) *et freq* with variant spellings *-bur-, batch*

Conberbeche or *Conbrebeche* 1191–4 Facs 8 (transcription Facs p. 17 reads *Comberbeche*)

Cumberbach c.1200 (1654) Sheaf, e13 Tab, *-e* 1304 Chamb *et freq* with variant spellings *-bir-, -bur-, -bre-, -bage, -back*

'Valley or stream of the Britons', *v.* Cumbre (gen. pl. Cumbra), bece¹, bæce¹, but DEPN observes that the first el. could be the OE pers.n. *Cumbra* ('Welshman'). The village stands in a hollow beside a small brook running into Budworth Mere.

AVENUE FM.   BUDWORTH MERE, *v.* 108 *supra*.   CLAYPIT WOOD, 1831 Bry.   COMBERBACH GREEN, *v.* grēne².   HOME FM.   IVY LODGE, 1831 Bry.   KENNEL WOOD.   KIDBROOK, a house, cf. Kid Brook 1 30.   MANOR HO.   SENNA LANE, 1831 ib, cf. Senna Green 133 *infra*.

FIELD-NAMES

The undated forms are 1845 *TA* 128.

(a) Ankers; Brook Shoot (*v.* scēat); Cock Pit Garden (*v.* cockpit); Cog-shall Hile (*v.* hygel (ME *huyle*) 'a hillock'); Cribb (*v.* crib); Intack (*v.* inntak); Two Loonts (*v.* land); Moss Croft & Fd; Narrow Lane Fd; New Hey; Oak Dish ('oak enclosure', *v.* āc, edisc); Ox Heyes; Rag Leyes; Ridding(s) (*v.* ryding); Rough Heys; Serrors Yard; Slip (*v.* slipe); Smithy Fd; White Mdw; Wilcroft.

9. DUTTON (109–5977)

> Duntune 1086 DB, -ton 1247 Cl (p), 1254 P (p), *Duninton'* 1183 ib, -yng- 1223–7 Whall (p), *Donitona, Don'ttoina* 1153–81 Tab, *Doninton* c.1240 ib, *Doncton* 1269–1300 ib (p)
>
> Duttun, -ton 1150–76 Chest (p), *Dow* (p) *et freq* with variant spellings *Dut(t)on(a), Dutun, Duttone, -onia, Dutthon*
>
> Dotton(a) 1157–94 Chest, 1172 Facs, 1178 Bun (p), c.1200 *LRO* Dx (p) *et freq* to 1350 AD, with variant spellings *-tone, -tana' Doton'*
>
> Dudton c.1233 *Dow* (p)
>
> Dittun 13 Tab, -e 1343 ib, -ton(e) 1245 P (p), 1252 RBE (p), (lit. *Dicton*) 1349 Eyre, *Dytton* 1349 *ib*, 1350 Chamb (p), 1390 ChRR, 1653 Sheaf
>
> Duderton 1284 Ch, 1356 Plea
>
> Dinton 1301, 1392, 1427 Pat (p)
>
> Douton 1447 AD (p)

The spellings for this place-name represent two traditions, one with *Dun-, Don-*, the other with *Dud-, Dut-*. The principal series, leading to the modern form, represents 'Dudda's farm', from the OE pers.n. *Dudda* and tūn as stated in DEPN. The development from OE **Duddantune* proceeds by loss of inflexional *-an*, assimilation of *-dt-* to *-tt-*, and occasionally the same shift of *-u-* to *-i-* (*Dut- > Dit-*) as in Dutton La 144. The series *Dun-, Don-*, which appears earlier than the prevailing one, could only be related to it by supposing a process OE **Duddantūne > *Dudntūne > Duntūne*. It seems prefer-able to suppose that *Duntune* etc. represent OE **Dūntūn, *Dūningtūn* 'farm at or associated with a hill', *v.* dūn, -ing-[4], and that Dutton was alternatively 'Hill Farm' and 'Dudda's Farm'. Cf. Duttons 326 *infra*.

POOLSEY (lost, 109–584777)

> *Pulleseya, -eia* c.1154 (1329) Dugd, 1329 Ch, *Pullishey* 1315 Orm², *Pulseya* 1329 ib, *capella de Pulsey* 1344, 1477 *MinAcct*, 1500 Chol, *Pulsey Chapell* 1496 Orm², *the Chapell of Pulsey* 1498 AddCh, *chapel-* 1529 Orm², *Pulsay* (*Eghes*) 1410 ChRR
> *Poosey* 1216–72 (1666) Orm², 1639 Sheaf, 1724 NotCestr, *-chappel* 1315 (1666) Orm², 1534 (1666), 1666 ib, *Powsey alias Newbrugh* 1576 Saxton, *Powsey* 1611 Speed
> *Pulsty* c.1240 Tab
> *pastura vocata Poleseyes* 1344 *MinAcct*, *Polsay* 1410 (1591) ChRR
> *Poolesley* 1609, 1615 Sheaf
> *Poolsey* 1841 *TA*

'Island at a pool', *v.* pull, pōl¹, ēg. The chapel was built by, and belonged to, Norton Priory 173 *infra*. Leycester, 1666 (Orm² I 643) notes 'In the demain of Dutton is also another chapel of ease, called Poosey-chappel within the parish of Runcorne, but is now ruinate and in decay. It is seated between the river and the park-pool within the demain of Dutton, but not in the township of Dutton, for the town of Dutton is within Budworth parish'. The *park-pool* was presumably the dead arm of the R. Weaver under the bank on which lies Dutton Park *infra* (cf. Dutton Lodge *infra*) and the *Poolsey* estate included the water meadows on the north bank of the river here. *Newbrugh* is Newbrook *infra*, which is some distance to the north.

BROOK FM, named from Whitley Brook 1 39. DONES GREEN, 1842 OS, cf. *Dones Moor* 1831 Bry (in Bartington, 107 *supra*), named from the family *Done* of Utkinton, holding in Bartington 1312–13 Orm² II 244. DUTTON BOTTOMS, 1831 Bry, *the Bottoms* 1748 Sheaf, *v.* botm 'valley bottom'. This place is beside R. Weaver, partly in Acton township, *v.* Island Fm 326 *infra*. DUTTON DEAN, 1831 Bry, cf. Dean Brook & Fm 107 *supra*, *v.* denu 'a valley'. DUTTON DINGLES, *The Dingles* 1831 ib, *v.* dingle. DUTTON HALL, 1831 ib, *Dutton house* 1666 Orm². The old house was removed to East Grinstead Sx, in 1935, Sheaf³ 30 (6729). DUTTON HOLLOW FM, *Gerrards Brow* 1831 Bry, *v.* brū 'the brow of a hill', holh. DUTTON LODGE (109–580778), *Duttons Lodge* (*Pool*) 1841 *TA*, cf. *the park-pool* 1666 Orm², 1724 NotCestr, *v.* loge, pōl¹, cf. foll. and *Poolsey supra*. DUTTON PARK (109–580773), 1831 Bry, *parcum de Dutton* 1344 *MinAcct*, cf. prec. and *Poolsey supra*, *v.* park. EIGHT ACRE WOOD, *Seven Acre Rough* 1831 Bry. GARDEN WOOD. HIGHER LANE,

1831 ib.   HILL FM, *Bennets Brow* 1831 ib, *v.* brū, hyll, cf. Dutton Hollow *supra*.   LIGHTWOOD FM, *Lyghtwode* 1344 *MinAcct*, *lightwod* 1477 ib, 'bright wood', *v.* lēoht, wudu.   LONGACRE BROOK & WOOD, *Long Wood* 1831 Bry, *Long Acre Wood* 1842 OS.   MARSH HO & LANE, 1831 Bry, *v.* mersc.   NEWBROOK FM (109–584780), 1831 ib, *Newburghe* 1545–6 Orm², *-brough(e)* 1582 ChRR, 1559 Pat, 1686 Tab, 1706 *Surv*, *Powsey alias Newbrugh* 1577 Saxton, *Newborough (in Dutton)* 1629 Orm², 1673 ib, *-brooke* 1623, 1647 Sheaf, 'new manor-house', *v.* nīwe, burh, cf. *Poolsey supra*.   PARK BROW, 1831 Bry, *v.* brū, cf. Dutton Park *supra*.   PICKERING'S BRIDGE & CUT (109–576763), *Pickering's Cut* 1831 ib, a reach of the Weaver Navigation, *v. Pickerings o' the Boat* 1841 *TAMap* and 327 *infra*, at a ferry across R. Weaver.   PROSPECT FM.   RESERVOIR WOOD, *Dutton Woods* 1831 Bry.   RYE GRASS PIPES, cf. *Rye Grass (Hollow & Wood)* 1841 *TA*, from dial. *pipe* 'a small dingle or ravine issuing from a larger one' (EDD), *v.* rye-grass.   SEVEN ACRE WOOD, *Swains Firs* 1831 Bry.   SILVER PITS, 1842 OS.   STREET LANE (101–605775 to 614788), from Dones Green *supra* to Lower Whitley, cf. Whitley Brook 1 39, Whitleybrook Bridge *infra*, *v.* 1 42 IX.   THATCHED HOUSE FM.   UNION FM.   WADE GREEN, 1841 *TA*, *Wheat Green* 1831 Bry.   WHITLEYBROOK BRIDGE, *Streete Lane Bridge* 1618 Sheaf, *v.* Street Lane *supra*, Whitley Brook 1 39.

FIELD-NAMES

The undated forms are 1841 *TA* 153. Of the others, e13, 1748 are Sheaf, 1250–90 Tab, 1308 Misc, 1344, 1477 *MinAcct*, 1353 BPR, 1706 *Surv*, 1831 Bry, 1842 OS.

(a) Apple Fd (*v.* æppel 'an apple (tree)'); Backside; Barn Fd (*the* 1748); The Bight ('river-bend' *v.* byht); Black Croft; Blake Hey (*v.* blæc, (ge)hæg); Blakeley (probably 'dark clearing', *v.* blæc, lēah); Bogs (*v.* bog); Brook Hey(s); The Brows (*v.* brū); Broxes (perhaps the simplex form of the first el. in Broxton, *v.* 325 *infra*); Chapel Fd; Childermas Hill (from dial. *Childermas(s)* 'Holy Innocents' Day (December 28th)', but the significance is not apparent); Clays (*v.* clæg); Clod Hut 1831 ('hut of clods' *v.* clodd, hut); Clough Fd (*v.* clōh); Deer Barn Fd; Dutton Hall Lane 1831 (cf. Dutton Lane 107 *supra*, Dutton Hall *supra*); East Fd (*Estfeld* 1344, 1477, *v.* ēast, feld); Entry Close (*v.* entre(e)); Fody Acre (probably 'forty acre'); Glade Fd; Gorst(e)y Hey (*v.* gorstig, (ge)hæg); Hand Croft & Ridding; Harry Fd; Hemp Fd & Yard; Intake (*v.* inntak); Killing Fd; Kiln Croft & Fd; Knowl; Linney (perhaps 'flax water-meadow', *v.* līn, ēg); Lock Brow Wd (named from a lock on the Weaver Navigation); Long Shoot (*v.* scēat); Main Hay (*v.* main, (ge)hæg); Main Stones; Marl Croft, Fd (*freq*) & Hey;

Milking Brow Fd (*v.* milking); Moor (*le More* 1477, *v.* mōr[1]); Moss Fd; Moulsdale 1748 (*v.* dæl[1] 'a hollow, a valley'); New Hay Pickow (*v.* pichel); Nickle Fd; Nix Hey; Nook Fd (cf. *Nook House* 1831, 1842); Oller Carr ('alder marsh', *v.* alor, kjarr); Ox Hey; Paradise Hill (*v.* paradis); Parlour Croft (*v.* parlur); Parson Croft (*v.* persone); Pingot (*v.* pingot); Pitstead Garden (*v.* pytt, stede); Quisters hey ('bleacher's enclosure', from eModE *quister, whytstar*, 'a whitster, a bleacher'); Rails (*v.* reille); Riding Ford (probably a horse-ford, *v.* ford); Runges; Sandyway (*v.* sandig, weg); Sarrates 1706; Shaws (*v.* sceaga); Sowders Acre; Stones Fd; Tan House Slack (*v.* tan-hous, slakki); Town Fd (1748); Turn Yard (*v.* trun, geard); Wallet (*v.* walet); Weir Fd; Withins (*v.* wiðegn); Wood Hays, -Heys.

(*b*) *Berefeld* e13 (p), *Berfeld* 1250–90 (p) ('barley field', *v.* bere, feld); *Hoblowe* 1344, 1477 ('goblin hill', *v.* hob, hlāw); *Hoklowe* 1344 (perhaps an error for prec., otherwise 'hill at a hook', alluding to the great crook of R. Weaver at Dutton, *v.* hōc, hlāw); *Hulteslegh* 1353 (a wood, *v.* lēah. The first el. may be hulc 'a shed'); *le Lowe* 1308 (the name of a fishery in R. Weaver, probably from lagu 'sea, flood, water, stream, pond', confused with hlāw 'a hill'); *Milnehey* 1344, *My-* 1477 (*v.* myln, (ge)hæg); *pastur' voc' Stoneley-feld* 1344 ('(field at) the stone-clearing', *v.* stān, lēah, feld).

10. LITTLE LEIGH, formerly LEIGH IUXTA BARTINGTON (101–6175) [li:]

Lege 1086 DB, *Leia* 1199–1216 Orm[2], *Legha* e13 (1666) ib, Tab *et freq* with variant spellings *Leg(a)*, *Leye*, *Legh* (1295 Ipm *et freq* to 1724 NotCestr), *Leghth* (1344 *MinAcct*), *Leghe*, *Lee*, *Leigh* (from 1486 BodlCh, 1585 ChRR), and the additions *-in hundred' de Halton* (e13 (1666) Orm[2], Tab, 1295 Ipm, 1350 VR, 1475 *Clif*), *-iuxta Berterton* (1344 *MinAcct et freq* with forms as for Bartington to *Leigh iuxta Bartington* 1860 White), *-iuxta Halton* (1393 Orm[2]), *iuxta Dutton* (1406 (1471) ChRR, 1429, 1504, 1536, 1585 ib), *-near Acton Brygge* (1486 BodlCh), *-iuxta Acton* (1500, 1511 Plea)
Little Legh 1666 Orm[2], 1724 NotCestr, *-Leigh* 1831 Bry

'The wood or clearing', *v.* lēah. The affix lÿtel 'little', distinguishes this from High Legh 45 *supra*, as do the references to *Halton Hundred*, Bartington, Dutton 2, 106, 112 *supra*, Acton, Halton 325, 166 *infra*, Acton Bridge *infra*.

CLATTERWICK, *Clatre-*, *Claterwik(e)*, *-wick* 13 AD (p), *-wuc* 14 ib, *Claterwike in Legh* 1545 Orm[2], *Clatterwig(ge)* H3 (1666), 1244 Orm[2], *Claturwyk* 1416 AD, 'rubble hamlet', *v.* clater 'loose stones, a heap of boulders, a pile of ruins', wīc. Cf. Clatterdishes 325 *infra*, Whitley Brook 1 39.

ACTON BRIDGE, *v.* 325 *infra.*   BRADLEYMEADOW BRIDGE & WOOD, cf. *Bradley Meadow* 1841 *TA* (*freq*), either 'broad clearing', *v.* brād, lēah, or a surname *Bradley* from the same.   BRAKELEYBANK FM, BRAKELEY ROUGH.   CRUMLEYHEATH FM.   DENE COTTAGE. DESLAYHEATH, *Dereslegh* 1399 Plea, 1400 ChRR, probably 'Dēor's clearing', from the OE pers.n. *Dēor* and lēah, cf. Daresbury 148 *infra.*   FRIAR'S ROUGH, 1831 Bry.   HAWTON CLOUGH, 1831 ib, *Horton Clough* 1842 OS, *v.* clōh, cf. Ralph *Horton* 1728 White 932.   HEATH COTTAGES, *Lapwing Hall* 1831 Bry, cf. foll. HEATH FM, cf. *Bartington Heath* 1831 ib.   HILLTOP, 1831 ib. HOLE HOUSE, 1831 ib, cf. *Hole House Browe Bridge* 1831 ib, *v.* hol[1], brū.   THE HORNS, 1831 ib.   ISLAND COTTAGE.   LEIGH HALL FM, LEIGH LANE, LITTLE LEIGH POND (*-Pool* 1831 ib), cf. Little Leigh *supra.*   SHUTLEY COMMON & LANE, 1831 ib, cf. *Shutleys Lot* 1841 *TA.*   SMITHY LANE, cf. *Smithy Field* 1841 *ib.* STREET LANE, *v.* 114 *supra* 1, 42.   TAYLORS BRIDGE.   WHITLEY-BROOK BRIDGE, *v.* 114 *supra.*   WILLOW GREEN, 1831 Bry, *v.* wilig, grēne[2].   YEWTREE HO.

FIELD-NAMES

The undated forms are 1841 *TA* 238. Of the others, e13 is *AddCh* 49926, 13 AD, 1288 Court, 1327 Pat, 1348 Plea, 1391, 1421, 1433, 1436 ChRR, 1397 Tab, 1831 Bry, 1842 OS.

(*a*) Asp Tree Fd (*v.* æspe); Backside Fd; Ball Fd (*v.* ball); Barn Fd or Lady Hays (*v.* hlǣfdige, (ge)hæg); Birch Mdw; Birchen Fd (*v.* bircen[2]); Black Croft; Blakeley (*v.* blæc, lēah); Bowling Green; Boyl; Bradder Ailes (probably 'broad rails', from some kind of fence, *v.* brād, reille); Brine Sheath Mdw ('brine pit' *v.* brīne, sēað, cf. 193 *infra* and Salt House Fd *infra*); Brook Fd; Broom Fd; Brow; Butt Croft; Calvers Croft, Calves Croft (*v.* calver, calf, croft); Cappers Mdw; Cliptical Garden (an oval-shaped field, the form may be an error for *Eliptical*); Corn Green (*v.* corn[1]); The Cossack; Crab Tree Fd & Heys; Dace Acre; Danks Hill; Dock Hill (*v.* docce); Easy Heath (cf. Hasy Broom Fd *infra*); Flat Yards, Lower Flatt (*v.* geard); Great Heys; Little Haman, Hamans Hey; Hanging Bank (*v.* hangende); Hanks Hill; Hasy Broom Fd (*v.* brōm, cf. Easy Heath *supra.* The first el. in these two names, both heath-land names, may be hǣs 'brushwood', or a derivative); Hemp Yard; Hen Bank (*v.* henn); Hollins (*v.* holegn); Hollows; Holt (*v.* holt); Howley (Wd) (*v.* ūle, lēah); Intake (*v.* inntak); Jacks Lane, Jack Lane Croft (*v.* jack); Know Fd, Knowls (*v.* cnoll); Lady Hay(s), -Hey (*v.* Barn Fd *supra*); Lambs Skin; Lane End 1842; Leigh Fd; Long Acre; Lords Fd (*v.* hlāford); Marl Fd, Marls Heys (*v.* marle); Mean Hey (*v.* (ge)mǣne); Moat Mdw (*v.* mote); Moor Hey; Moss; Muckle Fd (*v.* mycel); New Hey(s); Nook Ho; Nook'd Fd; Oaken Clough (*v.* ācen, clōh); Old Mdw; Ox Hey(s); Peacock Lane 1831; Pecks Fd; Pickle, Pickows (*v.* pichel); Pingot (*v.* pingot); Pump Head 1831 (*v.* 107 *supra*); Reddish ('reed ditch' or 'rye enclosure', *v.* hrēod, dīc, or ryge, edisc); Rye Croft; Salt House Fd (*v.* salt-hūs, cf. Brine Sheath *supra*, Wicks *infra*); Sand Fd; Saunder Hey ('Alexander's enclosure', from the ME pers.n. *Saunder*, a short form of *Alexander*); Long Shea (*v.* sc(e)aga); Big & Little Strenshire; Sim Acre; Spark Croft (*v.* spearca); Spring Fd; Sun Shoot (*v.* sunne, scēat); Swans Hey (*v.* swān² 'a herdsman'); Sweet Fd; Titters Hill; Town Fd; Water Long; White Stubbs (*v.* stubb); Whorley Fd, Worley Hey, Worlish; Wicks, Wick Ho (*v.* wīc, hūs, cf. *wych*(e)-*hous*(e)); Wimseys (*v.* ēg 'a water-meadow'); Wood Heys; Wytches ('the wych-elms', *v.* wice).

(b) (*insula de*) *Lehee* 13 ('island at Leigh', *v.* ēg, Little Leigh *supra*); *del quitehockes* e13 (p) ('the white oaks', *v.* hwīt, āc, cf. White Stubbs *supra*); *Woluelegh'* e13, *Wolvelee* 13, -*legh* 1348, *Wlveleg'* 1288 (p) ('wolves' wood', *v.* wulf, lēah, cf. the surname *de Wolvylegh*, -*i*- 1391, 1433 ChRR).

11. MARBURY (HALL) (101–6576)

Merebir' c.1200 *AddCh* (p), -*birie*, -*ia* 1216–30 (1666) Orm², -*bury* 1216–30 *JRC* 1808 (p), 1411 Tab, -*bur'* 1252 Ch, 1283 P

Merbury 13 *JRC* 847, 1278 Fine *et freq* with variant spellings -*bur*(*i*), -*bure*, -*burye*; -*iuxta Buddeworth* 1326 Plea, -*nigh Comberbach* 1666 Orm²

Meresbur' 1280 P

Marbury 1411 ChRR (p) *et freq* with variant spellings -*burye*, -*burie*, -*bery*; -*iuxta Budworth* 1425 MidCh

Marbury Hall 1831 Bry

'Stronghold or fortified house by a lake', *v.* mere¹, burh, named from Budworth Mere 108 *supra*. Cf. Leycester (1666), 'This hamlet . . . comprehendeth onely the manor-house, with the demain lands thereunto belonging' after which he cites the etymology, quoting Verstegan, *v.* Orm² 1 633. The p.n. recurs at Marbury 326 *infra*.

BIG WOOD, *Marbury Wood* 1831 Bry. DAIRYHOUSE FM, 1831 ib. HOPYARDS, 1842 OS, *v.* hoppe, geard. KENNEL WOOD, cf. *Kennels* 1842 ib, *v.* kenel. MARBURY BROOK (Wincham Brook 1 39), cf. Cogshall Brook 110 *supra*. MARBURY LODGE, MILL & PARK, *Marbury Lodge & Mill* 1831 Bry, cf. *Merbury milne, Parke-milne* 1499 Plea (two water mills), *v.* myln, park, cf. Cogshall Brook 110 *supra*. WITTON FLASHES, *v.* 197 *infra*.

FIELD-NAMES

The undated forms are 1844 *TA* 251, and 1831 is Bry.

(*a*) Butterfinch Bridge 1831 (lost in Witton Flashes *supra*); Cut Fd (by the Trent and Mersey Canal, *v.* cut); Big Heath; Marl Pit Fd; Old Wd; Slip (*v.* slipe); Slope (*v.* slope); Wick House Fd ('field belonging to a "wich-house" or salt-works', *v.* wīc, hūs, wych(e)-hous(e), cf. 193 *infra*).

12. MARSTON (101–6676)

    Merstona 1188 Tab, *-ton* 13 ib, 1281 CRV (p), 1300 Tab, 1346 Plea, 1362 BPR (p), 1371 Cl (p), 1581 ChRR, *-tone* 1318 InqAqd

    Mereston' 1280 P

    Merschton 1316 Chamb, *Mershton* 1337 Plea *et freq* with variant spellings *Merssh(e)-, Mershe-, Merss-* to *Mershton* 1584 ChRR

    Marston 1330 MidCh, 1407 (1471) ChRR, 1434 Tab, 1515 Plea *et seq*

    Marshton 1349 (17) MidCh, 1675 Sheaf, *Marshe-* 1465 *Outl*

    'Farm at a marsh', *v.* mersc, tūn.

OLLERSHAW LANE (101–672766 to 669753), *Alreschagh* 112 (1230) Orm[2], Tab, *-schahe* e13 Tab, *-sahe, -sathe* 1228 ib, *Aldershaw Lane, Ollershaw Lane* 1842 OS, cf. *Hawdisher Meadow* 1845 *TA*, 'alder wood', *v.* alor, sc(e)aga, lane. Ollershawlane Works (salt) was *Newman's Works* 1831 Bry, cf. Neumann's Flashes *infra*. This factory and Adelaide Works (6″, 1910) were at 101–671607, now subsided into a lake.

DARK LANE.   FORGE BROOK, COTTAGE & POOL, *Marston Forge Cottage, Forge Pool* 1831 Bry, *v.* forge 'a forge'. The brook joins Peover Eye 33 *supra*.   LANE-ENDS FM.   MARSTON HALL, 1831 ib, gives name to MARSTONHALL MINE (101–663762), a disused salt-mine. On this estate rock salt was discovered in 1670, and production of salt by mining as an alternative to walling was introduced at MARSTON OLD MINE (101–668607).   MARSTON LANE, leading to Marston from Wincham.   NEUMANN'S FLASHES, a lake caused by Peover Eye flooding a subsidence of the ground over old salt-workings, cf. Ollershawlane Works *supra*. The el. flasshe 'a swamp', here 'a shallow water, a pool', is applied to lakes formed in this way along Peover Eye and R. Weaver in the area of the Ch salt-field, cf. Witton Flashes 197 *infra*, which begin as shallow encroachments of water upon the subsided banks of the stream, creating swamps which deepen into lakes as the ground sinks. The same phenomenon is named *The Flash* at Preesall La.   POOL MINE, a salt mine near Forge Pool *supra*.   SWAN HOUSES.   WHALEBONE FM.

FIELD-NAMES

The undated forms are 1845 *TA* 255. Of the others, 1627 is *Chol*, 1666 Orm[2], 1675 Sheaf and 1831 Bry.

(a) Blake Hey (v. blæc, (ge)hæg); Bog (v. bog); Bull Mdw (cf. *Bull Barn* 1831); Clay Croft; Coney Grove (v. coninger 'rabbit-warren'); Crankerry; Dock Fd (v. docce); Ferney Fd; Grimes; Heath Fd; Little Hough (v. hōh); Old House Fd; Kiln Shaw (v. cyln, sceaga); Knowl (v. cnoll); Marl Fd; Mere Fd & Mdw (named from Pick Mere & Budworth Mere); Moss; Parkmeadow; Pease Fd (v. pise); Pool Fd; Riddings (v. ryding); Sand Fd; Long Shoot (v. scēat); Ston(e)y Fd; Town Fd; Walleys Fd (cf. *Walleys tenement* 1675, from the surname *Walley*); Well Croft; Wood Fd (*the wood feild* 1627, v. wudu).

(b) *the broad feild* 1627 (v. brād); *the litle Cowe heye* 1627 (v. cū, (ge)hæg); *the Longe Lownd* 1627 ('the long selion', v. lang, land); *the milne Crofte* 1627 (v. myln, croft); *the Reed Wood* 1627 (v. hrēod, wudu); *Sim-fields* 1666 (from the ME pers.n. *Sim* (*Simon*) or a surname derived from it).

12a. MARSTON (detached part, now included in Wincham c.p.)

LEONARD'S BRIDGE, FM, LANE & WOOD (101–6976) [ˈlenərdz]
    Linwood 112 (1230) Orm[2], (*boscus de*) 1288, 1300 Tab
    Lindwood 112 Tab, *-wode* e13 ib, (*boscus de*) 1228 ib, *Lynde-* 1318
      Eyre
    Linwoods 1819 Sheaf
    Linnards Farm, Lane & Wood 1831 Bry, *Leonard's Wood* 1842 OS,
      Lennards 1845 *TA*
    'Lime wood', v. lind, wudu.

SMOKERHILL FM, SMOKER WOOD, v. Smoker Inn 93 *supra*.

FIELD-NAMES

The forms are from 1845 *TA* 255.

(a) Birchen Mdw; Brickiln Croft; Crooked Corners; House Fd; Long Fd; Outlet (v. outlet); Pingott (v. pingot); Pit Fd; Poor Fd; Rye Grass Fd (v. rye-grass); Stony Croft; The Weeds; Wood Mdw.

13. PICKMERE (101–6977)

> *Pichemere* 1154–89 MainwB, e13 Orm², *Pikemere* 1236 (1580)
> Sheaf, *Pyke-* H3 *JRC* 845 (p) *et freq* with variant spellings *Pike-*,
> *Pyke-*, -*mer*, -*meyre* to *Pikemere* 1512 Plea, *Pykemere* 1527 *ChCert*
> *Pickmere* 1209 Tab, 1340 MidCh, *Pic-* 1216–72 (1666) Orm²,
> *Pyckmere* 1283 Ipm, *Pyc-* 1333 Tab (p), *Pyk-* 1367 Plea, *Pik-*
> 1385 Cl *et freq* with variant spellings *Pic-* (1415 ChRR to 1724
> NotCestr), *Pyk-* (1419 Bark to 1554 Pat), *Pycke-* (1488 ChRR),
> *Pik-* (1511 Plea to 1532 AD), *Pick-* (from 1531 AD), *Pyck-* (1544
> Plea to 1620 Orm²), -*mer(e)*, -*meir(e)*, -*meyre*, -*meare*
> *Pekemere* 1273 IpmR, *Peckmeir* 1656 Sheaf
> *Bykemere* 1280 P
> *Pickameire* 1698 Tab

'Pike lake', *v.* pīc¹ 'a pike (the fish)', mere¹, named from Pick
Mere *infra*.

PICK MERE, *Pykmer* 1452 Tab, *Pikmere Meer* 1502 ChRR, -*Mere* 1506
Tab, *Pickmere Meyre* 1581 (1666) Orm², -*Mere* 1831 Bry, *aqua de
Pickmere* 1584 ChRR, *Pickmere* 1656 Orm², *v.* Pickmere *supra*. The
lake Pick Mere gave name to the township and was later named in
turn from the township as *Pickmere Mere*, *v.* mere¹.

BROOK FM, *v.* brōc.   CHURCH FM, *Over Church Farm* 1831 Bry,
v. uferra, cirice.   COMMON FM, *v.* commun.   CROWN FM.
FROG LANE, 1831 ib, *v.* frogga.   MILLEY LANE, 1831 ib.   MOUNT
PLEASANT, -*or Pickmere Lodge* 1831 ib.   PARK LANE, *v.* park, lane.
PICKMERE FM, PICKMEREHALL FM, PICKMEREMOSS WOOD, *Pickmere
Moss* 1831 ib, *Moss Wood* 1844 *TA*, *v.* hall, mos, cf. Pickmere, Pick
Mere *supra*.   PICKMERE LANE (101–686765 to 708785), in Wincham
and Pickmere townships, is *Pepper Street* 1831 Bry at 101–686765 to
692767 where it forms the boundary between them. Cf. Pepper St.
(Chester) 327 *infra*.   ROSES FM, 1831 ib.   TANYARD FM,
Knowles' Tan Yard 1831 ib, cf. *Tan Pit Meadow*, *Tan Yard Croft*
1844 *TA*, *v.* tan-yard, tan-pit.   WALLHILL FM, 'spring hill', *v.*
wælla, hyll.   WATERLESS BRIDGE, *v.* 62 *supra*.

FIELD-NAMES

The undated forms are 1844 *TA* 320. Of the others, 1545 is Pat, 1666 Orm²,
1831 Bry, and the rest Tab.

(a) Black Acre (cf. *Ackars* 1684, 1698, *v.* æcer); Bark Shade Croft (*v.*

bark(e), sceadu); Bench (*v.* benc); Bent(s) (*v.* beonet); Black Fd; Bonewaste (cf. bone-dust); Brandor; Bull Fd; Burland Fd (*v.* (ge)būr, land); Burnt Acre (*v.* brende[2]); Chapel Fd; Cobhall Fd; Cold Heys; Cote Fd (*v.* cot); Crabtree Croft; Cross Fd; Deepmoor Hill (*v.* dēop, mōr[1]); Eastfords (*v.* ēast, ford); Fetters Croft; Field Green; Goodmans Fd (*v.* gōd-man); Gorsey Fd; Heild (*v.* helde); Hemp Yard; Intake (*v.* inntak); Kiln Croft; Kitchen Croft; Knowl Fd (*v.* cnoll); Langerlaths; Lees (*v.* lǣs); Leonards (*v.* Leonard's Wood 119 *supra*); Longyard ('long enclosure', *v.* geard); Lumber Butts (*v.* lumber, butte); Main Mdw (*v.* main); Mare Fd (*v.* mere[2]); Marl Cliffe, Marl('d) Fd; Mere Fd (*v.* mere[1]); Middle Spring; Mill Hay & Hill (cf. *Mylneclouse* 1500, *v.* myln, clos); Millstone Fd (*v.* mylen-stān); Newhey; Poor Fd; Riddings (*v.* ryding); Rye Croft; Sandholes Mdw; Sandyfoot (*v.* sandig, fōt); Shippon Mdw; Simmister Croft (from the ME occupational name *Semester* 'a tailor, a seamstress'); Singland; Sprink Lane 1831 (*v.* spring 'a young wood'); Sweet Fd; Three Nook'd Piece; Tile Yard Fd (*v.* tigel, geard); Timber Mdw (*v.* timber); Verrills; Warrens Lake 1831 (*v.* lacu 'a stream, a water-course'); Weir Fd; Well Brow Croft; Wet Fd.

(*b*) *Highfilde* 1545 (*v.* hēah, feld); *Lindpole* 1493 ('lime-tree pool', *v.* lind, pōl[1]); *Newhalls Moss* 1639, *Newalls Moss* 1665 (cf. Robert *Newhall* of Pickmere 1526, *v.* mos); *Swyn(e)hey(e)* 1500, 1507, (*v.* swin[1], (ge)hæg); *Wiche's lands* 1666 (held by William *Wiche*, Orm[2] 1632); *the Yate* 1666 ('the gate', *v.* geat).

14. STRETTON (101–6282)

Stretton(*a*) H2 (17), John (17) Orm[2], 1259 Court, *Plea*, 1263 Whall *et freq*, -*tone* 1305 Lacy, *Stretton iuxta Hulle* 1308 Plea, -*Over-whitelegh* 1348 ib, -*Apelton* 1381 ib, -*Gropenhale* 1383 ib
Strathton 1281 Tab (lit. *Stathton*), *Stratton* 1287 Court (p), 1329 IpmR, 1368 Mere, 1384 Plea

'Farm on a Roman road', *v.* strǣt, tūn. Stretton is on the Roman road from Warrington La to Northwich, *v.* 1 43 X.

BRADLEY BROOK, BRADLEY BROOKHOUSE FM, *Bradley Brook House & Bridge* 1831 Bry, '(brook at) the broad clearing', *v.* brād, lēah, brōc. The brook becomes Norcot Brook 125 *infra*. COMMON LANE. FIR TREE HO, 1831 ib. HALL LANE, cf. Stretton Hall *infra*. LOWER HALL, *the-* 1666 Orm[2], *the Nether Hall* 1819 ib, cf. Stretton Hall *infra*. MOSS HALL 1819 ib. MOSSWOOD HALL, *Mossewod* 1536 Plea, -*wood* 1665 Orm[2], *v.* mos, wudu. NEW FM. ROAD SIDE FM. ROLLYMOORS, *Rowley* 1751 Sheaf, *Ruley Moors* 1831 Bry, *Roughley Moor*, *Ruley Moor or Boggy Field* 1845 *TA*, 'rough clearing', *v.* rūh, lēah, mōr[1]. SPARK HALL, cf. *Spark Field* 1845 *ib*, *v.* spearca. STOCKLEY FM, LANE & ROUGH, *Stokley* 1394 Pat (p), *Stockley Rough* 1831 Bry, 'tree-stump clearing', *v.* stocc, lēah, cf. 126 *infra*.   STORK HO, 1842 OS, *Stalk House* 1831 Bry. LOWER STRETTON, 1842 OS.   STRETTON HALL, 1831 Bry, *Overhall in Stretton* 1536 Plea, *the Overhall of Stretton* 1559 Orm², *Higher Hall* 1842 OS, *v.* uferra, hall, cf. Lower Hall *supra*.   STRETTON MOSS, 1831 Bry.   SUMMIT COTTAGE.   TANNER'S ROW.   TAN-YARD FM, *Tan Yard* 1831 ib, *v.* tan-yard.   TARPORLEY RD, leading towards R. Weaver at Acton Bridge, and into Eddisbury Hundred, cf. Tarporley 327 *infra*, Street Lane 114 *supra*.   WALLSPIT, 'pit at a well-spring', *v.* wælla (ModEdial. *wall*), pytt.   WELL LANE.

FIELD-NAMES

The undated forms are 1845 *TA* 374. Of the others 1393 is Pat, 1672 Orm², 1690, 1751 Sheaf.

(*a*) Alms Yard; Appleton Fd (cf. Appleton 96 *supra*); Blackridge (*v.* blæc, hrycg); Brow Fd, Browey Mdw (*v.* brū); Cappersley Mdw (from the ME surname *Capper* (Fransson 116) and lēah); Chapel Croft; Cow Boose Croft (*v.* bōs); Dial Fd (*v.* dial); Doblane Mdw; Dog Fd; Dry Hurst (*v.* drȳge, hyrst); Flash Brow (*v.* flasshe); Gin Flatt; Gorsey Brow; Gutter Fd (*v.* goter); Hawking- or Fleeting Mdw; Heyes (*Stretton Heyes* 1627, *v.* (ge)hæg); Hollin Hedge Mdw (*v.* holegn, hecg); House Fd; Hut Fd (*v.* hut); Intack (*v.* inntak); Knowl Fd (*v.* cnoll); Lime Fd; Loont(s) (*v.* land); Marl Heath; Mill Heys; Long Noons; Outlet (*v.* outlet); Ox Hey; Pendlebury's Mdw (cf. *Pendlebury's Crofts* 1751); Pinfold Croft (*v.* pynd-fald); Pye Riddings (*v.* pīe² 'a magpie', ryding); Sand Fd; Big Shaw (*v.* sceaga); Siddens; Sludge Fd (*v.* sludge); Stoney Fd; Swine Cote Fd; Town Fd; Vetch Fd; Weedals Croft; Wet Moor; Wheat Ridding (*v.* ryding); Whim Bush (*v.* whin, busc); Whitley Croft (cf. Whitley 124 *infra*).

(*b*) *Wrontay* 1393 Pat.

15. TABLEY INFERIOR (101–7177), *Stablei* 1086 DB, *Parva Tabbeley* e13 (1295) Orm², c.1270 Tab, *Nether Tabley* c.1270 ib, *-talbelegh*, *-Tabell'* 1295 ib, 1296 Orm² *et freq* with variant spellings *Nethre-*, *Nethir-*, *-ur-*, *Neither-*, and as for Tabley Superior 60 *supra*, *Tabbelegh Inferior* c.1230 Chol, *Tabbele Inferius* 1329 IpmR, *Lower Tabley* 1724 NotCestr, *v.* neoðera, cf. Tabley Superior 60 *supra*.

FLITTOGATE, 1831 Bry, *Fletow(e)* c.1290 Chol (p), 113 Tab, *Fletehowe* 1308 ib, *fleton* 1306, 1330 ib, *Flyton* 1338 ib, *the Flitton* 1716 ib, *v.* geat 'a gate'. Some of the examples quoted as *-ton* (*v.* tūn) may well be *-tou*, and the eighteenth-century form may represent a late corruption. The earliest spellings indicate OE flet 'a floor', or ON flet 'a floor, a bench', and haugr or hōh 'a hill, a mound'. The p.n. could mean 'a mound with a flat-top, or with a bench, or shaped like a bench', but there may have been a more definite archæological or figurative significance (v. flet BT, Cleasby-Vigf) such as 'house'.

RINKS POOL & WOOD, Ryng(e)-, Ringestude, -stede c.1220 Tab et freq to 1338 ib, e14 Mere (p), 1312 (1348) Pat (p), Ruggested 1308 Tab (p), Ryng (parcum de-, boscus de-) 1322 ib et freq to 1381 ib, Tabbeleyryng 1401 ib, Rinks Pool 1831 Bry, 'the ring', v. hring, stede, styde 'a site, a place', cf. Ringestede 166 infra. The nature of this circle or ring is unknown. It may have been a ring-fence; but in Scandinavia this type of name is often associated with prehistoric stone-circles or circular earthworks, and this could be the case in England, see Sørensen 105–6, DEPN s.n. Ringstead, Nth 195, Sandred 103 (where an el. OE *hring-stede is proposed).

ALLENS BRIDGE, v. 92 supra. BOTANYBAY WOOD, perhaps a derogatory name, after the Australian colony. CLAY HO, 1831 Bry. CROW WOOD. DAIRYHOUSE FM (lost), 1842 Mere. DOGKENNEL WOOD. GREEN LANE. THE HUT, Tan Yard 1831 Bry. MANOR FM. PARKSIDE FM. ROUND WOOD, 1831 ib. ROYD WOOD, Ride Wood 1831 ib, v. rod[1] 'a clearing'. SCHOOL WOOD. SUDLOW LANE, 1842 OS, leading to Sudlow 61 supra from Sudlow Wash 1842 OS, at Wash Fm 93 supra. TABLEY GRANGE, cf. una grangia (in vill' de Over & Nethertablegh), del Graunge (p), 1442, 1466 Tab, v. grange 'a barn, a manor'. TABLEY HALL, Newehall 1381 ib, Table c. 1536 Leland, Old Hall 1831 Bry, v. nīwe, hall, cf. foll. TABLEY HO, -Hall 1831 ib, cf. prec. TABLEY MERE, v. mere[1] 'a lake'. 'WATLING STREET', v. 1 40. WHITE LODGE, 1842 OS. WILLOWBED WOOD, cf. bosc' de Wythynys 1338 Tab (lit. Wych-), 'willow wood', v. wīðegn, wilig, bedd.

FIELD-NAMES

Forms dated c.1280 are Chol, 1666 Orm[2], 1724 NotCestr, 1842 Mere, and the rest Tab.

(a) Chappel Fd 1666, 1724 (the site of an ancient chapel, v. Orm[2] 1 471); Fenderscroft 1704 (v. fender, croft).

(b) Babbelachkton 1310 ('(tūn by) Babba's stream', from the OE pers.n. Babba and læc(c), with tūn); Blakfild 1537 (v. blæc, feld); Bottefildes 1556 (perhaps 'fields infested by botts', from ModE *bott* (1523 NED) 'a horse-fly', *v.* feld); *Callerhey, Nallerheye* 1381 ('calves enclosure', *v.* calf (gen.pl. calfra), (ge)hæg; the second form is erroneous); *le Greuelondes de Nether-tabbelegh* 1295, *le Grenelowdes* 1297, *le Grenelondes* 1338 (the name of a wood in 1338, probably 'grove-lands' from græfe and land, but the first element might be grēne[1] 'green', since *u* and *n* are similar); *Hadleg'* 1324, *Hauedleg'* 1338, *Hadley Haye* 1425, 1428, *Hadleyes* 1480, *-leys* 1556 ('clearing at a headland', *v.* hēafod, lēah, (ge)hæg); *Haleford* 1260, *le Halehurst* 1306, 1338 ('ford and wood at a nook', *v.* halh, ford, hyrst); *Hawclenghe* 1559 ('hawk hill', *v.* hafoc, hlenc); *le Holt* 1260 (*v.* holt); *Horssale* 1338 ('horse's corner', *v.* hors, halh (dat.sg. hale)); *Hurst* 1338 (*v.* hyrst); *Lanercrofte* 1300 (p), *Lanecroft* 1319 (p) (*v.* croft. The first el. is obscure); *Long(e)ford* 1380 (p) (*v.* lang, ford); *Luggefote(ssmythye)* 1315, 1316, *Lugfoote* 1653, *Loffatte* 1556 ('(smithy at) *Luggefote*', *v.* smiððe. A difficult name. The two earlier references are to Bexton 72 *supra*, the later ones to this township, so the place was probably near the boundary. Local geography does not clearly indicate fōt, fótr 'a foot' in the topographical sense. The form could be explained as a pers. by-name, e.g. a ME **Luggefot* 'drag-foot, a lame man', from ME *luggen* 'to lug, to drag' and fōt, but this would hardly be used as a p.n. This p.n. may have affected the form *Luggebrigge* 73 *supra*); (*le*) *Lynstrete* (*v.* 'Watling Street' I 40); *Marlersfield* 1318 (1653) ('field of one who digs marl', *v.* marlere (cf. *Marlere* Fransson 182), feld); *le More* 1381 (*v.* mōr[1] 'a moor'); *Mulnehul* c.1260 (*v.* myln, hyll); *Nallerheye* (*v. Callerhey supra*); *Ruyfeld* 1381, *the Great Rye Field* 1666 (*v.* ryge, feld); *Son(d)-, Sond(e)for(d)-ley(e), -legh* c.1300, 1306 *et freq* in Tab to 1453, *Sandfordlegh* 1334 ('(wood or clearing at) the sand-ford', *v.* sand, ford, lēah, the name of a messuage in 1453).

16. HIGHER WHITLEY formerly WHITLEY LORDSHIP, cf. 'Over Whitley is a great township, comprehending the hamlets of Norcot, Anterbus, Middle Walke, Seaven Oakes & Crowley within the same. It is commonly called by the neighbourhood, The Lordship', 1666 Leycester (Orm[2] I 656), *v.* lordes(c)hip, cf. Norcotbrook, *Middle-Walks infra*, Antrobus, Crowley, Seven Oaks 127, 131, 133 *infra*. The lordship was of the barony of Halton in the Duchy of Lancaster.

HIGHER WHITLEY (101–6180)

> *Witelei* 1086 DB, *Wit(t)eleia, -le(g)a, -leth* 1182, 1183 P, 1191 Facs (p), R1 (1666) Orm[2] (p), *-legh* e13 Tab, *-leigh* H3 (1666) Orm[2], *-leg'* 1288 Court (p), *-le* 1323 Cl, *-ley* 1465 AD, *Wyteley* 1247 Tab (p), *-le(gh)* 1288 Court (p), *-leye* 1322 AD, Pat
> *Wytheley* H3 Orm[2]
> *Whetel(eye)* 1284 Cl (p), 1303 Chamb (p), *-le(gh)* 1317 City (p), 1324 ChRR (p), *-lee* 1353 BPR (p), *-lei, -ley* 1360, 1361 ib (p), *Qweteley* 1327–8 Sheaf (p)

Whit(t)e-, *Whyt(t)eley*, *-legh* 1295 Lacy, 1306 ChF, *-leigh*, *-leye*
1311 Ipm, *-le* 1367 ChRR (p), *Qwy-*, *Qwitelegh* 1316 JRL (p),
1357 BPR (p)

Whit-, *Whytlay* 1305 Lacy, 1307 *MinAcct*, *Whete-* 1323 Fine (p),
Whitelagh 1336 Plea, *-lawe* 1361 Fine, *-lowe* 1577 AD

Whit-, *Whytleye*, *-legh* 1322 Fine, MidCh, *-ley* 1386 ChRR (p) *et
freq*, *-leigh* 1612 Sheaf, *Whittley* 17 (1724) NotCestr

Whitelle 1329 IpmR

Overwhytelegh 1346 Plea *et freq* with variant spellings *ut supra*,
Higher Whitley 1724 NotCestr

'White wood', *v.* hwīt, lēah. 'White' would allude to either the
bark or the blossom of the trees. *Over-* (*v.* uferra) distinguishes this
part from Lower Whitley 134 *infra*.

ALDEWYK(E) (lost), 1305 Lacy, 1307 *MinAcct*, *Aldewich* 1199–1216
AddCh, *Aldwic* c.1180 (17) Sheaf, 'the old hamlet', *v.* ald, wīc.

MIDDLE-WALKS (lost), *the hamlet of-* 1724 NotCestr, *Mid(d)le- walke*,
Middle Walke 1666 Orm², 1702 *Chol*, from middel and walk 'a tract
of land used for the pasture of animals' (NED, cf. *sheep-walk*).

NORCOTBROOK (FM) (101–610805), NORCOT BROOK (> Whitley Brook
39 *supra*)

Norchot(es) H3 Orm², *-cotes* 1351 Plea, *-cott(e)s* 1465 Orm², 1579,
1673 ChRR, *Norcoot* 1486 BodlCh, *Norcott(e)* 1578, 1579 Orm²,
1607 ChRR, 1702 *Chol*, *-cot* 1666 Orm²

Northcotes 13 Tab (p), 1288 Court (p) *et freq* to 1507 *MinAcct*,
Norht- 1306 *ib*, *Northecote* 1386 *ib*, *-cot* 1487 *ib*

Norhcote 1305 Lacy, *-s* 1307 *MinAcct*

Nercotts 1530 Plea, 1551 Sheaf

Norcet 1724 NotCestr

'North hut(s)', *v.* norð, cot. The district is the north-west corner
of the township. The singular and plural forms recur constantly, the
plural being slightly the more frequent between the thirteenth and
sixteenth centuries. The modern name is from the stream Norcot
Brook, itself named from this hamlet.

AARON'S WELL & COTTAGE. ASHFIELD FM. BENTLEY'S FM,
Bentley Farm 1831 Bry. BIRCH TREE LANE, cf. *Birch Tree Field*
1844 *TA*, *v.* birce. BOOTHS LANE (101–620806 to 622808), from
bōth or the surname *Booth*. This and Dark Lane *infra*, with a footpath (101–622808 to 623814) continue the line of Street Lane 114

supra towards Lower Stretton, cf. 143. BRADLEYBROOK COTTAGES, named from Bradley Brook 98 *supra*, cf. *Bradley Brook Bridge* 1831 Bry. CHAPELHOUSE FM, 1854 *EnclA*, near a Methodist Chapel in 1831 Bry. DARK LANE (101–618802 to 620806), cf. Booths Lane *supra*. FACTOR'S HO. GREEN BANK, 1831 ib. GROVE HO. LAKE FM, *La(i)ke* 1595 *Rental*, *Lake House* 1831 Bry, probably from lacu 'a stream, a water-course', there being no lake here. LIMES LANE, from a house The Limes (6″), *Lowes Cottage* 1831 ib, from the surname *Lowe*. MARBURY HO, *Thompson Farm* 1831 ib, *estate called Marburys* 1854 *EnclA*, from the surnames *Thompson* and *Marbury*. MORRISHILL, 1844 *TA*. NORMAN'S LANE, probably 'no-man's lane', common land, *v.* nān-mann. OLDMILL FM, *the ould milnes* 1595 *Rental*, cf. *molendinum de Whitteley* 1295 Lacy, *v.* ald, myln. PILLMOSS FM, *Pill Moss* 1854 *EnclA*, 'willow bog', *v.* pill, mos. RADDEL LANE, cf. *Raddill Lane Field, The Raddill, Raddell Meadow* 1844 *TA*, perhaps from dial. *raddle* 'a wickerwork frame or hurdle'. SCHOOL LANE, 1831 Bry, cf. *Whitley School* (lost, 101–622808) 1831 ib. SPRING VIEW, *Spring Mount* 1831 ib, *v.* spring 'a young wood'. STOCKLEY LANE, cf. *Stockley* 1844 *TA, v.* 122 *supra*. TARPORLEY RD, *v.* 122 *supra*. TOWNGATE HO, 1831 Bry, 'communal pasture', *v.* toun, gata. TOWN PIT (FM), *Starkeys Farm* 1831 ib, cf. *Town Pit Croft* 1844 *TA*, 'public pond', *v.* toun, pytt. *Starkey* is a surname. WHITLEY BROOK, *v.* 39 *supra*. WILLOWBANK.

FIELD-NAMES

The undated forms are 1844 *TA* 428. Of the others, E1, 1426, 1598 are AD, *AD*, 1284 Cl, 1295, 1305 Lacy, 1349 Plea, 1479, 1484, 1504, 1618 ChRR, 1481, 1491 Mere, 1486 BodlCh, 1568, 1591 *Rental*, 17 (1724) NotCestr, 1831 Bry, 1842 OS, and the rest *MinAcct*.

(a) The one Acre (cf. *le two acars* 1568, *v.* æcer); Ainscroft; Angle Fd; Ash Hey, Ashurst (*v.* æsc, (ge)hæg, hyrst); Barney Canowl (perhaps 'barn-acre knoll' from bere-ærn and æcer, with cnoll); Black Acre; Bow Acre; Brick Kiln Fd (cf. *Brick Kiln Brows* 1831, *v.* bryke-kyl); Brocklehurst (*Brocwalhurst* E1, '(wooded hill at) the brook-spring', *v.* brōc, wælla, hyrst, cf. *Brekwellehurst* 1 180); Brow Fd; Burial Fd & Ground (cf. *Friends' Burial Ground* 1831, 1842, cf. also Frandley 133 *infra*); Bush Mdw; Caldwell ('cold stream or spring', *v.* cald, wella); Cast Moor; Chapel Fd; Great & Little Clough (*v.* clōh); Cross Hey (*v.* cros); Cuquits; Fernley Flats (*Feeney Flats* 1831, cf. George *Fearneley* 1591, 1598, *v.* flat); Fierners; Fisher's Nook (*v.* nōk); Flanders; The Folly (*v.* folie); Gangway (*v.* gang-weg); Grass

Platt (*v.* plat[2]); Green Side (cf. *la Grene* 1295 (p), *v.* grēne[2]); Hemp Yard; House Fd; Intack, Intake (*v.* inntak); Kinsey; Kiss Croft (*v.* kjóss); Lawn (*v.* launde); Little Land; Long Hey; Loont (*v.* land); Lydiatte's Mdw (*v.* hlid-geat); Marl Fd; Meg Acre (*Megge acar* 1568, *v.* meg, æcer); Moor; Nan Heys; Nickow Fd; Old Hey; Old Mans Nook; Palace Croft (*v.* palis 'a palisade'); Pen (*v.* penn[2]); Pickow (*v.* pichel); Pingot (*v.* pingot); Platt Fd (*v.* plat[1]); Quiesty (another instance of the p.n. discussed under Queastybirch 150 *infra*); Ridding (*v.* ryding); Riley (*v.* ryge, lēah); Rundown Fd (probably a derogatory nickname); Great Sand, Sand Fd; Sheep Fd; Shire Hall Garden; Shooting Butts; Sin Fd; Smithy Fd; Soon Fd (*v.* sand); Sour Fd (*v.* sūr); Sparks (*v.* spearca); Stoney Acre; Tilley; Town Fd; Way Pits (*v.* weg); Windmill Fd.

(*b*) *Assheby* 1507, 1514 (perhaps also *Assebe* 1287 Court 74 but cf. Ashley 10 *supra*; 'ash-tree farm', *v.* æsc (perhaps for ODan ask, ON askr), bȳ, cf. *Storeby infra*); *Bren(d)wode* 1386, 1398 (*v.* brende[2], wudu); *the Broade lane* 1591 (*v.* brād, lane); *Colstonstok(e)* 1479 (p), 1504 (p), *Colstonshok* 1481 (p), 1491 (p), *Colstanehok* 1486 (p), *Colstansock* 1483 (p), -*oke* 1556 (p), *Colstonsoke* 1484 (p) (a local surname, from the Scand pers.n. ODan *Kolsten*, ON *Kolsteinn* (Fellows Jensen 179), and āc 'an oak' or stoc 'an outlying farm'. The surname *Colswaynesoke* 111 *supra* is confused with this one by the reduction of *Colswayn-* to *Colsan-*, -*on-* whence *Colston-* by analogy with p.ns. in -*eston*, e.g. Snelson 1 93, Austerson 325 *infra*); *Cranell* 1507, 1514; *Faldemor* 1353 ('fold moor', *v.* fald, mōr[1]); *Grenewode* 1423 (*v.* grēne[1], wudu, the entry is for *Bren(d)wode supra*); *le Hau-*, *le Hawkesherd* 1426 ('hawk's gap', *v.* hafoc-scerde, cf. *Hawkesyord* 1 166); *le Houere-*, *le Neþerlith* E1 ('the higher & the lower hill-slope', *v.* uferra, neoðera, hlið[1]); *Outwod* 1422, *Outewode* 1443, (*parcus de-*) 1487, 1507, *Owte-* 1514 ('outlying wood', *v.* ūt, wudu); *Ropershey* 1487, 1514 ('Rope-maker's enclosure', from the ME occupational surname *Ropere* (Fransson 85) and (ge)hæg); *Great Sendlakes* 1568 (*v.* lacu); *Smythes Grene* 1591 (*v.* grēne[2]); *Southwod* 1497 (*v.* sūð, wudu, cf. Ashwood 128 *infra*); *Sproscroft* 1295, 1306, *Sprouthescrofte* 1305, 1307 ('Sprot's croft', from the OE or Scand pers.n. *Sprot* (Feilitzen 370) and croft, cf. *Sprostorne* 54 *supra*); *Storeby* 1507 (p) (the surname of Hugo Storeby who held land in *Assheby supra*; perhaps 'the big farmstead', *v.* stórr[1], bȳ, but the material is late, the form unreliable (*MinAcct*), and the name does not recur); *Vikerhey* 1398 (cf. the family *del Vikers* 13 AddCh, *v.* vikere 'a vicar', (ge)hæg 'an enclosure'); *Whyteleghwode iuxta Seuenokes* 1353 (*v.* wudu, cf. Seven Oaks 133 *infra*); *Wykerley* 1422, *Weykerley* 1423, *Werkeley* 1443, *Wekerley* 1487, *Wakerley* 1507, *Werkerley* 1514 (perhaps from the ME surname *Wyker* 'one who dwells at a wīc' (Fransson 202) and lēah).

17. ANTROBUS (HALL) (101–6480)

Formerly a hamlet in Higher Whitley, *v.* 124 *supra*.

Entrebus 1086 DB, 1281 Orm[2]

Anterbos c.1247 Tab, -*bus* c.1250 CoLegh, 1281 Ch, 1353 *MinAcct et freq* to 1666 Orm[2], -*bous* 1357 ChFor (p), -*bush'* 1358 Eyre (p),

Anturbus 1356 *Indict* (p), 1358 BPR, 1526 *ChEx*, *-buz* 1529
Sheaf
Anderbusk(e) 1295 Lacy, 1306 *MinAcct*, *-bushe* 1329 IpmR
Andrebusk(e) 1305 Lacy, 1307 *MinAcct*
Antrobus 1457 Pat (p), 1501 MidCh *et freq*

From buskr, busc 'a bush' and the same pers.n., ON *Andriði*,
Eindriði, ODan *Endrithi*, *Andriði*, as is found in Anderton 95 *supra*.

ASHWOOD BROW FM (101–637803), ASHWOOD LANE (101–637803 to
642807)

> *Northwode* 1287 Court *et freq* with variant spellings *Norht-,*
> *Northe-, -wood, -wod*; (*boscus de-*) 1361 BPR, (*parcarius de-,*
> *parcum de-*) e15 Mere, Orm², 1426 Tab, (*le Fence parci de-*) 1487
> *MinAcct*, (*parcum vel clausum de-*) 1507 *ib*, *Northwood Parke*
> 1595 *Rental*, 1651 *LRMB*
> *Norwode* 1370 *MinAcct*
> (*parke d'*) *asshewod* 1349 (1400) *MinAcct*, *Aschewode* 1370 *ib*,
> *Asshewod(e)* 1386 *ib et freq*, (*unum clausum vocatum-, clausa de-*)
> 1507, 1514 *MinAcct*, (*boscum de*) *Ashewode* 1506 ChRR
> *Ashwood* 1595 *Rental*, 1651 *LRMB*, *Ashwoodlane* 1606 ChRR

'(The park of) north wood' and 'ash wood', *v.* norð, æsc, wudu,
park, fence. This woodland and park belonged to the barony of
Halton, and was a royal park of the Duchy of Lancaster. The identification rests upon *LRMB* 278, f.242, 'Ashwood parcell of the
mannor of Overwhitley . . . formerly knowne by the name of North-
wood Parke in the parish of Budworth within the Fee of Halton'
(1651). It was split up and farmed out by 1651, *op. cit.*, f.251, the
allotments being represented by the frequent f.n. *Ashwood(s)* 1844
TA, about 101–635810. *North-* distinguished this wood from *Southwod*
127 *supra*. Ashwood Lane, with Reed Lane *infra*, was *a certaine hygh-
way that leadeth out of the Moore* 1651 *LRMB*, cf. Whitley Reed *infra*.

HOLLINS FM, *Arleyhurst* 1386 *MinAcct*, *Arlehurst* 1423 *ib*, *Arley
Hurst alias dict' le Hollins iuxta Arley* 1573 *Rental*, *the Hollins* 1627
Orm², 'the wood of Arley' and 'the hollies', *v.* hyrst, holegn, cf.
Arley 101 *supra*.

MANLEY FM (101–642798)

> (*le*) *Manhay(outwode)* 1422, 1423 *MinAcct*
> *Menehegh'* 1443 *MinAcct*, *parcus de Menhey* 1487 *ib*, *Meanhey alias
> Manlegh'* 1573 *Rental*

Manheth 1487 *MinAcct*, *The Man Heath* 1591 *Rental*
Manlegh' 1507, 1514 *MinAcct*

'The common enclosure', 'heath', and 'glade or wood', *v.*
(ge)mǣne, (ge)hæg, hǣð, lēah, and the outlying wood (*-outwode*)
thereof, *v.* ūt, wudu.

WHITLEY REED (101–645820), REEDGATE LANE, REED HO *&* LANE,
le Reede, Whitley Reede 1573 *Rental*, -*Reed, Reed House* 1831 Bry, *the*
Moore, (*a certaine Moore comonly called*) *þe Moss* 1651 *LRMB*, 'the
reed-bed', 'the moor', 'the moss', *v.* hrēod, mōr[1], mos. For Reed
Lane (101–642807 to 643815), *v.* Ashwood Lane *supra*, and for
Reedgate Lane cf. Reedgate 132 *infra*.

ANTROBUS HALL, *the Hall of Antrobus* 1579 ChRR. ANTROBUS
HO, *Tan House* 1831 Bry. BARBER'S LANE, *Barbers Lane* 1842
OS, cf. William *Barber* 1651 *LRMB*. BROOK COTTAGES, from a
watercourse on the Great Budworth boundary. BROW FM, *v.* brū.
CLAY LANE. COBBLER'S GORSE, *Fox Covert* 1842 OS, -*called*
Coblers Gorse 1844 *TA*. COCKER'S HEYES, *Cockers Hey* 1844 *TA*,
v. cocker, (ge)hæg. DEAKIN YARD. FAIRBANK FM. FLASH
FM *&* LANE, *Flash Lane* 1831 Bry, *v.* flasshe 'a shallow water, a
swamp'. FOGG'S FM *&* LANE, *Fogs House* 1831 ib, *Fogs* 1842 OS,
cf. *The Fogge estate* 1854 *EnclA*, *v.* fogge. THE FOLLY, *Folly*
Plantation 1844 *TA*, *v.* folie. FOX FM, cf. *Fox Croft & Field* 1844
ib, *v.* fox, cf. foll. FOXLEYBROW, 1842 OS, *v.* fox, lēah, brū, cf.
Fields Fm 134 *infra*. GARNERSGATE LANE, *v. Cardenhurst* 131
infra. GLEBE COTTAGE. GRANDSIRES GREEN, 1831 Bry.
GREENFIELD COTTAGE FM. HADES NOOK, *Hads Nook* 1842 OS,
Hedge Nook 1844 *TA*, cf. *Haddemosse* 1573 *Rental*, *v.* mos 'a moss',
nōk 'a nook, a corner of land', perhaps with a pers.n. HILL HO.
KNUTSFORD RD, consisting of Pole Lane *infra* and Meg Lane *infra*,
leading to Knutsford 73 *supra*. MEG LANE, *Megg-* 1831 Bry,
probably 'wenches' lane', from meg 'a wench'. MORRIS FM.
MOSS-SIDE HO *&* LANE, beside Whitley Reed *supra*, *v.* mos.
NEWALL'S ROUGH, *Newers Rough* 1831 ib, *Newalls Field & Top Hey*
or Foscoe 1844 *TA*, from the surname *Newall* and rūh, cf. Foscoe
infra. NEW BANK. NEW ROAD, a new highway over Whitley
Reed. NOOK HO *&* LANE, 1831 Bry, *v.* nōk. PAYNE'S FM, cf.
Paynes estate 1854 *EnclA*. PEELHALL FM (101–642807), *Peel Hall*

1831 Bry, 1854 *EnclA*, probably near the pale of the park of Ashwood *supra*, *v.* pēl 'a palisade'. THE POLE (101–650788), OLD POLE (101–650794), POLE LANE (ENDS) (101–643797), *The Pole* 1678 Orm[2], *Pole* 1787 ib, 'the pole (perhaps a maypole)', *v.* pāl, cf. Knutsford Rd *supra*. POOLSPLATT LANE, *v.* 132 *infra*. POTTERNELL. PUMP HO, 1831 Bry. SHAWBROOK (a farm, 101–653797), 1831 ib, 'stream at a wood', from the unnamed stream in a copse at 650797, *v.* sceaga, brōc. WHEATSHEAF INN, *The Wheatsheaf*, at *Four Lane Ends*, 1831 ib.

FIELD-NAMES

The undated forms are 1844 *TA* 16, 1398 is *MinAcct*, 1520 Tab, 1651 *LRMB* 278.

(a) Acre Fd; Backside Fd; Barker's Hey; Barlow's Fd (cf. Peter *Barlow* 1651); Little Barrow (*v.* bearu 'a grove'); Bent (*v.* beonet); Big Land; Black Acre; Blake Fd (*v.* blæc); Bottoms (*v.* botm); Brow Fd; Cabin Fd ('field with a shed in it', *v.* cabane); Chapel Fd (land belonging to Whitley Chapel (Nether Whitley) in 1666 Orm[2] i 660); Dig Hole & Lake (*v.* dīc, hol[1], lacu); Eaton's Fd (named from the family *Eaton* of The Pole); Filley; Finckleys Fd or Mdw; Flanders; Flood Mdw (*v.* flōd); Fosshey or Foscoe (from (ge)hæg 'a fenced-in enclosure' and skógr 'a wood', perhaps with foss[1] 'a ditch'); Franley Croft (*v.* Frandley 133 *infra*); Goodiere Fd (*v.* gōd, cf. Blackeyer 1 265); Gorsty Hey (*v.* gorstig, (ge)hæg); Gravel Fd; Head Fd ('top field', *v.* hēafod); Heath Fd; Hemp Yard; Hollow Heath Mdw; Honey Mdw (*v.* hunig); Kitchen Mdw; Lawyers Croft; Leg of Mutton Fd (*v.* 326 *infra*); Lordship Mdw, Lord Mdw (*v.* lordes(c)hip, hlāford, Higher Whitley 124 *supra*); Mans Fd; Marbury Mdw (from the surname *Marbury*); Marl (Pit) Fd, Old Marl'd Fd; Mop Mdw; Moss Fd, Moss(ey) Mdw (cf. Whitley Reed *supra*); Nant Arms Hey; Nickoe-, Nicoll Fd (perhaps from nicor 'a water-sprite'); Nook Fd; Outclap; Outlet (*v.* outlet); Oven Acre; Palce Garden (*v.* palis); Paradise (*v.* paradis); Parlour Fd (*v.* parlur); Pickerings Fd (cf. Elizabeth *Pickering* 1651); Pingot (*v.* pingot); Poole Frets; Poor Fd; Priest's Fd; Pump Croft; Reach(y) Mdw; Ring Fd (*v.* hring); Rusty Fd or Wolf Fd; Sandy Platt (*v.* plat[2]); Shake Croft; Slip (*v.* slipe); Sough Fd (*v.* sogh); Sowery Fd; Spring Fd; Starkey's Croft (cf. George *Starkye* 1651); Thelwell Heath Mdw (cf. Thellow Heath 134 *infra*); Two Cote Fd ('field with two huts in it', *v.* cot); White Folly (*v.* folie); Wimpenny's Mdw; Withy Mdw; Wolf Fd (*v.* Rusty Fd *supra*); Wormstow (*v.* wyrm-stall); Yard Mdw (*v.* geard).

(b) *Anturbus Myln* 1520 (*v.* myln); *Baltrelandyate* 1398 ('(gate at) Beald-ðrȳð's selion', from an OE fem.pers.n. *Bealdðrȳð* with land and geat. The pers.n. occurs in Balterley St. The gate was an exit from the park at *North-wood*, i.e. Ashwood 128 *supra*).

18. CROWLEY (101–6682)

Formerly a hamlet of Higher Whitley, *v.* 124 *supra*.

> *Croule* 13 Whall (p), *Crouleycroft* 1295 Lacy (lit. *Cron-*), 1305 ib
> (lit. *Corn-*), 1306 *MinAcct*, *Croulegh* 1325 ChRR (p), *Croweleigh*
> 1353 *MinAcct*, *-legh* 1452 CoLegh, *Crowley* 1537 ArlB
> *Craueley* 1443 *MinAcct*, *-legh'* 1487 *ib*, *Crawley* 1548 Tab
> *Crauglegh'* 1487 *MinAcct*
> 'Crow wood', *v.* crāwe, lēah, croft.

CARDENHURST (lost)

> (terre appelle) *Sprauston* 1349 (1400) *MinAcct*, *-vel Cardenhurst*
> 1398 *ib*
> *Sprouston* 1350 *MinAcct*, (claus' de) *Sprowston*, *-vel Cardenhurst*
> 1507 *ib*
> *Sperston vel Cardynhurst(e)* 1422, 1423 *MinAcct*, *-yng-* 1443, 1507
> *ib*, *-ing* 1514 *ib*, *-Gardynghurst* 1487 *ib* (terra et pratum vocat'-)
> (pastura de) *Coldynghurst* 1487 *MinAcct*
> (clausa de) *Sproston*, *-vel Cardenhurst* 1514 *MinAcct*
> *Farthest- & Midle Cardenhurst, the Litle Carden* 1651 *LRMB* 278

'Sprow's farm', from the OE pers.n. *Sprow* (Redin 35), *v.* tūn.
The later name contains hyrst 'a wood, a hill', but the origin of the
first el. is uncertain. Analogy with Carden 325 *infra* is topographically
unlikely. It may be the gen.sg. of a wk.masc. OE pers.n. **Carda* as
in Cardington Sa (DEPN s.n. Cardeston). It is probably 'marsh
valley', *v.* kjarr, denu. The 'marsh valley' may be the depression
occupied by Park Moss *infra* (101–660817). Garnersgate Lane (101–
653817 to 653813) may contain *Cardenhurst* and gata, 'lane to
Cardenhurst pasture-allotment'.

THE BELTS, plantations round Arley Park 101 *supra*. BRICKFIELD,
cf. *Brick Kiln Field* 1844 *TA*. CALDWELLS-GATE FM, cf. *Caldwell's Gate Field* 1844 ib, cf. John *Caldwell* 1651 *LRMB*, *v.* gata 'an
allotment of pasture'. CHAPEL HO, 1831 Bry. CROWLEY
BROOK (Ganders Brook 1 26). CROWLEYGREEN FM, CROWLEY
HALL & LODGE, *Crowley Green & Lodge* 1831 ib, *-Hall* 1842 OS,
Lodge 1559 Pat, *the Greene, the Lodge* 1651 *LRMB*, *v.* grēne², loge,
hall, cf. Crowley *supra*. FIRTREE FM, *Halls Farm* 1831 Bry.
GALEBROOK FM, GALEMOSS FM, 'moss where bog-myrtle grows', *v.*
gagel, mos, cf. Gale Brook 1 26. GARLAND HALL, 1831 ib.

GARNERSGATE LANE, v. *Cardenhurst supra.*   LODGE LANE, cf.
Crowley Lodge *supra.*   PARK FM & MOSS, *Parkemosse* 1612 *Surv,*
v. park, mos, cf. *Cardenhurst supra.*   PENNYPLECK HO, *Penny
Pluck* 1831 Bry, probably 'a mere penniworth of land', v. pening,
plek.   POOLSPLATT FM & LANE, *Pools Plat (Lane)* 1831 ib, v. pōl[1]
'a pool', plat[1] 'a footbridge'.   RANGEHEAD FM, v. range, hēafod.
REEDGATE (FM) (101–658823), *Reed Gate* 1842 OS, 'pasture-allotment
at Whitley Reed', v. gata, cf. *Reades-Meadow, the Reedefeild* 1651
LRMB, v. hrēod, mǣd, feld, cf. Whitley Reed 129 *supra.*   ROAD-
SIDE FM.   SANDILANDS FM, *Sandy Land Farm* 1831 Bry, v.
sandig, land.

FIELD-NAMES

The undated forms in (*a*) are 1844 *TA* 138, and in (*b*) 1651 *LRMB* 278.
Of the others, 13 is ArlB, 1487, 1514 *MinAcct*, 1568 *Rental*, 1651 *LRMB* 278.

(*a*) Two Acre, etc. (cf. *the two Acres, Broad Acre* 1651); Arley Fd & Mdw
(cf. Arley 101 *supra*); Ashtons Fd (*-feild* 1651, named from Peter *Ashton*
1651); Backside Fd; Barn Croft & Fd (cf. *Neare- & Farther Barnecroft,
Barnefeild,* 1651, v. bere-ærn); Bean Hey; Bent ((*-close*) 1651, v. beonet,
clos); Black Fd; Boons Croft (*Boondscroft, the Boones Croft, Boones Meadowe*
1651, 'peasant's or bondman's croft', v. bóndi (ME *bonde*)); Breeches Fd
(cf. *le Brech(e)* 1487, 1514, 'a breaking-in of land' v. brēc); Briery Bank;
Broad Heys; Brook Mdw (1651); Brow Fd; Calf Coat Mdw (v. calf, cot);
Cockset (v. cocc-scyte); Cratch Croft (cf. *Cratchfeild* 1651, v. cracche 'a
hurdle'); Flatts; Forest Mdw (cf. *Forrestfeild* 1651, v. forest); Garner Mdw
(v. garner); Gate Hey (*Yeate Hay* 1651, v. geat); Gin Croft; Glade Fd
(*-feild* 1651); Golden Close & Croft (named from Thomas *Golding* 1651);
Goodmans; Gorsty Fd (*Gorsey Feild* 1651); Great Mdw (cf. *Greatfeild, the
Greate Meade, -Meadow* 1651); Guest Fd; Hallons Croft (perhaps from
hēafod-land); Hemp Croft & Yard (*the Hempgarth, þe Hempeyard* 1651, v.
hemp-yard, hænep, garðr, geard); Heron Hey (v. (ge)hæg); Lower Heyes
(cf. *Middle Hay, Higher Hayes* 1651, v. (ge)hæg); Further-, Little- &
Nearer High Fd (*þe Highfeilds* 1651, v. hēah); Hob Hey (cf. *Hobcroft* 1651,
from hobb(e) 'a tussock' or hob 'a hobgoblin'); Hole Fd (*-feild* 1651, v.
hol[2]); Horse Pasture; House Fd (*freq,* cf. *House-, Howsfeild* 1651, 'field near
a house', v. hūs); Hurst (v. hyrst); Kiln Croft & Mdw (cf. *Kilnefeild* 1651,
v. cyln); Knowl, Knowl Fd (cf. *the Knowles, the sandy-knowles, Little No
Feild* 1651, v. cnoll); Lady Fd (v. hlǣfdige); Lettuce Fd; Level Fd; Lion
Hey (*Lyons Hay* 1651); Little Croft & Mdw (1651); Lodge Moss (cf.
Crowley Lodge *supra*); Long Mdw (*Longmead* 1651, v. lang, mǣd); Marl
Fd, Marl'd Hey (*Marle feild, Marlehay, Oldmarle hay, Marled grounde* 1651);
Middle Fd (*-feild* 1651); Big & Little Moss, Moss Fd, Hey & Mdw(s)
(*Greate & Little Mosse, Mossefeild, -hay & -pasture* 1651, v. mos); (Higher
& Middle) New Fd, New Field Mdw ((*Hygh-, Midle-*) *Newfeild, Newfeild
Meadow* 1651); Ouler Fd (v. alor); Outlet (v. outlet); Ox Heys ((*Great-,*

Little-) *Oxhay* 1651, *v.* oxa, (ge)hæg); Pike, Pike Mdw (*the Picke, Pick(e)-, Pikemeadow* 1651, *v.* pīc[1]); Poolste(a)d (*Powsteede Poolested Mead* 1651, 'the site of a pool', *v.* pōl-stede); Rye Croft (*Rycroft, the Ryfeild* 1651, *v.* ryge); Sand Fd; Long Shoot (*Longsute* 1651, *v.* lang, scēat); Shrogs (*the Scroggs* 1651, 'the shrubs', *v.* scrogge); Slack, Slack Fd (cf. *Slackmeade* 1651, *v.* slakki); Stepping Stone Fd; Three Nook(ed), -Nooks; Train Mdw; Turf Cot Fd (*v.* turf, cot); Big & Little Weir (*v.* wer); Wheat Fd (*the wheatfeild* 1651); White Fd (*Whitefeild* 1651); Wood Fd (*the Woodfeild, the Woode-pasture, Greate-, Higher-, Little-* & *Lower woode(s)* 1651).

(*b*) *Apeltreehalch* 13 ('apple-tree corner', *v.* æppel, trēow, halh); *Cavereald hay* ('calves' hillside', *v.* calf (gen.pl. calfra), helde); *Drinkwaterfeild* (probably a thirsty field, *v.* 326 *infra*); *Fence-croft* (*v.* fence 'a fence'); *Ferneles Meadow(s)* (*v.* fearn, lēah); *Geldfeild* (perhaps subject to a tax or payment, *v.* geld); *Gomesfeild*; *Goosefeild* (*v.* gōs); *the Harrclose* ('the higher close', *v.* hērra, clos); *Hattons Hay*; *Hay Meade* (*v.* hēg, mǣd); *Hemhay, Emhey* (*v.* hemm, (ge)hæg); *Hogg Hay* (*v.* hogg 'a hog', (ge)hæg); *Hordsfeild*; *the Lands* (*v.* land); *Littlefeild*; *Madge Acre* (*v.* madge); *Meane Acre* (*v.* (ge)mǣne); *Moor Mead* (*v.* mōr[1], mǣd); *Parkyeate meade* ('(meadow at) the park gate', *v.* park, geat, mǣd); *þe Persons feild* (*v.* persone 'a parson'); *Pitinthemidest* ('pit in the middle'); *Ravenfeilds* (*v.* hræfn, feld); *Richardsons Parke* (Peter *Richardson* tenant 1651, *v.* park); *Rish Close* (*v.* risc, clos); *Rounde Meadow* (*v.* rond, mǣd); *rushey* 1568, *Rushyhay* 1651 (*v.* risc, riscig, (ge)hæg); *Sandyway Croft* & *Meadow* (*v.* sandīg, weg); *the Scholehousefeild* & *meadow* (*v.* scōl, hūs, feld, mǣd); *Sisly Flat* (*v.* flat); *the Sparkye Meade* (*v.* spearca, mǣd); *Sparth* (*v.* sparð); *Springeclose* (*v.* spring, clos); *Stock Meade* (*v.* stocc, mǣd); *Woodes Close* (*v.* wudu, clos); *Yeatons Croft* ('Eaton's croft', from the surname *Eaton* and croft).

19. SEVEN OAKS (FM), SENNA GREEN (101-6379)

Formerly a hamlet of Higher Whitley, *v.* 124 *supra.*

> *Seuen okes* 1353 *MinAcct*, 1477 *Dav*, 1702 *Chol*, *Seven Oakes* 1591
> *Rental*, *-Oaks* 1757 *Sheaf*, *Seaven Oakes* 1666 *Orm*[2], 1702 *Chol*
> *Senokez* 1500 *CoLegh*
> *Senna Green* 1831 Bry

'Seven oaks', *v.* seofon, āc, grēne[2].

FRANDLEY (FM, HO & BROW) (101-636793)

> *Franley* 1514 *MinAcct* (p), *Franley Stocks* 1690 *Sheaf*, *Franley Croft* & *Field, Long Franley* 1844 *TA* 16
> *Frandley* 1663 *Sheaf*, (*-Stocks*) 1831 Bry, (cf. *Stocks* 1775 Sheaf),
> *-ly* 1714 *Sheaf*

The second el. is lēah 'a wood, a glade'. The first el. may be an ON pers.n. *Fráni* (Feilitzen 252) borne by the DB tenant of Chorlton 325 *infra*, or the ODan pers.n. *Frændi*, cf. DEPN s.n. Fransham Nf,

Fellows Jensen 88. A popular etymology associates the p.n. with OE *frēond* 'a friend', on account of a Quaker meeting-house here, *Quaker Meeting House* 1713 Sheaf, *Friends' Meeting at Frandley* 1811 Sheaf, *Quakers Meeting* 1831 Bry, cf. Burial Field 126 *supra*. The stocks were whipping stocks, *v.* stocc.

BARROW LANE, 1595 *Rental*, *v.* bearu 'a grove'.   COMBERBACH Ho, cf. Comberbach 111 *supra*.   FIELDS FM, *Foxley Brow* 1831 Bry, cf. Foxleybrow 129 *supra*.   GIB HILL, 1831 ib.   GOOSE-BROOK (LANE), *Goosebrook Farm* 1831 ib, cf. *Goose Brooke Meadow* 1651 *LRMB* (Crowley), 'goose brook', *v.* gōs, brōc, cf. Goose Brook 1 26.   THE KILN.   LESTER HO.   NEW HO.   SANDIWAY FM & LANE, *Sandiway* 1831 Bry.   SCOTCH HALL & LANE. THELLOW HEATH FM (101–643788), *Thillegh'* 1386 *MinAcct*, *The Waale Heathe* 1591 *Rental*, *Thelwall Heath* 1831 Bry, 'wood where planks were got', *v.* þille, lēah, hǣð, the later forms arising from metathesis and confusion with Thelwall 138 *infra*.   WELL FM & LANE, *Well House* 1831 ib, *v.* wella.

FIELD-NAMES

The forms are 1844 *TA* 350.

(a) Brickiln Fd; Brocklehurst Fd (cf. Brocklehurst 126 *supra*); Catch Moor Mdw; Cow Lane; Old Mdw; Plaster Fd (perhaps pleg-stōw); Sand Fd; Saw Pit Fd (*v.* saw-pytt); Tanyard Croft (*v.* tan-yard); Wear Croft.

20. LOWER WHITLEY (101–6178)

> *Nether Witelegh* H3 (1666) Orm[2], -*Whitelegh* 1306 ChF *et freq*, with variant spellings as for Higher Whitley 124 *supra*, and *Nethir-*, *Neyther-*, *Neither-*; *Whitelegh Inferior* c.1320 Chol, *Lower Whitley* 1544 *AD*

'The lower part of Whitley', *v.* neoðera, cf. Higher Whitley 124 *supra*.

GRIMSDITCH HALL & MILL (101–606803), 1831 Bry, *Grimisdich* e13 Tab, (terra de) *Grimsdich* H3 (1666) Orm[2], -*e* 113 Sheaf (p), *Grimes-*, *Grymesdyche* e14 ib (p), 1345 *Eyre et freq* with variant spellings -*dich(e)*, -*dik*, -*dych*, -*dick*, -*ditch(e)*, *Grymys-*, *Gryms-*, 'Woden's ditch', *v.* Grīm, dīc, presumably alluding to some lost earthwork. The p.n. recurs 49, 58, 66 *supra*.

BROOKHOUSE FM. CRIMWELLPOOL FM, *Crimhill Pool* 1831 Bry, *Crimwell Pool* 1842 OS, *v.* crymel 'a small piece of water', pōl[1]. GOOSEBROOK LANE, *v.* 134 *supra*. GREEN HILL (COMMON), GREENHILLS FM, *Grenehilles* 1515 ChEx, *Greenhills* 1551 Sheaf, *-Hill* 1666 Orm[2], 'green hill(s)', *v.* grēne[1], hyll. HALL LANE, cf. Cogshall Hall 110 *supra*. BIG & LT MERRYFALL, MERRYFALL WOOD, *Moryvale* 1597 ib, *Great & Little Merryfall, Merryfall Fox Cover* 1831 Bry, 'pleasant clearing', *v.* myrge, (ge)fall. NORCOT LODGE, *v.* Norcotbrook 125 *supra*. RED LANE, *v.* rēad 'red', from the colour of the soil. STREET LANE, cf. *Street Field* 1845 *TA, v.* 1 42 IX. TARPORLEY RD, *v.* 122 *supra*. WHITLEYBROOK BRIDGE, cf. Whitley Brook 1 39. WHITLEY GORSE, *Fox Cover* 1831 Bry, *v.* gorst. WHITLEY HALL, *the hall of Netherwhytley* 1561 ChRR. WHITLEY LODGE, 1831 Bry.

FIELD-NAMES

The undated forms are 1845 *TA* 429. Of the others, 1561 is ChRR, 1666 Orm[2], 1831 Bry, 1842 OS.

(a) Four- & Three Acre(s) (*Three Acres, The Fowre Acres Meadowe* 1561, *v.* æcer); Ball Fd (*v.* balle); Black Acre; Blackhurst (*-e* 1561, *v.* blæc, hyrst); Blake Butts (*v.* blæc); Cackows; Chapel Croft, Mdw & Yard (named from *Whitley Chappel* 1666); Cobby Fd (*v.* cobb(e), -ig[3]); Common Croft & Piece (cf. *Whitley Common* 1831, 1842); Cow Hay; Crowhalt Fd ('crow wood', *v.* crāwe, holt); Endshoot (*v.* ende[1], scēat); Gilbert Fd & Rough; Gorsey Moor; Greens (cf. *The Grene* 1561, *v.* grēne[2]); Griffiths Fd (*Gryffythesfelde* 1561, from the MWelsh pers.n. *Gruffud* (ModE *Griffith*) and feld); Hanging Crows; Hannock's Lane; Hemp Yard; Horse Pasture; Iley (perhaps 'yew glade', *v.* īw, lēah); Intake; Keys; Leet (dial. *leat* 'a conduit', cf. (ge)læt); Light Ash (*v.* lēoht, æsc); Long Loont, -Lound (*v.* land); Marl Fd; Moors; Moss Fd; Newtake (probably a new intake, *v.* nīwe, inntak); Orchard Flatts (*v.* flat); Outlet (*v.* outlet); Ox Pasture; Great Park; Pingot (*v.* pingot); Pit Fd & Mdw (*The Pyttes* 1561, *v.* pytt); Pretty Fd; Raby Lights (*Raby* is either a surname, perhaps from Raby 327 *infra*, not otherwise noted in this district, or an original p.n., 'boundary farmstead', from rá[2] and bȳ. *Lights* is 'light places', from OE *līhte, the Angl. form of the OE *līehte, 'a light place, a glade in a wood where the trees are more sparse', deduced for *Lighte* Sx (Löfvenberg 122). The el. appears also at Light 1 58 (*le Lyght*' c.1414). Cf. WRY 7 221, 2 xi s.n. Horbury Lights); Rose Moor (*Rodesmore* 1561, *v.* rod[1], mōr[1]); Rough; Rush Lane Mdw; Rye Croft; Sand Croft & Fd; Shaw Moss (*v.* sceaga); Sheep Heys; Shippon-, Shippun Mdw (*v.* scypen); Slang (*v.* slang); Snail Hays, -Hey (*v.* snægl, (ge)hæg); Sparks (*v.* spearca); Sprinks (*v.* spring); Sweet Fd; Tan Crows ('tanning huts', *v.* tan, crew); Three Nooks; Twiggery; Wair Fd (*v.* wer); Wall Fd (*v.* wælla);

Wete Butes ('wet selions', v. wēt, butte); Whitley Fd; Will Fd; Windmill Fd.

(b) *Brakefelde* 1561 ('field at a brake', v. bræc[1], feld); *The halfe meadow* 1561 (v. half, mǣd); *The (Lang) herbal(l) felde* 1561 (perhaps 'herbal field', v. *herbal* (NED)); *Meane Hey Croftes* 1561 ('crofts at a common enclosure', v. (ge)mǣne, (ge)hæg, croft); *The tree Croftes* 1561 (v. trēow).

21. WINCHAM (101–6875) [ˈwinʃəm]

> *Wimundisham* 1086 DB, *Wymundsham* 1306 Orm[2], (*Wymincham alias*) *Wymundysham* 1581 ChRR
>
> *Wy-, Wimingham* 112, 1209 Tab, *Wymyng-* 1695 ib, *Wymmincham(a)* c.1270 JRC 843, 1541 AD, *Wymincham* 1306 JRC 857 *et freq* with variant spellings *Wymyn-* to 1641 Sheaf, (-*alias Wymundysham*) 1581 ChRR, (-*Wyminaysh'm*) 1581 Orm[2], *Wimmincham alias Wincham* 1721 Chol, *Wemyncham* 1331 Tab, *Wymyngcham* 1353 *Indict*
>
> *Wemecham* e13 Tab, *Wimesham* 1234 ib, *Wymmycham* 1501 ib
>
> *Wimigham* 1228 Sheaf
>
> *Wymundham* 1281 Court 36
>
> *Wyningham, -incham* 1281 Court, -*yncham* 1286 IpmR, *Wynn-* 1540 AD
>
> *Wyvincham* c.1300 Chol (p), 1568 Tab
>
> *Wyncham* 1435 Chol, *Wi-* 1687 Sheaf, *Wy-, Winsham* 1651 Tab, 1666 Orm[2]
>
> *Wynmyncham* c.1490 Sheaf
>
> *Wyminaysh'm* 1581 Orm[2]
>
> *Wyminshaw near Northwich* 1608 Sheaf

'Wīgmund's homestead', from the OE pers.n. *Wīgmund* (Feilitzen 413) and hām. The earlier form of the p.n. is compounded by the gen.sg. of the pers.n., uninflected in 1281 Court 36. The later form appears to contain -ing-[4], but the palatalization is analogous with the -inga or -ing[2] formation of the other Ch -*ingham* p.ns., v. Altrincham 7 *supra*. The development of the form *Wincham* was noted by Leycester (1669), 'This township in Dooms-day book is written Wimundesham, . . . In old deeds it is written Wimingham, but now usually called and written Wincham, or Winsham', Orm[2] 1 627. Wincham formerly included the hamlet of Twambrook 195 *infra*, on the south side of Peover Eye, in Northwich Hundred.

BANK FM, *Friars Farm* 1831 Bry.   CRANAGE MILL, 1842 OS, *Grange Mill* 1831 Bry, one of the *molendina de Witton* 1228 Sheaf,

cf. Wittonmill Bridge 197 *infra*.   EARLES LANE.   GREEN LANE.
HALL LANE, cf. Wincham Hall *infra*.   HEATH FM & LANE.
HOPLEY'S PIPES, a wood, *v.* pipe[2].   KEEPERS WOOD & COTTAGE,
Gamekeepers House 1831 Bry.   LODGE WOOD. cf. *Lodge Field* 1844
TA.   MILL WOOD, cf. *le mulne heye* 1306 *JRC* 857, *Mill Croft &*
Field 1844 *TA*, named from Cranage Mill *supra, v.* myln, (ge)hæg.
PEARTREE FM, cf. *Pear Tree Field & Meadow* 1844 *ib.*   PICKMERE
LANE, *Pepper Street* 1831 Bry, *v.* 120 *supra*.   SHORESGREEN FM,
Shaws Green or Pig Lane 1831 ib, probably from the surname *Shaw*
and grēne[2]; the other name is 'lane frequented by pigs', *v.* pigga.
WINCHAM BRIDGE, 1618 Sheaf, *Peover Eye Bridge* 1831 Bry, cf. Peover
Eye 1 33.   WINCHAM COTTAGE, HALL & LANE, 1831 ib, *the Newe*
Hall 1604 Orm[2], *Wincham Hall* 1690 Sheaf.   WITTON BROW,
1842 OS, a road descending to Wittonmill Bridge 197 *infra, v.* brū
'a brow, a hillside'.

FIELD-NAMES

The undated forms are 1844 *TA* 437. Of the others, e14 is Orm[2], 1306 *JRC*
857, 1307 Tab, 1407 *Chol*, 1463 ChRR, 1490, 1512, 1675 Sheaf, 1541 AD.

(*a*) Acre; Backside; Bank; Blake Fd (*v.* blæc); Breaches (*v.* brēc); Brook
Fd (cf. Wincham Brook 1 39); Cadlings; Cafta; Common Fd, Lot &
Piece (*the common of Wincham* 1675 Sheaf[1] 3, 185, at which date it was
enclosed, *v.* hlot); Cow Hey; Ferney Fd; Gate Fd (*v.* gata); Hams Fd (*v.*
hamm); Hill Eyes ('meadows under a hill', *v.* ēg); House Fd; Near How
(*v.* hōh); Land Fd; Linnard's Fd (*v.* Leonard's Wood 119 *supra*); Lostock
Mdw (named from Lostock Gralam 189 *infra*); Mare Fd (*le Meyr-feld* 1490,
le Meirefeld 1512, 'the mere field', *v.* mere[1], feld, from Pick Mere 120
supra); Marl Fd; Meadow Eyes (*v.* ēg); Moor Fd; Oat Hay; Old House
Yard ('the curtilage of an old house', *v.* geard); Outlet (*v.* outlet); Ox Hey;
Pitts (*v.* pytt); Platts Hill; Pyd Acre; Rock Pit Fd ('field at a rock-salt pit',
v. roke, pytt); Sheep-cote Mdw (*v.* scēp, cot); Slip (*v.* slipe); Stean Hills (cf.
Stevens Hyll 1541, from the ME pers.n. *Steven* and hyll); Tan Mdw, Tan
Yard Fd (*v.* tan, tan-yard); Wincham Hill.

(*b*) *Albardestre* e14, *Olbardistre* 1307, *Olblastr'* 1463 ('Albert's tree' from
the ME (OGer) pers.n. *Albert, -berd* and trēow); *Boterlache* 1306 ('boggy
place providing rich pasture', *v.* butere, læc(c)).

xiii. Daresbury Chapelry

Thelwall township (now included in Grappenhall c.p.) was separated from
the rest of Daresbury Chapelry 146 *infra* by Grappenhall parish 140 *infra*.
Detached parts of Thelwall, cut off by meanders of R. Mersey, lay in Latchford, and are now included in Warrington County Borough La. Place-names

from these parts are marked +. The part between the Manchester Ship Canal and R. Mersey is now included in La.

1. THELWALL (101–6487)

(to) þel wæle 923 ASC (A), *Thealwæle* 920 (c.1118) FW

Thelewella 1154–60 (1329) Ch, 1190–1211 *Cott* Nero C III, *-well*, 1240 P, *-welle* 1294 ChF, *-vale* e13 *AddCh* (p), *-wall(e)* 1255 Plea, 1260 Court *et freq* to 1499 ChRR, *-wal* 1384 AD

Thelwall 12 (17) Orm², 1289 Court *et freq*, with variant spellings *-walle*, *-wal*; *Thelwella* c.1200 Dugd, *-well* 1325 ChRR (p), *Thellwalle* 1255 Plea

Thidewell' 1240 P

Thellewelle 1295, 1305 Lacy, 1306 *MinAcct*, *-walle* 1311 IpmR, *-wall* 1355 BPR

Felewelle 1295 Lacy, 1306 *MinAcct*

Thelowell 1304 Chamb

Thlewall 1355 BPR

Tolwell' 1487 *MinAcct*

Thylwal 15 Trev (Cx)

'Deep pool at a plank' probably 'pool with a plank bridge', v. þel, wēl². The second el. has been confused with wella, wælla 'a well, a spring'. ASC refers to a *burh* established here in 922 by Ēadward the Elder, presumably to guard the crossing of the Mersey at Latchford 143 *infra*, cf. Saga Book XIV 314. The deep pool would probably be a place in R. Mersey.

BANKHOUSE FM (101–657886), *Bank House* 1831 Bry, v. banke. BELL LANE.   BORHOLM.   BYE WASH (101–627885), 'flooding land at a river-bend', v. byge¹, (ge)wæsce.   CUERDEN HALL, probably named after Cuerden La.   DEAN'S LANE, cf. *Dean(s)*, *Dean Bog & Fields* 1843 *TA*, v. denu 'a valley'.   THE EYES, EYE LAND (101–640880), *The Ees* 1842 OS, 'the water-meadows', v. ēg. GALLOWS CROFT, 1843 *TA*, v. galga.   GREENFIELD HO, *Greenfield* 1831 Bry.   HALFACRE LANE, cf. *Half Acre* 1843 *TA*.   HOME FM.   LASKEY HO (101–657876) & LANE (FM), cf. *Laskey Meadow* 1843 *TA*; the lane extended to 101–657885. *Laskey* seems to have been the name of the meadows beside Mersey here. It may be 'island, or water-meadows, where salmon are taken', v. leax, ēg.   MASSEY HALL, cf. *Massie Fields* 1569 Orm² and Thelwall Grange *infra*. + MILES'S BITE (101–627887), a bend of R. Mersey, v. byht.   OAT-

LAND EYE (101–635886), -*Eea* 1842 OS, *Outland Hey* 1843 *TA*,
'island of outlying land', *v.* ūt, land, ēg.   OLD HALL FM.
+THE OLD WARPS (101–617879), *Old Warps* 1842 OS, cf. *Ol(l)er-*
warp(e) 1541, 1557 *Rental*, and 144 *infra*, *v.* ald, alor, wearp (dial.
warp) 'land built up by the deposit of silt', the place being beside
R. Mersey.   POWDER MILL COTTAGES (101–656885), named from
a lost *Powder Mill* 1831 Bry, 1842 OS, (101–654885) beside R.
Mersey.   SHEPHERD'S BANK COTTAGES, cf. *Shepherds Hey* 1843
TA.   THELWALL BRIDGE.   THELWALL BROOK (R. Mersey), cf.
Thelwall Brook Croft 1843 *ib.*   THELWALL COTTAGE, *Percy House*
1831 Bry.   THELWALL EYE (101–655885), -*Ees* 1842 OS, *v.* ēg 'a
water-meadow'.   THELWALL GORSE.   THELWALL GRANGE,
Massey Green 1628 Orm[2], 1842 OS, from the surname *Massey* and
grēne[2] cf. Massey Hall *supra.*   THELWALL HALL, 1831 Bry.
THELWALL HEYS, cf. *The Hey* (4x) 1843 *TA*, *v.* (ge)hæg 'a fenced-in
enclosure'.   THELWALL RD.   WASTE LANE, 1831 Bry, *West Lane*
1842 OS, cf. *The Waist, Great Waste* 1843 *TA*, *v.* waste.   WOOL-
STON WEIR (101–654885), a weir across R. Mersey to Woolston La,
v. wer.

FIELD-NAMES

The undated forms are 1843 *TA* 389. Of the others, 1289 is Court, 1308
Plea, 1354 *Indict*, 1382 ChRR, 1524 AD, 1544 Mere, 1637 *Chol*, 1666 Orm[2]
1 748, 1674, 1750 Sheaf, 1842 OS.

(a) Long Achors, Long Acre (*v.* æcer); Antlers; Bills Grave & Green;
Bank; Boot Fd (*v.* bōt); Broad Hey; Broadhurst (*v.* brād, hyrst); Brook Fd
(1750); Brows Fd (*v.* brū); Burling; Butty Mdws (*v.* butty); Cabin Croft;
Carry Mdw (*v.* kjarr); Chapel Fd; Court Fd; Long Croft Mdw (cf. *the*
further croft 1637, *v.* croft); Diglake (*v.* dīc, lacu); Discovery; Dovehouse Fd
(*v.* dove-house); Ellenhurst ('hill covered with elder-trees', *v.* ellen, hyrst);
Elton Hurst; Five Quarters; Foglane (*v.* fogge); Ford Orchard; Furlong;
Gig Mdw (*v.* gigge); Greaves Mdw (*v.* græfe); Grimsditches 1750 (perhaps
a parallel instance of the p.n. Grimsditch 134 *supra*, but probably land
belonging to the family named from that place); The Heath(s); Hell Hole (*v.*
hell, hol[1]); The Hey (cf. *the lower Hey* 1637); Hills, -Brow; Hommer Half
Acre; Hongs; Hough (*v.* hōh); Hows Shoot Fd (*Howshoots* 1750, *v.* hōh,
scēat); Knowl Fd; Leigh (*v.* lēah); Limekiln Fd; Loont (*v.* land); The Lum
(*The Lumm* 1750, *v.* lum(m)); Marl Fd (cf. *the marled croft, the ould marled*
Earth 1637); Marphany Mdw 1842 (101–635883, cf. *Little Marfeny* 1748
and Morphany Hall 154 *infra*, perhaps 'fen-meadow or -island', *v.* marr[1]
'a fen, a marsh', fenn, ēg. Orphany *infra* may be another of the type); Mean
Eyes & Hey (*the Mean Hey* 1637, 'common water-meadows and enclosure',
v. (ge)mǣne, ēg, (ge)hæg); The Moors, Moorshaw(s) (*Thelwallmore* 1544,

v. mōr[1], sceaga); New Hay, -Hey(s); Orphany Fd (cf. Marphany *supra*); Outlers; Pickoe (*v.* pichel); Pinfold Croft (*v.* pynd-fald); Pingot (*v.* pingot); Pockett Fd (*v.* poket); Poole Warthe ('pool marsh', *v.* pōl[1], waroð); The Raws (*v.* rāw); Renhill and Hurst, Renhill Hurst Fd; Ridding(s) (*v.* ryding); Ridg(e)way (*v.* hrycg, weg, cf. Cartridge Lane 141 *infra*); Rose Hey; Round Hey; Shaw Fd (*v.* sceaga); Middle Shorts; Short Butes (*v.* butte); Siddall Fd, Sidow (*v.* sīd, halh); Slap Fd (*v.* slæp); Slates (*v.* slæget); Sparrow Croft; Stone Delph Fd (*v.* (ge)delf); Sutch (*v.* sīc); Sutton Hey (*v.* sūð, tūn); Three Shoots (*v.* scēat); Tinkers Fd; Tomers End; Twampers; Twig Bank (*v.* twigge); Ware Fd (*v.* wær); Warehouse Fd; Weir Yard (*v.* wer, geard); West Fd; Wetwood (*v.* wēt, wudu); Widows Hey; Wilmoss Heath ('wild moss (heath)', *v.* wilde, mos); Windle Straw Fd (*v.* windle, strēaw); Windmill Hill; Withers Rough (*v.* víðir); Within Bank, Withins (*v.* wiðegn); Birch & Broth Yoart (*v.* geard).

(*b*) *Clayton* 1289 (p), *et freq* as a surname to 1534 with variant spellings *Claiy-* 1289, *Cley-* 1308, 1534 ('clay enclosure', *v.* clæg, tūn); *the longe flat* 1637 (*v.* lang, flat); *Martynescroft* 1354 (p), 1382 (p), *Martinscroft* 1666 (from the ME pers.n. *Martin* and croft); *the short Earth* 1637 ('short ploughland', *v.* sc(e)ort, erð).

xiv. Grappenhall

The ancient parish of Grappenhall comprised 1. Grappenhall (now a c.p. including Thelwall 138 *supra*), 2. Latchford (the part north of the Manchester Ship Canal is now included in Warrington county borough La, and the part south of the canal, called Latchford Without, is now included in Stockton Heath c.p. 145 *infra*).

1. GRAPPENHALL (101–6386) ['grapənɔːl, 'grapnəl]

> *Gropenhale* 1086 DB, *Gropen(h)ale* 112 Tab, Facs *et freq* with variant spellings -(*h*)*al* to *Gropenhale* 1519 Plea, -*hall* 1349 (1576) ChRR, 1448 ib *et freq* to 1677 Sheaf, -*elle* 1384 AD, -*all* 1436 Pat (p), 1673 *AddCh*, 1705 Sheaf, *Gropenehalle* 1295 Lacy, *Groppenhale* 1313 CRC, -*hall* 1554 ChRR, -*hull* 1633 Sheaf
>
> *Gropinhale* 1260 Court, 1291 Tax, -*yn-* 1458 ChRR
>
> *Grapenale* H3 *JRC* 845 (p), -*hale* 1353 BPR, *Grappenhall* 14 Mere, 1382 ChRR, 1724 NotCestr, *Grapenwall* 1752 Sheaf
>
> *Cropenhale* 1297 CRV, *Croppenhalle* 1536 Dugd, -*hall* 1739 *LRMB*
>
> *Grepenhale* 1338 Pat, -*hall* 1504 Sheaf
>
> *Gropnall* 1428, 1528, 1542, 1623 ChRR, 1637 *Chol*, -*ale* 1528 ChRR
>
> *Grovenhall* 1433 Tab (p)
>
> *Grapnall* 1554 Sheaf, 1660, 1670, 1698 ib, *Grapnell* 1593 (1656) Orm[2], *Grapnoe* 1690 Sheaf

'Nook at a ditch or drain', *v.* grōpe (gen.sg. grōpan), halh (dat.sg. hale). Cf. Gratton D 230.

CARTRIDGE LANE, REDDISHALL FM, *Caterich* E1 (1666) Orm², 1304 ib, (*the hall of*) 1581, 1593 ib, *Caterich alias Reddish* 1624 ib, *Caterich Lane* 1666 ib, *Catterugge* 1342 Plea, *Cattrich* 1522 Mere, *Catterich* 1550 Orm², *Catrych* 1550 EatonB, *Catterish alias Reddish* 1721 *Chol*, *Cartridge Lane* 1831 Bry, *the Hall of Reddish* 1696 Sheaf, *Reddish Hall* 1724 NotCestr, 'cat's ridge', *v.* catte, hrycg. The later name is taken from the family of Hugh *Reddish* of *Caterich* 1417 (1666) Orm² 1 596, from Reddish La, cf. Orm² 1 584n, 596, 11 846, *v.* hall, lane.

DERWALSHAWE (lost)

> *Derewelshagh* 1288 Court (p), *Der(e)wallescagh'* 1316 JRL (p), 1360 Orm², JRL (p), *-wa(l)l(e)shaw(e)* 1335 (17) Orm², Tab (p), 1348 *Eyre*, *Derwalshagh* 1350 *MinAcct* (p), *-shawe* 1360 BPR (p), JRL (p)
> *Derewardishawe* 1288 Court (p)
> *Derwallhagh* 1349 Sheaf (p)
> *Derwoldes(s)hagh* 1350, 1351 Chamb (p)

A surname found originally in Grappenhall, and afterwards frequent at Chester. Leycester (1666) cites the place as '*Derewallshaw, id est Thelwallshaw*', Orm² 1 472, cf. Thelwall 138 *supra*. The p.n. is either 'wood at the spring used by wild animals', from dēor, wella, wælla (cf. Wilderspool 145 *infra*), or 'Dēorwald's wood' from the OE pers.n. *Dēorwald* and sceaga.

TWEMBROKE (lost), 1504 Plea, *Twenebroke(s)* John Orm², 1310 Plea (p), *Thenebroc* 1260 Orm², *Twen(e)brok'*, *Twenebrokisheth* 1288 Court, *Twunbrokes* 1308 Orm² (p), *Twenbrokes* 1403 ChRR, *Tuwanbrokes* 1328 *LRO* Dx (p), 'between the brooks', from betwēonan, brōc, with hǣð. This is liable to confusion with Twambrook 195 *infra*, but the separate identity is proved by Court 121, §54, Orm² III 894 (addendum to p. 629).

BARRY'S COVERT, *Parks Wood* 1831 Bry, *Park-* 1842 OS, cf. *Parkfields* 1748 Sheaf and *the park of Gropenhale* mentioned 1352 BPR III 70–71, *v.* park 'a park'.   BELLHOUSE FM & LANE.   BRADSHAW'S LANE.   BROAD LANE.   BUTTYFOLD FM, 'a fold in joint ownership', *v.* butty, fald.   CARRHOUSE FM, *v.* kjarr 'brushwood, marsh'.   CHURCH HO & LANE.   CLAYBANK, 1831 Bry.   CLIFF LANE (FM), *Cliff Lane* 1748 Sheaf, cf. *Cliff Bank* 1748 ib, 'lane to a

steep bank', *v.* clif, cf. 1 44. The modern road runs along the
Thelwall boundary and into Lymm at 101–658850, north of Bradley
Hall 97 *supra*, whereas the farm is at 101–655848, a quarter of a mile
to the west, suggesting an older line of road, 101–643842 to 655850,
now a footpath, passing nearer to Bradley and touching Bradley
Cross.   COMMONSIDE FM.   CROSS LANE, *v.* cros 'a cross'.
DAMHEAD COVERT, *Dam Wood* 1831 Bry, cf. *Dam Side* 1748 Sheaf,
(*House*) 1831 Bry, *v.* damme, hēafod.   DAYBANK, 'dairy-house
bank', *v.* dey, banke.   THE DUNGEON, cf. *Dungeon Lane* 1842 OS,
v. dongeon.   THE GORSE, *Grappenhall Fox Cover* 1831 Bry, *v.*
gorst.   GRAPPENHALL HEYS, 1831 ib, cf. *Old Heys* 1748 Sheaf, *v.*
ald, (ge)hæg.   GRAPPENHALL LODGE, 1842 OS, *v.* loge.   GREEN-
BANK.   HALLBROW FM, HALL LANE, *Reddish Hall Lane* 1831 Bry,
cf. Reddish Hall *supra*, *v.* hall, brū.   KNUTSFORD RD, leading to
Knutsford 73 *supra*.   LUMBBROOK BRIDGE, cf. Lumb Brook[2] 1
30.   MANOR FM.   MARLFIELD, *the* (*new*) *marled Earth* 1637
Chol, *v.* marlede, eorðe.   MIDDLEHURST, 1359 (17) Orm[2], *le
Middilhurst* 1308 Ipm, 'the middle wooded-hill', *v.* middel, hyrst,
the origin of a local surname, Orm[2] 1 597.   MORRIS BROOK,
MORRISBROOK FM, *v.* brōc, cf. William *Morris* of Grappenhall 1666
Orm[2].   MOSSHOUSE FM, *v.* mos.   MOUNTAIN FM.   NARROW
LANE.   PEMBERTON'S LANE.   PICHAEL NOOK, 1842 OS, *v.*
pichel 'a small enclosure, a croft'.   STANNY LUNT BRIDGE, 'stony
selion', *v.* stānig, land.   THELWALL RD, *Tankards Lane* 1831 Bry.
TONGS COVERT, *v.* tang, tong 'a tang, a spit of land'.   WHITE-
HOUSE FM.   THE WILLOWS.   WOOD END FM (lost), 1831 Bry,
cf. *Gropenhale-wood* 1352 (1666) Orm[2], *Gropenhall Wood* 1519 ChRR,
v. wudu, ende[1].   YEW TREE FM.

FIELD-NAMES

Of the forms, 1504, 1696, 1748, 1750 are Sheaf, 1512 ChRR, 1593 (1656)
Orm[2], 1611 *AddCh*, 1637, 1668 *Chol*.

(*a*) The Backside or Cow Pasture 1696; the Booty Sandy Fd 1696 ('sandy
field in joint ownership', *v.* botye); the Britches Hay 1696 (*v.* brēc); the
Lower & the Upper Clapper 1696 (*v.* clapere); Green Side 1748; Heath
Side 1748 (cf. *Grapnell Heath* 1593 (1656)); the Holt 1696 (*v.* holt); Threap-
Meadow 1750 ('meadow in dispute', *v.* þrēap).

(*b*) *Abraym Parke* 1504, *Abramwode* 1512 (park and wood named after
the *Abram* family, of Abram La, cf. John *Alburgham* 1404 Orm[2] 1 596, *v.*
park, wudu); (*the*) *Caps hey, -Haye* 1637, 1668; *Cow-, long- & round Hey*

1637 (*v.* (ge)hæg); *Readishe Pyttes* 1611 ('Reddish's pits', *v.* pytt, cf. Reddishall *supra*); *weet wood* 1637, *Weate Wood* 1668 ('wet wood', *v.* wēt, wudu).

2. LATCHFORD (101–6187)

> *Lachford* R1 (1666) Orm², Tab, *Lach(e)ford* 1250–55 Whall, 1288, 1289 Court, 1305 Orm², Tab *et freq* with variant spellings *-forth* (c.1310 *Chol*), *-forde* (1399 Cl) to *Lachford* 1622 Earw, (*-iuxta Werynton, -Werington, -Warington*) 1417 *Vern*, 1436, Tab, MidCh, *Latch(e)ford* 1382, 1391 ChRR
> *Lechefordia* 13 Bun, *Leccheford* 1499 ChRR
> *Lachisford* 1288, 1289 Court
> *Lachiford* 1289 ib
> *Locheforde* 1391 ArlB (p)
> *Liccheford* 1499 ChRR

'Ford at a boggy place', *v.* læc(c), lece, ford. An 'ancient ford' is marked in 1842 OS at 101–619876 at an isthmus formed by a loop of the Mersey to 101–622875, in the south part of Old Warps, now Victoria Park, Warrington, *v.* 139 *supra*. It was superseded by Warrington Bridge *infra*. The ford carried across the Mersey the Roman road from Warrington to Northwich, *v.* 1 43. The ford and the bridge formed a medieval *passagium* into Ch, cf. *cheminum de Lachford* R1 (1666) Orm² 1 603, *passagium pontis de Weryngton* 1397 Orm², *le chemin de Lacheford* 1519 ChRR (DKR xxxix 154), *passagium in villa de Lacheford* 1250–55 Whall *et freq*, cf. Wilderspool Causeway *infra*.

ACKER'S LANE.   ARPLEY BRIDGE, named from Arpley La.   ASH-FIELD.   BLACK BEAR BRIDGE.   BROOK HO & -FIELD.   CHESTER RD, *Stanney Lane* 1831 Bry, 'stony lane', *v.* stānig.   COMMON LANE.   CROSS LANE.   GRAPPENHALL RD, leading to Grappen-hall 140 *supra*.   GREENBANK, *Green Bank* 1831 Bry.   GREEN-FIELD HO.   HIDE YARD.   HILLTOP, 1831 ib.   KNUTSFORD (OLD) RD, the road from Warrington La to Knutsford 73 *supra*.   LATCHFORD GRANGE, *Old Quay* 1831 ib.   LATCHFORD TANNERY, *Broadbents Tan Yard* 1831 ib, *v.* tan-yard.   LOUSHER'S LANE.   LOWER WASH (FM), *v.* (ge)wæsc 'a flood, land subject to flooding'.   LUMBROOK (BRIDGE), named from Lumb Brook² 1 30.   MANOR LOCK & TANNERY, site of *Manor House* 1831 ib.   MILL HO & LANE, named from *Stockton Mill* 1831 ib, cf. Stockton 145 *infra*.

OAK BANK.   OLDFIELD.   OLD WARPS LODGE, cf. Old Warps 139
supra.   POACHER'S LANE.   RADDON COURT, *Blackburn House*
1831 Bry, cf. Thomas *Blackborn(e)* 1630, 1666 Orm². THELWALL
LANE, leading towards Thelwall 138 *supra.* WARRINGTON BRIDGE,
pons de Werynton 1354 Plea, cf. Warrington La 96; referred to as *the
bridge over the Mersey* 1304 Orm² I 604n, *a bridge between Weryngton
and Lacheford* 1367 Pat; possibly the same as *Le Stubbrugge* 1354
Plea, 'bridge built of stubs', possibly the stubs or piers of an older
bridge, *v.* stubb; cf. *the Bridge End* 1740 Sheaf, a place in Latchford.
WASH LANE, *v.* (ge)wæsc, cf. Lower Wash *supra.*   WESTY LANE.
WILDERSPOOL CAUSEWAY, *v.* caucie; replacing the lost ancient road
(*via magna* 13 Orm² I 615) from Warrington Bridge to Wilderspool,
v. 145 *infra*, Latchford *supra.*   WILLOW BANK.

FIELD-NAMES

Of the forms, 13 is *LRO* Dx, 1354 Plea, 1397 ChRR, 1696, 1748 Sheaf,
1842 OS.

(*a*) The Broom Croft 1696 (*v.* brōm); Clay Pits Nook 1842; The Crabtree
Loond 1696 (*v.* land); House on the Green 1748; the Nearer & the Further
land Field 1696 (*v.* land); Latchford Eye 1696 (*v.* ēg 'a water-meadow');
Lords Sparth 1748 (*v.* hlāford, sparð); the Pike Loond 1696 (*v.* pīc¹, land);
Stockton Meadow 1748 (*v.* Stockton 145 *infra*).

(*b*) *Bervhefeld* 13 ('hill field', *v.* beorg, feld); *Lachefordyorde* 1397 (from
geard 'a fish-yard', a pound in which fish were trapped, probably connected
with the *piscarium* here in 1349 Orm² I 604); *Oldefeldesyate* 1354 ('gate of
an old field', *v.* ald, feld, geat; a place on the right-of-way of the road from
Warrington La to Northwich, DKR XXVIII 55); *le Stauriesford* 1354 (probably
a crossing of Lumb Brook into Appleton, *v.* ford). The first el. is difficult.
The name is a genitival composition, *v.* -es². The basis depends on the
reading of *u* which is ambiguous. If *u* is read as *u*, the first el. might be the
gen.sg. of the ME pers.n. *Story* (ON *Stóri*), but the orthography would be
unusual for this. If the *u* represents *v*, Dr von Feilitzen suggests a p.n.
'island at a pole or stake', *v.* stæfer, ēg. This would indicate a ford with a
marker, cf. Stapleford 327 *infra*, Handforth I 254. However, local topography
does not suggest ēg and some other el. would have to be supposed. Professor
Löfvenberg would read *n* for *u*, and derive *Stanries-* from a p.n. 'stony
stream', *v.* stān, rīþ, -es². This is an attractive solution.

xv. Runcorn

Cf. 159 *infra*. Stockton Heath township (now a c.p. including Latchford 143 *supra* and part of Appleton 96 *supra*) was separated from the rest of the parish by Daresbury Chapelry 146 *infra*. The part between R. Mersey and the Manchester Ship Canal is now included in La .

1. STOCKTON HEATH (101–6186)

> *Stoketon(a)* 1190–99 Facs, 13 *LRO* Dx, Orm², ArlB, Tab
> *Stocton* c.1200 *LRO* Dx, (*the commyne on the backsyde of-*) 1569 *ib*,
> *Stok-* 1220–40 Whall (p), *Stock-* 1217–32 (17) Orm² (p), 1444
> Mere, (*-infra Hull*) 1626 Orm², *-Heath* 1831 Bry, *Stocketon* 1557
> Mere (p)
> *Stoaken Heath* 1682 Sheaf, *Stocken* 1690, 1775 Sheaf

'Enclosure at an outlying hamlet', *v.* stoc, tūn. The heath which gives the township its modern name was near Heath Street (6″) and extended to the boundary of Appleton 96 *supra*, *v.* hǣð, commun, cf. *Hull* 96 *supra*.

WILDERSPOOL (CAUSEWAY), 1831 Bry, *Wildrespul* 1190–99 Facs, e13 Orm², *Wyldrespoll* 1307 *LRO* Dx, *-pol* (*Spytel*) 1354 Plea, *Wilders Poole* (*Bridge*) 1618 Sheaf, *Wilderspoole* (*Bridge*) 1625 ChRR, '(bridge, causeway & hospital at) the wild beast's pool', *v.* wilder, pōl¹, brycg, caucie, spitel. Cf. 144 *supra*, 1 43, and Orm² 1 602.

BLACK LION BRIDGE, named from *Black Lion* 1831 Bry, a p.h. BROOK HO, 1831 ib, named from the un-named brook on the eastern boundary of Walton Superior 158 *infra*. GREENBANK. OLD LONDON RD, *via que descendit a Wyc ad Weryngton* 1307 *LRO* Dx, 'the road which goes from Northwich to Warrington La', cf. London Road 99 *supra*, *le Saltlydehyate infra*. LUMBROOK (BRIDGE), *v.* 143 *supra*. MILL HO, *Stockton Mill* 1831 Bry. SANDY LANE. STOCKTON LODGE & MOUNT, 1831 ib.

FIELD-NAMES

Forms dated 1190–99 are from Facs, the rest are *LRO* Dx .

(b) *Croneberyhalvch* c.1250 (recurring in *Croneberehalgh'* (1353 *AddCh*) 315 *infra*, apparently 'cranberry nook', from halh and ME **crone-bery, -bere* 'a cranberry (cf. cran 'a crane' (the bird), berige, beger 'a berry'), cf. G *kran(ich)beere*, LG *krônbere, kron(es)bere, kraneber*, Swed *tranbär*, Dan *tranebær*. This p.n. suggests a lost early English form of the fruit-name, although the term *cranberry* ('crane-berry') is not recorded in English until 1672 NED, when it was introduced, with the fruit, from North America where NED supposes it had been adopted from some LG source. The fruit-name appears in *Cranberry Moss*, a modern p.n. in several parts of Ch, at places where it grew); *le Lavedicroft* c.1250 ('the (perhaps Our) Lady's croft', *v.* hlæfdige, croft); *le Myddylfurlong* 113 (*v.* middel, furlang); *sale* 1190–99 ('at the willow', *v.* salh, dat.sg. sale); *le Saltlydehyate* c.1250 ('gate through which salt is carried', *v.* salt, hlid-geat. This was on the Northwich-Warrington road 1 43, cf. Old London Road, Wilderspool Causeway *supra*); *Stanilode* (*v.* 1 40); *Weryntonforlong* 113 (named from Warrington La, *v.* furlang).

xvi. Daresbury Chapelry

The parochial chapelry of Daresbury, a member of Runcorn Parish 159 *infra*, comprised 1. Thelwall 138 *supra*, 2. Acton Grange (*v.* Walton *infra*), 3. Daresbury (now a c.p. including Keckwick and Newton by Daresbury), 4. Hatton, 5. Keckwick (*v.* Daresbury *supra*), 6. Moore, 7. Newton by Daresbury (*v.* Daresbury *supra*), 8. Preston on the Hill (now Preston Brook c.p.), 9. & 10. Walton Inferior & Superior (now Walton c.p. including Acton Grange *supra*). Those parts of Walton Inferior, Acton Grange and Moore between the Manchester Ship Canal and R. Mersey are now included in La.

2. ACTON GRANGE (109–5884)

> *Acton* 1194–1211 Whall, *LRO* Dx (p) *et freq*, *Actona iuxta moram* 1202 Whall, *Hacton* 1315 Plea
> *Aketon* 13 *LRO* Dx, 1397 ChRR
> *grangia Actone* 1249–61 Whall, *grangia de Acton* 1263 ib, *Acton Grange* 1308 ib, *graungia siue manerium de Acton* 1554 *MinAcct*, *-Graing* 1673 *AddCh*
> *Agden alias Agson alias Acton* 1599 Orm[2]

'Oak-tree farm', *v.* āc, tūn, grange. This manor was a grange of Norton Priory 173 *infra*. It adjoins Moore 153 *infra*. Cf. Agden 42 *supra*, 325 *infra*.

GRANGE MILL (109–594854), 1831 Bry, *molendinum* (*de Acton quod est*) *inter Acton et Wal(e)ton* 1195–1211 Whall, 1220–40 *LRO* Dx, (*stagnum*) *Wodemylne de Acton* 1263 Whall, 'mill (at a wood)', *v.* myln, wudu, cf. Acton Grange *supra*, Pool Bank *infra*, Walton Brook 1 37.

BIG HURST (lost), 1843 *TA*, *Hurst* 1194–1211 Whall, *(le)* 1263 ib (p), *(in Acton)* 14 ib, *(le)Hurstes* 1328 *LRO* Dx, *Dow*, cf. *Hurstebrok* 13 Whall, 'the wooded hill', *v.* hyrst, brōc.

ACTON GRANGE BRIDGE, *Grange Bridge* 1831 Bry, on the Bridgewater Canal.   BAXTER'S BRIDGE, *Wright's Bridge & Lane* 1831 ib, on the Runcorn and Latchford Canal.   BELLHOUSE BRIDGE & FM, 1831 ib, *Bellhouse Lane* ib, probably 'house with a bell', *v.* belle. BIRCH WOOD, 1831 ib.   CANAL FM, cf. *Canal Moss* 1843 *TA*. THE ELMS, 1831 Bry.   GRANGE GREEN FM, 1831 ib, *v.* grēne², cf. Acton Grange *supra*.   HOBB LANE, *Hob-* 1843 *TA*, *v.* Uplands *infra*.   HOLLYHEDGE FM, *Holly Hedg(e)* 1690 Sheaf, *v.* holegn, hecg.   MOSS WOOD, formerly in this township, *v.* 157 *infra*. OUTER WOOD, 1831 Bry.   PORCH-HOUSE FM, *Porch House* 1831 ib, 'house with a porch', *v.* porche.   RICHMOND BANK, a mud-bank in R. Mersey, cf. *Richmond Marsh* 1842 OS.   ROW'S WOOD, *Rose Wood* 1831 Bry, *Rows Wood* 1843 *TA*, *þe Roose* (lit. *Roofe*) c.1554 Whall, 'the rows', *v.* rāw. An earlier spelling may lie behind *le Bawes* 159 *infra*.   THOMASON'S BRIDGE, *Wilsons Bridge* 1831 Bry, on the Bridgewater Canal.   UPLANDS, *Hobs Hillock* 1831 ib, cf. *Hob Field (freq)* 1843 *TA*, Hobb Lane *supra*, *v.* hob 'a hobgoblin'. WALTON BROOK (lost), *v.* 1 37.

FIELD-NAMES

The undated forms are 1843 *TA* 3. Those dated 13, 1208–29, 1223–7, 1249–61, 1303, 1554 are Whall, 1831 Bry, 1842 OS.

(*a*) Acton Hoo Fd (*v.* hōh); Acton Wall (*v.* wælla 'a spring, a well'); Backside; Black Acre; Bongs (*v.* banke); Bottom Hey; Butty Meadow (*v.* butty); Calves Hey; Causeway Lake ('watercourse at a causeway', *v.* caucie, lacu); Cockfight Fd (*v.* cock-fight); The Cop (*v.* copp 'an embankment'); Cross Fd; General Wd 1842; Gorst(e)y Brow & Hey (*v.* gorstig); Heath Fd (*þe Grange heats* 1554, *v.* hǣð); Hemp Pit; High Lane 1831 (a lane running down into the meadows beside R. Mersey north of Walton Inferior, possibly identical with 'the way which leads from the grange of Acton towards Mersee and is called *fossatum monachorum*, henceforth to be the boundary of Acton and Walton' 1303 Whall, *v.* foss¹, munuc; the modern name is either hēah 'high', perhaps alluding to some embankment, or ēg 'an island, a water-meadow'); Intack (*v.* inntak); Kiln Croft; Long Nook; Markets Hay; Marl Fd; Nickow Fd; Old Road; Oxen Hey (*v.* oxa, (ge)hæg); Perch Ho; Pickows (*v.* pichel); Pike Mdw (*v.* pīc¹); Pool Bank, Pool Stead (*þe Polested* 1554, *stagnum de Acton* 1223–7, *stang de Aketon* 13², cf. Grange Mill *supra*, *v.* pōl-stede, pōl¹, cf. *caueas nanorum infra*); Quay Moss & Wd; Reedy Marsh; Middle Ridding, -Rydding, Ridding Mdw (*v.* ryding); Rye

Fd, Hill & Moss; Salt Mdw (v. salt); The Shaws (v. sceaga); Slack (v. slakki); Stoney Hill (v. stānig, hyll); Stringers Moss; Two Butts (v. butte); Wall Pool (v. wælla); Wat Hey; Wood Hey.

(b) *caueas nanorum* 1249–61 (ChetOS xi 397, 399. This could be translated 'dwarfs' caves' or 'little horses' enclosures', Lat *cavea* 'a cave, a den, an enclosure, a pit, an amphitheatre', *nanus* 'a dwarf, a little horse'. The context is *terra de Waleton iuxta Grangiam Actone contra caueas nanorum* 'land of Walton next to Acton Grange opposite . . .', granted to Stanlow Abbey for a mill-pond for the mill of Acton (Grange Mill, Pool Stead *supra*). This mill-pond was to be *infra caueas* 'below-, downstream of-', or 'within-' the *caueas*. The mill-pond of Grange Mill extended 109–594854 to 595852. This locates *caueas nanorum* about Higher Walton Bridge 109–595849. Hereabouts a supposed Roman road (1″ OS) crosses the stream. The 'caves of the dwarfs', as also *le Bawes* 159 *infra*, may refer to the old arches or culverts of a lost Roman bridge or causeway. There are no natural caves here); *Hassil* . . . 1554 (v. hæsel); *le Holdebrok* 13 ('the old brook', v. ald, brōc, perhaps in Walton 158 *infra*); *hollots way* 1554 (a capital messuage); *terra Hospitalarium* 1208–29 ('the Hospitallers' land', presumably referring to the Knights Hospitallers, v. hospiteler); *Lefsies croft* 13[2] ('Lēofsige's croft', from the OE pers.n. *Lēofsige* and croft).

3. DARESBURY (109–5882)

   Deresbiria 1154–89 (17) Orm[2], *-beri*, *-buri*, *-bury* 1194, 1200 Facs, Whall *et freq* with variant spellings *-bir(i)*, *-byre*, *-byry*, *-buyri*, *-burye*, *-burie*, *-bere*, *-bbury*, *Der(r)is-*, *-us-*, *-ys-*, *-es-*, *Ders(e)-* to *Deresbury* 1599 AD

   Darisburi c.1200 LRO Dx (p), (*-in Hal(y)ton(e)sire*) 1I3 AD, *Daresburi* 1220–40 LRO Dx (p), *-bury* 1434 ChRR *et freq* with variant spellings *-bery*, *-burye*, *-burie*, *Darus-*, *Darres-*, *Dars(e)-*; *Dasbury* 1660 Sheaf

   Doresburi c.1200 Tab (p), *-bury* 1537 AD, *Dosebury* 13 Tab

   Derebury 1281 Court (p)

   Dursbury 1571 AD

   Dearesburye 1594 AD

   Dueesbury alias Daresbury 1739 LRMB 264

'Dēor's stronghold', from the OE pers.n. *Dēor* and burh. Cf. Deslayheath 116 *supra*.

COMMON SIDE, 1831 Bry, cf. *the Common Wood* 1291 (17) Orm[2], *-e* 1576 AD, *the Comenwoode* 1548 ib, (*the*) *New(e) Com(m)en Wood(d)e* 1567, 1574 ib, *the Lytle Common Wood* 1581 ib, v. commun, wudu, nīwe, lȳtel.   DARESBURY DELPH, a quarry, v. (ge)delf.   DARESBURY HALL, *the Hall of Deresbury* 1541 AD.   DARESBURY LANE,

-*Field* 1844 *TA* 196 (Hatton).   Daresbury Lodge, *þe Lodg* 1660
Sheaf, *v.* loge.   Hall Lane Fm, 1831 Bry.   Morts Wood.
Village Fm.

FIELD-NAMES

The undated forms are 1843 *TA* 142. Of the others 1291 (17) is Orm[2], l13
(17) Tab, 1557 *Rental*, 1623 *AddCh*, 1690 Sheaf, 1831 Bry, and the rest AD.

(a) Aldershaw (*v.* alor, sceaga); Backside; Bench Moors (*Benche More*
1573, *v.* benc, mōr[1]); Big Heys; Bottoms ((*the Bothoms* 1541, 1542, *v.* botm);
Bowling Green Fd; Brook Fd & Mdw (cf. *Daresbury Brook* 1831); Chester
Fd; Church Fd & Mdw ((*the*) *Churche Filde* 1541, 1542, *v.* cirice); Cliff Hay
(*Daresbery Cliff* 1291 (17), *le Cliff* 1541, *The-* 1623, *Cliffe Buttes* 1580, *v.*
clif, butte); Clough (*v.* clōh); Cross Fd; Daniels Yard (from the local family
Daniels and geard); Big & Little Dareley (*the two Darleyes* 1576, *the too
Darlies* 1581, perhaps from the OE pers.n. *Dēor* as in Daresbury *supra* and
lēah); Gelding Pasture; Gold Hay (cf. *Goldy Croft* 1541, *v.* goldig 'growing
with marigolds', golde 'a marigold'); Grandmothers Hole (1831); Hall Croft
(1541, cf. Daresbury Hall *supra*); Hemp Croft; Jack Mdw (*v.* jack); Keakwick Lane 1831 (leading to Keckwick 151 *infra*); Kiln Croft; Lamber Hey
(1541, 'lambs' enclosure', *v.* lamb (gen.pl. lambra), (ge)hæg); Marks (*the
Markes* 1541, 1542, 'the boundary marks', *v.* mearc); Marled Hey (cf.
Marled Filde 1541, *v.* marlede); Mill Ridding (*the Mylne Ryddinge* 1576,
v. myln, ryding); Pinfold Croft (*v.* pynd-fald); Pool Mdw & Stead (cf. *the
Poole Hey* 1567, *v.* pōl[1], pōl-stede, mæd, (ge)hæg); Round Hay; Scotchmans
Well 1831; Shop Croft; Sour Pasture; Spodes Croft; Stumperley; Thur-
shaugh Brook 1690 (a stream near Daresbury Lodge *supra*, crossing the
Warrington road); Town Fd (*the towne filde* 1576, *v.* toun); Wall Fd (cf. *the
the Wall Croft* 1576, 1581, *v.* wælla); Welshman's Common (cf. *the Welch-
mans lytle croft* 1581, also *Walshemansheth* 179 *infra*, *v.* Wels(c)h-man);
Windmill Fd; Wood, Wood Fd & Hey.

(b) *Bircheley Wodde* 1541, *Byrcheley Woodde* 1567, *Burchelez Woode* 1574
('(wood at) birch-wood', *v.* birce, lēah, cf. Bearchleys Mdw, *Bircheley Hey*
151, 155 *infra*); *the Brome Filde* 1544, (*lee*) *Brom(e)feild* 1573–4 (*v.* brōm,
feld); *the Cow(e) Hey* 1577, 1582 (*v.* cū, (ge)hæg); *Hobbe Acre* 1541 ('tussock
field', *v.* hobb(e), æcer); *Mawgers felde* 1594 (cf. Blackeyer 1 256); *the
two shorte fildes, the lyttyll shortfild* 1576 (*v.* sc(e)ort); *Wallmore* 1291 (17),
the Wall(e) Mo(o)re 1577, 1581 ('moor at a spring', *v.* wælla, mōr[1]); *Wite-
field* l13 (17) (*v.* hwīt, feld).

4. Hatton (109–5982)

(*grangia de*) *Hattun* 13 Tab, c.1275 *Chol* (p), *-ton* c.1230 Orm[2] *et
freq* with variant spellings *-tona, -tone, Hatthon*; (*-iuxta Stretton*)
1288 ChF, (*-Haulton*) 1312 Plea, (*-Deresbury*) 1346 ib *et freq*,
(*-Apulton*) 1386 Plea, (*-in Deresbury*) 1500 ib
Hattne 1663 Sheaf

'Farm at a heath', v. hǣð, tūn, cf. Stretton, Appleton, Daresbury 121, 96, 148 supra, Halton 166 infra.

QUEASTYBIRCH HALL, LITTLE QUEASTYBIRCH FM [ˈkwiːsti-]

Quisty (quadam terra quæ vocatur) H3 Orm², (the mansion of, . . . occasionally . . . called Hatton Old Hall) 1882 Orm² 1 744n, Qisty 13 Tab (p), Custy 1288 ChF, Kuysty (lit. Kn-) 1306 Plea (p), 1436 ChRR (p)

Quystybirches 1533 LRO Dx, Quisty Birches 1616 Mere, Quistie Byrches 1654 Orm², Quisty Birch Farm 1819 ib

Coystiberches 1604 AddCh

Kyisty-Birches 1649 Tab, Kisstie Birches 1654 Sheaf

Questy Birch Hall, Little Questy Birch 1831 Bry, (Little) Queesty-birch 1842 OS

This is a Scand or a hybrid p.n. The first el. is either ON kví 'a pen, a fold', as in Whaw YN 296, Wheyrigg Cu 140, or ON kvíga (WRY 7 216, We 2 269) 'a heifer' (cf. ME qui 'a heifer' 1374 NED), as in Quiby YW 1 273, Wye Gill YW 6 136, 7 61n, Wyegarth We 2 38. The second el. is ON stía 'a sty, a kennel', or the equivalent OE stigu 'a sty, a pen'. The p.n. means 'sty fold', 'sty in a fold', or more likely 'heifer pen'. Cf. Quiesty 127 supra. The later name 'birches at Quisty' seems to indicate a popular interpretation—'birches frequented by wood-pigeons', from dial. quist, queest 'the wood-pigeon', with -ig³, v. birce.

GOOSE LANE.   GREENSIDE FM, Greenside 1844 TA, 'the side of the green', v. grēne², sīde.   HATTON COTTAGE, 1831 Bry.   HATTON HALL, cf. Queastybirch Hall supra.   HATTON LANE, 1831 ib. OAKTREE FM.   OWL'S NEST (WOOD), Owl's Nest 1831 ib, Owlets Nest 1842 OS.   PEARTREE FM.   PEPPER STREET FM (101–600822), cf. 327 infra.   PILLMOSS FM & LANE, Moss Farm, Pill Moss Woods 1831 Bry, (Lane) 1844 TA, cf. nearby Pilgreaves Meadow & Moor, Pilgrim Moor, Pilridge Moor 1844 ib, from píll 'a willow', with mos, grǣfe, hrycg.   WARRINGTON RD, Hannots Lane 1842 OS, perhaps from a pers.n. or surname, cf. the ME fem. pers.n. Annote, diminutive of Anna, or Hannot may be a diminutive of the ME pers.n. Hann (Reaney 153).

FIELD-NAMES

The undated forms are 1844 *TA* 196. Those dated 13 (17) are Tab, e14(?) Sheaf³ 23 (5319), 1367 *Tourn*, 1423, 1552 AD, 1842 OS.

(a) The Acres; Arms Lane Fd; Backside; Bear Fd; Bearchleys Mdw (cf. *Bircheley Wodde* 149 *supra*, *Bircheley Hey* 155 *infra*); Bell Flat; Black Acre; Blackshaw (*v.* blæc, sceaga); Blamborough Hey; Bog Rough Fd; Brickiln Fd; Broad Acre & Hey; Broom Hey (*v.* brōm, (ge)hæg); The Brundrett (*v.* branderith); Clay Lanes & Moss (*v.* leyne); Clough (*v.* clōh); Common (Side) Fd; Coney Grave (*v.* coninger); Cowhey; Cross Hey; Dingle Fd (*v.* dingle); Dun(n) Hey & Mdw (*v.* dunn); Eastage, Hestage; Farthing Croft (*v.* fēorðung); Fleam Hay, Hey (*v.* flēama 'a stream', cf. dial. *fleam* 'a conduit'); The Gales, Gales Wd ('places where bog-myrtle grows', *v.* gagel); Gorsey Fd; Hatton Hey (*Hattonheye* 1367, *v.* (ge)hæg); Heath Fd (cf. *Hatton Heath* 1842); Hemp Yard; Hestage (*v.* Eastage *supra*); Heys Acres (perhaps 'brushwood lands', *v.* hǣs); Jenkins Riddings (*Jankenesruding* e14(?), 'Jankin's clearing', from the ME pers.n. *Jankin*, diminutive of *John*, and ryding); Know Hey, Knowl Hay (*v.* cnoll, (ge)hæg); Bottom, Little & Top Land (*v.* land); Lawn (*v.* launde); Long Hey; Lougher Hey ('lower enclosure', *v.* lower); Mean Hey (*le Meane hey* 1423, *the Meane Heye* 1552, 'the common enclosure', *v.* (ge)mǣne, (ge)hæg); Mill Bangs (*v.* banke); Mizzy Fd ('boggy field', *v.* misy); The Moss; Nickoe Fd; Oucring Hey; Pigeon House Mdw; Pilling Hey (perhaps from ModEdial. *pilling* 'grazing'); Radshall, Radshaw ('red wood', *v.* rēad, sceaga); Ridding(s) Scow ('wood at the clearing(s)', *v.* ryding, skógr); Round Hey; Rye Hey; Sand Fd; Sankey Lane; Back Shew, Middle Shaw (*v.* sceaga); Slough Lake ('watercourse at a slough', *v.* slōh, lacu); Sour Mdw; South Fd; Spout Mdw (*v.* spoute); Stretton Fd (cf. Stretton 121 *supra*); Sutton Fd, Suttons Croft (cf. Sutton 180 *infra*); Swallows Acre; Tableys Acre (named from Tabley 60 *supra*, a seat of the Daniels family, lords of Daresbury); Toads; Towns Croft, Town Fd (*v.* toun); Twambrook Mdw & Townfield (possibly connected with *Twembroke* 141 *supra*); Wind(y) Mill Fd; Wisons Flash (*v.* flasshe 'a swamp'); Wood Fd & Croft.

(b) Steniber 13 (17) (perhaps 'stone hill' *v.* steinn, berg).

5. KECKWICK (109–5783)

Kekwic 1154 (1329) Dugd, 1329 Ch, *Kecwyk* 1287 Court (p),
  Keckwyk 1295 Cl *et freq* with variant spellings -*wyke*, -*wik*, -*wick*
  (from 1375 Tab), -*wich*
Kekewyc e13 *AddCh*, -*wike* 1295 IpmR, -*wycke* 1295 Lacy, -*wyck*
  1306 *MinAcct*, -*wyk* c.1320 *Chol*, -*weke* 1454 *AddRoll*, -*wik* 1479
  ChRR, -*wyke* 1536 Orm², -*wicke* 1554 *MinAcct*, -*wick* 1581 AD
  (lit. *Leke-*), *Kecke-* 1594 AD
Kequik 1288 Court (p), *Kequick* c.1703 *Chol*, *Kecquick* 1635 Sheaf

Keekwicke 1534 *Chol*, *Keeck-* 1673 *AddCh*
Keakwick 1831 Bry

The second el. is wīc 'a dwelling, a building or group of buildings, a hamlet'. For the first el. Dr von Feilitzen suggests the ON pers. by-name *Keikr* (MDan *Kegh* < *keikr* 'bent backwards'), as in Kexby YE 272 (cf. Fellows Jensen 164). DEPN suggests an OE pers.n. *Cæfca* for Keckwick and Kenswick Wo. Wo 147 draws an analogy between the two p.ns., citing a ME pers.n. *Keke*, a by-name or surname, which is there derived from the OE pers.n. *Cēc* (Redin 27, s.n. *C(a)ec*) but this is formally unlikely, and Dr von Feilitzen observes that ME *Keke* probably represents ON *Keikr*. Kenswick, an -*inga*- name or an -*ing*[2] compound, is unlikely to contain an ON pers.n., and Ekwall's *Cæfca* is correct for that p.n., but not for Keckwick.

CROW'S NEST, 1842 OS, *Northwodehey* 1360 *AddCh*, *Northwode* (a close) 1446 ChRR, *North Wood Farm* 1831 Bry, cf. *Big & Little Norwood* 1844 *TA*, '(enclosure at) the north wood', *v.* norð, wudu, (ge)hæg. BENNETT'S FM. BRICKFIELD COTTAGES, cf. *Brick Kiln Field*, *Brick Yard* 1844 *ib*. DARESBURY FIRS, *The Hill Plantation* 1831 Bry, cf. Keckwick Hill *infra*, Daresbury 148 *supra*. GEORGE GLEAVE'S BRIDGE. HATTON FM (lost), 1831 Bry, cf. Hatton 149 *supra*. KECKWICK BRIDGE, *Hattons Bridge* 1831 Bry, carrying *Keakwick Lane* 1831 ib over the Bridgewater canal, cf. Hatton 149 *supra*. KECKWICK BROOK (> *Warford Brook* 174 *infra*), *Kekewick Brook* 1842 OS, cf. *The Grimsditch* 1 28. Preston Brook 156 *infra* may preserve another name for this stream. KECK-WICK HILL, *Kekewick Hill* 1842 ib, cf. Daresbury Firs *supra*. PITTS HEATH, *Pits on Heath Wood* 1831 Bry, *v.* pytt, hæð.

FIELD-NAMES

The undated forms are 1844 *TA* 219. Of the others 1581 is AD, 1842 OS.

(a) The Acre; Boozey Moor (*v.* bōsig); Broad Hey; Calf Patch; Church Fd; Cistern Fd; Coach Nook ('corner growing with couch-grass', *v.* cwice, nōk); Crooked Acre; Cross Fd; Dole Mdw (*v.* dāl); Gorsey Brow; Hay-, Heybedore ('enclosure by the door', *v.* (ge)hæg, bī, duru); Holywell (*v.* hālig, wella); Intake (*v.* inntak); Kekewick Ford 1842 (*v.* Keckwickford Fm 174 *infra*); Kitchen Mdw; Lower & Upper Moor (*Keckewick Moore* 1581 (lit. *Lecke-*), *v.* mōr¹); New Hey; Peel Hay ('palisade enclosure', *v.* pēl); Pinfold Fd (*v.* pynd-fald); Push Ploughed Fd (*v.* push-plough); Ridding (*v.* ryding); Rye Croft; Sand Bank; Springs (*v.* spring); Sweet Fd; Wilds Croft; Wood Hey.

6. MOORE (109–5784)

Mora e12 (17) Orm², l12 ib, Whall (p), *More* e13 ib, 1295 Lacy
et freq to 1560 Sheaf, (*le-*) 1398 ChRR (p), (*the-*) 1517 AD, *Mor*
1311 Ipm
le Moer 1357 *Eyre*
Moore 1517 *Chol*, 1594 AD *et freq*, *Moor* 1715 ChetOS VIII
'The marsh', *v.* mōr¹, cf. foll. and Halton Moss *infra*.

BIG, LT. & NEARER MARSH (lost), 1843 *TA*, *mariscus qui dicebatur de
Mora* 1208–29 Whall, *mariscus de More* 1211–32 ib, *le Mersch'* 1340
MinAcct, 'the marsh', *v.* mersc, cf. prec. and Halton Moss *infra*.

THE BEECHES. BOB'S BRIDGE (109–567851), *Fleetway Bridge* 1831
Bry, on Moss Lane *infra*, leading towards R. Mersey, *v.* flēot, weg.
HALTON MOSS, 1842 OS, *Mo(o)re Mosse* 1517, 1630 *Chol*, *the common
called Halton or Moore Moss* 1882 Orm² 1 740, cf. *Moss Side* (lost,
109–570850) 1842 OS, (*Mosse-end* 1666 Orm²), *v.* mos, ende¹, sīde,
cf. Moss Side 174 *infra*. LAPWING LANE, 1842 OS. MILNER'S
COTTAGES. MOORE BRIDGE, *Heron Bridge* 1831 Bry, on the Runcorn & Latchford Canal. MOORE BRIDGE, *Grange Bridge* 1831 ib,
crossing the Bridgewater Canal towards Acton Grange 146 *supra*.
MOORE HALL, HO, & LANE, *Moore Hall, Moss Lane* 1831 ib, cf.
Halton Moss *supra*. MOOREFIELD BRIDGE. MOSS LANE (109–
577847 to 567851), 1842 OS, *Gig Lane* 1831 Bry, perhaps also
Fleetway, cf. Bob's Bridge *supra*, *v.* mos, gigge.

FIELD-NAMES

The undated forms are 1843 *TA* 272. Those dated 1370, 1386, 1398, 1487,
1507, and 1547 are *MinAcct*, 1630 *Chol*, 1842 OS.

(*a*) Aldersea; Bent (*v.* beonet); Broomy Knowl (*v.* brōmig, cnoll); Brown
Hill; Chad Hey (*v.* (ge)hæg); Clough Hey (*v.* clōh); Dear Bought (*v.* 326
infra); Gate (*v.* gata 'a pasturage'); Hanging Brow (*v.* hangende); Intake
(*v.* inntak); Jack Hey (*v.* jack); Kircock Hey; Lea Hey; Libbenend; Ridding;
Shaw(s) (*v.* sceaga); Sniddle or Snoddle (cf. snid(e), snād); Stone Tree
Flatt; Temperlands (*Templecroft* 1547, *Temples alias Templin's Crofts* 1630,
'croft belonging to the Knights Templars', *v.* tempel, croft); Town Fd &
Hey; Wall Hey (*v.* wælla); Walton Way (*freq* in an area north-west of the
village, 'the way to Walton', *v.* weg, Walton 157 *infra*).

(*b*) *the Heath* 1630 (*v.* hǣð); *piscaria super le Mersch' vocata Moresherd*
1370, *piscaria de Moresyerd* 1386, 1487, 1507, -*ʒerd* 1398 (a fishery upon the

Marsh, called 'the yard belonging to Moore', from *geard*, in the sense 'fish-pond', alluding to pounds in which fish were trapped, cf. *fisc-geard*); *Park House* 1630 (*v.* park).

7. NEWTON BY DARESBURY (109–5881)

Neuton 12 (17) Orm² (p), 1288 Court *et freq* to 1542 AD, (*-iuxta Deresbur*') 1302 Plea *et freq*, (*-Preston*) 1306 ib, (*-Hatton*) 1362 ib, (*-in hundredo de Halton*) 1433 ChRR, *Neuton inferior iuxta Deresbury* 1504 Plea

Neweton (*iuxta Preston*) 1290 Pat, IpmR

Newton 1423 AD *et freq*, (*-iuxta Darresbury*) 1488 *MinAcct et freq*, (*-nigh Daresbury*) 1673 ChRR

'The new farm', *v.* nīwe, tūn, cf. Daresbury, Hatton, *Halton Hundred* 148, 149, 2 *supra*, Preston 156 *infra*.

HALLAMHALL FM (109–586810)

Hallum 13 Tab, 1302 Plea (p) *et freq*, (*-in Newton iuxta Daresbery*) 1337 (17) Orm², *-Hall* 1831 Bry

Hallam 13, 1338 HMC x

Hallom 1343 Chamb (p), *-e* 1452 *CoLegh* (p)

Halum 1437 ChRR, *-om*(*e*) 1534 AD

'At the slopes', from hall² (dat.pl. hallum). Cf. *Great & Little Hallam, Hallam Meadow* 1844 *TA* (*Hallum meadowes* 1423 AD, *v.* mǣd), also Great & Little Hallam 157 *infra*.

MORPHANY-HALL FM (109–591808) ['mɔːrfəni]

Mortwayt 13 Tab (p), *Morthwayt*(*e*) l13 ib (p), 1285 AD, *-weyt* 1289 Court (p), e14 Mere (p), *Morethwayth* 1308 Whall (p), *Morthtwayt* 1310 *Chol* (p), *Morthwait* e14 Mere (p), Sheaf (p), (Rafe Starky of) *Morthwait in Newton* 1666 Orm² 1 741.

(Ralph Starkey of) *Morfanny* 1673 Sheaf³ 5 (824), *Marphoney Hall* 1831 Bry, *Murphany-* 1842 OS, cf. *the Morphoney Estate* 1854 *EnclA* (Whitley Reed 129 *supra*)

'Meadow at a marsh or moor', *v.* mōr¹, þveit, cf. Moorthwaite Cu 79, 335. The modern form is similar to *Marphany* 139 *supra*, *Foulfeney* 163 *infra*, and is probably '(water-meadow at) the moor-fen', *v.* mōr¹, fenn, ēg.

BLACK JANE FM, *Black Jane* 1831 Bry.   BROOK HOUSE FM. CROWHOLT FM & WOOD, *Crow Holt* (*Rough*) 1831 ib, *Cow Haught*

Cowholt 1844 *TA*, cf. *les Holtes* 1423 AD, 'the crow woods', *v.* crāwe, holt. DAIRY FM, 1842 OS, *Dairy House* 1831 Bry. GLEBE FM. LT. MANOR FM. NEWTON BANK (FM), 1831 ib, *v.* banke. NEWTON CROSS, 1831 ib, the site of a standing cross at a crossroads, (109–588816), *v.* cros. NEWTON GORSE. PENK-RIDGE LAKE FM (109–595812), *Penkridge Lake* 1831 Bry, cf. *Penksiche* 13 (17) Tab (perhaps for *Penkriche*). *v.* lacu 'a stream', referring to the watercourse 109–595812 to 592808. This p.n. may be, like Penkridge St, 'place by the chief mound', *v.* penn[1], cruc[1]. The p.n. recurs at Pancridge Field 289 *infra*. SLAUGHTER'S ROUGH. SUMMER LANE (FM), *Summer Lane* 1831 Bry, 'lane used in summer', *v.* sumor.

FIELD-NAMES

The undated forms are 1844 *TA* 293. Of the others, 13 (17), l13 (17) are Tab, l13 Sheaf, 1285 Court, 1306 Plea, 1488 *MinAcct*, 1831 Bry, and the rest AD.

(*a*) Abberdrill Fd (*v.* affadille); Alder Fd; Barn Hey; Barnett Mdw; Big Mdw (*le Greate meadowe* 1423, *v.* grēat); Black Butts (*v.* blæc, butte); Big & Little Brockless (*Brocholas* 1488, 'badger-holes', *v.* brocc, hol[1]); Brook Mdw; Cellars, Sellers Fd; Cutlings; Dove House Mdw; Galens Bower; Glade Fd; Green Hey(s) (*le Grenehey* 1423, (*the-*) 1540, *Greyne Heye* 1577, 'the green enclosure', *v.* grēne[1], (ge)hæg); Hammond Heys (*Hamondes Heyes* 1423, from the ME pers.n. *Hamond* (OG *Hamon*) and (ge)hæg, cf. Ammons Hey 156 *infra*); Hans Fd; Haslam Moss; Heath Fd; Hemp Croft & Yard; Hurst (*v.* hyrst); Intake; Kiln Fd; Leese (*v.* lēah, cf. Leese 229 *infra*); Little Mdw (*le Lyttle meadowe* 1423, *v.* lȳtel); Big & Little Margraves; Marl Pit Fd; Mayors Fd; Moor Acre; Newton Lane 1831 (109–576820 to 599806); Outlett (*v.* outlet); Owls Nest Mdw; Ox Pasture; Park Heys; Piece; Pigeon House Mdw; Pinfold Fd (cf. *Pinfold* 1831, *v.* pynd-fald); Pit Fd; Priors Fd (*Pryors Feild* 1423, belonging to Norton Priory 173 *infra*, *v.* prior); Radisher; Rushey Fd; Rye Grass Fd; Spark Heys (*v.* spearca); Stack Fd & Yard; Stone House Mdw; Stoney Fd; Thatch Croft; Walstow; Well Fd; Willow Bed; Within Platt ('willow patch', *v.* wiðegn, plat[2]).

(*b*) *Byrchleyhey* 1423, *Bircheley Hey* 1541 ('(enclosure at) the birch-wood', *v.* birce, lēah, (ge)hæg, cf. Bearchleys Mdw 151 *supra*, *Bircheley Wodde* 149 *supra*); *Brend Garth* 1423, *Brendeyorthe* 1541, *Brende Yearthe* 1579 ('enclosure cleared by burning', *v.* brende[2], garðr, the later forms confuse geard and eorðe); *Burnelee* l13 (17) 'Brūna's wood', from the OE pers.n. *Brūna* and lēah); *Caldewall* 1285 (p), *-welle* 1306 (p) ('cold spring', *v.* cald, wella, wælla); *Fulford* 13 (17), 1293 (p) ('dirty ford', *v.* fūl, ford); *Haukeserde* 13 (17), *Hawkesherde* 1488 ('hawk's gap', *v.* hafoc-scerde, cf. *Hawkesyord* 1 166)); *Meddowe Plek* 1541 ('meadow plot', *v.* mæd, plek); *Oxehey* 1423 (*v.* oxa, (ge)hæg); *le Pelecroft* 1423, *Peele Crofte* 1579, *Pele Hey* 1541 ('palisade enclosure', *v.* pēl, croft, (ge)hæg); *Pyckeringes Heyes* 1423 (from the surname *Pickering* and (ge)hæg); *Schawerudinge* 13 (17) ('clearing at a wood', *v.* sceaga, ryding); *Swaynesrudinge* l13 (17), *Swaynisruding* l13 ('Sveinn's clearing', from the ON pers.n. *Sveinn* and ryding); *le Upper meadowe* 1423 (*v.* upper).

8. PRESTON ON THE HILL, now PRESTON BROOK, cf. *Preston-on-the-Hill, usually called Preston Brook* 1860 White, *v.* Preston on the Hill, Preston Brook *infra.*

PRESTON ON THE HILL (109–571808)

> *Prestun* 12 (17) Orm² (p), *Prestona* 1157–94 Chest, *Prest'* 1175 Facs, *Preston* John (17) Orm², 1223 ClR *et passim*, (*-iuxta Dutton*) 1353 BPR, (*-Kekewyk*) 1440 ChRR, (*-near Daresbury*) 1573 AD
>
> *Prestanton* 1361 Tab
>
> *Preston super le Hill* 1373 Pat, *-super Montem* 1514 MinAcct, *-upon the Hill* 1560 Sheaf, *-of the Hill* 1775 ib, *-o' th' Hill* 1953 Index

'Priest's farm', *v.* prēost (gen.pl. prēosta, with one form showing a new ME wk.gen.pl. *prestene*, *v.* -ena), tūn. The hamlet stands on a hill, *v.* hyll, cf. foll.

PRESTON BROOK (109–567807), 1819 Orm², 'at the brook of Preston' or 'the part of Preston at a brook', *v.* brōc, cf. prec., Keckwick Brook 152 *supra*. This hamlet became the more important part of the township because it is on the Trent & Mersey Canal, the Bridgewater Canal, and the railway.

BARKER'S HOLLOW (109–576797), *Dods Wood* 1831 Bry, cf. *Barkers Brook* ib, (109–573808 to 574797, joins Keckwick Brook), 'tanner's brook and valley', *v.* barkere, hol¹, brōc. *Dod* is probably the Ch surname.   NEW MANOR FM, *the New Mannor* 1526 (1666) Orm², replacing *aula de Preston* 1414 Sheaf, cf. *Old Manor Field* 1843 *TA*, from ME maner 'a manor-house'.   RED BROW, 1842 OS.   RED-HOUSE FM, *Red House* 1831 Bry.   SUMMER LANE, *v.* 155 *supra*. TANYARD FM, *Tan Yard* 1831 ib.   WHITEHOUSE FM, *White House* 1842 OS.   WINDMILL FM, cf. *Preston Mill* 1831 Bry, *Windmill Hill* 1843 *TA*.

FIELD-NAMES

The undated forms are 1843 *TA* 330. Of the others 1384 are *AddRoll* 51504, 1560, 1743 Sheaf, 1599 Cre, 1831 Bry.

(*a*) Alder Fd; Ammons Hey (cf. Hammond Heys 155 *supra*); Backside; Brook Hays; Burn Heath (*v.* brende²); Buttey Hongrels (*v.* butty, hungor, hyll); Cockshill Mdw (*v.* cocc[1], hyll); Crank Fd, Cranks Mdw (*v.* cranuc); Dale Hay (*v.* dæl[1]); Dumpy and Houch (cf. *Hall's Houtches* 1743, probably ME hucche 'a hutch'); Fingerpost Croft; The Flatts; Gilbert Riddings (*v.* ryding); Hall Knights; Big & Little Hallows (*v.* halh); Great & Little Hallum (*v.* hall[2], cf. Hallamhall 154 *supra*); Haswell Fd; Heath; Hemp Yard; Hodges Way; Houch (*v.* Dumpy *supra*); Hurry Fd; Kirkway ('the way to church', *v.* kirkja, weg); Light Ash ('pale ash-tree', *v.* lēoht, æsc); Long Loons (*v.* land); Marl Fd; Old Marled Fd; Moat Mdw (*v.* mote); Monsdale Hay; Moss Fd; Old House Fd; Oldershaw (*v.* alor, sceaga); Oller Fd (*v.* alor, cf. Alder Fd *supra*); Oxhay (*v.* (ge)hæg); Pickow (*v.* pichel); Pinfold Croft (*v.* pynd-fald); Rhinos; Old Rush Hay (*v.* risc, (ge)hæg); Rustages Fd; Sheetway; Sith Fd; Sweet Fd; Towngate ('communal pasture-allot-ment', *v.* toun, gata); Tunnel Fd (cf. *Tunnel Mouth* 1831 Bry, at Preston Tunnel); Turngate Loons (Dern Gate 1743, 'hidden gate', *v.* derne, geat, land); Wades Green Fd (*v.* Wade Green 114 *supra*).

(*b*) *Auardesfelde* 1384 (from the pers.n. ON *Hávarðr* or ODan *Hawarth* and feld); *Crosseley* 1560 ('cross clearing', *v.* cros, lēah); *the Magdelenis near Preston* 1599 (a capital messuage and free chapel, the dedication presumably to St Mary Magdalene).

9. WALTON INFERIOR (101–6085)

Waletun 12 *Dow* (p), John *AddCh*, *-tona* 1154–60 (1329) Ch, 1190–99 Facs, *Cott.* Nero C III, *-ton'* 1191 Facs *et freq* with variant spellings *-thon*, *-tone* to 1331 Pat, (*-iuxta grangiam Actone*) 1249–61 Whall, *parua walet'* 1190–99 Facs
Walton 1190 Orm[2] (p) *et freq* with variant spellings *tona*, *-tone*; (*-in Haletonshir*) 1263 Whall, *-inferior* 1270–90 Mere, (*-in Haltonshir*) 1303 Whall, *Inferior Walton* (*in Haltonshir*) 1286 ib, *Nether-* 1295 Cl, *Neyther-* 1557 Mere, *Neither-* 1673 *AddCh*, *Neather-* 1673 ChRR, *Lower-* 1642 Mere, *Low-* 1775 Sheaf
Wall' 1200–63 Whall (p)

'The Britons' or the serfs' farm', *v.* walh (gen.pl. wala), tūn, also neoðera, lower, inferior.

BARONET FM. CHESTER RD, leading to Chester. FORD HOUSE FM (101–602863), EASTFORD RD, WESTFORD RD, from some lost ford in the brook below Walton Mill. MORLEY COMMON, *Mosley House & Common* 1831 Bry, *Malley Common* 1842 OS, *Morley* (*Common & Field*) 1843 *TA*, 'marsh clearing', *v.* mōr[1], lēah. MOSS WOOD, *Moswod* 1544 Mere, *v.* mos, wudu; this place was in Acton Grange, 1831 Bry. WALTON HEY FM, *v.* (ge)hæg. WAL-TON BROOK (lost), *v.* 1 37. WALTON MILL, *molendinum de Waletona* 1154–60 (1329) Ch, *v.* myln.

FIELD-NAMES

The undated forms are 1843 *TA* 411. Of the others, 13, 1307, 1393 are *LRO* Dx, 1249–61 Whall, 1361 BPR, 1433, 1434 Mere, 1751 Sheaf.

(*a*) Backside Fd; Bongs (*v.* banke); Brook Holland ('low-lying selion by a brook', *v.* brōc, hol², land); Brow Mdw; Cantliffe (*v.* clif); Cress Broom (3x) (*Cressebrokis* 1307, 'brooks where cress grows', *v.* cresse, brōc); Eye Mdw (*v.* ēg 'a water-meadow, an island'); Grange Mill Fd (*v.* Grange Mill 146 *supra*); Grantley; Grasshook (*v.* gærs, hōc); Gutsford, The Gutsfords ('ford over a channel', *v.* gote, ford; the name of water-meadows near R. Mersey); Heys (*v.* (ge)hæg); High Lane (*v.* 147 *supra*); Hodge Fd (*v.* hocg, cf. *Hodg Croft* 1 158); The Island, Islands (cf. *insula de Waleton* 13, *v.* ig-land); Knowl Fd; Linnow; Loont (*freq*, *v.* land); Marsh Moor; Mill Stone Fd; Moss, -Fd, -Mdw (*mosse* 1393, *v.* mos); Mossack; Pingos, Pingot (*v.* pingot); Pocket Patch (*v.* poket, pacche); Pool Ditch & Stead (*v.* pōl¹, dīc, pōl-stede); Quag Mdw (*v.* quag); Shaw (*le Shagh* 1433 (p), *v.* sc(e)aga); Snig Hole (from ModEdial. *snig* 'an eel'); Stanbridge Hey (*v.* stān, brycg or brēc); Town Fd; Turf Pits; Warthe (*v.* waroð); Well Rushes (*v.* wella, risc); The Wharf Mdw; (*v.* waroð or hwearf); White Fd; Will Fd; Withins (*v.* wiðegn); Old Yards (*v.* ald, geard).

(*b*) *Esthale* 13 ('east nook', *v.* ēast, halh); *le Holdebrok* (*v.* 148 *supra*).

10. WALTON SUPERIOR (109–5984), *Superior Walton'* l¹3 *AddCh*, *Walton Superior* E2 Orm², *Over Walton* E2 Mere, (*-in parish of Daresbury*) 1566 Hesk, *Oure-* 1309 Plea, *Overe-* 1312 ib, *Ovre* 1324 ib, *Upper-* 1498 AD, *High-* 1774 Sheaf, with other spellings as for Walton 157 *supra*, *v.* uferra, superior, upper.

BEECHTREE FM. BOG ROUGH, 1831 Bry. HOUGH'S BRIDGE & LANE, *Hough's Bridge* 1831 ib. PARK LANE. ROWSWOOD FM, named from Row's Wood 147 *supra*, cf. *le Bawes infra*. WALTON BROOK (lost), *v.* 1 37. WALTON HALL, 1843 *TA*. WALTON LEA (BRIDGE), *Lee Farm & Bridge* 1831 Bry, *v.* lēah. WALTON OLD HALL, *Walton Hall* 1831 ib. WALTON-WOOD, 1831 ib, *in bosco de Waleton* 1263 Whall. WARRINGTON RD, *Walton Lane* 1843 *TA*, cf. Warrington La.

FIELD-NAMES

The undated forms are 1843 *TA* 410, 1263 is Whall.

(*a*) The Birches; Brierly Linnow; Butty Croft (*v.* butty); The Court (a meadow, *v.* court); Flatts (*v.* flat); Gallantry Bank (probably 'gallows-tree hill', *v.* galg-trēow, banke); Gorsty Hey (*v.* gorstig, (ge)hæg); Gravestone

Fd; Green Hey; Heyes (*v.* (ge)hæg); Home Park; Kitchen Fd; Lambray ('lambs' enclosure', *v.* lamb (gen.pl. lambra), (ge)hæg); Linnow (*freq*, perhaps 'flax knoll', *v.* līn, hōh); Long Butts; Marl Fd; New Earth (*v.* eorðe); New Hurst (*v.* hyrst); The Pockett (*v.* poket); Pool Stead (*v.* pōl-stede); Priest Croft; Purseland (*v.* purs, land); The Ridding (*v.* ryding); Short Hill; Short Tail (*v.* tægl).

(*b*) *le Bawes* 1263 (ChetOS xi 406, part of 'the wood of Walton towards Acton Grange', perhaps in Walton Inferior. The form may represent the pl. of boga 'a bow, a bend, an arch', cf. *caueas nanorum* 148 *supra*. But it is probably a bad copy of *le Rawes* (*v.* rāw 'a row'), an early form for Row's Wood 147 *supra*, Rowswood *supra*).

xvii. Runcorn

The ancient parish of Runcorn comprised the detached chapelry of Poolsey, in Dutton township 113 *supra*, the parochial chapelry of Daresbury 146 *supra*, and the following townships, 1. Stockton Heath 145 *supra*, 2. Aston Grange (*v.* foll.), 3. Aston iuxta Sutton, including Middleton Grange (now a c.p. including Aston Grange), 4. Clifton (*v.* Sutton *infra*), 5. Halton (part now included in Runcorn c.p.), 6. Norton (now a c.p. including Stockham), 7. Runcorn (now a c.p. including Weston and part of Halton), 8. Stockham (*v.* Norton *supra*), 9. Sutton (now a c.p. including Clifton), 10. Weston (*v.* Runcorn *supra*). The part of Norton between the Manchester Ship Canal and R. Mersey is now included in La. Aston iuxta Sutton, Aston Grange, Middleton Grange and Sutton were formed into the parochial chapelry of Aston in 1635 (Orm ² i 721).

2. ASTON GRANGE (109–5677)

> *Mauricas Eston* 1178 Whall, *Mauriches Eston* 1178–82, 1194–1211 ib, *Mauricaceston* 1178 Orm² ii 400, *Mauricaceseston* 1187 Dugd, *Maurich Eston* 1187–91 Whall, *grangia de Maurikeseston* 1202 ib, *Meurik Aston in hundredo de Halton* 1316 ib, *Mauricaston(a)* 1334 Pat, 1344 AddCh
>
> *Eston* 1194–1211 Whall (p), c.1200 ib *et freq* and as for Aston 160 *infra*
>
> *grangia de Aston* 1291 Tax, -*alias Aston grange in Aston* 1553 Pat, -*Graunge* 1581 AD, -*Graing* 1673 AddCh
>
> *Ashton Grange* 1554 Whall

'Maurice's part of Aston', 'the grange at Aston', from the ME pers.n. *Maurice* (MedLat *Mauricius*) and grange 'an outlying farm belonging to a religious house', with the p.n. Aston 160 *infra*. Dr Barnes draws attention to a *Morice* witnessing a charter 1153–60

Chest 23, who may be the person referred to. The spellings in *-ik-* are probably due to Welsh influence, cf. *Meurik-* 1315 for Welsh *Meurig*. This township belonged to Whalley Abbey (cf. Stanlow 327 *infra*).

BANKFIELD FM. BANK ROUGH, 1843 *TA*, *the Bankropts* 1743 Sheaf, 'the rough land on the hillside', *v.* banke, rūh, rūhet. QUICKWOODS, *Quick Wood Roughs* 1831 Bry, *Wickwood Rough* 1842 OS, '(rough ground at) the live wood', *v.* cwicu, wudu, rūh. TOWNFIELD FM, *communis pastura que pertinet ad villam de Eston* 1200 Whall, *Aston-town-field* 1671 Orm[2], *the Fields* 1681 Sheaf, *Aston Grange Town Field* 1743 ib, *v.* toun, feld.

FIELD-NAMES

The undated forms are 1843 *TA* 26. Of the others, 1200, 1271, 1272, 14, 1554 are Whall, 1537 Dugd, 1547 *AddCh*, 1575, 1743 Sheaf, 1831 Bry.

(*a*) Alder Hey & Rough; Backside; Bank Hay (*Banks Hey* 1743); Birches; Cornhill Hay (*v.* corn[1], hyll); Aston Grange Cribs 1743 (*v.* crib); Cross Fd (*the-* 1743, *v.* cros); Dudgemoor (*Duddesmore* 1547, *Dudgmores* 1743, 'Dudd's moor', from the OE pers.n. *Dudd* and mōr[1]); Eye (*v.* ēg 'a water-meadow'); Flatt Wd (*v.* flat); Flax Croft Wd (cf. *Flax Wood* 1831); Glade Fd & Rough; Grange Hey (1743, cf. Aston Grange *supra*); Green Hay; Hill Hay (1743); Hop Yard 1831; Maddock Hey; New Hay, -Hey (*the New Hay* 1575, *v.* (ge)hæg); The Oaks; Outshot ('outlying corner of land', *v.* ūt, scēat); Sun Croft (*v.* sunne); Town Wd, Wood Lane (*Wood Lane* 1831 Bry).

(*b*) *le allis* 1271; *Aston Springs* 1537, *Ashton spring* 1554 (*v.* spring 'a young wood'); *Holteschagh* 1200 ('wood copse', *v.* holt, sc(e)aga); *Itley* 1554 (a parcel of ground included in Dutton Park 113 *supra*, *v.* lēah); *Rougehay(e)* 1271, 1272, *-in Eston* 14 (apparently an OFr form, 'red enclosure', from rouge and OFr haie (cf. (ge)hæg)); *Rughschagbrok*, *Rughschagwall* 1200 ('(stream at) the rough wood', *v.* rūh, sc(e)aga, brōc, wælla).

3. ASTON BY SUTTON (109–5578)

 Estone 1086 DB, *Eston* 1178 Whall *et freq* to 1397 ChRR, *Heston(a)* 1185–90 Facs (p), 1191 ib, *Estun* 1190–1200 ib (p), *Estona* 1190–1211 *Cott*. Nero C III, 1194 Facs (p)

 Astona 1135–54 (17) Orm[2], *-tun* 1185 Chol (p), *-ton* 1190–99 Facs (p), e13 Whall (p) *et freq*, (*-iuxta Sutton*) 1191 ArlB *et freq*, (*-super Wevre*) 1280 Ipm, (*-iuxta Crewode*) 1287 Court, 1315 Chol, (*-sub Cruwode*) 1398 AddCh, (*-iuxta Dutton*) 1312 Plea, *Haston* 1311 AddCh (p), *Astoun* 1347 *ib*, *Aston Towne* 1594 AD As(s)h(e)ton iuxta Sutton 1381 Plea, Orm[2], *Ashton* 1554 Whall

'East farm', *v.* ēast, tūn, lying east of R. Weaver, and in the south-east corner of Runcorn parish, cf. Norton, Sutton, Weston 173, 180, 182 *infra*. The later forms show confusion with æsc 'an ash-tree'. The suffixes refer to Sutton and to R. Weaver 1 38, Dutton 112 *supra*, Crewood 326 *infra*. For earlier forms, *v.* Middleton Grange *infra*. Aston by Sutton, Aston Grange and Middleton Grange are frequently comprehended by the name *Eston, Aston*, without addition, and it is not always possible to distinguish between the parts of what must have been originally one territory. Aston was a parochial chapelry of Runcorn parish, *v.* 159 *supra*.

MIDDLETON GRANGE (109–5577)

> *Eston* 958 (13) (17) BCS 1041, Dugd, KCD 473, Chest, *-tona, -e,*
> *-æ* 1096–1101 (1280), 1150 Chest, *-tuna* 1188 (17) ib
> '*E*'[*A*]*ston* 958 (13) (17) BCS 1041
> *Midestune* 1086 DB
> *Middel-Estona* c.1236 (17) Orm², *Middlaston* 1291 Tax, *Middleston*
> 1301 Chamb' (p), *Midl(e)aston* 1338 VR, *grang' de Medelaston*
> 1538 AOMB 399, *Aston vel Middle Aston* 1547 AddCh, *the*
> *Grange called Mydleaston in Aston* 1552 Orm², *Middle-Aston-*
> *Grange* 1668 ib, *Midle Aston* 1673 AddCh
> *Middelton* 1314 ChRR, *Middleton* 1325 ib (p) *et freq* with variant
> spellings *Midle-, Midel-, Middel-, Mydle-;* (*-iuxta Aston*) 1427
> ChRR, *-Grange* 1594 AD, (*-called also sometimes Middle-Aston-*
> *Grange*) 1668 Orm², (*-within Aston iuxta Sutton*) 1800 *Chol*

'The middle part of Aston', 'the grange at Middle-Aston', from the p.n. Aston 160 *supra*, with **middel** and **grange**, cf. Aston Grange 159 *supra*. Middleton Grange was a manor of St Werburgh's Abbey, Chester, with an ancient chapel, *Middleton Chappel* 1671 Orm², *ecclesia de Estona* 1096–1101 (1280) Chest, at a moated site 109–556771, *The Moat* 1842 OS, *the graunge ground* 1547 AddCh. This manor and its lands (cf. Parkside *infra*) formed an extra-parochial township, distinct in 1831 Bry, included in Aston by Sutton in 1843 *TA* 27.

MARE CLOUGH, 1743 Sheaf, *the Meere Clough pool dam* 1590 *AddCh*, *the Mareclough Pool* 1590 (1680) Sheaf, *the mearclough poole* 1621 (1680) ib, *Mare Clough Pool* 1743 ib, cf. *le Merebrock* 1307 *AddCh*, *the Mear brook* 1590 (1680) Sheaf, *le Maremore* 1538 AOMB 399,

1547 *AddCh*, *Mare Hey* 1743 Sheaf, all referring to an area along the boundary with Sutton 180 *infra*, 'brook and dell on a boundary', *v.* (ge)mǣre, brōc, clōh, pōl¹, damme, mōr¹, (ge)hæg. Cf. also 'an assart at *le mere de Astun* which is called *Kette Ruding*' m13 *AddCh* 51043, 'twenty acres of land in *le Mere* called *le Dich*' 1421 *ib* 51150, *v.* dīc.

ASTON HALL, 1831 Bry, *the maner place of Aston* 1546 *AddCh*, cf. *the Hall Croftes* 1580 *ib*, *Hall Croft* 1674 *ib*, *v.* hall.   ASTON HEATH, 1831 Bry, cf. *le hethfelde* 1538 *AOMB*, *the heythe Fylde* 1547 *AddCh*, *le hethe fieldes alias Briddes fieldes* 1556 *ib*, *Heath Field* 1743 Sheaf, *v.* hǣð, feld, cf. Bird's Wood *infra*.   BECKETT'S WOOD, *Beckets-* 1831 Bry.   BIRD'S WOOD, *Burd(s) Wood(s)*, *Birds Wood(s)* (*Lane*) 1743 Sheaf, *Birds Woods* 1831 Bry, cf. *le hethe feildes alias Briddes fieldes* 1556 *AddCh*, 'bird's wood', *v.* bridd, wudu.   BLACKAMOOR WOOD, *Blackmoor Wood* 1831 Bry, *v.* blæc, mōr¹.   BOUNDARY FM, on the boundary with Preston 156 *supra*.   CHAPEL WOOD, cf. *Chapelfelde* 1538 *AOMB* 399, *Chapell Heye* 1547 *AddCh*, *the great Chappel hey* 1679 Sheaf, *Chapel Lane & Plantation* 1831 Bry, 1843 *TA*, named from the chapel of Aston built in 1425 to replace Middleton Chapel *supra*, and replaced by a new one near Aston Hall, t. Henry VIII, cf. ChetOS VIII 354, *v.* feld, (ge)hæg, cf. Chapel Lane 182 *infra*.   CHESTER LANE (lost, 109–555797 to 559799), to 1743 Sheaf, 1746 *Chol*, cf. 181 *infra*, 1 40.   THE COPPICE.   DELL WOOD, cf. *Dell Plantation & Pond* 1843 *TA*, *the Dale* 1580 *AddCh*, *Dale Lount* 1674 *ib*, *v.* dæl¹, dell, land.   HATTON'S HEY WOOD, *Hatton Hey Wood* 1831 Bry, probably containing a surname from Hatton 149 *supra*.   KIDNEY PLANTATION, named from its shape. PARKSIDE, 1831 *ib*, *Aston Parks* 1745, 1750 Sheaf, cf. *the parke of Aston* 1546 *AddCh*, *the Parke Pool* 1637 Sheaf, *the upper Park* 1743 Sheaf, *the Higher- & the Old Park* 1767 *ib*, *v.* park, pōl¹, sīde. STRETCHES GORSE, from the Ch. surname *Stretch*.   WHITEHOUSE FM.   WHITTLE'S CORNER, *Corner Hey* 1743 Sheaf.

FIELD-NAMES

The undated forms are 1843 *TA* 27. Of the others, 13 (17), 1590 (1680), 1621, 1621 (1680), 1628 (1680), 1632 (1680), 1634 (1680), 1637 (1680), 1683 and 1743 are Sheaf, 1272, e14, 1554 Whall, 1287, 1290 Court, l13 (14) Chest, 1307 *Eyre*, 1312 Plea, 1381–2 (17), c.1385 (17), 1417 (17) Orm², 1427 ChRR, 1538 *AOMB* 399, 1594 AD, 1831 Bry, 1842 OS, and the rest *AddCh* 51023–51502.

(a) The Acres; Aston Gate 1831 (v. geat 'a gate', at a cross-roads 109–562798); Aston Lane; Backside; The Bank; Basnetts; Bathing Pit Fd; Brick-Kiln Plantation; Calf Croft; Childermoss Lane (perhaps 'children's moss', v. cild (gen.pl. cildra), mos, but cf. Childermas Hill 114 supra); Coney-gree Pond (Conyngre 1546, the Conniegree 1621 (1680), 'the rabbit warren', v. coningre); Crewd Lane 1743 (perhaps 'Crewood Lane', leading to Crewood 326 infra by Kingsley Ford infra, v. lane); the Crooked Lount 1674 (v. croked, land); Deans Fd; Eye 1743 (cf. the three Eez 1546, Middleton Eyes 1547, the great eyes 1621, v. ēg 'a water-meadow', cf. Middleton Grange supra); Glade Rough 1743; Gorsey Fds 1743; Habekirkum 1743; Hatchells; Intake; Kiln Pond (the Kill Pool 1637 (1680), v. cyln, pōl¹); Kingsley Ford 1842 (a ford across R. Weaver into Kingsley 326 infra, at 109–557764, v. ford); Long Croft, Fd & Mdw (cf. longe Furlonge 1580, Common Longfurlong 1674, Long Furlongs 1743, v. lang, furlang, commun); Nave Acres (v. cnafa); New Brook 1743; New Road Fd; Newotts; Norman's Acre & Ditch 1743 ('no-man's acre and ditch', v. nān-mann, æcer, dīc); Old Lane; Outlet (v. outlet); Pingot (v. pingot); Roughsedge's Fd; Rough Fd; Runjoe (perhaps another example of ear, with rond 'round', cf. Blackeyer 1 265); Ryders Hays (Pits) (Ryder's Hey, Ryder New Hey, Ryder Hey Pit 1743, probably from a surname, v. (ge)hæg, pytt); The upper Sidnall 1683 (Sidnall Lands 1621, perhaps 'spacious corner', v. sīd, halh); Sutton Lane 1743 (v. Chapel Lane 182 infra); Tan Yard Fd & Mdw (v. tan-yard); Three Cornered Piece; Town Fd (1743, the Townefield 1580, 'field common to the town', v. toun, feld); Town Mdw (-s 1743, cf. prec.); Tunnel Fd (named from Preston Tunnel on the Trent & Mersey Canal); Well Croft & Fd (cf. Well Banks 1743); Willow Walk (v. walk); Within Pit 1743 (v. wiðegn); Withy Croft (v. wiðig); Wood Fd (the Woddefyld 1547, cf. Middleton Wood 1621 (1680), v. wudu, feld, Middleton Grange supra).

(b) Bancroft 1547, the- 1628 (1680) (v. bēan, croft); the Barne pool 1634 (1680) (v. bere-ærn, pōl¹); blakebroc 1209–29, blakescich m13 (v. blæc, brōc, sīc); le Blakefeld 1370 ('black or dark field', v. blæc, feld); blakenhallbroc m13 ('(brook at) the dark nook', v. blæc (wk. dat.sg. blacan), halh (dat.sg. hale), brōc); blakescich (v. blakebroc supra); blakestub m13 ('the black stump', v. blæc, stubb); the great Brake 1632 (1680) (v. bræc¹); Catenall Medowes 1547 ('meadows near Catten Hall (325 infra)', v. mæd); Clangreve 1580 (v. græfe. The first el. could be clǣgig (wk.dat.sg. clǣgigan) 'clayey', or clǣne 'clean, clear of weeds, etc.'); le Dich' 1421 (twenty acres of land in le Mere, probably a boundary-ditch, v. dīc, cf. Mare Clough supra); Domelawe 1427 (p) (a surname at Middleton Grange, apparently from dōm 'judgement' and hlāw 'a mound, a hill'); Doncroft 1307–27 ('hill croft', v. dūn, croft); Dowehill 1546, the Dowsehyll (medowe) 1547, Dowce hill 1621 (1680) (perhaps 'allotment hill', v. dāl (ME dole), hyll, but the first el. could be the ME pers.n. Dow(e) (Reaney 99)); Drosse Fylde 1547 ('rubbish field', from ME dros (OE dros)); farenhurst 13, Pharinhurst l13 ('ferny wood', v. fearn, hyrst); Foulfeney 1275 ('(water-meadow at) the foul fen', v. fūl, fenn, ēg, cf. Morphany 154 supra); Gattlaff Field 1590 (1680) (perhaps 'goat clough', v. gāt, clōh); Haliwallebroc m13 ('holy-well brook', v. hālig, wælla, brōc);

Halton Heye 1547 ('enclosure belonging to Halton 166 *infra*', *v.* (ge)hæg);
holomesheie e13, (*piscarium de*) *holmesyard* 13, 13 (17), -*yerd* m13, -*gurd* e13,
Holmisclyf 1275 ('enclosure, fish-pond and cliff at an island', *v.* holmr,
(ge)hæg, clif, geard, cf. fisc-geard 'a fish pond, a fish-trap'); *the horsey* 1546,
Horse Hey 1621 (1680) ('horse meadow', beside R. Weaver, *v.* hors, ēg); *le
houenestude* l13 ('the site of an oven', *v.* ofen, styde); *Kette Ruding* m13
('Kett's clearing', from the ME pers.n. *Ket(t)e* and ryding); *Marland* 1272
('marl land' or 'marsh land', from marle or marr[1] and land); *Mobacres* 1538,
the mabacre 1547; *Mulnebroc* (a mill upon) e13, 13, *broca molendini* 1209–29,
cf. *le Mulnefeldesende* 1370 ('the mill stream', 'the end of the mill-field', *v.*
myln, brōc, feld, ende[1]); *Perifelde* 1538, *Pyers Fylde* 1547 ('pear-tree field',
v. pirige, feld); '*a parcel of land called a Ryland*' 1481 ('a selion on which rye
is grown', *v.* rye-land); *Ryngey* l13, 1301, 1417, *Ringey* a.1385 (17), 1417
(17), *Rengey* 1417 ('the circular enclosure', *v.* hring, (ge)hæg, cf. Ringway
28 *supra*); *the shorte buttes* 1580 (*v.* sc(e)ort, butte); *le Spert* c.1300 (*v.*
spyrt); *Stokeseye, Stocesheie* 1209–29, *piscaria de Stocisyerd* m13, *Stokkes-
medewe, -more* 1370 (*v.* stoc, ēg, (ge)hæg, geard, mǣd, mōr[1]); *the Thriche
wayne flatt* 1580 ('plot of ground where a cart has to be pushed from behind
(either a steep or a muddy place)', from wægn and flat, with dial. *thrutch,
thritch* 'to push, to rush something along, a push' (OE *þryccan*, (*of-*) *þrycce*,
ME *þrucchen, þrucce*, and cf. *þryȝt* pa.t., *þrich, Sir Gawayn* 1443, 1946, 1713),
especially applied to pushing a cart in an instance in EDD s.vv. *thrutcher,
rush-cart*); *Wallesyche* m13 ('watercourse from a spring or well', *v.* wælla,
sīc, perhaps *le Waterwalesiche* ?13 (17) Sheaf[3] 18 26, '*walesiche* from which
water is drawn', *v.* wæter, cf. wēl[2]); *Witefeld* 1209–29, *Whitefeld* 1211–29,
Wytfelt l13 (14), *Whitfield* 1621 (1680) (*v.* hwīt, feld, cf. *Blakefeld supra*);
Witters Riddinge 1580, *Withers riding* 1621 (1680) (*v.* ryding); *Woodhouses*
1381–2 (17), *le Wodehouses* 1390, *Wodhousefeld* 1454 ('house(s) in a wood',
v. wudu, hūs, feld); *wollehille* 1538 (perhaps 'wool-hill', a place where sheep
were shorn, *v.* wull, hyll); *the Wosehyll* 1547 ('muddy hill', *v.* wāse, hyll).

4. CLIFTON (109–5280)

   Clistune 1086 DB, -*tona* 1150 Chest

   Cliftona, -thona 1096–1101 (1280) Chest, 1163–90 ib, -*ton* 1154–89
     (17) Orm[2], c.1190 *Chol et freq*, (-*in Halton*) l13 AddCh, (-*now
     Rock-Savage*) 1672 Orm[2], (-*alias-, -or Rocksavage*) 1819 Orm[2],
     -*tun* 1247 Chest, -*tone* 1295 Lacy (p), *Clyfton* 1282 Court (p)
     et freq to 1599 Earw, -*tona* (*in Haltonshire*) 1310 Chest, *Cliffeton*
     1496 Orm[2], *Clyffe*- 1553 ib

   Clufton 1325 Chol

   Clefton 1534 Chol

'Farm at a cliff', *v.* clif, tūn. The *Clis-* form is due to scribal
substitution of *st* for *ft*, rather than to genitival composition. 'This
town or place hath its name from the cliffs or broken rocks therein',
1666 Leycester (Orm[2] I 771). Cf. Rock Savage *infra*.

ROCK SAVAGE, 1574 (1669) Orm², 1581 Sheaf, (-*in Clyfton*) 1599 Earw, *Rockesavage* 1598 Orm², *Rocksavage alias Clifton* 1626 *Chol*, *Rocksavage Park* 1630 *ib*, (-*alias Clifton Park*) 1721 *ib*, 'Savage's rock', from *rokke* and the surname of Sir John *Savage*, who built a mansion here in 1565 to replace Clifton Hall *infra*, v. Orm² 1 711. As the township comprises only the demesne of Clifton, it came to be known by the name of the new hall.

CLIFTON HALL, 1720 *Chol*, *The Old Hall* 1666 Orm², cf. Rock Savage *supra*.

FIELD-NAMES

The undated forms are 1844 *TA* 22. Of the others, 1288 is Court, 1310² ChRR, e14 Sheaf, 1505 AD, 1523 Orm², 1599 Earw, and the rest *Chol*.

(a) Actons Nooks 1777 (*Nookes* 1724, *Actons Corner* 1700); Ash Croft 1798; Ash Walks (1777); Barn Flatt; Big Wd; Birch Crofts-, Birch Fd or Brick Fd (*Further & Nearer Birch Field* 1777); Butty Nineacres 1777 (*v.* butty); Coppice (*The* 1777); Crabtree Fd (1777); the (long) Croft 1777; Higher Cross Fd 1777; Dear Bolt 1777 (probably a euphemism for 'dear-bought', a disparaging f.n. occurring elsewhere in the county); Big & Lt. Demesne 1777; Flood Brook Wd (*v.* Flood Brook 1 24); Grass Mdw or Grass Moss (*Grass Moss* 1777, *v.* gærs, mos); Haltonyate 1700 (*Clifton Gate* 1573 'gateway to Halton', *v.* geat, cf. Haltongate 169 *infra*); Higher & Lower Holts, Holt Plain (*le holt* c.1275, *the Holts* 1569, *Hole Lane* 1700, *Higher & Lower Holt*, *Holt Plain* 1777, *v.* holt, plain); Big Lea 1777 (*v.* lēah); Lower & Top Long Fd (*Higher & Lower Long Field* 1777); Long Hey 1794; Marled Julls 1798 (*Marl Julls* 1777, *v.* marlede, cf. Blackeyer 1 265); the Marsha 1798; Marsh Mdw (1777, *the Marsh Medows, Clifton Marsh* 1685); Big & Little Mill Fd (1798, *two Millfields* 1685, *Great & Little Mill Feild* 1692); Oak Hey (1777, *Oakley* 1798, *v.* āc, (ge)hæg, lēah); Old Orchard 1777; Outlet 1798 (*v.* outlet); Park Mdw (1724, cf. *Clyfton Parke* 1523, *the Parke* 1700, *Park Bridge Field* 1697); Pingard 1724 (*v.* pingot); Runcorn Plains (1798, *v.* plain, cf. Runcorn 176 *infra*); Rye Fd 1777; Sand Fd (1777); Tack Acre 1794; Tarrind 1697; Thistle Hey 1777; Far, Middle & Near Town Fd (1798, *Towne Fields* 1685, *Further Townfeild* 1692); Trolly Lolly (1798); The Wast 1720 (*v.* waste); Westons Lound 1794 ('selion belonging to Weston (182 *infra*)', *v.* land); Whins Glade (*Winns-, Wynns Glade* 1777, 1798, from ModE *glade* 'a glade', with either whin 'whin, gorse' or the surname *Wynn*).

(b) *Bridgehowse farm* 1641 (*v.* brycg, hūs); *Brownett's Marsh* 1685; *boscus de Clifton'* c.1275, *nemus de Cliftona* 1309, *Clifton grove* c.1310 (*v.* grāf); *le cloyt* 1275; *Elmerescholes* c.1275, *Elmeresscholes, helmarisscolis, -ys* c.1310 (from skáli 'a temporary hut or shed', with a pers.n. form *Almer, Elmer* (Feilitzen 147–9, from OE *Æðelmær* or *Ælfmær*); *Le Uvere Eueses, superior*

hevese c.1275, *le Overe Euese* c.1310 ('the higher edge', *v.* uferra, efes);
Farford Heye 1685 ('(enclosure at) the far ford', *v.* feor, ford, (ge)hæg);
Goselawe 1275, *Gos(e)lowe* 1275, 1314 ('goose hill', *v.* gōs, hlāw); *le Grene-
meneweylond* 1310 ('green selion at a common road', from (ge)mǣne and
weg, with land and grēne[1]); *Gunnildiscroft* 1275, *Gunnildescroft* 1288, *Gunnyl-
discrofte* 1415 ('Gunnhildr's croft', from the ON fem.pers.n. *Gunnhildr, v.*
croft); *Harstanistile, Harstandesfeld* c.1275 ('Herestān's stile and field', from
the OE pers.n. *Herestān* and stigel, feld); *Hirpishil, Irpeshul* 1275, *Hirpilhul*
1314 (the second el. is hyll 'a hill'); *Hokelond* 1310 (either 'oak land' or
'selion at a hook', from āc or hōc and land, cf. *Okelondis infra*); *le Homormor*
c.1310 (from mōr[1] 'a moor, *&* marsh', apparently with hamor or hamarr,
though the sense is not apparent and the first el. could well be amore,
omore the name of a bird, cf. ModE *yellow-hammer*); *Croft' Hugonis* ('Hugo's
croft', from the ME pers.n. *Hugo (Hugh)* and croft); *Lythelondes, Lethelondis*
1275, *le Lithelondes* c.1310 ('selions on a hill-side', *v.* hlið[1] (gen.pl. hleoða),
land); *le Merebroc* (*v.* 172 *infra*, cf. Flood Brook I 24); *Okelondis* c.1310
(*v.* āc, land, but cf. *Hokelond supra*); *(le) O(a)ldefeld* c.1275 (*v.* ald, feld); *le
Portewey* c.1310 (*v.* I 49); *Radelstones, radilstonis* c.1275, *radilstonys,
-stones, le Radelstones* c.1310 ('(stones or rocks at) the red hill', *v.* rēad, hyll,
stān); *Ringestede* c.1310 (p), *-stude* 1314 (p), *Ryngested(e)* 1310[2] (p), e14 (p)
(a surname appearing among witnesses to local deeds, etc. 'place where there
is a ring', *v.* hring, stede, cf. Rinks Pool 123 *supra*); *le Rugges* c.1310 ('the
ridges', *v.* hrycg); *Skalgreue, Scalgreue* 1275, 1310 ('copse at the sheds', *v.*
skáli, grǣfe, cf. *Elmerescholes supra*); *Schovilbrode, le Schouele brodys* c.1275
('the shovel-breadth(s)', i.e. narrow strips of land, *v.* scofl-brǣdu); *Smale-
brokeheued* c.1275, *Smalbrokesheuid, le More- & firresmallebrok, le Smalbrokes*
c.1310, *le Smallebrok* 1314 ('(the top end of, the greater and farther fields at)
the narrow brook', *v.* smæl, brōc, hēafod, māra, feor (comp. firra Angl); *(le)
s(o)urerthe* c.1275 ('the sour ploughed-land', *v.* sūr, erð); *le Wallebrockes*
c.1310 ('(fields at) the well brook', *v.* wælla, brōc); *Witefeld* 1310 ('white
field', *v.* hwīt, feld); *le Wodeway (vocat' Lodeway et Rodeway)* c.1310 ('(right
of) way to a wood, either to lead or to ride', *v.* wudu, weg, lād (ME *lode*)
and rād (ME *rode*)); *Twinne Mills* 1641 ('double mills', *v.* twinn, myln).

5. HALTON (109–5381) [ˈhɔltən]

Heletune 1086 DB, *Heltun* 1199–1216 *AddCh*, -ton 1305 Lacy
Haltona 1135–1154 (17) Orm[2], 1190–1211 *Cott.* Nero C III, -thon(a)
    1185–90 Facs, H3 Orm[2], -ton 1185–90 Facs *et freq*, (le-) 1334
    VR (p), (*West-*) 1574 Sheaf, (*-near Deresburye*) 1581 AD, -tone
    c.1277 ib, 1295, 1305 Lacy, *Alton(a)* c.1154 Tab, 1260 Court
Haulton(a) c.1154 (1329) Dugd, c.1190 *Chol et freq*, -tun c.1185
    Chol, Hauleton(e) 1252 RBE (lit. *Hanle-*), 1338 Pat
Hethelton 1174 Orm[2], *Hadelton* c.1200 Whall, *Hathelton* m13 (17)
    Orm[2]
Haleton 1194–1211, e14 Whall

Hauton c.1200 Facs, 1240 P *et freq* to 1306 *MinAcct*, *-tone*
   1295 Lacy, *Hau(g)hton, Haghton* 1287 Court, *Hawton* 1398
   Orm²
Haw(e)ltun 1240 P, *Hawelton* m13 Orm², *Hauil-, Hauelton* c.1270
   AddCh, 1287 Court
Halyl'thon 13 Tab
Hehylthon 13 Tab
Halyton c.1277 AD
Halgton' 1295 *AddCh, Halghton* 1301 (1344) Pat, *Halughton* 1397
   JRC 1664
Holton 1296 Plea (p)
Hailton l13 *AddCh*
Hathton 1304 Chamb
Hallton' 1487 *MinAcct*

Probably 'farm at a heathery place', from tūn and the p.n. el. OE
*hāðel, *hǣðel, supposed for *Halton* (near Bingley) YW (*Hatelton*
1086, *Hathelton* 1156, *Ageltunum* 1160, *Hageltune* 13, *Hadelton*
1203–6, *Halton* 13) and Haddlesey YW, *v.* WRY 4 163, 18–19.
Ekwall (Studies³ 62–3) suggests that the Yorkshire *Halton* may contain the OE pers.n. *Haðuwulf*, and the same might be said of Halton
Ch. There is no certain evidence in the forms and an occasional
gen.sg. form in *-es-* might have been expected. His other proposal
(DEPN) that Halton Ch is from halh must be rejected. That el.
may have been substituted for *hāðel in some forms, and it would
be relevant to Halton's position on the peninsula between Mersey
and Weaver. The village and castle stand on a very bold and prominent hill, so that el. OE *haðol 'a hollow', proposed in Studies³ 62–63,
WRY 4 xi, for Haddlesey YW, does not apply here. For the development of the forms of Halton cf. WRY 4 163, ANInfl 100–7, Feilitzen
102–3. A greater degree of AN influence is to be expected in the
forms of the Ch p.n. since Halton was the head of the Norman
barony of *Halton Hundred 2 supra*.

Astmoor Fm & Marsh (109–5383)

Estmor 1190–1211 *Cott.* Nero c iii, *Hestemor* H8 *Rental*
   Astmore 1305 Lacy, *-mor* 1380 *Chol*, *-moore* 1581 AD, *Astemore*
      1370 *MinAcct, Hastmore* 1443 *ib*
   Astonmore alias Astmore 1594 AD, *Aston Moore* 1650 *ParlSurv*
      Ashmoor (Bridge) 1843 *TA*

'The eastern marsh', v. ēast, mōr[1], lying east of Runcorn 176 *infra*. Cf. *Astemorelone, Astmore lane* 1398, 1422 *MinAcct, Go(r)st(e)ast(e)more* 1443, 1452 *MinAcct, Gorsteamore* 1487 *ib, Astmorefeld(e), -filde* 1536 Orm², 1560 Sheaf, *Aston Mooreheyes* 1650 *ParlSurv, Astmore Hey* 1695 *Chol, Astmorefield* 1739 *LRMB* 264, v. lane, gorst, (ge)hæg, feld.

HALTON CASTLE, *de Castello* 1172 Facs (p), *castrum-, castellum de Haulton, -Hawelton'* 1240 Pat *et freq* with spellings as for Halton *supra, Haulton castel* c.1536 Leland, *the Castell of Halton* 1564 *Rental, the Old Castell* 1661 *Surv*, v. castel(l), ald. This was the seat of the constables of Chester, barons of Halton, and an honour of the Duchy of Lancaster, cf. *Halton Hundred* 2 *supra*. Various parts of the castle are recorded as follows: in 1295 Lacy, *falda castri de Haltone*, 'the castle fold', probably the bailey, v. fald; in 1422 *MinAcct* (DL 29, 5, 58), *camera vocata Erleschaumbre*, 'the Earl's room'; *purifaldum regis*, 'the King's lavatory'; *orreum infra castrum*, 'the barn within the castle'; *le Bordehous*, 'the boarded house'; *porta Castri*, 'the castle gate'; in 1452 *MinAcct* (DL 29, 7, 84), *noua turris ad introitum Castri de Halton*, 'the new tower at the entrance of the castle'; in 1507 *MinAcct* (DL 29, 10, 136), *murus Castri*, 'the castle wall'; in 1695 *Chol, Earles House*, 'the Earl's house'. Here also belongs *parcella terre supra Halton hull, -hill infra antiquos muros de Halton'* 1443 *MinAcct*, 'a piece of land on Halton hill within the ancient walls of Halton', which suggests older works than the medieval castle's curtain-wall, enclosing a space of land. It may in fact be *Old Castle* (109–535823, marked CAMP in O.S. 1") 1811 *Sund*, 1843 *TA*.

HALTON HILL, *le Hyl* 1113 *AddCh* (p), *le Hill* 1443 *MinAcct, Haltonhill, -hull, mons de Halton* 1386, 1423, 1443 *ib*, v. hyll, cf. Halton *supra*.

HALTON PARK (lost, about 109–535815), *parcum de Haltona* 1190–1211 *Cott*. Nero c III, *-Hauton'* 1241 Cl *et freq* with spellings as for Halton *supra, Halton park* 1557 Sheaf, *-Parck* 1565 *Chol*, cf. *Parke Lane howse, -house* 1650 *ParlSurv*, 1658 *Chol*, v. park.

THE HEMPSTONES (109–535848), HEMPSTONES POINT (109–535846), (*piscaria inter Haltonyerde et*) *Emmeston'* (*in aqua de Mercy*) 1452, 1507 *MinAcct, Hemneston* 1487 *ib, Hemmeston* 1489 *ib, Hempstones* 1811 *Sund, Halton Point* 1842 OS, the name of a bank in R. Mersey and a point of land near it, probably 'the flat rock', v. emn, stān, point.

MARSH FM, cf. *mariscus* 1295 Lacy, *le Mersch* 1380 *Chol* (p), *le Marsshemore* 1395 *AddCh*, *le Mereschmore* 1409 *ib*, (placea herbagii vocata) *Merssy et Eggere* 1452 *MinAcct*, *Marsh and Egar* 1661 *Surv*, *Marsh and Eger* 1698 Sheaf, *The Marsh* 1811 *Sund*, *Halton Marsh* 1831 Bry, *v.* mersc, mōr[1]. The *MinAcct* forms refer to pastures washed by the flood-tides, *v.* ēg, ēgor.

MEADOW LANE BRIDGE (lost, 109–537838), 1831 Bry, cf. *Medewemor* 113 *AddCh*, *Halton Mede* 1536 Orm[2], *-Meade* 1554 *MinAcct*, *-Meadowe(s)* 1650 *ParlSurv*, *Halston Meadow* 1739 *LRMB* 264, 'the meadow-marsh, the meadow of Halton (*supra*)', *v.* mǣd, mōr[1].

HADDOCK'S LODGE & WOOD, *Haddocks Wood* 1842 OS, *Fir Wood* 1811 *Sund*, 1831 Bry, cf. the surname *Haddock* 1811 *Sund*. HALLWOOD, 1681 *Rental*, *Hall of the Woodd* 1608 *AddCh*, cf. *boscus de Haltone* 1295 Lacy, 'hall at the wood of Halton', *v.* hall, wudu. HALTON COMMON. HALTONGATE FM, *Haltongate* 1353 *MinAcct*, cf. *þe Clapyate* 1650 *ParlSurv*, 'gateway to Halton', *v.* geat, clap-gate. HALTON GRANGE, cf. Pool Dale *infra*. HALTON LODGE, 1831 Bry, *logium infra parcum* 1423 *MinAcct*, *Lodge Farm* 1777 *Chol*, *Rock Savage Lodge* 1842 OS, *v.* loge, cf. Halton Park *supra*, Rock Savage 165 *supra*. HALTON RD, *via regalis que ducit versus Runcor'* 1315 *AddCh*. THE MOUNT, cf. Monks Mdw *infra*. PICKERINGS ROUGH, *Pickering Field* 1843 *TA*, *v.* rūh. POINT TURN BRIDGE (109–534839), *The Turnbridge* 1811 *Sund*, at a bend on the former Runcorn and Latchford canal, near Hempstones Point *supra*, was *Marsh Bridge* 1831 Bry, cf. Marsh Fm, Astmoor Marsh *supra*. POOL DALE, FM & HO, with Halton Grange *supra*, were *Gill's Ground* 1842 OS, in Runcorn township 1831 Bry, cf. Big Pool 178 *infra*, 'valley with a pool in it', *v.* pōl[1], dæl[1]. SEA-LANE, 1845 *TA*, *v.* sǣ, lane. STENHILL LANE (lost, 109–526822 to 517818), 1831 Bry, cf. Stonehills 177 *infra*. HIGHER & LOWER STREET (lost), *alta strata ville de Halton* 1379, 1407 *Chol*, *-& inferior strata* 1506 *AddCh*, the upper and lower streets of the village.

FIELD-NAMES

The undated forms are 1843 *TA* 184. Of the others, 1190–1211 is *Cott.* Nero c III, 1260, 1288 Court, c.1270, 113, E2, 1315, 1326, 1328, 1377, 1397, 1400, 1409, 1410 (Jas I), 1424 (Jas I), 1506 *AddCh* 51047–51178, 1295, 1305 Lacy, 1306, 1370, 1386, 1398, 1422, 1423, 1437, 1443, 1452, 1487, 1489,

1507, 1514, 1547 *MinAcct*, 1391, 1532, 1534 *JRC* 1662–1665, 1418, 1536 Orm², H8, 1595, 1681 *Rental*, c.1547, 1661, 1685 *Surv*, 1560, 1840 Sheaf, 1593, 1594 AD, 1650 *ParlSurv*, 1724 NotCestr, 1739 *LRMB* 264, 1811 *Sund*, and the rest *Chol.*

(*a*) Augars Fd (*Augur's-* 1811, at 109–539812, probably *Nauegerfeld infra*); Backside 1811; Banner Studge-, Bonner Stitch Mdw (*Banner Sludge Mdw* (109-542809) 1811, *v.* Holding Brook 1 29); Barn Fd 1811; Briers 1811 (*le Breres* 1487, *le Brerers* 1507, *v.* brēr 'a briar'); Brickiln Fd 1811; Bolton's Fd (*Belton's field* 1724); Bongs (cf. *le Litelbangfeld* 1288, *v.* lȳtel, banke, feld); Broken Cross (approx 109–542848) 1811; Brook Hay 1811 (cf. *Halton Brook, the Brook Field* 1794, *le Brookefeild* 1695, *v.* brōc); Brow Mdw (1811, *v.* brū); Calvers Clough (cf. *the Calverwell Clough, Culverwell-, Claiderwell Clough* 1661, '(dell at) the calves' spring', *v.* calf (gen.pl. calfra), wella, clōh); Calver's Croft (*the Calver Croft* 1702, cf. *le Callermedwe* 1328, 'the calves' croft & meadow', *v.* calf (gen.pl. calfra), croft, mǣd); Carrs (*Carr* 1811, *v.* kjarr); Cherry Tree Walk (1811); Chester Lane Fd (1811 (109–542805), cf. *Chester Lane* 1650, 'lane leading towards Chester'); Cote Mdw (1777, 1798, *v.* cot); Crook Lane ('lane with a bend in it', *v.* krókr); Crow Nest (1695, 1794, 1811, *Crowenest* 1377, *Cravnest* 1400, *v.* crāwe, nest); Deer Cote Hey (cf. *Deer Cote Lea* 1777, '(enclosure and meadow at) the deer-shed', *v.* dēor, cot, (ge)hæg, lēah); Edge Hey (1695, *Egge* 1370, *le-* 1443, *le Yegge* 1452, *the Hedge Heyes* 1811, 'enclosure at the edge of a hill' *v.* ecg); Ferney Brow (*Fearney-* 1777); Flash Quarter 1840 (1811, *v.* flasshe); Fox Holes (1811); Big Gate Fd (*Big & Little Gate Field* 1777, (*Big*) *Gate Field* 1798, *v.* gata 'a cow-gate, a pasture'); Goldsmith's Hey (1811); The Gosses (1811, cf. *le Gosswall* 1695, *Goswell* 1794, 'goose well' *v.* gōs, wælla, wella); Grass Moss (*v.* gærs, mos); Green Heyes 1811; Halefield 1739 (*v.* halh); Hales Crib 1811; Hall Fd 1811; The Hancocks in the Marsh (1811, *Hancocke Meadowe* 1695); Heesoms Fd 1811; the Hemp Yard(s) 1747, 1794 (*le Hempyoard* 1695, *v.* hemp-yard); The Holdings 1811; Kiln Croft 1811; Lammas Bridge 1811; The Lands 1811; the Lakes 1695, 1794, 1811 (*v.* lake or lacu); Land Stile Mdw (*Land Style, -Stile* 1777, 1798, *v.* land 'a selion', stigel 'a stile'); Lane Fd (cf. (*the*) *Lane End*(*s*) 1695, 1794, 1811); Lenage Pool (*Linage-* 1811); Little Hey 1794 (1695); Lords Acre 1699 (*v.* hlāford); Monks Mdw 1699 (*Mountesmedowe* 1507, *Muncks-, Monckes Meadowe alias Mountes Meadow(e) or Mountaynes Meadowe* 1607, 1650, from munt 'a mount, a hillock' and munuc 'a monk' cf. The Mount *supra*); (Big & Little) Moss (1777, cf. *Halton Moss* 1640, *Mosse-side* 1724); Mouldy Croft (1811, 'croft infested with moles', from dial. *mouldy* 'a mole'); New Fd 1811; New Hey (1811, *le-* 1695); Nine Butts (1811); Oat Hey; Old Castle (*v.* Halton Castle *supra*); Overshotts 1811; Orchard Fd 1811; Page Croft 1794 (*Padge Croft* 1695, *v.* pacche 'a patch of land'); Pig Ridding (1811, *v.* pigga, ryding); Pike Nook (1777, *v.* pīc¹); Priest Croft (1811); (Near) Rushy Pasture (*Rushey Pasture* 1724, *Further, Middle & Nearer Rush(e)y Pasture* 1777, 1798, *Rushey Mdw* 1811); Sales (1811, *v.* salh); School Lane 1811; Shades 1811; Short Butts (-*But*(*t*)*s* 1724, 1777, *le Shortbuttes* 1377, 'the short strips', *v.* sc(e)ort, butte); the Shut Greave 1794 (*le Shuttgreave* 1695, 'wood at a corner of land', *v.*

scēat, grǣfe); Six Acres 1811; Slower Fd; Sludge Croft (1811); Smithy Croft 1811; Sower Fd 1811; Springall; Stedham 1724; Stockham Fd (1811, *v.* Stockham 179 *infra*); Street Moors (1811, at 109–537812 to 535807, *le Stret(e)more* 1370, 1378, 1398 'moor or marsh beside a paved road', *v.* strǣt, mōr[1], cf. *Stretemore* 182 *infra*); Summer Lane Croft (1811, *Somerlane* 113, -*land* 1487, 'land-, lane-, used in summer', *v.* sumor, lane, land); Tan House Fd (1777); Three Butts 1695; Three Nooks (1724, cf. *Three Nook'd Lea* 1777); Under Town Mdw 1811; Wall Hey (1811, *v.* wælla); Well Mdw 1811; Wharf Mdw (*v.* waroð); Whins Glade (cf. 165 *supra*); Whirley Rents 1724; White Field Gate (*v.* gata); White Lands (*Whitlands* 1777, 1811, 'white selions', *v.* land); Winter Croft (1811, *v.* winter[1]).

(b) *le Bakehous(e)* 1487, 1507 (the bakehouse', *v.* bæc-hūs); *Barkers brooke* 1610 (*v.* barkere, brōc); *Birche howse* 1681 (*v.* birce, hūs); *Bondeth* 1296, -*heth* 1305, *bonde*- 1400 ('the peasants' heath', *v.* bóndi, hǣð. Professor Sørensen suggests that the final el. could have been ODan *heth* 'a heath'); *Bosewalle* 1397 ('well-spring at a cow-stall' *v.* bōs, wælla); *le Brenker* 1443, *le Brouker* 1422, 1423, *v.* kjarr 'marsh, brushwood'); *Brodeland Moore, Bradelandes* 1573 ('(moor or marsh at) the broad selions', *v.* brād, land, mōr[1]); *Bradewallescroft* 1378, *Brades*- 1407, *Bradewallestyle* 1379, *Brades-wallestele* 1407, *Broadwellfeild* 1661 ('(croft, stile and field at) the broad well', *v.* brād, wælla, wella, stigel, feld, croft); *Byland* 1386, *Biland apud le Broke* 1398 ('land, or a selion, in the bend of a stream', *v.* byge[1], land); *Canons Way* 1506 (*v.* canoun, weg); *Channell way* 1661 (*v.* chanel, weg); *Chyrchefeld* 1295, 1306, *Chirchefeld* 1305, (*superior*-) 1326, *le Netherchurchefeld* 1315, *the Churchfeild* 1661 (*v.* cirice, feld, uferra, neoðera); *le Cleyacre* 1409 (*v.* clǣg, æcer); *the Crooked Lound* 1661, *v.* croked, land); *le Crosseway* 1506 (*v.* cros, weg); *le Crymbe* 1506, *the Crime*-, *Cryme Hay(e)*, -*hey & Lane* 1650, 1661, 1661[2] (*v.* (ge)hæg, lane. This f.n. belongs to a series including C(h)rimes 1 233; 325 *infra*, (Mdw, Fd, Hey, Lane) 191, 200, 203, 325, 326 *infra*, Crimes Brook 326 *infra*, Crimbucks 1 238, Crimbabent 1 245, *Chanon-crymbre* 175 *infra*, C(h)rimbers 40 *supra*, 272 *infra*, The Crime 326 *infra*, Crime Fd 326 *infra*, *le Cruymbes* 326 *infra*, and perhaps also Crinsey 1 315, *Crimlow* 201 *infra*, Crimmer Lane 326 *infra*. The common el. in these appears to be OE **cryme* 'a crumb, a small piece', i.e. 'a little plot of land', related to cruma, crymel (ME *crimble*, cf. La 167), cf. cryming Db 723, and to OE *gecrymian, gecrymman* 'to crumble' (BTSuppl), cf. *crim* NED, *creem* EDD); *Conyngyerd'* 1487, *Conygarth* 1507, *Cony-Greene Close* 1650, *Cunnygreene* 1661[2] ('rabbit warren', *v.* coninger, coning, coni, geard, garðr, grēne[2], clos); *Ernysbuttes* 1409 (from butte 'a balk, a selion' with a pers.n., either OE *Earnwīg*, or *Earne* (Feilitzen 163) from ON, ODan *Arni*); *le Fence* (*infra Parcum*) 1452, 1487, 1507 ('the fenced-in place', *v.* fence, cf. *Halton Park supra*); (*piscaria de*) *Halton Fissh(e)garth* 1443, 1452, 1487, 1507, -*Fyshgarth* 1607, *le Fysshe*-, *Fisshepole* 1443, 1452, *Haltonyerd(e)* 1452, 1487, 1507) 'the fish-pond', *v.* fiski-garðr, fisc-geard, fisc-pōl, geard); *þe geylde* H8, *Gyld* 1547; *le hall feld* 1506, *Halfeld(e)* 1560 (*v.* hall, feld); *the Hay*-, *Hey Lane* 1661 (*v.* (ge)hæg, lane); *Herons* 1534 (perhaps 'the corners', from hyrne, cf. Heronbridge 326 *infra*); *le Highefeld* 1547, *þe hyfellde* H8 (*v.*

hēah, feld); *Holepul* c.1270, *le holghpole* 1390 ('pool in a hollow', *v.* hol[1], pōl[1]); *le Horston* l13 ('the hoar stone', *v.* hār[2], stān); *le Hullimore* 1288 ('the hilly moor', *v.* hulli, mōr[1]); *le Kynges Acr'* 1507 and *le Kyngesgap* 1487 ('the king's acre and opening', *v.* cyning, æcer, gap); *Ladder* 1610 ('a ladder, a flight of steps', *v.* hlǣd(d)er, cf. The Lader 179 *infra*. There may have been a ladder-stile here); *Longacre yate* 1532 (*v.* lang, æcer, geat); *Longham* 1443, 1487, 1507 ('long meadow', *v.* lang, hamm); *fossatum vocatum le Marelake* 1437 ('boundary water-course', *v.* (ge)mǣre, lacu); *le Mar-*, *le Merketsted* 1398, 1422 ('place where a market is held', a piece of waste land on Halton hill, *v.* market, stede); *þe marled earthe* 1650 (*v.* marlede, eorðe); *le Merebroc inter Halton' et Clifton* c.1275 ('the boundary brook', *v.* (ge)mǣre, brōc, cf. Flood Brook 1 24); *le milnehull* 1386, *-hill* 1443 (*v.* myln, hyll); *Morley* 1386, *Moreley in Halton* 1422, *Morley More, Hyll & Crofts* H8, 1536 ('clearing at a moor', *v.* mōr[1], lēah); *Nauegerfeld* l13, *Naugerf(i)eld* 1370, 1398, *Naugre -*1409, *Nawgerfeld* 1547, (?)*Nawgreuefeld* 1377, *Naugeresfeld* 1409, *-gresfe(i)ld* 1410 (Jas 1), 1424 (Jas 1), *Nawger's Field* 1593, *Nawgars Field* 1594, *Little Nawgers Field* 1661, *Nogerfeld* 1506 ('auger field', from OE *nafu-gār, nafegār* 'an auger' and feld. This may be Augars Fd *supra*. The el. recurs at Naugerhill 63 *supra*, Noger Croft, Nogars Moor 305, 313 *infra*, but the significance is unknown); *le Newstede* 1418 ('the new place', *v.* nīwe, stede); *Nungreeue* 1595 (probably 'nun's wood', *v.* nunne, grǣfe); *le Olerfyeld* 1424 (Jas 1), cf. *Ollers* 1514 ('alder-tree field', 'the alders', *v.* alor, feld); *þe Pale* 1650 (*v.* pale 'a fence (round a park)'); *stansile vocata pater noster Style* 1532 ('a stone-stile called Paternoster Stile', probably from the recitation of the Lord's Prayer at Rogation processions or the like, *v.* stān, stigel); *Poole Bridge* 1681, 1685 (*v.* pōl[1], brycg); *Proud(e)-*, *Prowdebridge* 1650, 1661, 1661[2] (perhaps 'splendid bridge', *v.* proud, brycg); (*le*) *Remersch* 1370, *-mers(s)h(e)* 1452, 1487, 1507 ('roe-deer marsh', *v.* rǣge 'the female roe-deer', mersc); *Rilond* 1422, 1423, 1443 (*v.* rye-land); *Rogerescroft* 1190–1211 (perhaps in Norton, cf. 175 *infra*, from the ME pers.n. *Roger*, after Roger Lacy, baron of Halton 1190–1211, who granted it to Norton Abbey, *v.* croft); *le Roncorn'feld* 1506 ('the field towards, or belonging to, Runcorn (176 *infra*)', *v.* feld); *Runcoreyat, -ʒate* 1386, 1398, 1422 ('the gateway to Runcorn', *v.* geat); *Saltpleck* 1650 ('salty plot', probably saltings, *v.* salt, plek); *le Sedich* 1437 ('the sea-ditch', *v.* sǣ, dīc); *Sefton hey* 1506 (probably from the surname from Sefton La 118 and (ge)hæg); *Sheire Okes* 1573 ('shire oaks', oak-trees where a shire-meeting was held, *v.* scīr[1], āc, cf. Halton Hundred 2 *supra*); *le soppetgreneflat* 1409 ('the water-logged green plot', from a ME **soppet*, the pa. part. of OE *soppian* 'to sop, to soak', *v.* grēne[1] or [2], flat); *Squonridyng'* 1400 ('peasants' clearing', *v.* swān[2], ryding); *le Touneyat(e), -gate* 1487, 1489, 1507 ('gate leading to the town', *v.* toun, geat); *Vnderhull'* 1423 (cf. *subtus le hull* 1422, *v.* under, hyll, cf. Halton Hill *supra*); *le Wallesiche* l13 ('stream from a well or spring', *v.* wælla, sīc); *le Weende subtus le hill* 1386, *le Wende-* 1422, *leʒ Wendes* 1443, *le Wynde subtus Haltonhull* 1391 ('winding road(s)', *v.* wende, (ge)wind[2], cf. Halton Hill *supra*); *Whitley Moore* 1573 ('(moor at) the white clearing', *v.* hwīt, lēah, mōr[1]); *Wodecokeslond* E2 (from wodecok 'a woodcock', perhaps as a pers. by-name, and land 'a selion').

6. NORTON (109–5582), *Nortune* 1086 DB, *-tun'* c.1200 *AddCh* (p) *et freq* to 1285 *Chol*, *-ton* 1134 (17) Orm[2] *et freq* with variant spellings *-tona*, *-tone*, *Nort'*, *Northon*, *Northtton*; *Northon iuxta Haulton* 1298 Chol, *Norton super le Mores* 1418 *ib*, *-cum Stock(h)am* 1663 Sheaf, 1724 NotCestr, 'the north farm', *v.* norð, tūn. The township lies north of Sutton 180 *infra*, from which it was separated by Stockham 179 *infra* (now included in Norton), and extends to R. Mersey on the north side of the peninsula between that river and R. Weaver. Cf. Weston 182 *infra*.

(LOWER) EANLEY WOOD FM (109–553814) [ˈiːnli, ˈiːɘnli]

> *Enlelei* 1086 DB
> *Hendeleia, -ley* John (17) Tab, Orm[2], *Hendley (or Endley)* c.1230 (17) Orm[2], *Endel(e)y* 1325 (1594) *Chol*, 1329 IpmR, *Endley* 1666 Orm[2], *(Higher) Endley Wood* 1688 *Dep*
> *Enleywod(d)* H8 *Rental*, 1538 *AOMB* 399, *Henley Wood alias Endley Wood* 1691 *Dep*
> *Hemley-, Enley Wodd* 1538 *AOMB* 399
> *Eanl(e)y Wood* 1709 LCWills, 1842 OS
> *Danely Wood* 1831 Bry
> *(Lower) Hindley Wood* 1842 OS

'Lambs' clearing or wood', *v.* ēan (gen.pl. **ēana*), lēah, cf. Yeanley 327 *infra*. The DB form duplicates the final el., probably a copyist's error, and the forms in *Hend-* contain an infixed *-d-* between *-n-* and *-l-* as in Handley 326 *infra*, 1 98. The Bry form is either erroneous, or derived from one with the definite article prefixed. The lower farm at Eanley Wood is called *Ashley Bridge Farm* 1831 Bry, probably from an older name of Borrow's Bridge *infra*.

NORTON PRIORY (109–5483)

> *Ecclesia sanctae Mariae de Norton et Canonici ibidem Deo regulanter servientes* 1134 (17) Orm[2], *domus-* 1359 *Chol*, *monasterium-* 1410 Cl
> *prior(atus) de Norton(a)*, etc., 1178–90 *Bun et freq*, *a priory of canons cawllid Northtton* c.1536 Leland, *Norton Priory* 1724 NotCestr
> *abbas-, abbatia de Nortun, -ton*, etc., 1253 Cl, 1396 ib, *the abbay of Norton* 1521 Life, *Norton Abbey* 1553 Pat
> *monasterium de Norton* 1549 Pat
> *Hall Graunge* 1569 Orm[2], *the hall of Norton* 1634 ib, *Norton Hall* 1646 Sheaf

The priory was established in Runcorn c.1115 and transferred to Norton c.1134 (*v.* Orm[2] 1 691, Facs 24). The priory became an abbey at an unspecified date—it is called an abbey in 1253 Cl but more regularly from 1396 ib, yet it is more frequently called a priory down to the dissolution. *v.* hall, grange.

BIG WOOD, 1811 *Sund.* BOB'S BRIDGE, *v.* 153 *supra.* BOG WOOD, *Haughtons Bog* 1842 OS, *v.* bog. BORROWS BRIDGE, (Bridgewater Canal), *v.* Eanley Wood *supra.* CAWLEY'S BRIDGE (Bridgewater Canal), *Platts Bridge* 1831 Bry. FIDDLER'S FERRY, 1831 ib, a ferry across R. Mersey. GREEN BRIDGE (Bridgewater Canal) & WOOD, 'at a green', *v.* grēne[2]. HAYSTACK LODGE, 1831 ib, cf. *Hay Stack Bridge* ib. KECKWICKFORD FM (101–564837), *Keakwick Ford Farm* 1831 ib, *Kekewick-* 1811 *Sund*, a ford at 101–565837 on Keckwick Brook 152 *supra*, the boundary of Keckwick 151 *supra*, *v.* ford. LODGE FM, *v.* Norton Lodge *infra.* MANOR FM, 1842 OS. MARSHGATE FM, *Norton Farm* 1831 Bry, 'marsh pasture', *v.* mersc, gata, cf. Norton Marsh *infra.* (UPPER) MOSS SIDE FM, *Moss Side Farm* 1811 *Sund*, (2x) 1831 Bry, cf. *the Moss* 1536 Orm[2], *Mosseside* 1705 ChetOS VIII, *v.* mos, sīde. NORBURY'S WOOD, *Norbury Wood* 1842 OS, *Old Bog Rough* 1831 Bry, *v.* bog, rūh. *Norbury* is a surname. NORTON BRIDGE, *Languish Bridge* 1831 ib. This is on the Bridgewater Canal. The name may be a lost f.n. *Lang-wish* 'long marsh', *v.* lang, wisc. NORTONHILL, 1842 OS. NORTON LANE (lost), 1811 *Sund.* NORTON LODGE, cf. Lodge Fm *supra.* NORTON MARSH, 1811 *Sund*, cf. Marshgate *supra.* NORTON TOWN BRIDGE (Bridgewater Canal), *v.* toun. NORTON TOWNFIELD, 'the common field'. NORTON WAREHOUSES, *New Warehouse* 1831 ib. OXMOOR WOOD, 1842 OS, *the Oxmoor* c.1536 Orm[2], *Generals Wood* 1831 Bry, 'moor or marsh where oxen are pastured', *v.* oxa, mōr[1]. SANDYMOOR WOOD, 1811 *Sund*, *Sondewall Moor* c.1536 Orm[2], '(marsh at) the sandy spring', from sand(ig) and wælla, with mōr[1]. STONEDELPH DOCK, 'stone quarry', *v.* stān, (ge)delf. WEIR'S GORSE. WHATFORD FM (109–563821), *Watford* 1636 ChRR, *Walford House* 1709 LCWills, *Warford (Farm)* 1831 Bry, 1842 OS, *Warford Brook* 1831 Bry, from a ford of Keckwick Brook 152 *supra*, at 109–565821, *v.* ford. The first el. may be vað 'a ford'. The brook was the lower course of Keckwick Brook and joined R. Mersey. WINDMILL HILL, & *Wood* 1811 *Sund*, cf. *the Windmill* c.1536 Orm[2]. WOOD LANE, 1811 *Sund.*

FIELD-NAMES

The undated forms are 1811 *Sund*. Of the others, 1190–1211 is *Cott*. Nero c III, c.1200, 1536 Dugd, 1291 Tax, 1353 *MinAcct*, 1433, 1543, 1560, 1618 Sheaf, H8 *Rental*, c.1536, 1568 Orm², 1538 *AOMB* 399, 1831 Bry, 1843 *TA* 301.

(a) (The) Eight, Five, Seven-, Ten-, Three-, Two Acre(s); Backside; Barn Fd & Head (*v.* heáfod); Great & Little Bent (*v.* beonet); Broad Fd; Brickiln Fd; Brook Fd, Mdw & Yard (*v.* geard); Butts (*v.* butte); Calf Yard 1843; Calyard (perhaps 'calf enclosure', *v.* calf, geard, cf. prec., but 'vege-table garden' is possible, *v.* cǎl); Church Fd (c.1536, *v.* cirice); Churner; Clover Fd; Cock Shot (*v.* cocc-scyte); Coneygreaves (*Coney Graves* 1843, *v.* coningre); Cow Pasture; Cowslips; Crab Tree Fd; Damas' Acres; Dog-kennel Mdw; Fryers Moors (*-Moor* 1843); Garden Fd; Big Gate Fd (*v.* gata); Gig Fd (*v.* gigge); Gorstey Fd; Gorsty Lane; Green Fd; Green Hays 1843; Half Acre(s); Hall Moor; Halton Fd (cf. Halton 166 *supra*); Hasteel; Heath Gate Fd ('gate leading on to a heath', *v.* geat); Hole; Hoo Row (*The Horrow* 1843); Horse Pasture (cf. *Horselownes* c.1536, *v.* hors, launde); Great & Little Humphrey (*Great Humprey* 1843); Isle of Man (a field shaped like a three-pointed star); Kells Acres; Kiln Croft; The Lawn (*v.* launde); Long Duck 1831 (the south shore of a reach of R. Mersey); Madge Intake (*v.* madge, inntak); Mares Hey (*Mareshay* 1843, *v.* mere², (ge)hæg); Marsh Nook; New Hey (*-Hay* 1843); Norton Fd; Old Mdw; Outlet (*v.* outlet); Pear Tree Croft; Pecked Fd; Penketh Bar 1842 (a bank in R. Mersey opposite Penketh La, *v.* barre 'a bar, a barrier'); Pike Fd (*v.* pīc); Riggot(t)s, Riggotts Parks (*Priggots* 1843); Rough Mdw; Rushey Mdw; The Rushes; Salt Mdw (*v.* salt); Sander's-, Sanders Heys (cf. *Saunders-field* c.1536, 'Sander's field', from the ME pers.n. *Sander*, a short form of *Alexander*, *v.* feld, (ge)hæg); Sandy Heys; Sankey Mdw; School Fd & Mdw; Shroggs (*v.* scrogge); Sower Mdw; Stable Fd; Stubbs (*v.* stubb); Syllylow(s) (109–555832, 'little mounds', *v.* (ge)sǣlig (ModE *silly* 'insignificant, little'), hlāw); the Three Quarters; Vicar's Heys (*Vicar Hays Plantation* 1843, 'the vicar's enclosures', *v.* vikere); Wharf (*the warth* c.1536, *v.* waroð); Withers Wd, Wither's Little Wd ('willow wood', *v.* víðir); Wood Fd; Wood Hatch (*v.* hæc(c)).

(b) *Barlowe* c.1536 ('barley hill', *v.* bere, hlāw); *Chanoncrymbre* 1353, *þe cryme* H8, c.1536, 1538, 1543 ('the canon's bit of land', *v.* canoun, cryme, cf. *le Crymbe* 171 *supra*); *Crop Field* c.1536 (*v.* crop); *Dendhow* 1433; *Halfelde* 1560 (perhaps 'field at a nook', *v.* halh, feld); *þe Lyttell hye felde* H8, *littell high felde* 1538 (*v.* hēah, feld); *littell mede* 1538, *Litell Medowe* 1543 (*v.* lȳtel, mǣd); *Mosse Moor* c.1536 (*v.* mos, mōr¹); *the Park* c.1536 (*v.* park); *Radford Field* c.1536 (perhaps 'red ford', *v.* rēad, ford); *Rogerescroft* 1190–1211, c.1200 (*v.* 172 *supra*); *ryddynge more* H8 ('moor at a clearing', *v.* ryding, mōr¹); *the Sheephouse* c.1536 (*v.* scēp, hūs); *Stotfeld Shawe* 1536 ('(wood at) the ox field', *v.* stot, feld, sceaga); *the Lower Swyne Park* c.1536 ('swine enclosure', *v.* swīn¹, park); *Through Bridge* 1618 ('bridge over a drain', v. þrūh, brycg); *Venables More* 1538, 1543 ('moor belonging to the Venables family', v. mōr[1]); *the water Mill* c.1536; *the Weldmare Flatts* c.1536 ('the wild mare's flats', v. wilde, mere[2], flat).

7. RUNCORN

RUNCORN, formerly LOWER RUNCORN or RUNCORN ABBOTS (109–5983)
> *æt Rūm cofan* 915 (c.1000) ASC (B), (m11) (C)
> *Runcofan* c.1118 FW, 15 Trev, -*cofam*, *Rucofan*, *Rouncofan* 14 Higden, *Runcoua* 1115 Runc (lit. -*cona*), 1154–60 (1329) Ch (lit. -*cona*), 1190–1211 *Cott*. Nero C III, *Runcovan, but now called Runcorne* 1672 Orm[2] I 5
> *Runcorna* c.1134 (17) Orm[2], 14 Higden, -*corne* 1172 (17) Tab, 1420 Plea *et freq* to 1549 AD, -*corn* 1262 ArlB, 1354 Sheaf (p), *et freq*, (*Nether*-) 1430 Sheaf, 1527 ChRR, (-*inferior*) 1672 Orm[2], (*Lower*-) 1831 Bry, (-*abbatis*) 1536 Dugd, (-*Abbatt*(*e*)) 1607, 1619 Chol, *Rungcorne* 1487 *MinAcct*, *Runckorne alias Runckorne Abatis* 1635 Chol, *Rounckorne* 1681 *ib*
> *Roncoueria* 1172 Facs, -*cover* 1178–90 Orm[2], -*couer* 1186–90 Whall (lit. -*coner*), (-*inferior*) 1306 *MinAcct*, -*couere* 1291 Tax (lit. -*conere*), -*cour* 1242 Cl, -*kor*(*e*), -*core* 1311 Cl, Ipm, 1312 Plea, 1322 Whall, AD
> *Runcouer*(*e*) 1245 P, 1295 Ipm (lit. -*conere*), Lacy, -*covere* 1295 Cl, -*cour'* 1245 P, -*core* 1255 Plea *et freq* to 1370 *MinAcct*, -*kore* 1303 Chamb (p)
> *Rancovere* 1249 Lib
> *Runcar* 1329 IpmR
> *Roncorne* 1464 *LRO* Dx, -*corn* 1535 VE
> *Rencorn* 1475 ChRR (p), -*e* 1554 Pat
> *Ronkhorne* 1500 Chol, (*Nether*-) 1655 *ib*, *Ro*(*u*)*nck*- 1630 *ib*, *Run*(*c*)*khorn*(*e*) 1577 Saxton, 1656, 1660 Sheaf, (*Nether*-) 1665 Chol
> *Romcorne* 1507 *MinAcct*
> *Ronnakherne* 1534 Chol
> *Runkon* 1692 Sheaf

'At the roomy cover', v. rūm, cofa. This would aptly describe the part of the Mersey estuary above Runcorn Gap *infra*, where the constriction of the channel by the promontories of Widnes La 106 and *Castle Rock infra* caused river and tide to form a wide lagoon. This pool was *le creke de Runcorne* 1481 ChRR (cf. *Runcorn, now a poore townlet by a salt creke* c.1536 Leland), a creek of the port of Chester.

Runcorn was the site of a *burh* made by Æþelflæd, lady of the Mercians, *v. Saga Book* XIV 313. The location of the fortification is not certain, but it has been supposed to be *the castle rock* 1817 Orm² 1 675, which was removed in 1862 to improve the navigation of the R. Mersey. In 1845 this site was 'a triangular piece of ground opposite the gap (Runcorn Gap *infra*) which juts out into the river, by which it was defended. It was cut off from the land by a ditch six yards in breadth', ChetOS VIII 353n. A fortification at this point would command the narrow passage from the lower estuary into the upper reaches of R. Mersey, a strategic requirement, *v. Saga Book loc. cit.*

The lower part of Runcorn was associated with Norton Priory, originally founded here, cf. 174 *supra*, *v.* neoðera, inferior, abbas, abbat, cf. Higher Runcorn *infra*.

HIGHER RUNCORN, *alterior Roncover* 1178–90 Orm², *Runcoure superior* 1295 Lacy, *Over-Runcorn* 1428 ChRR, *Upper Runckhorne* 1684 *Chol*, *Higher-* 1724 *ib*, with variant spellings as for Runcorn *supra*, 'the higher part of Runcorn', *v.* superior, uferra, upper.

THE FERRY (lost), 1860 White, *passagium navis de Widnesse* 1178–90 Orm², *passagium de Merse apud Runcouam* 1190–1211 *Cott.* Nero C III, (lit. *-conam*) c.1200 Dugd, *batella vocata le Ferybote* 1507 *MinAcct*, *Runcornboate* 1618 Sheaf, *Runkhorne Bote* 1715 ib, *Runcorne Ferryboat* 1729 *Chol*, cf. *boateland* 1592 *ib*, *the-* 1619 *ib*, *-s* 1638 *ib*, *Boat Lands* 1729, 1757 *ib*, 'the ferry-boat' and 'land belonging to the ferry', *v.* ferja, bāt, land. This ferry at Runcorn probably also gave name to *Chiplode* 1290 (17) Tab, a fishery, and to a place of waste called *Shepelodmanwey* 1370, *Shiplod(e)manway* 1388, 1398, 1423, *Sheplondmanley* 1443, *-lye* 1452, *Shiplandmanley* 1514, *Shipland* 1487, *Shiplandenale* 1507 all *MinAcct*, 'the ship passage and the common way to it', from scip 'a ship' (confused with scēp 'a sheep') and (ge)lād (confused with land 'land'), (ge)mǣne and weg (confused with lēah 'a clearing').

RUNCORN HEATH, HEATH HO, 1831 Bry, *Runcoreheth* 1370 *MinAcct*, *Runcorne Heath* 1685 *Chol*, *v.* hǣð, hūs.

STONEHILLS, STONEHILL'S LANE, *Stenehul* 1315 *AddCh*, *Stenhill Lane* 1831 Bry, *the Stenhills* 1842 OS, 'stony hill', *v.* stǣnen, hyll.

BATE'S BRIDGE, *Knights Bridge* 1842 OS. BEACON HILL, *Runcorn Hill* 1831 Bry, site of *The Beetle Rock* 1842 OS, 'the overhanging

rock', v. NED s.v. *beetle* 'to project, to overhang'.   BRICKFIELD
COTTAGES, cf. *Brickfield, Brickiln Field* 1843 *TA*.   BRIDGEWATER
Ho, cf. *Dukes Dock* 1842 OS, and Bridgewater St., named from the
Duke of Bridgewater's Canal.   BROOKSIDE, v. brōc, sīde.   CHURCH
BANK, a bank in R. Mersey at Runcorn Gap, opposite Runcorn
church, v. banke.   COCK & HEN LANE, cf. *Cock & Hen* 1843 *TA*.
DOCTOR'S BRIDGE.   GREENWAY RD, *the green(e)way* 1672, 1729
Chol, v. grēne[1], weg.   GROVE HO (lost), 1831 Bry, the site now
of Grove St.   HIGHFIELD HO & TANNERY, *Tan Yard* 1831 ib.
HILL COTTAGES, named from Beacon Hill *supra*.   HOLLOWAY,
'road in a hollow', v. holh, weg.   IRWELL LANE, named from the
old Mersey and Irwell Navigation canal.   LOCKFIELD COTTAGE,
named from the locks on the Duke of Bridgewater's Canal.   MILL-
BROW, *Milhill* 1612 *Chol*, cf. Windmill St. and *molendinum de Haltona*
c.1134 (17) Orm[2], (*-quod est iuxta ecclesiam de Runcoua*) 1190–1211
Cott. Nero C III, 'mill hill', v. myln, hyll, brū.   MOUGHLAND
LANE, *the Mothland, Moughland, Mouth Lount* 1681, 1702, 1729 *Chol*,
Mow Land 1843 *TA*, 'land or selion at a mound', v. mūga, land.
No MAN'S LAND, a piece of land isolated by the Manchester Ship
Canal, v. nān-mann, land.   PENKETH'S LANE, from the surname
from Penketh La 106.   PEWITHALL, 1842 OS, from the bird-
name pewit.   PICKOW FM, cf. *Pickow* 1843 *TA*, v. pichel.   POOL
LANE, BIG POOL, cf. *þe Poole bridge in Runcorne* 1650 *ParlSurv*, v.
pōl[1], brycg, cf. Pool Dale 169 *supra*.   RUNCORN GAP, 1842 OS,
the narrow strait of the Mersey estuary between Runcorn and Widnes
La, v. gap.   RUNCORN SANDS, a bank in R. Mersey, v. sand.
SEA LANE, leading down to the Mersey estuary, v. sǣ.   WELL HO.

FIELD-NAMES

The undated forms are 1843 *TA* 344. Of the others, 1134 (17), 1178–90,
1350–61 (17) are Orm[2], c.1250 *LRO* Dx, 1290 (17) Tab, 1295 Lacy, 1322
Whall, 1353, 1370, 1380, 1386, 1398, 1423, 1443, 1452, 1487, 1507, 1514
MinAcct, 1420 Plea, 1668 Sheaf, 1831 Bry, 1842 OS, and the rest *Chol*.

   (a) Ackers (*The Acres, Acres Hey Meadow* 1672, v. æcer); Backside; Bank
Fd; Bann Croft 1773 (1741, 'bean croft', v. bēan); Barn Flat 1798 (*Barn(e)
Flat(t)* 1672, 1729); Big Harrows Stile (v. stigel); Black Riding (v. ryding);
Bow Croft 1752 (1690); Bradow Fd 1729 (1681); Brook Fd (1794); Broom
Fd (cf. (*the) Broom(e) Croft* 1672, 1754, v. brōm); Long & Short Butts;
Carr (v. kjarr); Churchway Butt 1773 (1741, '(selion at) the way to the
church', v. cirice, weg, butte); Cow Hay; The Dale (v. dæl[1]); Delf (v.

(ge)delf); Dobhill 1729 (*Dobb Hill* 1681, probably 'clay hill (a place where daub was got)', *v.* daube, hyll); Dodfelount 1773 (*Dadofelount* 1672, *Dadefe-* 1729, *Dadfe-* 1741, probably contains land 'a selion'); The Hill Acres 1741 (1672); Hough (*the-* 1640, *Higher Hough* 1757, *v.* hōh); Hursts Croft (cf. *Higher Hurst* 1684, 1702, *v.* hyrst); the Kirkfield, the Kirke Hadland 1754 (1672, 'the church field and head-land', *v.* kirkja, feld, hēafod-land); the lader at Runkorne 1700 (probably a flight of steps, *v.* hlǣd(d)er 'a ladder', cf. Ladder 172 *supra*); Long Ridding; Lords Heath 1798; Lowfield 1754 (*Feild* 1672); Marl Fd (cf. *the Marled Yords* 1724, *v.* marlede, geard); New Hey (1627, *The-* 1702); Nuncroft 1754 (*Nancroft* 1672, cf. *Nungreeue* 172 *supra*, *v.* croft); Oldershaw ('alder wood', *v.* alor, sceaga); Parkers britch ('the park-keeper's breach' from ME *parkere* 'a park-keeper' (perhaps here a surname) and brēc 'a breaking, land broken in for cultivation'); Piggs-hadland 1729 (1702, 'pig's headland', *v.* pigga, hēafod-land); Poop Ridding; Po(p)y Butts 1729 (1681); Rales (*v.* rail(e)); Rough Riding (*v.* ryding); Shawcroft 1729 (1681, 'croft at a wood', *v.* sceaga); Smith(y) Fd; Snayle Hadland 1754 (1672, 'head-land infested with snails', *v.* snægl, hēafod-land); Spout Fd (*v.* spoute); Sprinch, Sprint (*the Sprinch* 1640, *the Sprink* 1729, 'young copse', *v.* spring); the Town Fd 1754 (*the Townefeild* 1640); Triangle; Vetch Croft; Waterfall; West Fd (1729, *-Feild* 1672, *v.* west); Wills Lane 1831; Wood Dale (*v.* dæl[1]); Woodwards-, Woodworths Hill (*Woodwards Hill* 1681, cf. *Wothershall* 1672, 1741 *-hill* 1672, 1729, *-feild* 1702, 1729 which seem to be the same piece of ground, probably 'the wood-keeper's or forester's hill', from ME *wodeward* (perhaps as a surname) and hyll); Lower Yard 1752 (*-Yord* 1690, *v.* geard).

(*b*) Annotryding 1353, *Annot(t)esryd(d)yng(e)* 1487, 1507 ('Annot's clearing', from the ME fem. pers.n. *Annot*, diminutive of *Anna*, and ryding); le Breck 1353 ('the slope', *v.* brekka, cf. foll.); le3 Brenk' 1487 ('the bank-edges', *v.* brink, cf. prec.); Frespoole 1350–61 (17), *Freschpole* 1380, *Frisshe-* 1398, *Fresshepole* 1423 *et freq* ib to 1514, *Fisshepole* 1487 (the name of a pool in R. Mersey at Runcorn, the limit between the fishery of Runcorn (*piscaria de Runcouer* 1295, which extended downstream as far as Liverpool La) and the free water upstream, 'the freshwater pool', *v.* fersc, pōl[1]); le Heye 1353 (*v.* (ge)hæg); la hoc 1178–90 (*v.* hōc); le3 lake3 1487 ('the watercourses', *v.* lacu); le milnepit 1398 ('the pit at the mill', *v.* myln, pytt); le Moremersch 1322 (14), *Moremosse* 1353, *Runcorne Moss* 1640 (*v.* mōr[1], mersc, mos); *campus vocatus le porte* 1487, (*-iuxta fordam*) 1514 ('the market-place (near a ford)'; *v.* port[2], ford); Walshemansiche (a parcel of land) 1386, *Walsmanheth* 1423, *Wals(s)hmanheth(e)* 1443, 1452, 1487, *Walshemansheth* 1507, 1514 ('Welshman's heath', *v.* Wels(c)h-man, hǣð, cf. Welshman's Common 149 *supra*. The earliest form may contain sīc 'a watercourse', or hiche 'an enclosure of hurdles').

8. STOCKHAM (109–5480) ['stɔkʌm]

Stoccum 112 Facs 11, 1288 Court, *Stockum* 1288 ib (p), H8 *Rental*, *Stochum* 1289 Court (p)

Stokcum 1289 Court (p), *-com(e)* 1535 VE, 1536 Dugd, 1538
   AOMB 399, *-combe* c.1547 *Surv*, *Stokecombe* 1553 Pat, *Stocome
   alias Stockecombe* 1568 Orm²

Stockham 1594 AD *et freq*, (*-alias Stockcombe*) 1634 Orm², (*Norton
   cum-*) 1724 NotCestr, (*Norton cum*) *Stockam* 1663 Sheaf

'At the tree-stocks', *v.* stōcc (dat.pl. stoccum). In the earliest
reference the place is an assart. The dative plural in *-um* is confused
with cumb 'a hollow, a valley' and hām 'a homestead'.

HIGHER & LOWER GREENHOUSE FM, (*The*)*Higher Green(House)* 1811
Sund.   NORTON LANE, cf. Norton 173 *supra.*   WOOD LANE.
WOODFALLS FM, *Woodfalls* 1811 *ib*, *Woodfall Tenement* 1831 Bry,
probably contains the surname *Woodfall.*

FIELD-NAMES

The undated forms are 1811 *Sund*; 1842 is OS, 1843 *TA* 368.

(a) Abbey Hey ('the abbey's enclosure', named from Norton Priory 173
supra; Great Acre; Backside; Banyards Mdw; Barn Mdw; Celler Mdw;
Eanley Mdw & Wd (*Eanly-* 1843); Goulders Nook 1843; Halls Croft;
Halton Fd (cf. Halton 166 *supra*); Hay (*freq, v.* (ge)hæg); Heath Hey; Horse
Pasture; Kings Fd; Kitchen Fd; Marl Fd; Nanns Croft (*Nans-* 1843); New
Hey; Pickow (*v.* pichel); Pinfold Fd (*v.* pynd-fald); Poor Land (*Poorland*
1843); Ridding (*Rydding* 1843, *v.* ryding); Rough Fd; Rushey Fd; Lower
Sideway (*v.* sīde, weg); Sower Mdw; Stockham Wd 1842 (cf. The Gorse 181
infra); Well Mdw; Wheat Fd; Higher Yard (*v.* geard).

9. SUTTON, formerly -IUXTA FRODSHAM, lately SUTTON WEAVER (109–
5479), *Sutton* 112 Facs, c.1271 Whall (p) *et freq*, (*-in Halton hundred*)
1348 ArlB, (*-beside Frodsham Brugge*) 1447 CoLegh, (*-iuxta Aston*)
1511 Plea, (*-negh Froddesham*) 1537 AddCh, (*-iuxta Halton*) 1539
Plea, *-tune* e13 Orm², *Sotton* e13 ArlB (p), 'south farm', *v.* sūð, tūn.
Sutton is on the north bank of R. Weaver opposite Frodsham 326
infra, and on the south side of the peninsula between Weaver and
Mersey. The place is south of Norton 173 *supra*, south-east of Weston
182 *infra*, north-west of Aston 160 *supra*. These four places are
named from their position relative to each other, to Halton 166 *supra*,
or to the peninsula. *Sutton Weaver* (perhaps a contracted form of
Sutton on Weaver), is the name of the old L. & N.W. Railway station
in this township and appears to be the official name of the township
in the 1953 Index and on county council road-signs.

MURDISHAW WOOD [mə:diʃə], 1842 OS, *Murder Shaw* 1746 *Chol*, *Mottershaw Wood* 1831 Bry, *Mattershaw Wood* 1843 *TA*, probably 'spokesman's wood', v. mōtere, sceaga, the first el. confused with *murder* 'murder' or exchanged for it after some unrecorded killing. The wood was at the boundaries of Aston, Norton, Preston, Stockham and Sutton, a position suitable for local assemblies. The place may be the origin of the surname *Modershale, Modreshale* 1333, 1339 ChRR, in which case the second el. is halh (dat.sg. hale) 'a nook, a corner', confused with sceaga through a ME form *(-s)haugh* from the nom.sg.

ROSAM GRAVE (lost), 1843 *TA*, *Rosumgrese iuxta Stretemore in territorio de Sutton* 1400 *AddCh* 51136, perhaps the origin of the Ch surname *de Rosinenegreue* 1318 *Chol*, *Rosmegreue* (lit. *-grene*) 1330 Plea *et freq* to 1357 BPR, *Rosemgreue* (lit. *-grene*) 1344, 1354 ChRR, *Rosumgreue* 1350 *Eyre*, (lit. *-grene*) 1358 ChRR *et freq* to 1414 ib, *-greve* 1415 ib, *Rosomgreue* 1357 *Eyre*, *Rosungreue* (lit. *-grene*) 1392 Pat. The second el. is grǣfe 'a wood, a thicket, a grove'. The first is uncertain. It might be an older p.n. containing ros, 'a moor, a heath'. However, Professor Löfvenberg states 'In my opinion there can hardly be any doubt that the first el. is OE hramsa, hromsa 'wild garlic', with metathesis and development of a svarabhakti vowel in ME: *hromsa- > rosm(e)- > rosem-* or *rosum-* (cf. Jordan §147 Anm. 1). The same development has obviously taken place in the dial. form *rosems* 'wild garlic' in Yorkshire and Staffordshire (v. EDD s.v. *rosems*).' Cf. *Stretemore infra*.

BEECH WOOD, 1842 OS, *-Cover* 1831 Bry.   CHESTER LANE (lost), v. 162 *supra*.   CLOUGH WOOD, 1843 *TA*, *Rough Clough* 1831 Bry, v. rūh, clōh.   THE GORSE, *Stockham Wood* 1842 OS, v. gorst, cf. Stockham 179 *supra*.   HIGHER HO.   LOWE'S WOOD.   MARSH-GATE FM, cf. *Marsh Gate Lane* 1843 *TA*, 'pasture allotment at a marsh', v. mersc, gata.   PARK FM, cf. *Sutton Parke* 1621 (1650) Sheaf, v. park.   SPRINGFIELD.   SUTTON BRIDGE, 1831 Bry. SUTTON CAUSEWAY, v. caucie.   SUTTON FIELDS FM, *The Fields Farm* 1831 Bry, v. feld.   SUTTON HALL, 1831 ib.   SUTTON LOCKS, cf. *Lock House* 1831 ib, named from canal locks.   SUTTON MILLS, cf. *Mill Field Plantation, Millers Hays* 1843 *TA*.   WOOD-SIDE, 1831 Bry.

FIELD-NAMES

The undated forms are 1843 *TA* 378. Of the others, 112 is Facs, ?13 Orm² (1 729), 1249–60 Orm², E2, 1400 *AddCh*, 1424 ChRR, 1430, 1511 AD, 1712 *Chol*, 1743 Sheaf, 1831 Bry, 1842 OS.

(a) Adder Fd & Shoe (*v.* scēo 'a shelter'); The Bank; Bark Mill Brow; The Beach (*v.* bece¹); Bean Butts; Birkill field 1743 ('birch hill field', *v.* birki, hyll); Blake Flat (*Blak(e) Flat(t)* 1712, *v.* blæc, flat); The Bog; Briery Hay (*Breerey Hey* 1712); Buck Croft; Calf Park (*v.* park); Chapel Lane 1831 (109–558783, *Sutton Lane* 1743, cf. 162 *supra*); Cooks Hays; Crab Mill Ho 1842 (*v.* crab-mill); Crow's Nest (*v.* nest); Crumper Land; Deep Lake (*deeplake* E2, *Depe-* 1400, 'deep watercourse', *v.* dēop, lacu); Duck Lake ('duck stream', *v.* dūce, lacu, cf. *Henedelake infra*); the Farley(e)s 1712 (*v.* feor, lēah); Foredrift; Frame Hay; Frogland Brow (*v.* brū); Halton Lane (cf. Halton 166 *supra*); Hays Leys; Hen Ridding (*v.* henn, ryding); Holding Brook (*v.* 1 29); Intake (*v.* inntak); Kell's Acre (*Kell(e)s Acres* 1712); Lady Acre (*v.* hlǣfdige); Lee Brook Croft; Lower Loons (*v.* land); Low Nook; Mare Clough (cf. Mare Clough 161 *supra*); Old Marl Fd; Meeting House Mdw; Moor; Orleys; Outlet (*v.* outlet); Ox Hays; Paddocks Moor (from mōr¹ 'a moor, a marsh', with either paddock, pearroc 'an enclosure', or padduc 'a frog'); Ridding Lane (*v.* ryding); Rocksavage Wd (named from Rock Savage 165 *supra*); Rodge Bushel; Rye Croft; Schooleys; Sinny Pool (*v.* pōl¹, cf. Sinepool 327 *infra*); Slack (*v.* slakki); Spark(s) (*v.* spearca); Stamperley; Stones (*v.* stān); Sutton Gate (2x) 1831 (*v.* geat 'a gate', probably turnpikes); Tan House Fd (*v.* tan-hous); Town Mdw (*v.* toun); The Wayside (*v.* weg, sīde); Wingery Fd.

(b) the tend Bearne of Bold 1511 ('Bold's tithe barn', from the surname of John *Bold* 1511, cf. *Bold(e)* 1424 (p), 1430 (p), and teōnde, bere-ærn); *Fernclogh* ?13 ('fern dell', *v.* fearn, clōh); *the iiii acre* 1511 (*v.* fēower, æcer); *Gayel More* 1249–60 ('marsh where bog-myrtle grows', *v.* gagel, mōr¹); *le hethfeld* 1400 (cf. *brueria eiusdam Sutton* 112, 'field at a heath', *v.* hǣð, feld); *Henedelake* 112 ('duck stream', *v.* ened, lacu, cf. Duck Lake *supra*); *Stretemore* 1400 ('moor at a paved road', *v.* strǣt, mōr¹, cf. Street Moors 171 *supra*, *Rosam Grave supra*).

10. WESTON (109–5080), *Westone* 1086 DB, *-tona* 1154–60 (1329) Ch, 1170 Facs, *-ton* 1260 Court *et passim*, (*-iuxta Haghton*) 1287 Court, (*-Frodesam*) 1324 *Dow*, (*-Runkore*) 1353 BPR, *Westan* 1287 Court (p), *Windy Weston* 1678, 1709 Sheaf, 'west farm', *v.* west, tūn. Cf. Sutton 180 *supra*, and Halton, Runcorn 166, 176 *supra*, Frodsham 326 *infra*. The place was called Windy Weston from its exposed position at Weston Point overlooking the Mersey Estuary, *v.* windig.

BANKES' LANE. CAVENDISH FM. CHESHYRE'S LANE. GORS(E)Y ACRE(S), 1846 *TA*, cf. *Gorstiacra* 1156–60 (1329) Ch, 1190–1211

Cott. Nero c iii, 'the gorsey ploughland', *v.* gorstig, æcer. HEATH
RD, leading to Runcorn Heath 177 *supra*, cf. *Heath Croft & Field*
1846 *TA*. QUARRYBANK, *Weston Hill* 1842 OS, cf. Weston
Quarries *infra*, *v.* quarriere, banke, hyll. WESTON HO. WESTON
MARSH, 1846 *TA*, *v.* mersc. WESTON POINT, 1831 Bry, the pro-
montory between the R. Mersey and the R. Weaver, *v.* point.
WESTON QUARRIES, *Weston Quarry* 1842 OS, cf. Quarry Bank *supra*.

FIELD-NAMES

The undated forms are 1846 *TA* 420. Of the rest, 1384 is *AddRoll* 51504,
1419, 1433, 1443 ChRR, 1477 *MinAcct*.

(*a*) Acres; Balk(s) (*v.* balca); Banks alias Bongs (*v.* banke); Briery Loons
(*v.* land); Britch (*v.* brēc); Cockshute (*v.* cocc-scyte); Cow Hey; Crimboe
(*v.* crymel); Crowland Hey (*v.* crāwe, land); Farthing (*v.* fēorðung); Gratt-
ledge; Guilt Flatts (*v.* flat); Hen Croft; Holms Mdw (*v.* holmr); Lamb
Sickle, Lamsittle (final el. perhaps sīcel 'a small stream'); Lee Head &
Wood (Hey), Leewood (*v.* lēah, hēafod); Longreaves ('long woods', *v.* lang,
grǣfe); Mantle; Mare Gates ('pasturage for mares', *v.* mere^2, gata); Mickley
('big wood', *v.* micel, lēah); Mill Field Hey; Moors; The Nabs (a marsh,
occasionally flooded by the tide, probably from nabbi in the sense 'projecting hummocks'); Big & Little Ridding (*v.* ryding); Salt Mdw (*v.* salt);
Stanley Hay; Stubbs (*v.* stubb); Summerland Hey ('(enclosure at) the
summer-land', *v.* sumor, land, (ge)hæg); Town Fd; Weston Hey; Wills
Lane (*v.* 179 *supra*).

(*b*) *Brerewood* 1419 (p) (*v.* brēr, wudu); *Caldewalle, Caldewalle oke* 1384
('(oak at) the cold spring', *v.* cald, wælla, āc); *le Netherhalleorcharde* 1384
('the lower orchard belonging to the hall', *v.* neoðera, hall, orceard); *le
Warthes* 1477 (*v.* waroð).

III. NORTHWICH HUNDRED

Mildestuic(h) Hundred' 1086 DB, *hundred' de Nor(t)wic, Nor(t)wic Hundred'* 1260 Court *et freq passim* with spellings as for Northwich 192 *infra, v.* hundred. The original hundred was dependent upon Middlewich 240 *infra,* where the justices in Eyre continued to hold court even after the transfer of the hundred to Northwich. The circumstance of the change is not recorded—it was probably part of the general re-organization noticed under Bucklow Hundred 1 *supra.* In the process, the old Hundred lost the township of Weaver 232, 327 *infra* to Eddisbury Hundred 326 *infra,* Church Minshull, Betchton, Alsager and Hassall 325, 325, 325, 326 *infra* to Nantwich Hundred 326 *infra,* and gained Cranage, Twemlow, Kermincham and Swettenham 223, 230, 281, 283 *infra* from *Hamestan* (Macclesfield) Hundred 1 51, and Nether Peover 220 *infra* from *Bochelau* (Bucklow) Hundred 1 *supra.* Northwich Hundred is bounded to the south-east by St and the millstone-grit edges of Mow Cop, The Cloud and Congleton Edge, to the east by Macclesfield Hundred and the R. Dane, to the north by Peover Eye and Bucklow Hundred, to the west by R. Weaver and Eddisbury Hundred, and to the south by Nantwich Hundred and R. Wheelock. It contains a plain of boulder clay and glacial sands and gravels sloping evenly down from the foot of the millstone-grit scarp north-westwards to the Weaver valley, and drained by the Rivers Dane and Wheelock. The south-eastern half of the hundred lies between these rivers, the north-western half extends beyond them to the R. Weaver and Peover Eye and includes the secondary drainage area of Wade Brook 1 37, one of heathland represented by the waste of Rudheath 1 11.

i. Witton Chapelry

The parochial chapelry of Witton, a member of Great Budworth parish 95 *supra,* contained the townships of Castle Northwich, Winnington, and part of Hartford in Eddisbury Hundred, *v.* 327 *infra,* and in Northwich Hundred the townships 1. Birches (*v.* Lach Dennis *infra*), 2. Hulse (now Hulse Heath, *v.* Lach Dennis *infra*), 3. Lach Dennis (now a c.p. including Stublach 255 *infra* from Middlewich parish, Newall 208 *infra* from Davenham parish, Birches and Hulse *supra,* and Earnshaw and Kings Lane Fm from Rudheath

Lordship 198 *infra*), 4. Lostock Gralam (part now included in Northwich c.p.), 5. Northwich (now a c.p. including Castle Northwich and Winnington *supra*, Witton cum Twambrook *infra*, part of Leftwich 205 *infra* from Davenham parish, and Wallerscote 327 *infra* from Weaverham parish), 6. Witton cum Twambrook (*v.* Northwich *supra*). Part of Rudheath Lordship was tithed within this parish, *v.* 198 *infra*.

1. BIRCHES (HALL) (110–701725), (*le*) *Birches* 1265–1291 Chest (p), *et freq* with variant spellings *Byrchys, -es, -is, Burches*; (*-iuxta Shibbrok*) 1308 Orm[2], (*-super Rodeheyth iuxta Lostock Gralam*) 1314 AddCh, (*-juxta Schidbrok et Lostock Gralam*) 1321 *ib*, *Birches Hall* 1690 Sheaf, 'the birch-trees', *v.* birce, cf. Shipbrook, Lostock Gralam 208, 189 *infra*, Rudheath 1 11.

HANGMAN'S LANE, 1842 OS, the boundary of Birches, Hulse and Lostock Gralam, cf. *Hangsmans Field* 1844 *TA*, perhaps named after an executioner or a gibbeting, cf. 239, 246 *infra*, *v.* hangeman.

FIELD-NAMES

The undated forms are 1844 *TA* 51.

(*a*) Blake Flatt (*v.* blæc, flat); High Knoll; Loons (*v.* land); Outlett (*v.* outlet); Red Fd; Rundle Fd (*v.* rynel); Stump Fd (*v.* stump).

(*b*) *le Grenefeld* 1284, 1313 *Chol* (*v.* grēne[1], feld); *le Quykedyche* c.1380–90 ChRR (*sepes et fossatum de Birches* 1284 *Chol*, the boundary between Birches and Hulse 186 *infra*, 'the quick-set ditch', *v.* cwic, dīc, cf. ModEdial. *quick-dyke* EDD).

2. HULSE (FM, HEATH & HO) (110–700720, 710720)

The township is now Hulse Heath, a hamlet in Lach Dennis c.p.

> (*le*) *Holes* c.1270 *Chol*, Chest *et freq* to 1480 ChRR (p), (*-super Ruddeheth, -iuxta Lostok*) 1330 Pat, *Holesheth* 1353 BPR, *le Hols* 1433 ChRR (p)
> (*le*) *Huls* 1350 ChRR (p), *et freq* to 1535 VE, *le Hules* 1359 ChRR (p), *Hulles in Lostokgrauenham* E3 Surv, *Hulse* 14 ChRR, 1465 ArlB *et freq*, (*the Hall of-*) 1614 ChRR, *Hulsse* c.1539 Dugd *Houlesheth* 1353 BPR, *Househeath* 1650 *LRMB* 278

'The hollows', from holh 'a hollow, a hole', with hǣð. The name is ME nom.pl. *holis, -es* (OE *hōlu* with the ME pl. *-es*, cf. DEPN). Cf. Rudheath 1 11, Lostock Gralam 189 *infra*.

COMMON LANE, *Hulse Lane* 1842 OS, *v.* commun, lane, cf. Hulse Lane *infra*.   THE GREEN (lost 110–705720), 1842 OS, 1845 *TA*, *v.* grēne², a hamlet now named Lach Dennis, cf. 188 *infra*, on the boundary of the two townships.   HANGMAN'S LANE, *v.* 185 *supra*. HULSE LANE, *v.* 1 46, cf. *Le Wyteweye infra*.   PORTFORD BRIDGE, *v.* 218 *infra*.   SNIG HALL, cf. ModEdial. *snig* 'an eel'.

FIELD-NAMES

The undated forms are 1845 *TA* 212. Of the others, c.1300 is JRL, E2, E3 Orm², 1380–90 ChRR, and the rest Chest.

(*a*) Acres; Apron; Blake Flatt (*v.* blæc); Butty Piece ('piece of land in butts', *v.* butty); Day Math (*v.* day-math); Fitch Fd (*v.* ficche); Kidd Butts ('calf headlands', from ModEdial. *kid* 'a young calf'); Mad Hadlent (cf. *le Hallond* c.1300, *v.* hēafod-land); Mickley (probably 'big enclosure', *v.* micel, (ge)hæg); Ovel Croft (*v.* hovel); Pingott (*v.* pingot); Silver Loons (*v.* land); Stubbs Common (perhaps 'tree-stumps', *v.* stubb, but cf. Stubb's Fm 255 *infra*); Town Fd; Two Withens, Withens Croft (*v.* wīðegn 'a willow (copse)').

(*b*) *Bacforlong* 1269–91 ('back furlong' or 'furlong on a ridge', *v.* bæc, furlang); *le Hallom* E2 (probably 'at the nooks', *v.* halh (dat.pl. halum), but cf. Hallamhall 154 *supra*); *Le Leueth* 1269–91 (perhaps 'the head of the clearing', *v.* lēah, hēafod, but Professor Löfvenberg suggests reading *Leneth*, from hlēonoð 'a shelter', as in Lent Bk 233); (*Le*) *Lomylathe* E3, 1380–90 (probably for *-lache*, 'boggy stream in clayey or loamy ground', *v.* lāmig, læc(c), like *lamilache* 232 *infra*); *Pilotescroft* 1269–91 ('croft where pill-oats are grown', from pil-āte (with a ME nom.pl. in -*es*) and croft); *Platforde* E3, 1380–90 ('ford with a bridge', *v.* plat¹, ford, cf. Portford Bridge *supra*); *le Quykedyche* (*v.* 185 *supra*); *Sulinesfeld* 1267–70, *Sulinfeld* 1269–91 (*v.* feld. For the first el. Professor Löfvenberg suggests an OE *sylen (from sol, -en²) 'muddy, dirty', which would also explain *Solmegrenes* 215 *infra*, *Sullunhull* 323 *infra*. This is attractive, but does not explain the genitival *Sulines-* unless this represents a substantival use of the adj.); *Le Wyteweye* 1265–91, 1291–1316 ('white way', *v.* hwīt, weg; perhaps Hulse Lane *supra*).

3. LACH DENNIS (100–705719) [latʃ]

  Lece 1086 DB (ff. 266, 267b)
  Lache 1190–1220 Chest (p), 1259 Plea *et freq* with variant spellings *Lach* (from 1287 AD), *Lace*; (-*apud*-, -*iuxta*-, -*super*-, -*in Rudhethe*) 1277 Dugd, Orm², (14) VR, 1301–7 ChFor, 1312 Ch
  Lache Deneys 1260 Court, c.1294 ChFor, -*deyneis* (lit. *deyeis*) c.1294 ChFor, -*deyneys* E3 Surv, -*nys* 1332 Chol, -*nes* 1534 Plea, -*deins*

1579 ChRR, -*Dennis* 1312 AD, -*ys* 1595 *Chol*, -*denys* 1332 *ib et freq* to 1619 ChRR, (-*super Roddehed'*) 1332 *Chol*, -*Denis* 1570 ChRR, -*denes* 1598 *Chol*

Lache Maubanc c.1270 Chest *et freq* with variant spellings -*ban(k)*, -*Malbanc*, -*banke*, -*Mabaunk* to *Lachemaubank super Rudeheth* 1362 Plea

Lache Merton E3 *Surv*

'The boggy stream', *v.* lece, læc(c), cf. *The Green*, Great Booth Fd *infra*. There are problems concerning the identification of the DB names with this place (*v.* Tait 175, 215, notes 159, 237), and the occasion for the two suffixes -*Dennis* and -*Maubanc*. The suffix -*Merton* is derived from the family of Randle de *Merton* (Marton 326 *infra*) who had land here of Vale Royal abbey c.1301 (Orm² III 168, II 179), still held by David and Stephen de *Merton* E3 *Surv*, 1356 BPR. *Maubanc* can only be the name of the *Malbank* family, barons of Nantwich, but there is no record except the p.n. of their connection with Lach Dennis (*v.* Orm² III 168, cf. Nantwich 326 *infra*). *Dennis* has also been supposed a surname, *v.* Orm² III 168. The surname *Deneys* occurs in Ch sources (1288, 1289 Court, 1309 ChRR, 1354 BPR), but, as with *Maubanc*, there is no proven connection with this place, and no family of the name held in fee in the county. This problem is bound up with that of the identification. The DB entries are tentatively identified with Lach Dennis by Tait, but on formal grounds he rightly rejects identification of either with Leese 229 *infra*. *Lece* DB f.266 was held 1086 by William fitz Nigel, but Lach Dennis does not appear in the records of the Halton barony (nor does Leese) and this is an obstacle to the identification with Lach Dennis. However, Norton Priory had a manorial interest in Lach Dennis (*Lache* 1535 VE 209), which may represent an unrecorded grant out of the fitz Nigel barony. *Lece* DB f.267b was held TRE by one *Colben* (ON *Kolbeinn*, ODan *Kolben*). If he were a Dane, or of Danish stock, his part of the vill could have been distinguished from the fitz Nigel part by the adj. 'Danish' (OE *Denisc*, ME *denshe*, *danais* (OFr *daneis*), but *denez* in *Sir Gawain* 2223) and the forms -*Deneys*, -*deyneis*, -*deynys*, -*deynes*, -*deyneys* from this adj. could be confused with the common ME pers.n. *Denis*, *Dennis* (Lat. *Dionysius*). This would do away with any need to identify this *Lece* with Stublach 255 *infra* (Tait 215), it would explain a mysterious manorial suffix, and would distinguish between two manorial interests, -*Dennis* (*Lece* DB f.267b) and -*Maubanc* (*Lece* DB f.266). Tait 175, introduces the unhistorical form *Lach St Dennis*, cf. Mottram St Andrew 1 202.

EARNSHAW HALL (110–727702)

Formerly a detached part of Rudheath Lordship 198 *infra*, and in Sandbach parish.

> *Erdscagh* 1349 Tab, -*shaw* 1457 Orm[2], 1758 Sheaf, -*schawe* 1475 MidCh, *Erdeshawe* 1532 Plea, *Eard-* 1677 *LRMB* 211, -*shaw* 1736 Sheaf, (*Hall*) 1819 Orm[1]
> *Ernshaghe* 1353 *MinAcct*, *Earnshaw Hall* 1831 Bry
> *Erdestlegh* 1494 MidCh
> *Herdescha* 1529 MidCh
> *Yerdshagh* 1532 Plea, -*sha'* 1539 Orm[2], *Yerde-* 1540 MidCh, -*shawe* 17 ib, *Yeardshaw(e)* 1615 *ChCert*, 1624 Earw, *Yardshaw* 1740 Cre
> *Earnslow Grange* 1845 ChetOS VIII
> *Heronshaw Hall in Rudheath . . . commonly called Yarnshaw Hall* 1880 Sheaf

Perhaps 'herdsman's wood', from hirde and sc(e)aga, but a pers.n. is possible and likely, such as OE *Ēarēd*, *Ēanrēd* or *Ēorēd*, cf. NoB XXXIII 79 n.27, SNPh XL 8, *v.* Yeardsley 1 176. The forms show popular confusion with earn 'an eagle', and he(i)roun (ModEdial. *yarn, earn*) 'a heron'. Cf. Eardswick 247 *infra*.

CROWDER'S LANE, *v.* 199 *infra*.   THE GREEN (lost), 1842 OS, *Lachgreene* 1609 *Rental*, *Leach Greene* 1650 *LRMB* 278, *Lachegreene alias Lache domus* c.1662 *Surv*, *Lach Green* 1690 Sheaf, *v.* grēne[2] 'a green', cf. Lach Dennis *supra*, Newhall, Oldhall *infra*. This hamlet lies on the boundary with Hulse, *v.* 186 *supra*.   KING'S LANE (FM), *King's Lane* 1650 *LRMB* 278, 1831 Bry, *v.* cyning, lane. Rudheath Lordship was a royal demesne. The farm (110–726705) was in the same detached part of Rudheath Lordship as Earnshaw *supra*. It is now in Allostock township 216 *infra*, but was in Lach Dennis 1911 6″ OS. The lane runs 110–727706 to 740699 into Cranage, cf. 218, 224 *infra*.   NEWHALL FM, 1831 Bry, OLDHALL FM, cf. *Lachegreene alias Lache domus* under *The Green supra*, in which *domus* may be Lat sg. or pl., 'houses', both farms being at *The Green*.

FIELD-NAMES

The undated forms are 1845 *TA* 299. Of the others, 1288 is Chest, c.1380–90 ChRR, 1529 Plea, 1560 Sheaf, 1841 *TA* 154 (Earnshaw Hall Fm), and the rest *Chol*.

(a) Great Booth Fd (*Lachebothe, le Bothe* c.1300, *Le Lachebothe, Lachebothdych* c.1380–90, *the Laches otherwise Boowefyeldes* 1595, *The Laches* 1654, 'the herdsmen's huts at the Laches', *v.* bōth, feld, læc(c), cf. Lach Dennis *supra*); Long Butts 1841; Carthouse Fd 1841; Cloaths Hedge Croft (a hedge on which clothes are dried); Foxley Field ('fox clearing', *v.* fox, lēah); Griffith Green 1841; Hall Green 1841; Hocknells 1841; Holfords Croft (so named from the family of Holford 91 *supra*, cf. *le Sixpeniwurthe infra*); Horse Pasture 1841; Intake (*v.* inntak); Knoll; Great & Little Manor 1841; Marl Fd (*v.* marle); Muck Fd; Oak Croft 1841; Orchard Bank 1841 (*v.* orceard, banke); Outlet (*v.* outlet); Rough 1841; Rushey Plat (*v.* plat[2]); Sweet Fd 1841; Swine Lane 1841 (*v.* swīn[1]); Well Fd & Mdw 1841; White Fd; Windmill Fd 1841; Winter Pasture (*v.* winter[1]).

(b) *Ammerlache* 1288 (from the bird-name amore, perhaps 'bunting' or 'yellow hammer', and læc(c) 'a boggy stream'); *Lacheparke near Rudheth* 1529 (*v.* park 'a park'); *le Meresiche, -syche* c.1300 ('the boundary stream', *v.* (ge)mǣre, sīc); *Shacrofte* 1560 ('croft at a wood', *v.* sc(e)aga, croft); *le Sixpeniwurthe of lande* 1548 (a plot of land probably rented, purchased or valued at sixpence, belonging to the Holford family, cf. Holfords Croft *supra*, *v.* sex, peni(n)g-weorð).

4. LOSTOCK GRALAM ['lɔstɔk 'greiləm] (110–690748)

Lostoch(e) 1096–1101 (1280), 1150 Chest, c.1230 *JRC*, e14 *AddCh* (p), *Lostock(e)* 1154–89 Tab, 1257 (17) Chest (p), 1288 Court (p) *et freq* with variant spellings *-stoc, -stok* (l12 *Dow* to 1353 BPR); (*-super Rudhethe*) 1316 Orm[2], *Lostoke* 1277 Dugd (p) *et freq* to 1532 AD, *Losstoc* 1280 *AddCh* (p), *Losthoke* 1281 Tab (p)

Lastoc c.1200 Facs (p), 1202–10 Sheaf, *-stock(e)* 1690, 1775 ib

Lodestock e13 Dieul (p)

Loustoc e13 Tab, *Louestok* 1355 BPR (p)

Lachestoke 1277 VR (p)

Lustok 1287 Court

(*le*) *Lostoke Graliam* 1288 Court *et freq* with variants *ut supra*, and *-Gralan, -Gral(y)am, -Garlam, -Gralum, -Grulam; Gralam Lostock'* 1323 *Chol*

Lostok Grau(en)ham E3 *Surv*, 1334 *JRC*

Lostock Granam 1673 Sheaf

Nether Lostock 1386 Orm[2], *Nethir-, Neither Lostock Gralam* 1505, 1548 Tab

Loston' 1514 *MinAcct*

'Pig-sty hamlet', *v.* hlōse, stoc, and neoðera 'lower'. The p.n. may allude to the pasturage of swine in the waste of Rudheath. Lostock is supposed to be the name of a manor divided c.1070–1101. This moiety was granted to Hugh de Runchamp (Lat. *de Rotundo Campo*), whose grandson *Gralam, Graland* held the manor from 1194 (Facs 8 (2), Orm² III 163, Morris 139). The other moiety is Allostock 216 *infra*, to which some of the unmodified forms apply.

BANCROFT (lost), *Banecroft* c.1294 *ChFor et freq* to 1357 *Eyre* (p), *Bancroft(e)* 1357 *Eyre* (p), 1397 Plea *et freq*, (the manor of-) 1494 ChRR, (a messuage called-) 1561 ib, (-*in Lostok*) 1417 ib, Plea, cf. *Bancroft Moss* 1845 *TA*, 'bean croft', *v.* bēan, bēanen, croft.

LANGFORD FM (110–705740), *Longford* c.1260 Tab, 1362 ChRR (p), 1427 Plea (p), 'the long ford', *v.* lang, ford, presumably the crossing of Crow Brook at 110–705733.

LOSTOCK GREEN, 1842 OS, *Parva Lostock* E2 Orm², -*lostok* 1514 *MinAcct*, *Lostock* 1531 AD, 1775 Sheaf, -*stoke* 1534 AD, *Robin Hood Green* 1831 Bry, 'little Lostock', *v.* lȳtel, grēne², cf. Lostock Gralam *supra*, Robin Hood Fm *infra*.

BEAUTYBANK, *v.* botye, banke.   BIRCHES LANE, *v.* Birches 185 *supra*.   CAPE OF GOOD HOPE FM, 1842 OS, *v.* 325 *infra*.   CASTLE-CROFT.   COMMON MOSS (lost), 1831 Bry, *v. Sandlow Moss* 91 *supra*.   COOKE'S LANE, *Cooks Lane* 1831 ib.   CROWBROOK BRIDGE, 1831 ib, *Croebridge* 1619 Sheaf, *v.* Crow Brook 1 20.   FIELDHOUSE FM, 1842 OS, *Holfords of the Field* 1663 Mere, cf. *Holford Field* 1845 *TA*, from feld with the surname from Holford 91 *supra*.   GRALAM FM, commemorating *Gralam* de Lostock, *supra*.   GRIFFITHS RD.   HAME FM, commemorating *Hame*, the reputed eleventh-century lord of Lostock, cf. Orm² III 163.   HANG-MAN'S LANE, cf. *Hangman's Croft & Field* 1845 *TA*, *v.* 185 *supra*.   HEATH FM (110–694723), a detached part of this township near Birches 185 *supra*.   HIGHBANK HO.   HOLFORD MOSS, *v.* 91 *supra*.   LIMEKILN FM, *Bonners Green* 1831 Bry, cf. *Banners Field* 1845 *TA*.   LOSTOCK GRALAM BRIDGE (110–691742), LOSTOCK HOLLOW, *Lostock Hollow (Bridge)* 1831 Bry, *v.* holh 'a hollow'. This might be the site of *Loweforth infra*.   LOSTOCK LODGE (lost), 1831 ib, 1842 OS.   MANCHESTER RD, *regia strata* 1310–30 *Chol*, cf. 'Watling Street' 1 40.   MOSS LANE (FM), *Mosse Lane* (lit. *Mope*) 1622 Sheaf³ 10, 18, *Moss Lane* 1741 Sheaf, (*Farm*) 1831 Bry, cf. *Moss (Field)* 1845 *TA*, *Mossefield* c.1240 (17) Sheaf, -*feld* 1494

ChRR, *v.* mos, lane, feld. OVER STREET (lost, 110–681743), 1842 OS, -*Farm* 1831 Bry, *Overstreet(e) (House)* 1652, 1666, 1672 Mere, (-*in Lostock Gralam*) 1679 ib, (-*near Northwich*) 1700 *Chol*, cf. *Street Field* 1845 *TA*, 'above the street', *v.* ofer[3], strǣt, named from its position overlooking 'Watling Street' 1 40 and very nearly on the presumed line of King Street 1 44 northwards from Broken Cross 199 *infra.* PARK FM. PASTURE LANE (lost, 110–695748 to 101–705752), 1831 Bry, 1842 OS, by *Pasture Wood* 1831 Bry, cf. 94 *supra.* RIDGE FM. ROBINHOOD FM, probably from an inn-sign. SPRINGBANK FM. WADEBROOK BRIDGE, 1619 Sheaf, *v.* Wade Brook 1 37. WINCHAM BRIDGE, 1619 ib, *Peover Eye Bridge* 1831 Bry, cf. Wincham 136 *supra*, Peover Eye 1 33. WINNINGTON WOOD, 1831 ib, *v.* 92 *supra.*

FIELD-NAMES

The undated forms are 1845 *TA* 243. Of the others, John is Orm[2], c.1220 (1400) CASNS XIII, c.1240 (17), 1619, 1741 Sheaf, 1321–26 *AddCh*, E3 *Surv*, 1346 VR, 1354 *Eyre*, 1385 AD, 1439, 1462, 1494, 1589 ChRR, 1663 Mere, and the rest *Chol*.

(*a*) Armyshire Hill; Higher & Lower Banks (*the banke* c.1550, cf. *the halfe bancke* 1549, *v.* banke, half); Barn Croft (cf. *barnecroftes* 13 (p), *v.* bere-ærn, croft); Blake Flatt (*v.* blæc); Blind Hole Fd; Bongs (*v.* banke); Brickley; Brirey Low ('briary mound', *v.* brērig, hlāw); Brook Hey; Burton Ley; Castles Croft; Chrimes Mdw (*v.* cryme, cf. *le Crymbe* 171 *supra*); Cockshaw Oakes ('(oaks at) the woodcock wood', *v.* cocc[2], sceaga, āc); Crib (*v.* crib); Dockey Fd (cf. *Dokkefeld* 1494, *v.* docce 'a dock'); Foxleys (*v.* fox, lēah); Goddles, Goddess; Hall Hey; Hanging Hill (*v.* hangende); Hemp Yard; Holcroft Fd (cf. *Ocrofte heathe* 1604, *Hollcroft Heath* 1741, cf. *Holcroft* 1385 (p), 1439 (p), 1462 (p), -*e* 1589, '(heath by) the croft in a hollow', *v.* hol[1], croft, hǣð); Horse Pasture (cf. *Litle Horse Closse Yate* 1604, *v.* hors, clos, geat); Intack, Intake (*v.* inntak); Knowles (*v.* cnoll); Lord's Mdw (1741 Sheaf, *v.* hlāford); Lostock Fd & Mdw (cf. *pratum de Lostok* 1276); Great & Little Lowe (*v.* hlāw 'a mound, a hillock'); Marl Fd (*freq*) & Yards (*v.* geard); Moor; Oular Croft (*v.* alor); The Oulton (perhaps 'old enclosure', *v.* ald, tūn, cf. Oulton 326 *infra*); (Great & Little) Pingott (*the ly-, lityll* & *the more pyngolt, -pynghold* 1549, 1550, *v.* pingot); Wheat Fd (*the wetefelde* 1549, *v.* hwǣte, feld); White Fd & Moors (*Whitfield* c.1240 (17), *the whitte feld* 1550, *v.* hwīt, feld); Wincham (Lane) Fd (cf. Wincham 136 *supra*).

(*b*) *Beuer'feld* 1483 (perhaps 'beaver field', *v.* beofor, feld, though this would be unusual unless the land was near a stream); *Bircherowe* E3 ('row of birch-trees', *v.* birce, rāw); *le Breches* 1310–30 ('lands newly broken in', *v.* brēc); *le Brocholes* 13 ('badger holes', *v.* brocc-hol, cf. 197 *infra*); *Caldecote*

John ('at the cold hovel', v. cald, cot); *Claye acr'* 1483 ('clay acre', v. clǣg, æcer); *the Cow(e)hey* 1549, 1550 ('cow enclosure', v. cū, (ge)hæg); *Hasschuluestre forde* (v. 94 *supra*); *Honeford* 1260–80 (perhaps 'ford at a stone', from hān and ford, cf. Handforth 1 254); *Hordawic* c.1220 (1440) ('the herd farm', v. heorde-wīc); *Livildesforde* John ('Lēofhild's ford', from the OE fem. pers.n. *Lēofhild* (Feilitzen 312), with a ME masc.gen.sg. *-es*, and ford); *Loweforth* 1346 ('the low ford', v. lágr, ford, a bound of Rudheath heath cf. 1 12. The location was either 110–682742 where a lost road crossed Wade Brook, or at Lostock Gralam Bridge *supra*); *campus de Monchehull* E3 (probably 'nun's hill', v. mynecen (gen.pl. mynecena), hyll, representing the field between *Holedene* (The Holdings 119 *infra*) and *Ruhasale* (*infra*) near *Hordawic* (*supra*), granted c.1220 to the nuns of Chester by Gralam de Runchamp (of Lostock), CASNS XIII 98); *Mosingislowe* 1321–26 (from hlāw 'a mound', and the gen.sg. of a p.n. or pers.n.); *le Oldefeld* 1310–30 (v. ald, feld); *Oueneford* 1260–80 (perhaps 'ewes' ford', v. eowu (gen.pl. eowena), ford); *le quercover haystowe* 1300–30 ('enclosure site', from (ge)hæg, and stōw, with an adj. probably meaning 'twisted over, turning across', cf. thwert-over, þvert, or *quirk* NED, EDD, and ofer[3]. Professor Löfvenberg would read *quertover*, and observes *quart* EDD, a Y dial. form of *thwart*); *Robinsons Bridge* 1619 (a horse-bridge, Sheaf[3] 22 (5258)); *Ruhasale* c.1220 (1400); *Shauintonfeld* 1310–30 (perhaps from a surname from Shavington 327 *infra*, but cf. Shannock 1 64, v. feld); *Sporneschaghalgh'* 1310–30 ('(corner of land at) a wood at a spur', v. spurn, sc(e)aga, halh); *le stygate* 1328 ('the path-way', v. stīg, stígr, gata; the name of a path towards Hulse 185 *supra*); *Syminecroft* 1310–30 (perhaps 'Simon's croft', from the ME pers.n. *Simon* (ON *Sigmundr*, ODan *Sigmund* or Hebrew *Simon*) and croft).

5. NORTHWICH (110–657738) [-witʃ]

> *Wich* 1086 DB, *le Wiche* 1299 Tab (p), *Wych* 14 Whall, *Wycus* 1258 ib, *Wicus* 1320 Mere (p), *Wyc* 1307 *LRO* Dx, *Wiz* 1351 BPR
>
> *Norwich* 1086 DB, 1184 P *et freq* with variant spellings *Nore-* to 1646 Sheaf, *Norht-*, *Northwich* 1119 (1150), (1280), 1150 Chest *et freq* with variant spellings *Nort(he)-*, *Nord-*, *Northt-*, *-wy-*, *-wich(e)us*, *-(i)us*, *-wic(h)e*, *-wic(us)*, *-wiz*, *-wyhh*, *-wyk*, *-wi(c)ke*, *-wys*, *-wics*; *le-*, *the-* 1296 Plea, 1375 Tab, 1458 *AddCh et freq* to 1656 Orm[2], *Northwich(toun)*, *-apon Wyver* c.1536 Leland, *Northoyche* 1571 Sheaf

'The northern wīc, v. norð, wīc. This was the northern-most of the Ch salt towns, the 'salt-wiches'. The special use of wīc in relation to the salt-works in Ch & Wo is discussed in EPN s.v. wīc (3, iii). Cf. Middlewich, Nantwich, & Fulwich 240, 326, 326 *infra*, Leftwich 205 *infra*, Sheath Street, *Wich House Streete infra*. Northwich, Middlewich & Nantwich are collectively known as 'The Wiches', *les Wyches* c.1200 Orm², *tres villae de wyz* 'the three towns of wich' 1282 CRV, *villae de Wichis* c.1304 *AddCh, the Wiches* 1355 BPR, and the two former as *les deux Wiz* 1351 BPR, the two latter as *ambo Wyci* ('both Wiches') 1317 *AddCh*. Northwich in Northwich Hundred was originally only a few acres in extent (Orm² III 159), an enclave in Witton township, cf. Newton 243 *infra*. The parish church was Witton Chapel, just outside the town boundary. The wīc at Northwich would be the 'industrial estate' and the wīc-tūn at Witton the residential quarter in this district, cf. the parallel in Droitwich and Witton Wo 289, 285. Castle Northwich 325 *infra* in Eddisbury Hundred does not appear to have been part of the town. Cf. *Condate* 195 *infra*.

STREET-NAMES

APPLE MARKET ST., 1860 White.

CROSS ST., cf. *Cross* 196 *infra*.

HIGH ST., *regalis via* e14 *JRC, le Kynges Strete* 1499 Adl, *the kynges hey strete* 1546 *Chol, the heyghe streete* 1556 *ib, v.* hēah, strǣt, cyning.

SHEATH ST., 1860 White, cf. (*una salina iuxta*) *le seth de Norwyco* c.1260–70 *JRC, the salt water pitte harde by the brinke of Dane River* and *the salt springg-ing pitte* c.1536 Leland, *a salt-spring, or brine-pit, in the bank of the river of Dane* 1656 Orm² (ValeR), *v.* sēað 'a pit, a hole' (*seath* NED), cf. *Wich House Streete infra*, and *Lunseth*, etc. 243 *infra*.

WITTON ST., *v.* Witton 194 *infra*.

LOST STREET-NAMES. *The Crannie hill* 1556 Chol (perhaps from *crannock* (NED) 'a measure of salt' and hyll); *le Cromehill* 1499 Adl (*le Gromhyll*' 1295 Chol, *the Cromhill*' 1458 *AddCh*, 'boy's hill', *v.* grome, hyll); *Holloway Head* 1821 Sheaf (*le holow wey hed* 1538 *AOMB*, '(the top end of) the sunken way', *v.* holh, weg, hēafod); *Schoolmaster's Lane* 1536 Sheaf; *The Swine Market Street* 1786 Sheaf (*The Swine Market* 1712, 1725 ib, *v.* swīn¹, market, cf. Apple Market St. *supra*); *le Twychele* e14 JRC (*v.* twitchel 'a narrow passage'); *the Yate Strete* 1556 Chol (cf. *le Northyate* 1354 *Indict*, apparently '(the street to) the north gate', *v.* geat, strǣt, norð, but there is no evidence of a town-wall, and geat may have been confused with gata 'a roadway').

LOST BUILDINGS: *le Bakehouse* 1506 AD (*v.* bæc-hūs); *le Leadsmythye* 1580 Orm² (*Ledesmythe* 1415 ChRR, *le Ledesmyth(e)* 1460 ChCert, 1514 Orm², 'the lead-smithy', where leaden salt-pans were made for the salt-houses, *v.* lēad, smiððe, cf. 241 *infra*); *le Petithall*' 1355 *Indict* ('the little hall', *v.* pety, hall, cf. 243 *infra*).

THE WICH HOUSE STREETE (lost), 1695 JRL, named from the factories of the salt-wich, known as *wich-houses*, where the salt-boiling industry was carried on, *v.* wych(e)-hous(e), cf. wīc, hūs, cf. Northwich, Sheath St. *supra, Wich(e) House Street(e)* 242 *infra*. The more notable salt-houses are named—*salina de Catenale* c.1350 *JRC* (cf. Catten Hall 325 *infra*); *-de Clauerton'* c.1350 *ib* (cf. Claverton 325 *infra*, to which DB f.268b ascribes 'una salina' in North- wich); *Cockeshull-*, *Cog(g)eshil(l)wychehous* 1380, 1386, 1507 *MinAcct*, *Cogeshull' Whichous* 1487 *ib*, *Coggshall Wich-howse* 1650 *ParlSurv* (cf. Cog- shall 109 *supra*); *una salina que vocatur Condalehous* c.1306 *JRC*, 1342 Orm² (this belonged to the *Leftwich* family, cf. Leftwich 205 *infra*, v. Sheaf² 1, 33; the origin of *Condale-* is not known); *salina de Crouton* 1235–40 Sheaf (cf. Crowton 326 *infra*; the connection suggests that this might be part of the Weaverham manor salt-works mentioned in DB f.263b, assigned by Tait to Nantwich); *le Tolfrewychehous* 1342 Sheaf, *le Frewichehouses* (in Middlewich and Nantwich) 1352 BPR, 1420 *MinAcct* ('salt-works free of Friday-tolls (customs levied on a salt made on Fridays)' v. tol-frēo, cf. Tait 42, 223, DB f.268); 'a wich of twelve leads (*xii plumborum*) called *Walmez*' 1536 Plea ('a salt-factory with twelve leaden boiling-pans called "the boiling pans"', v. wælm, cf. *walm* NED); *Whitleighwychehouse* 1370 *MinAcct*, *le Whitelegh- wichous* 1354 BPR, *Whitele Wichouses* 1355 *ib*, *-wychehous* 1386 *MinAcct*, *Whytewych house* 1423 *ib*, *Whitewich* 1507 *ib*, *Whitley Wich-howse* 1650 *ParlSurv* (cf. Higher Whitley 124 *supra*, which, like this salt-house, belonged to the Duchy of Lancaster).

DANE BRIDGE, (lit. *Leane*) 1619 Sheaf³ 22 (5258), crossing R. Dane into Leftwich 205 *infra*.   TOWN BRIDGE, *le pont de Northwiz* 1351 BPR, *pons de Northwich* 1392, 1408 ChRR, *Northwich bridge* 1619 Sheaf, *Weaver Bridge* 1831 Bry, crossing R. Weaver from the middle of the town into Castle Northwich 325 *infra*.

FIELD-NAMES

(a) Kiln Meadow 1849 *TA* 300 (cf. *le Kylnehose* 1547 *MinAcct*, v. cyln, hūs).

(b) *ly Wenall'* 1295 Chol; *le Oldeyordes* 1368 *JRC* ('the old enclosures', v. ald, geard); *Shawes crofte* 1554 Pat (probably 'croft belonging to one Shaw', v. croft).

6. WITTON CUM TWAMBROOK, 1860 White, *-Twembrook* 1819 Orm², *Wytton et Twembrok'* 1430 Dav, v. Witton, Twambrook *infra*.

WITTON (110–660737)

Witune 1086 DB, *Wytton alias Wytune* 1581 ChRR

Witton c.1200 Peov *et freq* with variant spellings *Wyt-*, *Whit-*, *Whyt-*, *-tune*, *-tonia*; *Witton-Crosse* 1343 (1471) ChRR, *-(et) le Crosse* 1367 (1582) ib

Woton 1504 Pat

'Village with a wīc', v. wīc-tūn, the wīc being Northwich 192 supra.
Witton Chapel is Northwych Chapel 1718 ChetOS VIII, cf. 193 supra.
Witton was manorially joined with Cross infra.

STREET-NAME. WITTON ST., one street called Wytton 1621 Orm², Witton-
street 1814 Sheaf, the street from Witton to Northwich, v. strǣt.

TWAMBROOK (110–672743)

Tynebroc 112 Tab
Twi, Twynebrokes 1228 Sheaf, Tab
Tromebrokes 1228 Tab
Twenebrokys c.1270 JRC, -is, Twen(e)brokes e14 Orm², JRC, 1322
   Plea et freq with variant spelling Tuene- to 1386 IpmR, (-in
   territorio de Wymyncham, -iuxta Wytton) e14 JRC, 1317 Plea,
   (-within Wymyncham) 1328 Orm², (-hamelettum de Wymyncham)
   1334 JRC, -brok 1357, 1358 BPR
Twanlbrooke 113 Tab
Twnnebrokes 1308 Plea (p)
Thembrokes 1398 ChRR (p)
Twembroke 1424 Plea, -brok 1519 ib, -brooke 1641 Sheaf, -brokes,
   (-in Wymmyncham) 1426 JRC, 1539 Plea
Twambrookes 1673 ChRR, -brook 1831 Bry

'Between the brooks', v. betwēonan, brōc, between Peover Eye
and Wade Brook, eastward of Dunkirk infra. This hamlet was
formerly part of Wincham 136 supra, and seems to have been transferred to Witton between 1426 and 1430. A place of the same name
existed in Grappenhall, v. 141 supra. Cf. Condate infra.

CONDATE (lost), 7 RavGeog, 4 (8) AntIt (twice), 'the confluence'. As
to the form, Professor Jackson points out that it is the source of the
French p.ns. Condé, Condat, Condes, and that it consists of Brit *com-
'with', and either -da- from *də from the root *dā- 'give', or -da-
from *dhə from the root *dhē- 'put', according respectively to J.
Vendryes in Mémoires de la Société de Linguistique de Paris XIII (1906)
394, or R. Hertz (reported by K. H. Schmidt) in Zeitschrift für
Celtische Philologie XXVI (1957) 189. The final el. -te is Brit -*tĭ, neut.
participial suffix, according to Vendryes loc. cit. Condate would then
be Brit (and Gaul) *Condati 'the giving-together-(place)', neut.,
according to Vendryes, or 'the putting-together-(place)', neut.,
according to Hertz. Professor Jackson observes, however, that it is

possible that the -*te* in *Condate* might represent Brit *-*t-is* (masc. *i*-stem) as a noun (as in the pl. folk-names *Atrebates*, *Nantuates*, etc.) or adjectival (as in *Namausatis* 'of Nîmes', or *Dunatis*, *Randosatis*, epithets of Mars), and if this were so, *Condate* would be a Lat ablative-locative form for the Celt dative-locative *Condati, which would not, however, affect the meaning. As to the location *v.* Archæologia XCIII 29, where the association with Harbutt's Field 238 *infra*, is adequately dismissed. AntIt (II and X) places *Condate* eighteen Roman miles from Manchester, twenty from Chester, and nineteen from *Mediolanum* (*v.* 326 *infra*). RavGeog names it as the next place of note after *Salinis* (*v.* 238 *infra*) from *Mediolanum*. It must have been near Northwich 192 *supra*, and it was probably in Witton cum Twambrook township, which is at the confluences of Dane *&* Weaver, Weaver *&* Peover Eye, Peover Eye and Wade Brook. Near Twambrook (the meaning and location of which invite comparison with *Condate*), the Manchester–Chester Roman road ('Watling Street' 1 40), Iter II of AntIt, crossed the Warrington–Middlewich road (King Street 1 43), Iter X, about 110–678745, cf. *Over Street* 191 *supra*. This intersection is the most likely site of the place *Condate*.

CROSS (lost), (*le*)*Cros*(*se*) 1343 Plea, 1346 (1471) ChRR (p) *et freq*, *Cross* 1407 ib, *villa de Cros* 1353 Indict, *maner' de-* 1401 ChRR, *maner de Witton Crosse* 1343 (1471) ib, *Wy-*, *Witton et Cros*(*se*) 1367 (1582) ib, *Le Cros iuxta Northwicum* 1377 Eyre, *the cross* (*by the Northewiche*) 1541 AD, 1557 Sheaf, 'the cross', *v.* cros, from which Cross St. 193 *supra* was probably named, cf. Witton *supra*, Northwich 192 *supra*.

ASHTON'S FLASHES, a lake formed by subsidence along Peover Eye near a factory called Ashton's Works, *v.* flasshe, cf. Witton Flashes *infra*.   BARON'S QUAY (MINE), *Ballance Quay* 1845 *TA*, *v.* kay. DUNKIRK, 1842 OS, *-Works* 1733 Dep (a salt-works), cf. Dunkirk 326 *infra*; this hamlet is called *Twambrook* 1831 Bry, 1842 OS.   ISLAND SALT WORKS (lost), 1842 OS, cf. *Island* (*Works*) 1845 *TA*, at the tip of the peninsula between R. Weaver *&* Peover Eye, *v.* ēg-land. LIMEKILN LANE.   MANCHESTER RD, *v.* 'Watling Street', 1 40, cf. 190 *supra*.   MIDDLEWICH RD, *Pennys Lane* 1831 Bry, 1842 OS, cf. *Penneys Field* (6x), *Penneys Lone Field* 1845 *TA*, *v.* 199 *infra*.   PARKFIELD.   WADEBROOK BRIDGE, *-brook*(*e*)- 1619 Sheaf, cf. Wade Brook 1 37.   WARRINGTON RD, leading towards

Warrington La. WITTON FLASHES, a lake like Ashton's Flashes *supra*, on the boundary with Marbury, Anderton and Marston, cf. 118 *supra*. WITTON HALL (lost, 110–663742), 1831 Bry. WITTONMILL BRIDGE, *Witton Bridge* 1426 Tab, 1831 Bry, cf. *Witton Mill* 1831 ib, lost under Ashton's Flashes *supra*, one of the *molendina de Witton* 1228 Sheaf, cf. Cranage Mill 136 *supra*.

FIELD-NAMES

The undated forms are 1845 *TA* 442. Of the others, c.1294 is *ChFor*, 1304 Chamb, 1308–17 *JRC*, 1407–1627 *Chol*, 1490, 1512, 1765 Sheaf, 1503, 1558 Orm[2], 1507[1] AD, 1507[2], 1515 *MinAcct*, 1539 Plea, 1831 Bry.

(a) Bear Park (perhaps alluding to bear-baiting, cf. Cock Pit Fd *infra*); Boot Mdw (*v.* bōt); Block Shop; Church Fd; Cock Pit Fd (*v.* cock-pit, cf. Bear Park *supra*); Commissary; Dods Yard 1831; Gastry Fd; Green Hay; Holdings (cf. The Holdings 199 *infra*); Intake; Kitchen Fd; Leech (*v.* lece 'a boggy stream'); New Cross Fd; Rock Pit (Fd) (alluding to the mining of rock-salt); School Croft 1765 (belonged to Witton Grammar School); Sweet Fd; Townend Fd (*v.* toun, ende[1]); Town Fd; White Acre(s); Wittons (*v.* wīc-tūn, cf. Witton *supra*); Yates (*v.* geat 'a gateway'); Yealds ('hill-sides, slopes', *v.* helde).

(b) *the ould barne feild* 1627 (*v.* ald, bere-ærn, feld); *le brocholes* 1407 ('the badger-holes', *v.* brocc-hol, cf. 191 *supra*); *Claycrofte* 1304 (p), *-croft* 1503, 1507[1], [2], *Cleycroft* 1515, *-e* 1539, 1558 (*v.* clǣg, croft); *the Duffehowse Crofte* 1627 (*v.* dove-house); *le Fendesers clogh*' 1407 (*v.* clōh 'a dell, a ravine'. The first component may be merely a figurative description of the valley itself, or it may be a figurative p.n. 'Devil's Arse', *v.* fēond, ears, cf. Peak Cavern Db 56 (*Divillsarse* 1630), *Trollesers* YN 324 ('troll's arse'). Such 'arse' names may refer to a buttock-shaped hill, but the Ch and Db instances probably have a more fundamental allusion to a cleft or orifice. This Ch p.n. means either 'dell at The Fiend's Arse' or 'dell like the devil's backside'); *Herberdisgreue* 1308–17 ('Herbert's wood', from the ME (OFr) pers.n. *Herbert*, *-berd* and grǣfe); *the bigger & lesser Heywood* 1627 ('enclosed wood', *v.* (ge)hæg, wudu); *le hullis* 1308–17 ('the hills', *v.* hyll); *the longe loundes* 1627 ('the long selions', *v.* lang, land); *(le) Lyn(t) Strete* (*v.* 'Watling Street' 1 40, cf. Manchester Rd *supra*); *Le Pyncher Clogh* 1490, 1512 (perhaps 'miser's dell', from *pincher* (NED from 1440) 'a miser' and clōh); *the Reed ground* 1627 (*v.* hrēod 'a reed-bed'); *le sondiflatte* 1308–17 (*v.* sandig, flat); *Wyttonheth* c.1294 (*v.* hǣð cf. Witton *supra*).

ii. Rudheath Lordship (extra-parochial)

RUDHEATH (110–690717), -*Lordship* 1819 Orm², *v.* lordes(c)hip, cf. Rudheath 1 11, of which this township represents that part retained in royal demesne with Drakelow *infra*, and distinguished as *balliva-, ballivus de Drakelowe et Rudheth* 1365 Orm², 1378 Pat *et freq, manerium regis de Drakelowe et terræ Rudheth* 1378 Cl, *Rudheth infra dominium de Drakelowe* 1386–7 Orm², *dominium de Rudheth* 1394 Pat, (-*Drakelow et-*) 1417 ib, *Readheath lordship* 1751 Sheaf, *terrae dominicales et tenementa de Rudheth* 1391 Pat, (-*Drakelow et-*) 1465 ChRR, *lez demeynes in Drakelowe et Rudeheth* 1468 *MinAcct*, *le(s) Demaynes-* 1474, 1510 ChRR. Rudheath c.p. includes part of Shurlach cum Bradford 210 *infra*, from Davenham parish, but excludes the detached portions of the Lordship at Earnshaw and Kings Lane 188 *supra* and No Town Fm 230 *infra*.

DRAKELOW HALL & FM (110–700700) ['dreiklou]

>   *Drakelow(e)* 1310–30 *Chol*, 1346 BPR, 1357 ChRR *et freq* with variant spellings -*lew, -loth, -lowes, -lo(o), Drak-, Drack(e)-, Drac-*; (*manerium de-*) E3 *Surv*, (*le demaynes de-*) 1391 ChRR, (-*in Ruddehethe*) 1441 Orm², *Draclo Hall* 1724 NotCestr
>
>   *Drakeslowe* 1351 BPR (p), 1378 Pat
>
>   *Drakenlowe* 1359 BPR

'Dragon's mound', *v.* draca, hlāw. Cf. Db 633. The name alludes to the ancient folk-belief in the dragon which guards the burial-treasure, as in *Draca sceal on hlæwe, frod, frætwum wlanc* 'it is for the dragon to be on the burial mound, to be old and wise, and resplendent with treasure' (*Maxims II* 26–27, in Dobbie, *Anglo-Saxon Minor Poems* 56), and in *Beowulf* (ed. Klæber) 2212 *et seq.* Cf. *Hordfeld infra*. The earliest reference is *campus quod vocatur Drakelowe* 1310–30 *Chol*, a field which probably contained the tumulus, cf. *Drakeloweflat'* 1350 *MinAcct*, E3 *Surv, Long- & Three Nook'd Drakelow* 1841 *TA*, *v.* flat, lang, three-nooked. There was another *Drakelowe* in Lower Bebington, 325 *infra*.

BILLINGE GREEN (110–677713) [-indʒ] *Bellynge* (lit. *Mell-*) 1534–47 Dugd, 16 *AOMB* 397, *Billings Greene* 1650 LRMB, *Billing(e) Greene* 1650 (18) *Surv, Billinge Green house* 1687 Sheaf, *v.* grēne², cf. Billinge Hill 1 138.

THE HOLDINGS (110–676736), 1650 *LRMB, Holedene* c.1220 (1400)
CASNS XIII, *Holenden(e)* 1288 Court (p), Plea (p), *Holden(e)* 1300–30
Chol, E3 *Surv et freq* to 1650 *Surv,* (*-iuxta Shurlach*) 1346 VR,
Holdyn 1334 VR (p), 'at the hollow valley', *v.* hol² (dat.sg. holan),
denu. For the development of the form cf. Holding's Drumble 276
infra.

ASHBROOK FM. BROKEN CROSS (110–684732), *Old Broken Cross*
(p.h.), *Broken Cross Farm* 1831 Bry, cf. *the Cross(e) feild* 1650 *LRMB,*
(18) *Surv,* from a wayside cross formerly standing at the intersection
of King Street and Penny's Lane *infra.* It appears to have been broken
in the seventeenth century, cf. Broken Cross 1 118. Crump 96
associates it with a salt-way from Northwich to Macclesfield, *v.* 1
46, 49. BROWNHAYES FM, *Browne heys* 1650 *LRMB,* 'brown enclosures', *v.* brūn¹, (ge)hæg. COOKE'S LANE, 1650 *LRMB.*
CROSS LANES, 1842 OS, *Crosslanes Farm* 1831 Bry (at 110–719695),
named from a cross-roads. CROWDER'S LANE, 1831 ib, cf. *The
Crowders feildes* 1650 *LRMB, Crowders Fields* 1841 *TA,* from
crowdere 'a fiddler', or the derived surname. DRAKELOW GORSE
FM, *v.* gorst, cf. *Fox Covert* 1831 Bry, *Coppice* 1842 OS.
DRAKELOW LANE, 1842 ib, formerly *Occleshaw Lane* 1831 Bry,
cf. *Ackersey* 1841 *TA,* from a p.n. which may contain sc(e)aga
'a copse, a wood'. FOURLANE ENDS, the crossing of Crowder's Lane *supra* and King Street *infra.* GADBROOK FM, *Gad-
broke* 1514 ChEx, cf. *þe Gadfield* 1650 *LRMB, v.* gad, Gad Brook
1 26 HEATH HO, cf. Rudheath 1 11. HIGGINSLANE
FM, 1831 Bry, cf. *the Higgings field* 1650 *LRMB, the Higgenes Feild*
1650 (18) *Surv,* probably from a pers.n. *Higgin(s),* from ME *Higgin,*
diminutive of *Higg,* a voiced side-form of *Hick,* a pet-form of *Richard*
(Reaney 164), but hecing is possible, cf. Higginbotham 1 266.
HIGH HO, 1609 *Rental, The-* 1677 *LRMB.* KING'S LANE, *v.* 188
supra. KING STREET, *v.* 1 44, cf. foll. KINGSTREET FM &
HALL, *Kingstreete* 1609 *Rental,* 1650 (18) *Surv, Kings-streete* 1619
Sheaf, 1650 *LRMB, v.* prec. LANE END FM, cf. *Lane End Field*
1841 *TA.* MARSHALL'S GORSE, *Millingtons Gorse* 1831 Bry, *v.*
gorst. MELVIN HO, *Pennys Lane House* 1831 ib, *v.* Penny's Lane
infra. MIDDLEWICH RD, *Pennys Lane* 1831 ib, cf. 196 *supra, v.*
Penny's Lane *infra.* NINEHOUSES, 1831 ib, self-explanatory.
PENNY'S LANE (110–675734 to 705720), 1831 ib, *Pen(n)ies-* 1650
LRMB, extending from the Witton boundary at Ninehouses *supra,*

cf. Middlewich Rd *supra*, to Broken Cross *supra* and the green at Lach Dennis 188 *supra*. The name is from ME peni (OE peni(n)g) 'a penny', and probably alludes to a toll, perhaps one levied on salt carried from Northwich, cf. *Halfepenihill* 242 *infra*. PUDDINGLAKE BROOK, *v.* I 34. SHIPBROOK RD, *v.* 211 *infra*. WHATCROFT LANE, 1831 Bry, *v.* 215 *infra*, I 12. WITTON LODGE, cf. Witton 194 *supra*.

FIELD-NAMES

The undated forms are 1841 *TA* 343. Of the others, 1310–30 is *Chol*, E3, 1650 (18) *Surv*, 1346 VR, 1351 Chamb, 1387 ChRR, 1468, 1488, 1507, 1515 *MinAcct*, 1560, 1768 Sheaf, 1609 *Rental*, 1630 *AOMB* 380, 1650, 1677 *LRMB* 278 and 211.

(a) Antrobus (the Venables family of Antrobus 127 *supra* held land here e17, Orm² III 169); Bakehouse Fd; Barn Croft & Fd (*the Barnefield, the Barne close* 1650); Bent, Bently (*v.* beonet, lēah); Big Mdw (cf. *the great meadow* 1650 (18)); Blake Fd (*the litle blacke field* 1650, cf. *the blacke acre* ib, *v.* blæc); Blay Croft; Brick Kiln Fd; Brook Fd (*the Brooke field (meadow)* 1650); Chrimes Fd (*v.* cryme, cf. *le Crymbe* 171 *supra*); Cote Mdw (*v.* cot); Cow Hey; Crab Tree Fd (*the* 1650); Crymbo (perhaps for ModEdial. *crimble, v.* crymel 'a small piece of land'); (Seven- & Three-) Daymath (*v.* daymath); Dog Croft (cf. 'a cottage called the Dogge builte for a watche house' 1630, 'a cort of Survey houlden ... att *the Dogg in þe Wall* within the said Mannor' 1677); Feather Bed Fd (1650, cf. Featherbed Moss I 323); Garden Fd; Hall Fd (1650); Hanging Fd (*v.* hangende); Hinds Croft (*the Hindes Croft* 1650, *-Hyndes-* 1650 (18), 'servant's croft', *v.* hine); Horton Fd & Mdw (*Horton Felde* 1560, *-Feild* 1630, *-Fields* 1768, *Hortons fields* 1650, perhaps 'dirty enclosure' from horu and tūn, but *Horton* may be a surname, cf. Horton 326 *infra*); Hulse (*v.* Hulse 185 *supra*); Hunger Hill (*v.* hungor); Hunts Hey (*the Hunt Heys* 1650, cf. *Stephen le Hunt's lane* 1346, a boundary of Rudheath heath, cf. I 13, against Shipbrook, *v.* (ge)hæg); Intake (*v.* inntak); Jumpers Hey; Kiln Croft (*Kill Croft(e)s* 1650, 1650 (18), *v.* cyln); Far & Near Lady Hey (cf. *le Lauedyfeld, le Leuedys-, -iesfeld* 1346, *the great & litle Lady(s) field* 1650, 'the lady's field', *v.* hlǣfdige, feld); Big & Little Lidgate (*the (litle) Lidyates* 1650, *the Litle Ladyates* 1650 (18), cf. *Yate Meaddow* 1650, *Yeates meadow* 1650 (18), *v.* hlid-geat); Little Mdw (*the litle-* 1650); Long Acre (cf. *le Longacre* 1346, near the Witton–Rudheath boundary I 13, *v.* lang, æcer); Long Butts (*the long & the short Butts* 1650, *-Buttes* 1650 (18), *v.* butte); Lordship Fd (*v.* lordes(c)hip, Rudheath Lordship *supra*); Lostock Fd (*v.* Lostock Gralam 189 *supra*); The Lound (*v.* land or launde); Marl Fd (*the marled field* 1650, *Marldfeild, the marled Earth* 1650 (18), *v.* marlede, eorðe); Mere Fd (*Mare Field* 1650, *v.* (ge)mære 'a boundary'); Big & Little Mickle Hey (*the great & litle Mickle Hey* 1650, 'the big enclosure', *v.* micel, (ge)hæg); Milking Brows (*v.* milking, brū); Moat Croft (at a moat-site near Drakelow Hall, *v.* mote); Moss Croft & Fd (*le mos* 1310–30, *Moss Field* (*Lane*) 1650, *Mossefeild* (*Land*) 1650 (18), *v.* mos); Nook Fd; Outlet(t) (*v.* outlet); Ox Fd; Pavement Fd (*v.* pavement); Pear Tree Fd (*the Peare tree field* 1650); Pingots (*v.* pingot); Pit Fd (*the Faire Pittfield* 1650, *v.* pytt); Poolstead (*v.* pōl-stede); Push Plow'd Fd (*v.* push-plough); Raw Fd (*Raufflat* E3, 'the raw plot', from OE *hrēaw* (inflected **hraw-* > ME *rawe*) and flat); Rough Rans; Rudheath (*a close called Rud-heath, the litle Rudheath* 1650, (*the litle*) *Rudheath* 1650 (18), cf. *Redheath hay* 1609, *Rudheath Hayes* 1768, *Rudheath Close Haie* 1768, *v.* clos, (ge)hæg, cf. Rudheath *supra*); Salt Lake ('salty stream', *v.* salt, lacu); Seven Acre (*the seaven Acres* 1650 (18)); The Such (*v.* sīc); Swans Neck; Ten Pound Fd; Twelve Butts; Whatcroft (cf. Whatcroft 215 *infra*); White Acre & Fd (cf. *Whitcroft* 1609, *v.* hwīt); Big & Little Will.

(*b*) *Battens Earth Close* 1650; *Bradefordeswey iuxta le Lauedyfeld* 1346 ('the way to Bradford', *v.* weg, cf. 1 13, Bradford 210 *infra*, Lady Hey *supra*); *the Higher & Lower Broadfield* 1650, *Broadfeild End* 1650 (18) (*v.* brād, feld); *Carters Meaddow* 1650; *Crimlow* 1650 (perhaps 'crumbled mound', *v.* crymel, hlāw, cf. Crymbo *supra*, but the first el. may be cryme as in *le Crymbe* 171 *supra*); *the Croftes* 1650 (18); *the Dungfeld* 1650, *-feild* 1650 (18) (*v.* dung² 'dung'); *Eliuereslach'* 1310–30 (a watercourse, the second el. is læc(c) 'a boggy stream'; the first may be a compound of æl, ēl 'an eel' and OE *ge-fær* (gen.sg. *-es*) 'a going, a course, a march', cf. *eel-fare* NED (from 1533) 'the migration of elvers'. The stream-name would mean 'boggy stream in which the elvers run'); *fayre acre* 1650 ('the fair acre', *v.* fæger, æcer); *the Garlands Croft* 1650; *the goulden Crofft* 1650, *the Golden Croft* 1650 (18) (*v.* gylden 'golden', cf. golde 'a marigold'); *Haresfelde* 1560 (*v.* hara); *le heye* 1310–30 (*v.* (ge)hæg, cf. *Rudheath Hayes supra*); *The Hay Croft* 1650, *-Haycroft* 1650 (18) (*v.* hēg); *the headlands close, the litle Hudland* 1650 ('(close at) the headlands', *v.* hēafod-land, clos); *the heathfield* 1650 (*v.* hæð, feld); *Hitch Close* 1650 ('hurdled enclosure', *v.* hiche, clos); *Hobbefeld* 1387 (from either hob 'a hobgoblin', or hobb(e) 'a tussock'); *Hordfeld* 1488 ('treasure field, hoard field', *v.* hord, feld, perhaps from the discovery of buried treasure, cf. Drakelow *supra*); *Hulkokeshey* E3 (from a ME pers.n. *Hulcock*, a diminutive of *Hulle*, a pet-form of *Hugh*, and (ge)hæg 'an enclosure'); *the Kings Croft* 1609, *-s* 1650, *-Feildes* 1630 (*v.* cyning, cf. King's Lane *supra*); *Leafeild* 1650 (18) (*v.* lēah); *the meadow field* 1650 (*v.* mæd); *Morbarwe* 1310–30 ('wood at a moor', *v.* mōr¹, bearu); *le Newefeld* 1310–30, *-field, -feild* 1650, 1650 (18) (*v.* nīwe, cf. foll); *le Oldefeld* E3, *Oldefeldesdyche* 1346 ('(the ditch of) the old field', *v.* ald, feld, dīc, cf. prec. and 1 13); *Ormilow* 1650 (18); *the Pease Croft Meadow* 1650 (*v.* pise); *the Ryd(e)ing(e)* 1650, *Riding* 1650 (18) (*v.* ryding); *þe Seruer* 1650 (*v.* server); *Simmesfeld* 1346 ('Sim's field', from the ME pers.n. *Simm*, a short form of *Simon(d)* and feld, cf. 1 13); *Slack field* 1650 (*v.* slakki); *del Snabbes* 1351 (p) (from snabbe 'a steep place, a projection on a hill', not topographically suited to this district, so the surname may not belong here); *Stubbesclose* 1507, *Stubbeslese* 1515, *Stubbests* 1560 (Sheaf³ 23 (5349)), *Stubbs Field* 1650 ('close, meadow & field at the tree-stumps', *v.* stubb, clos, læs, feld, cf. Stublach 255 *infra*); *Sumpter Feild* 1630, *-es* 1650 (18), *-s* 1768, *Sumptersfields*

1650 ('pack-horse field', from *sumpter* (NED) 'a sumpter horse'); *Suntfelde* 1560 (perhaps 'sand field', *v.* sand, feld); *Thunlowe* 1560 (Sheaf³ 23 (5342); if not a mistake for *Twemlow* 230 *infra*, probably 'mound by a *tūn*', *v.* tūn, hlāw, cf. *Tonlowe* 3 *supra*); *the Wayfield* 1650, -*Wey*- 1650 (18) (*v.* weg, feld); *the widdow Hey* 1650, -*Hay* 1650 (18) ('widow's enclosure', *v.* (ge)hæg, which belonged to Ann Buckley, widow, 1650 *LRMB* 278); *the Yard Croft Meadow* 1650 (*v.* geard, croft, mæd).

iii. Davenham

Davenham parish contained the townships, 1. Bostock, 2. Davenham (now a c.p. including Eaton and part of Leftwich *infra*), 3. Eaton (*v.* Davenham *supra*), 4. Leftwich (now included in Davenham and Northwich c.ps., *supra* and 192 *supra*), 5. Moulton, 6. Newall (now included in Lach Dennis c.p. 186 *supra*), 7. Shipbrook (*v.* Whatcroft *infra*), 8. Shurlach cum Bradford (now included in Rudheath c.p. 198 *supra*), 9. Stanthorne, 10. Wharton (now included in Winsford c.p. 327 *infra*), 11. Whatcroft (now a c.p. including Shipbrook *supra*). Part of Rudheath Lordship 198 *supra* was tithed in Davenham parish.

1. BOSTOCK (110–670680)

> *Botestoch* 1086 DB
> *Boristok* c.1180 *AddCh*, 12 (17) *Chol*
> *Bostoc* c.1200 *AddCh* (p), -*sto(c)k*, -*stocke* c.1250 MidCh (p) *et freq*
>   with variant spellings -*stock*, -*stocsk*; *Bostoke* 1281 Tab, 1304
>   Chamb (p), 1385 Cl (p), 1463 ChRR *et freq* to 1536 ib, -*sthoke*
>   1281 Tab (p)
> *Bustok* 1287 Court
> *Bostestok* 1335 MainwB
> *Poystok* 1408 ChRR (p)
> *Boxtok* 1421 Tab (p)

'Bōta's hamlet', from the OE pers.n. *Bōta* and stoc, cf. Bosley 1 54.

ADAMSHEATH FM, cf. *Adams Heath* 1831 Bry, in this and Moulton townships, perhaps named after *Adam* de Bostock 1341 ChRR, 1398 Cl, *v.* hǣð.   BOSTOCK GREEN, 1666 Orm², *Hall Green* 1838 *TA*. BOSTOCK HALL, 1724 NotCestr, cf. Oldhall Fm *infra* near which is the moated site *Old Hall Moat* 1842 OS, of the original hall, *manerium de Bostok* 1486 *MinAcct*, *v.* mote.   BRICK-KILN LANE, *Cow Lane* 1831 Bry, cf. *Brickiln Field* 1838 *TA*.   BROOK HO, 1842 OS. BULL'S WOOD, 1831 Bry.   FIDDLE CLUMP, a wood.   HILL

WOOD, 1842 OS. HOME FM. JACK LANE (FM), *Jack Lane* 1831 Bry, cf. *Jack Croft* 1838 *TA*, *v.* jack. OLDHALL FM, *Dairy House* 1842 OS, cf. Bostock Hall *supra*. PECKMILL BRIDGE, BROOK & FM, *Peck Mill* (*Brook*) 1831 Bry, *Peck Bridge* 1839 *TA* 140, cf. *molendinum de Bostok'* 1354 Eyre, *v.* myln, brycg, brōc. For the first el. *v.* Peckmill 84 *supra*. Cf. 204 *infra*. PENNEL'S WOOD. SHEEPSGREEN WOOD, 1842 OS, *Sheep Green Wood* 1831 Bry, *v.* scēap, grēne[2]. SMOKEHALL LANE, *v.* 207 *infra*. THE WILLOWBEDS, *Willow Bed Piece* 1838 *TA*.

FIELD-NAMES

The undated forms are 1838 *TA* 62. Of the others, 1333 is Plea, 1350, 1375 *Eyre*, 1509 ChRR.

(*a*) Banks; Bedsomes Fd; Blake Fd (*v.* blæc); Bottoms (*v.* botm); Brown Heath Fd; Far & Near Buckley (probably named after the *Bulkeley* family, of Eaton 204 *infra*); Butney; Cockshutes (*v.* cocc-scyte); Cote Fd (*v.* cot); Creswell Fd (*v.* cærse, wella); Crimes Mdw (*v.* cryme, cf. *le Crymbe* 171 *supra*); Dane Mdw (*v.* R. Dane 1 20); Davenham Fd (*v.* Davenham 203 *infra*); The Deans (*v.* denu); Dingle Hill (*v.* dingle); Dirty Lane; Little Eye (*v.* ēg); French Fd; Gib Greave (*v.* græfe); Glade (*v.* glǣd[3]); Hobbinsways (*v.* Earls Wood 204 *infra*); Hongrill (*v.* hungor, hyll); Hough Mdw (*v.* hōh); Improved Mdw; Intake (*v.* inntak); Jack Croft (*v.* jack); Kiln Mdw; Lady's Mdw (*v.* hlǣfdige); North & South Ley, Ley Fd (*v.* lǣge); Lousey Fd (*v.* lowsy); Marl(ed) Fd; Mill Fd & Hill; Big Moss; North Hill; Old Hey(es) (*v.* (ge)hæg); Picco (*v.* pichel); The Riddings (*v.* ryding); Rogers Eye ('Roger's water-meadow', from the ME (OFr) pers.n. *Roger* and ēg); Sand Fd; Sour Milk Fd; Standaloons; What Croft (*v.* hwǣte 'wheat', but cf. Whatcroft 215 *infra*); White Fd; Wilbraham Fd (after the *Wilbraham* family); Wood Oak Pit (probably a pit near a wood in which to soak oak-bark for tanning).

(*b*) *Balshagh* 1333, 1350 (p), *-shawe* 1375 (p) ('rounded wood', or 'wood at a rounded hill' *v.* balg, sceaga, cf. Balshaw La 7); *Dichefeelde* 1509 (*v.* dīc, feld).

2. DAVENHAM (110–660710) ['deivnəm]

Deveneham 1086 DB, *Deuenham* c.1190 (1400) CASNS XIII (p)
Dau-, Davenham 1178 Facs, 1278 Ipm *et freq*, (*-or Daneham*) 1621 Orm[2], *Dauenham* 1285 ChFine, *Davenaham* 1295 Ipm
Dau-, Davennam 1215 (1299) Chest (p), e13 (1300) Pat (p), *Dauenam* 1284 CASNS II
Daueham 1325 AddCh, *Dav(eh)am* 1536 ChRR

Daneham 1330 (1662) VR, 1430 *AddCh et freq*, (*-alias Davenham*) 1599 Orm², *Danam* 1443 JRL, *Danham* 1554 Pat

Denham 1402 ChRR, 1739 *LRMB* 264, *Deneham* 1536 Dugd, *Dename* 1548 Pat

Daynum 1691 Sheaf, *Deynam* 1696 ib

'Village on the R. Dane', *v.* hām, R. Dane 1 20.

BRIDGE END FM, 1839 *TA*, named from Shipbrook Bridge *infra*. DAIRY FM, *New Farm* 1839 *TA*.   DAVENHAM COTTAGE, *The Cottage* 1831 Bry.   DAVENHAM MILL, 1831 ib.   EARL'S WOOD, 1839 *TA, Hanging Banks Wood* 1831 Bry, *Hanging Bank & Wood* 1839 *TA, Hobbinsways* 1838 *TA* 62 (203 *supra*), 'steep banks', *v.* hangende. The later name may be weg 'a road', with the ME pers.n. *Hobbin*, diminutive of *Hobb*, a pet-form of *Robert*.   ELDERSBRIAR BROOK, *v.* 1 22.   HARTFORD RD, leading to Hartford Bridge 205 *infra*. IVY HO, -*Farm* 1839 *TA*.   JACK LANE, *v.* 203 *supra*, cf. *Jack Lane Field* 1839 ib.   LONDON RD, *Davenham Pavement* 1537 Sheaf, *v.* pavement.   MEREBANK, MERE HEATH (FM), *Mereheath Farm* 1839 *TA, Mare Heath* 1831 Bry, 1842 OS, near the Bostock and Moulton boundaries, *v.* (ge)mære.   NEW HALL, (*Farm*) 1839 *TA, Hall Farm* 1831 Bry.   PECKMILL BRIDGE & BROOK, *v.* 203 *supra*. SHIPBROOK BRIDGE, *v.* 209 *infra*.

FIELD-NAMES

The undated forms are 1839 *TA* 140. Of the others, 1538 is ChRR, 1539 Plea.

(*a*) Childs Grave; Cowhey; Dane Mdw (*v.* R. Dane 1 20); The Deans (cf. *Gynes Deynes* 1539, *v.* denu 'a valley'); Dove House Fd; Hall Green; Mill Fd (cf. Peckmill Bridge *supra*); Tan Yard (*v.* tan-yard).

(*b*) *Brett' lands* 1538 (named from the family *le Bret*, landowners here, *v.* land).

3. EATON (110–646704) [ˈiːtən, ˈeitn̩]

Yeiton 1290 Ipm (II 459), *Eyton'* 1299 P (p), 1312 Plea *et freq*, (*-iuxta Multon*) 1313 Plea, (*-by-, -nigh Davenham*) 1351 AD, 1669 Orm², *Heyton* 1481 Tab, *Eiton* c.1536 Leland

Eayton 1321 (18) Orm²

Ayton' 1354 *Eyre et freq*, (*-iuxte le Valroyal*) 1357 AddCh, (*-alias Yeaton alias Eaton*) 1576 ChRR, *Yayton* 1547, 1561 ib

Eton 1364 BPR (p), c.1536 Leland

Eaton 1378 Plea, 1431 MidCh, 1576 ChRR, 1724 NotCestr,
   Yeaton 1576 ChRR
   Yatton 1471, 1486, 1488 *MinAcct*

'Farm by a river', *v.* tūn. The first el. is ēg 'water-meadow, land
by a river', interchanging with ēa 'a river', cf. DEPN. The place
is beside R. Weaver. Cf. E(a)ton 326 *infra*, 1 61, Vale Royal,
Moulton 327, 207 *infra*, Davenham 203 *supra*.

EATON HALL, 1831 Bry.   HARTFORD BRIDGE, HILL & RD, *v.*
206 *infra*.

FIELD-NAMES

The undated forms are 1838 *TA* 157. Of the others, 1504, 1521 are AD,
1831 Bry.

(a) The Acres; Billy's Wall (*v.* wælla); Black More Eye (*Blackemeyr
Eghde* 1521, '(island-meadow at) the black pool', *v.* blæc, mere[1], ēg, ēgeð);
Blake Fd (*le Blakefeld* 1504, *v.* blæc, feld); Crab Hill Wd 1831; Crabtree
Green; Gorsty Fd (*v.* gorstig); Lords Mdw (*v.* hlāford); Marled Fd (*the
Marlfild* 1504, *v.* marle(de)); Nannys Hill Wd 1831; Nestases (*Nestall heath*
1504, *v.* hǣð); The Okenthorpe or Okentrap (named from John *Okynthrop*
1504); Sand Fd; Stocktons Spring (*Stockton Wood* 1831, *v.* stoc, tūn); Walk
Wd (*v.* walk); Ware Eye(s) ('island-meadows at a weir', *v.* wær, wer, ēg);
Windmill Fd; Wychhouse Mdw (*v.* wych(e)-hous(e), cf. 193 *supra*).

(b) *the lowne* 1504 ('the lane', *v.* lane); *the Newfild* 1504 (*v.* nīwe, feld);
Plumley deyne 1504 ('(hollow at) plum-tree clearing', *v.* plūme, lēah, denu).

4. LEFTWICH (GREEN) (110–660725)

Wice 1086 DB f.265
Leftetewych 1278 Ipm, -*wich* 1284 CASNS II, 1321 *AddCh* (p),
   Lefted(e)wich 1311 Ipm, *Leftatewych*, -*wich* (lit. *Lest*-) 1350–1400
   (1615) ChRR
Lestowhec E1 *AddCh* (p)
Left(e)wich(e), -*wych(e)*, -*wyk*, -*wike* 1278 IpmR (lit. *Leftewith*),
   1284 Tab (lit. *Lostwych*), 1295 Ipm, 1296 Plea *et freq* with
   variant spellings *Lestewyth*, *Lestwike* (1295 IpmR), *Loste*-,
   Lostowych, -*wiche* (1331, 1381 Tab), *Leftwitch* (1352 Orm[2] (p)),
   Lestewytche, -*wiche* (1534 Dugd, 1557 Pat), *Lestwich* (1610
   Speed, 1673 Sheaf); *Lyftwich* 1458 ChRR (p), *Leaftwyche*
   1554 Pat (lit. *Least*-)
Letewich c.1536 Leland

'Lēoftǣt's wīc', from the OE fem. pers.n. *Lēoftǣt* (ASCharters 375) and wīc, v. also grēne². The spelling of this p.n. is complicated by scribal confusion of *s* and *f*, *t* and *c*, *o* and *e*.

THE BROCKHURST, *Brokholes* 1439 Cl (p), *Broke Holl* 1523 AD, *Brocklehurst* 1840 *TA*, *Brockhurst* 1831 Bry, '(wooded hill at) the badger holes', v. brocc-hol, hyrst, cf. 197, 191 *supra*.   DANEBANK FM, DANE BRIDGE, cf. *Higher & Lower Dane, Dane Eye & Meadow* 1840 *TA*, named from R. Dane 1 20, v. ēg, cf. 194 *supra*. DOBELL'S FM, 1842 OS.   ELDERSBRIAR BROOK, v. 204 *supra*. GREENBANK, *Nursery* 1831 Bry.   GREENLANE FM, *Brasseys Farm* 1831 ib, from the Ch surname *Brassey*, as in Brassey Bank, Green & Hall 325, 325, 325 *infra*.   HARTFORD BRIDGE, HILL & RD, *Hartford Bridge* 1619 Sheaf, -*Lane* 1831 Bry, -*Hill* 1838 *TA* 157, named from Hartford 326 *infra*, cf. foll. and Poor's Wood *infra*. Hartford Hill may be *Sandywaye hill infra*.   HARTFORDHILL (a farm), *Poors Land Cottage* 1831 Bry, *Hill Farm* 1842 OS, cf. prec. and Poor's Wood *infra*.   LEFTWICH GRANGE, *Bancrofts Farm* 1831 Bry, from the surname *Bancroft*.   LEFTWICH HAYES & MOUNT. LEFTWICH OLD HALL, 1842 OS, *Leftwich Hall* 1724 NotCestr, 1831 Bry, a house demolished in the nineteenth century, ChetOS VIII 244n. POOR'S WOOD, *Cottage Wood* 1831 Bry, 1842 OS, cf. Hartfordhill *supra*, probably land held in trust for charitable purposes, perhaps by the local Overseers.   WOOD COTTAGE, cf. prec.

FIELD-NAMES

The undated forms are 1840 *TA* 236. Of the others, 1354 is ChRR, 1506, 1523 AD, 1537 Sheaf, 1546 Chol, 1547 MinAcct, 1553 Pat, 1831 Bry.

(a) Acres (cf. *Long Acre* 1506, v. lang, æcer); Black Butts (v. butte); Butty Mdw (v. butty); Chapel Mdw; Church Moss (cf. *the Chirchemosse of Davenham* 1354, 'moss belonging to Davenham church', v. cirice, mos. The parish church of Davenham stands in Leftwich township); Coppice Loons (v. land); Cow Banks; Dirty Croft; Elder Acres; Fearny Butts; Haddirick, Haddrick's Mdw (cf. *Halkeriek Lane* 1831, at 110–655723); Hick Croft & Hill (*Hycke Crofte* 1523, perhaps from the ME pers.n. *Hick*, a pet-form of *Richard*, and croft); Hill Fd (cf. *Hylle Heye* 1523, v. hyll, (ge)hæg); Honey Hurst (v. hunig, hyrst); Horton Eye (*Horton Egh* 1523, named from Horton 326 *infra*, v. ēg); Intake (v. inntak); Marled Fd; Moors; Mote Fd (v. mote 'a moat'); Mow Flatt ('flat piece of ground where a stack stands', v. mūga, flat); Nabo; New Lane Mdw & Moss (cf. *the New Lane* 1537); Parsons Eyes (v. persone, ēg); Pavement Fd (v. pavement); Pingot (v. pingot); Rector's Fd (cf. Parsons

Eyes *supra*); Riddings (*v.* ryding); Rough Hill; Sand Fd & Hill; Sparks (*v.* spearca); Stockley Croft (perhaps from stocc and lēah); Stone House Mdw; Welch Bank Mdw; Whalebone Mdw; White Fd; Willow Moss; Winnington (Moss) (named from the family of Winnington 327 *infra*); Wood Fd; Yusley Croft.

(*b*) *Claye Gape* 1523 (*v.* clǣg, gappe); *Meane Meadow* 1546 ('common meadow', *v.* (ge)mǣne, mǣd); *Pykmercrofte* 1523 (perhaps manorial after Pickmere 120 *supra*, but possibly 'pike pool croft', *v.* pīc¹, mere¹, croft); *Sandywaye hill* 1523 (*v.* sandig, weg, hyll. This could be Hartford Hill *supra*); *Tarbockes Eye alias Pavers Eye alias Leftwich Eye* 1546 (*v.* ēg 'a water-meadow'. The family *de Torboke* held land in Northwich 1295 *Chol*; *Paver* may be the surname from Peover 85 *supra*, 220 *infra*); *le Whetefyld* 1547, 1553 (*v.* hwǣte).

5. MOULTON (HALL) (110–650690) ['moultən, 'mou(l)tn̥, 'mouʔn̥]

> *Moletune* 1086 DB, *-ton* c.1602 *Chol*
> *Multon* 1260 *Court et freq* to 1579 ChRR
> *Molton* 1375 *Eyre* (p), 1544 AD (p)
> *Moulton* 1519, 1596 AD *et freq*, *-Hall* 1831 Bry

'Mūla's or Múli's farm', from the OE pers.n. *Mūla* or ON *Múli* and tūn, but mūl 'a mule' is equally possible, hence 'mule farm', cf. Moulton NRY 286.

EATON BANK WOOD, on the boundary of Eaton 204 *supra*, *v.* banke. FIELD COTTAGES. HILLSIDE FM. JACK LANE, *v.* 203, 204 *supra*. MOULTON BANK & LODGE, *Moulton Farm*, *The Lodge* 1831 Bry. NEW BRIDGE, 1831 ib, a bridge across the Weaver Navigation, cf. Newbridge 326 *infra*. SMOKEHALL LANE (110–653689 to 663682), cf. 203 *supra*, 214 *infra*. This leads past Moulton Hall to the bank of R. Weaver. The name may be from a derogatory allusion to that house, or to the river-valley (i.e. 'smoke-hole'), on account of the industrial smoke from the neighbouring river-side salt-factories, numerous here in 19th century.

FIELD-NAMES

The forms are 1840 *TA* 280, with 1831 Bry.

(*a*) Adams Heath 1831 (*v.* 202 *supra*); Adfield; Bakehouse Fd; Birchen Fd (*v.* bircen²); Flash Mdw (*v.* flasshe); Glade Fd (*v.* glæd³); Gorsty Bank (*v.* gorstig); Lower Head (*v.* hēafod); Big & Little Heys; Holdfords Eye (from ēg 'a water meadow', with either the surname *Hol(d)ford* from Holford 91 *supra*, or the name of a ford from hol² or ald and ford); Hough (*v.* hōh); Lords Park (*v.* hlāford); Mill Fd; Moss Flat; Moultons Wd (*Moulton Wood*

1831); Old Man's Mdw; Outlet(t) (*v.* outlet); Ox Pasture; (Little & Long) Patch; Pike Fd; Ricker Fd; Rye Eddich (*v.* edisc); Sand Fd; Slutch Croft; Snail (Hole) Fd; Stocktons Fd (from either a surname, or stocc, tūn); Swine Cote Mdw (*v.* swin[1], cot); Turnstools (cf. 215 *infra*).

6. NEWALL (FM) (110–699709), *Noua Aula* 1284, 1297 *Chol* (p), *New(e)hall(e)* 1310–30 *ib*, 1391 *AddRoll*, 1430 *Dav*, Neuhall 1375 *Chol* (p), *Newall* 1579 ChRR, *Nual, New-Hall* 1724 NotCestr, 'the new hall', *v.* nīwe, hall. The farm is now *Boundary Farm* 1″ OS, cf. Drakelow Lane *infra*, Stubb's Fm 255 *infra*.   MARSH FM (110–700714).

FIELD-NAMES

The forms are from 1838 *TA* 286, with 1842 OS.

(*a*) Brickiln Croft; Drakelow Lane 1842 (110–698707 to 702706, formerly the south boundary of Newall, now of Lach Dennis c.p., cf. 202 *supra*, hence *Boundary Farm* for Newall Fm *supra*, cf. Drakelow 198 *supra*); Marl Fd; Ovan Fd (*v.* ofen); Sand Fd; Swannick (probably 'swain's dairy-farm', *v.* swān[2], wīc, cf. 256 *infra*).

7. SHIPBROOK (-HILL) (110–674710)

> *Sibroc* 1086 DB, *Sybbroc Major et Minor* 1278 Ipm, *-brok* 1348 *MinAcct*
>
> *S(c)hi(b)broc, -brok(e)* 13 AD, 1248 (1384) Pat, 1311 Ipm, 1325 Plea *et freq* with variant spellings *Shy(b)-, -brock, -brook(e)* from 1287 (18) Sheaf, 1295 Ipm to 1581 ChRR; *Schiberoc* 1284 CASNS II, *Schibbroke Major* 1295 Ipm, *Litelshibbrok* 1410 Plea
>
> *S(c)hyp-, S(c)hipbrok(e)* 1252 RBE, 1254, 1277 P, 1295 Ipm *et freq* with variant spellings *Scip-, -broc, -brouk, -brook(e)* (from 1287 Orm[2]); *Shipbrok on Rudheth* 1346 BPR, *Lytelshipbrok* 1348 *Eyre*, *Litel-* 1422 ChRR, *Shipbrook Hill* 1831 Bry
>
> *Siphpbroc* 1288 Court
>
> *Chippebroc* 1288 Chest
>
> *Schubbrok'* 1311 *Chol*
>
> *S(c)hilbrok(e)* 1311 IpmR, 1312 Misc, Fine
>
> *Schelbroke* 1312 InqAqd
>
> *S(c)hidbrok(es)* 1321 AddCh, 1354 *MinAcct*
>
> *Skipbrok* 1370 *MinAcct*
>
> *Shebroke* 1407 Cl (p), (*Litel-*) 1478 ChRR, (*Magna-, Parva-*) 1514 Plea, *She(a)brook(e)* 1624 Earw, 1637 ChRR
>
> *Shribbroke* 1530 AD
>
> *Seabrook(e)* 1624 Earw
>
> *She(e)pbrooke* 1650 LRMB 278, (18) *Surv*

'Sheep-brook', perhaps a brook where sheep were washed, v. scēap, brōc, and hyll, maior, minor, lȳtel, cf. Rudheath 1 11. Some forms show confusion with *scell, *scille 'noisy' (as in Shell Brook 1 67), and scīd 'a beam (possibly a foot-bridge)'. Shipbrook was the seat of the Vernon family's barony *baronia de Schipbrouk* 1317 Misc *et freq*. *Castle Hill* (110–672712) 1819 Orm² III 253, from which the remains of a castle were removed c.1789, marks their stronghold. A later house was near Manor Fm *infra*.

BROOK FM, cf. *Brook Field* 1838 *TA*.   DAVENHAM RD, leading to Davenham.   MANOR FM, near 110–679708, the site of *Shipbrook Hall* 1724 NotCestr, 1842 OS, cf. *Hall Plantation* 1831 Bry.   OLD LANE.   PARK FM.   SHIPBROOK BRIDGE, 1831 ib, *Shipbrooke-*, *Longe Bridge* 1619 Sheaf, crossing R. Dane into Davenham, v. lang, cf. Bridge End Fm 204 *supra* and *Birdge Cliffe* 1598 Orm², v. clif. SHURLACH LANE (110–675711 to 673720), *Shipbrokeslone* 1346 VR, *Shipbrook Lane* 1831 Bry, from Shipbrookhill *supra* to Shurlach 210 *infra*. Part of it was the boundary of Rudheath heath in 1346, v. 1 12.

FIELD-NAMES

The undated forms are 1838 *TA* 352.

(a) Acres; Bank(s); Big Hill (cf. Shipbrookhill *supra*); Bottoms (v. botm); Brickiln Fd; Canons Acre; Coney Grays ('rabbit warrens', v. coningre); Cop Mdw (v. copp); Corn Hill; Cow Hay; Crabtree Eye or Bridge Mdw (v. ēg, cf. Shipbrook Bridge *supra*); Dane Eye or Town Mdw (cf. prec., v. toun, ēg, R. Dane 1 20); Dry Pits; Ed Fd; Flakes ('hurdles', v. fleke); Hand Fd; Hollis; Hungerhill (v. hungor, hyll); Big & Little Lands (v. land); Marstow (*le Morstal* 1346 VR, *Marstow Meadow* 1650 LRMB 278 'stall or place on a moor', v. mōr¹, stall, a bound of Rudheath heath, v. 1 13); Mile Fd; Milking Bank (v. milking); Moss Fd (cf. *Shipbrokesmos* 1346 VR, a bound of Rudheath heath, v. 1 12 and mos); Muffolands (may contain furlang); North End Mdw (at the northern end of the township); Old Hay; Overflatt (v. uferra, flat); Oxens; Radcliff (v. rēad, clif); Rushy Reans ('rush-grown strips of land', v. riscig, rein); Steand Mdw; Stock Mdw; Tong Shaft (v. Tongue Sharp Wood 1 162); Town Fd (cf. Dane Eye *supra*); Yels Croft.

(b) *Mamhills Yard* 1581 Dep (v. geard); *Millne Lane Bridge* 1619 Sheaf, cf. *Shibbrok mill* 1352 Orm², *molendinum aquaticum in Shipbrok*, etc., 1362 BPR, c.1362, 1393 ChRR, 1410 Orm² (v. myln, lane, brycg); *Polsych* 1346 VR ('watercourse to or from a pool', v. pōl¹, sīc, the boundary of Rudheath heath, v. 1 12).

8. SHURLACH CUM BRADFORD, 1597 *Dav*, *Syrlache et Badeford* 1278 Ipm, *Schorlach et Bradforth'* E3 *Surv*, *Shurlache et Bradford'* 1430 *Dav*, *v.* Shurlach, Bradford *infra*.

BRADFORD FM (110–682731)

> *Bradefort* 1119 (1150), 1150 Chest, (*-iuxta Shibbrock*) 1331–6 *JRC*,
> *-ford* 1119 (1280) Chest, 1278 Ipm (lit. *Bade-) et freq* to 1360
> ChRR, BPR, (*-iuxta Schipbrok*) 1311 Plea, (*-Shurlache*) 1360
> ChRR, BPR; *-forth* 1291 Tax
>
> *Bradforth* E3 *Surv*, *-ford* 1346 VR *et freq*, (*-juxta Shipbrok*) c.1350
> Orm², (*-Shurlache*) 1360 ChRR
>
> *Botford* 1346 BPR, *Botte-* 1347 ib
> *Bradefeld* 1360 BPR

'At the broad ford', *v.* brād (wk.dat. brādan), ford, cf. *Bradfordes-brok*, *Bradeford moor* and 'the field of Bradford' 1346 VR, *Bradeford-feld*, *Bradefordmerefeld* 1310–30 *Chol*, *v.* brōc, feld, mōr¹, (ge)mǣre, and cf. 1 12–13 *supra*. This place is sometimes confused with Bradford in Whitegate, cf. 325 *infra*. The location of the ford is not clear.

HIGHER & LOWER SHURLACH (110–670730, 670720), SHURLACH FM & FIELDS [ˈʃurlatʃ]

> *Suruelec* 1086 DB, *Survaleche* 1154–60 (1329) Ch, (Dugd VI 314
> reads *Surnalethe*)
>
> *S(ch)yrlach(e)* 1278, 1295 Ipm, 1281 Tab, *Shir-* 1424 ChRR, 1527
> Chol, *Shirlacs* 1671 *AddCh*
>
> *S(c)hurlach(e)* c.1284 CASNS II, (17) Tab, 1325 Plea, E3 *Surv*,
> (*-dyche*) 1346 VR *et freq* with variant spellings *-leche*, *-leidge*,
> *-lacs*, *-lack*, (*-iuxta Northwich*) 1381 Plea; *Surlach* 1536 Dugd
> (lit. *-lath*), *-e* 1553 Pat, *-leidg*, *-lidge* 1650 *LRMB* 200, 278
>
> *Shorlache* 1287 Court, 1342 ChRR (p), 1517 Plea, 1552 Tab, 1563
> Sheaf, 1592 ChRR, *Schorlach'* E3 *Surv*, *Shorlachesiche* 1310–30
> Chol
>
> *Ch'rlache'ude* 1310–30 *Chol*

'Bog, or muddy stream, with a scurf on it'. Shurlach is at the confluence of Puddinglake Brook and R. Dane. The second el. is læc(c), lec(c), lece 'a stream, a bog'. The first is OE sc(e)orf, scurf, scyrf, 'scurf' (BT & Suppl *scorf*, NED *scurf*), here probably with the sense 'an incrustation', alluding to a bog with a crust on its surface, or a sluggish stream whose sides are encrusted with dried scum.

The various derivative forms -*'ude*, -*dyche*, -*siche*, and -*Fields*, are 'wood, ditch, water-course and town-fields of Shurlach', *v.* **wudu, dīc, sīc, feld**, higher, lower. For the ditch, see also 1 13.

ASH BANK.   BLEAKHOUSE FM.   SHIPBROOK RD, *v.* Shurlach Lane
209 *supra*.   TANYARD FM.

FIELD-NAMES

The undated forms are 1841 *TA* 355. Of the others, 1346 is VR, 1391 *AddRoll* 5230, 1648, 17 Tab.

(*a*) Abbotts Mdw (perhaps named after the abbot of Dieulacres, *v.* Orm² II 866); Barn Flatt (*Barne Flatt* 1648, *v.* flat); Blanch Fd; Breeches (*v.* brēc); Briery Hill; Bugmoor Hill (perhaps 'goblin's moor', *v.* **bugge, mōr**¹); Gilhill; Gooseledge (*Goslache* 1346, 'goose stream', *v.* **gōs, læc(c)**, a boundary of Rudheath heath, *v.* I 13); Little Lees (*v.* **lǣs** or **lēah**); Marl Fd; Mere Mdw (*v.* (ge)mǣre, cf. *Bradefordmerefeld supra*); Mill Hill (1648); Nields Hill (cf. *Neliscrofte* 1391, 'Nel's croft', from the ME pers.n. *Nel* (cf. *Nigel, Neil, Njáll*) and croft); Pingot (*v.* pingot); Ridding (*v.* ryding); Sid(e)land(s) (*v.* sīd 'wide', land); Swallow Fd; Town Fd; Were Mdw (*v.* wer 'a weir').

(*b*) *caldewalheye* 1391 ('(enclosure at) the cold spring', *v.* **cald, wælla, (ge)hæg**); *collecrimhull* 1391 (the reading -*crim*- is doubtful, but this name may be from the ON pers.n. *Kolgrímr* and hyll); *Dunsmore* 17 ('hill moor', *v.* dūn, -es², mōr¹); *uno molendino aquatico* 1391 (a watermill, site unknown); *Oxeʒe* 1391 ('ox meadow', *v.* **oxa, ēg**); *le Oxeʒung*, *le Oxʒunges* 1391 (*v.* ox-gang); *Philips Hill* 1648; *le Sperh* 1391 (*v.* spearca 'brushwood').

9. STANTHORNE (-HILL FM) (110–690660 and 692668)

(*Magna-, Parva-*) *Stanthirle* 1277 Dugd, (14) VR, 1299 Orm², -*thur(l)l(e)* 1278 Ipm, 1280 IpmR, 1296 Plea (p) *et freq* with variant spellings *Stane-, -thorl* to 1581 ChRR, (*Magna-*) 1315 Plea, (*Great-*) 1353 VR, (*parua-*) 1353 *Indict*, (*Mecul-*) 1369 Tab, (*Mukel-*) 1374 ib, (*Litel-*) 1385 Cl

Stanthorn(e) 13 MidCh (p), 1284 CRC, Ch *et freq* with variant spellings -*thorhn, -thorin, -thirn, -thurn, -turn, Staun-*, (*Parua-*) 1321 AddCh, (*Great-*) 1364 (1484) ChRR, (*Litel(l)-*) 1459 ChRR, Orm², (*Magna-*) 1537 MidCh, (*Over-*) 1541 Orm²; *Stonthorne* 1545 Orm²

Stanitill 1291 Tax

Stanhurle 1291 (1338) VR, -*hurl* 1420 AddCh

Stanton 1347 BPR, *Little Stanton Hill* 1375 Orm², *Spital Hill* latterly *Stanton Hill* 1819 ib (III 262), cf. *The Hill* 1831 Bry, 1842 OS, *Spittle Hill Field* 1841 *TA*, *Letel Stanshurl* 1385 IpmR *v.* **magna, parva, grēat, lȳtel, mycel, uferra**. This p.n. is from **stān** 'a stone' and **þyrel** 'an opening, a gap, a passage-way', (DEPN has 'door'). The final el. gives way to **þorn, þyrne** 'a thorn-tree'. The -*thurl* forms are more frequent until m15, and thereafter the -*thorn* forms. *Stānþyrel* is an unusual name, which led to the substitution of **þyrne**, whence **þorn**, before the date of the earliest record. The significance of *stān-þyrel* is not certain, but 'stone passage' or 'stone doorway' or 'opening in a stone' looks like an allusion to a megalithic monument, perhaps even a burial-chamber of the 'port-hole' type, *v.* Varley 34, cf. The Bridestones 291 *infra*. Little Stanthorne is obviously Stanthornehill, *v.* **hyll**, cf. Whatcroft 215 *infra*. This may have been the site of the lazar-house belonging to Vale Royal abbey mentioned in 1291 Tax (cf. Orm² II 171, 173), *v.* **spitel** 'a hospital'. The form *Stanitill* 1291 Tax may mean 'hill at a stony place', *v.* **stǣniht, hyll**.

WALLANGE BRIDGE & FM (110–690655), [ˈwɔlənd͡ʒ], *Walleng Bridge* 1619 Sheaf, *Wallange Farm* 1842 OS, *Wall-inch-bridge* 1643 Orm², *Wall Inch* 1883 Sheaf (road and land in Newton, cf. 245 *infra*), perhaps 'well bank', *v.* **wælla, hlinc, hlenc**. However, it may be an old -**ing²** formation meaning 'place where water springs', though the forms are too late for certainty. The name obviously extends either side of R. Wheelock near the bridge. It may be original to Newton, giving name to the bridge which gave name to the farm.

BANK FM, cf. *Buckleyes Banckes iuxta aquam de Dane* 1622 ChCert, -*Bancke* 1630 ChRR, held by Richard *Bulkeley*, knight, d.1621, *v.* **banke** 'a hill-side, a bank'.   BROWN BROOK (lost), 1831 Bry, the boundary of Clive, cf. *Big-, Further-* & *Great Browns* 1841 *TA*, *v.* **brún², brōc**, cf. 235 *infra*.   DAIRY HO, 1842 OS, -*Farm* 1831 Bry, both maps have it at 110–680645 in Wimboldsley 257 *infra*.   GREEN-HAYS FM.   MIDDLEWICH RD, *Gravel Road* 1831 Bry, cf. I 47, Middlewich 240 *infra*.   PARK FM, *Stanthorne Farm* 1831 Bry. STANTHORNE BRIDGE, *pons de Quelok* c.1300 Chol, *Wheelock Bridge* 1619 Sheaf, crossing R. Wheelock I 38, into Middlewich. STANTHORNE HALL & MILL, 1831 Bry.   STANTHORNEMILL FM, *Moor House* 1831 ib, *v.* **mōr¹**, cf. Stanthorne Mill *supra*.

FIELD-NAMES

The undated forms are 1841 *TA* 365.

(a) The Acres; Birchin Bank (v. bircen[2]); Black Fd; Braddy; Brains Fd (perhaps from brægen); Brom Fd (v. brōm); Carp Pip Fd (? for -*Pit*-); Cow Moss (v. cū, mos); Crabtree Knowl; The Croft (cf. *the Croftes* 1418 Tab, v. croft); Cross Fd; Dane Mdw (v. R. Dane 1 20); Davenham Flatt (v. flat, Davenham 203 *supra*); Day Math (v. day-math); Digbite; Little Eace (perhaps for *ees*, v. ēg 'an island, a water-meadow', but a derogatory name 'little-ease' is possible); Flatts (v. flat); Friars Fd; Glade Fd; Hall Fd; Hamp Yard (v. hemp-yard); Horse Moss; Kiln Fd; Little Lay (v. lēah); Marl Fd; Moss (cf. *mussetum de parua Stanthorne* 1333 MidCh, v. mos (MedLat *mossetum*) cf. Moss, etc. 214 *infra*); Muck Fd; The News; Nitch Fd; Oat Rough; Orchard Mdw; Ox Pasture; Riddings (v. ryding); Sand Fd; Sprink (v. spring); Way Fd (v. weg); Wham House Fd (cf. *Mawhouse* 1637 Sheaf).

(b) *Westcroft* 1277 (1350) VR, *Westcrofte* (lit. *Wert*-) 1299 Orm[2] II 169 (v. west, croft).

10. WHARTON (GREEN) (110–660660) ['ʌ-, 'wɔːr-, 'waːrtən]

Wanetune 1086 DB

(*vetus*-, *Old(e)*-, *alter*-) *Waverton* 1216 MainwB, c.1230 & 1269 (1400) CASNS XIII, 1415 Orm[2], ChRR, *Wav*-, *Wauerton* 1259 Plea *et freq* to 1628 Orm[2], (-*iuxta Bustok*) 1288 Court, (-*Medium Wicum*, -*Overe*) 1535 VE, (-*alias War(e)ton*) 1599, 1628 Orm[2]; *Wauirthon* 1281 Tab

Wal-, *Wollverton iuxta Bostok* 1287 Court, 1288 Plea

(*Vetus*-, *Old(e)*-) *War(e)ton* 1288 Court, 1315 Plea, Orm[2] (p) *et freq* to 1633 ib, (-*iuxta Middlewich*, -*Clyve*) 1315 Plea, (-*Bostok*) 1369 ib, (-*Over*) 1441 MainwB, (-*in hundredo de Northwich*) 1418 Plea, (-*alias Waverton*) 1499 Orm[2]

Oldewarden 1382 Plea (-*on* Orm[2])

Wharton 1398 ChRR, Pat, 1724 NotCestr, -*Green* 1831 Bry

Werton 1420 Orm[2]

Little Warson 1553 MainwB

v. wæfre, tūn. The significance is uncertain, but is probably either 'farm at a waving tree' or 'farm at a quaking bog' (cf. Moss *infra*). The same name appears at Waverton 327 *infra*, Warton St (Duignan 160), Wa 23, Wharton He (DEPN), La 43, and cf. Waverley Sr 174. DEPN s.n. Waverley suggests from analogous continental p.ns. that the el. *waver*- means 'brushwood'. The forms rule out a derivation from R. Weaver 1 38, beside which Wharton stands. It is distinguished from Waverton by relation to Bostock 202 *supra*, Over, Middlewich and Clive 326, 240, 234 *infra*. 'The other' (Lat *alter*) or 'Little-' (*v.* lȳtel) is distinguished from 'Old-' Wharton (*v.* ald). There were two manors here TRE, *v.* Orm² III 264.

STREET-NAMES. GRAVEL HILL, *Winsford Hill* 1842 OS, leading down to Winsford Bridge, cf. Station Rd *infra*, Winsford 327 *infra*, *v.* hyll; MARKET PLACE, *v.* market; STATION RD, *Gravel Lane* 1842 OS, cf. Gravel Hill *supra*, Gravel Fm and Middlewich Rd 235 *infra*, Redestrete 235 *infra*, all in the same line of road, 110–656663 to 685667, and presumably alluding to the gravel with which it was metalled, cf. 1 47.

BOTTOM FLASH, a lake formed by subsidence of a reach of R. Weaver, *v.* flasshe, cf. *Flash Meadow* 1838 *TA* and Witton Flashes 197 *supra*. CROOK LANE, from a twist in its course, *v.* krókr.   DONEFIELDS, cf. *Done's Works* 1831 Bry, from the surname *Done*.   GREVILLE LODGE, probably a euphemism for *Gravel*, *v.* Station Rd *supra*. NUN HO, *le Nunhouse* 1554 Pat, *Nunehowse* 1554 *MinAcct*, (*the*) *Nunhouse* 1621 Orm², 'the nun-house', belonging to the Nuns of Chester, cf. 1554 Pat 507, *v.* nunne, hūs.   OAKLANDS, *The-* 1831 Bry.   THE PARK.   RILSHAW (LANE), 1838 *TA*, *Ryelshall* 1536 (1574) ChRR, 1562 Orm², *-shaw* 1562 ib, *Raleshawe* (lit. *Kale-*) 1599 ib III 216, *Relshaw's tenement* 1749 Sheaf, 'wood at rye-hill', *v.* ryge, hyll, sceaga.   SMOKEHALL LANE, *v.* 207 *supra*.   TANNER'S WELL.   WINSFORD BRIDGE & LODGE, 1831 Bry, cf. Winsford 327 *infra*.

FIELD-NAMES

The undated forms are 1838 *TA* 424. Of the others, c.1230, c.1240 are (1400) CAS NS XIII, 1333 MidCh.

(*a*) Bakehouse Fd; Bank; Blake Fd (*v.* blæc); Bow Ridding (*v.* ryding); Broom Fd & Yards (*v.* brōm, geard); Catherine Croft; Old Chapel Fd; Clapperhangs; Cliff Moss (*v.* clif, mos, cf. Clive 234 *infra*); Cow Hill; Crooked Fd (cf. *Crokedeforlong* c.1230, *v.* croked, furlang); Daymath (*v.* day-math); Fallow Fd; Fitch Fd (*v.* ficche); Glade Fd & Mdw; Gravel Fd (*v.* gravel, cf. Gravel Hill *supra*); Green Fd ('field at Wharton Green *supra*', *v.* grēne²); Hastage; Herons (*v.* hyrne); Hobb Croft (*v.* hobb(e) 'a tussock'); Kiln Fd; Kitchen Fd; Milking Bank (*v.* milking); Moss (Fd & Flatts) (*mussetum de Veteri Warton* 1333, the same as 'a plot of moss in Oldwaverton and Stanthorne' mentioned 1415, 1460 ChRR, *v.* mos (MedLat *mossetum*),

flat, cf. Wharton *supra*, Moss 213 *supra*); National Patent; Nunners' Wall
Fd ('field at a well or spring belonging to Nun Ho *supra*', *v.* wælla); Orchard
Fd; Over Fd (cf. *Overe Forlong* c.1230, 'the higher furlong', *v.* uferra,
furlang); Ox Hayes, -Heyes; Paddock; Little Patch; Pingow (*v.* pingot);
Riddings (*v.* ryding); Saggs; Sand Fd; Shambles (*v.* sceamol); Long Slang
(*v.* slang); Town Fd; Turning Shoots (*v.* scēat); Turnstools (cf. 208 *supra*);
Wall-, Well Croft & Fd (*v.* wælla, wella); Welshman's Acre; Whistleys.

(*b*) *Fridaieslake* c.1230, *-lache* c.1240 ('the Friday stream', perhaps
because the Friday diet was caught here, *v.* Frīgedæg, læc(c), lacu. Professor
Sørensen points out the parallel Danish stream-name *Fredagsbæk* in Jutland
(DaSN IX 123), from which the bishop of Viborg got his fish for fast-days);
Solmegrenes, *Solme Greneforlong* c.1230 (for the first el. *v.* *Sullunhull* 323
infra. The second is either grēne[2] 'a green' or grǣfe 'a grove, a copse', *v.*
furlang).

11. WHATCROFT (HALL) (110–681698) ['wɔt-, 'ʍɔt-]

    Watecroft(e) 1255 Sheaf, E3 *Surv*, *Qw-*, *Quate-* 1289 Plea, Court,
    Whate- 1310–30 *Chol et freq* to 1388 AD, *Whatcroft(e)* 1346 VR,
    1390 Orm[2], 1426 ChRR *et freq*, *Whatcroft Hall* 1724 NotCestr
    W(h)etecroft 1288 Court, Plea
    Whitcroft 1560 Orm[2]

'The wheat field', *v.* hwǣte, croft. Orm[2] III 262 identifies this with
Little Stanthorne, but *v.* 212 *supra*.

BRIDGE FM, *Bridge House* 1831 Bry, near a bridge over an unnamed
stream, *v.* brycg.   BROOK HO (110–691698), 1831 ib, near Puddinglake Brook, which crosses King Street nearby, and is probably *le
Hethlach* 1346 VR, 'the boggy stream from the heath', *v.* hǣð, læc(c),
one of the bounds of Rudheath heath, *v.* 1 12, 34.   DAIRY
FM, 1831 Bry.   WHATCROFT LANE, 1831 Bry, *Whatcrofteslone*
1346 VR, a bound of Rudheath heath 1 12, *v.* lane.   YEWTREE
HO, 1831 Bry.

FIELD-NAMES

The undated forms are 1838 *TA* 425. Of the others, 1255 is Sheaf, 1310–30
Chol. 1346 VR, 1461 Orm[2], 1622 *ChCert*, 1630 ChRR, 1677 *LRMB* 211,
1831 Bry.

(*a*) Adam's Eye Mdw (*v.* ēg, cf. Adamsheath 202 *supra*), Bancroft ('bean
croft', *v.* bēan); Bear Fd; Broom Fd (*v.* brōm); Chairs Yard; Char Coal Fd
(*v.* charcole); Crab Tree Bridge 1831 (over Trent & Mersey Canal); Crooks
(*v.* krókr); Cuttings; Dove House Fd; Gib Fd; Gladerow; Hall Bridge 1831,

Hall Fd (cf. Whatcroft Hall *supra*); Hay Greaves (*v.* (ge)hæg, grǽfe); Heath Croft (cf. *Hethwode infra*); Intack (*v.* inntak); Kiln Fd; Land Croft (*v.* land 'a selion'); Ley Fd (from ModE *ley* 'a piece of pasture', cf. lēah); Long Shute (*v.* scēat); Lord's Mdw; Marl Heys (*v.* marle, (ge)hæg); Mill Mdw; Moss Fd; Outlet (*v.* outlet); Oven Fd (*v.* ofen); Ox Hey; Rough Riddings (*v.* ryding); Sand Fd; Slutch Fd; Stander Fd (7x), Knowl *&* Mdw (from standard 'the standing stump of a tree'); Sword Wd (first el. obscure, perhaps the same as in *Swerdwode, Werdswode* 1278 Pat 255, 256, a wood between Kinnerton and Mold Fl, and cf. *Sworwde, Swordwud* 1247 P (p), *v.* wudu); Town Fd; Underwood (*v.* under, wudu); The Way Fd; Wood.

(*b*) *Alstan Thornsyche* 1346 ('(watercourse at) Alstan's thorn', from the ME pers.n. *Alstān* (Feilitzen 152) and þorn, with sīc, *v.* 1 12); *le Hethwode* 1255 ('wood at a heath', *v.* hǽð, wudu, cf. *Wodehouses infra*); *Pertreleghes -lyes* 1310–30, 1346, -*Lee* 1461, *Pearetree lee* 1622, 1630 ('clearings, or meadow, at the pear-tree(s)', *v.* peru, trēow, lēah or lǽs, *v.* 1 12); *Stonyfeilds* 1677 (*v.* stānig, feld); *le Whitesych* 1346 ('the white stream', *v.* hwīt, sīc; the colour may have come from a brine spring. This was a bound of Rudheath heath, *v.* 1 12); (the lane of) *Wodehouses* 1346 (on the boundary of Rudheath heath, cf. 1 12, probably leading to houses in a wood, cf. *Hethwode supra, v.* wudu, hūs).

iv. Nether Peover Chapelry

Nether Peover was a parochial chapelry of Great Budworth parish 95 *supra*. It contained the townships 1. Peover Inferior 90 *supra*, 2. Plumley 90 *supra*, in Bucklow Hundred, and 3. Allostock, 4. Nether Peover (now a c.p. including part of Peover Inferior), in Northwich Hundred. Allostock was not mentioned in DB, Nether Peover was included with the other Peovers under *Bochelau* (Bucklow) Hundred.

3. ALLOSTOCK (110–750710) [ɔ:(l)ˈlɔstɔk]

    Allostok 13 MainwB, 1312 Misc *et freq*, -*stock(e)* 1234 (17) Tab, 1534 AD, 1539 ChRR *et freq*, (-*or Over Lostock*) 1819 Orm²; -*stoke* 1503 ChRR

    Allelostock' 1310–30 *Chol*

    Alstoke 1312 InqAqd, -*stok* 1515 *MinAcct*

    Albostok, Albe- 1312 Fine, Orig

    Superior Lostok 1331 Tab, *Over Lostocke* 1386 Orm²

    Alastoke 1547 *MinAcct, Allastock* 1594 Tab

    Alwastocke 1554 *MinAcct,* -*stock* 17 Tab

    Allestocke 1673 ChRR

    All Lostock 1724 NotCestr

'The higher part of Lostock', *v.* superior, uferra, and cf. Lostock Gralam 189 *supra* where the earlier material is given. The difficult initial el. *Al(le)-*, an affix distinguishing this township from the other Lostock, might be taken to be hall (gen.sg. halle) 'a hall', also appearing as an affix in *Allom* 275 *infra* (*Halle-*, *Allehulm(e)* H3) and Little Sutton 327 *infra* (*Hallesutton* 1278). However, in view of the absence of *H-* spellings, Ekwall's suggestion (DEPN) of ald 'old', would suit Allostock, with loss of *-d* before *-l*; but ald would not suit Little Sutton or *Allom* with their *Halle-* forms. Moreover, *Allom* might then be expected to show a similar development to Oldham La 50 (from ald, hulm). The prefix 'hall' would be an appropriate distinction between Little Sutton and Great Sutton 327 *infra*. The ancient manors of Hulme and Bradshaw are in Allostock, while Lostock Gralam has no manor-house. Nor is there now a hall at *Allom*, but there probably was, for the place was 'a vill' in 1296 (Ipm III 271, No. 408), it gave rise to surnames, and is distinguished from 'Church' Hulme 278 *infra*. The persistent *Al(le)-* form in Allostock, with absence of initial *H-*, is analogous with that in *Allom*, perhaps also with Allgreave, Allmeadows 1 168. The *Alb-* forms are orthographic sports for *All-*.

BRADSHAW (BRIDGE, Ho & BROOK FM) (110–738725), *Bradshawe* 12 Tab, *-shaw* 1234 ib *et freq* with variant spellings *Brade-* (c.1300 *Chol* to 1378 *Pat*), *-s(c)hawe*, *-s(c)hagh*, *-saghe*, *-scawe*, *-schewe*, *-chawe*, *-shagh(e)*; *Bradshaghfeld* 1465 Tab, *-fild* 1472 ChRR, *Bradshaw-brooke* 1554 Orm², *a horse bridge over Bradshawe* 1619 Sheaf, *Bradshaw House, Bradshaw Brook Bridge* 1831 Bry, *Bradshaw Bridge* 1842 OS, *Bradshaw hey* 1845 *TA*, 'the broad wood', from brād and sc(e)aga, *v.* also brycg, hūs, brōc, feld, (ge)hæg. Cf. Bradshaw Brook 1 17. The bridge might be the site of *Hardeshagheforth*, a bound of Rudheath heath, *v.* 1 12.

HULME (COVERT, HALL, LANE & MILL) (110–720720), *Hulm* c.1212 Morris, 1219 *Chol*, *-e* c.1233 Orm², (*maner' de*) 1430 ChRR, *Holme* 1292 Orm², (*le*) *Holm* c.1294 ChFor, c.1320 *Chol*, *Houlme* (*in Allostock*) 1464 (17) Orm², (*-juxta Nether-Pever*) 1666 ib, *Hoome* c.1662 *Surv*, 'the water meadow', from hulm, holmr, *v.* also hall, lane, myln. Hulme Covert is *Hulme Sprynge* 1549 *Chol*, *v.* spring 'a young wood'. Hulme Mill was *the water milne of Hulme called Hulme mylne* 1549 *Chol*, cf. *Mill Pool, Field & Meadow* 1845 *TA* and Millgate Fm *infra*. Various parts of the ancient hall of Hulme are named in 1429 Orm² III 149, '*the lesser chamber, le Pantre, le Buttre, the Larder, le*

Deyhouse, le Malthous, le . . . *berne, le Hayberne, le Vyne Yorde, le Night'gale Erber* ('the Nightingale Arbour'), *le Lytell Erber, the bridge'*. This bridge crossed the moat, cf. *maner de Hulme et aqua circumeund' vocata le Pele* 1465 Tab, 'the peel, the moated site', *v. peel* (NED, sb[1]), cf. pēl, and Peel 327 *infra*. For Hulme Lane cf. *Saltway* 222 *infra*.

PORTFORD BRIDGE & FM (110–716728), *vadum de Porteford'* 1291–1316 Chest, *Le Porteforth, -forde* E3 ChRR, *Portforth* 1346 VR, *-forde* 1445 ChRR, *-ford* 1650 *LRMB* 278, *Portford Bridge* 1831 Bry, *Peckford Bridge* 1619 Sheaf, 'the market ford', *v.* port[2], ford. This carried the highway from Macclesfield to Northwich (*v.* 1 46, 49) across Crow Brook 1 20 (cf. ChetNS LXXXII 731, DKR XXXVI 496, Orm[2] III 167); it was probably a salt-way (*v.* Crump 96); and it was a bound of Rudheath heath, *v.* 1 12.

ALLOSTOCK BRIDGE, 1831 Bry, *v.* brycg, cf. Oldbridge Fm *infra*. AXON'S SMITHY, 1842 OS.   BAKER'S LANE, 1831 Bry, cf. *Saltway* 222 *infra*.   BOOTHBED FM & LANE, *Booth Beds* 1842 OS, *Rough Bed* 1831 Bry, *Bowbedd House* 17 Sheaf, *v.* bedd 'a bed, a plot of ground where plants are grown', cf. foll.   BOOTS GREEN, 1831 Bry, cf. *le Bothe* 1381 *Chol*, *v.* bōth 'herdsman's hut or shelter', grēne[2] 'a green', cf. prec.   BROOKHOUSE FM, *Bull's Head* (*Inn*) 1831 Bry, 1842 OS.   CHAPEL FM & HO.   CHARITY FM. CLAY BANK, cf. *Clay Croft & Hill* 1845 *TA*, *v.* clǣg.   CROSS LANES FM, *Cross Lanes* 1831 Bry, a cross-roads where the Holmes Chapel–Knutsford road crosses the Northwich–Macclesfield route, cf. 1 44, 46, *v.* cros, lane.   DRAKELOW FM, probably named after Drakelow 198 *supra*.   FULLERS GATE, 1842 OS.   THE GULLET (a stream), *Gullet* 1842 ib, *v.* golet.   HALES PASTURE.   HEATH FM, cf. *Heath croft & Field* 1845 *TA*, cf. Rudheath *infra*.   HIGH-FIELD HO, *High Field* 1842 OS.   HOLE HOUSE (WOOD) & LANE, *Hole House* 1845 *TA*, *v.* hol[1] 'a hollow'.   KING'S LANE, 1831 Bry, *v.* 188 *supra*.   MILLGATE FM, 1831 ib, 'gate or road to a mill' named from Hulme Mill *supra*, *v.* gata, geat.   MILL HO, named from Over Peover Bridge & Mill 88 *supra*.   NEW PLATT (FM, LANE & WOOD), *New Plat* 1831 Bry, *The Gall Plantation* 1831 Bry, 1842 OS, 'the new plot of ground', an intake from Rudheath *infra*, *v.* plat[2]. The other name presumably refers to a plantation where oak gall was obtained.   OLDBRIDGE FM, named from Allostock Bridge *supra.* Old Mill Fm. Old Wood, 1842 ib, *Old Plantation* 1831 Bry. Over Peover Bridge, cf. 88 *supra.* Racecourse Wood. Rudheath, 1831 ib, cf. *Rudheath Field* 1845 *TA*, a tract of heath in this and neighbouring townships, the remnant of the ancient heath of Rudheath 1 11. Sandhole Fm, cf. *Sand Hole Field* 1845 *TA.* Sculshaw Green & Lodge, 1831 Bry. Shakerley Wood, named from the *Shakerley* family of Hulme Hall *supra.* Townfield Fm, cf. *Town Field* 1845 *TA.* Wash Lane (Fm), 1842 OS, *v.* wæsce 'a place for washing', e.g. a sheep-wash. Widow's Home Fm. Woodland Fm & Ho, Woodside Fm.

FIELD-NAMES

The undated forms are 1845 *TA* 9. Of the others, 1219 is *Chol*, c.1294 *ChFor*, 1346 VR, 1464, 1465 (17) Orm², 1465, 1474, 1768 Tab, 1474² *JRC*.

(a) Bakehouse Fd (*v.* Oven Fd *infra*); Bank; Barn Flatt; Barrows Lake (*v.* bearg, lacu); Bent Fd (*v.* beonet); Big Sprink (*v.* spring 'a young wood'); Birch Hall Fd, Birchin Flatt & Hay (cf. *Bircheles* 1219, *Birchels* c.1294, 'little birches', and 'flat plot of land, enclosure, growing with birches', *v.* bircel, bircen²); Birds Eye; Black Fd, Blake Fd (*v.* blæc); Blind Hole (cf. 221 *infra*); Bottoms (*v.* botm); Bower End (*v.* būr¹, ende¹); Brick Hill, Brick Kiln Fd (*v.* bryke-kyl); Burnt Lane Croft; Calvey Croft (cf. *Callecroft* 1465, 'calves' croft', *v.* calf (gen.pl. calfa), croft); Clough (*v.* clōh); Cockle Fd (*v.* coccel); Cooks Stool (*v.* cucke-stole); Coppice; Cow Hey; Cross Fd (*the two Cross fields* 1768, *v.* cros); Cuttings; The Danes (*v.* denu); Dovehouse Fd; Fallow Fd; Firplatt; Flash Fd (*v.* flasshe); Four Lane Ends; The Gaw, Gaw Fd & Mdw (*v.* galla 'a wet or barren spot'); Gighole (*v.* gigge, hōl¹); Green (cf. *le Grene* 1465, *v.* grēne²); Guinea Fd; Hat Fd; Hobb Lake & Mdw (*v.* hob 'a goblin', or hobb(e) 'a tussock', lacu 'a watercourse'); Horse Hey; Hunger Hill (*v.* hungor); Intack, Intake (*freq, v.* inntak); Kiln Croft & Fd; Knock Acres (*v.* cnocc); Lady Hey (*v.* hlǣfdige, (ge)hæg); Lands Fd (*v.* land); Lane Stead (*v.* lane, stede); Lays, Leys (*v.* lēah); Loft Acre; Long Butt(s); Long heys (cf. *Longhey* 1465, *v.* lang, (ge)hæg); Long Shoot (*v.* scēat); Lostock hursts (*v.* hyrst); Main Wd (*v.* main); Marl Croft & Fd; Mean Wd (*v.* (ge)mǣne); Milkin(g) Bank & Croft (*v.* milking); Moss on Peover Heath (*v. Common Moss* 220 *infra*); Muck Fd; Ness Fd (*v.* nes² 'a headland, a promontory', here probably 'a projecting piece of land'); Nickow Fd; Noggin Brow (perhaps a hill where clay was got for making wattle and daub, *v.* nogging, brū); Old Lane; Oulery Fd (*v.* alor); Outlet (*v.* outlet); Oven Fd or Bake house Fd; Ox Rough (*v.* oxa, rūh); Pam Hills Mdw; Park Mdw (cf. *Parkefeld* 1465, *v.* park); Pickow Fd (*v.* pichel); Pinfold Fd (*v.* pynd-fald); Pingot(t) (*v.* pingot); Push Marl Fd; Putty Fd; Rail Croft (*v.* rail(e)); Ripstitch; Rough Moss; Senex Mdw; Seven Shilling Worth (*v.* shillingworth); The Shaws (*v.* sceaga); Shippon Fd (*Sheponfeld* 1465, *v.* scypen); Skin Fd; Slate Gate Fd (*v.* slæget, gata); Slutch Fd; Spath (probably *Sparth*, i.e. from sparðr 'sheep droppings'); Spring Shaw Butts ('selions at a young wood', *v.* spring, sceaga, butte); Sprink Fd (*v.* spring, cf. prec.); Stay Fd (perhaps from stæg 'a pool'); Storkey Flatt; Stubbs Green (*v.* grēne², cf. Stublach 255 *infra*); Swine Cote Mdw; Tan House Mdw, Tan Pit Mdw (*v.* tan-hous, tan-pit); Three Nook(s); Warren Fd; Way Fd; Wheat Fd (cf. *Whete Crofte* 1564, *v.* hwǣte); Whithymore Mdw (*v.* wiðig, mōr¹); Work House Fd.

(*b*) *Chikenshagh in Ruddeheth* 1346 ('chicken wood', *v.* cicen, sceaga, a bound of Rudheath heath 1 12, probably near Rudheath *supra*); *Hard-shaghforth* (*v.* Bradshaw *supra*); *le Oldhey* 1465 (*v.* ald, (ge)hæg); *Ormesforth* (*v. Ormesforde* 222 *infra*); *Py(e)greve* (*Wood*) 1464, 1465, 1474, 1474² ('magpie wood', *v.* pīe², grǣfe); *Rynesforth* (*v.* 222 *infra*); *Stubbyngeffeld* 1465 ('field at the place where trees have been stubbed up', *v.* stubbing, feld).

4. NETHER PEOVER (110–730730) [pi:vər]

Pevre 1086 DB, -*u*- 1194 Facs, 1295 Lacy, (*Inferior-, Nether(e)-, -ir-*) *Pev(e)re, -er, -u-* 1288 Court, 1292, 113 Tab, 1302 ChF, 1310 Plea, 1375 *AddCh, le Nether Peuere* 1345 *Eyre, Netre-, Inferior P(h)efre* 1317 *Chol, Nether Pevor* 1507 *ib*
Peua c.1200 Tab
Inferior Peuerhe 113 Tab
Piuer Inferior 113 Tab, *Nether Pyver* 1540 Dugd
Nether Peover 1508 Tab, *Great-* 1641 Sheaf, *Lower-* 1724 NotCestr
Nether Peever 1621 Orm², *Greater-* 1676 Tab, *Neither-* 1702 *ib*

'The lower, or greater, part of Peover', *v.* neoðera, grēat, Peover Eye 1 33, Peover Inferior & Superior 90, 85 *supra*.

BACK LANE (FM), *Back Lane* 1831 Bry, 'the lane at the back of the township', *v.* back.   BAKER'S LANE, 1831 ib, cf. *Saltway infra*.
CHEADLE LANE, 1831 ib, cf. Back Lane 93 *supra*.   COMMON MOSS (lost), 1831 ib, *v. Sandlow Moss* 91 *supra*.   CROWN LANE (FM), *Crown Lane Farm* 1842 OS, named from *Crowne Inne* 1702 Tab, *The Crown* 1831 Bry, a public house here.   FOX COVERT FM, COTTAGES & LANE, *Peever Heath* 1677 Tab, *Peover Heath Covert* 1831 Bry, cf. foll., *v.* hæð, covert.   HEATH FM, *v.* prec.   HULME LANE, 1831 ib, cf. 217 *supra, Saltway infra*.   LOWER PEOVER MILL, *Coppocks Mill* 1831 Bry, from the surname *Coppock*.   MILLBANK FM.   PATMOS.   PUMP HO, 1842 OS.   PURCHASE LANDS (110–748730), 1831 Bry, *the purchased lande* 1491 Tab, (*Graveners Bankes alias-*) 1564 ib, from the purchase of a moiety of Nether Peover by Robert Grosvenor of Hulme in Allostock from William

de Mobberley, c.1320–27 Orm² I 668.   Swan Green, 1769 Tab.
Trouthall Bridge, *Wooden Bridge* 1831 Bry, named from Trouthall 93 *supra.*   Yewtree Fm, *Yewtree House* 1831 ib.

FIELD-NAMES

The undated forms are 1844 *TA* 318. Of the others, e13 (17) is Dieul, 1232
Dugd, H3² MainwB, c.1300, 1507 *Chol*, 1346 VR, 1554, 1557 Pat, and the
rest Tab.

(*a*) Bakehouse Croft; Barrows Fd (cf. *Barrowe's Greene & intake* 1702,
from the surname *Barrow*, *v.* grēne², inntak); Big Mdw (cf. *Greate Medowe*
1557, *v.* grēat); Birchen Flat (cf. *le Birchen(e)lond* 13, e14, *v.* bircen², land);
Blind Hole (*the* 1695, cf. 219 *supra*, *v.* blind, hol¹); Bridge Croft; Broad Fd
((*le*) *Bradefeld* l13–e14, *v.* brād, feld); Brook Fd (*le Brocfeld* 1317, *v.* brōc,
feld); Butty Mdw (*v.* butty); Church Fd (*Chyrchefeld* H3, *Chirchefeld in
Inferior Peuere* l13, *v.* cirice, feld); Common Lane Fd; Copy (*v.* copis); Dig
Fd (*v.* dīc); Dilseymoor; Dog Lane Fd; Ducking Stook (cf. cucke-stole);
Eyes (*v.* ēg); Fair Pleck (*Feyre Plek* 1535, 'the fair plot', *v.* fæger, plek);
French Fd; Frodsham Fd (cf. Frodsham 326 *infra*); Hatch Fd (*v.* hæc(c));
Heath Fd; Hillikin Fd; Horse Hey (*le Horseheye* l13–e14, *v.* hors, (ge)hæg);
Intake; Kirk Fd (*v.* kirkja); Kite Clough (*Kyd Clough* 1695, cf. *Cuythylcroft*
l13–e14, 'kite dell, croft at kite-hill', *v.* cȳta, clōh, hyll, croft); Mainwarings
Fd (named from the *Mainwaring* family of Peover); Marl Eyes & Fd (*v.* ēg);
Modus; Moss, Moss Fd; Ouzleden (*v.* ōsle, denu); Pleck (*v.* plek); Plumley
Moor Fd (cf. Plumley Moor 91 *supra*); Poolstead (*v.* pōl-stede); Priest
Ridding (*Preyst Rydding* 1545, cf. *the Rydding, -Riddyng* 1556, 'priest's
clearing', *v.* prēost, ryding); Shackerley's Mdw (named from the *Shakerley*
family of Hulme 217 *supra*); Shaws (*v.* sceaga); Smithy Fd (1718); Sour Fd;
Stairs Croft (perhaps from stǣger 'a stair'); Sweet Fd; Tentry Croft (*v.*
tentour); Three Nooks; Town Fd; Wag Fd; Wrights Croft (cf. *Wrightes
Hedge* 1564, *v.* hecg).

(*b*) *bornecroft* 1293 ('croft by a stream', *v.* burna, croft); *bouirflat* l13–e14
(from flat 'a piece of flat level ground', *v.* būr¹ 'a cottage' or (ge)būr 'a
peasant'); *Bowkerscroft* 1501 (from the occupational surname *Bowker* (Fransson 109) and croft); *le Bradebrugge* e13 (*v.* brād, brycg); *Dandecroft* l13–
e14 ('Dande's croft', from the ME pers.n. *Dande*, a pet-form of *Andrew*,
v. croft); *le ford, fordeforlong'* 13 (*v.* ford, furlang); *Gatelond* e13, *le Catelond*
l13–e14 ('selion at a road', *v.* gata, land); *le Gleyde heye* 1507 ('kite enclosure',
v. gleoda, (ge)hæg); *Hardeshagh(e)forth* 1346 (*v.* Bradshaw Bridge 217 *supra*);
Hemmyngilcroft l13–e14 ('croft at Hemming's hill', from the ON, ODan
pers.n. *Hem(m)ingr* and hyll, with croft); *le heye* l13–e14, *le iii heys* l13,
Lytlehey l13–e14 (*v.* (ge)hæg); *Hiccocke landes* 1651 (one *Hiccock* owned them
in 1509 Tab, *v.* land 'a selion'); *Pever Holmes* 1554, 1557 ('water-meadows
in Peover', a detached part of the demesnes of Rudheath 198 *supra*, *v.* holmr);
le Homiseuest, le Howeseuse c.1290 (the second el. is efes 'eaves, an edge or
border', the first is either hōh 'a spur of land' or hamm, homm 'an enclosure,

a meadow, a water-meadow'); *Horsley* e14 ('horse clearing', v. hors, lēah); *houchecroft* l13–e14 (v. croft); *houereforlong* l13–e14, *houerforlone* e14 (v. uferra, furlang); *Humsolnscroft* l13 (v. croft); *Hunstablissache* e13, *Hunstablesawe* H3², *Hunstablesscalie* e14 (from sceaga 'a wood', skáli 'a temporary hut or shed', and perhaps læc(c) 'a boggy stream' (if -ss- for -sl- rather than -sch-), with a first el. which may be a mis-copy of *Cunstable* 'a constable', v. conestable; the Lacy family, constables of Chester, held land here in the thirteenth century, cf. NRA 3636, No 450 etc.); *le Medulon* l13–e14 ('meadow lane', v. mǣd, lane); *Ormesforde* l13–e14, *-forth* 1346 ('Orm's ford', from the ON pers.n. *Ormr* (ODan *Orm*) and ford; a bound of Rudheath heath, v. 1 12); *Peuere lee* l13 ('the wood of Peover', v. lēah, cf. *boscus-*, *nemus de Pevere* e13 (17), 1232, c.1290); *Raleg, le Roeleg* l13 ('roe-buck's clearing', v. rā¹, lēah); *Rismeford* l13–e14, *Rynesforth* 1346 (perhaps 'ford at the brushwood', v. hrīsen, ford, cf. 1 12); *Saltway* l13 (v. salt¹, weg, probably Baker's Lane and Hulme Lane *supra*, cf. 1 46); *Swyneheueyt* H3 ('swine hill', v. swīn¹, hēafod); *Turnecroft* l13–e14, H3 (v. trun, croft); *Twysilmeford* H3 ('ford at the fork(s)', v. twisla, ford, the -me- probably representing the OE gen.pl. -ena inflexion of *twisla*); *Wedwodd, Wetwode* 1501 (v. wēt, wudu); *Wych Mosse* 1535 (from wīc 'a hamlet' or wice 'a wych-elm' and mos 'a moss'); *Wyngyl'mor* l13 (possibly 'moor at a corner', v. wincel, mōr¹).

v. Goostrey Chapelry

Goostrey was a parochial chapelry of Sandbach parish 264 *infra* created in 1350, ChetOS VIII 257n. There was an ancient chapel at Barnshaw 226 *infra* t. Edward I, belonging to Chester Abbey, *op. cit.*, 254. The chapelry contained the following townships, 1. Blackden (v. Goostrey *infra*), 2. Cranage (now a c.p. including Cotton 280 *infra* from Church Hulme chapelry, and Leese *infra*), 3. Goostrey cum Barnshaw (now Goostrey c.p., including Blackden *supra*), 4. Leese (v. Cranage *supra*), 5. Twemlow (now a c.p. including No Town Fm, a detached part of Rudheath Lordship 198 *supra*). Cranage was listed under *Hamestan* (Macclesfield) Hundred in DB, as was Kermincham 281 *infra*, which suggests that Twemlow, between them, was probably in that Hundred, though not mentioned in DB.

1. BLACKDEN (HALL, HEATH & LANE) (110–780700), *Blakedenebroc* 1287 Chest, *Blakedene in territorio de Kerthingham* 1308 AddCh, *Blak(e)den(e)* 1414 JRL, 1423 Plea, 1455 Tab, *-don* 1442 Orm², 1479 ChRR (p), *Blackden* 1548 MainwB, *Blacke-* 1573 LCWills, *Blagden* 1621 Orm², 'dark valley', v. blæc (wk. obl. blacan), denu. Cf. Blakeden 325 *infra*, Kermincham 281 *infra*, Brookbank *infra*.

BROOKBANK FM, cf. *Blakedenebroc* 1287 Chest, v. brōc, banke.
BULLMARSH LANE (lost), 1831 Bry, cf. *Big & Little Bommish* 1841

TA, *v.* Bellmarsh Ho 227 *infra*.　　JODRELL BANK (FM), *Jodrell Bank* 1831 Bry, *v.* banke 'a hill-side', cf. Jodrell Hall 231 *infra*, which is adjacent.

FIELD-NAMES

The undated forms are 1841 *TA* 53.

(a) Acre; Bank; Bent (*v.* beonet); Bottom(s) (*v.* botm); Broomy Fd (*v.* brōmig); Calf Croft; Common Dean (*v.* commun, denu, cf. Blackden *supra*); Crofts; Crow Bar; Deal Fd (*v.* dæl²); Four Day Work (*v.* day-work); Goostrey Mdw (*v.* Goostrey 226 *infra*); Hare Heys (*v.* hara, (ge)hæg); Havadrill Bank ('daffodil, or asphodel, bank', *v.* affadille); Heath Heys (cf. Blackden Heath *supra*); Homestead; House Fd; Intake (*v.* inntak); Lecters; Lime Fd; Man Croft; Old Mdw; Outlet (*v.* outlet); Ox Hey; Pingot (*v.* pingot); Pool Flats; Road Heys (from either rād 'a roadway' or rod¹ 'a clearing'); Big & Little Rogery Fd (perhaps associated with *Rogereswey* 229 *infra*); Rough; Round Mdw; Rushy Fd; Sand Fd; Sanders Yard (*v.* geard); Saw Pit Fd (*v.* saw-pytt); Shippon Fd; Sour Fd; Stockey Mdw (*v.* stocc); Thisley-, Thistle Fd; Three Nooked Fd; Watering Pool Mdw; Well Mdw; Old Wheat Fd.

2. CRANAGE (110–750680) ['krænidʒ]

Croeneche 1086 DB

Cranlach(e) 12 *Dav*, H3 Orm² (p), c.1259 AD

Crau(e)-, Craw(e)-, Crav(e)nach(e) l12, e13 Orm², Chest (p), H3 Orm² (p), 13 *AddCh* (p), 1260 MidCh, 1284 Cre, 1312 ChRR (p), *Craunac'* 1249–65 Chest, *-athe* 14 AD (p), *-eche* 1346 VR (p), *Crauonach* 1288 Court (p), *Krawnache* e14 *Dav* (p), *Crauenhach* E3 *Surv*, *Crav(e)nage* 1417 *Eyre*, 1422 ChRR (p), *Craunidg* 1690 Sheaf

Croulach 1188 Tab (p), *-e* 1249–61 Chest, 1260 ib, Plea, Court, *Crowelach* 1259 *Plea* (p)

Cran(n)ach(e) e13 (17) Orm², 1246–60 MidCh (p), Chest (p), c.1300 *Dav*, (*-in Ruddeheth*) 1346 VR, *Crannage* 1318 Plea, *-adge* 1621 Orm², *Cranage* 1399 ChRR (p), (*-Green*) 1752 Sheaf, (*-alias Craunidg*) 1690 ib

Cronlach e13 Tab

Crau-, Crawlach(e) 1220–30 *AddCh*, 1233–44 (17) Chest (p), a.1240 MidCh (p), (*-cum Ermitagio*) 1245–9 Chest, *Crawe-* 1259 Plea (p), *-lacht* 1260 Court (p)

Crounach(e) 1284 *Chol* (p), 1287–91 Chest, 1291 (1338) VR (p)

Cronnache c.1290 *Chol* (p)

Grannage 1353 BPR (p), *Granage* 1553 Pat

Craumache 1354 BPR (p)
Cran(n)enach(e) 1359, 1398 ChRR, *-age* 1423 ib
Carnage 1775 Sheaf

'Boggy place, or stream, frequented by crows', *v.* crāwe (gen.pl. crāwena), læc(c). The name developed in two forms, one with loss of *l-* after *-n* and reduction of *crawen-* to *cra(u)n-*, the other with loss of the inflexion *-ena*, retaining *l-*. The former has prevailed. The confusion of *-n-* and *-u-*, e.g. *Cranl-*, *Craul-*, obscures some stages of development, but the reduced forms *Cran-*, *Craun-* may easily have been associated with similar forms of OE cran, cron 'a crane'.

HERMITAGE (110–766682)

> *Ermitage* l12–e13 Chest (p), (*le*) (*H*)*Ermitag(e)*, *-agium* 1245–9 ib, c.1247 Tab, 1259 Court (p), 1260 ib, *Plea*, l13 Tab *et freq* with variant spellings *Her(e)myt-* (from 1513 Earw, 1515 *ChEx*); (*Craulach-*, *Craunach cum-*) 1259 Court, (*-nigh Holmes Chappel*) 1666 Orm[2], (*the-*) 1548 AD, (*the hall of-*) 1631 ChRR
> *Hermitorium* e13 Chest (p)
> *le Ermites*, *-myt-*, *-met-* 1333 *Vern* (p), 1334 Plea (p), 1348 *Eyre* (p)
> (*le*) *Armytage*, *-mit-* 1504 ChRR, 1510 MidCh, *the-* 1540 AD

'The hermitage', *v.* ermitage (MedLat *heremitorium*). The place adjoins Cranage *supra*, Holmes Chapel 278 *infra*.

CRANAGE BRIDGE, *pons de Cranlach(e)* 12 *Dav*, 1656 Orm[2]. CRANAGE HALL, 1831 Bry, *Cranage manor and place* c. 1536 Leland. CRANAGE MILL, 1831 Bry. GOOSTREY LANE FM, *v.* Goostrey 226 *infra*. HALL FM, 1842 OS, cf. Cranage Hall *supra*. HERMITAGE THORNS, *Hollins Clough* 1831 Bry, cf. *Hollins Wood Field* 1844 *TA*, 'the thorn-trees', formerly 'dell growing with holly-trees', *v.* þorn, holegn, clōh, wudu, cf. foll. and Hermitage *supra*. HOLLINS FM, 1831 Bry, *v.* holegn, cf. prec. KING'S LANE (FM), *King's Lane* 1831 ib, *v.* 188 *supra*. MILL LANE FM, cf. Cranage Mill *supra*. MOUNTPLEASANT. NEW FM. NOOK FM & WOOD, *Nook House* 1831 ib, *v.* nōk. ROSEBANK, *The Hitch* 1831 ib, *v.* hiche 'an enclosure of hurdles for penning sheep'. RUDHEATH LODGE, 1831 ib. This part of Cranage was within the bounds of Rudheath heath 1 12. Probably hereabouts was *minera de Ruddheth infra metas de Craulach* 1270–71 Chest, *minera de Ruddehet*, *-super Rudeheth* c.1277 ib (ChetNS LXXXII 740, 750), 'the mine of Rudheath within

the bounds of Cranage'. There is no record of what was mined here.
SPRING BANK, cf. *Spring (Field)* 1844 *TA*, *v.* spring 'a young wood'.
SWAN FM, *Swan* 1831 Bry, probably a p.h. TWEMLOW LANE,
leading to Twemlow 230 *infra*. WARRINGTON COMMON. This is
beside the Knutsford road, on the way from Newcastle St to Warrington La. WOODSIDE FM.

FIELD-NAMES

The undated forms are 1844 *TA* 134. Of the others 1274–81, 1281–1300,
1295–7 are Orm², 1307–27 *Dav*, 1346 VR, 1540 AD, 1609 *Rental*, 1677
LRMB 211, 1831 Bry, 1842 OS, and the rest Chest.

(a) Old Ancient Fd; Bakehouse Croft; Bear Croft; Black Croft; Bradwall,
Bradwall Wharf ('(meadow at) the broad spring', *v.* brād, wælla, waroð);
Breach (*v.* brēc); Brickiln Fd; Briery Hills; Brook Fd; Clay Hill; Far &
Near Clitheroe (*lands called Cletherowes* 1609, *Clithe-* 1677, probably from
the surname from Clitheroe La 78); Cuckoo Oak 1831 (a tree on the boundary
with Allostock, probably named in allusion to the popular tradition of the
'cuckoo-tree'); Dane Mdw (cf. R. Dane 1 20); Daul Mdw (*v.* dāl);
Six-, Nine Day Math (*v.* day-math); Dukespiece Waste; Big & Little Flat;
Flax Eye (*v.* fleax, ēg); Far & Near Hays (*v.* (ge)hæg); Hazlehurst Wd (*v.*
hæsel, hyrst); Heath Croft & Fd (cf. *bruerium de Craunach*' 1287–91, *v.*
hǣð); Hig Fds; Hol(l)y Bank; Holt (*v.* holt); Hop Yard (*v.* hoppe, geard);
Hough Fd (*v.* hōh); House Fd; Intake (*v.* inntak); Kiln Croft; Lane Fd
(*v.* lane or leyne); Big & Near Lees (*v.* lēah or lǣs, cf. Leese 229 *infra*);
Long Butts; Lowes Pool 1831, 1842 (*v.* 255 *infra*); Marl Fd; Moss Acre,
Fd & Rooms (*v.* rūm); New Hay(s); New Years Eye (cf. *the Neweyerthe*
1540, *v.* nīwe, eorðe, ēg; but the modern form suggests analogy with Black-
eyer 1 265); Nine Butts; Oaken Fd (*v.* ācen); Old Land Hern ('(corner
at) the old selion', *v.* ald, land, hyrne); Outlet (*v.* outlet); Pickows (*v.* pichel);
Polly; Rail(s) Fd (*v.* rail(e)): Higher & Lower Ridding (*v.* ryding); Rix
Mdw; Round Bank; School Fd; Scotch Fd; Shay Fd (*v.* sc(e)aga); Sheep
Fold; Sour Mdw; Strine (*v.* strind); Swine Butts; Three Nooked Wd; Toll
Bar Fd (probably named from a turnpike); Vetch Croft & Yards (*v.* fecche,
geard); Wall Fd (*v.* wælla); Weir Mdw; Well Croft; White Fd; Widney
('wide water-meadow', *v.* wīd (wk. dat.sg. wīdan), ēg); Wood Fd, Great &
Nearer Wood (cf. *le Nether & Ouerwode de Craunac(h)* 1265–91, *boscum de
Craunache* 1346, *v.* wudu, neoðera, uferra, cf. 1 12).

(b) *le Bradeclif* 1265–91 ('the broad cliff', *v.* brād, clif, cf. foll.); *Clif* e13
(lit. *Elif* ChetNS LXXXII 764), *le Cliff* 1307–27 (*v.* clif, cf. prec.); *Clow* e13
(*v.* clōh, cf. *Saxirudingesclow infra*); *Croked(e)lac(he)* 1245–9, 1288, c.1310
('crooked stream', *v.* croked, lǣc(c), cf. *Windgates infra*); *le Oldedyche* 1346,
cf. *vetus fossatum* 1265–91 ('the old ditch', *v.* ald, dīc; a bound of Rudheath
heath, *v.* 1 12); *Redlache* 1346 ('the red stream', or perhaps 'reedy
bog', from rēad or hrēod and lǣc(c); a boundary of Rudheath heath, *v.* 1

12); *Saxiruding(esclow)* e13 ('(dell at) Saxi's clearing', from the ON, ODan
pers.n. *Saxi* and ryding, with clōh); *Serlecroft* 1270–1 ('Serlo's croft', from
the ME pers.n. *Serlo* and croft); *Slaccum* 1265–91 (*v.* slakki, here in a Lat
acc.sg. form); *Stan(i)land(e)s* 1270–1, 1274–81, c.1277, 1281–1300 ('the stony
selions' *v.* stānig, land); *Windgates* 1295–7, *Wint-, Wyntgat'* 12, *Winegat'*
l12–e13, *Windhgates, Wyngat'* 1245–9, *Wingates* 1288 (in Cranage or Leese
229 *infra* with *Croked(e)lac(he) supra*, where topography is against wind-geat
'windy gap', thus indicating wind-geat 'swing-gate', from OE *windan* 'to
wind' and geat, as in Wingate(s) K 446, La 44); *le Witesiche* 1287–91 (*v.*
hwīt, sic).

3. GOOSTREY CUM BARNSHAW, *Gostre et Berneshagh'* 1430 Dav,
Goostree cum Barneshawe 1597 ib, *Barnshaw cum Goostrey* 1845
ChetOS VIII, *v.* Barnshaw Hall, Goostrey *infra*.

BARNSHAW HALL (110–770710)

> *Bernulisah'* 1190–1220 Chest, *Bernul(e)s(c)hawe* 1249–65 ib *et freq*
> with variant spellings *Bernolschaue, Bernulssage* to e14 Chest
> *Berlesshawe* 1244 Chest (lit. *Herl-*), *-schawe* 1291–1305 (17) ib,
> *-shaw(e)* 1295 Ch, CRC
> *Bernulue(s)s(cag')* 1248 Dav (p), 1249–65 Chest (p), *Bernulf(e)-
> sh(ah)'*, *-schawe* 1249–65 Chest *et freq* ib to e14; *Bernulhessahe*
> 13 AD, *Bernulphshaw* 13 Chest (p)
> *Berne(s)s(c)hawe* 1249–65 Chest, 1291 Tax, 1291–1305 Chest,
> *-shagwe* 13 Tab, *-shagh(e)* 1353 Indict (p), 1396 ChRR
> *Barneshagh* 1483 MidCh, *-shaw(e)* 1535 VE, *Barnshawe* 1579 Dugd,
> (*the hall of*) 1654 AddCh, *-shaw* 1621 Orm²
> *Baronshaw* 1541 Dugd
> *Burneshawe* 1553 Pat

'Bernulf's wood', from sc(e)aga with a pers.n. derived from OE
Beornwulf or ON *Biǫrnulfr* (Feilitzen 200), cf. Barnston 325 *infra*. A
man of this name was tenant TRE of Gawsworth and North Rode
1 66, 59. An unnamed stream running from Barnshaw Hall into
Peover Eye, was *aqua de Bernulschawe* 1249–65 Chest, *v.* wæter.

GOOSTREY (110–770700) ['gu:stri]

> *Gostrel* 1086 DB, *Gostrey* 1119 (17) Chest, 14 Tab (p), (*-Chapel,
> a great township*) 1621 Orm², *Gostre* 1190–1220 Chest *et freq* to
> 1553 Pat, *-tree* 1539 Dugd
> *Gosetro* 1119 (1150), 1150 Chest, *-tre* 1119 (1280), 1249–61 ib *et
> freq*, *-tree* 1361 Eyre, *le Gosetr'* 1468 MinAcct

Gorestre(e) 1192–1208 Chest, (17) Orm², *Goristre* c.1220–30 *AddCh*,
    1233–9 Chest, *Gorstre(e)* 1265–91 ib, 1267 Ch (p), 1283–8 Chest
Goostre 1258 Chest, *-trey* 1272–1305 MidCh (p), *-tree* c.1536 Orm²,
    Goosetrey 1579 Dugd, 1831 Bry
Goustree 1265–91 (17) Chest, 1352 Orm²
Gortre 1283 Chest
Coystre alias Gostre 1554 Pat
Gossetre 1560 Sheaf
Goulstry 1650 *LRMB* 278
Goestre 1653 Sheaf

This name appears to be OE *gorst-trēow, from gorst 'gorse' and
trēow 'a tree'. Ekwall (DEPN) rejects this as giving no sense, but cf.
OE *gorst-bēam* 'a bramble'. A *gorst-trēow* need not be a furze bush,
for OE *gorst, gost* also means 'juniper' (BT), and ME *gorstes tre* is
'butcher's broom, *Ruscus aculeatus*' (MED s.v. *gorst*). The compound
occurs in Goosetree(s) 1 68, 161, and probably in the hundred-name
Gostrow Sx 514.

BARNSHAWBANK FM, *v.* banke.   BELLMARSH HO, *Bullmarsh Farm*
1831 Bry, *Bomish House* 1842 OS, cf. *Bell Marsh Croft & Wood* 1838
TA, and Bullmarsh, Bomish 222 *supra*, 1 90. These names refer to a
district in this, Lower Withington and Blackden townships, which
seems to be *Bolemos* 1307 *Eyre* (p), 'moss in which tree-trunks are
found', *v.* bola or bolr, mos, mersc.   BLACKDEN LANE, cf. *Blackden
Meadow* 1838 *TA*, named from Blackden 222 *supra*.   THE BONGS,
Bongs Wood 1831 Bry, 'the banks', *v.* banke.   BRICKBANK FM, cf.
Brickiln Field 1838 *TA*, *v.* bryke-kyl, bryke, banke.   BUCKBEAN
PIT (FM), a pond in which the buck-bean *Menyanthes trifoliata* grows,
v. pytt.   CORNBROOK HO.   CROOK HALL, *Crooks Hall Farm*
1831 Bry, cf. *Crooks Field* 1838 *TA*, probably from the surname
Crook, and hall.   DROMEDARY LODGE.   GALEY WOOD, *Gailey-*
1831 Bry, *v.* gagel 'gale, bog-myrtle'.   GOOSTREY LANE, cf. *Lane
Field* 1838 *TA*.   GOOSTREY MILL, 1831 Bry, *molendinum de
Gorestre* 1249–65 Chest.   MANOR HO.   MILLBANK FM, MILL
LANE, *Mill Farm* 1831 Bry, *Pool Head* 1842 OS, cf. *stagnum de
Bernolschawe* 1249–65 Chest, and Goostrey Mill *supra*, *v.* banke, pōl¹,
hēafod.   POOR HOUSES, 1831 Bry.   RIBBLE BRIDGE, 1831 ib, cf.
Ribble Meadow 1838 *TA*. The bridge crosses Peover Eye. The name
may be from rippel 'a strip of land, a boundary strip'. Cf. discussion
of the r.n. Ribble YW 7 135–6.   SANDY LANE (FM), cf. foll.

SHAWCROFT HALL, LT. SHAWCROFT, *Shawcroft* 1831 Bry, cf. Shear Brook 1 35, *Saghemor* 232 *infra*, also *Shaw Bridge* 1831 Bry (carrying Sandy Lane *supra* over Shear Brook at 110–768700, at the probable site of *le Sondyforth* 1346 VR, a bound of Rudheath heath, *v.* 1 12), and *Shaw Wood* 1838 *TA* (*Gostreschawe* 1291–1305 Chest), *v.* sc(e)aga 'a wood', croft, brycg, sandig 'sandy', ford. SWANWICK HALL, *Swanwich-* 1860 White, if an old name, this is 'peasants' hamlet', *v.* swān[2], wīc, cf. Swanwick Green 327 *infra*, Swannick 208 *supra*. WINTERBOTTOM, *-Farm* 1831 Bry, 'bottom land usable in winter', *v.* winter[1], botm. WOOD CORNER, WOOD-END FM (*Wood End* 1831 ib), WOODSIDE FM, *v.* wudu, corner, ende[1], sīde.

FIELD-NAMES

The undated forms are 1838 *TA* 178. Of the others, E3 is *Surv*, 1346 VR, 1419 Orm[2], 1499 Sheaf, 1540 AD, 1842 OS, and the rest Chest.

(*a*) Alder Bottom (*v.* alor, botm); Alley (*v.* aley); Allostock Hurst (*v.* hyrst, cf. Allostock 216 *supra*); Birchen Row (*v.* bircen[2], rāw); Black Fd; Bowsey Fd (*v.* bōsig); Bradley (*v.* brād, lēah); Broomy Croft (*Bromicroft* 1287, *v.* brōmig, croft); Buck Fd; Butty Mdw (*v.* butty); Calves Croft; Cats Croft (*v.* catte); Cinder Hill (*v.* sinder); Colts Hey (*v.* colt, (ge)hæg); Coughers Fd; Cow Hey; Dale Park (*v.* dæl[1] or deill); Dial Fd (*v.* dial); Face Croft; Fallow Fd; Ferny Fd; Finisher (cf. *Fenshaw* 1540, *v.* fenn(ig), sceaga); Flash Mdw (*v.* flasshe); Fulwood (*v.* fūl, wudu); Goostrey Mdw (cf. *campus de Gorstre* 1287, *v.* Goostrey *supra*); Gorsey Bottom (*v.* gorstig, botm); Hatchet (*v.* hæcc-geat 'a wicket-gate'); Hazle Cover (1842); Hill Park; Hollins Crofts (*v.* holegn); Kiln Fd; Kitchen Fd; Knowl Fd (*v.* cnoll); Lands (*v.* land); Marl Pits; Midgrave (perhaps 'middle wood', *v.* middel, græfe); Mooley; Oven House Croft; Palace Fd (*v.* palis 'a palisade'); Pinfold Fd (*v.* pynd-fald); Porch Fd; Privy Mdw; Rough; Rush Fd; Shippon Fd; Spring, Sprink (*v.* spring 'a young wood'); Sun Croft; Sweet Fd; Town Fd; Walk Mdw (*v.* walk); Withen Croft (*v.* wiðegn); Woodfent Mdw; Yervis Park (perhaps from a pers.n. or surname, *v.* park).

(*b*) *Bernulisah' croft* 1190–1220 (*v.* croft, cf. Barnshaw *supra*); *Bystou(we)-snabbe* 1291–1305, c.1294–6, *Bistouisnabbe* 1291–1305 (17), cf. *Byshonsuabbe* 1249–65 MainwB (the spellings are unreliable, and probably represent original forms *Bysc-, Bisc-, Bysh-,* -(*h*)*ou(we)-, -snabbe* 'bushy hill', from (ge)bysce and hōh, with nabbi 'a knoll' or snabbe 'a steep place, a projecting part of a hill'); *Brerehey, -hay* 1287, 1291–1324 (*v.* brēr, (ge)hæg); *Chikenshagh* 1346 ('chicken wood', *v.* cīcen, sceaga, a bound of Rudheath heath, *v.* 1 12); *Dedishay* 1291–1305 (p) ('Ded's enclosure', from the ME pers. by-name *Ded* (Reaney 92 s.n. *Deed*) and (ge)hæg); *le Ewode* 1291–1305 (*v.* ēa, wudu); *Gostraleghes* 1499 ('the clearings belonging to Goostrey', *v.* lēah); *the Grene* 1419 (p) (*v.* grēne[2]); *le Longesthayecloch* 1287 (apparently '(the dell at) the longest enclosure', from OE *langost* (superl. of lang), (ge)hæg, with clōh; but possibly a misreading for *Longeschaye-* '(dell at) a long wood', *v.* lang, sc(e)aga, clōh); *Rogeriswey(e)* 1249–65, 1287, 1291–1323, *-es-*, *-way* 1291–1305, 1346, E3 ('Roger's road', in Barnshaw, probably named after *Roger de Bernulphshaw* 13 Chest, *v.* weg. This was a boundary of Rudheath heath and may have been a saltway, cf. 1 12, 46, 47, 49. The road-name may survive in Rogery Fds 223 *supra*); *Salteriswey* 1287 (in Goostrey, 'salter's way', *v.* saltere, weg, cf. 1 47, 49); *Sercroft* 1190–1220 ('dry, barren croft', *v.* sēar, croft); *Syddenale* 1190–1220 ('at the wide nook', *v.* sīd (wk. dat.sg. sīdan), halh (dat.sg. hale), cf. Siddenhall, Sydney 327 *infra*).

4. LEESE (110–730680) [li:s]

> *Ley(e)s* e13 Chest, *Lehges*, *Leyg'* 1244 ib, *(le(s))* *Leghes* c.1271 ib
> *et freq* with variant spellings *Leg'*, *Leigh(e)s*, *Leghs*, *Leyghes*,
> *Leghez* to 1659 ChRR, *(-super Ruddehet)* 1271 Chest, *Leighes-*
> *Rudheath* 1659 ChRR; *Lees* 1546 Dugd, *Leese* 1860 White
>
> *Loges* 1244 Chest
> *le Layes* 1351 Chamb
> *Lyes* 1549 JRL

'The clearings', *v.* lēah. Part of the township fell within Rudheath heath 1 11, cf. Whishaw *infra*.

CROSS LANES, *v.* 199 *supra*.   EARNSHAW HO, *-Hall* 1842 OS, cf. Earnshaw Hall 188 *supra*.   HOLLY BANK.   MANOR HO.   MOSS LANE, 1842 ib, *v.* mos.   PEARTREE FM, *Peartree* 1831 Bry. PUDDINGLAKE, 1831 ib, named from Puddinglake Brook 1 34. PUMP HO.   ROUND HO, 1831 ib.

FIELD-NAMES

The undated forms are 1842 *TA* 235. Of the others, 1226–8 (17) is Dieul, E3 *Surv*, 1346 VR, 1375, 1378, 1380 *Eyre*, 1407, 1408 ChRR, 1666 *ChCert*, 1831 Bry, 1842 OS, and the rest Chest.

(a) Barrows (*v.* bearu 'a grove' or beorg 'a hill'); Corb Pasture; Four Butts; Heath Fd (cf. *le Heth-*, *Hed-*, *Hetfeld* c.1271, c.1281, c.1287 (*v.* hǣð, feld); Hemp Yard (*v.* hemp-yard); Great & Little Hill; Lill(e)y Fd & Lane (*v.* Lily Fm & Lane 234 *infra*); Little Eye (*v.* ēg); Lowes Pool 1831, 1842 (*v.* 255 *infra*); Maple Fd; Meg Fd (*v.* meg); Moorsbarrow (cf. Mooresbarrow 251 *infra*); Big Mow Fd (*v.* mūga); Parliament; Pool Bank; Ridding (*v.* ryding); Rooley Fd (cf. *Rohe-*, *Ruhelawe* e13, *Releywood* 1666, 'rough mound', *v.* rūh, hlāw); Slack Fd (*v.* slakki); Tit Fd; Turf Fd; Walley Wd; Whishaw (*Wystelyng-*, *Swhistelying-*, *Whistelingschawe* E3 (p), *Whystelhaghe* 1346, *Quystelshagh* 1375 (p), *Whistelschawe* 1378 (p), *-shagh'* 1380 (p), 1407,

1408 (p), cf. Hugh *Whishall* 17 Orm² III 172, and Whishaw's Meadow 281 *infra*, 'whispering wood', from ME *whisteling* (OE *hwistlung*, cf. hwistle and *whistling* (NED)), 'a hissing, sibilant, whispering noise, a whistling' (presumably from the sound of the wind in the trees), *v.* sc(e)aga. In 1346 this was a bound of Rudheath heath, *v.* I 12); Withy Croft.

(*b*) *la Bruch* e13 (*v.* bryce 'a breaking-in of land'); *le Claycroft* c.1271 (*v.* clæg, croft); *Derneleygreue* e13, *-lehegreene* e13 (17), *-greue* 1244, *-lekegreve* 1226–8 (17) ('(grove at) the secluded clearing', *v.* derne, lēah, grǣfe); *Jurdanes-rydding* 1346 ('Jordan's cleared-land', from the ME pers.n. *Jordan* and ryding. This was a bound of Rudheath heath, *v.* I 12); *Legheslone* 1346 ('Leese lane', *v.* lane; a bound of Rudheath heath, *v.* I 12, cf. Byley Lane 234 *infra*); *Littlecroft* c.1271 (*v.* lȳtel, croft); *molendinum de Leyes* 1265–91 (*v.* myln); *Perde iuxta Rohelawe* e13 (named in the bounds of *Derneleygreue supra* (ChetNS LXXXII 753n.), cf. Rooley Fd *supra*. *Perde* is obscure).

5. TWEMLOW (110–780680)

> *Tu-*, *Twam(e)lou(e)*, *-law(-e, -a)*, *-low(e)*, *-l(au)* 12 *Dav* (p), c.1185 *Chol* (p), l12–e13 Facs, *AddCh* (p), Chest, ChRR, Dieul, (1300) Ch (p), n.d. AD (IV 105), 1299 Orm², *Twamlag* 1277 Chest (p), *Thwamlawe* l12 (1300) Pat (p), *Twham-* 1281 CRC, *Twanlawe* H3 Orm² (p)
>
> *Twemlowe* l12–e13 *Fitt* (p), 1291 Misc *et freq* to 1640 ChRR, *-low* 1408 VR, *-loe* 1697 *Dow*, *Twem(e)lawe* 1259 Court, 1284 Ch, *-lowe* 1336 VR, *Thuemelowe* 1281 Plea, 1282 Court, *Tweemlow* 1842 OS, *Twemlowe* 1358 BPR, 1549 ChCert
>
> *T(h)am-*, *T(h)omlawa*, *-lawe*, *-low(e)* l12–e13 Chest, Dieul, (1425) Pat (p), 1266 Chest, *Taumeleg'* H3 JRC (p), *Themlowe* 1278 Ipm, *Thume-* l13 MidCh
>
> *Twymelawe* 1259 Court (p), *Twymlawe* 1475 VR
>
> *Twomlowe* 1266–7 Chest (p), 1291 VR, 1468 *MinAcct*
>
> *Twelowe* 1345–53 MidCh

'By, or at, the two mounds', *v.* twēgen (dat. twǣm), hlāw. Cf. *Little Twemlow, Four Twemlows* 1839 *TA*, f.ns., and Blueslates Fm *infra*, also Twamlow I 58. Orm² III 3 reports that in 1819 there were five tumuli in a line in this township, Jodrell Hall *infra* standing between the second and third. In view of the eccentric position of that house in the township, it is not clear whether these particular mounds gave rise to the p.n.

No TOWN FM (110–771687), 1831 Bry, *No Town* 1842 OS, probably 'Thomas Hardy's house in Rudheath' 1346 VR, cf. I 12, for this farm was a detached part of Rudheath Lordship, v. 198 *supra*, down to 1831 Bry. Being, therefore, extra-parochial, it was in no township of any parish, *v.* nān, toun.

SALTERSFORD BRIDGE (110–773677), FM & COTTAGE, *Salterisforde* c.1300 *Dav*, *Salteresford* 1331 Pat (a grant of pontage for building a bridge), *Saltersford Bridge & Farms* 1831 Bry, 'salter's ford', *v.* saltere, ford, cf. *Salter's Hay* 1839 *TA*. This ford of R. Dane lay on a salt-way from Middlewich to Macclesfield, *v.* 1 47.

BANK FM, cf. *The Banks, Bank Field* 1839 *TA, v.* banke. BLACK-YARD FM, *Black Yards Farm* 1831 Bry, 'black enclosures', *v.* blæc, geard. BLUESLATE FM, *Twemlow Farm* 1831 Bry, 1839 *TA, Blue Slates* 1860 White, cf. Twemlow *supra*. BOWSHOT WOOD. BROADLANE FM, *Gilead Farm* 1831 Bry, *Glead Farm* 1842 OS, cf. *Gilead Field, Glade Croft, Gleads Meadow* 1839 *TA*. JODRELL HALL (110–795702), 1831 Bry, named after the *Jodrell* family, land-owners here, cf. Edmund *Jodrell* of Twemlow 1697 *Dow*, and Jodrell Bank 223 *supra*. MANOR FM. OLD FARM. TWEMLOW GREEN, 1831 Bry. TWEMLOW HALL, 1831 ib, *grangia de Twem(e)-lowe* 1336 VR, *v.* grange.

FIELD-NAMES

The undated forms are 1839 *TA* 405. Of the others, 1220–30 is *AddCh*, 1277 (14), 1335–8, 1346 VR, 1299 Orm², 1468 *MinAcct*, 1623 Dav, 1650 *LRMB* 278, 1831 Bry.

(a) The Acre; Backhouse Fd (*v.* bæc-hūs); Barrows Wood (perhaps from beorg 'a hill, a mound' (cf. Twemlow *supra*), but bearg or bearu are possible); Birchen Row, The Birches (cf. *the Birchin Crofts* 1650, *v.* birce, bircen², rāw); Bird Eye; Black Croft; Broad Hay (*þe-* 1650, *v.* brād, (ge)hæg, cf. foll.); Broady Way (cf. prec., *v.* brād, (ge)hæg); Broom Fd; Clay Acre; Dane Mdw (named from R. Dane 1 20); Four Day Work (*v.* day-work); Ten Days Math (*v.* day-math); Dean Mdw (*v.* denu); The Dingle (1831, a clough in Bowshot Wood *supra, v.* dingle); Donkin's Knowl (*v.* cnoll); Dry Fd; Ferny Hay; Flax Eye (*v.* fleax, ēg, cf. *Linney infra*); Gat Croft; Goostrey Fd (*v.* Goostrey 226 *supra*); Gulver Croft (probably culfre 'a dove'); Hazle Croft; Henbury Hay (perhaps connected with Henbury 1 78); Hob Fd (*v.* hob or hobb(e)); Hollock Bottom (*v.* holoc 'a hollow', botm 'a valley bottom'); Horse Hills; Jack Fd (*v.* jack); Kettleshall (perhaps from the ON pers.n. *Ketill*, ODan *Ketil*); Kiln Ground; Middle & Near Knowl; Lane Hey (cf. *the Land Hay* 1650, *v.* leyne, land, (ge)hæg); Long Shutt (*þe long shutts* 1650, *v.* lang, scēat); Moss Fd; Nu(n)n Fd (*v.* nunne); Old Man's

Croft; Outlet (v. outlet); Pattenhall Knowl (v. cnoll, cf. the Warburton family of *Patenhall* 1533 *LRO* Dx); Pingot (v. pingot); Porridge Fd; Reap Fd; Big & Master Ridding (v. ryding); Rush(e)y Hay (v. riscig, (ge)hæg); Sand Fd; Great Singlehurst ('wood where shingles were got', v. shingel[1], hyrst); Town Fd (cf. *Tounemedowe* 1277 (14), 'public, or common, meadow & field', v. toun, mæd); Way Fd ('field at a road', v. weg); Well Fd; The Wood, Little Wood Fd (cf. *boscum de Twamlowe* 1299, 1346, a bound of Rudheath heath, cf. I 12, v. wudu).

(b) *Breriforlong* 1220–30 (v. brērig, furlang); *chirchelond* 1220–30 (v. cirice, land); *feltiard-, feltjard de Tuamlawe* 1220–30 (probably from feld and geard 'a yard, an enclosure'); *Goldewey* 1346 ('golden way', v. golde 'a marigold', weg; a bound of Rudheath heath, v. I 12); *les Greves* 1299 ('the groves', v. grǣfe); *mucle hakennesholtland* 1220–30 ('(big selion at) Hakon's wood', from the ODan pers.n. *Hákon* and holt, with land, mycel); *campus de Horefeld* 1468 ('the hoar field', v. hār[2], feld); *hutlone, athutlonishende, -es-* 1220–30 ('the out-lane, at the end of the out-lane', v. æt, ūt, lane, ende[1]); *lamilache* 1220–30 ('boggy stream in clayey or loamy ground', v. lāmig, læcc, cf. *Lomylathe* 186 *supra*); *the peece in Lynney* 1623 ('(the piece of ground in) flax-meadow', v. līn, ēg, cf. Flax Eye *supra*); *Marliol'* 1335–8 ('a marl-hole', v. marle, -ig[3], hōl[1]; this form antedates the first record of the adj. *marly* 'abounding in marl', c.1420 NED); *mucclefeld* 1220–30 (v. mycel, feld); *Saghemor* 1346 ('moor at a wood', v. sc(e)aga, mōr[1], cf. Shawcroft, Shear Brook 228 *supra*, I 35. This was a bound of Rudheath heath, v. I 12); *uinterhedis* 1220–30 ('winter pasture', v. winter[1], edisc).

vi. Middlewich

This parish contained 1. Byley cum Yatehouse (now Byley c.p. including Croxton and Ravenscroft, *infra*, and part of Rudheath Lordship 198 *supra*), 2. Clive (now included in Winsford c.p., 327 *infra*), 3. Croxton (v. Byley *supra*), 4. Kinderton cum Hulme (v. Sproston, Middlewich *infra*), 5. Middlewich and Newton (now Middlewich Urban District c.p., including Sutton *infra* and part of Kinderton *supra*), 6. Minshull Vernon, 7. Mooresbarrow cum Parme (v. Sproston *infra*), 8. Occlestone (v. Wimboldsley *infra*), 9. Ravenscroft (v. Byley *supra*), 10. Sproston (now a c.p. including Hulme, Mooresbarrow cum Parme and part of Kinderton *supra*), 11. Stublach (now included in Lach Dennis c.p. 184 *supra*), 12. Sutton (v. Middlewich *supra*), 13. Wimboldsley (now a c.p. including Occlestone *supra*), 14. Weaver 327 *infra* (now in Eddisbury Hundred, but in *Mildestvic* (Northwich) Hundred DB).

1. BYLEY CUM YATEHOUSE, *Byveley et les Yatehouses* c.1536 Orm[2], *-cum Yatehouse* 1597 Dav, *Biley cum Yatehouses* 1724 NotCestr. In 1819 Orm[2] III 204, the township consisted of Higher & Lower Byley and Higher & Lower Yatehouse, representing Byley Hall *infra*,

Higher Green (lost, 110–716687) 1842 OS, Yatehouse Fm and Yatehouse Green *infra*.

BYLEY HALL (formerly HIGHER BYLEY), LOWER BYLEY (lost), BYLEY FM & HILL (110–710670–680) [baili]

> *Bevelei* 1086 DB, *Beueley* 1291 Tax (lit. *Bene-*)
>
> *Bifle* 1208–29 (17) Orm[2], Dieul, *Byu-*, *Biuley*, (*graungia de*) 1547 MinAcct, (*manor or grange of*) *Byvley* 1560 Sheaf, *Biuly Graunge* c.1662 *Surv* (lit. *Bin-*)
>
> *By-*, *Bivel*(*eh*), *-le*(*ye*), *-ley*(*a*), *-leg*(*h*), *-le*(*gh*) 112–e13 Ch, Dieul, Dugd *et freq* with variant spellings *-le*(*e*), *-lega*, *-lie*, *Biu-*, *Byu-*, *Bivi-* to *Byvelegh* 1499 Orm[2], (*grangia de*) e13 Dieul, (*Magna-* & *Parua-*) 1253 Cl
>
> *Bygele* 1304 Chamb
>
> *Byle* 1304 Chamb (p), *-leych'* E3 *Surv*, *-ley* 1410 ChRR *et freq*, (*-Hall*) 1724 NotCestr, (*Higher-* & *Lower-*) 1819 Orm[2], *-ly* 1619 Sheaf, *Bilegh* 1351 BPR, 1621 Orm[2]
>
> (*grang' de*) *Byurley* c.1536 Orm[2]

'Bēofa's clearing', from an OE pers.n. *Bēofa* (as in Bevington Wa 220, DEPN) and lēah, *v.* also **grange** and cf. Byley cum Yatehouse, *Higher Green supra*. Byley was a grange of Dieulacres Abbey.

YATEHOUSE FM & GREEN, formerly HIGHER & LOWER YATEHOUSE (110–700680) ['jeitaus]

> *Byuele gate* 1310–30 *Chol*
>
> *Byleych' yathuses* E3 *Surv*, *Yatehouses* 1535 VE, *the Yatehouses* 1609 Rental, *Over* & *Nether Yat*(*t*)*howses* c.1554 Orm[2]
>
> *the Yatehouse* c.1427 Orm[2], 1650 *LRMB* 278, *Yatehouse* 1513 ChEx, (*the towneshipp of-*) 1650 *LRMB* 278, (*-Green*) 1785 Sheaf, (*Higher-* & *Lower-*) 1819 Orm[2]

'The houses at the gate at Byley', *v.* **geat**, **gate-hous**, **uferra**, **neoðera**, **grēne**[2], cf. Byley cum Yatehouse *supra*. The earliest form may have been influenced by ON **gata** 'a road'. *Byuelegh-lydeyate* 1346 VR ('swing-gate', *v.* **hlid-geat**), a bound of Rudheath heath, may have been here, but was probably on the boundary of Leese township, on *Legheslone*, i.e. Byley Lane *infra*, cf. 1 12. Gates at Byley would be access-points to grazing rights in the waste of Rudheath.

BYLEY BRIDGE, 1655 Orm[2], crossing R. Dane into Kinderton, probably *le Boghbrugge* 1349 *Eyre*, 'arched bridge', *v.* **boga**, **brycg**, giving

name to *le Bouhous infra*.   BYLEY LANE, an unnamed bridle-path
in 1842 OS (110–717675 to 730682) from Byley Hall to Leese.
Byley Lane 1831 Bry, 1842 OS ran from Byley Bridge to Puddinglake
229 *supra* to the west of Byley Hill Fm *supra* (110–715675 to 722696),
v. lane. The modern Byley Lane may be *Legheslone* 1346 VR, a
bound of Rudheath heath, *v.* 230 *supra*, 1 12.   KING STREET, *v.*
1 44.   KING STREET FM, *Lane Ends* 1831 Bry, at the junction
of Croxton Lane 236 *infra* with King Street *supra*, *v.* lane, ende[1], cf.
foll.   LANE END COTTAGES, at the junction of Yatehouse Lane
infra and King Street *supra*, *v.* prec.   LILY FM & LANE, *Lilly
Lane* 1831 ib, cf. Lill(e)y Fd 229 *supra*, *v.* lilie.   YATEHOUSE LANE,
leading to Yatehouse Green *supra* was *Pinfold Lane* 1831 Bry, cf.
Pinfold Field 1842 *TA*, *v.* pynd-fald, lane.

FIELD-NAMES

The undated forms are 1842 *TA* 50. Of the others 1208–17, 1217–29 are
Dieul, E3 *Surv*, 1346 VR, 1471, 1484, 1529 ChRR.

(*a*) Abbotts Croft (probably named from the abbots of Dieulacres, lords
of Byley, *v.* abbat); The Acre; Boatman's Fd; Bowl Fd; Brownley Fd
('brown clearing', *v.* brūn[1], lēah); Cat Croft; Coats Croft (*v.* cot); Cog Fd
(cf. *del Cogges* E3 (p), perhaps from cogge 'a cog-wheel, a mill'); Colley
Croft (*v.* colig, cf. *Coliescloch* 1208–17, *Colreseloch* 1208–17 'charcoal-
burner's dell', *v.* colere, clōh); Cow Hey; Coxey Hill (perhaps to be associated
with *Cocsuche* 1217–29, 'watercourse from a hill', *v.* cocc[1], sīc, ēa); Dung
Fd (*v.* dung[2]); Dunnock; Eddish Fd (*v.* edisc); Elbow Fd (*v.* elbowe); Feat;
Flat(t); Furlong Croft (*v.* furlang); Gallamus; Gin House Bank; Forsty Fd
(*v.* forst); Green Heys; Hoorick; Intack (*v.* inntak); Keightley; Lords Fd;
Mag Acre; Marl Croft & Fd; Meaney Fd; Moss Fd; Nook Fd; Northwich
Flatt (*v.* flat, cf. Northwich 192 *supra*); Oaken Flatt (*v.* ācen); Owlery Fd
(*v.* alor); Pet Fd; Pingot (*v.* pingot); Poverty (*v.* 327 *infra*); Price Gout;
Riot; Rooley Fd (*v.* 229 *supra*); Rushy Reins (*v.* rein); Long Shoot (*v.* scēat);
Sink Croft (*v.* sinke); Spring Croft; Sproston Mdw (cf. Sproston 254 *infra*);
Sweet Fd; Three Nook'd Fd; Welchman's Croft; White Fd.

(*b*) *Thepprovement of Rudheth* 1471, *ThappROMent-* 1484, *the Approwment
of Rudheth* 1529 (land 'approved' out of the royal waste of Rudheath 1
11 by Dieulacres Abbey, whose lands were at Byley and in Goostrey 226
supra, *v.* approvement[2] NED); *le Bouhous* 1346 ('house at a bridge-arch', *v.*
boga, hūs, cf. Byley Bridge *supra*; a bound of Rudheath heath, *v.* 1 12).

2. CLIVE (110–670650) [klaiv]

Clive 1086 DB, e13 Tab (p), Facs (p) *et freq* with variant spellings
Cliue, Clyve, Clyue; (*le-*) 1411 ChRR (p)

Clywe H3 (1578) ChRR
Cleve 1312 Plea, 1360 BPR (p), *-u-* 1376 *Eyre* (p), *Cleave* 1621 Orm²
Clyf, -i- 1327, 1330 Cl (p), (*le-*) 1335 AD (p), *Clief* 1375 *Eyre* (p),
   Clyff(e) 1415 ChRR, 1421 Tab, *-i-* 1527 Orm², 1538 ChRR,
   Clyfe 1493 ib
Clive, Cliff or Cleave 1860 White
'(At) the steep bank', *v.* clif (dat.sg. *clife*).

BROWN BROOK (lost), 1831 Bry, *v.* 212 *supra*, cf. *Big & Little Browns*
1841 *TA*, *v.* brún². CLIVE FM. CLIVE GREEN, 1625 *Chol.*
CLIVE HALL, 1724 NotCestr. CLIVE HO, 1831 Bry. DOLE HO,
cf. *Dole Croft* 1841 *TA*, *v.* dāl 'a share, an allotment'. DOUBLE
WOOD, *Middle Wood* 1831 Bry. BOTTOM & TOP FLASH, lakes
formed by subsidence of the valley of R. Weaver, *v.* flasshe, cf. 197,
214 *supra*, 326, 326, 257 *infra*. GRAVEL FM, *v.* gravel, cf. foll., to
which it is adjacent. MIDDLEWICH RD, *Gravel Lane* 1842 OS,
cf. prec., *v.* 1 47. RILSHAW LANE, cf. *Higher & Lower Rilshaw*
1841 *TA*, *v.* Rilshaw 214 *supra*. This would be on the line of
redestrete infra.

FIELD-NAMES

The undated forms are 1841 *TA* 123. Of the others, c.1233 is *AddCh*,
1233-4, 1299-1300 Orm², 1269 IpmR, 1371, 1414 MidCh.

(*a*) Add Croft; Banks; Black Way Fd (*v.* weg); Bully Mdw; Bunn Croft;
Burn Fd; Colleys Croft; Cross Green; Dudfins Moss (*Dudfynmosse* 1371,
Dudfenmosse 1414, from the surname of Gilbert or Henry *Dudefin, Dodefyn,*
1281, 1289 Court, *v.* mos); Flid Croft; Frenche's Bank; Gadbridge; Ghorsty
Fd (*v.* gorstig); Haggard Croft; Hallet Mdw; Halors Acre; Heads Croft;
Hill Greave (*v.* grǣfe); Hoogreave Fd (cf. Hoolgrave 248 *infra*); Hum (*v.*
hamm, homm); Intake (*v.* inntak); Kiln Croft; Knaves Acre (*v.* cnafa, æcer);
Litters; Load(s) Croft (*v.* (ge)lād); Long Clough (*v.* clōh); Marl Fd; Oaklet;
Oldsworth, Oldsworths Bank, Oldworth Fd (either from a surname, or from
ald 'old' and worð 'an enclosure', with banke); Outlet (*v.* outlet); Poolstead
(*v.* pōl-stede); Ravens Croft; Sand Croft & Fd; Siddows Croft, Suddows
Mdw; Supers Clough; Three Nook'd Fd; Town Fd; Weir Fd; Within
Croft (*v.* wiðegn); Wood Fd.

(*b*) *molendinum de Cliue* c.1233, *a water-mill in Clyve* 1299-1300 (*v.* myln);
Clive parcus 1269 (*v.* park); *via que vocatur redestrete* 1233-4 Orm² III 214
('the red street', *v.* rēad, strǣt. It was near the mill *supra*, on R. Weaver.
It would be Rilshaw Lane *supra* leading to Welsh Lane 327 *infra*, cf. 1
47).

3. CROXTON (110–690670) [ˈkrɔkstan, ˈkrɔkssn̩]

> Crostune 1086 DB, -ton 13 Chest (p), Crouston 1370 MidCh (p)
> Crocstun e12 Orm² (p), -ton(a) l12 ib, e13 Tab, 13 Chest (p),
>   Crokeston' 1247 Chest (p), -tone l13 Orm² (p)
> Croxtun c.1200 AddCh, -ton e13 Chest (p), Dieul et freq with
>   variant spelling -tona
> Croxdone e13 Dieul
> Croxon 1400 ChRR (p)

'Crōc's farm', from the late OE pers.n. Crōc (from ON Krókr or
ODan Krók), v. tūn. This township stands upon the rivers Weaver
and Dane, so it is unlikely that the place is named from R. Croco 1
19, cf. Orm² III 9, Sheaf³ 50 (9962).

BLUESLATES FM, Blueslate 1831 Bry, -s 1842 OS.   CROXTON
BRIDGE, 1619 Sheaf, crossing R. Dane into Middlewich, cf. the platt
1619 ib, v. brycg, plat¹.   CROXTON HALL, 1724 NotCestr, Croxton
House 17 MidCh.   CROXTON LANE.   DAIRYHOUSE FM, Croxton
Dairyhouse Farm 1831 Bry.   HELL KITCHEN BRIDGE (lost, Trent
and Mersey Canal), 1831 ib.   KING STREET, v. 234 supra.

FIELD-NAMES

(b) Woodhouse l13 MidCh (p), Wode- 1489 ChRR (p), Woodhouses 1328
MidCh, le- 1377 ib, le Wodehouses 1330 ChRR (p) ('house(s) at a wood', v.
wudu, hūs).

4. KINDERTON CUM HULME, Kynderton cum Hulm 1430 Dav, v.
Kinderton, Briaryhulme etc. infra.

KINDERTON (110–709670) [kind-]

> Cinbretune 1086 DB, (Kynderton alias), -tume 1581 ChRR
> Kindreton 1240 Cl, (-by the Midle Wiche) c.1536 Leland, Kyn-
>   c.1560 Sheaf, Kin-, Kynderton 1246–60 MidCh, c.1300 AD, 1304
>   Chamb et freq with variant spellings -dir-, -dyr-, -dur-, -da-,
>   -tone; (Lytil-) 1557 Tab
> Kylderton 1347 BPR
> Kynnerton 1403 Pat
> (Little) Kunderton 1557 Tab
> Kenterton 1566 Sheaf
> Kindetton 1800 Wil

'Cyneræd's farm', from the OE pers.n. *Cyneræd* and tūn. The DB form has *b* for *d* by scribal error. The modern form arises from OE *Cynered(es)tūne* > **Kindredtun* (with inorganic *d* between *n* and *r*, and loss of inflexional *-es-*) > *Kindreton* (with assimilation of *-dt-* to *-(t)t-*) > *Kinderton* (with metathesis). There is no connection between this name and *Condate*, *v.* 195–6 *supra*.

STREET-NAMES. KINDERTON ST, *v.* 241 *infra*; NEW KING ST., on the line of King Street *infra*.

LOST STREET-NAME. *Cow Lane* 1710 Cre, *Cowlane* 1260 MidCh *et freq*, *-lone* 1260–92 ib, 'lane along which cows are driven', *v.* cū, lane. This was a turning off Kinderton St. *supra*, and appears as a Middlewich street-name in 1656 Orm² 1 138.

BRIARYHULME (110–733653), CURTISHULME (100–732643), KNIGHTS-HULME (110–735644) [-ju:m]

> *Hulm(e)*, *Holme* 112 MidCh *et freq* to 1581 ChRR, *-u-* predominat-ing, with variant spelling *Hollme*; *Hulme iuxta Bradwall* 1406 ChRR, *-near Middlewich* 1415 ib
> *Curte(i)s-*, *Curteys(e)hulm(e)*, *-holm(e)* c.1280 *Vern*, 1295, 1298, 1314 Cre, c.1300 *Chol*, 1306 Orm², 1312 Plea, *Curtis-* 1314 MidCh, *Curteholme* 1415 ChRR, *Curteiseholme* 1575 Sheaf
> *Bretherhulme(e)* 1312, 1313 Plea, Orm², 1606 ChRR, *Brother-* 1581 ib, *-holme alias Breryholme* 1665 Sheaf, *Breary-*, *Brearishulme* 1581 Orm², ChRR, *Breryc-*, *Brerye-* 1590 ib, *Briary Holme* 1831 Bry, *Briery Hulme* 1842 OS
> *Knetisholm* 1311 Orm², *Knyghtesholme*, *-hulme* 1385 Cl, IpmR, *Kny(th)teshulm(e)* 1386 ib, ChRR, *Knythes-* 1388–9 Orm², *Knightes-* 1581 ChRR, *Knight's Holme* 1671 AddCh, 1884 Sheaf, *-Hulme* 1831 Bry

'The marsh', *v.* hulm, holmr, spellings in *-u-* predominating. The affixes are from ME *brether* (ON brœðr(s), brœðra, gen.sg. and pl. of broðir) 'brother's, brothers'', cniht 'a youth, a youngster' and the ME surname *Curteis* (OFr *curteis* 'courteous'). Ranulph *le Curteis*, e13 ChetNS cviii 256, held a third part of Hulme. He is the same as Randulf son of Henry *Litecurteis* ib 156, 255, 'hardly courteous'. Other parts of Hulme were *Silk(e)hulme* 1284 (18) Sheaf, 1288 AD, from either the ON pers. by-name *Silki*, or sēoluc 'a gulley, a small drain', cf. Silkby L (DEPN, Fellows Jensen 240); and *Will(i)ames-hullme, -hollme* 1294–1307 MidCh, *Williamsholme* 17 ib, from the ME pers.n. *William*, perhaps the Sir William Venables who held half of Hulme in l12 Orm² III 187.

CLEDFORD HALL & LANE (110–710650)

> *Clateford* e13 Cre
> *Cleytford* e13 Dieul, *Cleyte-* 1303 Orm²(p), *Clait(e)-, Clayt(e)ford(e)*
>   1230 Tab (p), 13 MidCh *et freq*, *Cleatford* 1621 MidCh
> *Cleyford* e13 Dieul
> *Cleadford (or Claytford)* 1771 Wil, (*-Farm*) 1775 ib
> *Cletford in Newton* 1771 Wil

'Clayey ford', from an OE adj. *clǣgiht (*v*. clǣg, -iht) and ford. Professor Löfvenberg points out that the diphthongal ME forms are against clǣte 'burdock' as first el. The ford was probably at 110–715651, where Cledford Lane crosses Sanderson's Brook, *v*. Cledford Bridge 245 *infra*.

HARBUTT'S FIELD (110–703670), *the Harbour's Field* 1819 Orm², *Harbour Field* 1883 Sheaf, 'a place of shelter or refuge', *v*. here-beorg. This is the site of the earthworks of a rectangular camp near the confluence of the rivers Croco and Dane near Middlewich, *v*. Orm² III 2–4, at the intersection of three, perhaps five, Roman roads (1. King Street *infra*, 2. towards Nantwich, 3. towards Sandbach, and perhaps 4. towards Chester and 5. towards Nether Peover). It was probably a Roman station, but its identification with *Condate* is untenable, *v*. 196 *supra*. It could be the location of *Salinis* 7 RavGeog, 'at the salt-pans or salt-works' (Lat. nom.pl. *salinae*, dat.pl. *salinis*), presumed to be Nantwich 326 *infra* (*Archæologia* XCIII 44). RavGeog names *Salinis* next before *Condate* on a route from *Mediolanum* (near Whitchurch Sa, *v*. 326 *infra*). Harbutt's Field is a nodal site, it is next to *Condate* along King Street, and it is near the salt-works of Middle-wich & Kinderton. The importance of Nantwich as a salt-wich in DB, which prompted its identification with *Salinis*, is in fact no greater than that of Middlewich, which, moreover, was then the capital of a Hundred named after it (*v*. Northwich Hundred 184 *supra*).

BRIARPOOL FM, *Briary Pool* 1831 Bry, *Brier Pool* 1842 OS, *v*. brēr, brērig, pōl¹. BROOK HOUSE (FM), named from Sanderson's Brook

I 34.   BYLEY BRIDGE, 1831 Bry, *v.* 233 *supra.*   HIGHER &
LOWER DALEACRE (110–730637), a detached part of Kinderton, in
Bradwall, cf. 267 *infra, v.* Daleacre 261 *infra.*   DANE HO, named
from R. Dane.   DAWFIELDS, 1831 Bry, probably from dāl 'a share,
a dole, an allotment'.   FENDER WOOD, 1831 ib, *v.* fender.
HANDSFIELDS FM, cf. *the feilds called Hanfeildes* 17 *MidCh, Handfields*
1848 *TA* 265, probably the same as *Hannefeld Dobbeson* 1366 MidCh,
'the field belonging to Hann son of Dobb', from a ME pers.n. *Hann*
and feld.   JONES'S LANE, JONESLANE BRIDGE, *Joan's Lane* 1831 Bry,
Jones Lane (*Bridge*) 1842 OS, cf. 267, 252 *infra,* apparently from the
fem. pers.n. *Joan.*   KINDERTON HALL & LODGE, 1724 NotCestr.
KING STREET, cf. Harbutt's Field *supra, v.* 1 44.   LODGE
LANE, *Gallows Lane & Gate* 1591 Sheaf, cf. *Gallows Field* 1819 Orm²,
1883 Sheaf, *v.* galga; named from a place of execution kept by the
barons of Kinderton, last used in 1596. Cf. Hangman's Lane & Fd
185 *supra,* 246 *infra,* Hangeman's Butts 254 *infra.* The fields lie at
the south end of Lodge Lane (110–723655).   POLE COTTAGE.
POOLHEAD FM, 'the head of a pool', *v.* pōl¹, hēafod.   RAVENSCROFT
BRIDGE, 1831 Bry, carrying King Street *supra* across R. Dane from
Harbutt's Field *supra, v.* 253 *infra.*   ROOKERY WOOD, *Gorsty
Wood* 1831 ib, *Gorsy Coppice* 1842 OS, *v.* gorstig.   SEA BANK.
SPRING COVERT, *v.* spring 'a young wood'.   TRUBY COTTAGE,
Truby's 1883 Sheaf, cf. Daniel *Truby* 1685 ib.   WALKER'S GREEN,
1831 Bry.

FIELD-NAMES

The undated forms are 1842 *TA* 222. Of the others, e13 is Cre, 13 AD,
c.1272, c.1351, c.1464 Orm², 1316² Chamb, 1355, 1504, 1505 ChRR, 1360
(17) Tab, 1504² Plea, 1591, 1619, 1879, 1883 Sheaf, 1653 *Vern,* 1831 Bry,
1842 OS, and the rest MidCh.

(a) Briary-eye 1883 (*v.* brērig, ēg); Butty Fd (*v.* butty); Coney Greave
1883 (*v.* coningre); Cordell Hill 1883; Crowley 1883 (*v.* crāwe, lēah);
Croxton Wd (cf. Croxton 236 *supra*); Foldstead (*v.* fald, stede); Footage;
Great Hard Fd 1883; Big & Little Hay Fd (*Hays* 1883, *v.* (ge)hæg); Isle of
Man 1883 (*v.* 326 *infra*); Kinderton Croft (cf. *le furlange de Kinderton* 1367,
v. furlang); Lampun (*Lompon* 1879, a field in the confluence of Sanderson's
Brook and R. Croco, probably a swampy place named from dial. *lompond* 'a
refuse-pit, a cess-pit'); Little Croft (*the little crofte* 1653); Lord's Eye 1883
(*v.* hlāford, ēg); Middle Fd (cf. *the Middlecroft* 1653); Milking Bank (*v.*
milking); Moon Fd 1883 (perhaps from dial. *moon-daisy* 'the large Ox-eye
Daisy or *Chrysanthemum leucanthemum*'); Nun Yard 1883 (*the Nunyoardes*
1653, 'nun's enclosures', *v.* nunne, geard); Ox Pasture; The parks 1883

(Sheaf[1] 3 80 describes it as part of an old deer-park at Kinderton, created in 1355 Orm[2] III 189, *v.* park); Pinfold 1831, 1842 (*v.* pynd-fald); Pingle 1883 (*v.* pingel); Ravenscroft (cf. 253 *infra*); Roundabout Fd (*v.* 327 *infra*); Saltersford 1883 ('salter's ford', *v.* saltere, ford, land next to a brook southeast of Middlewich, perhaps towards Cledford *supra, v.* Sheaf[1] 3 80); Sawpit Fd (*v.* saw-pytt); Silverpit Fd 1883; Stubborn Oryon 1883 (*the stubborne Iron* 1653 'intractable corner', *v.* hyrne, and 327 *infra*); Well Greaves 1883 (*v.* græfe); White Fd (*the further & nearer Whitefield* 1653); Wood Fd.

(b) *Adcoksfeild* 1316, *-feld*, *At(t)coksfe(i)ld* (*-iuxta Kellrudding*) 1365, 1366, *Hadcoks-* c.1592, *At(t)co(c)k(e)s-*, *Atcock-* 17 ('Adecock's field', from the ME pers.n. *Adecoc*, a per-form of *Adam*, and feld. This and *Kellrudding*, placed variously in Kinderton, Cledford and Middlewich by the Vernon MSS. and MidCh, were in Kinderton, near Handsfields *supra*); *Adyfurlonge* 1336 (*v.* furlang); *Bond(e)croft* 13, a.1287, (*Little-*) c.1300, *-crofte* c.1592, 17, *Bownecroftes* 1590 ('peasant's or bond-man's croft', *v.* bóndi, croft. This field also lay near Handsfields *supra*); *Brademedue* 1316[2] ('at the broad meadow', *v.* brād, mæd); *Broadhalflone* 113 ('broad half-selion', *v.* brād, half-land, the final *-d* mistaken for *-e* in a late copy); *Carters Croft* c.1592; *Cokesacre* 1504, 1505, *Cokescre* 1504[2] ('the cook's acre', *v.* æcer, cf. Cooks Croft 246 *infra*); *Douleghtorne* 1326 (*v.* lēah, þorn); *the higher & lower Flatte* 1653 (*v.* flat); *Fullsich(furlonge)* 1240–46 ('(furlong at) the foul stream', *v.* fūl, sīc. This was near *Adcoksfeild supra*); *Halwinscroft, Halmescroft, Hawnscroft* 1281, *Hawns-* 17 ('Alwin's croft', from the ME pers.n. *Alwine* discussed by Feilitzen 158 (< OE *Ælf-, Æðel-* or *Ealdwine*), and croft); *the great Heathfield* 1653 (*v.* hæð); *High Aspes* c.1464 (perhaps elsewhere, 'the high aspens', *v.* hēah, æspe); *Highlane* 1506 (*v.* hēah, lane); *Kelrridding* 1260–82, *Kellridding* 1366, *-rudding* 1362, c.1592 (from the same first el. as *Kelmeadow* 247 *infra* and ryding); *Kinderton Bridge* 1619 (Sheaf[3] 22 (5260), 'a horse bridge over Dane in Kinderton . . . built for the use of a mill there now in decay', apparently different from Ravenscroft Bridge *supra*, cf. *molendinum de Kinderton* 1330, *v.* brycg, myln); *Lortborne* a.1281 ('muddy stream', *v.* lort(e), burna); *Qecokedehalflone* 113 (a half-selion, *v.* half-land, cf. *Broadhalflone supra. Qecokede-* is unintelligible); *the Richcrofte* 1653 (from *rich* adj. 'fertile, full of goodness' and croft); *Rusford* c.1272, 1340 (lit. *Rufford*), 1360 (17), *Rush-* c.1351 ('ford growing with rushes', *v.* risc, ford. It was towards Sproston 254 *infra*); *Stockelache* e13 ('boggy stream at the tree stumps', *v.* stocc, læc(c)); *Stone Lake Lane* 1591 ('(lane near) a stony watercourse', *v.* stān, lacu, lane).

5. MIDDLEWICH (110–704662) [ˈmidḷwitʃ]

(seo) *wic* 1002–4 (c.1100) ASWills

> *Wich* 1086 DB, e13 Dieul, 1260 Court (p), *le Wych* 1367 ChRR (p),
> *Wicus* e13 Dieul, 1537 MidCh, *Wiz* 1351 BPR

> *Mildestuich* (Hundred) 1086 DB, *le Mydlestwych* 1394 MidCh, *the-*
> 1517 ib, *Medlistwich* 1420 ib, *Medelest-*, *the Mydellest Wyche*
> 1489 *Dav*, *the Mydelstwyche* 1504 MidCh

Mideluuiche 1070–1101 (1302) Ch, *Mildeluuichus* 1153–81 (1346)
ib, *Middelwich'* 1184 P, *Middlewich* 1217–28 (1427) Pat, 1273
Misc *et freq* with variant spellings *Midle-, Mydle-, Midele-,*
Myd(d)il(l)-, Middil-, Myddel(l)-, Middell-, Medle-, -wych(e),
-wiche; *le-* 1459 Orm², *the-* 1483 AD
Medius Wichus 1205–15 Facs, *-Wicus* e13 Dieul, 1237 P *et freq* with
variant spellings *-wyc(h)(i)us, -wikus, -vicus, -wicheus, -wicius,*
-vich(i)us; *Medeius Wycus* 1291 P
Memwich 1275 Cl, *Mienwyz* 1330 *AddCh*, *Menewys* 1331 Pat, *-wiz*
1351 BPR, *-wich* 1367 ChRR, *le Mesnewiche* 1339 MidCh,
Meenewych 1353 Tab, *Meisne wiche* 1428 ib
Middewiz 1351 BPR
Medewicus, -wycus 1376 Cl

'The (salt-)works', 'the middlemost wīc', *v.* middel (Lat. *medius*,
ME *mene*, OFr *mesne*), midlest, wīc, cf. Northwich (Hundred) 192,
184 *supra*, Nantwich 326 *infra*. For a possible connection between
Middlewich and *Salinis* 7 RavGeog, *v.* Harbutt's Field 238 *supra*.
Cf. Newton *infra*, which is 'Newton at the Wich', *Niwantun æt*
þære wic 1002–4 (c.1100) ASWills, from which the earliest reference
is derived.

STREET-NAMES

CHESTER RD., cf. *regia via que se ducit versus Cestriam* 1373, 1482 MidCh,
v. Chester 325 *infra*, cf. 1 47 and Wheelock St. *infra*.

DOG LANE, 16 MidCh, 1643 Orm², 'lane frequented by dogs', *v.* dogga,
lane.

HIGHTOWN, *the Kinges high streete* 1474 MidCh, *the Kings way* 1566 ib,
the High Streete 1587, 17 ib, *King-street* 1656 Orm², *publica via regis* a.1271
MidCh, *via regalis de Mediowico* c.1300 ib, *alta via* 1320 ib, *regia strata* 1380
ib, *alta strata* 1486 ib, *alta via regia* 1509 ib, 'the high part of the town', 'the
high-street', 'the king's street', *v.* hēah, toun, strǣt, cyning, weg. Hereabouts was the town place, 'a broad place in the middle of the town, in
mannor of a market place, called *the King's Mexon*' 1656 Orm², 'the king's
midden', *v.* cyning, mixen 'a dung-hill'.

KINDERTON ST., 1656 Orm², *Kinderton streete* 1414 MidCh, *Kynderton-* 1517
ib, cf. *via que vadit versus Kinderton* c.1300, *semita que-* 1308, *vicus ducens*
versus Kinderton 1309, *le lone que ducit uersus Kinderton* 1320, *regalis via que-*
1356 all MidCh, *v.* lane, strǣt, cf. Kinderton 236 *supra*.

LEAD SMITHY ST., cf. *letsmit* 1316 MidCh, *le leadsmithie* c.1320 ib, (*the-*)
1321 *et freq* ib, *-smithy* 1344 ib, (*le-*) 1482 ib, *Ledesmythe* 1436 Sheaf, named
from the lead-smithy where the salt-pans were made, cf. 193 *supra*, *v.* lēad,
smiððe.

LEWIN ST., *Lewenstreete* c.1300 *et freq* MidCh to 17, -*Strette* 1489 Dav, *Lewinstreete* 1315 *et freq* MidCh to 1597, *Lewyn-* 1315 ib, -*street* 1412 ib, *Lewynestreete* 1321 ib, *Lewon* (*or London*) *streete* 1643 Orm², *Lewis-street* 1658 Orm², 'Lēofwine's street', from the OE pers.n. *Lēofwine* and stræt.

PEPPER ST., *Pepperstreete* 1463 MidCh, (regia via vocata) *Peper Lane* 1487 ib, *Pep(p)erlane* 1567 ib, *peperstane* 1592 Sheaf² 1, 41 (for *pepere-* or *pepers-lane*), *Pepper-lane* 1656 Orm², cf. 327 *infra*, *v.* stræt, lane.

WHEELOCK ST., 1656 Orm², 1703 Cre, *Waleckstrate* e13 Dieul, (alta strata vocata) *Quelockstreete* 1260 MidCh (seven times to 1320 ib), *Wheelockstreete* 1317 ib *et freq* to 17 ib, *Whelockstreete* 1408 ib, *Wheleck strete* 1378 AD, 'the street leading to the R. Wheelock', *v.* stræt, R. Wheelock 1 38. This also was probably the road to Chester mentioned under Chester Rd *supra*.

LOST STREET-NAMES

Bawardeslone n.d. (17) MidCh 234, *Bagardelone* 1487 ib, *Bagardlone* 1518 ib, *Beggars Lane* 1533 ib ('beggar's lane', from ME *baggard* 'one who carries a pack, a migrant craftsman, a beggar' (MED; OFr *bague* 'a bundle', *baguer* 'pack up'), *v.* lane); *paruus pons* 1320 MidCh, *pons magnus* 1326 ib *et freq*, *Littlebridge* c.1536 Orm², *Litilbrige* 1547 *MinAcct* (lit. *Witil-*), *the bridg* 1602 MidCh, *the great bridge, the little bridge ende* 17 ib (cf. *le great ford* 1485, 1492 ib, (-*of the Wichebrooke*) 1565 ib, *v.* grēat, lȳtel, brycg, ford); *the churchyard side* 1558, 17 MidCh (cf. *the waye leading from the churchyarde to the streete* and *the churchsteele* 17 ib, *the Churche streete* 1544–80 ib, and *cemiterium* c.1300 ib *et freq*, *the Kirkeyorde* 1474 ib, *the churchyard* 1566 ib, *v.* cirice, geard, (ME *chirche-ȝeard*, with *k* due to Scand. influence), stigel 'a stile', stræt. The churchyard had houses abutting upon it and opening into it in the fourteenth century, cf. Churchyard Side 325 *infra*); *Cow Lane* (*v.* 237 *supra*); *le Halpenyhill* 1309 MidCh, -*Hyll* 1491 JRL, *Halpenihill* 1414 MidCh, -*penie-* 1504 ib, *Halfpeny-* 1498 ib, *Halfe-* 1557 ib, *Halfpenihil* 1506 ib, *Hal(fe)penihill* 17 ib ('halfpenny hill', *v.* halfpeny; perhaps named from some toll levied upon salters, cf. Penny's Lane 199 *supra*); *Hamlone* 1366, 1367 ib (this led off Lewin St. *supra*, perhaps to a meadow, *v.* hamm, lane, cf. foll.); *the lytyll strette* 1489 Dav (running east out of Lewin St. *supra*, perhaps identical with prec., cf. *Petitlone infra*, *v.* lȳtel, stræt); *Market Streete* 1524, 1600 MidCh (*v.* market, stræt); *le Milne waye* (*que ducit versus Kinderton*) e14, 1414 ib ('the way to the mill', *v.* myln, weg); *Petilone* (*ducens versus le Holt*) 1335 ib, *Petitlone* 1408 ib ('the little lane', *v.* petit, pety, lane, cf. *Holt, le Petit Halle infra*); *the Stywaye* 16 ib ('the pathway', *v.* stīg, weg); (*le*) *Warners lane* 1541 ib ('the gamekeeper's lane', *v.* warener (perhaps as a surname here), lane).

(THE) WICH(E)-HOUSE-STREETE(E) (lost), 17 MidCh, 1656 Orm², 'the street of the wich-house(s)', cf. *le wychouses* 1482 MidCh, 'the factory buildings, the salt-works houses', *v.* wych(e)-hous(e) (wīc, hūs), stræt, cf. 193 *supra*. Various wich-houses are named, as at Northwich 193–4 *supra*, usually after the manor to which they appertained or the family owning them (the references are all MidCh except where stated): *Bostock house* 17 (cf. Bostock 202 *supra*); *salina de Wico pertinens ad manerium de Bivele* e13 Dieul (cf. Byley 233 *supra*); *Crabtreefields salthouse* 1713 Cre (*v.* Crabtreefields *infra*); *una salina vocata Craunach house* 13, *Cranach house* 17 (cf. Cranage 223 *supra*); *the wichehouse belonging to Croxton house* 17 (cf. Croxton Hall 236 *supra*, Croxton-bank *infra*); *the eight leade house* 1591 (a salt-house with eight leaden boiling-pans); *Elworth house* 1290–1300, 17, *salina de Elworth* 1314, *salina vocata Elworth house* a.1340, *unum wicum vocatum Elworthouse* 1504 ChRR, *Elworth wichhouse* 1512, *Elworthe House* 1536 (cf. Elworth 266 *infra*); *salina de Kinderton* 13, *Kinderton House* 1643 Orm², 17 (cf. Kinderton 236 *supra*); *le Longe Wichehouse* 13 (*v.* lang); *Occleston house* 17 (cf. Occlestone 252 *infra*); 'a wichhouse lying in Ollerpool' 1517 (*v. Ollerpool(e) infra*); *Pages wichhouse* 17 (probably named after the family *le Page* of Earnshaw 188 *supra*, Hugh le Page was a lessee in Middlewich in 1367 Orm² III 169, 172); *Sandbach house* 17 (cf. Sandbach 269 *infra*); *salina de Sproston* 1321, *Sproston House* 17 (cf. Sproston 254 *infra*); *le Stock wichehouse* n.d. (17) (the sense of *stock* is not clear); *salina de Lunton* 13 (17) (ChetNS CV 112 suggests a mistake for Sutton 256 *infra*); *Tetton House* 17 (cf. Tetton 260 *infra*); *Unwens wichhouse* 1525 (from the surname *Unwin*). The brine for these factories was drawn from brine-pits (cf. Sheath Street 193 *supra*), some of which are named: *Lunseth* e13 Dieul (344, 127, lit. -*sech*'), *Lonseyth* 1328 *et freq* to 1371, -*seth* 1340, -*seith* 1484, *Lynseth* 1367, *Linseath* 1504, *Londseth* 1414 ('pit at a wood', *v.* lundr, sēað. This name may be connected with *Holt infra*); *Little Seyth* 1250–71, *the little bryne pitt* 1582, 17 (*v.* lȳtel, sēað, brīne, pytt); *le scheyth* 1260–90 (*v.* sēað with *sch*- for *s*-); *Newset* 1260–90, 1320, -*sed* c.1270, *New(e)sed* 1277 (1350) VR, 1299 Orm², -*seth* 1385, 1396, (*le*-) 1428 ('the new brine-pit', *v.* nīwe, sēað); *Brynseth* 1444 Orm² (III 175, lit. -*sech*; 'brine-pit', *v.* brine, sēað); *the great seth* 1512 (*v.* grēat, sēað).

Lost Buildings. *Burden Hall* 17 MidCh (a house-name at *the Churchsteele supra, v.* hall); *le motehall* 1468 MinAcct (*v.* (ge)mōt, hall); *le Petit Halle* 1365 BPR, *Petehall* 1378 Orm², *le Pety Hall* 1454 ChRR, 1489 ib, *Petihall* 1547 Orm², *Petehall* 1586 ib ('the little hall', *v.* pety, petit, hall); *Thornehall* 1587 ChRR (a house, 'thorn hall', *v.* þorn, hall).

Newton (110–700650)

> *Niwantun æt þære wic* 1002–4 (c.1100) ASWills
> *Neutone* 1086 DB, 1295 Cre, -*ton* e13 Tab, Dieul *et freq* to 1538 ChRR, -*tun* e13 Cre, *Newtona* a.1245 MidCh, -*ton* 1250 ib *et freq*, (-*iuxta Medium Wicum*) 1317 Plea, 1320 MidCh *et freq* with spellings as for Middlewich *supra*, (-*iuxta Kinderton*) 1498 MidCh
> *Noton* 1592 Sheaf
> *Nuton* 1698 Sheaf

'The new farm', *v.* nīwe, tūn, cf. Middlewich *supra*, Kinderton 236 *supra*. It is possible that the relationship between Newton and the wīc at Middlewich is similar to that between Witton and the wīc at Northwich, i.e., that the salt-works were in an enclave of the larger township, but through economic importance achieved an independent status, cf. 193 *supra*.

BOOTH LANE, BOWFIELDS (110–710640), cf. *in Bot(h)is de Medio Wico* 1240 P, *bothis regis in Medio Vico* 1241 Lib, *le Boþis*, *le Bothe* l13 *Vern* (p), *Booth Lane* 1515 MidCh, *(le) Booth(e) lane* 1541 ib, 'the herdsmen's shelters', '(the lane to-, and the fields at) the booths', *v.* bōth, lane, feld. Cf. 1 44.

HOLT (lost), 1440 Orm² III 209, *(le-, la-) Holt(e)* e13 Dieul, 13, 1280 MidCh *et freq* to *(manor of-)* 1424 Orm², *Holth* 14 *Sotheby* (p), 'the wood', *v.* holt, cf. *Lunseth, Petilone supra*.

MUGSALE IN NEWTON (lost), 17 MidCh, *Mugesle* c.1215 MidCh (p), *Mu(g)g(e)s(h)ale* c.1250, 1250–1300 MidCh (p), 1310 ib, *AddCh*, 1316 *HarlCh*, *(tenementum de-, -cum Pulforlonge)* e14 MidCh, *(villa de-)* 1313 ib, *Midsale* 1374 Orm², (a brooke called) *Mydsallbrooke* 1533, 1538 MidCh, 'at the midge-infested clearing and nook', *v.* mycg (gen.sg. *-es*), lēah (dat.sg. lēa), halh (dat.sg. hale), brōc.

OLLERPOOL(E), -POL (lost), 1517, 17, *Woluernepoole* 1260–90, *Wolrenpoole* c.1271, 1315, *-rem-* c.1300, *Wollernepoole* 1284–94 (twice), *Wollerpoole* 1406 all MidCh, the site of a wich-house of six leads near *le Hyppyngstonys infra*, in 1517, ChetNS CVIII 325, probably a pool and a brine-spring in R. Croco, *v.* pōl¹. The first el. may be an OE **hwalf-ærn* 'vaulted house' or 'house with or at a vault arch', *v.* hwalf, ærn, cf. *wholve* (NED) 'a short arched or covered drain under a path'. The allusion might well be to a wich-house with a conduit for brine, or with a vaulted roof. However, there is a lack of *Wh*-spellings to support this derivation. The note in WRY 3 xi, s.n. *Wormald* (WRY 3 59), refers to this p.n. Nevertheless, it is possible to derive *Ollerpool(e)* and *Wormald* from the OE fem. pers.n. *Wulfrūn* (rejected by Professor Smith WRY *loc. cit.* in favour of an appelative on account of the co-incidence of water-names—another example is found in an old name for Valley Brook 1 37). It would be interesting to maintain this pers.n. derivation for *Ollerpool(e)* on account of the Middlewich association of Wulfric Spot, whose mother was called *Wulfrūn* and who held land at Newton by Middlewich (ASWills 152, 156). But it would perhaps, be mischievous to observe that

Lewin St. (Middlewich) contains the OE pers.n. *Lēofwine* (*v.* ASWills 153 ll. 26 ff.).

WARIHULL (lost), *Warihullfeild* 1287 MidCh (143, a field outside Middlewich bought from Robert de *Warihull*), *Warehullfeld in villa de Newton* 1377 ib, from the Middlewich surname *de Warihul(l)* 13 ib *et freq* to 1482 ib, *Wary-* 1328 ChRR, *Warihill* 1488 ib, *Wayrhull* 1250–1300 ib, *Warehull* 1396, 1412 ib, 'felon hill', *v.* wearg (Angl werg, Merc *wærg, cf. Campbell §223) 'a felon, a criminal, an out-law', hyll, feld.

BANKQUAY FM, *Bank Hey* 1831 Bry, cf. *del Bonk* 1357 *Chol* (p), 'enclosure at a bank', *v.* banke, (ge)hæg.   BROOKFIELD, near R. Wheelock.   BROOK COTTAGES, named from Sanderson's Brook 1 34.   BROOKS LANE, crossing Sanderson's Brook and R. Croco. CHADWICKFIELDS.   CLEDFORD BRIDGE & COTTAGES, *Cledford Bridge* 1842 OS, *v.* Cledford 238 *supra*.   CROXTONBANK & BRIDGE, *v.* Croxton 236 *supra*. The bridge spans R. Dane. Croxtonbank is on the south bank, in an area in the north end of Newton and Middle-wich which seems to have belonged to the manor of Croxton, cf. *terra Ricardi de Croxton* 1407 MidCh 277, and *Croxton house supra*. EDGEFIELDS FM, *Edgefields* 1831 Bry, on Sanderson's Brook, the old boundary with Kinderton cum Hulme, at 119–718649, perhaps 'fields at the town's edge', *v.* ecg, feld.   FINNEY'S LANE, probably from the surname *Finney*, but cf. Finney 326 *infra*.   HADDONHURST. HANNAH'S WALK.   KITFIELD COTTAGE.   LONG LANE.   MANOR HO, *Manor Hall* 1831 Bry, *Middlewich Manor* 1″ OS.   MOUNT PLEASANT.   NEWTON BANK, FM & HALL.   NEWTON HEATH, *bruerium* 1287 MidCh 143, *v.* MedLat *bruerium*, *bruera* 'a heath'. ST ANNE'S COTTAGE & RD, cf. *St Anne's Field* 1848 TA, 1883 Sheaf[1] 3 80, supposed the site of *St Anne's Chappell* 1666 Sheaf *loc. cit.* STANTHORNE BRIDGE, *v.* 212 *supra*.   SUTTON COTTAGE, 1831 Bry, *v.* Sutton 256 *infra*.   WALLANGE BRIDGE, *v.* 212 *supra*.   WARDLE BRIDGE & LOCK (Shropshire Union Canal), perhaps from a surname *Wardle* (cf. Wardle 327 *infra*).   WARMINGHAM LANE, *v.* Warming-ham 262 *infra*.

FIELD-NAMES

The undated forms are 1848 *TA* 265. Of the others, e13 is Dieul, 1269 IpmR, l13, c.1281, 1307 AD, 1315 *Chol*, 1316, 1612, 1668, 1688, 1693, 1702, 1703, 1706, 1708, 1713, 1739 Cre, 1354 *Indict*, 1365[2] BPR, 1378, c.1536,

1547, 1586 Orm², 1454, 1489, 1504, 1536, 1584, 1587 ChRR, 1468, 1471, 1486, 1515 *MinAcct*, 1511 Plea, Eliz *Surv*, 1592, 1619, 1883 Sheaf, and the rest MidCh.

(*a*) The Four Acres (cf. *the Half Acre(s)* 1668, 1713, *v.* half, æcer); The Attwoods 1883 (cf. Peter *Attwood* tenant 1663 Sheaf); Bateson's Crofts 1706 (*-Croftes* 1517, (*le*) *Batesons croft* 1541, *Batteson's Crofts* 1703, from the surname *Bateson* and croft); Big & Little Berms; Briar Pool Mdw (*v.* Briarpool 238 *supra*); Fur Butts ('the further butts', from dial. *furr*, *v.* firre, butte); Butteyfeild 1702 (*v.* butty); Cock Fd; Cooks Croft & Fd (cf. *Cokesacre* 240 *supra*); The Coppice; Crabtreefields 1713, Crab Tree Croft 1703 (*Crabtreecroft(e)* 1589, 1602, *v.* crabbe, trēow, croft, cf. *Crabtreefields salthouse supra*); The Cross Bank 1713 (1668, *v.* cros, banke); Flashy Fd (*v.* flasshe); Hangman Fd (cf. Hangman's Lane, Gallows Field 185, 239 *supra*); Kills Fd (cf. foll. and *Kelmeadow infra*); Kiln Croft (cf. terra vocata *le Kilneyard* 1470, *v.* cyln, geard); Kitchen Croft; Lane Place (*v.* lane, place); Mud Pool; Nook Fd (cf. *Nook Farm* 1739); the Pingott 1713 (*the Pingate* 1668, *v.* pingot); Quaker House Fd; Reddish Fm 1706 (*le Redys* 1364, *Reddysh* 1502, *Redich* 1531, *the Rey Eddish* 1668, *Reddish tenement* 1696, perhaps 'the rye enclosure', *v.* ryge, edisc, but in view of the uniform *Re-*spellings, Professor Löfvenberg prefers as first el. rǣge 'the female roe-deer' as in *Remersch* 172 *supra*); Shippon Fd; the Short Land 1713 (*-lands* 1668); Smalwoods Fd 1713 (*Smallwood Field* 1693, probably from a surname, cf. Smallwood 316 *infra*); Stony Fd & Flatt (cf. *Stanforlong* e13, *Stanifurlung* l13, *Stamfurlong* c.1281, *v.* stān, stānig, furlang); Thorney Croft; Tinkers Croft ((*le*) *Tinkers croft(e)* 1528, *v.* tink(l)ere, croft); Wheelock Banks (cf. R. Wheelock 1 38).

(*b*) Agasseyord(*e*) c.1340, 1341 ('Agatha's yard', from the ME fem. pers.n. *Agasse* (OFr *Agace*, Lat *Agatha*) and geard); Banners Stoope 1619, Boners stoope Jas 1 (a boundary mark between Middlewich and Kinderton, probably the limit of salt-boiling rights in Middlewich, *v.* ChetNS CV 182. The second el. is stolpi (dial. *stoop*) 'a post, a pillar'. The first el. might be either a surname as in Banner Cross WRY 1 197, or from ON *bœn*, *bón* (gen.sg. -*ar*) 'prayer, request, boon', the stoop being a place at which requests were to be made, e.g. for permission to proceed to the salt-works. Cf. *le Tolstok* 327 *infra*, Banners Style 325 *infra*); le south boys de Birdlehirst 1394 ('(hill or wood at) bird's clearing', *v.* bridd, lēah, hyrst); le Blacklawe 1301 ('the black mound', *v.* blæc, hlāw); Brooke(s)meadow 1590 (*v.* brōc, mǣd); Burdmoscrofte 1504, Boardmanscrofte 1520, Bordmoscroft 1536 (from croft, perhaps with the surname *Boardman*); Cadmons crofte 1283 (perhaps 'Cædmon's croft', from the OE pers.n. *Cædmon*, but the first el. may be the ME surname *Cademan*, *v.* croft); le Church ground 1538, le Kyrke-, le Kirkefeld 1541, cf. terra ecclesie a.1274 (*v.* cirice, kirkja, feld, grund); (Le) Dromble 1536 ('the clough, the ravine', *v.* drumble 'a wooded ravine'); the Gorsty Croft 1668 (*v.* gorstig, croft); le Greene 1412 (p) (*v.* grēne² 'a green'); Greynes ground 1522 (probably from the surname *Green*, cf. prec.); le Hallyard 1321, -yord 1325 (*v.* hall, geard); le Hyppyngstonys 1517, Tippingtone c.1536, the typping stones, Hipping stones 17 ('the stepping stones', *v.* hypping, stān); the horse

mill 17 (*v.* horse-myln); *Intak* 1471, 1486, *the entack(e)-, -intake lane* 1592
(*v.* inntak, lane); *Jarewell* 1269 (possibly 'winding stream', *v.* ceare, wella,
as in R. Cherwell O 6, PNE 84, with *j-* for *ch-* as in Cholmondeley 325 *infra*;
but the *J-* probably represents *i-*, and this p.n. is like Yarwell Nth 209
(*Jarewelle* 1166 to 1289), 'spring by the yair(s) or fishing-pool(s)', *v.* gear,
(gen.pl. geara), wella); *Kelmeadow* 1407, *Kelemedowe* 1413, *Kellmeadow* 17
(probably from the surname *Kel(l)* which also appears in *Kellridding* 240
supra, cf. Robert *Kel* 13 AD IV 382, MidCh *et freq, v.* mǣd); (porta vocata)
Lacheyate 1515 (perhaps 'gate with a latch', *v.* geat); *Lampcroft* a.1365,
Lampecroft or Lampeyord 1590 (perhaps a croft (or enclosure) dedicated to
the upkeep of a lamp in church, from ME *lampe*, though lamb 'a lamb' is
possible, *v.* croft, geard); *le Lamputt* 1250–1300 ('the loam pit', *v.* lām, pytt);
Littecroft a.1274, *Littlecrofte* 1360 (*v.* lȳtel, croft); (*le*) *Lowe* 1333 (p), 1396
(p) ('the mound', *v.* hlāw); *Nineteen Selions* 1307 (from *selion* (NED) 'a
land, a strip or ridge between two furrows in an open field'); *the noon-heyes*
Eliz ('the nuns' enclosures', *v.* nunne, (ge)hæg); *le Oldgar* 1310 ('the old
corner', *v.* ald, gāra); *the Little Padocke* 1572 (*v.* lȳtel, paddock); *Pulforlonge*
e14, 1396, *-long(e)* 1572 ('furlong at a pool', *v.* pull, furlang); *Redemore* 1315
('moor where reeds grow', *v.* hrēod, mōr[1]); (*le*) *Rosemedow* 1373, *Roes land*
1589 (*v.* mǣd, land); *Shepefurlonge* 1303 (*v.* scēp, furlang); *Skadegreen londes*
1373 (probably from skeið 'a course, a track, a race-course', *v.* grēne[2] 'a
green', land 'a selion'); *Stanford* 1584 ('stony ford', *v.* stān, ford); *le
Wallecroft* 1316 ('well croft', *v.* wælla, croft); *Weaver Banks* 1612 (*v.* banke.
The name may refer to Weaver 327 *infra*, or a surname from it, but cf. dial.
weaver, waver 'a young tree left standing after a wood is felled', *v.* wæfre);
Weyrefelds 1511 Plea ('fields at a weir', *v.* wer, feld); *Wibardesdiche* 1274,
Wybardussedche 1360 ('Wibert's ditch', from the ME pers.n. *Wibert, Wyberd*
(OFr *Guibert*, OGer *Wigbert*, cf. OE *Wīgbeorht*) and dīc); *Wuchefeld* 1281,
cf. *Wychefurlong(e)* 1320, 1353 ('field and furlong at a wīc', or 'belonging to
Middlewich', *v.* wīc, feld, furlang); *Yardleys banckes* 1572 (*v.* banke, cf.
Hugh *Yardley*, tenant. The surname is *freq* at Middlewich from 1412, with
variant spelling *Erdley*).

6. MINSHULL VERNON (110–670600), *Manessele* 1086 DB, *Muneshull'*
c.1200 *AddCh et freq* with variant spellings as for Church Minshull,
and *Moinshull iuxta Wermingham* 1287 Court, *Munshulvernoun* 1308
AddCh, *Munschuluernon'* 1311 *ib*, *Minshull Vernon* 1394 ChRR,
-Varnon 1607 *AddCh*. For other spellings cf. Church Minshull 325
infra. The suffix is the surname of Warin *de Vernon* lord of this moiety
of Minshull c.1200 *AddCh* 50671.

EARDSWICK HALL (110–673599) [ˈɛːrdzwik]

    Erdeswich c.1200 *AddCh, Erdes-, Erdiswik* 1289 Court (p) *et freq*
    with variant spellings *Erdus-, Erdys-, Erds-, -wick(e), -wike,
    -wek, -wyk(e)* to 1640 Sheaf, *Erdswick Hall* 1724 NotCestr

Herdes-, Herdiswic(k) c.1220–30 *AddCh*, -*wik*, -*wyke* 113 *ib* (p),
　-*weke* 1369 *Dav* (p)
Ordeswyke 1331 Tab (p)
Eerdeswyk' 1336 *AddCh* (p), *Eardswicke* 1621 Tab, -*wick* 1673
　Sheaf, (-*Hall*) 1831 Bry
Ardeswyk 1346 BPR (p)
Herdewike 1356 MidCh (p), *Erddewike* 1369 ib, *Erdewick* 1629 Cre
Yardeswyk 1550 *MinAcct*
Hardwick 1615 Tab
Erswicke 1619 ChRR

Perhaps 'herdsman's sheds', *v.* hirde, heorde, wīc, cf. heorde-wīc;
but the first el. is probably a pers.n. OE *Ēorēd* or *Ēa(n)rēd*, cf.
Yeardsley 1 176, Earnshaw 188 *supra*.

NEW & OLD HOOLGRAVE (110–672589, 663599)

Hulegraua, -greue c.1200, e13 *AddCh*, -*gr(e)ave* 1231 (1580) Sheaf,
　-*greave* (*Hall*) 1617 *AddCh*, *Hulgrave* c.1262 *Dav* (p), (*Old- &
　New-*) 1846 *TA*, -*greue*, -*v*- 1278 *AddCh*, 1294 Ipm (p) *et freq*
　to 1819 Orm[2], (*mansio de-*) 1336 *AddCh*, (-*iuxta Erdeswyk*) 1410
　ib, *Ulgreve* 113 Tab (p), *New Hullgrove* 1842 OS
Holegraue c.1220 *AddCh*, -*gref* 1275–82 *ib* (p), -*greve* 1322 Fine (p),
　Holgreve 1294 Ipm (p), -*grave* 1390 ChRR (p), *Hollegreve* 1325
　Mere (p), *Hoolegre(e)ve* Hall 1611, 1615 *AddCh*, *New- & Old
　Houlegreave* 1831 Bry
Olograve, Oul(e)greve, -*grave* 1287 Court (p), *Owlegreue* (lit. -*grene*)
　1330 ChRR (p)
Hugreue 1290–1310 *Chol* (p)
Halgreve 1369 Bark (p), *New Hall Grove* 1860 White
Howgreve 1581 *AddCh*, -*grave Hall* 1724 NotCestr, *Hoograves* 1621
　Orm[2]

'Wood with a hovel in it', *v.* hulu, grǣfe, nīwe, ald, hall.

HIGHER ELMS, LOWER HAMS (110–667613), *le hem* 1308, 1347 *AddCh*,
1348 Eyre, *la-* 1353 BPR, *le hemme* c.1335, 1454, 1475 *AddCh*, *legh'
hemme* 1498 *ib*, *the hemme* 1565 *ib*, *Higher & Lower Hams* 1831 Bry,
-*Elms* 1842 OS, 'the edge, the border', *v.* hemm. The place is on a
bank over R. Weaver. The spelling *legh-* represents the OFr def.art.
le, cf. Bradfield Green *infra*.

BEECH WOOD, *Eardswick Wood* 1831 Bry. BRADFIELD GREEN, 1831 ib, *Ligh Bradfield* 1595 *AddCh*, *Leighe Bradfyeld* 1598 *ib*, *Bradfield within Minshull Vernon* 1652 Sheaf, 'the broad field', v. **brād, feld**, and **grēne**[2] 'a green'. The OFr def.art. *le* is formally confused with **lēah** as in Higher Elms *supra*. BROOK FM, 1842 OS, named from a stream in Polestead Wood *infra*. CHAPEL FM, cf. *Chapel Field* 1846 *TA*. CHURCH FM. CHURCH MINSHULL BRIDGE, v. 325 *infra*. DAIRY FM. EARDSWICK BRIDGE & WOOD, *Eardswick Wood* 1831 Bry, cf. Beech Wood, Eardswick *supra*. HIGH FM. HOLE HO, 1831 ib, v. **hol**[1]. KEEPER'S FM. MINSHULLHILL, 1831 ib. MOAT FM, 1831 ib, near a deserted moat. MOSS LANE, 1831 ib, cf. *Minshull Moss* ib, Leighton Moss 326 *infra*. NEWFIELD HALL. PARKFIELD, -HALL & HO, *Park Fields, Hall & House* 1831 ib, named from *Mynshull Parke* c.1602 *Chol*, v. **park**. POLESTEAD WOOD, *Pool-* 1831 Bry, *Brook Wood* 1842 OS, cf. *Big & Little Poolstead* 1846 *TA*, Brook Fm *supra*, v. **pōl-stede**. SPRING FM, *Spring House* 1831 Bry, cf. foll. SPRING PLANTATION, *Spring Wood* 1831 ib, cf. prec., also *Springs Bank* 1846 *TA*, v. **spring** 'a young wood', **banke** 'a hill-side'. WALLEY'S GREEN, 1831 Bry, probably from the surname *Walley*, v. **grēne**[2]. WEAVER BANK, *Weever-Bank* 1745 Sheaf, v. **banke**, cf. foll. and R. Weaver 1 38. WEAVER WOOD, 1831 Bry, cf. prec. WORSLEY COVERT.

FIELD-NAMES

The undated forms are 1846 *TA* 267. Of the others, 1231 (1580), 1671 are Sheaf, 1308 Mere, 1394, 1527 ChRR, 1666 *ChCert*, 1831 Bry, 1842 OS, and the rest *AddCh, AddRoll*.

(*a*) Bakehouse Croft; Bank; Bean Fd; Beggars Croft; Bell Fd; Black Wd; Brick (Kiln) Bank; Brook Flatt (*v.* flat); Butty Fd (*v.* butty); Clemley Fd (cf. Clemley 326 *infra*); Coach Croft (*v.* cwice 'couch-grass'); Cote Fd; Cow Ridding; Cross Lane 1842; Crownfield; Five-, Six- & Three Day Math (*v.* day-math); Dumbello Mdw (probably from dumbel and hol[1]); Eachus Plan; Ear Wd; Fat Pasture ('rich pasture', alluding either to lush grass or to rich soil, *v.* fætt); Fender Fd (*v.* fender); Flaxfield; Foxley (*v.* fox, lēah); Gore-field (*la Gore* c.1220, *Le Gare* c.1230, *v.* gāra 'a gore, a triangular piece of land'); Green Lane 1831; Hake Yards (*lez hakysyardes* 1569, cf. Hawkers Head *infra*); Hall Lane 1831 (named from Eardswick Hall *supra*); Ham Fd (*v.* hamm); Hatch Fd (*v.* hæc(c)); Hawkers Head (*le haukeserd* 1311, 'the hawk's gap', *v.* hafoc-scerde, cf. *Hawkesyord* 1 166 and Hake Yards *supra*); The East & West Hays; Hoose Bank (*v.* hōh); Intake (*v.* inntak); Kitchen Croft; Lodge; Loughton Croft; Maall Wd, Marl Fd (*v.* marle);

Mews (v. meuwe); Milking Bank (v. milking); Millfield, Mill Mdw (cf.
pratum molendini 13, *le Milneheye* 1391, v. myln, (ge)hæg. There was a mill
upon R. Weaver beside Old Hoolgreave *supra* in 1336 *AddCh* 507814. Cf.
Mill Lane 1831 Bry); Ox Hill; Park Fd & Land; Patch; Penny Oak; Poolstead (v. pōl-stede); Priest Fd; Radda's Croft (possibly from a surname
Radway, cf. dial. pronunciation of Radway Green 327 *infra*, [ræda]); The
Rang (v. range); Ravens Close (cf. *Rauenisheye* c.1230, from hræfn 'a raven'
or the OE pers.n. Hræfn, and (ge)hæg 'an enclosure', or, since the source
describes it as an 'insula', ēg 'an island, a water-meadow'); Rushy Flatt;
Sawtree; Sein Acre ('seven-acre', v. seofon, æcer); Serral Croft; Shoulder
of Mutton (v. 327 *infra*); Smithy Croft; Sour Fd; Thieves Clough (v. þēof,
clōh); Tinkers Hill v. (tink(l)ere, hyll); Tongue Shaft (v. 1 162); Twist
Bank (cf. *le Sichetwisse* 1315, 'the fork of the stream', v. sīc, (ge)twist); Two
Stylefield (v. stigel); Great & Little Warburton (probably from the surname
from Warburton 34 *supra*); Weaver Mdw (named from R. Weaver); Weir
Fd, Hill & Mdw (cf. *unum Wer' super aquam de Weuere* 1395, v. wer);
Windmill Fd; Within Fd (v. wiðegn).

(b) *Aldalesiche* c.1220, c.1230 ('(watercourse at) the old corner', v. ald,
halh, sīc); *profundum Bache uersus Munessulf* c.1220 ('the deep valley
towards Minshull', v. bæce 'a stream, a valley', cf. Church Minshull 325
infra); *le Barndepol* 1324 ('the brownish pool', v. brende[2], pōl[1], cf. Brindle
Heath La 41); *le Birchenehul* 1324 ('hill growing with birch-trees', v.
bircen[2], hyll); *Blake Lake* c.1230 ('the black watercourse', v. blæc, lacu);
Burrowes (Hall) in Minshall Vernon 1671 (Sheaf[3] 39 (8378), cf. Barrow's
Green 325 *infra*); *Burtonisheye* c.1230 ('the enclosure belonging to a burh-
tūn', v. (ge)hæg); *le Clyf (iuxta aquam de Weuere)* 1311, 1315 (v. clif); *paruum
Cloch* c.1230, *le Clogh* 1310 ('the (little) dell', v. lȳtel, clōh); *le Croft* 1527
(v. croft); *Crowe Bache* 1581 ('crow valley', v. crāwe, bæce[1]); *le Flodȝate-
medewe* 1339 ('meadow at a flood-gate', v. flōd-yate, mǣd); *Forthacres*
c.1220, *Furdacs* 1231 (1580) ('plough-lands at a ford', v. ford, æcer); *le
hauetlant* c.1220 ('the head-land', v. hēafod-land); *le Hayberne* 1339 ('the
hay barn', v. hēg, bere-ærn); *Heldohedach* c.1230 ('ash tree at the top of a
slope', v. helde, hēafod, æsc); *porta del Hewe, fossatum del Olde hewe* 1329
('gate and ditch of (place called after) the old yew-tree', v. īw, ald); *Ince's
House* 1602, -*Farm* 1611 (cf. Randolph *Ince* 1607); *Mannis heis, -hayiis* c.1230
(probably 'common enclosures', v. (ge)mǣnnes, (ge)hæg); *Mayonesegh* 1394,
Mayoegh 1454 (v. *Mayowse* 326 *infra*); *Menihincwey* c.1220 (a road-name
discussed at *Grene Mening Wei* 326 *infra*. The line of a Roman road from
Middlewich towards Nantwich has been traced through this township, cf.
1 47); *Merei* 1308 ('boundary water-meadow' or 'water-meadow at a
pool', (ge)mǣre or mere[1], ēg); *Pearetree feild* 1666 (v. peru, trēow); *Shidhard*
c.1230 ('enclosures made of palings', v. scīd-geard); *ad slaccum* 1310 (v.
slakki 'a slack, a hollow'); *þornisiche, Thornishiche, -sihche* c.1230
('thorny stream', v. þornig, sīc); *leȝ vigint' acr'* 1569, *the twentie Acres Bache*
1582, *The Twenty Acres Farm* 1611 (v. twēntig, æcer, bæce[1]. Here bæce[1] 'a
valley, a stream' refers to a wooded dell, 'all that bache or parcell of wood . . .
called-' 1582 *AddCh* 50921); *Wilmesheye* 1315 (from a pers.n. such as OE

Wīghelm, OGer *Willelm*, and (ge)hæg 'an enclosure'); *Wynebaldisheye* c.1230 (described as an 'insula', hence from either (ge)hæg 'an enclosure' or ēg 'an island, a water-meadow', cf. Raven's Close *supra*); with the OE pers.n. *Winebald* which also appears in the adjacent Wimboldsley 257 *infra*).

7. MOORESBARROW CUM PARME, *Moresbarwe cum Parme* 1430 *Dav*, *Moresbury et Perme* 1535 VE (lit. *P'ine*), *Moresbury cum Parme* 1538 Orm², *Moorsbarrow with Parm* 1846 *TA*, *v*. Mooresbarrow, Parme, *infra*.

MOORESBARROW HALL (100–748652)

> *Moresbarrow* c.1215 MidCh (p) *et freq* with variant spellings *Moris-*, *-bar(r)ow(e)*, *-baru(e)*, *-bar(e)w(e)*, *-baruwe*; *Moresbury* 1535 VE, 1538 Orm²
>
> *Merisbarew* e13 Tab, *Meresborwe*, *-boru* (lit. *-born*) 1291 Tax
> *Moriebaruwe* 1260 Court
> *Morebarwe* 1350 VR
> *Mosbarue* 1547 *MinAcct*, *-borue* 1554 *ib*, (*-alias Mosbarowe*) 1568 Orm², *Mosebarue* (lit. *-barne*) 1553 Pat, *Mosseberre* m16 *AOMB* 397
> *Mooresborrowe* 1652 Sheaf, *-barrow* 1791 Orm², (*Hall*) 1831 Bry
> *Moulsbrowe* 1663 Orm²

'At the wood on the moor', *v*. mōr¹ (gen.sg. *-es*), -es², bearu (dat.sg. bearwe). The form *parua Mosborue* 1554 *MinAcct* stands for *Parm in Mosborue*, *v*. Parme *infra*. For the genitival composition, cf. Mosborough Db 248.

PARME FM (110–746647) [pa:m]

> *Perme* 1309–12 VR (p), 1430 *Dav*, 1535 VE (lit. *P'ine*), 1597 *Dav*, (*-in Mosbarue*) 1547 *MinAcct*, cf. *Permebrok'* 1349 *Vern*
> *Parme* 1538, 1544 Orm², 1553 Pat, and five examples to 1724 NotCestr, *Parm* 1554 *MinAcct*, 17, 1791 Orm², *The Parm(e)* 1842 OS, 1882 Orm²
> *Perve alias Pervie* 1568 Orm² 1680

The origin of this p.n. is obscure. It is recorded late and infrequently, there is no diversity of form, and an etymology is hard to discern. There would be formal difficulty in deriving the p.n. from OE *pirigum*, dat.pl. of pirige, i.e. 'at the pear-trees', for this would require palatal *g̊* before the back-vowel of the inflexional *-um*. Dr von Feilitzen suggests OE peru 'a pear', in the sense 'a pear-tree' (not

recorded until c.1400). This would produce the locative OE (*æt*)
perum > ME *Perm(e)* with syncope of the *u* as in Yarm YN 172
(OE *gearum*, dat.pl. of gear 'a yair, a fishing-pool'). This is an
attractive solution. Professor Löfvenberg suggests an OE **peren* 'a
place where pears grow, a pear-orchard', a substantivized form of the
adj. peren 'growing with pears' (cf. EPN s.v., DEPN s.n. Parndon
Ess), parallel with the substantive use (bircen[1] 'a place overgrown
with birches, a birch copse') of bircen[2] 'growing with birch-trees,
birchen', as in Birkin YW 4 16 (cf. DEPN, EPN s.v. bircen[1], [2]).
OE **(æt) per(e)ne* would lead to ME *Perne*, and the change *n* > *m*
would have to be explained as distant assimilation, as in ME *brimston*
< *brinston*, *pilegrim* < *pilegrin* (*v.* Jordan §§173, 254). Unless further
evidence comes to light, the best guess which can be made at this
p.n. is that it probably has something to do with pear-trees, but that
the spellings do not certainly indicate the precise nature of the
allusion. *Permebrok* is unidentified, *v.* brōc.

JONESLANE BRIDGE, *v.* 239 *supra*.   MOORESBARROW LODGE, *The*
Farm 1831 Bry.

FIELD-NAMES

The undated forms are 1846 *TA* 273. H3 is (1585) ChRR.

(*a*) Black Croft; Cow Hay; Daw Fd; Four- & Six Day Work (*v.* day-
work); Fifteen Butts ('fifteen selions', *v.* butte); Fourley Fd; Kiln Lane
Fd; Marl Fd & Hay; Old Fd & Hey; Rogers Eye (from the pers.n. *Roger*
and ēg 'a water-meadow'); Sample Field Nook; Silver Fd.

(*b*) *vadum de Wemustr'*, *-Weumstr'* H3 (perhaps '(ford at) Wīgmund's tree',
from the OE pers.n. *Wīgmund* and trēow).

8. OCCLESTONE (GREEN) (110–695629) [ˈɔkəlstan]

Aculuestune 1086 DB, *Ac(c)ulueston*, *-is-* e13 Facs (p), Tab (p),
  Chest (p), *Hacwluest'* c.1230 AddCh (p), *Akulueston* 1238 (1580)
  Sheaf (p), *Haculuiston* a.1245 MidCh (p)
Acleston c.1165 Chol, *-is-* H3 Tab (p), Orm[2] (p), ChRR (p), *Accles-*,
  -is- 1233–44 (17) Chest (p), MidCh (p), *Haccles-* 1260–70 MidCh
  (p)
Acul(l)uston e13 Dieul, c.1233 AddCh (p), *-es-* c.1240 (1400) Pat
Alunueston c.1209 Tab (p)
Hoculfustun (lit. *Hot-*) e13 Cre (p)
Aucleston 1230 Tab (p)

Oc(c)liston e1233 *AddCh*, *-es-* 1246–60 MidCh (p) *et freq* with
variant spellings *Ok(k)les-, -is-*; *Occleston Green (Farm)* 1831 Bry
Akeliston 13 MidCh (p)
Okeleston l13 MidCh (p)
Akelweston 14 Tab (p)
Occulston 1458 Orm², 1518 MidCh, *-toune* 1553 Pat
Hogeleston 1550 *MinAcct*

'Ācwulf's farm', from the OE pers.n. *Ācwulf* and **tūn**. The form
Sutton by Eccleston 1316 Plea is an error for *Occleston*, cf. Sutton 256
infra.

NORCROFT (110–693649), *Nortcrofte* 13 MidCh (p), *Northcroft* 1420
Chol, Norcroft 1482 *ib et freq* with variant spelling *-crofte*; *Norcroft
Hall* 1831 Bry, 'the north croft', *v.* **norð, croft**. The place is at the
north end of the township.

FIELD'S FM.   HOPLEY HO.   LEAHEAD, *Leehedd* 1544 Pat, 'the
top end of the wood or clearing', *v.* **lēah, hēafod**, cf. Wimboldsley 257
infra.   MANOR FM, *Manor House* 1831 Bry, cf. *Sir John Savage's
mese place called Occleston* 1515 AD.   NEWFIELD FM.   PETTY-
WOOD FM, *Pettywood near Middlewich* c.1700 *Cross*, 'little wood', *v.*
pety.

FIELD-NAMES

The undated forms are 1845 *TA* 302. Of the others, 1553 is Pat, 1734 *Dep*,
1831 Bry.

(*a*) The Bank 1831; Barrows Lane 1831 (perhaps from **bearg**); Bell Fd;
The Brundocks 1734 (*Bryndockes Herne* 1553, perhaps 'corner at the burnt
oaks', *v.* **brende², āc, hyrne**); Cocksey Fd; Furrows Fd; Hand Croft; Heath
Fd; House Fd; Sutton Hollow 1831 (a sunken way down to Sutton Bridge
256 *infra*, on the line of a Roman road, cf. 1 47, *v.* **holh**).

(*b*) *Sharpesfeldes* 1553 (from a surname *Sharp* and **feld**).

9. RAVENSCROFT BRIDGE & HALL (110–700670)

Rav-, Rauen(e)scroft(e) 13 Dieul, 1287 Orm², 1291–1311, 1301
MidCh *et freq* with variant spelling *Raunes-*; *the Hall of-* 1598
Orm², *-Bridge* 1619 Sheaf
Ranncroft 1357 Eyre (p)
Rencroft 1377 Eyre (p)
Raynscroft 1504 *Chol*

'Hræfn's enclosure', from the OE pers.n. *Hræfn* (cf. **hræfn**) and **croft**.

FIELD-NAMES

(a) Hangeman's Butts 1819 Orm[2] III 201 (v. hangeman, butte. The tenure of this land was by service of providing an executioner to the barony of Kinderton, cf. Lodge Lane 239 *supra*).

(b) *Ravenescroftes-lach* 1346 VR ('boggy stream at Ravenscroft', v. læc(c). This was a boundary of Rudheath heath, v. 1 12, probably from 110–708676 northwards).

10. SPROSTON (110–730660) ['sprɔstən, 'sprɔssṇ]

> *Sprostune* 1086 DB, -*ton* 1240–6 MidCh (p) *et freq* ib, 1503 Plea
> *Sprouston* 1230 Tab (p), 1271–4 Chest (p) *et freq* to 1621 Orm[2],
>   *Sprow(e)s-* 1425 ib, 1429 *Chol*, 1561 ChRR, 1784 Sheaf, *Sprous-*
>   *towe* 14 Chest, *Sprovstou'* 1444 Cre
> *Sproxton* 1299 Fine (p), 1397 Pat (p), -*tun* 1351 Chamb (p)
> *Sprauston* 1407 ChRR

'Sprow's farm', from the OE pers.n. *Sprow* and tūn. Cf. *Cardenhurst* 131 *supra*. Some spellings show confusion of -*ston* with -*stou* (cf. stōw).

PARKSIDE FM (110–731659), *Bidomley* 13 MidCh, *Bedeneleye* 1301–3 Vern, *Budenleys* 1588 MidCh, *Bidam Leys* 1591 Sheaf, *Billum Leys* 1831 Bry, cf. *Billow Lees* 1839 *TA*. The earliest form is that recorded by *Vern*. The first el. appears to be byden (gen.sg. -*e*, gen.pl. -*a*) 'a tub, a vessel', also 'a hollow', though the place stands on rising ground. The second is lēah 'a clearing, a wood'. Cf. Boden Hall 307 *infra*.

BACK LANE FM, *Cinder Hill (Farm)* 1831 Bry, 1842 OS, v. sinder, hyll, cf. Broad Lane, Cinderhill *infra*.   BRERETON LANE, cf. Brereton 274 *infra*.   BROAD LANE (FM), *Back Lanes* 1842 ib, 'lanes on the out-skirts', v. back, cf. Back Lane Fm *supra*.   CINDERHILL, *Breaches Barn* 1831 Bry, cf. *Breach Meadow*, *Breech(es)* 1839 *TA*, v. brēc 'a breaking-in of land for cultivation', cf. Back Lane Fm *supra*, Near Bruch *infra*.   DAIRYHOUSE FM, *Yewtree House* 1831 Bry.   DOCKBANK FM, *Dockbank* 1831 ib, v. docce, banke.   DRUMBLE LAKE, cf. *Drumble* 1839 *TA*, 'watercourse in a dell', v. drumble, lacu, cf. Holding's Drumble 276 *infra*.   FLASH FM, *Donkin Fields* 1831 Bry, probably from a surname *Donkin*. The later name is from flasshe 'a shallow water, a swamp'.   MANOR FM.   POOLFORD

LANE, *Poolsford Lane* 1842 OS, cf. *Pulford Meadow* 1839 *TA*, named from *Pool Ford* 1831 Bry, on R. Croco at 110–740666, 'ford at a pool', *v.* pōl¹, ford.   SPROSTON GREEN & HALL, 1831 Bry.   SPROSTON WOOD, 1842 OS, -*Cover* 1831 Bry.

FIELD-NAMES

The undated forms are 1839 *TA* 362. Of the others a.1281, 1366, 1588 and 17 are MidCh, 1831 Bry, 1842 OS.

(*a*) Aldhouse Fd, Old House Croft (*v.* ald, hūs); Back o' the Kiln; Baggage Fd; Bakehouse Croft; Barnstead (*v.* bere-ærn, stede); Barons Lane Fd (alluding to the barony of Kinderton); Battle Bank (perhaps alluding to a site where juridical battle took place, *v.* bataille, banke); Bean Butts; Big Doach; Bill Fd; Black Croft & Fd; Near Bruch (*le Bruch* a.1281, 'a breaking-in of land', *v.* bryce, cf. Cinderhill *supra*); Butty Mdw (*v.* butty); Childs Croft (*v.* cild); Crickland Croft; Crumbly Land; Dane Mdw (*v.* R. Dane 1 20); Four & Three Daymath (*v.* day-math); Dunstall (*v.* tūn-stall, but this may be 'site on a hill', *v.* dūn, stall); Dyal Croft (*v.* dial); Elton Yards (*v.* geard, cf. Elton 258 *infra*); Footway Fd; Gig House Croft (*v.* gigge); Hare Croft; Heath Fd; Hen Acre; Hewn Wd; Jack Fd (*v.* jack); Long Acre & Butt(s); Great & Little Long Kellant (*v.* land, cf. *Kelmeadow* 247 *supra*); Loont (*v.* land); Lowes Pool 1831, 1842 (a pool in R. Dane, from pōl¹ and a surname *Lowe*, cf. 225, 229 *supra*); Macklick Croft; Marl Fd; Moor Fd; Old House Croft (*v.* Aldhouse Fd *supra*); Outlet (*v.* outlet); Ox Hey (*v.* oxa, (ge)hæg); Pole Croft; Ridding, Riddings Hough (*v.* ryding, hōh); Rye Bank; Sanbachs Fd (from the surname from Sandbach 269 *infra*); Stern Croft; Sweet Fd; Swine Meadow Plantation (*v.* swin¹); Turnhurst ('round wood', *v.* trun, hyrst); Wallnut Croft; Wich Fd (a group of seven fields, perhaps so named from wic in the special meaning 'salt-works', i.e. the wīc at Middle-wich 240 *supra*, cf. 192–3 *supra*); Wood Fd (*le Wodefeld* 1366, *v.* wudu, feld); Woolery Croft; Wych Fd (from wice 'a wych-elm' or wīc as in Wich Fd *supra*).

(*b*) *le Gadday* 1366; *Puddinges yord* 1588 (from the surname *Pudding* 13 NotCestr 297 and geard 'a yard, an enclosure'); *Ticklettes croft* 1588, *Trickleys crofte* 17 (*v.* croft).

11. STUBLACH, consisting of STUBB'S FM, STUBLACH FM (110–710700)

> *Stubbs* 1245–9 Chest (p), (*le*) *Stubbes, -is, -us* 1250 MidCh, 1260,
> 1311 Chol et freq, le Stubbus super Rudhet 1331 Chol, Stubbes alias
> Stubbes Lach 1560 Orm², Stubbes Green or Pains Green 1578 Dep
> (*la, le*) *Stobbis, -es* 1246–60 MidCh (p), 1271, 1281 Chest (p), 1302,
> 1311 Chol
> *Stubbes et Lache* 1480 Dav

Stublache 1480, 1528 Plea, 1598 *Chol,* 1607 ChRR, *-lach* 1706 Cre,
   -lage 1675 Sheaf
Stubbeslache 1534 *Chol,* (*Stubbes alias-*) 1569 Orm², 1570 ChRR,
   1626 *Chol, Stobeslache* 1534 Plea (DKR xxx reads *Stokes-*)

'The tree-stumps', *v.* stubb. The later name is 'the boggy stream
at Stubbs', *v.* læc(c) 'a boggy stream, a muddy place', cf. Lach
Dennis 186 *supra,* and *Lachefield, Mukelstubbes, Stubbeleg' infra.*
Stubb's Fm, also now in Lach Dennis, was included by Bryant (1831)
in Rudheath Lordship 198 *supra,* and tithed in Newall 208 *supra* in
1838 *TA* 286, cf. Stubbs Green 220 *supra. Pain* is a surname.

FIELD-NAMES

The undated forms are 1848 *TA* 376 (Stublach). Those dated 1838 are *TA*
286 (Stubb's Fm), 1842 OS, 1426 *Chol,* 1288 Court.

(*a*) Abbots Fd & Flatt (probably named from the abbots of Chester, *v.*
abbat); Breeches Croft & Mdw (*v.* brēc); Cheadle; (Three) Day Math (1838,
v. day-math); Edgrew Fd 1838 (*v.* hecg-rǣw); Leicesters Croft (from the
Leycester family); Marl Fd (1838); Mere Hey ('enclosure at a boundary',
v. (ge)mǣre, (ge)hæg); Moss Fd; Newall Mdw 1838 (cf. Newall 208 *supra*);
Old Woman's Mdw; Ovan Fd 1838 (*v.* ofen); Ox Pasture; Ridings (*v.*
ryding); Long Shoot 1838 (*v.* scēat); Sour Fd; Street Fd (*v.* strǣt 'a street,
a road, a paved road'. This is at 110–721701, which suggests that the Roman
road marked 110–725700 in 1″ OS 7th edn., might have been aligned from
Crosslanes Fm 110–720694 by Sculshaw Lodge 110–725716, to 110–731731
in Nether Peover, a line marked by hedgerow and footpath in 6″ OS); Great
& Little Swannick, Swannick Mdw 1838 (perhaps 'peasant's dairy-farm',
v. swān², wīc, cf. Swannick 208 *supra,* Swanwick 327 *infra*); Tope Croft
1838; Two Penneworth (*v.* 327 *infra*); Way Fd (1838); Yards (*v.* geard).

(*b*) *lachefield* 1426 ('field at a bog', *v.* læc(c), feld, cf. Stublach *supra*); le
Mukelstubbes 1426 ('the great stubbs', *v.* mycel, cf. Stublach *supra*); *Stubbeleg'* 1288 (p) ('clearing full of stubs', *v.* lēah, cf. Stublach *supra*).

12. SUTTON (110–700640), *Sudtune, Sutone* 1086 DB, *Sutton* 1291
(1338) VR *et freq* with variant spelling *-tone*; (*-iuxta Oc(c)leston*) 1316
Plea (lit. *Eccles-*) *et freq* to 1585 AD, (*-iuxta Neuton* 1421) Cre, (*-iuxta
Medlewich*) 1521 Plea, *Sotton* 1592 Sheaf, 'the southern farm', *v.* sūð,
tūn. The township is on the south side of Newton and Middlewich
243, 240 *supra,* and adjoins Occlestone 252 *supra* across R. Wheelock.
SUTTON BRIDGE, 1619 Sheaf.   SUTTON HALL & LANE, 1831 Bry.
Sutton Lane is on the line of a Roman road from Middlewich south-

eastwards towards Nantwich crossing R. Wheelock near Sutton Bridge, *v.* 1 47 cf. Sutton Hollow 253 *supra.* SUTTON MILL, 1656 Orm².

13. WIMBOLDSLEY (110–680630) [ˈwɪmbouzli, -bəːzli]

Wibaldelai 1086 DB
Winebaldesleg' 1216–30 *AddCh, -legh* 1295 Cre, *Wynbaldeleg'* c.1232 *Fitt, Winelboldel'* 1262 *AddCh*
Wymbaldesle(ye) 113 *ChFor*, Cre, *-legh* 1314 ib, *-ley* 1375 *Eyre et freq* with variant spellings *Wimbald(e)s-* (from 1402 MidCh), *-is-*, *-ly, -leigh, -lewe* to 1594 ChRR, *Wimbalddelegh* 1310 *AddCh, Wymbaldelegh* 1313 *ib, Wym-, Wimbold(e)slee, -ley* 1418 Cre, 1544 ChRR, 1642 *ChCert*
Wymbasley 1629 Sheaf, *Wimbersley* 1724 NotCestr, 1860 White, *Wimbosley* 1759 Tab

'Winebald's clearing or wood', from the OE pers.n. *Winebald* and lēah, cf. *Wynebaldisheye* 251 *supra* in Minshull Vernon, probably named from the same man, since Wimboldsley itself is described as *in bosco de Moneshull*, 'in the wood of Minshull (part of Mondrem forest)', 113 *ChFor*. The chief house in Wimboldsley is Lea Hall *infra*, whence the township is sometimes referred to as *Ley et-, Ley alias Wimbolds-, Wymbaldesley* 1544, 1561, 1569 ChRR, *Wimbersley cum Lee-Hall* 1724 NotCestr, *Lea otherwise Wimboldsley* 1762 Orm².

LEA HALL (110–680640), *Lee, Lea* 1230–40, 1240–46 MidCh (p), *le-, la Lee* 1410 Orm², 1414, 1433 ChRR (p), *Lee-Hall* 1724 NotCestr, *Le* 1283 Pat (p), (*the hall of*) *Ley* 1494 Orm², 1531 MidCh, *the manor or capital messuage of Ley and Wimbaldesley* 1561 ChRR, *Lay* 1621 Orm², cf. spellings under Wimboldsley *supra*, 'at the clearing or wood', *v.* lēah (dat.sg. lēa), hall.

BELLSMITHY, 1842 OS, *Ball Smithy* 1831 Bry, *v.* smiðõe. BOUND-ARY WOOD, *v.* Weaver Bank Wood *infra*. DAIRY HO, *Dairy Farm* 1860 White, now in Stanthorne 212 *supra*, shown as in Wimboldsley 1831 Bry, 1842 OS, at 110–679648, a site now covered by the Shrop-shire Union Canal. THE DINGLE, 'the deep dell', *v.* dingle. TOP FLASH, cf. Bottom Flash 214 *supra, v.* flasshe. ROOKERY WOOD. STORE ROOM WOOD, probably the site of an ice-house. TWELVE ACRES, 1842 OS, *Twelve Acre Farm* 1831 Bry. WEAVER

BANK WOOD, with Boundary Wood *supra*, was *Wimboldsley Wood* 1831 ib, *v.* banke, R. Weaver 1 38.   WIMBOLDSLEY HALL, *Stocks Farm* 1831 ib, *-House* 1860 White, *le Stokks de Wimbaldesley*, *le Stokes* 1402 MidCh, *The Stocks* 1734 *Dep*, 'the tree-stumps', *v.* stocc.   WIMBOLDSLEY WOOD, cf. Weaver Bank Wood *supra*. YEWTREE FM, *Yew Tree House* 1831 Bry.

FIELD-NAMES

(*a*) Barrows Lane 1831 Bry (*v.* 253 *supra*).

(*b*) *del Croftes* 1402 MidCh (p), cf. *Torkinton's croft* 1734 *Dep* (*v.* croft); *Nikerespool* 1309 *AddCh* ('water-sprite's pool', *v.* nicor, pōl[1]. This was near foll.); *pons de Wynbaldeslegh'* 1309 ib, *Wartons bridge* 1619 Sheaf (a cart-bridge over R. Weaver in 1619, probably at 110–672630 the site of a wooden bridge shown 1831 Bry).

vii. Warmingham

Warmingham parish contained the townships 1. Elton, 2. Moston (*v.* foll.), 3. Tetton (now a c.p. including Moston), 4. Warmingham. In DB only Tetton is mentioned, from which Orm[2] III 225 supposed it included the other places. The shift of capital township could well be the result of the Mainwaring family's keeping house in Warmingham.

1. ELTON (110–720590), *Elton* 1289 Cl *et freq*, (*-juxta Wyrmyncham*) 1385 Ipm, *Helton* 1290 Ipm, *v.* tūn. The first el. may be the OE pers.n. *Ella*, which DEPN adduces for this p.n. and Elworth 226 *infra*, which is partly in this township. However, the absence of *Elle-*forms suggests that this Elton is 'farm where eels are got', *v.* ēl[2], tūn, cf. Elton 326 *infra*.

BOOTHLANE HEAD, 1831 Bry, the top end of Booth Lane 1 44, *v.* hēafod.   BROOK FM, *v.* 262 *infra*.   CRABMILL FM, 1842 OS, *Crabmill* 1831 Bry, 'mill for crushing crab-apples', *v.* crab-mill.   ELTON BRIDGE & HALL.   FIELDS FM, *v.* 262 *infra*.   FLASH FM, *v.* flasshe 'a shallow water, & swamp'.   HALL LANE, 1831 Bry.   LONGFOLD, *v.* lang, fald.   RAILWAY FM, *v.* 263 *infra*. RED LANE, 1842 OS, *v.* rēad, lane.   WATCH LANE, 1831 Bry, cf. Watchlane Fm 260 *infra*.

FIELD-NAMES

The undated forms are 1838 *TA* 164. Of the others, 1619 is Sheaf, the rest Cre.

(*a*) Berringtons Fd (perhaps named after John de *Beryngton* of *Ewode* (Yeowood 271 *infra*, cf. Yeowood *infra*) 1465 ChRR); Brick Kiln Fd; Broad Butts; Brook Fd; Butt (*v.* butte); Charming Fd; Big Coppenhall, Coppenhall Croft, Copnall Fd (from Coppenhall 326 *infra*); Crabtree Croft; Three Day Math (*v.* day-math); Drumble (*v.* drumble); Ferny Lee (*v.* lēah); Gate Fd (cf. *Yate Field* 1722, *v.* geat); Golders; Ham Mdw (*v.* hamm); Hays Fd (*v.* (ge)hæg or hǣs); Head Berry; Hitch Croft (*v.* hiche); Hough Bridge (cf. Old Hough 262 *infra*); Knibling Yard (*v.* geard); Little Daylight; Moss Piece; Nook Patch; Oven Fd; Ox Flatt; Phythians Close (cf. Bridge Fm 261 *infra*); Red Hill; Far-, Near-, Old- & Stony Ridding (*v.* ryding); Roundabout (*v.* 327 *infra*); Sand(y) Croft; Sand Hole; Side Sands (*v.* sīd, sand); Sideway Croft; Sim Butts; Sun Croft; Tilladore; The Tongue (*v.* tunge); Town Fd; Great Warmingham (cf. Warmingham 262 *infra*); Wele Croft; Well Lands (*v.* land); Wilfow Nickow; Woodhouse Fd (cf. (*the*) *Woodhouses* 1637, 1671, 1689, 1742, *-house* 1704, 'house(s) at a wood', *v.* wudu, hūs); Yeowood Croft & Ridding ('yew wood', *v.* īw, wudu, cf. Yeowood Fm 271 *infra*).

(*b*) *Fynns Bridge* & *Watter Lane Bridge* 1619 (bridges over R. Wheelock, the former from the surname *Fynn*, the latter 'bridge at the lane to the water', *v.* wæter, lane).

2. MOSTON (110–720610), *Moston* e13 Dieul *et freq*, (*-iuxta Wermyncham*) 1319 Plea, *-tun* 1351 Chamb (p), 'farm at a bog', *v.* mos, tūn.

RYECROFT (110–717615), *Rycroft* 1283 Cl (p), *Ruycroft(e)* 1332, 1334 ChRR (p) *et freq* to 1415 ib (p), *Ricroft* 1586 Sheaf, 'the rye field', *v.* ryge, croft.

SPARROWGROVE (110–719625)

> *Sparchgreue* (lit. *-grene*) 1348 Plea (Orm[2] III 236 reads *-greve*)
> *Sparwegreve* 1348 Orm[2], *-grene* 1387 ChRR
> *Sparrogreve* 1482 Chol, *Sparowgreue*, *Sparowe Gravue* 1486 MinAcct, *Sparrowgrene*, *-greve* 1527 Orm[2], *-greave* 1528 Plea, 1838 *TA*, *-greaue* 1638 Orm[2], *-Grave Hall* 1800 Sheaf, *-grove* 1831 Bry

'Wood frequented by sparrows', *v.* spearwa, grǣfe, cf. Sparrow Greaves 17 *supra*. Some forms show *-n-* for *-u-* in *-greue*. The unique spelling *Sparch-* is probably *-ch-* for *-th-* for þ.

BOOTH LANE, *v.* I 44.   CROWS NEST FM, CROW NEST BRIDGE, *Crow's Nest Bridge* & *Farm* 1831 Bry, *v.* crāwe, nest.   DRAGON'S

LANE, named from *Dragons Lake* 1839 *TA*, 1842 OS, *the Dragon's pool* 1819 Orm[2], so called from its association in popular tradition with the dragon of the Venables family (a wyvern as their crest, Orm[2] III 236), *v.* lake, pōl[1].   FIELDS FM, *The Fields* 1842 OS.   GREEN-BANK.   HOLLYBANK, cf. *Hollen Hurst* 1839 *TA*, *v.* holegn, banke, hyrst.   MOSS LANE, cf. *Moston Moss* 1632 *Vern*, 1831 Bry, *le Mos* 1284 Cre (p), 1289 Cl (p), *v.* mos.   MOSTON GREEN & HO, 1831 Bry.   MOSTON MANOR & MILLS, *v.* myln, cf. *Mill Field* 1839 *TA*. STUDGREEN BRIDGE, cf. *Stud Green Field* 1839 *ib*, *v.* Stud Green 261 *infra*.   WALNUT-TREE HO, *Weathercock House* 1831 Bry.   WATCH LANE (FM), *Watch Lane, Moston Fields* 1831 ib, cf. *Town Fields* 1839 *TA*. What kind of watch was kept here is not apparent. The first el. could be wæsce 'a place for washing', e.g. a sheep-wash.

FIELD-NAMES

The undated forms are 1839 *TA* 276.

(*a*) Ash Wall (*v.* æsc, wælla); Aze Wd; Barley Shanks (probably 'long narrow fields where barley is grown', from bærlic and *shank* (OE scanca) 'a leg, a shank', cf. Db 747); Bask Croft; Bean Fd; Beggars Greaves (*v.* beggere, græfe); Bents (*v.* beonet); Birchen Flatt; Bonny Greaves (*v.* bonny, græfe); Brick Kiln Fd; Broom Fd; Catgreaves (*v.* cat(t), græfe); Clay Butts; Cranks Moor ('crane's marsh', *v.* cranuc, mōr[1]); Crow Fd; Fish Fds; Foxholes; Green Lane; Hanging Wd (*v.* hangende); Harper; Hen Croft; Hill Fd; Kiln Croft; Kirk Mdw (*v.* kirkja); Kitchen Fd; Ley Fd, Leys (*v.* lēah); Limeric Hill (*Limbrick Hill* 1831 Bry, perhaps 'lime-tree hill', *v.* lind, brekka, hyll); Match Croft; Middle Piece; Mill Fd; Old Man's Mdw; Oliery Fd (*v.* alor, -ig[3]); Patch; Pleck(s) (*v.* plek); Reaps (*v.* reap); Ridding (*v.* ryding); Top & Bottom Rose (*v.* rāw 'a row'); Roundabout (*v.* 327 *infra*); Row Moor (*v.* rūh, mōr[1]); Rug Fds; Sallow Platts (*v.* salh, plat); Sand Fd; Sheep Fd; Shippon Fd; Shoulder of Mutton (*v.* 327 *infra*); Throps Mdw (either from þrop or a surname); Town Intake ('communal intake', *v.* toun, inntak); Twelve Pence; Wall Croft (*v.* wælla); Wheel Ridding ('circular clearing', *v.* hweowol, ryding); White Fd; Wood Mdw.

3. TETTON (110–710630)

> *Tadetune* 1086 DB
>
> *Tettona* 1284 Cre, *Tetton* 1287 Court, *et freq, passim*, (*-iuxta Ettelegh*) 1407 (1471) ChRR, (*-et Wermyncham*) 1417 ib

'Tæta's farm', from the OE pers.n. *Tæta* and tūn.

BOOTH LANE, 1772 Cre, cf. *Booth Lane Croft* 1729 ib, *v.* 1 44.
BOWFIELDS, cf. *Big, Little & Near Booth Field* 1838 *TA*, 'fields at the

herdsman's shelter', *v.* bōth, feld, cf. 244 *supra*. BRIDGE FM,
Phytians 1831 Bry, cf. Phythians Close 259 *supra*, from the surname
Phythian. DALEACRE, 1842 OS, 'allotted plough-land', *v.* dæl²,
æcer. Adjacent are Higher- & Lower Daleacre 267 *infra*, a detached
part of Kinderton cum Hulme township. FORGEMILL COTTAGES,
cf. *Forge Meadow* 1838 *TA*, *v.* Forge Mill 262 *infra*. GLEBE FM,
1842 OS, *Minshull Glebe Farm* 1831 Bry, named either from Church
Minshull 325 *infra* or from the local surname *Minshull*, *v.* glebe.
HALFWAY HO. NEW BANK, *Pear House* 1831 Bry, *Pear Tree
House* 1842 OS. SPARROWGROVE, *v.* 259 *supra*, the place is on the
boundary of Tetton and Moston, and is recorded in both townships,
cf. Orm² III 237. STUD GREEN (BRIDGE), *Stud Green* 1842 OS,
v. stōd, grēne². TETTON BRIDGE, HALL (1831 Bry), HALL COT-
TAGES (*Old Hall* 1831 ib), LANE, & LEY FM (*Tetton Farm* 1831 ib),
v. lēah. WITHINSTREET FM (110–713626), *Withinstreet* 1831 ib,
'road growing with willows', *v.* wīðigen, strǣt, cf. 1 44. YEWTREE
FM, *Yew Tree House* 1831 Bry.

FIELD-NAMES

The undated forms are 1838 *TA* 388. Of the others 1693 is *Dep*, the rest
Cre.

(a) Acres; Ange Fd; Bancroft (*v.* bēan, croft); Big Fd (cf. *the Great Field*
1693); Far & Near Bing (dial. *bing* 'a receptacle, a heap', cf. ON *bingr* 'a
stall'); Blackhouse Croft; Blake Fd (cf. *Blach Butts* 1650, *v.* blǣc, butte);
Brick Kiln Croft; Brook Fd; Cam Hays; Coppy (*v.* copis); Cow Hays;
Coxhead (*v.* cocc-scyte); Cross Lane Fd; Dales Fd; Danford Fd; Two-,
Three-, Four-, Five-, Seven-, Eight-, Nine Day Math (*v.* day-math); The
Ell; Fish Pond Yard (*v.* geard); Fitch Fd (*v.* ficche); Flash Mdw (*v.* flasshe);
Fodderlings; The Greene 1693 (*v.* grēne²); Green Fd (cf. *the Green Close*
1722); Gutter Crofts (*v.* goter); Hays (*v.* (ge)hæg); Hills; Hunger Hill (*v.*
hungor); Kelsey Fd (*Kelsale fieldes* 1568, *-feld* 1591, *the two Great-* & *the
next Kelsall Field*(s) 1693, *Great-* & *the two little Kelsal Field*(s) 1705, 1722,
1729, *Kelsals Fields* 1730, probably from the surname from Kelsall 326 *infra*);
Kiln Croft; the Long Meadow 1722 (*the longe Meadowe* 1693); Dry Marlpit
Fd; Moss Croft; (Little) Oatlands (*the Higher* & *Lower Outland* 1650, 'outlying plots', *v.* ūt, land); Orchard Fd; Oven Crofts; Ridding (*v.* ryding);
Round Mdw 1661 (*the-* 1650); Sand Fd; Shoulder of Mutton (*v.* 327 *infra*);
Spink Croft (perhaps dial. *spink* 'a finch', but cf. Swettenham's Spink *infra*,
which suggests that the origin is dial. *sprink* for spring 'a young wood');
Stavegate Fd (probably 'a gate made of staves', *v.* stæf, geat); Sutton Fd
(cf. Sutton 256 *supra*); (Far & Near) Tetton (Fd); Wall Fd (*v.* wælla); Wasp
Fd; Well Fd; Yards (*the Yords* 1693, *the two Yard Closes* 1722, *v.* geard, clos).

4. WARMINGHAM (110–700610) [-iŋəm] older local [-intʃam]

Warmincham 1259 Sheaf *et freq* to 1879 Sheaf, *Wermyncham* 1315
ChRR *et freq* with variant spellings *Warmyn-, Wermin-* to 1581
ib, *Warmincham alias Warming(e)ham* 1574 ib, *Warmyncham
alias Warmingham* 1580 Cre, *Wyrmyncham* 1385 IpmR
Wermingham 1260, 1287 Court *et freq* with variant spelling *-yng-*
to 1336 Pat; *Worm-* 1307 Plea, *Werem-* 1327 ChRR (p), *Warm-*
1488 *Chol*, 1555 Cre *et freq*, *Wharm-* 1671 Sheaf
Worchingham 1265 Ch, *Wrchincham* a.1272 (1285) ib
Wermincheam 113 *AddCh*
Werbincheam 113 *AddCh*
Werningham, -yng(e)- 1290 Ipm, 1291 Tax, *-ycham* 1478 ChRR (p)
Warmengeham 1306 Pap, *Wermynge-* 1342 Sheaf, 1397 Pat, *Warm-*
1492 *Chol, -inge-* 1574 ChRR
Werminsham 1489 MidCh, *War-* 1647 Cre
Warmyngcham 1492 *Chol, -e-* 1595 Sheaf
Warringham 1554 *MinAcct*
Warmisham 1629, 1660 Sheaf
Warmincsham 1656 Orm[2]
Warminckham 1669 *AddCh*

This p.n. also appears in the f.ns. *Warynsamhillis* 1500, *Warencham
hills* 1515, 1 75. The p.n. is either 'the village of Wærma's, or
Wærmund's, people', from the OE pers.n. *Wærmund* (cf. Nantwich
Hundred 326 *infra*) or its derivative **Wærma*, with -ingahām; or,
'the village *Wærm(und)ing*', from hām and an -ing[2] formation on the
pers.n., *v.* Altrincham 7 *supra*. For the pers.n. cf. Warmsworth
WRY 1 62, Warndon Wo 175, Warmington Wa 274. The forms
W(o)rch-, Werb- are inexplicable save as scribal sports.

OLD HOUGH (110–699624) [uf, ʌf], *le How* 1282 Cl, *-e* 1426 *Chol* (p),
Oldhaugh c.1580 Orm[2], *The Old Hough* 1734 *Dep*, 'the spur of land',
v. hōh, ald 'old'. The place lies on a spur between R. Wheelock and
Hoggins Brook.

BOTTOMS FM, 1831 Bry, *v.* botm 'low-lying land'.   BROOK FM,
-House 1831 ib, named from R. Wheelock.   CHURCH HO, 1831 ib.
DONKINSON'S OAK, *v.* 326 *infra*.   DRURY LANE, if not an allusion
to Drury Lane in Westminster Mx 178, this might be 'love lane'
from ME (OFr) *druerie* 'love, friendship', cf. *Sir Gawain* 1507, 1517
(*drury*), 2450 (*drwry*).   FIELDS FM, twice, *v.* feld.   FORGE MILL

(HO), MILL POND, *Warmingham Forge House* 1806 Cre, *Forge Pool Farm* 1823 ib, *Forge Mill* 1831 Bry.   HILL FM, HILL TOP, *the Hill Top Farm* 1793 Cre.   LANE ENDS, 1831 Bry, cf. *the Lane End* 1750 Cre. LEESE FM, cf. Leese 229 *supra*.   MILL HO, named from an old corn mill, *Warmingham Mills* 1780 Cre, cf. *the Mill Bridge* 1619 Sheaf. There was a mill here 1289 Cl.   MOSS FM, cf. Warmingham Moss *infra*.   OAK TREE FM.   RAILWAY FM, *Fields Farm* 1831 Bry, cf. Fields Fm *supra*, *v.* feld. This farm adjoins a railway.   RIDDING FM, *Riddings Farm* 1831 ib, 'the clearing', *v.* ryding.   STOCIA FM, 1800 Cre, *Stocal* 1672 ib, *Stotiall House* 1697 ib, -*Farm* 1709 ib, *Storeshaw Farm* 1831 Bry, presumably named from *Stotiall Mosse* 1637, 1662 Cre, *v.* mos 'a moss'. The 1831 spelling probably represents the traditional form, which may be a wood-name, from storð 'a plantation' and sceaga 'a copse, a wood'.   WARMINGHAM BRIDGE, *Saters bridge* 1619 Sheaf. The first el. may be saltere 'a salter'.   WARMINGHAM MOSS, (*Lane*) 1831 Bry, cf. Moss Fm *supra*, *Moss Croft* 1661 Cre, 1838 *TA*, *Moss(e) Riddings* 1555, 1731 Cre, *Moss Piece* 1768 ib, 1838 *TA*, *v.* mos, ryding.   WARMINGHAM WOOD, 1831 Bry, cf. *Wood Lane* 1831 ib and John *de Bosco* 1289 Cl, *v.* wudu.

FIELD-NAMES

The undated forms are 1838 *TA* 414. Of the others, 1289 is Cl, 1352, 1588 *AddCh*, 1608 ChRR, 1619 Sheaf, 1831 Bry, and the rest Cre.

(*a*) Aston (either 'ash-tree farm' or 'east farm', from æsc or ēast, and tūn); Bache (*v.* bæce[1]); Barnetts Lane 1831; Bostock Fd (*v.* Bostock 202 *supra*); Breach Fd & Piece (*v.* brēc); Brick Kiln Fd & Wd; Butty Mdw (*v.* butty); By Leys; Causeway (*v.* caucie); Close (*v.* clos); Coat Field Mdw (*v.* cot); Conway's Croft (cf. *a cottage called Conways* 1742, from a surname *Conway*); Cote Fd (*v.* cot); Cross Lane Croft & Fd; Half-, Six-, Seven-, Eight Day Math (*v.* day-math); Dumelow, Dumilow Mdw & Wd (cf. *Dumbells Wood* 1831, *v.* dumbel, hol[1]); Fall Fd (*v.* (ge)fall 'a fall, a felling of timber'); Flax Yard (*v.* fleax, geard); Four Lane Ends; Gate Fd; Glead Wd (*v.* gleoda); Gorsley Green Mdw (*Gosely green* 1661, *v.* gorst, lēah, grēne[2]); Green Lane (*the-* 1742); Hall Fd (cf. *Hall Grounds* 1716, 1742); Hempbutt 1784 (*v.* hænep, butte); Hill Fd; Horse Pasture (1661); Horse Wash Croft (*v.* wæsce); The Hough (*v.* hōh); Hurst (*v.* hyrst); Jack Fd (*v.* jack); Kiln Croft; King's Fd & Mdw; Kinsey's Croft & Piece (*Kemshey* 1608, *Keyneshey* 1616, *the Kinsey's croft* 1782, originally a p.n. from (ge)hæg 'an enclosure', and a pers.n. *Keyne* (*v.* Reaney s.n. *Cain*), which gives rise to a surname *Kinsey* 1597 ChetNS cviii 245, cf. Bardsley s.n.); Kirk Croft (*v.* kirkja); Lady Mdw (*v.* hlǣfdige); Ledge Wd (1716, perhaps from ME *leche* 'a stream, a bog, a muddy place', *v.* læc(c)); Lee Wd (*v.* lēah); Marl

Fd; Meadow Butts; Mode Croft; Mott Wd; Little Nun Mdw; Great Oats Wd; Park Fd; Pingle (v. pingel); Poolstead Mdw (v. pōl-stede); Potatoe Pleck (v. plek); Red Hill (this is adjacent to Brick Kiln Fd *supra*); Ridding, Ridding Fd & Moss (*The Ridding Moss* 1779, v. ryding, mos); Rough Wd ((*the*) *Rough Wood*(s) 1700, 1782); Rushy Acre (*Rushie Acre* 1661, v. riscig); Rye Croft; Sand Fd (cf. *Sandy Field* 1661); Scotch Croft; Seckup; Sheep-cote Fd; Middle Shoot (v. scēat); Long Slang (v. slang); Slum; Sparrow Greave (cf. Sparrowgrove 259 *supra*); Spike Fd; Big & Little Spring (v. spring 'a young wood'); Swine Croft; Tubary Fd, Turbary-, Turbury Croft (v. turbarye 'land where turf or peat is got'); Twopenny Pasture; Washing Fd (1661, probably a field where washing was done); Watt Fd; Well Croft & Fd (*Wall Croft* 1661, cf. *la Welle* 1289 (p), v. wella, wælla); Wheat Eddish (v. hwǣte, edisc); Wheat Wd ('wet wood', v. wēt); Whitley Mdw (either a surname from Whitley 124 *supra*, or 'white clearing' v. hwīt, lēah); Wingreaves (v. grǣfe); Woodhouse Fd (v. wudu, hūs).

(b) *Aldford Bridge* 1619 ('(bridge at) the old ford', v. ald, ford, brycg); *Calverffield* 1661 ('calves' field', v. calf (gen. pl. calfra), feld); *Depe Clohu* 1289 ('deep dell', v. dēop, clōh); *Dodcote* 1588 (from cot 'a cote', perhaps with dodde 'a rounded hill-top', but the topography is not conclusive, cf. Dodcott 326 *infra*); *Dowfeild* 1661 (probably 'dole field', v. dāl, feld); *le Holtes* 1362 (v. holt); *the Intack* 1683 (v. inntak); *Little Hall* 1661 (v. lytel, hall); *le Newehaye* 1289 ('the new enclosure', v. nīwe, (ge)hæg; the name of a wood); *Werminghamfeld* 1289 (presumably common- or town-land, v. feld); *Wetenhay* 1289 ('wet enclosure', v. wēt (dat.sg. wētan), (ge)hæg).

viii. Sandbach

The ancient parish of Sandbach (Orm ^{2} III 95), consisted of the parochial chapelries of Goostrey 222 *supra* and Church Hulme 278 *infra*, the townships of Hassall and Betchton 326, 325 *infra* (now in Nantwich Hundred, but in this hundred in DB), and in Northwich Hundred the townships 1. Arclid, 2. Bradwall, 3. Sandbach (now a c.p. including Wheelock, and parts of Elton and Bradwall at Elworth 266 *infra*), 4. Wheelock (v. prec). Earnshaw Hall 188 *supra*, a detached part of Rudheath Lordship, was in Sandbach parish.

1. ARCLID (110–780610)

 Erclid 1188–1209 MidCh (p), *-lide* 1547 *MinAcct*, *-led* l12–e13 Tab (p)

 Arclid a.1240 MidCh (p) *et freq* with variant spellings *-lyd(d)*, *-lidd*, *-lide*, *-lyde*, *-lude* (1498, 1611 AddCh, 1619 Sheaf), *-liud* (1671 AddCh), *-luyd* (1595 *ib*), *-luid* (1699 *ib*)

 Arcleyt 13 Dav, *-led(e)* c.1260 Tab (p), 1298 Cre (p), 1611 AddCh

 Arkelid 1357 (1579) ChRR, 1399 *Sotheby* (p), *-led* 1558–79 ChancP, *Arkilydd* 1551 AddCh

 Artcluyt 1385 Cl, *-cluyd* 1386 IpmR, *-clid* 1690 AddCh

Arclad 1662 *Surv*
Archlade 1647 Cre
Arctlyd 1673 *Chol*
Arkley 1690 Sheaf

'Arnkell's hill-side', from the ON pers.n. *Arnkell* or ODan *Arnketill* with hlid[1] (Löfvenberg 123, cf. OE hlið[1], ON hlíð[2]). The pers.n. appears as *Archil* DB f.266b, the TRE tenant of Byley 233 *supra*, *v.* Feilitzen 163, cf. Fellows Jensen 14–16.

FAR & NEAR ARCLID BRIDGE, *Arclude brooke bridge* and *Fordbridge* 1619 Sheaf, *v.* brōc, brycg, ford.   ARCLID BROOK (R. Wheelock), *Alcomlowe Brook, Arclude Brooke* 1619 ib, *v.* brōc, cf. Alcumlow 304 *infra*.   ARCLID COTTAGE & GREEN, 1831 Bry.   ARCLID HALL, *the Hall of Arclide* 1671 *AddCh*.

FIELD-NAMES

The undated forms are 1839 *TA* 18. Of the others, 1547 is *MinAcct*, 1673 *Chol*, 1831 Bry, 1842 OS.

(a) Ancient Land; Barn Fd (cf. *Barne-croft* 1673, *v.* bere-ærn, croft, cf. *Erclide graunge* 1547); The Birches (1673); Blake, Blake Fd (*v.* blæc); Boosey (*v.* bōsig); (The) Broom (*Broome(medow)* 1673, *v.* brōm, mæd); Cowshade Fd; Far Bank (cf. *Banck-medow* 1673, *v.* banke); Gorsty Flatt 1673 (*v.* gorstig, flat); Grass Fd (*Gresse-field* 1673, *v.* gærs); Hall Flat & Walk (cf. Arclid Hall *supra*); Heath Fd (1673, cf. *Arctlyd Heath* 1673, *Arclid Heath* 1831, *v.* hǣð); Hemingshaw (*v.* sceaga 'a wood, a copse'. The first el. might be the ODan pers.n. *Hem(m)ing* or its borrowed form ON *Hem(m)-ingr*); Further & New Hillage (*Lower & Higher part of Illidge, Little Illidge* 1673, *v.* Illidge 276 *infra*); Bottom & Top Holding (*Houldens* 1673, *v.* Holding's Drumble 276 *infra*); King Tree Fd; Linn Lund (perhaps 'lime-tree grove' *v.* lind, lundr); Long Moss; The Marsh; The Meadow (cf. *Higher-, Lower & New Medow* 1673, *v.* mæd); Mill Croft ((*Little*) *Mill Croft* 1673); Morning Fd; The Moss; Pool Stead ('the site of a pool', *v.* pōl-stede); The Ridding (*v.* ryding); Sand Fd; Shaw Fd (*v.* sceaga); Smithy Fd (cf. *Smithy-croft* 1673); Town Fd & Mdw (*freq*); Wall Croft (*v.* wælla); Wash Fd (probably from wæsce 'a washing-place'); Whitish.

2. BRADWALL. *Bradwall et Hollins* c.1662 *Surv*, *Bradwall cum Hollins* 1819 Orm[2], *v.* Bradwall, Hollinsgreen *infra*.

BRADWALL (110–750630)

Bradwall a.1226 MidCh (p) *et freq* with variant spellings *Brade-*, *-wal, -wal(l)e, -wale; Bradewalle iuxta Hulm, boscus de Brade-walle* 113 *Vern*

Brad(e)well(e) 1281 Court (p), 1307 Plea, 1385 Cl, *Bradwell* 1724
  NotCestr
Brod(e)wall 1324 Bark, 1356 Tab, *Broadwall* 1415 ChRR
Beatwall 1326 Tab
Bardwell 1438 ChRR

'The broad spring', *v.* brād, wælla (occasionally wella). Forms in
-*wale* (1359 *Vern*, 1362 BPR) are rare, but may arise from confusion
with wēl² 'a deep pool', cf. the reverse process in Thelwall 138 *supra*.

HOLLINSGREEN (FM), HOLLINS WOOD (FM) (110–730630), *del Holyns*
1344 *Eyre* (p), *Holyns* 1503 Plea, c.1540 Orm², *the Hollins, -yns*
1555, 1559 *Vern, Hollins (Green)* 1589 *ib*, (-*Pool & -Wood*) 1831 Bry,
Hollens c.1568 Orm², 1581 ChRR, (-*Mill*) 1586 *Vern, Holynhaye* 1359
Eyre (p), *Holynwode* 1435 ChRR, *Hollin Green* 1831 Bry, 'the holly
trees', *v.* holegn, grēne², pōl¹, wudu, (ge)hæg, myln. The pool was at
Barlow Wood *infra*.

BRINDLEY LANE (110–756632), *Brunleghmor'* 113, 1330, 1345, 1349
Vern, -more 1349 MidCh, *Brundelegh Moore* 1307 Orm², *Little
Brindley, Brindley Moor* 1839 *TA*, *v.* mōr¹ 'a moor, a marsh' and
Brindley Green 275 *infra*.

ELWORTH (110–740615), now included in Sandbach c.p., but formerly
a hamlet in the several townships of Elton 258 *supra*, Bradwall, and
Sandbach 269 *infra*.

   Ellewrdth, -worke 1282 Court (p), -*worthe* 1305 Plea (p), (*campus
     quod vocatur-*) 1308 *Vern, -worth* 1318 *ib, -wurth* 1391 *AddRoll*
     (p), *Hell(e)wr(the)* 113 *Vern, Helleworth* E1 Orm² (p)
   Elworth 113 MidCh (p), 1527 *ChCert et freq*
   Ellesworth 1325 ChRR (p), 1335 Orm² (p)
   Eltworth 1621 Orm²

'Ella's enclosure', from the OE pers.n. *Ella* and worð. One spelling
indicates confusion with (ge)weorc 'a work, a structure, a fortification',
so the 'enclosure' may possibly have been an earthwork. The same
pers.n. appears in *Ellebrugehet infra*.

FOUSLEY FM, 1831 Bry, *Fouleslegh'syche* 1349 *Vern, Fouleslegh* 1353,
1358 *ib, Fowles-* 1355 *ib, Farther- & Nearer Fousley* 1839 *TA*,
'(watercourse at) the bird's clearing', *v.* fugol, -es², lēah, sīc.

HOPE(S)HILL, HOPES FIELD 1839 *TA*, *Hope* 1281 Court, (the hamlet called) 1580 Orm[2], *le Hope* 1295 *Vern*, (*campus de-, -dil-, -in Brade-wall(e)*) 1308, 1317 *ib*, *le Hoope* 1342 *ib*, *the Hope in Bradwall* 1585 *ib*, 'at the hollow', *v.* hop[1], cf. Sour Field 273 *infra*.

BARLOW WOOD, *v.* Hollins Pool *supra*.   BRADWALL COTTAGE, GREEN, HALL & WOOD, 1831 Bry, *Bradwell Hall* 1724 NotCestr. The original hall was in a moat in *Hall Field* 1819 Orm[2] III 110, 1839 *TA*, cf. *Hall Bank* 1839 *TA*.   BRADWALL MANOR, 1″ OS, *v.* Wellbank *infra*.   CHESWORTH FM (lost), 1842 OS, *Tythe House Farm* 1831 Bry, cf. *Chesworths Field* 1839 *TA*, from a surname *Chesworth*, *v.* tēoða.   DAIRY FM.   HIGHER & LOWER DALEACRE, *v.* 239, 261 *supra*.   DENMAN WOOD.   FIELDS FM, *Field Farm* 1831 Bry, *The Fields* 1842 OS, *v.* feld.   FOXCOVERT FM, 1842 *ib*.   GREEN FM, 1842 *ib*, *v.* grēne[2], named from Bradwall Green *supra*.   THE HILLTOP, 1831 Bry.   HOLEHOUSE FM, *Hole House* 1842 OS, 'house at a hollow', *v.* hol[1], cf. Hope *supra*.   JONES'S LANE, *v.* 239 *supra*.   LEAHEAD FM, 1842 *ib*, *Ley Head* 1831 Bry, cf. *le Legh* 1353 *Vern*, 'the top end of the clearing', *v.* lēah, hēafod.   LONDON RD, *v.* Booth Lane 1 44.   MARSH GREEN, 1831 Bry, 'green at a marsh', *v.* mersc, grēne[2].   PLUMTREE FM, 1842 OS.   SPRING-BANK FM, SPRINGFIELD, *Spring Bank & Field* 1831 Bry, *v.* spring 'a spring of water'. Springfield and Wellbank Fm *infra* are at the head of Small Brook.   UNION GORSE, *New Gorse Cover* 1831 *ib*.   WALNUT TREE FM, 1831 *ib*.   WARD'S LANE, 1831 *ib*, cf. *Wards Land* 1839 *TA*, from the surname *Ward*.   WELLBANK (FM), *the Well Bank* 1673 Cre, 'bank at a spring', *v.* wella, banke, cf. Spring-bank *supra*. Wellbank (110–756630) is now called Bradwall Manor.   WHITENING HO, 1831 Bry.   WOOD LANE (FM), *Wood Lane Farm* 1831 *ib*, cf. Bradwall Wood *supra*.

FIELD-NAMES

The undated forms are 1839 *TA* 66. Of the others, 1232, 1310–11 are Orm[2], 1666, 1667, 1669 Cre, 1831 Bry, 1883 Sheaf, and the rest *Vern*.

(a) Acre Fd; Antrey Lee (*Antreleg'siche, Hontreleg'* 113, 'lone tree clear-ing', *v.* ān, trēow and lēah, sīc 'a watercourse'); Aspin Mdw (*v.* æspen); Bakehouse Fd; Barn Fd (*freq*, cf. *Barn Field* 1598, *the three barn fields* 1669, *v.* bere-ærn); Beech Fd (*v.* bēce[2]); Big Mdw (cf. *the great meadow* 1667, *v.* grēat); Bird Eye; Black Croft (twice, cf. *the two Black Fields* 1669, *v.* blæc); Boosey Pasture (*v.* bōsig); Booth Lane Croft (*v.* Booth Lane 1 44); Briary

Wood Fd; Brick (Kiln) Fd; Broomy Croft (*the-* 1669 ,*v.* brōmig); Buttey Hey (*v.* butty); Big-, Cross-, Five-, Little- & Long Butts (*v.* butte); Calf Croft; Clay Flatt; Colliers Croft (*v.* colere 'a collier, a charcoal burner'); Common Lot ('an allotment of common-land' *v.* commun, hlot); Coxheads (*v.* cocc-scyte); Crooked Croft; Cross Lane Fd; Cuckoo Fd; Dams (*v.* damme); Day Math (*v.* day-math); Degs Mdw; Dip Moor (from mōr[1] 'a moor, a marsh' with either dēop 'deep' or ModE *dip* 'a depression, a hollow'); Eardleys Wd (cf. *Yardleys Banckes* 247 *supra*); Fold Croft; Forty Acre; Frog Pool; Golden Fd (*v.* gylden); Goose Fd; Gorsey Croft, Gorsty Fd (*v.* gorstig); Great Fd; Green Fd (*the grene Fylde* 1547, *v.* grēne[1]); Gutter Croft & Hey (*Gutter Haie* 1598, *v.* goter); Hall Croft; Hassleshaw ('hazel wood' *v.* hæsel, sceaga); Heath Fd; Hendlack (*Hendlach* 1883, probably 'duck stream', *v.* ened, lacu); Hey, Long Heyes (*le Hay* 1311, cf. *le Hayeyate* 1349, *v.* (ge)hæg, geat); Hobs Croft (cf. *Hobfield* 1598, *v.* hob 'a goblin'); Holly Moor (*v.* mōr[1], cf. Hollins *supra*); Hop Fd; Hurstfield Croft (*v.* hyrst, feld); Intake (*v.* inntak); Kiln Croft & Fd; Kitchen Croft; Land Fd (*v.* land); Lane Fd (*v.* lane or leyne); Long Croft (1598, cf. *Long Field* 1669); Madams Wd; Marl Fd; Modes Croft; Moor; Mooresbarrow Fd (*v.* Mooresbarrow 251 *supra*); Nook Fd; Oulery (probably 'growing with alders', *v.* alor, cf. Woollery Croft *infra*); Outlet (*v.* outlet); Ox Hey (*v.* oxa, (ge)hæg); Parkers Fd (cf. *Bradwell park* 1669, *v.* park); Partridge Hill; Peovers Moor (from the surname from Peover 220 *supra*, *v.* mōr[1]); Pinfold Inclosure (*v.* pynd-fald); Pipers Croft (cf. Pipers Lane 272 *infra*); Pool Eye, Poolstead Bank & Mdw (*v.* pōl[1], ēg, pōl-stede); Rates Croft; Riding(s) (*le Rudyng* 1350, *le New(e)rudyng* 1355, *v.* nīwe, ryding); Rough Fd & Hays (*the rough croft & heys* 1669, *the four rough heys* 1667, *v.* rūh, (ge)hæg); Round about (*v.* 325 *infra*); Sand Fd; Sandersons Mdw (cf. Sanderson's Brook 1 34); Seven Acre Fd & Mdw (*the vii aker* 1547, *the seven acres* 1588, *Senacre* 1625, *v.* seofon, æcer); Shady Fd; Sindertons Mdw (perhaps 'cindery enclosure', *v.* sinder, tūn); Sorrel Croft; Sprink (*v.* spring 'a young wood'); Stack Yard; Stubbs Croft (*v.* stubb); Tenter Croft (*v.* tentour); Tom Field, Town Field ('communal field', *v.* toun); Little Tunstall (cf. *Tunstudemor* 1330, *v.* tūn-stede, tūn-stall, mōr[1]); Warmer Hold (cf. *le Holt* l13, *v.* holt); Watery Moor; Way Croft; Well Fd; Wich Fd (*le Wychefeld* 1355, 1358, *v.* wic or wice); Wit Croft (*le Wyte-*, *-Qwytecroft* l13, *v.* hwīt, croft); Woman's Acre; Wood Fd (cf. *the great-* & *-little wood* 1667, 1669, cf. Bradwall Wood *supra*); Woollery Croft (i.e. 'owlery croft', *v.* alor, -ig[3], croft); Yard Croft (*v.* geard); Yate Moor (*v.* geat).

(b) *Bradeleg' forde* l13 ('(ford at) the broad clearing', *v.* brād, lēah, ford); *le bredin-*, *-bredynyate* 1308 ('gate of planks', *v.* breden, geat); *Brodmeadowe* 1232 (*v.* brād, mǣd); *Chircheleiis* 1308 (p) ('church clearings', *v.* cirice, lēah); *Le Copmor* l13 ('moor at a ridge', *v.* copp, mōr[1]); *Cumbircroft* 1311 (*v.* croft). Cumbre 'the Britons', is possible but unlikely in such a minor name. The first el. is probably cumber 'an encumbrance, a pile of stones', but the OE pers.n. *Cumbra* is possible); *Ellebrugehet* l13 (perhaps 'heath at *Ellebruge* ('Ella's bridge')', from the OE pers.n. *Ella*, as in Elworth *supra* and brycg with hǣð); *le Fairefeld* 1350, *the Fairefylde*, *-felde medowe* 1547 (*v.* fæger, feld); *the Fox Meadow* 1666, *the two Fox Fields* 1669 (*v.* fox); *the Glade croft* 1669; *Haytelegh'croft* 1353 ('(croft at) the heathy clearing', *v.* hǣðiht, lēah, croft); *the lane* 1669 (*v.* lane); *Holcroft* 1310–11 (*v.* hol[1], croft); *Hulmesbrok'* 1349 (*v.* Sanderson's Brook 1 34); *the two lockshutt Fields* 1669 (if not an error for *cockshutt* (*v.* cocc-scȳte), perhaps from loc, loca 'a fold' and scēat 'a corner of land'); *le Merestal* l13 (probably 'the pond' *v.* mere-steall, but Professor Sørensen thinks this could be a parallel to the Danish p.n. *Marstal* 'a stable for horses', *v.* mere[2], stall); *the Outer croft* 1669; *Le Siche* l13 ('the stream', *v.* sīc); *Silkemedwe* 1349 (*v.* mǣd, cf. *Silkhulme* 237 *supra* adjacent to this); *Sclauelokeshurst* l13 ('(hill or wood at) the muddy fold', *v.* slæf, loc, hyrst); *the Yonkeshae* 1547 ('the young wood', *v.* geong, sceaga).

3. SANDBACH (110–750600) ['sanbætʃ]

Sanbec, -becd 1086 DB, -bache 1308 Ipm (p), -bach 1647 Cre, -bage 1539 Dugd, -bitch c.1703 Chol, Sonbach(e) 1210–20 Chest (p), c.1260 Tab (p), -bac c.1230 AddCh, -baghe 1455 Vern, Sanebache 1308 Fine (p), Sone- 1434 Cre

Sand-, Sond(e)bach e13 Chest (p), Dieul (p), Whall (p) et freq with variant spellings Sande-, -bac(c)h(e), -bage, -batch, -bich, -back, -bah, -bayche; -bech(e) c.1233 Earw (p), m13 Orm[2] (p), 1365 Pat (p), Sondabache 1498 ChRR

Santb' e13 Dieul, Sontbach(e) c.1233 Whall, Orm[2] (p)

Sambage 1255 Pat, -bach 1474 Cl (p), -bache 1560 Sheaf, -beche 1607 Cre, -bech 1629 ib, -bitch 17 Chol

'Sandy valley-stream', *v.* sand, bæce[1], bece[1]. Cf. Betchton 325 *infra*, which is nearby.

STREET-NAMES

CHAPEL ST., 1840 *TA*; CHURCH ST., cf. *Church Steps Cottage* 1787 Cre; CREWE RD., *Whelock Lane* 1775 Wil, 1840 *TA*, leading to Wheelock 273 *infra*. The later name is from the Crewe family, landowners here; ELWORTH ST., 1842 OS, *v.* Elworth 266 *supra*; FLAT LANE, cf. *Flat Lane House* 1730 Wil, *Flatt Lane Field* 1840 *TA* 'level lane', *v.* flatr; GREEN ST., named from the green at Scotch Common *infra*, *v.* grēne[2]; HIGH ST., HIGHTOWN, the main street, the centre of the town, *v.* hēah, toun, cf. Hightown 241 *supra*; NEWFIELD ST., cf. *Newfield Gardens* 1840 *TA*, New Field *infra*; SMITHFIELD LANE, cf. *Smith Field* 1699 Cre, 1840 *TA*, *v.* smið or smiððe. LOST STREET-NAMES: *Back Street* 1780 Cre (*v.* back); *School House Lane* 1749 Cre.

ABBEYFIELD, 1819 Orm[2], a house named from *Abbey Field, the Abbot's Field* 1819 ib, *Abbey Field & Land* 1840 *TA*, land owned by Dieulacres Abbey, *v.* abbaye. ASHFIELDS. BANK HO (lost),

1831 Bry, *Cliffs of the Bank* 1681 Cre, *Cliffes Bank* 1700 ib, named from a family called *Cliff*, v. banke. BLACK ACRES, cf. *Black Acre* 1840 *TA*. BRICKHOUSES, 1842 OS, *Brick House Farms* 1831 Bry, 'houses built of brick'. THE BROOK, BROOK MILL, *Sandbach brook* 1619 Sheaf, cf. *the brook(e) field(es)* 1637, 1692 Cre, *Brook Meadowe* 1727 ib, v. brōc. COLD MOSS HEATH, 1831 Bry, *Coldmosse* 1598 Cre, *Colemoss* 1731 ib, v. cald, mos, hǣð, cf. Oldhouse Fm *infra*. COLLEY LANE, v. colig 'pertaining to charcoal', lane. CRABMILL HO, *Crabmill* 1831 Bry, v. crab-mill. CROSSFIELDS, cf. *Great & Little Cross Field* 1840 *TA*, *Crosses* 1589 Sheaf, *the Crosses Croft* 1630 Cre, perhaps named from the famous Anglo-Saxon crosses at Sandbach. COOKSMERE LANE, *Cooksner Lane* 1831 Bry, cf. *the Cook(e)snow(e)* 1637, 1692 Cre, *the Cocksnow(e) (Croft)* 1692, 1727 ib, *Cooks Knoll Croft* 1687 ib, *Cocksure Lane Croft, Cooksnall's Croft, Cookson Lane Field* 1840 *TA*, 'the cook's hill', v. cōc, -es², cnoll. DINGLE FM & LAKE, cf. *the large Dingle* 1723 Wil, *the Dingle* 1751 Sheaf, *the Dingo tenement* 1799 Cre, v. dingle 'a dell', lacu 'a water-course'. ELTON RD, v. Elton 258 *supra*. EAST ELWORTH, ELWORTH HALL, *Elworth Hall* 1787 Sheaf, named from Elworth 266 *supra*, with ēast, hall. ETTILEY HEATH (110–730600), *Ettelegh* 1407 (1471) ChRR, *Le Hethes* within the lordship of *Echill'y* 1527 ib, *Etelegh Heathe* 1581 ib, *Etteley Heath* 1611 Wil, 1813 Cre, *Ettiley-* 1629, 1801 Cre, *Ettylie-* 1689 ib, *Ettily-, Italy Heath* 1840 *TA*, v. hǣð 'a heath'. *Ettiley* is probably 'grazed clearing', from ete-, eten- 'grazing, pasture' (cf. eting) and lēah, but Professor Löfvenberg offers an alternative first el., the OE pers.n. *Ēata* or **Etti*, as in Etloe Gl 3 251, DEPN. Cf. Ettily Wood 1 86, probably similar. THE FIELDS, *Skerrotts of the Fields* 1702 Cre, named from a family *Skerrott, Skerratt*, cf. *Skerratts Croft* 1840 *TA*, and Sheroddes 280 *infra*, v. feld. FORGE FIELDS, *Iron Works* 1831 Bry, v. forge. GOOSELAKE, cf. *Wildgoose Lake* 1647, 1720 Cre, fields called after a watercourse, 'wild-goose stream', v. wilde-gōs, lacu. HASSALL RD, v. Hassall 326 *infra*. HEATH FM, cf. *Great Heath, Heath Croft & Field* 1840 *TA*, and Sandbach Heath *infra*. THE HILL, 1842 OS, *Sandbach Hill* 1831 Bry, cf. *the Hills* 1723 Wil, *the further hills* 1585 Cre, v. hyll, cf. foll. HILLSIDE COTTAGE, *Hill House* 1842 OS, *The Hill* 1819 Orm² III 103, v. hyll, cf. prec. and Top o' th' Hill *infra*. (LITTLE) HINDHEATH, *Hindeheath* 1410 Orm², (*Farms*) 1831 Bry, -heth 1423 Plea, *Hynde-* 1437 ChRR, *Hind Heath Farm* 1812 Sheaf, apparently from hind 'a female deer', but

the first el. could be ME *hine* (cf. OE hīwan, hine), 'a servant', *v.* hǣð.
HOUNDINGS LANE, *Howning's Lane* 1612 Cre, *Hardings Lane Farm*
1831 Bry, perhaps from hegning 'a fenced-in enclosure', but cf.
hounding (NED) 'a fabulous animal, half dog and half man'.
LIGHTLY HILL, 1831 ib. MALTKILN FM, *Malt House* 1831 Bry.
THE MEADOWS. MIDDLEWICH RD, cf. Booth Lane 1 44,
Middlewich 240 *supra.* MILLHILL HO, *Mill Hill* 1831 Bry.
NARROW LANE. OAK FM, 1831 ib, *Oke* 1589 Sheaf, *v.* āc.
OFFLEY HO & WOOD. OLDHOUSE FM, *Cold Moss Farm* 1831 Bry,
cf. Cold Moss *supra.* PADDY'S WOOD. PARKHOUSE FM, *Park-
house* 1688 Cre, 1831 Bry, cf. *Parke* 1589 Sheaf, *v.* park. PARK
LANE, *Giddy Lane* 1831 Bry, cf. prec. and Giddy Fields *infra.*
THE PITTS, *The Pits* 1831 ib. THE POOL. PRISONBALL BANK,
Prison Bars 1831 ib, perhaps a playground for the game of Prisoner's
Base, *v.* prison-bars. REYNOLD'S FM. SANDBACH BRIDGE, cf.
the Bridge Croft 1665 Cre. SANDBACH HEATH, 1611 Wil, cf.
Heath 1589 Sheaf, *the nearer & further heath field* 1646 Cre, *the two
heath crofts* 1669 ib, *v.* hǣð, cf. Heath Fm *supra.* SANDBACH MILL,
1831 Bry, *-Mills* 1771 Cre. SCOTCH COMMON, 1843 ib, *-Commons*
1735 Wil, 1819 Orm[2], supposed to be named from a party of
Scottish troops defeated here by the townsfolk in 1651, Orm[2] III
104. SMALLBROOK, 1842 OS, named from Small Brook[1] 1 35.
SWEETTOOTH LANE, cf. *Sweet Tooth* 1840 *TA.* TAXMERE (FM),
Taxmere Pool & Farm 1831 Bry, *Tastmere* 1630 Cre, a lake, now
mostly drained, *v.* mere[1]. The first el. also appears nearby in the lost
p.n. *Taxley* 1686 Cre, 1673 ib, *Toskeley* 1618, 1684 ib, *Task(e)ley*
1630, 1631 ib, *v.* lēah 'a clearing, a wood'. It may be ME *taske* 'a tax,
a duty, exacted work' (*task* NED), here alluding to places on which
service-labour or tax-payments were due. But a pers.n. is possible,
such as that in Taxal 1 172. TOP O' TH' HILL, cf. The Hill,
Hillside Cottage *supra.* Here were *Wellstone* 1831 Bry, 1840 *TA* (a
house) and *Wilfield* 1630 Cre, *the Will feild*, *-field(s)* 1637, 1692 ib,
1840 *TA, v.* wella 'a spring, a well'. WEST FIELDS. WHEELOCK
BRIDGE & HO, *Wheelock House* 1842 OS, named from R. Wheelock
1 38, or Wheelock 273 *infra.* YEOWOOD FM, 1665 Cre, *Euwode*
1454 *Eyre, Ewode* 1465 ChRR, *Yewoods House* 1612 Cre, *Yeawood-*
1665 ib, 'the yew-wood', *v.* īw, wudu.

FIELD-NAMES

The undated forms are 1840 *TA* 347. Of the others, 1307 is *Eyre*, 1589 Sheaf, 1723, 1755 Wil, 1724 NotCestr, 1831 Bry, 1842 OS, 1845 ChetOS VIII, and the rest Cre.

(*a*) Far & Near Adder Mdw (*Two Adder Meadows* 1665); Arclid Fd (*v.* Arclid 264 *supra*); Back Fd; Bakehouse Croft; Bankfield (*v.* banke); Barn Fd (*the barne feild* 1637, *the Barnfield* 1666, *v.* bere-ærn); Bent (*v.* beonet); Bletch Fd; Boat Bridge Fd (probably from bōt and brēc, bryce, alluding to land broken in for cultivation, in which some privilege was used); The Bolshaw (*v.* bola, sceaga); Bosmoor (*v.* mōr¹); Bowling Alley; Breach Fd (*v.* brēc); Brick Fd, Brick Kiln Fd (cf. *Brick Kilns* 1831, *Brick Bank* 1842); Brine Pit Fd (*v.* brīne, pytt, cf. Wich House Fd *infra*); Broom Fd; Brown Fd; the four Butts 1723 (cf. *the Butt* 1637, *v.* butte); Caltens Bottom ((*the*) *Katerines-, Catherine(s) Bottom* 1665, 1669, 1673, *v.* botm); Clay Flatt; Cockpit Fd; Cordry Fd; Cow Lazor ('cow leasowe', *v.* cū, lǣs); Cranks Moor Moss (*v.* cranuc, -es², mōr¹, mos); Great & Little Crimbers (*v. le Crymbe* 171 *supra*); Daddys Croft; Four Day Math (*v.* day-math); Dobbins Hill; Great Dowry (*v.* dowarie); Drumble (dial. 'a wooded dell', cf. dumbel); Flash Mdw (*v.* flasshe); Foot Road-, Foot Way Fd; Great & Little Giddy Fd (*the lytell giddiefyeld* 1585, *Giddy-yards or Needhams* (*Lands*) 1694, cf. Needams Croft *infra*, Park Lane *supra*); Gorsty Croft (*the two gorstye croft* 1585, *v.* gorstig, croft); Gow Mdw; Grannums Croft ('granddam's croft'); The Green Stitches (*v.* sticce¹); Hackley; Near Hall Fd, Great Hall Flat, Hall Mdw ((*the*) *Hall Flatt* 1621, 1637, *the little Hall Flatt*, 1637, *the Great-* 1692, *the Hall Meyn* 1621, *the hall meanes* 1637, *-means* 1687, cf. *Sandbach Hall* 1724, 1845, *v.* hall, flat, main); Hays (*v.* (ge)hæg); Hemp Butt; Hen Croft (*the-* 1673); (Little) Highs (*the Great & Little High* 1651, *v.* grēat, lȳtel, ēg); Holly Stile Fd (*v.* holegn, stigel); Holt Fd (*v.* holt); Hursteads (*v.* hyrst, stede); Intake (*the further & nearer Intacke* 1651, *v.* inntak); Kelsea Marsh & Mdw, Kelsey Fd; Kibble Ditch, Kidden-, Kitten Ditch (*the Kyddendych* 1585, *v.* dīc); Kiln Croft & Fd (*the Kiln Meadow* 1673); Knackey Piece; The Knowl (*v.* cnoll); Lady Mdw (*v.* hlǣfdige); Leak's Fd (cf. *Lake* 1589, *the lake* 1606, *v.* lacu); Leas Mdw (cf. *Leas of the Lane* 1680, 1725, 1729, from the surname *Lea*); Long Fd (*the Long Field* 1665); Long Mdw (*the-* 1665); Lowders Garden (cf. *Lowther's cottage* 1772); Mark Fd; Marlpit Croft (cf. *the marle pitt flatt* 1646); Marsh Green Fd (cf. Marsh Green 267 *supra*); Mere Ground & Mdw (named from Taxmere *supra*, *v.* mere¹); Mode(s) Fd; The Moor(s), Moor Mdw (*del Moor* 1307 (p), (*the*) *Moore croft & meadow* 1651, 1665, *v.* mōr¹); Moss Croft 1711 (*v.* mos); Needams Croft (*v.* Giddy Fd *supra*); New Fd (*the new fyeld* 1585, *-field* 1621, *-feildes* 1637, *v.* nīwe, feld); Nub Fd; Ox Pasture; Park(s); The Patch; Penny Croft; Pickow (*v.* pichel); Pinfold Fd (*v.* pynd-fald); Great Pink Fd (*v.* pinca); Pipers Lane 1831 (extending from 110–770624 along the Brereton boundary and north-westward into Bradwall to 762628, perhaps from pipere or the surname *Piper* and lane, cf. Pipers Fd 278 *infra*, Pepper Street (Chester) 327 *infra*); Pithow Fd (probably pichel); Puddle Fd (*v.* puddel);

Rathbones tenement 1780 (cf. *Rathbone Barn* 1605, *Rathbones Barne* 1607, from the surname *Rathbone*, cf. John *Rathebon* 1362, *-bourn* 1353); (Further-, Near-) Ridding(s) (*the two rid(d)ding(e)s* 1637, 1692, *the further & nearer Ridding* 1651, *the Riddings* 1687, *v.* ryding); Rocher Bank (*v.* rocher); Roundabout (*v.* 327 *infra*); Round Fd (*the-* 1665); Roundow; Sand Fd (*Great & Little Sountfield* 1651, *v.* sand); Sender Fd; Shaw's Cottage 1797 (*Shawes of the Sidneys* 1681, *Shaw's tenement* 1755, from the family *Shaw* of Sydney 327 *infra*); Shoulder of Mutton (*v.* 327 *infra*); The Slum (a plantation, *v.* Slum Wood 321 *infra*); Snigtail Mdw (*v.* snygge, tægl); Sour Fd or Big-, Near- & Sour Hope (*v.* sūr 'sour', hop[1], cf. Hope(s)hill 267 *supra*); Spaw Fd (*v.* spa); Stanway Croft (cf. *Stanwayes cottage* 1726, (fields called) *Stanways* 1794, from a surname *Stanway*); Stock Acre (*v.* stocc); Stony Croft (*v.* stānig); Sugar Cane; Sun Fd; Tan Yard 1772 (*the Upper-* 1769, *v.* tan-yard); Town Fd; Trubshaw; the Tythe Barn 1724 (cf. *Town Barn* 1605, *v.* toun, tēoða); Wall Fd (*v.* wælla); Wash (*v.* wæsce); Weilding; Well Bank; Welshden, Welsh Dens (*v.* Welisc, denu); Wheat Fd & Hill (*the wheate feild* 1646, *the wheathill* 1651, *v.* hwǣte); White Fd; Wich-, Wick-, Wych House Fd ('field at a "wich-house" or salt-works', cf. *Old Salt Works* 1831, and Brine Pit Fd *supra*, which were adjacent, *v.* wych(e)-hous(e), cf. 193 *supra*); Widenor Flatt (*Widney flatt* 1651, 'at the wide meadow', *v.* wïd (dat.sg. widan), ēg, and flat); Within Fds (*v.* wīðegn); The Wood; Woolley Fd (*the Wo(o)lley feild* 1665).

(*b*) *the bigger Cockshade*, *-Cockshed fields* 1666, 1670, *the Cockshoote field* 1667 (*v.* cocc-scyte); *the Barley Field Wood* 1665; *the Long & Little Beames* 1630, *the Long Beam* 1633 (*v.* lang, bēam); *the great & little birches* 1646 (*v.* birce); *Byrshdoore* 1589; *Corner* 1589 (*v.* corner); *the diddye Borwsmore* 1585; *the Fal(l)ings* 1665, *the Fouleings* 1673 (*v.* felling, fælling); *the Grange Moore* 1665 (*v.* grange, mōr[1]); *the Herne croft* 1669 (either 'heron croft' or 'croft in a corner', *v.* heiroun or hyrne, croft); *the two hurler crofts* 1666; *Mickefeild* 1651 ('big field', *v.* mikill, feld); *Watfeild* 1651 (perhaps 'wheat feild' *v.* hwǣte, feld).

4. WHEELOCK (110–750590) ['wiːlɔk]

Hoiloch 1086 DB

Weloc e13 Dieul, *-oke* e13 *JRC* (p), *-ok* 1260 Court (p), *-ock* 1290 *AddCh*, *Geloke* E1 *JRC* (p) (a French spelling)

Wolok 1235 *Mainw*

Wehlok 1260 Court (p), *Weylok* l13 *AddCh* (p)

Wulok 1275 Cre

Que-, *Qwelo(c)k* l13 *Vern* (p), MidCh (p), c.1300 *Chol*, 1316, 1321 AD, *-oc* e14 ChRR, (*-iuxta Sondbache*) 1319 Plea, *Cwelock* 1284 Tab (p)

Whelok 1288 Court *et freq* with variant spellings *-oc(k)*, *-o(c)ke*, *Whelhoc* E3 *Surv* (p), *Whelek* 1404 ChRR (p), *Whelk* 1434 ib (p)

Welokes 1364 AD (p)
Whyllok 1377 (1672) Orm[1], *Whillock(e)* 1581, 1586 Cre, (-*near Sambitch*) 17 Chol
Wheelock 1387 ChRR, -*ocke* 1538 Orm[2]
Whylock 1586 *Rental*

Named from R. Wheelock 1 38. It adjoins Sandbach 269 *supra*. Wheelock Heath is partly in Haslington township 326 *infra*.

CREWE RD, *v.* 269 *supra.*   GROVE HO, cf. *Grove* 1839 *TA*, *v.* grāf. MILLHOUSE FM, cf. Wheelock Mill *supra.*   MILL POND, *Mill Pool* 1839 ib, *a milne domme . . . in Whelok* 1440 *AddCh*, named from Wheelock Mill *infra*, *v.* myln, damme.   WHEELOCK BRIDGE, *pons de Quelok* c.1300 *Chol.*   WHEELOCK HALL, 1724 NotCestr. WHEELOCK HEATH, 1831 Bry.   WHEELOCK MILL, 1656 Orm[2], *molendinum de Quelok* 1316 AD.   WHITE HALL, 1831 Bry.

FIELD-NAMES

The undated forms are 1839 *TA* 426, 1831 is Bry, 1842 OS.

(*a*) Bakehouse Croft; Bent Mdw (*v.* beonet); Bidner (possibly analogous with Boden Hall 307 *infra*); Bridge Fd *&* Mdw (cf. Wheelock Bridge *supra*); Broom Fd; Calves Croft; Ditch Moor; The Flash 1831, 1842 (*v.* flasshe); Gorstey Croft (*v.* gorstig); Halves; Hill Fd; Malkins Bank; Marl Fd; Mill Mdw (cf. Wheelock Mill *supra*); Mucklow ('big mound', *v.* mycel, hlāw); Oakley (*v.* āc, lēah); Old House Bank; Old Intake (*v.* inntak); Orchard; Outlet (*v.* outlet); Penn Croft (*v.* penn[2]); Pinfold Croft (*v.* pynd-fald); Pit Croft *&* Fd; Podmore Mdw ('toad marsh', *v.* pode, mōr[1]); Pool Head (*v.* pōl[1], hēafod); Rough Fd; Ryle (*v.* ryge, lēah or hyll); Rye Croft; Sand Leys (*v.* lēah); Sprink (*v.* spring); Tentrey Fd (*v.* tentour); Wash Pool End (*v.* wæsce); Wheat Fd; Wickhouse Fd ('field at a wich-house', *v.* wych(e)-hous(e), cf. Wich House Fd 273 *supra*).

ix. Brereton

The parish of Brereton contained one township, Brereton cum Smethwick, and was originally part of Astbury parish 285 *infra*, from which it was separated t. R1, *v.* Orm[2] I 400, III 81, 92. It is not noted in Tax. The modern c.p. of Brereton includes Davenport 301 *infra*.

1. BRERETON CUM SMETHWICK, 1724 NotCestr, *v.* Brereton Green, Smethwick Green *infra*.

BRERETON GREEN *&* HALL (110-770640) ['briətən] locally ['brɛətən] *Bretone* 1086 DB, (*Brereton alias*) *Breton* 1581 ChRR

Brereton c.1100 Orm² (p), *Brer(e)ton* e13 Facs (p), MidCh *et freq*
with variant spellings *-tune, -toun, Brerre-*; (*-alias Bruerton alias
Bruton, -alias Bruerton Grene*) 1559 Pat, (*-Hall*) 1724 NotCestr
Breartun e12 (17) Orm² (p), *Breirton* 1392 Chol (p), *Breerton* 1461
Pat, (*-Green*) 1656 Orm²
Brureton 1408 ChRR (p), 1552 AD (p), *Bruerton* (*hawle*) c. 1536
Leland, (*-Grene*) 1559 Pat, (*-Green*) 1775 Sheaf, *Brewrton* 1548
Pat (p), *Brewerton* 1589 ChRR (p), (*-Green*) 1690 Sheaf
'Briar farm', *v.* brēr, tūn, with grēne² and hall.

SMETHWICK GREEN, HALL & LANE (110–800630) ['smeðik]
Smethewik(e) 1312 ChRR (p), 1313 *Dav* (p), *-wyk* 1331 Plea, *-weke*
1432 ChRR, *Smethwike* 1371 MidCh (p) *et freq* with variant
spellings *-wick(e), -wyk, -wik, -weke*; *Smethwick Green & Hall*
1831 Bry
Smythwike 1530 ChRR
'The smiths' hamlet', *v.* smið (gen.pl. smeoða), wīc, grēne². Cf.
Spark Lane *infra.*

ALLOM (lost), ALUM BRIDGE (110–765665)

Hallehulm H3 Orm² (p), 1287 Court (p), *Halhulm* 1289 ib (p)
Allehulm(e) H3 Orm² (p), 1260 Court, 1296 *Vern*, 1300 Tab,
Alhulme l13 MidCh (p), *-holm* 1296 Ipm, *Allhullme* l13 *MidCh*
(p), *-holme(bridge)* 1619 Sheaf
Holme iuxta Brereton 1391 MidCh, *Hulme-* 1419, 1431 ib, 1429
Plea, *Holme* 17 MidCh
Allum 1425 Orm², *-Bridge* 1831 Bry, *Alum Bridge* 1842 OS,
Allom Meadow & Pits 1847 *TA*
For further instances of the name cf. R. Croco 1 19, Doglane Fm
infra. The principal el. is hulm 'a water-meadow', as in Church
Hulme 278 *infra*, with variant forms from holmr. Church Hulme is
adjacent, and may have included part of this manor, cf. Allum Mdw
279 *infra.* The location of the meadows and the bridge suggest that
the old manor occupied the north-western corner of the township
against the Church Hulme boundary. The affixed (*H*)*alle-* is probably
hall 'a hall', *v.* 217 *supra.*

BRINDLEY GREEN (110–770627), 1831 Bry, *Brunlegh* 1349 Plea (p),
-ley 1489 ChRR, *Brundelegh* 1393 ib, *Brenley* 1519 Plea, 'burnt
clearing', *v.* brende², lēah. The name refers to a district extending

into Bradwall township, cf. Brindley Lane 266 *supra* (*Brunleghmor'*
l13).

ARCLID WOOD, 1848 *TA*, *v.* Arclid 264 *supra*.   BACK LANE (FM),
Back Lane 1831 Bry.   BAG MERE (LANE), BAGMERE (BANK) FM,
BAGMERE LANE, *the Bagmere* 1621 Orm[2], *Bagmer(e)* (*-Mear*) 1656 ib,
formerly an extensive lake, drained and brought into cultivation in
the eighteenth century (Orm[2] III 86). The name may be 'bag lake'
either from its original shape or from its acting as a trap for water,
v. bagga, mere[1]. However, 'bog pool', *v.* bog, mere[1], is more likely,
cf. Orm[2] III 86.   BRERETON HEATH, 1831 Bry, cf. *Hetcroft* 1306
Plea, *v.* hǣð, croft.   BRERETON POOL, *Brerton Mere* 1445 ChRR,
Blackmere, *Brereton's Lake* 1612 Polyolbion, *v.* pōl[1], mere[1], lake,
blæc 'black'.   BROWNEDGE, 1831 Bry, *-Egge* 1519 Plea, *Brounegge*
1402 Pat (p), either 'brown edge' or 'the edge of the brow(s)', from
brūn[1], or brū (gen.pl. *brū(we)na*), or brún[2] and ecg.   COURTHOUSE
FM, *Court House* 1842 OS, *Cote House Farm* 1847 *TA*, from either
court 'a court, a courtyard', or cot 'a cote, a cottage' with hūs.
DAIRYHOUSE FM, 1831 Bry.   DOG LANE (FM) (110–767657), *Dog
Lane* 1831 ib, *v.* dogga, lane. The farm was *Deers Green* 1842 OS,
Deans Green 1847 *TA*, *Allum Brook Farm* 1949 OS 1″, *v.* grēne[2] 'a
green'. *Dean* is a surname, cf. Roger *del Dene* 1393 ChRR, *v.* denu.
Deers- may be a form for this, but may be analogous with Deers-
green 316 *infra*. *Allum Brook* is R. Croco 1 19, cf. *Allom supra*.
DUKE'S OAK (FM), named from a tree, *Dukes Oak* 1831 Bry, cf.
Dukes Croft & Meadow 1847 *TA*, from the surname *Duke* and āc.
DUNKIRK FM, *Dunkirk* 1831 Bry, cf. 326 *infra*.   HANDFIELD FM.
HARELANE ROUGH, 1831 ib, *v.* hara 'a hare', lane, rūh.   HAZEL-
SHAW FM, 1842 OS, *Hassell Shaw Farm & Lane* 1831 Bry, 'hazel
copse', *v.* hæsel, sceaga.   HOLDING'S DRUMBLE (FM), *Holden's
Drumble* 1831 ib, cf. *Drumble Lake* 1831 ib, *Drumble Meadow* 1847
TA, 'the dell of *Holden* ("deep valley")', *v.* hol[2], denu, dial. *drumble*,
cf. dumbel 'a wooded dell', a valley with a stream on the boundary
with Sproston and Arclid, cf. 254, 265 *supra*.   ILLIDGE GREEN,
1831 Bry, *Yelegge* 1519 Plea, *Ilich(brook)* 1619 Sheaf, *Illege Green*
1842 OS, *Holige* (*Bank*), *Illidge Field & Meadow* 1847 *TA*, 'boggy
stream, or bog, near yew-trees', *v.* īw, læc(c), lec(c), cf. 265 *supra*.
JILLION COVERT.   LEA COTTAGE.   LIGHTFOOT GREEN FM, *Lightfoot Farm* 1831 Bry, *-Green* 1842 OS. *Lightfoot* is probably a surname.
MEDHURST GREEN, 1842 ib, *Merehouse or Medhurst Green* 1831 Bry,

Merehouse Green 1848 *TA*, *Meyrhowse* 1519 Plea, 'house near a boundary', i.e. the eastern boundary of the township, *v.* (ge)mǣre, hūs.   MILL LANE, *Park Mill Lane* 1831 Bry, cf. *Mill Cotch* 1847 *TA*, named from Park Mill *infra*, with dial. *couch* 'couch-grass'. MOORHEAD FM & LANE, *Moorhead* 1831 Bry, 'the top end of a moor', *v.* mōr[1], hēafod.   THE MOSS, MOSS FM & LANE, *Moss Farm* 1842 OS, *v.* mos.   PARKHOUSE FM, *Pack House* 1831 Bry, cf. *Park Field*, *Knoll & Meadow* 1847 *TA*, *v.* park.   PARK MILL, 1831 Bry, *the Parke Millne bridge* 1619 Sheaf, *le mulne* 1400 ChRR (p), 'a watermill in Brereton', 1445 ChRR, *v.* park, myln, cf. Mill Lane *supra*. PECKLOW, 1831 Bry, named from Pecklow Cob 319 *infra*.   PEWIT FM.   SANDLOW GREEN, 1831 ib, *Seynlow* 1519 Plea, 'burnt-off mound', from sænget or OE (ge)senged, pa.part. of OE *sengan* 'to singe', with hlāw.   SPARK LANE (BRIDGE), *Smethwick Lane* 1831 Bry, cf. Spark Lane 317 *infra*.   WILACRE LANE, probably 'wild acre', *v.* wilde, æcer, cf. 317 *infra*.   YEWTREE HO (lost), 1831 Bry.

FIELD-NAMES

The undated forms are 1847 *TA* 69. Of the others, 1306, 1519 are Plea, 1619, 1690, 1775 Sheaf, 1650 *ParlSurv*, 1831 Bry, 1848 *TAMap*.

(a) The Acre; Alderley Croft ('alder wood', *v.* alor, lēah); Alasager Fd (cf. Alsager 325 *infra*); Arecumlow Fd (named from Alcumlow 304 *infra*); Great & Little Bath, Moss Bath Pits (*v.* bæð); Baileys Knoll, Baileys Knowls pits; Bake House Croft; Bear Fd (named from the Bear's Head, *Bear's Head Inne* 1690); Bent Mdw (*v.* beonet); Birchen Fd; Black Fd & Flatt; Blake Fd (*v.* blæc); Bog(g) Fd (*Buggfeilde* 1650, 'boggart-, hobgoblin field', *v.* bugge, feld); Boosey Pastures (*v.* bōsig); Bowling Green Ley, Bowling Hey; Broad Hey; Broom(e)y Fd & Croft (*v.* brōmig); Brown Fd; Burnt Earth & Heath (*v.* brende[2], eorðe, hǣð); Butts Fd (*v.* butte); Calf Croft; Cheapoak Hey (perhaps 'oak at which dealers met', *v.* cēap, āc); Church Fd & Mdw; Cinder Hill, Cinderland Mdw (cf. *Sindersych in le Stockes* 1306, 'cindery stream', *v.* sinder, sīc, cf. Stockings *infra*); Clay Flatts; Clulow Heys, Clulows (from a surname *Clulow*, cf. Cleulow 1 165 and (ge)hæg); Coney Greaves and Green (*v.* coningre); Cow Hey; Doe Fd & Greaves (from dial. *doe* 'to do well, to thrive, to fatten (of cattle etc.)', or dāl 'a dole, an allottment'); Driving Road (a drove-way for cattle); Fenny Lane (*v.* fennig); Five Day Work (*v.* day-work); Gorsey-, Gorsty Fd (*v.* gorstig); Grammarian's Fd; The Hale Hey (*v.* halh, (ge)hæg); Harrow Acre; Henbury Croft; Heys (*v.* (ge)hæg); Hollin Fd (*v.* holegn); Holloway (*v.* hol[2], weg); Homestead; Hop Yard (*v.* hoppe, geard); Horse Leasure (*v.* lǣs (dat.sg. lǣswe)); Intake (*freq*, *v.* inntak); Jones Earth (cf. Jones's Lane 267 *supra*); Kiln Fd; Knowle Pits, Knowls (*Knoles* 1690, 1775, *v.* cnoll); Lady Lane (*v.* hlǣfdige); Lepers Hey ('enclosure belonging to, or dedicated to the care of, a leper or lepers', from

ME *leper* and (ge)hæg); Long Butts (*v.* butte); Long Furlong; Long Shoot (*v.* scēat); Marled Earth (*v.* marlede, eorðe); Marsh Fd *&* Lane; Mere Fd (cf. Bagmere *supra*); Mickle Fd (*v.* mikill); Milking Bank (*v.* milking); Missicke (dial. mizzick (EDD) 'a boggy place', (cf. misy), perhaps from an OE *mēosuc, from mēos and -uc, cf. Mossocks Moor 326 *infra*); Nick Fd; Oakley Fd (*v.* āc, lēah); Old House Croft; Ox Hey; Paradise (*v.* paradis); Petty Fd (*v.* pety); Pingott (*v.* pingot); Pink Fd; Pipers Fd (cf. Pipers Lane 272 *supra*); Prison Bar Fd (cf. Prisonball Bank 271 *supra, v.* prison-bars); Ridding Mdw (*v.* ryding); The Rough; Salting Fd; Sand Field; Seven Day Work (*v.* day-work); Sharp Fd; (Long) Slang (*v.* slang); Slatern Fd *&* Mdw; Slaters Fd; Slope; Snail Fd; Sooty Hill (*v.* soti); Sound Fd (*v.* sand); Spring Green; Sprink (*v.* spring); Stockings (cf. *le Stockes* 1306, *v.* stocc, stocting, cf. Cinder Hill *supra*); Stoney Lake (*v.* lacu); Teeming Croft; Titty Mouse Green 1848 (a dial. form of *titmouse*); (Further *&* Middle) Tyrants, (Little, Long *&* Round) Tyrant (cf. *Tyrant Farm* 1848 and Tyron I 58, Tyrant 327 *infra*. The basis of these forms may be *iron* from hyrne 'a nook, a corner, a secluded place' (cf. Heronbridge 326 *infra*) with a reduced def. art. By popular rationalization *t'iron* becomes *tyrant*); Wall Fd (*v.* wælla); Well Fd; Westons Edge Pits (cf. Whetstonedge 288 *infra*); Whitledge ('white boggy stream, *v.* hwīt, læc(c)); Wich Fd (cf. *Witch Lane* 1831, probably from wice 'a wych-elm'); Wilk Fd; Wing Flat; Far *&* Near Yards (*v.* geard).

(b) *Foxley* 1619 ('fox clearing', *v.* fox, lēah); *Twyford* 1519 ('double ford', *v.* twī-, ford).

x. Church Hulme

Church Hulme was a parochial chapelry of Sandbach parish 264 *supra*, and contained the townships 1. Church Hulme or Holmes Chapel, 2. Cotton (now included in Cranage c.p. *v.* 222 *supra*).

1. CHURCH HULME, HOLMES CHAPEL (110–7667) [ˈhjuːm, ˈhoumz]

   Hulm 12 *Dav*, *Hulm(e)* H3 Orm[2] *et freq*, (*le-*) 1288 Court (p), (*-iuxta Crannache*) 1335 *Dav*, (*-iuxta Daneport*) 1353 *ib*, (*-alias Church Hulme*) 1621 Orm[2]

   Holm(e) 1278 Ipm, 14 *Dav*, 1671 *AddCh*, *Holmes* 1775 Sheaf

   Church(e) Hulm, -Hwlm c.1292 Orm[2] *et freq* with variant spellings *Chirche-, -hulme, -holm(e)*; *Church Hulme or Holmes Chapel* 1831 Bry

   Holme chapell 1400–5 PremIt, 1463 ChRR, *capella de Hulme* c.1536 Orm[2], *Hulme Chapel(l)* 1687 ChetOS VIII, 1707 Sheaf

   Hulmesschapell 1483 AD, *Holmes Chapel* 1591 Sheaf *et freq*, *Holme's-* 1621 Orm[2], *Holmschapple* 1658 Sheaf, *Hulms Chappell* 1681 ib

'The water-meadow', *v.* **hulm** (with variant spellings from **holmr**). The affix is **cirice** 'a church', from the parochial chapel, distinguishing this from *Allom* 275 *supra*, cf. 217 *supra*. The later name is 'chapel of Hulme', *v.* **chapel**(1). In modern usage, Church Hulme is the township-name, Holmes Chapel being that of the village.

SALTERSFORD BRIDGE, cf. Bridge Fm *infra*, and *Saltersford House* 1842 OS, later an Agricultural College, *v.* 231 *supra*.

SANDIFORD COTTAGE (110–762672), cf. *Sondifort* H3 Orm², *Sandiford* c.1292 ib, *le Sondyforth* 1351 *Eyre*, *Sandyford Brook* 1831 Bry, 'the sandy ford', *v.* **sandig, ford**. The brook is a watercourse from 110–772672 joining R. Croco at 743667.

ALUM BRIDGE, *v. Allom* 275 *supra*.   BACK LANE (FM), *Back Lane* 1831 Bry.   BANK FM, 1831 ib.   BRIDGE FM, *Saltersford* 1842 OS, cf. *Bridge Field & Meadow* 1840 *TA*, Saltersford Bridge *supra*. BROOKLANDS (FM), near a watercourse, *v.* **land**.   THE CROFT. DANE BANK, 1831 Bry, 'bank over-looking R. Dane', *v.* **banke**, R. Dane 1 20.   DEANE CROSS, cf. *Dene* 1358 *Eyre* (p), *Dean Hey* 1840 *TA*, '(cross and enclosure at) the valley', *v.* **denu, cros, (ge)hæg**. HERMITAGE BRIDGE, *v.* Hermitage 224 *supra*.   IRONBRIDGE FM. IVY COTTAGE, *The Cottage* 1831 Bry.   LANE-END FM, *Lane-Ends* 1784 Sheaf.   LONDON RD, the main road to London.   MANOR FM & LANE, *Manor House* 1842 OS.   MARSH LANE (FM & COTTAGE), *Marsh Lane (House)* 1831 Bry, *v.* **mersc, lane**.   NICKER'S WELL, cf. *Nicho Well Field* 1840 *TA*, 'haunted well', *v.* **nicor** 'a water-sprite', **wella**.   OAK HOUSES, *Oaktree House* 1831 Bry, *Oak House* 1842 OS, cf. *Oakhouse Field* 1840 *TA*.   PARKMILL FM, named from Park Mill 277 *supra*.   RYECROFT WOOD, 1831 Bry, *Ruycroft'* 1307–27 *Dav*, *Rycroft* c.1350 ib, *Rie Croft* 1840 *TA*, *v.* **ryge, croft**.   SADDLERS CLOSE.

FIELD-NAMES

The undated forms are 1840 *TA* 116. Of the others, 12, c.1300, e14, 14, 1335, 1568 are *Dav*, e13 Dieul, 1328, 1338, 1507 MidCh.

(a) Alderley (*v.* **alor, lēah**); Allum Mdw (cf. Alum Bridge *supra*, *v. Allom* 275 *supra*); Bakehouse Fd; Bent (*v.* **beonet**); Black Croft; Big & Little Bode (*v.* **bold**); The Bottoms (*v.* **botm**); Big & Little Bratt; Brick Kiln Fd; Broad Hay; Brook Fd; Cackow; Chapel Fd (cf. *Churchfeld* 1507, *v.* **cirice, chapel(e)**); Coach Lane Fd; Cockpit Fd; Crib Mdw (*v.* **crib**); Dane Mdw (named from R. Dane 1 20); Dry Croft; Flax Fd; Gorsty Green (*v.* gorstig); Granary Croft; Hare Shot (*v.* hara, scēat); Hen Acre (*v.* henn); Hill Fd; Houghs Acre; The Knowl; Marl Fd; Mill Mdw (cf. *mulney* 12, *molendinum de Hulm* e13, *v.* myln, ēg); Newale, Newall; Ox Hay (*v.* oxa, (ge)hæg); Park Fd; Parlour End; Pinfold Croft (*v.* pynd-fald); Pingot (*v.* pingot); Red Rose; Ridding (*v.* ryding); Rough Bank; Sandlow Green (*v.* 277 *supra*); Shilsbury Croft; Snape ('a boggy piece of land', *v.* snæp); Spath (*v.* sparð); Spoon Mouth; Stepping Stone Fd; Strithits Croft; Well Croft *&* Fd; Westmoreland; Within-, Withy Fd (*v.* wiðig, wiðegn); Woodhouse Fd (cf. Woodhouse Fm 302 *infra*).

(*b*) *le Furmost Ashwallfeld* 1507 ('spring near an ash-tree', *v.* æsc, wælla); *le Bertiknoll* 1328, 1338 (*v.* cnoll. First el. obscure); *Betriche eie* 14 ('Beadurīc's water-meadow' from the OE pers.n. *Beadurīc* and ēg); *le Clef* 14 ('the cliff, the bank', *v.* clif); *Estedis* 12 ('east enclosure', *v.* ēast, edisc); *nemus del Hee* c.1330, 14 ('grove at the river', *v.* ēa, probably R. Dane 1 20); *Holcineden* 12 ('valley of the hollows', *v.* holce (gen.pl. *holcena*), denu); *Hopes Sprinke* 1507 (*v.* spring 'a young wood'); *Louingishey* 12 (a messuage and land held by one *Louinch*', from the OE pers.n. *Lēofing* and (ge)hæg); *le Pekusfeld* e14 ('field at the hill', *v.* pēac, feld); *Sheroddes* 1568 (the gen.sg. of the surname *Sherott*, *Sher(r)ard*, cf. The Fields 270 *supra*); *Sladehurst* 1335 (p), ('wood or hill at a valley', *v.* slæd, hyrst); *le Whitsiche* c.1300 ('the white stream' *v.* hwīt, sīc).

2. COTTON (HALL) (110–7467)

Cotes c.1230 *AddCh* (p)

Coten c.1230 Orm² (p), 1260 Court, 1295 Lacy, 1314 Plea, -*e* l13 Tab (p)

Coton c.1230 Bark (p), 13 MidCh (p), c.1278 *AddCh* (p) *et freq* to 1540 MidCh, -*a* c.1294 Tab (p), *Cotton* c.1296 MidCh *et freq*, (*the hall of*) c.1260 Orm²

Cotyn 1260 Court (p)

Cotun a.1274 MidCh (p), 1299 Orm² (p), c.1320 *Chol*, 1277 Dugd (p), c.1380 ChRR (p)

Cotum 1305 Lacy

'(At) the cotes', *v.* cot, (dat.pl. *cotum*). *Cotes* is a new ME nom.pl. replacing OE *cotu*; the -*en*, -*un* forms represent ME reductions of the OE dat.pl., *v.* Studies³ 30. Cf. Cotton 326 *infra*.

COTTON FM, *Jointress Farm* 1831 Bry, presumably land held in jointure by an heiress, cf. jointure.   COTTON WOOD, cf. *Wood Field*, *Big Wood* 1839 *TA*.   POOLFORD LANE, *Poolsford Lane* 1842 OS, cf. *Pool Ford* 1831 Bry, a crossing of R. Croco at 110–740666, *v.* pōl¹, ford.   PRIMROSE HALL.

FIELD-NAMES

The undated forms are 1839 *TA* 131.

(*a*) The Bank; Brickkiln Fd; Brook Fd (cf. Sandyford Brook *infra*); Cotton Fd; Dane Mdw (from R. Dane 1 20); Ford Eye (*v.* ford, ēg); Holly Dish (from edisc with either hol² 'hollow, in a hollow' or holegn 'a holly-tree'); Lilly Fd(s) (*v.* lilie); Macklish; Marl Fd; Mill Bank, Fd & Mdw; Old Fd; Ox Fd; Pigeon Croft; Pinfold (*v.* pynd-fald); Pool Fd (*v.* pōl¹); Big & Little Ridding (*v.* ryding); Rushy Hays (*v.* riscig, (ge)hæg); Sandyford Brook 1831 Bry (*v.* 279 *supra*); Small Thorn ('narrow field at a thorn-tree', *v.* smæl, þorn); Swine Cote Bank & Fd ('pig-cote', *v.* swīn, cot); Tony Gold Fd; Way Fd; The Wharf (*v.* waroð); Wheat Eye (*v.* hwǣte, ēg); Whishaw's Mdw (cf. 230 *supra*).

xi. Swettenham

The parish of Swettenham contained the townships 1. Kermincham, 2. Swettenham (now a c.p. including Kermincham). It appears to have been taken out of Astbury parish 285 *infra*, for it is not separately mentioned in Tax, *v.* Orm² III 21, 72, ChetOS VIII 260 n.2. Kermincham was in *Hamestan* (Macclesfield) Hundred DB, cf. 222 *supra*, and since Swettenham lies north of R. Dane, between Kermincham and Macclesfield Hundred, it was probably in the same Hundred.

1. KERMINCHAM (110–7968) [ˈkəːrmintʃəm] older local [-idʒəm]

   Cerdingham 1086 DB, *Cherd-* 1278 Ipm, *Kerthyngham, -ing-* 1275 ib, 1288 Court, 1307 *Eyre*, 1308 *AddCh*, 1673 Sheaf, *-inham* 1312 *Dav*, *-incham, -ynch-* 1345 *ib*, 1350 VR *et freq* to 1561 ChRR, *Certingham* 1307 *Eyre* (p), *Karthyncham* 1522 Plea, *-inch-* 1580 ChRR

   Kermincham, -ynch- 1286 Court, 1341 *Eyre et freq, (or Carincham)* 1819 Orm², *-yngham* 1312 *Dav*, *-ing-* 1564 ChRR, 1745 Sheaf, *-ynge-* 1464 *Dav*, *-yngcham* 1514 *ChEx*, *Karm'cham* 1393 (17) MidCh, *Carmyncham* 1553 Pat, *-ycham* 15 Rich, *-yngam* 1580 *AddCh*, *-ingham* 1784 Sheaf, *Kyrmingham* 1451 ib, Orm², *Kirmincham* 1459 ib

   Kernincham 1286 *Eyre*, *-yn-* 1375 VR, *-yngham* 1310 Plea, *-ycham* 1307 *Eyre* (p), *-icham* 1422 Plea

   Kerincham, -yn- 1353 *Dav*, *Indict et freq* to 1547 Orm², *(-alias Kermyncham)* 1434 Plea, *-yngham* 1394 Cl, 1510 ChRR, *-ynge-* 1401 *Dav*, *Kiryncham* 1465 *Outl*, *-ingham* 1652 BM, *Keyryncham* 1515 *ChEx*, *Kerr-* 1534 Orm², *Caryngham* 1517 *ChEx*, *-ing-* 1559 Orm² *et freq* to 1675 Sheaf, *-inge-, -ynge-* 1579 ChRR, *AddCh*,

-yncham 1517 *ChEx*, *-inch-* 1559 Pat, *Karingham* 1520 *Sotheby*, *Kar(r)yncham* 1522 Plea, 1538 *AddCh*, *Karingham* 1724 NotCestr, *Carryngham* 1574 *Dow*, *-ing-* 1621 Orm², *Charyngcham* 1553 Pat, *-incham* 1597 *Dav*
Callingeham 1650 *ParlSurv*, *Calingcham* 1682 Plea
Kimmincham 1839 *TA*

Either 'the home of Cēnfriδ's people', from *-ingahām* and the OE pers.n. *Cēnfriδ*, as suggested in DEPN, or 'the village *Cēnfriδing*', from *hām* with an *-ing²* formation upon the pers.n., *v.* Altrincham 7 *supra*. Dr von Feilitzen suggests that the various forms of this p.n. have evolved from two developments of OE **Cēnfriδing(a)-hām*, (a) late OE **Kenverδingham* (metathesis of *-friδ* to *-ferδ*, voicing of *f*), (b) late OE **Kemverδingham* (*-n-* > *-m-* before *f*, *v*). From (a) would come **Keverδing-* (loss of *-n-* before *f*, *v*) > **Kevṛδingham* (*-er-* > *-ṛ-*) > *Kerδing-* (reduction of *-vṛδ-* to *-rδ-*) whence *Kerthingham*, *Kerdingham* and *Kerringham* (*-rd-* > *-rr-*). From (b) would come **Kemṛδing-* (with reduction of *-er-* to *-ṛ-* and loss of interconsonantal *-f-*, *-v-*) > **Kemṛing-* (with reduction of *-mṛδ-* to *-mṛ-*) > *Kerming-* (with metathesis) > *Kerning-* (with assimilation of nasals).

ROWLEY HALL & HO, *Rouheleg'* 1274–81 *Dav*, *Rouley* 1309 Pat (p), *-legh* 1342 ChRR (p), *Row-* 1335 AD (p), *-ley* 1393 ChRR (p), *Rolegh* 1353 *Dav*, *-ley* 1396 Orm² (p), *Rowe-*, *Rouelegh* 1373 ib, Plea (p), 'rough clearing', *v.* rūh, lēah.

BESWICK'S RUNDLE, cf. *Bissex Field* 1839 *TA*, from the surname *Beswick* and dial. *rundle* 'a small stream', *v.* rynel. Cf. 284 *infra*. BROOK FM, named from Swettenham Brook 284 *infra*. CROSS LANE (FM). THE FIELDS FM, 'farm in the fields'. THE FOLLY, *v.* folie. FORTY ACRE LANE, 1831 Bry, cf. *Frosty Acre Meadow* 1839 *TA*. GREENHEY WOOD, *Green Hey* 1839 *ib*, 'green enclosure', *v.* grēne¹, (ge)hæg. (LOWER) HEATH FM, cf. *Heath Inclosure &* *Plantation* 1839 *ib*, Kermincham Heath *infra*, Swettenham Heath 284 *infra*, *v.* hǣδ. KERMINCHAM HALL, HEATH & LODGE, 1831 Bry, *Karingham Hall* 1724 NotCestr, *Carmingham Hall* 1784 Sheaf. KERMINCHAM WOOD. LANE END FM. LONGHOUSE FM. LONG LANE FM. OLDHOUSE FM. PIGEON HOUSE CLOUGH, 1831 Bry, *v.* clōh. SAWPIT FM, *v.* saw-pytt. SHINGLAR WOOD, perhaps a wood where a shingler got shingles. WHITE HO.

FIELD-NAMES

The undated forms are 1839 *TA* 226. Of the others, 1308, E2 are Orm²,
1464, 1560 *Dav*, 1308², 1648 *AddCh*.

(*a*) Acre Mdw; Barn Bank; Bottoms (*v.* botm); Brawshot Clough (*v.*
clōh); Broom Fd (*v.* brōm); Cattons (*v.* cat(t), tūn); Church Walk (*v.* walk);
Collin; Dane Mdw (from R. Dane 1 20); Two-, Four- & Seven Day
Work (*v.* day-work); Dry Pit Fd (cf. *Drye Pyttes* 1560, *v.* drȳge, pytt);
Furneys Croft (*v.* furneis 'a furnace'); Furnwall Bank ('(bank at) the ferny
spring', *v.* fearn, wælla); Gorsey Bank, Gorsty Fd (*v.* gorstig); Half Crown
Fd (probably named from a rent, *v.* 326 *infra*); Hall Heys (cf. Kermincham
Hall *supra*); Hockenhulls Wd (either from the surname *Hockenhull* or 'oak-
grown hill', *v.* ācen, hyll); House Acre; Intack, Intake (*v.* inntak); Longtons
Woods & Yards (from the surname Longton, *v.* geard); Marl Bank, Marle
Fd; Mawbanks Mdw (from the surname *Maubanc*, cf. Malbon's Croft 284
infra, Lach Dennis 186 *supra*); Muncorn Fd; Outlet (*v.* outlet); Oven Fd
(*v.* ofen); Park; The Patch; Peartree Bank; Plumbs (*v.* plūme); Rough
Banks; Sand Fd; Shaw Croft (*v.* sceaga); Spout Mdw (*v.* spoute); Sun Fd
(*v.* sunne); Tan Croft ('tannery croft', *v.* tan); Well Major (perhaps analogous
with the f.n. type *Marljurr* discussed under Blackeyer 1 265); Wood
Bank.

(*b*) *Blakedene within Kerthingham* 1308 ('the black valley', *v.* blæc, denu,
cf. Blackden 222 *supra*); *Boterlegh*' 1308² ('rich pasture' *v.* butere, lēah);
Bothefeld E2 ('field at a booth', *v.* bōth, feld); *Gylmyns londe* 1464 ('William's
selion', from the ME pers.n. *Gylmyn*, OFr *Guillemin*, diminutive of *Guillaume*,
and land); *the Mawde Croft* 1648 (from either the fem. pers.n. *Maud* or
molde 'mould' and croft); *the Killne Feilde* 1648 (*v.* cyln).

2. SWETTENHAM (110–8167) ['swetnəm]

> *Suetenham* 112 Chest (p), 1220–30 *AddCh* (p), *Swet-* e13 Chest (p)
> *et freq* with variant spellings *Schwet-, Squet-, Scwet-, Sweth-,*
> *Sueth-, -en(h)am* to 1621 Orm², (*-under Lyne, -subtus Linee*) 1335
> Pat, *Mont, Swetinham* 1260 Court (p), *-yn(g)-* 1390 Pat (p), 1391
> ChRR (p), *-ing-* (*near Marton*) 1551 ChRR, *Swetunham* c.1262
> *Dav* (p), *-on-* 14 *ib* (p)
> *Sweteham* 1278 Ipm (p), *Squete-* l13 *Dav* (p)
> *Swettenham* 1283 (17) Chest (p), l13 MidCh (p), 1343 VR, 1393
> ChRR *et freq, -an-* 1602 Cre (p)
> *Sweteneham* 1296 Ipm (p)
> *Swentenham* 1451 ChRR (p)
> *Swetnam* 1557 Sheaf, *Swettnam* 1576 *Dav*
> *Swittnam* 1660 *Dav*

'Swēta's homestead or village', from the OE pers.n. *Swēta* and hām. The form *Suetenhala* 1183 P quoted in DEPN belongs to Wettenhall 327 *infra*. *Lyne* is *The Lyme* 1 2.

BESWICK'S RUNDLE, *v.* 282 *supra*.   CHAPEL WOOD, *v.* chapel(e). CAWLEY FM, *Cowley Field House* 1839 *TA*, cf. *Cow Hill & Lane ib*, and *parwm Quehey* 1313 *Dav*, 'the cow enclosure, field, hill, lane and clearing', *v.* cū (gen.pl. cūa), (ge)hæg, hyll, lane, feld, lēah, parvus.   CLOUD HILL, 1831 Bry, 'the hill', *v.* clūd, hyll, cf. The Cloud 291 *infra*.   CLOUTERBROOK FM (1831 Bry), CLOUTER WOOD, named from Clouter Brook 1 19.   DAVENPORT HO, cf. *Davenport Flatt* 1839 *TA*, named from Davenport 301 *infra*, on the opposite bank of R. Dane, *v.* flat.   THE FOLLY FM, *v.* folie. FOX HALL, *v.* fox, hall.   HALL FM, named from Swettenham Hall. HOME FM, *v.* home.   MILL HO & WOOD, *Mill Clough, Field & Wood* 1839 *TA*, named from Swettenham Mill *infra*, *v.* clōh.   PIT FM, cf. *Pit Field* 1839 *ib*, *v.* pytt.   SANDY LANE.   SWETTENHAM BROOK (R. Dane), *-Brook* 1619 Sheaf.   SWETTENHAM GREEN, 1831 Bry.   SWETTENHAM HALL, 1724 NotCestr, *the Hall of Swettnam* 1576 *Dav*.   SWETTENHAM HEATH, 1831 Bry, *v.* hǣð, cf. Kermincham Heath, Heath Fm 282 *supra*.   SWETTENHAM MILL, 1724 NotCestr, *molendinum de Swetenam* 1345 *Dav*, cf. Mill Ho *supra*, *v.* myln.   SWETTENHAM RD, *Swettenham Lane* 1831 Bry, running into Somerford Booths, *v.* 1 65.   TRAP RD, running into Lower Withington, *v.* Trap St. 1 91 *supra*.

FIELD-NAMES

The undated forms are 1839 *TA* 381. Of the others, 13, 1313, 1607 are *Dav*, 1268 Tab, 1386 ChRR, 1570 Sheaf, 1831 Bry.

(a) The Bank(s); Black Fd & Hay; Bottoms (*v.* botm); Broad Eye ('broad water-meadow', *v.* brād, ēg); Broomfield Bank (*v.* brōm, feld); The Bulls; Church Fd; The Clough (*v.* clōh); Companow; Crabtree Farm 1831; Cross Butts ('selions lying athwart', *v.* cros, butte); Dane Bridge Mdw, Davenport Bridge Mdw (cf. Davenport Bridge 301 *infra*, R. Dane 1 20); Two-, Four- & Five Day(s) Work (*v.* day-work); Dolla Moor; Dry Fds; The Eye (*v.* ēg); Flax Eye (*v.* fleax, ēg); Gayley Mdw (*v.* gagel, and lēah or ēg); Gorsy Intack (*v.* inntak); Gravelly Bank; Grinding Stone Fd; Hall Croft Wd (1831); Hemp Yard (*v.* hemp-yard); Hole Bottom (*v.* hol[1], botm); Holmes Bank (*v.* holmr); Intack (*v.* inntak); Kitchen Mdw; Knowle or Bank (*v.* cnoll, banke); The Ley (*v.* lēah); Malbon's Croft (from the surname

Malbon, Maubank, cf. Mawbanks Mdw 283 *supra*); Missick (*v.* mizzick); Moslin Wd (cf. Moslin 313 *infra*); North Wd (1831); Big- & Little Oulton(s), Oultons Wd (*v.* ald, tūn); Oven Fd; Patch; Pearse Fd, Perkins Heath (perhaps from the ME pers.ns. *Piers, Perkin,* for *Peter, v.* hǣð); Pingot(t) (*v.* pingot); Sand Fd (cf. Sount Fd *infra*); Shear Wd (*v.* scīr²); Sheet Follow, Street Tullow Wd (*scitfoldeley* 13, *Shutfallow Wood* 1831, '(clearing at) the midden-yard', *v.* scite, fald and lēah, cf. *Westedis* 1 66); Sount Fd (*v.* sand, cf. Sand Fd *supra*); Sour Butts (*v.* sūr, butte); Tan Yard 1831 (*v.* tan-yard); Timber Bank (*v.* timber); Town Fd; Wall Bank Wd (*v.* wælla, banke, cf. foll.); Well Bank (cf. prec); White Ley (*v.* lēah).

(*b*) *Duddockes More* 1607 (from mōr¹, perhaps with a surname, cf. the OE pers.ns. *Duddac, Dudec, -uc*); *le Hethalle* 1386 ('heath nook', *v.* hǣð, halh); *Quitey* 13 ('white enclosure', *v.* hwīt, (ge)hæg); *Threphurstisclok* (*v.* 1 66); *Yeverleye* 1268, *Yerileg', Yerlleg'* 13, *Yherileth* 1313, *Yerlay* 1570 (perhaps 'heifers' clearing', *v.* hēah-fore, lēah, but Dr von Feilitzen suggests as first el. eofor 'a boar', which would account better for prosthetic *i̯-* (*y-*) and medial *-v-*, cf. Everley YN 115, Yearsley YN 193).

xii. Astbury

The ancient parish of Astbury comprised the townships 1. Eaton 1 61 and 2. Somerford Booths 1 63 in Macclesfield Hundred, and the following in Northwich Hundred, 3. Newbold Astbury, 4. Buglawton (*v.* foll.), 5. Congleton (a municipal borough chartered in 1272, 1624–5 and 1835, now a c.p. including Buglawton *supra*), 6. Davenport (*v.* Brereton 274 *supra*), 7. Hulme Walfield, 8. Moreton cum Alcumlow, 9. Odd Rode, 10. Smallwood, 11. Somerford cum Radnor. Also in Astbury parish, originally, were Brereton, Swettenham and Church Lawton, parishes, *v.* 274, 281 *supra*, 320 *infra*, Orm² III 21, 70.

3. NEWBOLD ASTBURY (110–8461), *Newbold & Astebury* 1320 Plea, *Astebur' Neubold* 1344 *Eyre*, *Newbold Astbury* 1348 ChRR *et freq*, *passim* with variant spellings as for Astbury and *Newbold infra*. It looks as though the original name of the township was *Newbold*. Astbury is not mentioned in DB, whereas Newbold appears there with a priest. Astbury seems to have been the name of a small manor within Newbold, including the site of the parish church, and belonging to St Werburgh's Abbey, Chester, *v.* Orm² III 21, cf. *ecclesia de Astbury cum medietate bosci et plani et omnium quæ pertinent ad Newbold* 1093 ib 25. The ecclesiastical and manorial importance of Astbury would have caused the name *Newbold* to be superseded by that of Astbury. However, there remains a possibility that Astbury is in fact the more ancient name, but that by 1086 the manorial

centre had been moved to a new site at Newbold, and that the old name and site returned to pre-eminence as a result of St Werburgh's possession of Astbury and the site of the parish church there.

ASTBURY (110–846616) [ˈæsbəri]

>Astbury 1093 Orm² (ecclesia de), 1162–82, 1265–91 Chest et freq
> with variant spellings Aste- (1174–84 Chest et freq to 1444 ChRR),
> -bur(i), bury(e), -burie, -byr(i), -biri, -biry, -beri, -bery(e), -br';
> Hastebury 1347 Eyre, Astbury & Newbold Astbury 1579 Orm²,
> the manor of Astbury 1580 ib, the capital messuage called Astbury
> demesne 1660 ib
>Est(e)buri(a) 1096–1101 (1280) Chest, 1154–8 (17) ib et freq to 1471
> MinAcct, with variant spellings -bury, -bur(ie), -birie, -beri
>Esebury 1355 MinAcct
>Asteabury 1393 Morris
>Ashebury 1510 Sheaf, 1527 ChCert, -burie 1579 AD
>Asbury 1544 Sheaf, -bery 1585 ib
>Askebery 1591 Sheaf
>Austbury 1621 Orm²

'The east manor or stronghold', v. ēast, burh. There is a rectangular earthwork at Glebe Fm infra, at the south-east side of the churchyard, which could represent the burh.

NEWBOLD (lost)

>Neubold 1086 DB, Neu-, Newbolt, -bold 13 AD, Dieul, 1259 Plea,
> 1268 (18) Sheaf et freq with variant spellings -bolde, -boldt,
> -bolte, -bould, (-iuxta Magna Morton sub Lymam) 1289 Court,
> (-subtus Lynam) 1350 Plea, (-under Lime) 1350 AD, (-by Astbury)
> 1446 ib, (-infra parochia de Astbury) 1536 Orm², (-in Astebery)
> 1539 Dugd, (-alias Newbold Astbury) 1591 ChRR, Newebold
> 1327 Cl, Newbald 1430 Orm², -balt 1535 VE
>Neobald, -bold 1096–1101 (1280) Chest
>Noubold 1354 AD, 1399 Surv

'The new house', v. nīwe, bold. Cf. Great Moreton 304 infra, The Lyme 1 2. The manor house may have been at Peel Fm infra. Cf. Newbold Wd infra.

BANK FM, Lower Holmes 1831 Bry, Lower Hulme 1842 OS, cf. Upper Hulme infra, v. holmr, hulm, banke, cf. The Bank 1831 Bry, 1842

OS. BAYTREE FM. BENT FM & LANE, *The Bent* 1593 JCJ, *Bent Lane* 1831 Bry, *Bent Farm & Fields* 1842 OS, from beonet 'bentgrass', with lane, mæd, feld. BLACK COB, an eminence on Mow Cop *infra*, 'the black knoll', *v.* blæc, cobb(e). BRICKHOUSE, 1831 Bry, *v.* bryke, hūs. BROOK FM & Ho, *The Brookhouse* 1636 *Dep*, *Brook Houses* 1842 OS, *v.* brōc. The farm is near Dairy Brook *infra*, the house is near an un-named stream under Edge Hill *infra*. BROWNLOW (FM & HEATH), (*the*) *Browne Low(e)* 1586 *Rental*, 1666 *Sheaf*, *Brownlow Common, Radnor Wood* 1831 Bry, *Brownlow Heath* 1842 OS, '(heath & common at) the brown mound', *v.* brūn¹, hlāw, hǣð, commun. CHARITY FM, *Reeves' Farm* 1724 NotCestr, *Reeves Farm* 1831 Bry, 1842 OS, from the surname *Reeve*. This is part of an eighteenth-century bequest to the poor of Middlewich, ChetOS VIII 250. CHESHIRE'S CLOSE, *inclosure adjoining Cheshires* 1839 *TA*, from clos and the surname *Cheshire*. CHILD'S LANE, 1831 Bry. CISS GREEN, *Siss Green* 1842 OS, cf. *Sess Lane* 1831 Bry, -*Field* 1839 *TA*, perhaps from cess 'a rate, a tax' (NED) and grēne² 'a green', but cf. *Syssocusfeld infra*. CORDA WELL, cf. *Cord Hay* (*Meadow*) 1839 *ib*, *v.* wella. *Cord(h)a(y)* might be 'cold stream' from cald and ēa. DAIRY BROOK (FM & BRIDGE), *Dairy Brook* 1831 Bry, (*Farm*) 1842 OS, 'brook named from a dairy', *v.* deierie, brōc. The brook joins Loach Brook 1 30. DOBB'S LANE, *Limekiln Lane* 1831 Bry, cf. Limekiln Fm *infra*. *Dobb* is a surname. DUBTHORN, 1831 ib, 'cropped thorn', *v.* dubbed, þorn. EDGE HILL, *Bilsbury Hill* 1831 ib, cf. *Edge Close* 1839 *TA*, *v.* ecg, hyll, clos, cf. Congleton Edge 297 *infra*. The earlier name is probably 'hill where bilberries grow', *v.* bilberry, but may be from bile or bill 'a promontory' with beorg or burh. FAIRFIELDS, *Fairfield* 1593 JCJ, *v.* fæger, feld. FENCE LANE, *Kirk Lane* 1831 Bry, probably from the surname *Kirk* and lane. FIELDHOUSE FM, *Field House* 1831 ib, *v.* feld. GLEBE FM, adjoining the churchyard, cf. Astbury *supra*, *v.* glebe. THE GORSE, GORSE LANE, *The Gorse* 1842 OS, *Gorse Green* 1831 Bry, *v.* gorst, grēne², lane. HILL FM, cf. *le Hulle house* 1399 *Surv*, *v.* hyll, hūs. HOLLY WOOD, 1842 OS, *v.* holegn, wudu. UPPER HULME, 1842 ib, *Higher Holmes* 1831 Bry, cf. Bank Fm *supra*, *v.* holmr, hulm 'an island, a water-meadow'. LIMEKILN FM, 1842 OS, named from *Newport Lime Works* 1831 Bry, cf. Dobb's Lane *supra*, *v.* līm, cyln. LOCKETT'S TENEMENT, *Shrigleys Smithy* 1842 OS, *v.* smiððe. MILLHOUSE, 1842 ib, cf. *Neubold mulne* 1404 *MinAcct*, *v.* myln, hūs. MORETON COTTAGES, cf.

Great Moreton 304 *infra*.   Moss Rd, cf. *the Mosse* 1586, 1594
Rental, *v.* mos, cf. Congleton Moss 297 *infra*.   Mow Cop, 1831
Bry, *v.* 308 *infra*.   Nick i' th' Hill, cf. *Nyckeredyng* 1399 *Surv*,
the Nickereadinges 1511 *Rental*, *the Nickryddinges* 1585 AD, *Nick-
ridinges* 1586 *Rental*, *nycckereddynges* 1594 *ib*, *Big-*, *Little-* & *Lower
Nickriding(s)* 1839 *TA*. The name alludes to a col on Congleton Edge
297 *infra* and Edge Hill *supra*, *v.* nick(e), ryding, hyll.   Oak Fm,
1831 Bry.   Peel Fm & Lane (110–854612), *Peel* (*Lane*) 1831 ib,
named from a moated site adjacent, perhaps the site of *the maner
house* 1586 *Rental*, *the manar-*, *manor howse*, *-hosse* 1594 *ib*, *Surv*, *v.*
pēl (*peel* NED), lane, cf. *Newbold supra*, Peel 327 *infra*.   Pot Bank.
Styeheath, *Sty Heath* 1831 Bry, from either stīg 'a path' or stigu
'a sty, a pen', and hǣð.   Wallhill Fm & Lane, *le Wallehull* 1399
Surv, *the Wallehill* 1586 *Rental*, *Walhill'* 1454 *Eyre*, 1475 MidCh,
1594 *Surv*, (*the*) *wall hill* 1475 MidCh, 1511 *Rental*, *-hyll* 1594 *ib*,
1603 Sheaf, *Brownhill Lane* 1831 Bry, 'hill at a spring', 'brown hill',
v. wælla, hyll, brūn[1], lane.   Watery Lane, *Water Lane* 1831 ib,
v. wæter, lane.   Weld House Fm, 1831 ib, *Hockerdilly* 1842 OS,
cf. John *Welde* 1593 JCJ.   Whetstonedge, 1831 Bry, *Wetstones
Edge* 1842 OS, cf. Westons Edge 278 *supra*, *Whetstone Corner Croft*
1839 *TA*, 'hill-edge where whetstones are got', *v.* hwet-stān, ecg.
Whitethorn, *v.* hwīt, þorn.

FIELD-NAMES

The undated forms are 1839 *TA* 287. Of the others, 1281, 1289 are Court,
1334 *AddCh*, 1399, 1594[2] *Surv*, 1404 *MinAcct*, 1446, 1575, 1585, 1596 AD,
1505 Sheaf, 1511, 1586, 1594[1] *Rental*, 1531, 1619 Orm[2], 16 *AOMB* 397,
1540 Dugd, 1636 *Dep*, and 1831 Bry.

(a) Acre; Apple French; Backhouse Fd (*v.* bæc-hūs); Back Lane Pringle
(probably 'a little plot of land on the back lane' from dial. *pringle* 'a small
coin', or pingel); Belshaw (probably from sceaga 'a wood, a copse'); Bentley
Leys, Benty Leys (cf. *le Bentileye Heye* 1399, '(enclosure at) the grassy
clearing', *v.* beonet, -ig[3], (cf. benty), lēah, (ge)hæg); Birchen Fd; Black
Dole (*v.* dāl); Black-, Bleak Fd (*le Blakefeld* 1399, cf. *le Blakeacur* ib, *v.* blæc,
feld, æcer); Black Hurst Head, Bleak Hurst (*v.* blæc, hyrst, hēafod); Boozey
Fd (*v.* bōsig); Breach Fd (*v.* brēc); Broad Fd (*le Brodeffeld* 1399, *v.* brād,
feld); Broad Oak Fd; Brook Flatt (*v.* flat); Broom Fd (*le Bromefeld* 1399,
1404, *v.* brōm, feld); Bulkley Flash 1831 (*v.* flasshe); Casshaw Croft ('cat's
wood', *v.* cat(t), sceaga); Carry Nothing (presumably a barren field); Castle
Fd; Cathrines Deans Croft, -Dour, -Dowle & -Intack (probably 'Catherine
Dean's croft, dower-land, allotment and intake', from croft, dāl, inntak and

dowarie, with the fem. pers.n.); Church Fd; Clay Flatt(s) (*v.* clǣg, flat);
Cobb Fd (*v.* cobbe); Cock Shute (*v.* cocc-scyte); Cooks Pit Croft (*v.* cockpit,
cf. Cookspit 326 *infra*); Corner Croft; Cow Hay; Crabtree Croft; Cross
Croft & Fd (cf. *Cross Heath* 1831, from a ruined cross at 110–845620 on the
Congleton boundary, *v.* cros, hǣð); Four-, Five-, Six- & Three Day(s)
Work (*v.* day-work); Dodder; Dowle (*v.* dāl); Drakes Foot Bottom, -Head
& -Nook (*v.* fōt, botm, hēafod, nōk. *Drakes* may be the gen.sg. of rake or
hraca prefixed by the reduced def. art.); Dry Leas (*Drylees* 1593 JCJ, *v.*
lǣs); East Bed (*v.* ēast, bedd); Big & Little Fall (*le Falle* 1399, *v.* (ge)fall);
Flash Fd (cf. *Flashecroft* 1593 JCJ, *v.* flasshe); Fox Fd; French Fd (*v.*
french-wheat); Gennetts Croft (*Gennettes croft* 1511, 'horse paddock', from
jennet 'a small Spanish horse' (NED) and croft); Gorsty Bank Lane 1831
(*v.* gorstig); Grandfathers Croft; Halfpenny Patch (*v.* halfpeny, pacche);
Hedlock; Hemp Yard (*v.* hemp-yard); High Hays (*the* (*High*) *Heighis* 1505,
the High Hayes 1531, 1619, *v.* hēah, (ge)hæg); Hollins Dole (*v.* holegn, dāl);
Hungary Hill (a variant of the common 'hungry hill', *v.* hungrig, hyll);
Intacks (cf. *the Intak* 1586, *v.* inntak); Jolly Hey; Kettle Croft (*v.* keddle-
dock); Kiln Fd; Knowl, Knowle Hill (*v.* cnoll); Leas Fd (cf. *le Leghes* 1399,
v. lēah); Long Shute (*v.* scēat); Loon (*v.* land); Many Ways (not near an
intersection of roads); Mark Fd (*v.* mearc); Marl Fd; Big & Little Marsh
(cf. *Marsh Gate* 1831 Bry, The Marsh 298 *infra*, *v.* mersc, geat); Moorton
Fd (*v.* Gt. Moreton 304 *infra*); Mossley (*Moseley Hey* 1505, *Mosseley-*
1596, *Moseley* 1586, *Mosley* 1594, 'clearing at a moss', *v.* mos, lēah, (ge)hæg);
Newbold Wd (1575, cf. *Neuboltfeld* 1446, *v.* feld, *Newbold supra*); New
Hay; Nine Butts (*v.* nigon, butte); Nook; North Fd; Odd Fd (*v.* odde); Old
House Croft; Old Womans Fd; Older Hays, Oldery Fd (*v.* alor, (ge)hæg);
Oven Fd; Ox Hay (*v.* (ge)hæg); Pancridge Fd (cf. Penkridge St, and 155
supra); Paradise (*v.* paradis); Park Fd; Parlour Fd (*v.* parlur); Parsons Croft
& Fd (*v.* persone); Pear Tree Fd (cf. *le Peretrihelondis* 1281, '(selions at)
pear-tree enclosure' *v.* peru, trēow, (ge)hæg, land); Pinfold Fd (*v.* pynd-
fald); Pingo (*v.* pingot); Poolstead (*the Poole Styddes alias Poole Place* 1585,
v. pōl-stede, pōl[1], place); Rye Croft & Fds (*the Rye Field* 1593 JCJ, *v.* ryge);
St Mary's Croft; Sanbach Lane Mdw (cf. Sandbach 269 *supra*); Spen
Green (*v.* spenne); Sprink Wd (*v.* spring); Stanniel (*v.* stānig, hyll); Stew
Fd (*v.* stewe); Stoney Flatt (*v.* stānig, flat); Stonniers Way (from the
occupational name *stone-hewer*, *stonier*, perhaps as a surname); Tenter Loon
(*v.* tentour, land); Three Butts (*v.* butte); Turf Pits ('peat diggings', *v.*
turf, pytt); Twin Acres (*v.* twinn); Wall Croft & Mdw (*v.* wǣlla, cf. foll);
Well Croft(s) (cf. prec.); Wheelock Close (cf. Wheelock 273 *supra*); White
Fd, Whitfields Mdw (cf. *le Whitemedo* 1399, *v.* hwīt, mǣd); Wickens Hay,
Wiggens Hay (from cwicen, dial. *whicken* 'a mountain ash' and (ge)hæg);
Winshaw Fd ('gorse wood', *v.* hvin, sceaga); Winter Fd (*v.* winter[1]);
Yardley Hay (*The Adderley Hayes* 1636, *v.* lēah, (ge)hæg; the first el.
cannot be ascertained).

(b) *Beyekefeld* 1399 (*v.* feld); *le Callurheye* 1399 ('the calves' enclosure',
v. calf (gen.pl. calfra), (ge)hæg); *the com(m)onclowghe* 1511, 1594, *-Cloughe*
1586 ('common dell', *v.* commun, clōh); *Cortusfeld* 1399 (perhaps 'court-

house field', *v.* court, hūs, feld); *The Eaves Farm* 1636 (*v.* efes 'a border, an edge', but a surname is possible here); *the Foure Acres* 1585; *the horsemyll, -mylne* 1594[1], [2] ('a mill driven by a horse', *v.* horse-myln); *Lynna* 16, 1540 (a hamlet, location not known, derivation obscure); *the poles wyndmill* 1511 (from pāl 'a pole, a stake' and **wind-mylne**); *Syssocusfeld* 1399 (perhaps for *Syssotus-*, from *Cissot*, diminutive of *Ciss*, a short-form of *Cecilia, Cecily*, and feld, cf. Ciss Green *supra*); *le Sourelondis* 1281 ('the sour selions', *v.* sūr, land); *le Stywardisheye* 1281 ('the steward's enclosure', *v.* stig-weard, (ge)hæg); *Wilshaw Howse, Wilshawe* 1511 (probably 'wild wood', *v.* wilde, sceaga); *Wodehuses* 1289 (p), *le Wodehouse(s) in Newbold* 1334 ('houses at a wood', *v.* wudu, hūs).

4. BUGLAWTON (110–8863) ['bug'lɔ:tǝn]

> *Lautune* 1086 DB, *Lauton* 1278 Ipm, l13 *Dav*, 1299 Ch, 1304 ChF, 1561 ChRR
>
> *Buggelauton* 1287 Court, 1312 *BW*, 1334 Plea, 1340 *Eyre*, 1359 Pat (p)
>
> *Boggelauton* 1337 Plea, 1343 Bark
>
> *Buglauton* 1357 *ChTourn*, 1399 Plea, *-laweton* 1434 ib, *-lawton* 1468 ib, (*-alias Buglaughton*) 1549 Orm[2], *-laton* 1516 Sheaf, *-laughton* 1526 ib, *Bugglaton* 1547 ChRR
>
> *Bucglauton* 1454 *AddRoll*
>
> *Bugleton* 1487 *MinAcct*
>
> *Buklawton* 1527 Plea
>
> *Bugland* 1547 ChRR
>
> *Burglawtone alias Burglaughtone* 1567 *AddCh*

'Farm by a mound', *v.* hlāw, tūn, cf. Lowe Fm *infra*. The original form survives in *Lawton Hollows* 1831 Bry, *v.* Hollows *infra*, and was current in local usage down to the nineteenth century. The affix is **bugge** 'a hob-goblin' and distinguishes this place from Church Lawton 320 *infra*, cf. Buglaw 1 191.

CROSSLEY (HALL)

> *Crossel(eg)*, *-le(gh)*, *-ley(e)* 13 Chest (p), 1271 *BW*, 1278 Ipm, 1282 Court, 1286 ib (p), 1289 Plea (p), *Superior Crosseleg* l13 *Dav*, *le Crosselegh* 1377 ChRR (p), *Croseley* 1278 IpmR, *-leg'* c.1370 *BW* (p), *Crossileg'* 1280 *AddCh* (p)
>
> *Crossleghe* 1283 MidCh (p), *-leg(h)* 1321 *BW* (p), 1353 MidCh (p), *-ley* 1394 ChRR (p), *Crosley* 1445 ib
>
> *Crossledge (Hall)* 1831 Bry

'Clearing with a cross', *v.* cros, lēah. The form *Crossledge* recurs in *Crosledge* 297 *infra*, and is probably incorrect for this place.

ACORN LANE. ALDERS FM, *v.* alor. BANK HO, *Bank Top* 1831 Bry, named from Hardings Bank *infra*. BATH VALE, cf. *Bath Wood* 1840 *TA*, 1842 OS, and *The Bath* 1882 Orm² III 42, a mineral spring in a coppice, good for scrofula and scorbutic cases, probably *fons Sancti Oswaldi* 1300 AD 'St Oswald's spring', *v.* bæð, val, wudu. HIGH BENT, 1842 OS, cf. *Bent* 1840 *TA*, *v.* beonet 'bent-grass'. BOUGHMOOR FM, *Bolemore* 1343 Bark, *Bullemor' howse* 1493 *AddCh*, *Bull Moor* 1840 *TA*, 'bull marsh', *v.* boli, bula, mōr¹. BRIDE-STONES, 1831 Bry, *The-* 1882 Orm², apparently from brȳd 'a bride' and stān 'a stone'; the remains of a megalithic burial-mound, *v.* Varley 34. There are, of course, local legends associated with the site (Orm² III 43 n., cf. also *Antiquity* XII 351–3), but the name is typical, occurring elsewhere in the country as a name for megalithic groups etc., cf. *bride-stones* (EDD and F. K. Robinson, *A glossary of words used in the neighbourhood of Whitby*, EDS 1873), also Bride Stones WRY 3 174, 7 73. BROCKSGREEN. BROOK HO, 1831 Bry, *v.* brōc. CAT STONES, *Cats Cliff* 1831 ib, probably 'rocks frequented by the wild cat', *v.* cat(t), stān, clif. THE CLOUD, CLOUD SIDE, cf. *Cloude Wod* H8 Sheaf, *Penket Cloud* 1656 Orm², *(the) Cloud hill, the Cloud* 1819 ib, 1831 *EnclA*, 'rocky hill', *v.* clūd, hyll, cf. Cloudberry I 232, Cloud Hill 284 *supra*. The Cloud is a prominent hill on the county boundary, rising to 1,125 feet. *Penket* is probably a British name, 'wood on a hill', *v.* penno-, cēto-, cf. Penketh La 106, Penge Sr 14. Cloud Side is a hamlet on the slope of the hill, *v.* sīde. COACH & HORSES (p.h.), *Fairhouse* (*Inn*) 1831 Bry, 1842 OS. COLLEYMILL BRIDGE, *v.* I 59. CROUCH LANE, 1831 Bry, 'lane with a cross', *v.* crouche, lane. LOWER DANE-EN-SHAW (lost), 1842 OS, *v.* Dane In Shaw 296 *infra*, Dane-enshaw *infra*. DIG-LAKE, 1831 Bry, 'watercourse in a ditch', *v.* dīc, lacu. EATON BANK, *v.* banke, cf. Eaton I 61. BIG FENTON, 1842 OS, *Great Fenton* 1831 Bry, *tenement called Fenton's* 1752 Sheaf, apparently from a surname *Fenton*. FINGERPOST FM, *-House* 1842 OS. FOLLY COTTAGE, *v.* folie. GOSBERRYHOLE LANE, *Big & Little Gosberry Hall* 1840 *TA*, perhaps alluding to either of the rural arts of Cheshire, raising show-gooseberries and playing chaperone, *v.* hol¹ 'a hollow'. J.C.J. observes that raising the fruit would be impossible at this altitude but a sheltered hollow might allow either sport.   GREENHOUSE, 1842 OS.   HARDINGS BANK, *Harding Bank* 1831 Bry, from an unidentified first component and banke 'a bank, a hillside'. J.C.J. observes that the surname *Harding* is not recorded in the district.   HAVANNAH, *The-* 1831 Bry, cf. 1 61, the site of a copper mill established 1761, the year the British captured Havana in Cuba (J.C.J.). White 455 reports the name as derived from a former cigar factory here.   HAVANNAH LANE (FM), *Clough House* 1831 Bry, 'house at a dell', *v.* clōh, hūs, cf. prec.   HINES-WOOD, *Hinds Wood (Farm)* 1831 ib, perhaps from *hind* 'a peasant, a labourer', *v.* hine, wudu.   HOLLY BANK.   HOOFRIDGE, HIGHER OVEREDGE, IRLAM HO, are respectively *High-, Low-, & Over Ridge* 1831 ib; the first two are *Ridge* and *Little Ridge* 1840 *TA*; the last two are *Lower Over Edge, Upper Edge* 1842 OS; from hrycg 'a ridge'. The later forms have ecg 'an edge' by metanalysis.   ISLAND HO, cf. *Island Croft* 1840 *TA*.   KEY GREEN, 1831 Bry, 'cattle pasture', *v.* cū, grēne², cf. another instance 1 56.   LIGHTHEY, 1831 ib, *-Hay* 1581 Sheaf, 'light enclosure', *v.* lēoht, (ge)hæg.   LOWE FM & HO, cf. *Lawton Low(e)* 1787 Sheaf, 1831 Bry, *Buglawton Low* 1842 OS, 'the mound at Buglawton', *v.* hlāw, cf. Buglawton *supra*.   MIDDLE LANE, 1831 Bry, *v.* middel, lane.   MOSSLEYVALE FM.   HIGHER OVEREDGE, *v.* Hoofridge *supra*.   PECKER POOL, *v.* 1 56.   PEDLEY HO & LANE, *Pedley House* 1831 ib, probably from the surname Pedley, cf. 1 182.   PEOVER, 1831 ib, perhaps called after Peover 220 *supra*, but the derived surname is possible, cf. Peavers Croft 314 *infra*.   POOL BANK, 1831 ib, *v.* pōl¹, banke.   QUARRY BANK.   RAINOW FM & HILL, *Rayney Hill* 1831 ib, cf. *Top of Rainer, Rainer Common, Rainows Inclosure* 1840 *TA*, obscure, unless 'raven's hill', from hræfn and hōh, analogous with Rainow 1 137.   ROOKERY FM, *Rookery* 1831 Bry, *v.* rookery.   SMITHY FM, *Smithy* 1831 ib, cf. *Smithy Plack* 1840 *TA*, le *Smethepleckis* 113 *Dav*, 'the smithy plot(s)', *v.* smiððe, smeðe², plek.   SPOUT, SPOUT-HOUSE FM, *Spouthouse* 1831 Bry, *v.* spoute, hūs.   SPRINGBANK (FM), 'bank at a spring', *v.* spring, banke.   TALL-ASH FM, *Tall Ash* 1831 ib, cf. *Tall Ash Wood* 1842 OS.   TANHOUSE FM, 1831 Bry, cf. *Tan Yard Croft* 1840 *TA*, a tannery, *v.* tan-house, tan-yard.   TIMBERSBROOK, *-Browk* 1840 *TA*, *Timber Brook* 1831, the name of a hamlet and a stream, 'brook running through timber-trees', *v.* timber, brōc.   VICARAGE, *Throstle Nest* 1831 ib, *v.* þrostle, nest.   HIGHER WASHFORD MILL, cf. *Lower Whashford* 1593 JCJ, 'ford at a washing-place', *v.* wæsce, ford, cf. *Wash Field, Meadow & Piece* 1840

TA. J.C.J. informs me of a flint-washing industry at this mill, where the flow of water is strong. Perhaps here was *Strongeford* 301 *infra.* WEATHERCOCK FM, 1831 Bry.   WOOD FM, WOODSIDE FM, *Wood Side* 1831 ib, *The Wood* 1842 OS, cf. *Woodfield* 1593 JCJ, *Wood House (Mill)* 1831 Bry, and *boscus de Lauton* 113 *Dav*, *v.* wudu, sīde, hūs, myln.   YEWTREE FM.

FIELD-NAMES

The undated forms are 1840 *TA* 82. Of the others 1831 is Bry, 1842 OS, and JCJ indicates forms reported by Mr J. C. Jones from local records.

(*a*) Acres (cf. *The Acres* 1831); Alm Flatt; Back Bone; Bank; Bean Roots (*v.* bēan, root); Beech (*v.* bece[1]); Biddulph Coppice (cf. Biddulph St); Birch Moss; Black Heath Common (*Black Heath* 1842); Blake Fd (*v.* blæc); Bogs (*v.* bog); Bottom (*v.* botm); Broad Hay & Lane; Broken Bank Waste (*v.* brocen, banke, waste); Broomaday ('(enclosure at) the broomy hill', *v.* brōm, hēafod, (ge)hæg); Broomy Bank; Bully; Butty Fd (*v.* butty); Calders (perhaps 'cold hill', *v.* cald, ears); Cheshire Brook Wd (*v.* Cheshire Brook 1 19); Clews, Clews Wd (*v.* wudu. The main el. may be clūs(e) 'a close, a narrow passage', cf. Clews Moors WRY 3 272); Coat(s) Fd (*v.* cot); Cobstarts (*v.* cobb(e), steort); Cobstow (*v.* cobb(e), stōw or stall); Cock Pit (*v.* cockpit); Cockshot (*v.* cocc-scyte); Cook Fd; Corn Pack; Cote Fd (*v.* cot); Cow Hay & Lane; Crumble Hay (*v.* crymel); Dairy (*v.* deierie); Dane Fd & Mdw (*v.* R. Dane 1 20); Dane(-)enshaw(s) Fd, Daneinshaw Fd (*Davenynsale Croft & Field* 1593 JCJ, cf. Dane in Shaw 296 *infra*); Day Croft (*v.* dey); Four-, Half-, Six-, Ten-, Three-, Twelve- & Two Days Work (*v.* day-work); Deanocks; Dean Wd 1842 (*v.* denu); Dear Bought (probably a poor field, a bad bargain, *v.* 326 *infra*); Denesons Wd 1842 (from a surname); Ditch Fd; Doe Croft (*v.* dāl); Driving Fd (a field across which cattle were driven to reach another one); Dunamay (perhaps from (ge)hæg 'an enclosure', with a p.n. *Dunhamm* 'hill enclosure', *v.* dūn, hamm, or the surname from Dunham 19 *supra*, 326 *infra*); Ferney Knowl House 1842 (*v.* fearnig, cnoll); Flash Mdw (*v.* flasshe); Flatt (*v.* flat); France (*v.* 326 *infra*); Gilders; Godhomsley (perhaps from the OE pers.n. *Godhelm* (as in Godalming Sr 195) and lēah); Gossey Hall (*v.* gorstīg, hol[1]); Gunbridge (probably a clearing where guns were stationed during a shoot, *v.* brēc); Gutter Fd (*v.* goter); Hackney (probably a horse-pasture, *v.* hakenei); Haggs (*v.* hogg); Haw Foot Wd, Howfoots (*v.* hōh, fōt); Hays Wd 1842 (*v.* (ge)hæg); Hob Croft (*v.* hobb(e) 'a tussock'); Hollows (*Lawton Hollows* 1831, *v.* holh, cf. Buglawton *supra*); Hook Heath (*v.* hōc, hæð); Howfoots (*v.* Haw Foot *supra*); Intake (*v.* inntak); Jack Stile (*v.* jack, stigel); Kei Croft (from ME kye, pl. of cou 'a cow', and croft); Kirk Stile (*v.* kirkja, stigel); Lady Croft (*v.* hlæfdige, croft); Lawton Howler (perhaps from alor 'an alder-tree'); Ley (*v.* lēah); Long Eye Bridge (*v.* lang, ēg, brycg); Long Shot (*Long Shoot Wood* 1842, *v.* lang, scēat); Madams Wd 1842; Marl Bank & Fd (*v.* marle); Matress Fd (perhaps a boggy or soft field, *v.* 326 *infra*); Mill Hill, Mdw &

Fd; Mop Mdw; Mope Fd; Mote Homestead (*v.* mote, hām-stede); Nan
Acre (perhaps 'Nan's acre', from the fem. pers.n. *Nan* (*Anne*), or 'knave's-,
boy's acre' from cnafa (gen.sg. cnafan, pl. cnafena), cf. Nangreave 1
297); Newings ('newly cultivated places', *v.* nīwe, -ing¹); Newton Land
(*v.* land; from a surname or from a place-name *Newton*, *v.* nīwe, tūn); Nick
House, Nickoth (Croft) (*v.* nick, hofuð); Oat o' Hay (probably 'enclosure
at *oat-halgh*', *v.* āte, halh, (ge)hæg); Ox Hay, -Hey (*v.* (ge)hæg); Park;
Parsons Fd; Patch; Peachley (*v.* piche, lēah); Pearl Hill (*v.* pyrl(e)); Pepper
Fd (cf. Pepper St. (Chester) 327 *infra*); Pinfold (*v.* pynd-fald); Pingle (*v.*
pingel); Pingot (*v.* pingot); Post Croft; Privy Garden; Ragg Acre; Roundabout (*v.* 327 *infra*); Rye Fd, Ryley (*v.* ryge, lēah); Saddle Back Fd (*v.* sadol,
bæc, cf. 327 *infra*); Sand Fd; Seed Fd; Shot Wd (*v.* scēat, wudu); Slack
(*v.* slakki); Slang Mdw (*v.* slang); Slew, Slough (*v.* slōh); Sprink ('a young
wood', *v.* spring); Stair Fd (*v.* stæger); Stay Field Bottom & Head (*v.*
stæg, cf. WRY 7 248); Swing Fd; Tom Hay (*v.* toun, (ge)hæg); Too Lail
('too little', from dial. *lile* (EDD) 'little', the name of a small field, cf. 327
infra); Town Fd ('common field', *v.* toun); Turn Hurst (*v.* trun, hyrst);
Turn Penny Fd (probably a field from which a quick profit could be raised,
v. turn-penny NED, cf. 327 *infra*); Twanley Mdw (perhaps 'at the two
glades', *v.* twēgen (dat. twǣm), lēah); Under the Wood; Wade Fd (*v.*
(ge)wæd); Wall Croft (*v.* wælla, croft); Way-, Wey Fd (*v.* weg); Webbs
Wd 1842 (from the surname *Webb*); Well Croft & Mdw (*v.* wella); Weston
Flatt (*v.* flat. The first component could be a surname, or hwet-stān, or a
p.n. 'west enclosure', *v.* west, tūn); Whittacar Lanes (*v.* hwīt, æcer, leyne);
Whittle (probably 'white hill', *v.* hwīt, hyll); Within Croft (*v.* wiðegn);
Wooll Mdw (*v.* wull); Wrias Mdw (probably 'Uriah's meadow', from the
pers.n. *Uriah*).

(*b*) *The Ryde Over* 1593 JCJ (probably a piece of ground with a right of
way through it, from the verb *to ride* and ofer³).

5. CONGLETON (110–8663) [ˈkɔŋ|tən, ˈkɔŋg|tn̩]

    Cogeltone 1086 DB, *-ton* 1355 ChRR

    Congun' c.1200 AddCh (p)

    Congulton c.1262 *Dav et freq* to 1498 AddCh, *-tone* 1465 Comb,
        Congilton E1 *JRC*, 1281 Court, *Congelton* 1281 Ch *et freq* to
        1433 ChRR

    Congletone 1295 Lacy, *-ton* 1322 Pat *et freq*, (*-apon Dane*) c.1536
        Leland, (*-or Congerton*) 1621 Orm², *-tun* 1347 Eyre, *-tonne* 1544
        Sheaf, *Conglton* 1318 AddCh

    Connkelton' 1307 Eyre (p)

    gowngulton c.1492 Dow

    Con(g)woton 1505 Sheaf

    Congerton 1547 Tab, 1553 Sheaf, 1558–79 ChancP, 1596 Sheaf,
        1621 Orm², 1629 Earw, 1690 Sheaf

Conglington 1694 Sheaf
Conghton 1819 Orm² (lit. *Cough-*)

A difficult name. The final el. is tūn 'a farmstead, an enclosure'. Ekwall (DEPN) suggests a first el. related to the PrGerm stem **kang-* found in ON *kengr* (< **kangi*) 'a bend', *kǫngull* 'a cluster (of grapes, etc.)', which he associates with Congham Nf. Wallenberg PNK 336 derives the first el. of Conghurst K, from the same stem, and suggests that the el. *cung-* means 'a turning, a bend'. Congleton town was formerly skirted by a great bend of the R. Dane. The place is in a hilly district, however, and the name could be analogous with *Conkhulle* 1400–5 PremIt (356–7, where Bruce Dickins suggests Cank Wo), 'a steep, rounded hill', *v.* canc, hyll, cf. Wa 292–3, Hrt xxxviii, 112. The development of Congleton would then be OE **canc-hyll* > ME **conk-hull*, with reduction of the final syllable in unstressed position (LMS I 148), *a* > *o* before *n* (although a few *Cang-* spellings would have been expected), voiced *-ng-* from *-nk-* by inversion of the more usual unvoicing *-ng-* > *-nk-* (Jordan § 193, § 178 n.2; although *-nk-* > *-ng-* is usually supposed a feature of the SE dial. of ME, and the *-nk-* spelling appears only once), cf. *Connkelton* beside *Gowngulton*. The p.n. would mean 'farm at *Cank-, Conkhill*'. This could refer to one of the big hills in the district, The Cloud 291 *supra* and Congleton Edge *infra*, or more particularly to the round-topped hill at the west end of the town, 110–850625, near The Mount *infra*.

STREET-NAMES

CANAL RD. & ST., 1843 *TA*, *Doglawne* 1484 *Dav*, *Dog Lane* 1504 *ib*, 1831 Bry, cf. *doglawne brucke* 1520 *AddCh*, 'lane frequented by dogs', *v.* dogga, lane, brōc.

HIGH ST., 1660 Wil, *v.* hēah.

HOWEY HILL & LANE, cf. *Further & Little Howey* 1843 *TA*, *Holway Brook* 1442 JCJ, *Holway* 1467 *ib*, *Howage Lane* 1599 *ib*, *Hollway Brook* 1660 Wil, '(brook at) the sunken road', from hol² and weg, with brōc, hyll, lane.

LAWTON ST., 1751 Sheaf, cf. Buglawton 290 *supra*.

MARKET ST., cf. *le marketstede* 1386 *MinAcct*, *-sted* 1487 *ib*, *le merketsted(e)* 1423, 1507, 1514 *ib*, *le markedsted* 1487 *ib*, 'the market place', *v.* market, merket, stede.

MILL GREEN & ST., 1843 *TA*, *le Mulnestrete* 1405 *AddCh*, *le Mylnestrete* 1409 JCJ, *Mill Streete* 1702 *Dav*, *v.* myln, strǣt, grēne². Cf. *Meelhall infra*.

MOODY ST., *Moodie-* 1641 JCJ, from the surname *Moody*.

Moor St., *Moor Lane* 1843 *TA*, cf. *(ley) Morelawne* 1520 *AddCh, le Moreway* 1393 *ib, v.* lane, weg, cf. *le More infra.*

Stonehouse Green 1860 White, *& Field* 1843 *TA*, cf. *le Stonehouse* 1589 *AddCh*, 'house built of stone', *v.* stān, hūs, grēne².

West Rd., *West Lane* 1843 *TA*, cf. foll.

West St., *le Westestrete* 1392 *AddCh, le Westrete* 1437 *ib, v.* west, strǣt, cf. prec.

Lost Street-Name. *Bagge Lone* 1264 DbA xxii, 'bag'lane', *v.* bagga, lane, but cf. George St. (Chester) 326 *infra.*

Lost Buildings. *Meelhall* 1443 *MinAcct (le Melhall* 1370, 1386 *ib*, *-hale* 1423 *ib, le Melehous, le Mel(l)ehall* 1386 *ib, le Meldhall* 1416 AD (a bakehouse), *le Molehale* 1423 *MinAcct*, 'the hall or house where meal was kept', *v.* me(o)lu, meldr, hall, hūs, melu-hūs, cf. *Melestrete* (Nantwich) 326 *infra.* In *MinAcct* this name alternates with *le Mylnhull* 1423, *-Milnehill* 1443, 1487, *-hilne* 1507, *-hyll* 1514, 'the mill hill', *v.* myln, hyll, cf. Mill Green *supra*, and the building is sometimes confused with the moot-hall (*v.* foll.), near which it stood. These confusions are the result of clerical error, frequent in the DuLa accounts for Congleton); *le Motehall* 1514 *MinAcct* (1443, 1487 *ib, -halle* 1507 *ib*, 'the moot-hall', *v.* mothall, called *aula placitorum* 'court house' in 1507, 1514 *MinAcct*, cf. prec.); *Old Mill* 1842 OS (*molendinum de Congleton* 1307–10 Orm², *v.* ald, myln); *Walk(e)myl(e)hous(e)* 1507, 1514 *MinAcct (Walkemilnehous* 1386, 1398 *ib, -mynlhous* (sic), *Walkynmylnhous* 1423 *ib, Walk(e)mylnehouse(e)* 1443, 1487 *ib*, cf. *molendinum fullonicum de novo leuata* 1353 *MinAcct*, 'house at a fulling-mill', *v.* walke-milne, hūs).

Dane in Shaw (Brook), *Danehynchill* 1407 JCJ, *Higher Dane-in-Shaw* 1843 *TA, Dane Henshaw* 1831 Bry, *(Lower) Dane-en-Shaw* 1842 OS, a p.n. better recorded in the stream-name derived from it, *Davenynsale, -in-* 1593 JCJ, *the Daningschow* c.1610 Camden, *Dane Inch* 1610 Speed, *the water called Dane-inch* 1621 (1656) Orm², also named *The Biddel* 1656 Orm² from Biddulph St, where it rises. The place-name *Danehynchill, Daneingschow* looks like hyll 'a hill', hōh 'a prominence', or halh 'a nook, a corner, a valley, land at a confluence', added to an assibilated sg. *-ing*-suffix formation upon the r.n. *Dane* (R. Dane 1 20), *v. -ing²*, cf. Altrincham 7 *supra*. The basis, OE **Dæfeninge*, would mean 'at *Dæfening*, the place or thing called after R. Dane'.

Mossley (Fm, Hall, Ho *& Moss*), *Moseleg'* E1 *JRC, -ley* 1594 *Surv, -Hall, -House Farm* 1831 Bry, *Mosley* 1404 *MinAcct, Mossley* 1593 JCJ, *Mossley Moss* 1586 AD, 'moss clearing', *v.* mos, lēah.

Parkhill, Park Lane, 1843 *TA, le Parkelo(o)ne* 1457, 1459 *AddCh, Parkelawne* 1520 *ib*, 1565 ChRR, *Park Lane Road* 1831 Bry, named from *parcum de Congilton* E1 *JRC*, *le Parke* 1443 *MinAcct*, *le perk(e)* 1487, 1507 *ib*, *v*. park, lane, hyll.

ASTBURY LANE END, -*s* 1842 OS, *Lane End* 1831 Bry, *v*. lane, ende[1], cf. Astbury 286 *supra*.   BACK LANE (FM), *v*. back, lane, the boundary with Radnor 318 *infra*.   BANK FM & TOP.   BELLE VUE HO, *Belle Vue* 1843 *TA*.   BERRY BANK, probably 'bank where berries grow', *v*. berige, banke.   BIDA RD, perhaps a form of Biddulph St, cf. foll., but JCJ reports the local pronunciation (baidə).   BIDDULPH RD, leading to Biddulph St.   BIRCH NOOK, *v*. nōk. BOUNDARY LANE, *Brick Bank* 1795 JCJ, 1831 Bry, 1842 OS, cf. *Brick Kiln Field*, *Brick Pit Field* 1843 *TA*, 'bank, pit and kiln where bricks are made', *v*. bryke, bryke-kyl, banke, pytt. The lane is on the edge of Congleton Moss *infra*.   BROMLEY FM, HO & LANE, *Banbury Lane* 1831 Bry, *Bramley Lane (Field)*, *Bramley Field & Hill*, *Bromley Field & Meadow* 1843 *TA*, 'broomy clearing', *v*. brōm, lēah. The form in Bry may represent a mishearing.   THE BROOKLANDS, *v*. brōc, land.   BROWNSWOLDS, *The-* 1595 JCJ *et freq* 1600 to 1650 *ib*, *Brownsoles* 1842 OS, from the surname of Thomas *Brownsworth* 1593 JCJ.   CANAL RD, *v*. Canal St. *supra*.   CONGLETON EDGE, 1602 JCJ, *Congleton (H)Edge* 1593 JCJ, *The Edge* 1595 ib, *Congleton Hedge (or Edge)* 1656 Orm[2], a great hill on the St boundary, giving name to a hamlet, *v*. ecg, cf. Congleton *supra*.   CONGLETON MOSS, 1831 Bry, *the mosse* 1511 *Rental*, cf. Moss Fm *infra* and *Mossehey* 1370, 1423, 1507 *MinAcct*, 1593 JCJ, (*le-*), *-heigh* 1353 *MinAcct*, *-hay* 1386 *ib*, *Mosehaye* 1423 *ib*, *-hey* 1487 *ib*, *Moshey*, *Moskehey* 1443 *ib*, from mos and (ge)hæg.   CROFTERS.   CROSLEDGE (lost, 110– 852631, along West Rd), 1860 White, *Crosslytch* 1555 JCJ (a stream near West Heath), *Crossledge Bank* 1831 Bry, 'boggy stream near a cross', *v*. cros, læc(c).   CROSS LANE, *v*. cros.   DANE BANK, 1831 Bry, *Hul super Dauene* (lit. *Daneno*) 1305 Lacy, *Davenhull* 1507, 1514 *MinAcct*, 'hill by the R. Dane', *v*. hyll, banke, R. Dane 1 20, cf. Eaton Bank 1 62.   DANE BRIDGE, 1619 Sheaf, *Congulton Bridge* 1407 JCJ, cf. *the bridge end* Eliz Orm[2], *v*. brycg, ende[1], R. Dane 1 20. There was an ancient chapel at the north end of the bridge (*the Old Chappell standing at Davon Bridge End* 1701 JCJ), *v*. Orm[2] III 38, ChetOS VIII 238, from which the present parish church was distinguished as *superior capella* 1437 *AddCh*, *Overchapell* 1521 *ib*, 'the higher chapel', *v*. uferra, chapel(e).   DANE MILL, *v*. R. Dane 1 20, myln.   FOL HOLLOW, 'muddy hollow', a stretch

of road, v. fūl, holh.   FORGE LANE, MILL & WOOD, *Forge Wood*
1831 Bry, v. forge.   GIRTHING BANK, on Congleton Edge, per-
haps an ascent where saddle-girths needed checking, v. banke.
GREENFIELD FM, cf. *Green Field* 1843 *ib*, v. grēne[1], feld.   HEATH-
FIELD.   HENSHALL HALL, probably from the surname *Henshall*.
HIGHTOWN, the upper hamlet of Congleton, cf. 241 *supra*.   HILLES-
DEN.   HILL FM, named from Congleton Edge *supra*, v. hyll.
HORSLEY BANK, *le Hertislip* 1413 JCJ, *Horslyppe* 1470 ib, -*Bank* 1601
ib, *Horsleys* 1583 ib, *Horsely-*, *Horsley Bank* 1599 ib, *Horsley Banck*
1702 *Dav*, 'deer's leap', v. heorot, hlēp, a steep hill. The modern
form may be due to some phonological development, (harts- > haːrs-
> hɔːrs), leading to a substitution of *horse* for *hart*, v. hors.   THE
HOWTY, *Howty* 1612 Polyolbion, *Howtie* 1621 Orm[2], a stream
running through the town into *Houghteth* 1443 *MinAcct*, *Heghtegh*
1487 *ib*, *Houghtith* 1507, 1514 *ib*, *the Howte Eye* 1595 JCJ, a parcel
of land beside R. Dane, from which the stream was named, cf. *Houty
Lane* 1790 JCJ. The final el. appears to be ēg 'a water-meadow, an
island', alternating with ēgeð 'a small island'. The first el. presents
difficulty. It appears to be ME *hought*, pa.part. of the verb *hough* 'to
hamstring' (NED), perhaps in a figurative sense here for a water-
meadow with a piece cut off, cf. the el. hamol.   THE LAKES, *Big &
Little Black Lake* 1544–1699 JCJ, *Lakes Farm, Big & Little Lake*
1843 *TA*, v. blæc, lacu 'a watercourse'.   LAMBERT'S LANE,
Lamberts Loone 1442 JCJ, *Lamber(s) Lane* 1593 ib, from the ME
(OFr) pers.n. *Lambert* and lane.   LEEK RD, leading to Leek, St.
LOACHBROOK BRIDGE & COTTAGES, v. Loach Brook 1 30.
LOVERS' WALK, v. lover, walk.   LOWER HEATH, 1582, 1593 JCJ,
v. hǣð.   THE MARSH, MARSH FM, *Marsh Gate* 1831 Bry, *The
Marsh* 1595 JCJ, v. mersc, geat, cf. 289 *supra*.   MORETON
MEADOWS, -*Meadowes* 1593 JCJ, also *Moreton Field* 1843 *TA*, cf.
William *Moreton* of Hulme Walfield 1593 JCJ.   MOSS FM & RD,
cf. *the house on the mosse* 1511 *Rental*, v. Congleton Moss *supra*.
THE MOUNT, v. mont, cf. Congleton *supra*.   PADGBURY FM, HO &
LANE, *Padgebridge* 1626 Sheaf, *Padgbridge Lane* 1593, 1595 JCJ, 1798
BW, *Padgebury Lane* 1831 Bry. The origin of this name is perhaps
'pads bridge', from dial. *pad* 'a path' (cf. pæð) with brycg and lane.
The pl. *pads* is used in north-west La to denote a continuous line
of footpaths across country, and the same usage may have held for
south-east Ch; but the name could also be 'patch of ground newly
broken in', from pacche and brēc, bryce.   PARNELLSCROFT, prob-

ably from the surname or pers.n. *Parnell.*   PRIESTY FIELDS, cf.
Farther-, Lower- & Near Priesty Field, etc., 1843 *TA*, perhaps
'priest's enclosure', *v.* prēost, (ge)hæg.   PRIMROSE VALE, 1842 OS.
PUDDLE BANK, 17 JCJ, 'bank near a dirty pool', *v.* puddel, banke.
THE QUINTA, a house-name, *v. quinta* (NED) 'a country villa'.
READE'S LANE, cf. Roger *Read* 1593 JCJ. This road was *Earlswaie*
1593 JCJ, 'the earl's road', *v.* eorl, weg, cf. route XVIII 1 46.
The p.n. Earlsway Ho (110–913617) in Rushton St James, St,
indicates that the road-name referred to a route from Congleton
towards Leek St (110–877618 to 939617). A similar road-name
appears in *Hyerlisweye* 1 83, cf. route XIII 1 45.   ROODHILL
FM, ROOD LANE, *Roade Lane* 1582 JCJ, *Rood(e)-, Rodde Lane*
1593 ib, *the Roade Lane* 1593 ib, from rōd[2] 'a rood, a cross' or rōd[3] 'a
rood of land', *v.* hyll, lane.   ROWSELEY.   SPRINGFIELD, (*-House*)
1843 *TA*, *v.* spring 'a spring'.   STONY LANE, *Stoney Lane*
1831 Bry, *v.* stānig, lane.   TIDNOCK HO, cf. Tidnock 1 68.
TOWN WOOD, 1831 ib, cf. *Congletonwode* 1386 *MinAcct.*   WAGG
RD & ST., *Wagges Lane* 1593 JCJ, *Wagg Street* 1843 *TA*, *Wagg's
Road* 1860 White, probably from the surname *Wagg.*   WEST-
BOURNE, a house.   WEST END COTTAGES, *v.* west, ende[1].   WEST
HEATH, 1593 JCJ, *v.* west, hæð.   WESTHOLM, a house.   WINDY
BANK, 1831 Bry.

FIELD-NAMES

The undated forms are 1843 *TA* 129. Of the others, E1 is JRC, 1295, 1305
Lacy, 1355, 1362 *Eyre*, 1347, 1392, 1393, 1407, 1437, 1520, 1589 *AddCh*,
1399 *Sotheby*, 1412, 1414, 1416 AD, 1505 Sheaf, 1511, 1586 *Rental*, 1512
ChRR, 1548 *Chol*, 1701 *Dav*, 1831 Bry, 1842 OS, 1843 *TA*, 1860 White,
and the rest *MinAcct*. JCJ indicates information by Mr J. C. Jones from
local knowledge and Congleton town records.

(*a*) Acre; Antrobus Croft & St. (from the surname from Antrobus 127
supra); Banks (cf. *the Bankes* 1593 JCJ, *v.* banke); Bent (*v.* beonet); Bob
Slack (*Babslack, Babbe's Slack* 1593 JCJ, *v.* slakki. The first el. is probably
a pers.n. or surname); Bog Mdw (*v.* bog); Bowling Green Mdw; Brook
Shoot (*v.* brōc, scēat); Brook Side (1860 st.n., *v.* brōc, side); Broom Fd (cf.
Broom Hill 1842, *v.* brōm); Bye Flatt (*Byflet(e)* 1423, 1507, 1514, *Bifflete*
1443, *Biflete* 1507, *Biflete* 1451 JCJ, *Byflatte* 1600 ib, two names, the later
one 'flat piece of land in a river-bend', *v.* byge[1], flat, cf. 1 170, and the
earlier one either 'beside the creek' or 'creek at a river-bend', from bī or
byge[1] and flēot); The Clough (*v.* clōh); Cock Shoot Fd (*v.* cocc-scyte); Cole
Hill (*Cole Hill Bank* 1860 st.n., 'charcoal hill', *v.* col[1], hyll, banke); Cot
Croft, Cote Mdw (*v.* cot); Cow Lane Mdw; Cunning Greave (*Cunning
Greaves Farm* 1843, *v.* coningre); Dane Eye (cf. *Davenhees* 1443, *Davenhes*

1507, 1514, *Danes* 1507, *Daines* 1514, *The Furmost-, The Great Eyes* 1593 JCJ, 'meadow(s) by the R. Dane', *v.* ēg, R. Dane 1 20); Dean Fd (*v.* denu); Drumble (dial., 'a wooded ravine, a dell', cf. dumbel); Flashes ((*le*) *Flaskes* 1295, 1305, 1306, 1414, *le Flasekes* 1512, 'the swamps, the shallow waters', *v.* flask, flasshe); Hall Mdw (cf. *Halmede* 1443, 1457, *Hallemede* 1507, *Halmete* 1514, *hallemedo* 1520, *Hallmeade* 1584, *v.* hall, mǣd); Head Lane (*v.* hēafod); Hey Wd (*v.* (ge)hæg, wudu); Hill Fd; Holts (*v.* holt); Hone Fd (*v.* hān); Kiln Fd (*v.* cyln); Kings Butt 1818 JCJ (*v.* cyning, butte); Knowl (*v.* cnoll); Lady Fd (*v.* hlǣfdige); The Lawn (*v.* launde); Liverpool Fd; Long Lych (*v.* lece); Long Shoot (*v.* scēat); Macclesfield Piece (*v.* pece); Marl (Pit) Fd (*v.* marle-pytt); Mill Fd (*Mylnefield* 1593 JCJ, *v.* myln); Monny Pits ('many pits', *v.* manig, pytt); Moor Lane (*v.* mōr[1], lane); Open Bank (*v.* open, banke); Overton Mdw (*v.* uferra, tūn); Ox Hey Mdw (*v.* oxa, (ge)hæg); Parson's Fd; The Patches (*v.* pacche); Pingot (*v.* pingot); Radnor Lane 1831 (*v.* Radnor 318 *infra*); Rope Walk Piece (at a rope factory, cf. the st.n. Rope Walk); Scarr (*v.* sker); Shippon Fd (*v.* scypen); Spout Mdw (*v.* spoute 'a spout, a spring'); Swamp; Swan Bank (1860 st.n., *v.* swan[1], banke); Tenter Croft (*v.* tentour); Toad Hole (*Toade Hole* 1593 JCJ, a meadow beside R. Dane, *v.* tāde, hol[1]); Tom Fd (*v.* toun, feld); Town's End Croft (*v.* toun, ende[1]); Two Day Work (*v.* day-work); Wallsall Wd (*Walsam* 1505, perhaps 'wood at a spring or well', from wælla, sceaga); Warfow Mdw; Watbiss Fd (the second el. may be beōs 'bent-grass'); Way Fd (*v.* weg); Weay Mdw, Wey Fd ('sour field', *v.* hwǣg); West House (1842); The Wharf (cf. *lez Warthes* 1443, *-Wrathes* 1487, *le Wrathes* 1507, 1514, 'meadow(s) by a stream', *v.* waroð); Whitmore Wood Gate 1831 (*v.* geat, cf. Whitemore, in Biddulph, St); Wood Drake & End (*v.* wudu, rake or hraca, ende[1], cf. Drakes Foot 289 *supra*); Wood Hay 1842 (*Wood hee* 1511, *-hey* 1586, *v.* wudu, (ge)hæg).

(b) *le Bakehousecroft* 1514 ('bake-house croft', *v.* bæc-hūs, croft); *le Breche* 1507, 1514 (*v.* brēc); (*le*) *Brod(h)ok'* 1347 (p), *le Brodok(e)* 1355 (p), 1361 (p) (*v.* brād, āc); *le Clyfe* 1362 (p) (*v.* clif); *Colleye* 1392, *Colay* 1437 ('charcoal enclosure', *v.* col[1], (ge)hæg, cf. Colleymill 1 59); *Dead Daven* 1593 JCJ (a dead arm of R. Dane at 110–855635, *v.* dēad); *Friarsmeadows* 1593 JCJ (*v.* frere, mǣd); *le Goandwerk* 1370 (apparently from ME *goande* (pres.part. of *go*) 'going, walking' and ME *werk(e)* 'work'); *Grisley* 1507, *Grysley* 1514 ('young pig's clearing', *v.* grīss, lēah); *Halond'* 1487, *le Hallande* 1507 (perheps 'selion at a nook', *v.* halh, land, but probably 'a half-selion', *v.* half-land); *Hardeshedebroke* 1423 ('(brook at) the angle of hard land', *v.* heard, scēat, brōc); *le longehurst* E1 ('the long wood', *v.* lang, hyrst); *Meerstall* 1442 JCJ (*v.* mere-stall); *Milneston(e)bargh', -bergh'* 1386, 1398 (quarrera vocata), *Mylnstanbergh'* 1423, *Mustanbargh' alias vocata Milnestonbergh'* 1443, *Mustanbach alias Milstonbargh'* 1507, *Mustanbath' alias Milstonbath'* 1514 ('mill-stone hill', the name of a quarry referred to in *firma rupe-, -rupis Molarium* 1295, 1305, *v.* mylen-stān, beorg); *Moggesgronde* 1520 (from the ME fem. pers.n. *Mogg* (< *Margaret*) and grund); *le More* 1443, 1487, 1507 ('the marsh or moor', *v.* mōr[1], cf. Moor St. *supra*); *Netherfield* 1423–42 JCJ (*v.* neoðera, feld); *Ouerwastfeld* 1407, *Overwestfield* 1423–42

JCJ ('the higher waste field', v. uferra, waste, wēste, feld); *The Rowhurst* 1593 JCJ (v. rūh, hyrst); *le Smythyepost* 1347 ('post at a smithy', v. smiðõe, post); *Sprowforde* 1507 (v. ford. If this is not merely a corrupt form for foll., the first el. may be the OE pers.n. *Sprow*); *Strongeford (iuxta Dane)* 1443, *(Walkeley) Strongford (iuxta Dane)* 1487, 1514, *Stronghford(e)* 1507, 1514, *Great Stronnforde alias Strongforde* 1516 ('strong ford', probably a ford where the current was strong (e.g. at Washford 292 *supra*), v. strang, ford, cf. *Whateleighbonk infra*); *le Threpehurst* E1 ('wood in dispute, or where disputes are held', v. þrēap, hyrst); *Tyrwhyn maior et minor* 1443, *Tyrwlyn-* 1487, *Thurwyn-* 1507, 1514 ('fuel gorse', v. tyri 'a resinous wood for fire-making', hvin 'whin, gorse'); *Wellacre* 1407 JCJ, *Wellscroft* 1442 JCJ (v. wella, æcer, croft); *Whateleighbonk* 1386, *Whaitlebonk* 1398, *Whateley* 1412, *W(h)atele(y)bonke (Croft)* 1416, *Watteley* 1443, *(le) Watley* 1487, *Whatley* 1514, *Whayleybanke, -bonk* 1423, *Weylebank* 1443, *Strongeford et Whitlegh* 1443, 1487, 1507, 1514, *Walkeley Strongford* 1487 ('(hillside at) the wheat clearing', v. hwǣte, lēah, banke, cf. *Strongeford supra*); *le Yate* 1393 (p), *le Ȝate* 1399 (p) ('the gate', v. geat).

6. DAVENPORT (110–7966)

Deneport 1086 DB, *Deynport* 1352 BPR (p)
Devennport c.1130 SD (s.a. 920), *Deueneport* 1304 Chamb (p)
Daun(e)-, Dauen(e)-, Daven(e)port(e) 1188 Orm² (p), MidCh (p), e13 (1608) ChRR, (1621) ib, c.1233 *Dow* (p), 1240–57 *AddCh* (p), Chest (p), l13 AD (p) *et freq* with variant spellings *-pord, -porth*; *Dafneport* c.1270 Tab (p), *Davinport* c.1330 *Fitt* (p), *-yn-* 1441 Cl (p)
Daueport 1237 P (p), *Dave-* 1318 Cl (p)
Daneteport 1238 P (p)
Daneport 1238 Lib (p), *Danport* 1350 JRL (p)
de Alneport 1242 Cl (p)
Damppord c.1318 *Dav* (p), *Damport* 1365 Pat (p), *-e* 1559 ib, *Daumport* 1373 ib (p)
Dau-, Davemport(e) 1512 ChEx, 1580 Orm², 1581 ChRR

'Market on the R. Dane', v. port², R. Dane 1 20. Symeon of Durham, II 93, 123, s.a. 920, reports 'Sihtric broke into *(infregit) Devennport*', v. Stenton 329–330. This suggests a town. There is neither a town nor any trace of one here now, and the place was never a borough, but the p.n. infers a commercial centre. It may have been a market-place for a Danish settlement area, v. Sagabook XIV 313.

BROWN'S BANK, 1842 OS from the surname *Brown*.   DAVENPORT BRIDGE, 1619 Sheaf, cf. Dane Bridge Meadow 284 *supra*, v. brycg,

R. Dane 1 20.   DAVENPORT HALL, *The hall of Davenport* 1652
Dav.   DAVENPORT HO.   DINGLE WOOD, *v.* dingle.   ENGINE
WOOD, *Wallfield Rough* 1831 Bry, *v.* wælla 'a well, a spring', feld,
rūh 'a rough place'.   HARE LANE ROUGH, 1831 ib, *v.* hara, lane,
rūh.   NORTH WOOD.   PINFOLD ROUGH, 1831 ib, *-ford-* 1842
OS, *v.* pynd-fald, rūh.   STOCKERY PARK FM, *Stockerys* 1831 Bry,
Stockery Park 1839 *TA*, perhaps a 'stockery', i.e. a place where
stockers work, *v.* dial. *stocker* 'a workman who fells or grubs up
tree-stocks' (NED).   WOODHOUSE FM, *(the) Wood House* 1751
Sheaf, 'house in a wood', *v.* wudu, hūs, cf. Woodhouse Field 280
supra.

FIELD-NAMES

The undated forms are 1839 *TA* 141. Those dated 1510 are ChRR, and
1623 *Dav.*

(a) Bean Stalk (a figurative name for a field good for growing beans); Cat
Yard (*v.* cat(t), geard); Clough Water (*v.* clōh); Corker's (Big, Little &
Long) Hay (*Corkers Crofts* 1510, from a surname *Corker* and croft, (ge)hæg);
Deer's Leap (*v.* dēor, hlēp); Gravelly Mdw (*v.* gravel); Heath Fd (*v.* hǣð);
Hough Mdw (*v.* halh); Intake (*v.* inntak); Ley Ground (*v.* lǣge); Lime Fd
(*v.* lim); Maiden's Hatch & Wd (*v.* mægden, hæc(c), wudu); Marl Pit (*v.*
marle-pytt); Mop; Odd Fd (*v.* odde); Overy Mdw (*v.* uferra, ēg); Rail
Mdw (*v.* rail(e)); Shippen Fd (*v.* scypen); Stockford (*Stokforthe* 1510,
perhaps 'ford marked by tree-stocks', *v.* stocc, ford); Town Fd (*v.* toun);
White Fd (*v.* hwīt); Wilsey Mdw; Wood Fd (*Wodfild* 1510, *v.* wudu, feld).

(b) Godams Ge 1510; Lynney 1623 ('flax meadow', *v.* līn, ēg, cf. Linney
Meadow 1 65).

7. HULME WALFIELD (110–8565) [ˈhjuːm ˈwɔːl-]

> *Wallefeld et Hulm'* c.1262 *Dav*, *-filde-* 1290 Ipm, *-Hulme* 1290
>   IpmR
> *Wallefeld* E1 Orm², 1307 Plea *et freq* to 1361 Orm², *-felt* 1344
>   ChRR, *Walefeld* 1290 Ipm, *Walfield* 1361 Orm², *-fyld*, *-fild* 1547
>   ChRR, *Watfield* 1724 NotCestr
> *Hulm* 1290 Ipm, *(-iuxta Wallefeld)* 1307 Plea, *Hulme* 1296 Tab,
>   1337 Plea, *(-iuxta Davenport)* 1458 Orm²
> *Hulle et Walmefeld* 1295 Lacy, 1306 *MinAcct*, *Hulm et Wallefeld*
>   *(iuxta Congelton)* 1319, 1337 Plea, *Hulme et Walfeld* 1430 *Dav*,
>   *-feild (alias Hulme Walfeild)* 1626 Sheaf, *Holme et Walfeld* 1527
>   Plea
> *Hulm-Wallefeld* 1338 Plea, *Hulme-* 1393 Orm², *Hulmewalfield* 1413
>   ChRR, *(-alias Welfield alias Walkfield)* 1591 Orm², *-feild* 1612 ib,

-felde 1489 ChRR, *-feld*, *-fild* 1513 ib, *Hulmwalfeld* 1576 ib, *-field* 1742 Sheaf, *Holm Wallfyld* 1515 Orm², *Holme Walfeld* 1543 Plea, *Homewalfeld, -fild* 1525 ChRR

'The island, the water-meadow', *v.* hulm; and 'the open land at a spring', *v.* wælla, wælm, feld. The township consists of two manors. The form *Walme-* argues against a derivation from wall 'a wall', suggested by the account of a fortification here in 1725 thought to be Roman and on a Roman road from Middlewich to Astbury, *v.* Orm² III 71.

BRICKHOUSE FM, *v.* bryke, hūs. CHIPHILL COTTAGES, cf. *Chip Hillock* 1840 *TA*, *v.* hylloc. CLAPHATCH, cf. dial. clap-gate, *v.* hæc(c). DAISY BANK, *(near Congleton)* 1747 Earw, *v.* dægesege, banke. GIANTSWOOD LANE, 1842 OS. HULME WALFIELD FM & HALL. HULME WALFIELD OLD HALL, *Hulmewalfield Hall* 1842 OS. MANORHOUSE FM. MOUNTPLEASANT FM, *Prospect House* 1831 Bry, *Mount Pleasant* 1842 OS. SANDHOLE FM, 1842 ib, *Sandy Farm* 1831 Bry, cf. *Sandy Hole Field* 1840 *TA*, *v.* sand, sandig, hol¹. SANDYLANE FM, *v.* sandig, lane. SHANNOCK BIG WOOD, *v.* Shannock 1 64. SMITHY COTTAGE, cf. *Smithy Lane* 1831 Bry, *v.* smiðõe, lane. SQUARE WOOD, *v.* squar(e). THORNLAW COTTAGE, cf. *Far-, Middle- & Near Thornlow* 1840 *TA*, 'thorn-tree mound', *v.* þorn, hlāw.

FIELD-NAMES

The undated forms are 1840 *TA* 211.

(a) Abbey Fd 1815 Orm² (perhaps after St Werburgh's abbey, Chester); The Acre; Bell Mdw (*v.* belle; perhaps this field was dedicated to maintain a church bell); Bent (*v.* beonet); Bleaching Croft; Broad Fd; Broomy Dale (*v.* brōmig, dæl¹); Cinderhill (*v.* sinder, hyll); Clough (*v.* clōh); Corn Hill (*v.* corn¹, hyll); Cote Croft (*v.* cot, croft); Cow Hey (Rough), Cow Lane (Field) (*v.* cū, (ge)hæg, rūh, lane); Crow Burrow ('crow's stronghold', *v.* crāwe, burh; an ironic name); Dane Mdw (*v.* R. Dane); Dove Bank; Drumble (dial., 'a wooded dell or ravine', *v.* dumbel); Elderley (*v.* ellern, lēah); Flatt (*v.* flat); Fox Fd (*v.* fox); Gammer, Gammers Rough (*v.* gammer, rūh); Gorsy Knowl (*v.* gorstig, cnoll); Gutter Fd (*v.* goter); Heatley, Heatley Moor (*Heytley* 1525 Orm², 1551 ib, *Haytley* 1612 ib, 'heath clearing', *v.* hǣð, lēah); Hill Top 1842 OS (*The Bank* 1831 Bry, *Near Bank* 1840 *TA*, *v.* hyll, topp, banke); Kiln Croft (*v.* cyln); Kiss Bank (*v.* kjóss, banke); Lunt (probably land 'a selion'); Mare Pit Fd; Mill Ridding (*v.* myln, ryding); Moss (*The-* 1831 Bry, *v.* mos); Nib Fd; Nine Day Work (*v.* day-work); Ox Close; Patch (*v.* pacche); Pickery; Piker Hill, Pikers Hill Wd; Pinion Hill;

Pit Fd; Ridding (v. ryding); Rogerley; Sand Fd; Spark (v. spearca); Spout Fd (v. spoute); The Stew (v. stewe); Stock Moss (v. stocc, mos); Stoney Butts (v. stānig, butte); Stych (v. sticce[1]); Tenterhill (v. tentour, hyll); Three Day Math (v. day-math); Toad Hole (v. tod-hole); Under Hill; Walker Hey ('tanner's enclosure', v. walcere, (ge)hæg); Wall Fd (v. wælla, cf. Walfield supra); Well Fd; Way (Pit) Fd (v. weg); Well Fd; Wheat Hays (v. hwǣte, (ge)hæg); Withimer ('willow pool', v. wīðig, mere[1]).

(b) Cattes Oak 1582 JCJ, Cattesoak(e) 1593 ib (v. cat(t), āc); Cathayes 1599 JCJ ('cat enclosures', v. cat(t), (ge)hæg. JCJ identifies this in a modern local name Catty Ward's Hole affixed to a p.n. from Ward the surname of the landowner c.1750, and hol[1]).

8. MORETON CUM ALCUMLOW, 1842 OS, (or Great Moreton) 1882 Orm[2], Moreton-Alcomlow(e) 1696, 1722 BW, 1724 NotCestr, cf. Alcumlow, Great Moreton Hall infra.

ALCUMLOW (110–828598) [ˈalkəmlou, ˈaːkəmlou]

> Alkmundelawe 13 AddCh, -mundley 1304 Chamb (p), Alkemonde-
> lowe 113 AddCh, Alk(e)mundelowe e14, 1308 ib et freq with variant
> spellings Alk(e)-, -mund(e)-, -mo(u)nd(e)-, -mont-, -lawe, -louwe
> to 1426 ChRR, Alcmondelowe 1398 Orm[2] (p), Alco-, Alcumunde-
> lowe e14, 1313 BW (p), Alkymondelow 1429 ChRR (p)
> Alcomdelowe 1318 BW (p), Alkumde- 1320 ib (p)
> Alkumlowe 1375 Eyre, Alcum-, -com(e)- 1386, 1389 Chol (p),
> Alcomlowe (Brook) 1619 Sheaf, Alcomlow alias Moreton Alcomlow
> 1722 BW
> Allemondlowe 1441 ChRR (p)

'Ealhmund's mound', from the OE pers.n. Ealhmund and hlāw. Cf. Arecumlow Field 277 supra. The brook is Arclid Brook 265 supra.

GREAT MORETON HALL (110–840595)

> Mortunia 12 Tab, -tune 1287 Court (p), -tona 1185–90 Facs, -ton
> 13 AddCh et freq to 1440 Cl (p), (-iuxta Newbold) 1316 Plea,
> (Magna Morton) 1289 Court (-sub Lymam), 1344 Plea, (Great-)
> 1350 AD, (Mikel-) 1349 Plea, (Mykel-) 1385 IpmR, -tone 1316
> ChRR
> Moreton 1265–91 (17) Chest (p) et freq, (Hall) 1724 NotCestr,
> (Mykill-) 1384 Orm[2], (Magna-) 1315 AddCh
> Moorton 1309 ChRR (p), (Great-) 1350, 1354 AD
> Mourton 1313 BW (p), 1370, 1373 AddCh

'Farm at a marsh', v. mōr[1], tūn, grēat, micel, cf. Little Moreton
Hall 306 infra, The Lyme 1 2, Newbold 286 supra. There is mention
of 'the peel and the mote of Great Moreton' in 1354 AD (C.6348),
v. pēl (cf. 218 supra, Peel 288 supra, 327 infra, and NED s.v. peel),
mote.

BROWNLOW FM & HEATH, Brownlow Common 1831 Bry, -Heath 1842
OS, 'the brown mound or hill', v. brūn[1], hlāw.   GROTTO WOOD,
Grotta Wood 1842 ib.   HALL FM, v. hall.   HANGING WOOD,
1842 ib, v. hangende, wudu.   HOME FM, Brook Farms 1842 ib, v.
brōc, home.   KINGSPOOL WOOD, Kings Pool 1842 ib, Keen's Pool
Wood, Keen's Meadow & Patch, 1839 TA, from the surname Keen,
v. pōl[1] 'a pool', wudu, mǣd, pacche.   LIMEKILN WOOD.   LODGE
FM, 1842 OS.   MORETON GREEN (lost) & MILL (lost), 1831 Bry,
near Great Moreton Hall, included in its park, as also is Far Moreton
Bridge 1831 Bry (110–835595), on the old road from Congleton to
Scholar Green.   MOW COP, v. 308 infra.   ROE PARK (FM),
Rawe Parke 1559 Pat, Roe Park, Park House 1831 Bry, 'roe-deer
park', v. rā[1], park.   ROUND PLANTATION, Round Wood 1842 ib.
THE WILDERNESS.   WOOD FM, cf. Wood House 1831 Bry, Low
Farm 1842 OS, v. wudu, hūs, lágr.

FIELD-NAMES

The undated forms are 1839 TA 274. Of the others, e14 is AddCh, 1831
Bry, and 1842 OS.

(a) Archy Field Lane; Black Bank Wd; Broad Hay (v. brād, (ge)hæg);
Button Cap Fd; Carters Lane 1831 (a lost road between Bogg Hall 310 infra,
110–826596, and Spen Green 317 infra, 110–817605, from the occupational
surname Carter); Clough Croft & Fd (v. clōh); Colley Croft (v. colig);
Cooksey Fd; Cow Hay (v. cū, (ge)hæg; Big Daw Hay; Four-, Nine- & Two
Day Math (v. day-math); Three Days Work (v. day-work); Far Knowl (v.
cnoll); Girlfield Lane 1831 (v. lane. Girlfield may be 'young person's field',
from girle or girl and feld); Holling grave fd (v. holegn, grǣfe); Knowl (v.
cnoll); Little Lands (v. land); Long Shute, Long Shutt Flat (v. scēat, flat);
Madge Mdw (v. madge); Marl (Pit) Fd (v. marle-pytt); Mill Fd & Mdw
(v. Moreton Mill supra); Moss (v. mos); First-, Second- & Far Nickbarrow,
Nickabarrow Mdw (cf. Nickalbarrows Lane 1831 Bry. This probably contains
the name of the mythical person or goblin Nicka-, Nickerbore, recorded in
Yorkshire dialect (EDD), but the final el. may be bearu 'a wood, a grove', cf.
nicor); Noger Croft (cf. Nogars Moor 313 infra, v. Nauegerfeld 172 supra);
Nook Fd (v. nōk); Ox Hay (v. (ge)hæg); Park Croft & Mdw; Penny Croft
(v. peni(n)g); Little Spath, Spath Mdw (v. sparðr); Spout Mdw (v. spoute);

Sprink (*v.* spring 'a young wood'); Tentrey Croft (*v.* tentour); Timber Hurst 1842 (*v.* timber, hyrst); Tinker Hill Wd 1842 ('hill frequented by tinkers', *v.* tink(l)ere, hyll); Well Fd.

(*b*) *Bolekroft* e14 ('croft full of tree-trunks', *v.* bola, croft); *Houllemor* e14 ('(marsh near) the glade at the hut', *v.* hulu, lēah, mōr[1]); *Longhacris* e14 ('the long ploughlands', *v.* lang, æcer).

9. ODD RODE, *Odrode*, or *Little Moreton cum Rode* 1882 Orm[2], *Rode et Parua Mortoun* 1342 *AddCh*, *v.* Rode Hall, Little Moreton Hall *infra.*

MORETON OLD HALL or LITTLE MORETON HALL (110–832589), *Parua Morton* 1271 *BW*, *-Moreton* 1320 Orm[2], *Little-* 1527 ChRR, (*-Hall*) 1845 ChetOS VIII, *Parua Mortoun* 1342 *AddCh*, *Mooreton Hall* 1614 *ib*, *Moreton Hall* 1724 NotCestr, *-Old-* 1831 Bry, cf. Great Moreton Hall 304 *supra*, Odd Rode *supra*, *v.* lȳtel, ald, hall.

RODE HALL, HEATH, CLOSE, MILL & POOL (110–8157)

> *Rode* 1086 DB, 1259 Court (p) *et freq* with variant spellings *Rod(a)*, *Roode, Rodde, Rowde, Road(e), Rhode*, (*-iuxta Morton*) 1349 *BW*, (*-iuxta Magna Morton*) 1380 Plea, (*-iuxta Chirchelauton*) 1422 Orm[2], (*-alias Odd Rode*) 1593 *BW*, *le Roode* 1509 *AddCh*, *Rodeheze* 1280 *ib* 37109 (BM reads *-hez*), *-Heath* 1741 *BW*, *-Hall* 1690 Sheaf, *Rodhethe* 1536 ib
> *Herode* 1278 Ipm
> *Hoderod(e)* 1258 Whall (p), 1286 Ipm (p), *Odderode* 1286 *AddCh et freq* with variant spellings *Od(d)-, Edde-, Ord-, Odroode* 1442 *AddCh*, *Odde Rowde* 1506 *ib*, *-Roode* 1509 *ib*, *Od(d)road(e)* 1581 ChRR, 1618 Sheaf, 1693 *Cross*, *Odd Rhode* 1668 *BW*

'The clearings', *v.* rod[1], hǣð, hall, cf. North Rode 1 59. Rode Heath is liable to confusion with Rudheath 198 *supra*, 1 11, since the Runchamp family of Lostock Gralam had manorial interests in both places. The affix *Hode-, Odde-* is a confusion of the by-name of a former tenant of the manor, 'Adam dictus Hod de Odderode' 1286 *AddCh* 37105 (from ME hod 'a hood', cf. hōd and the surname *Hood*), with the OE pers.n. *Odda* (cf. DEPN), or with ME odde 'odd, the odd one of three, the third', thence 'unique, standing alone' (from 1330 NED). It distinguishes this place from North Rode, and perhaps also between Rode Hall and Rode Heath. *Herode* is 'high Rode', from hēah. Rode Close was *Rode Field* 1774 *BW*, *Big Rode* 1839 *TA*, *v.*

clos. Rode Mill, 1831 Bry, was *molendinum (aquaticum) de Rode* 1315
AddCh, 1328, 1389 *BW*, *Rode Water-Mill* 1722 *ib*, cf. Millbank *infra*
and *le Milnelone* 1329 *AddCh, v.* myln, lane. Rode Pool, a lake, gives
name to *Pool End Meadow* 1651 *BW, Pool Head Rang* 1668 *ib, Pool
Head* 1786 *ib, Poole Place* 1651 *ib, (the) Pool(e) Stead or-* 1669 *ib,
the Poolstead* 1786 *ib, Pools Land* 1743 *ib, v.* pōl[1], ende[1], hēafod, pōl-
stede, place, land, range. Great Moreton is with Alcumlow 304 *supra*,
and Church Lawton 320 *infra* is adjacent to the south-west.

BIG BARR (110–817568), *le Barude* 1260 Court (p), *le Barud* 1265–91
Chest, *the Barr* 1605 *BW, two Barrs* 1663 *ib, Lower & Upper Barr,
Barr Bank* 1669 *ib, Bar Wood* 1842 OS, cf. *Lower & Over Barrowdish*
1839 *TA* 115 in Church Lawton (*Barwedes, -ys, -is, Barwehedys* 1265–
91 Chest). The basis of these names is bearu 'a wood, a grove', with
wudu 'a wood' and edisc 'a park, an intake', giving *Barud(e)* and
Barwedis respectively. Cf. *le Barude* 325 *infra*.

BODEN HALL (110–810588) ['boudən, 'budən]
> Butthenhale 1259 Court (p)
> Budenhal 1288 Court (p) (lit. *Dud-*), 1303 *BW* (p), -*hall* 1299 Ipm,
> -*hale* e14 *AddCh* (p), c.1330 *BW* (p) *et freq* to 1399 Tab (p), 15
> ChRR (p), *Budenale* 1317 *AddCh* (p), 1331, 1356 *ib* (p), *Budynnale*
> 1308 *ib* (p)
> Bydenhall 1312 *BW* (p), *Bydenal(e)* e14, 1315 *AddCh* (p), -*hale*
> 1354 Eyre (p), *Biden-* 1362 BPR (p), *three Bidnall Crofts* 1709
> Dav, *Bidenhall* 1831 Bry, *Biddenhall (Bank & Meadow)* 1839
> TA, 1842 OS
> Bedynhale 1327 ChRR (p), *Beden-* 1357 Eyre (p), *Bedenalehalle*
> 1387 *AddCh*, *Bedenall* 1499 Orm[2]
> Higher-, Little- & Lower Bignall Croft 1718 Dav

'Nook with a tub in it', or 'hollow nook', *v.* byden, halh. The hall
(*Bedenalehalle* 1387, *v.* hall) stands in a little valley. Cf. Parkside Fm
254 *supra*.

CUTTLEFORD (110–830590), 1727 *BW*, (-*Meadow*) 1658 *ib, Cudlesford*
1345 Eyre (p), *Codils-* 1354 *ib* (p), *Cod(e)lesford* 1356 *AddCh* (p),
Cuttelsford 1401 Orm[2] (p), *Cattleford Meadow* 1649 *BW, Cutleyford*
1831 Bry, perhaps 'Cūðwulf's ford', from the OE pers.n. *Cūðwulf*
and ford, but the first el. may be an OE pers.n. *Cud(d)el*, a diminutive
of OE *Cud(d)a*.

Mow Cop (hill and hamlet, 110–8557)

> *Mowl* 13 *Dav* (p), *Mowel* c.1270 *Dav* (p), (*rocha de*) 1280 *AddCh*
> 37109 (BM reads *rocha de Mowa*), 1320, 1330 *BW*, *Mowell* 1298
> Orm² (p), *Moul'* 1313 *BW* (p), -*e* 1631 *AddCh*, *Mole* 1437–68
> *ib* (p), 1657 *BW*, 1680, 1692 *ib*, *the-* 1720 *ib*, *Molehelle* 1320 *ib* (p),
> -*Hill* (or *Mole Copp*) 1692 *ib*
> *Mowhul* 1286 *AddCh* (p), -*hull* 1322 *ib* (p), 1329 *BW* (p), *Mouhul*
> e14 *AddCh* (p), 1313, 1321 *BW* (p), 1317 *AddCh*, -*hull* 1342,
> c.1360 *BW* (p), *Mowehul* 1374 *ib* (p)
> *Molle* 1524 *AddCh*, (-*alias Moolcop*) 1647 *BW*
> *Mowle-coppe* 1621 Orm², *Moolcop*, *Mol Copp* 1647 *BW*, *Mole Copp*
> 1692 *ib*, -*Cop* (*Hill*) 1819 Orm², *Mowcop Hill* 1656 ib, *Mow Cop*
> 1831 Bry

'Hill with, or like, a heap or stack', from **mūga** 'a stack, a heap,
a mound' and **hyll**, with **copp** 'a hill top', and, again, **hyll**. The *Mow*
may have been an outcrop or a cairn, cf. Old Man of Mow *infra*. The
hill gives name to a hamlet in Odd Rode, and to Mow Lane *infra*,
but extends along the St border into Moreton cum Alcumlow and
Newbold Astbury townships. It appears to have had a beacon on it
in 1329, *v*. Orm² III 47, *AddCh* 37046, Sheaf³ 29 (6482), cf. *Balgreuemor infra*. The form *rocha de Mowa* in DEPN from BM is an
error.

Scholar Green (110–8357) [ˈskɔlə(r)-]

> *Scolehalc*, -*haleth* E1 *AddCh*, *Scol(e)halg(h)* 1286 *ib* (p), 1300, 1307
> *BW* (p) *et freq* with variant spellings *Skol(e)-*, *Sc(h)ol-*, -*halges*,
> -*halk*, -*halch* to 1369 *Tourn*, *Scolaleg* 1303 *BW*, -*algh* 1354 *Eyre*
> *et freq ib* to 1359
> *Sc(h)ol(l)al* E1 *AddCh*, *Scolale* 1280 *ib* (p), *Scol(e)hale* 1363 BPR
> (p), 1376 Fine (p), 1379 Cl, *Cholale* 1398, 1399 ChRR (p),
> *Sc(h)olehall* 1308 *AddCh* (p), 1330 *BW* (p) *et freq* with variant
> spelling -*halle* to 1410 Pat, *Sc(h)olall(e)* 1312 *BW*, 1365 BPR (p),
> 1376 Fine (p), *Schol-*, *Scollhall Greene* 1653, 1674 *AddCh*
> *Scolegh* 1294 ChF (p), *Scoleh'* c.1300 *BW* (p)
> *Scalehalg(h)* 1313, 1360 *BW*, *Schalehald* 1360 *ib*
> *Scolhach* 1320 *BW*, *Scol(e)hagh*, *Scolagh* 1351, 1356 *Eyre*
> and eight instances to 1372 AD (p), *Schollah Greene* 1675
> *AddCh*
> *Scokehall* 1371 (1400) Pat (p)

Schollers Greene 1668 *AddCh*, *Scol(l)ar Green* 1767 *BW*, *Schollow
Green* 1704, 1741, (*alias Scholar Green*) 1813 *ib*, *Schallow Green*
1842 OS

'Nook with a shed', *v.* skáli, halh, with grēne[2] 'a green'. The
Norse influence in this p.n. may be connected with the possible OIr
pers.ns. in *Mekerleg*', *Rugonnyscroft infra*.

STREET LANE (110–805587 to 810578), 1831 Bry, *strata de Roda* 1184
P, *cheminum de Rod(a)* 1185, 1186 ib, possibly associated with *Rodesti*
c.1270 *AddCh*, *Rode Lydyate*, *-Lidyate* 1308 *ib*, since the reference
in P is to a toll, cf. Lawton-Gate 320 *infra*, *v.* stīg 'a path, a road',
strǣt 'a paved road', hlid-geat 'a swing-gate', and Rode *supra*. The
road may be part of a Roman road from Middlewich to Chesterton
St, but more probably part of the Chesterton–Warrington route, cf.
317 *infra*, 1 43, 44. Cf. Forge Mill, which is on this road, and
styfordlone infra.

THURLWOOD (110–803578), 1842 OS, *Thirlewode* 1288 Court (p),
-wood 1581 Orm[2], *Thurlewode* 1265–91 Chest (p), (*vetus-*, *vetus
campus de-*) 1342, 1346 *AddCh*, *-wood* 1634 *ib*, *Thirlwood Field* 1839
TA, *The Hallwood* 1831 Bry. Here belong *Thurlsmalwode* 1315 BW,
Thursmalwod(e) 1314–19, 1342 *AddCh*. 'The (narrow) wood at, or
with, a gap', *v.* þyrel, wudu, smæl, cf. Higher Smallwood *infra*,
Smallwood 316 *infra*, Stanthorne 211 *supra*. The nature of the gap
is not apparent.

WOOD FM (lost), 1842 OS, *Wood House* 1831 Bry, cf. *le Wodehusis*
1271 *BW*, *-hus* 1271 *AddCh*, *le Wodehusefeld & -yerd* l13 *ib*, *Wode-
houseyord & -orcheard* e14 *ib*, *le Wodehous(e)feld* 1329 *ib*, *Wodehouzes*
1320 *BW*, *-houses*, *le Wodehouse medewe* 1349 *AddCh*, *Wodehoue*
c.1370 *BW* (p), and *boscum de Rode* 1380 Plea, *Rode Wood* 1605 *BW*,
and *Wood Field* 1662 *BW*, 1839 *TA*, *the Great & Lower Wood* 1786
BW, 'house(s) at a wood', from wudu and hūs, with feld, geard,
orceard, mǣd, cf. Rode *supra*.

ALMA COTTAGE, reminiscent of the Crimean War.   ASHBANK FM,
Ash Bank 1842 OS.   THE BANK, (HIGHER & LOWER) BANK FM,
BANK HO, *The Bank* 1842 OS, *Bank House* 1685 *BW*, *Higher Bank
Fd* 1788 *BW*, 'the hill-side', *v.* banke.   BATH WOOD, cf. *Bath
Field* 1839 *TA*, *v.* bæð. There may have been a spa here.   BIRCH

TREE FM.   BLAKEMOOR COTTAGE, named from *Blakemere Moss* 1831
Bry, 1842 OS, 'black-pool bog', v. blæc, mere[1], mos.   BOARDED-
BARN, 1831 Bry, *New House* 1709 *BW, Newhouse or Boarded Barn*
1757 *ib,* named from a weather-boarded barn, v. borded.   BOGG
HALL, *the Bogg* 1798 *BW,* v. bog.   BRATT'S WOOD, 1842 OS.
BRICK HO, 1842 ib, v. bryke.   CHANCE HALL, 1798 *BW.*   CINDER
HILL (LANE), *Syndurhulla'* (sic), *le Syndurhullus* e14 *AddCh,* v.
sinder 'cinder', hyll.   CLAPHATCH, 'a clap-gate', v. hæc(c), cf.
clap-gate.   CLOSE FM, 1831 Bry, v. clos.   DIP, 'a hollow', v.
dip.   DRUMBER LANE, cf. *the Drumble* 1647 *BW, Drumbus* 1839
TA, Drumber House 1842 OS, from dial. *drumble* 'a wooded dell or
ravine', v. dumbel.   FORGE MILL, *Street Forge Mill* 1831 Bry, v.
forge, myln, Street Lane *supra.*   HALL GREEN, 1583 *BW, the
Green* 1786 *ib,* v. hall, grēne[2].   HATCHING CLOSE, *Acorns Close*
1831 Bry, *Acorn Close* 1839 *TA, Acorn Wood* 1842 OS, 'enclosure and
wood where acorns are got', v. æcern (ModEdial. *atchorn* gives
Hatching), clos, wudu.   HILL COTTAGE.   HOBSON'S WOOD.
HOLEHOUSE FM, *the Hole House* 1744 *BW,* 'house in a hollow', v.
hol[1], hūs.   KENT GREEN (FM), *Kent Green* 1583 *BW,* a hamlet
under Mow Cop hill, v. grēne[2] 'a green'. The first el. may be a
surname, as in *Kents Meadow* 1651 *BW, the further & nearer Kents
Croft* 1798 *ib.*   LAWTON SALT WORKS, 1831 Bry, cf. *Salthouse
Field, Whitchhouse field* 1839 *TA,* v. salt-hūs (salt[1], hūs), wych(e)-
hous(e), cf. 193 *supra* for 'wich-house' in the special sense 'a salt
factory'.   LION COTTAGE.   LOW FM, 1831 Bry.   MIDDLE
WOOD, v. middel.   MILLBANK WOOD, MILL POND, cf. *Little Mill-
field* 1786 *BW, Millfield, Mill Pool Meadow* 1839 *TA,* named from
Rode Mill *supra.*   MOOR'S FM, *The Moors* 1831 Bry, v. mōr[1] 'a
moor, a marsh'.   MOSS COTTAGE & WOOD, LITTLE MOSS,
mosseta de Rode 1329 Orm[2], *Mosse Croft & Field(s)* 1647 *BW,* 1839
TA, Little Mosse 1662 *BW, -Moss* 1842 OS, *Mosse Meadow* 1744
BW, the Further-, Middle-, Near-, Gorsey- & Long Moss 1798 *BW,*
v. mos.   MOTTERSTALL, 1831 Bry, *Motterstow alias-* 1810 *BW,
Matterstall* 1842 OS, *Maltonstall* l13 *AddCh, Mawtunstal* 1315 *ib,*
'enclosure where speeches are made, a council enclosure' from mǣl[2]
and tūn, with stall, or mǣl[2] and tūn-stall.   MOUNT PLEASANT,
Cheshire Fields 1831 Bry, cf. *Cheshire Croft* 1830 *TA,* 'fields in
Cheshire', from their proximity to the St boundary.   MOW LANE,
Mole Hollows 1831 Bry, cf. *Mow Close, Common & Field* 1839 *TA,
the great(e) close on Mo(u)le* 1631 *AddCh,* 1657 *BW,* v. holh, clos,

commun, Mow Cop *supra*.   OLD HOUSE GREEN, 1798 *BW*.
OLD MAN OF MOW, a prominence at the highest point on Mow Cop
hill *supra*. The name might be from dial. *man* 'a cairn' (EDD, NED),
cf. maen and La 194, but a figurative origin seems likely, for JCJ
explains that the Old Man of Mow is a pillar of rock left standing
by the millstone quarrymen in the nineteenth century.   OLD
WOOD.   PACKHORSE FM, 1831 Bry.   PARSON'S WELL.   PEAR-
HOUSE, 1842 OS, *Bank House* 1831 Bry, cf. Bank Ho *supra*.   POOL
WOOD, *v.* Rode Pool *supra*.   PORTLAND HO.   PRIZE PLANTATION.
PUMP FM, *Pump House* 1831 Bry, 1842 OS, cf. *Pump Field* 1651, 1747
BW, *Pumpe-* 1663, 1669 *ib*, *v.* pumpe.   QUARRY WOOD, 1842 OS,
Quarry Close 1831 Bry, *v.* quarriere, cf. Orm² 1 130, '... there are
very fair mill-stones digged up at Mowcop-hill' (King), and *the
millstone work called the Marefoot Work* 1647 *BW*, *Marefoot on Mole*
1684 *ib*, 'the foot of the boundary', *v.* (ge)mǣre, fōt, from the
position below the county-boundary ridge of Mow Cop hill *supra*.
RAMSDELL HALL, 1831 Bry, cf. *Big-*, *Little- & Long Ramsdale* 1839
TA, from ramm 'a ram' or hramse 'wild garlic', and dæl[1].
ROOKERY FM.   SHOULDER OF MUTTON WOOD, *v.* 327 *infra*.
HIGHER SMALLWOOD, *High Smallwoods* 1798 *BW*, *-Smallwood* 1831
Bry, cf. *Smalwode Heys* 1497 ChRR, *Smallwood Lane* 1728 *BW*,
'(lane and enclosures at) the narrow wood', *v.* smæl, wudu, (ge)hæg,
lane, cf. Smallwood 316 *infra*, Thurlwood *supra*.   SPRINGBANK,
v. spring 'a well-spring', banke.   SPRINK PLANTATION, *the Spring*
1651 *BW*, *the Sprinke* 1687 *ib*, *v.* spring 'a young wood'.   SQUIRES
WELL, *v.* wella.   STANMER HO (lost), 1842 OS.   STONE CHAIR
FM, *v.* stān, chai(e)re.   SUGAR WELL, 'sweet well', *v.* sugre, wella.
TOWNSEND COTTAGES, FM & LANE, *Rode Town* 1842 OS, *v.* toun,
ende[1].   WALKERS LANE, *Narrow Lane* 1831 Bry.   WILDERNESS
WOOD, *Wilderness* 1839 *TA*.   WILLOW PLANTING, a wood.

FIELD-NAMES

The undated forms are 1839 *TA* 303. Of the others, 1293 is BM, c.1260–70,
E1, l13, 1280, c.1291, e14[1], 1308, 1311, 1312[1], 1313[1], 1314[1], 1315, 1329,
1342, 1345, 1346, 1349, 1350, 1353, 1362, 1368[1], 1437–68, 1453, 1509, 1631,
1662[1], 1675, 1728[1], 1740 AddCh, 1265–91 Chest, 1316, 1369, 1450 Orm²,
1423 *Eyre*, 1581 ChRR, 1619 Sheaf, 1831 Bry, 1842 OS, and the rest *BW*.

(*a*) (Little & Long) Acres (*Lower Acres* 1656, *Over Acres* 1685, *The Acres*
1718, *the Long Acre* 1786, *v.* æcer); Aldrey Croft (*Ollery Croft* 1704, 1743,
Aldery Croft 1798, *v.* alor); Ashcroft 1728 (*v.* æsc); Audles (*the Audlays*,

-*lass* 1663, *Awdleyes* 1669, *Little Audlas alias Audlees* 1703, *the Audlass* 1750, probably named after the Tuchet family, lords *Audley*, who held Boden Hall *supra* in the thirteenth century, but 'old clearings or pastures' is possible, from **ald** and **lēah** or **lǣs**); Bach Bottoms, Great & Little Bach 1762 (*The Baches* 1651, cf. *Rodebache* 1265–91, 'the valley-brook', *v.* **bæce**[1], **botm**, cf. Rode *supra*); Banflatt 1720 (*v.* **bēan**, flat); Barley Croft & Fd (*Barliecroft* 1647, *Barley Field* 1774); Barn Croft & Fd (1786, 1647); Barren Fd; Black Croft (1720, cf. *Blake Field* (*Meadow*) 1668); Blakeley Wds 1774 (*v.* **blæc**, **lēah**); Blue Button Fd (1793, from dial. *blue-buttons* 'the cornflower *Centaurea*, or devil's-bit *Scabiosa succisa*'); Boozy Pasture (*the Boosey Pasture* 1798, *v.* **bōsig**); Bottom Mdw (cf. *Bottom Field* 1793); The Bottoms (1774, *v.* **botm**); Brad fd (1666, *v.* **brād**); Brick (Kiln) Fd (*Brickes Field* 1647, *Brick Field* 1720, *Brick Kiln Field* 1798, *v.* **bryke**, **bryke-kyl**); Brinne 1705 (*v.* **bryn**); Brinsells (*the Brinseys* 1647); Brittains Croft (*Britton's-* 1700, *Brittaines-* 1721, *Britain's-* 1728, from a surname *Britton*); Broom Croft & Fd (*the Brome feild* 1631, *Broome Field* 1648, *Broom Croft Meadow* 1668, *The Brooms* 1744, *v.* **brōm**); Broomy Fd (cf. *Broomy Croft* 1668, *v.* **brōmig**); Burnt Mdw (1798); By Flatt (*the Byflatts* 1786, cf. *Bye Field* 1668, *v.* **byge**[1] 'a corner, an angle, the bend of a river', flat); Caseless, Casel(e)y, Keasley (*þe Careslegh* c.1300, 1327, *Karylegh* 1314, *the Cawsley* 1786, 'the cress clearing', *v.* **cærse**, **lēah**); Cats Moss (*the-* 1798, *v.* **cat(t)**, **mos**); the Channellend Fd 1703 (*v.* **chanel**, **ende**[1]); Church Fd (1774, cf. *Church-way Field* 1668); Coal Fd (*v.* **col**[1]); Cobby Fd (*v.* **cobb(e)** 'a round lump, a cob'); Cock (Fd) (*v.* **cocc**[1] 'a heap, a hillock'); Cockshutts (*v.* **cocc-scyte**); the Collington 1685, 1788 ('charcoal enclosure', *v.* **col**[1], -**ing**[1], **tūn**); Colly Croft & Mdw (*v.* **colig**); Common Piece (*v.* **commun**, **pece**); Coppy (cf. *Coppice Bank(s)* 1747, (*Bottoms*) 1762, *v.* **copis**, **banke**, **botm**); Cote Fd (*v.* **cot**); Cow Hay (*the Cowhey* 1647, 1651, *v.* **cū**, (ge)**hæg**); Cow Leys 1788 (1685, *Broomie-*, *Gorsty-* & *Little Cowle(ye)s* 1647, *Great-* & *Little Cowles* 1744, 'cow pastures', *v.* **cū**, **lǣs**); Cow Pasture (1720); Dace-pit Fd; Dairy Pit Fd (cf. *the Dairy House* 1741, -*Dayrie-* 1651, *v.* **deierie**); Daw Hay (cf. *Daw(e)croft* 1605, 1663, 1669, 'jackdaw enclosure', *v.* **daw(e)**, (ge)**hæg**, **croft**); (Five-, Nine- & Ten-) Day Math (*Ten Day Math* 1662, *Five-* 1798, cf. *Two-* 1647, *Twelve-* 1662, *v.* **day-math**); Delf-, Delph Fd (*v.* (ge)**delf** 'a quarry'); Dicas Close; Dove House Mdw 1720 (1647, *v.* **dove-house**); Dram Fd; Dunns Fd (1669, *Dunsfield* 1605, probably from the surname *Dunn*); Ebbfield 1718 ((*Meadow*) 1709, cf. *le Bente hebfilde* 1509, perhaps 'bramble field', from **hēopa** and **feld**, with **beonet**, **mǣd**); Elbow Mdw (*Ellow Meadow* 1720, *v.* **elbowe**); Higher Flatt (*High Flatt* (*Meadow*) 1663, 1685, 1788, *v.* flat); Flower Croft (*Flowers Croft* 1647, 1744); Ford Sprink 1842 ('young wood at a ford', *v.* **ford**, **spring**); Four Pits 1831; Frog Pool (Mdw) (1720, (*the*) *Frogge Poole* (*Medowe*) 1631, 1649, *v.* **frogga**, **pōl**[1]); Garden Croft 1788 (1685); Geld Acres (perhaps 'marigold acres', *v.* **gylde**); Gennings; Goshan (probably biblical, named after the Land of Goshen, *v.* 326 *infra*); Little Grace (a derogatory name, *v.* 326 *infra*); Good Grass 1718 (1709, *v.* **gærs**); Gutter Croft (*v.* **goter**); Hall o' Lee Mdw (*v.* Hall o' Lee 321 *infra*); Hawsted 1786 (*the Hursteads* 1728[1], 'wood-site', *v.* **hyrst**, **stede**); Big-, Little- & Long Hay(e)s (*Great* & *Little Haies* 1647, *Great-*, *Little-* & *Long Heys* 1721, cf. *le heie* 1349, *the New Hay* 1666, -*Hey*

1722, *Heys Bank* 1721, *v.* (ge)hæg); The Hemmings Croft; Little Hemp-
croft 1720 (*v.* hænep); Hen Heath (*the Heane Heath* 1666, *Heam Heath* 1722,
perhaps from hegn or hægen 'an enclosure' with hæð); the Higgens Fd
1747 (1651, *the Hickens-* 1687, probably from the pers.n. or surname *Higgin(s)*,
Hickin(s)); High Fd (1685); Highermost Fd & Mdw (*Highmost Field* 1704,
1741, *Higmost-* 1743, cf. *Higher Meadow* 1662); Hill Fd (*Higher & Nearer
Hill Field* 1647, cf. *the three hills* 1798); Hog Grass (*v.* hogg, gærs); Holy
Croft (*v.* hol[1], -ig[a]); Holly Brow (*v.* holegn, brū); Horns Lane 1831 (1647, *v.*
horn); Horse Close (*New & Old Horse Close* 1663, cf. *New Horse Coppice,
Old Horse Croft* 1669); Horse Pasture (1605, 1720); Huines-, Hewnes Croft
1717 (*Huynusfeld* 1318, *the Huins Croft* 1662, 'the peasant's croft', *v.* hine,
feld, croft); The Hurber (*two Hurbers Croft* 1704, *two Harburs Crofts* 1741,
-*Hurburs-* 1743, perhaps from here-beorg 'a shelter'); (Lower & Upper)
Intake (*two Intak Yords* 1743, *v.* inntak, geard); Two Jack Yards 1741
(-*Yords* 1704, cf. *Jacke Croftes* 1509, *v.* jack, geard); Keasley (*v.* Caseless
supra); Kiln Croft; Knowl Fd & Pits, Near & Rough Knowl(e)s (*le Knoll*
1311, 1385, *le Knol* 1312, *Gorstie & Rough Knowles, the Knolle alias the
Knowe, Hill Knoll* 1647, *Knole Croft* 1717, *v.* cnoll 'a hillock', hyll, gorstig,
rūh, croft); Ladies Walk (*v.* hlǣfdige, walk); Lady Platt (*Bigg & Little Lady
Field* 1774, *v.* hlǣfdige); Lane Croft & Fd; The Leese (*Lees Pasture* 1605,
(*the*) *Lees* 1647, 1669, *v.* lǣs 'pasture, meadow-land'); Litch Field Flatt
(perhaps from līc 'a corpse'; but probably from lece 'a boggy stream'); Lite
Moor (*v.* lȳt); Long Flatt 1718 (1709); the Lunts Field Mdw 1830 (1647,
1767, *le Luntesfeld* 1385, *v.* feld. Dr von Feilitzen suggests a ME pers.n.
*Lunt, related to the OE pers.n. *Lunting*, ModE *lunt* 'spiritless, tame', and
an OE pers.n. **Lunta* the first el. of Luntley He, *v.* SNPh IX 9–10); Madge
Breeze (*the Magbrey feild* 1631, *v.* madge 'a magpie', and brēg (ModEdial.
bree 'the brow') 'the brow (of a hill)', cf. *Madgcroft* 1675, 'magpie croft', *v.*
croft); Man Mdw (*v.* maen, cf. Old Man of Mow *supra*); Margerts Fds 1719
(*Margret Fields* 1703, from the fem. pers.n. *Margaret*); Marl Croft & Fd
(cf. *le Marledecroft* e14, *Marled Hayes* 1647, *Marle Field* 1747, (*Bottom*) 1762,
v. marle, marlede, croft, botm); Marsh Mdw 1788 (1685); Martin Rutter;
Great & Little May Pool 1788 (-*poole* 1647, 1685, cf. *May-Pole Bank* 1680,
on Mow Cop hill, a place where a maypole was erected, *v.* maye-pole,
banke); Meadow Fd (cf. *Meadow Ridding* 1685, 1788, *v.* mǣd, ryding);
Mecca Fence, Mickow Pant (*Micclefonts, Mickle-, Micclefont Meadow, the
Micklefont* 1647, 'big spring', *v.* micel (with -*k*- from mikill), funta); Far &
Near Moslin (*Further & Near-* 1817, cf. *Moslin* 326 *infra*); (Little) Mosseley
1720 (*Great- & Little-* 1658, *Moseleg(h)* 1313, 1314[1], -*ley(hurst)* e14[1], 1316,
Moseleghacre 1345, *le Hedurmoslegh'* 1349, *Mosley* 1581, -*leyes* 1649, 'moss
clearing', *v.* mos, lēah, æcer, hyrst, and ME *hider, hedur* (OE *hider*), adv.,
used here as an adj., 'hither, nearer', recorded 1387 NED); New Fd (*the-*
1647); Nogars Moor (1831, cf. Noger Croft 305 *supra*, *v.* mōr[1]); Nook
Willings (cf. *Nookdale* 1647, *v.* nōk, wilegn, dæl[1]); Odd Fd (*v.* odde); Old
Mdw (cf. (*le*) *Oldemedowe* c.1300, 1314, 1327, *two Old Meadows* 1647, *v.*
ald, mǣd); The Outlett 1786 (*v.* outlet); Oven House Croft 1767 (*v.* ofen,
hūs); Ox Hay; Parsons Hey 1718 (1709, *le Persones Heye* 1329, *v.* persone,
(ge)hæg); Patches (*the Patch* 1744, cf. *Swinnertons Paches* 1651, *v.* pacche);

Pear Tree Flatt 1830 (1647, *v.* flat); Peas Flat (*Pease-* 1720, cf. *Pease Field* 1583 *et freq*, *Peasfield* (*Banke*) 1666, *Pease Croft* 1668, *v.* pise, feld, banke, croft, flat); Peavers Croft (cf. *Peevors Yate* 1605, probably from the surname from Peover 85, 220 *supra*, *v.* croft, geat, cf. Peover 292 *supra*); The Pickers 1786 (*v.* pichel); The Pingel (1774, *v.* pingel); Pit Mdw (cf. *Pit(t) Ridding* 1685, 1788, *v.* pytt, ryding); Plough Mdw; Poor Fd (1793); Pretty Fd; Rabel Fd; Rag Fd (*Ragge-* 1647); the Rathbone Close 1631; Red Bank & Lane (cf. *Ridlond* 1423, *Redland* (*Meadow*) 1605, *v.* rēad, banke, lane, land); Relicat Fd 1798; Riddings (*the Furthest-*, *Little-* & *Middle Riddinge* 1666, 1668, 1677, *v.* ryding); Rough Close, Fd & Mdw (*Rough Field* 1798, cf. *Middle Rough alias -Ruffe* 1647, *v.* rūh); Rushy Hay (*v.* riscig, (ge)hæg); Rye Fd 1788 (1605, *Rie Field* 1662, cf. *Ruykroft* e14[1], *v.* ryge, croft, feld); Saint John's Fd; Sand Hole Fd, Sandy Fd; School Fd (cf. *School Lane* 1831); Seven Butts (*Seaven-* 1668, *v.* seofon, butte); Silch-hurst Fd 1718; the two Sim Fds 1798; Smetherups (*Smith Rope* 1647, *Higher-*, *Lower-* & *the Lowest Smeadrope* 1662, 1662[1], *the Smethropes* 1720, *the lower Sneadrope field* 1728, *Lower Sirethorp or Cartwright's Field* 1786, 'smooth allotments', *v.* smēðe, rāp, cf. Rapdowl(e)s, Rope 327, 327 *infra*); Smithy Croft & Mdw (*Smithie Croft* 1651, *-Field* 1662, cf. *Smith Pool* 1786, *v.* smiððe); Snape Mdw 1722 (cf. Snape 321 *infra*); Spons (cf. *Spone Mosse* 1583, *Great Span* 1647, 'the strip', *v.* spann[1]); Spout Fd (1774, *v.* spoute); Squint Willings (*v.* squint, wilegn); Stocking Flatt (*Stockieflatt* 1728, *v.* stoccing, flat); Stone-pit fd; Styphers Fd (perhaps from *Styfordlone infra*); The Thistley Fd 1798; Three Corner Fd; Top Close & Fd; Turnip Bank; Wain-house Croft (*Waynhouse Yard* 1647, 'cart-house enclosure', *v.* wain-house, geard); Watfield Gapp 1750 (*v.* gap); Way Fd 1774 (*v.* weg); Well Fd (cf. *Wall Croft* 1647, 1675, *v.* wella); Wench Acre; Wheat Fd (1605, cf. *Wheat Croft* 1668, *the French Wheatfield* 1793, *v.* hwǣte, French wheat); Big & Little Whit Fd (*Great-*, *Higher-* & *Lower Whitfield* 1728, *v.* hwīt); Whithy Fd (cf. *the wytheney Feild* 1631, *v.* wiðegn, (ge)hæg, wiðig); Whittney's bridge 1619 (*v.* brycg, cf. Thomas *Quytteney* 1437–68); Wide Lane Fd (*Wade Lane Field* 1647, 1721, 'ford lane', *v.* (ge)wæd); Wildblood Croft; the Winnel (Bottom) 1863 (1718, 'valley-bottom where windle-grass grows', *v.* windle, botm).

(b) *Aleweynsacre* c.1330 (from the OE pers.n. form *Alwine* discussed by Feilitzen 158 and æcer 'an acre, a selion'); *Babacre* (*Green*) (*v.* grēne[2] 'a green'); *Baggelone*, *Baggemosse* 1329 ('badger's lane and moss', *v.* bagga, lane, mos); *Baklottes Ruyding* 1342 (*v.* ryding, 'a clearing'. The first el. may be a pers.n.); *Balgreuemor* c.1260–70, *Balgreue* (*medue*, *-medwe*) e14[1], 1313[1], *Balegreue* e14[1] (p), *the Balgreave medowe* 1631 ('beacon-wood marsh & meadow', *v.* bāl, grǣfe, mǣd, mōr[1], cf. Mow Cop *supra*); *beane holme* 1583, *-hulme* 1666 ('bean marsh-meadow', *v.* bēan, hulm); *le Blakeflat'* 1308 (*v.* blæc, flat); *ad nigrum lacum* c.1260–70, *le Blakelccu* 1320 ('black stream', *v.* blæc, lacu, lœkr); (*le*) *Blakelode* 1271, 1350 ('black water-course', *v.* blæc, (ge)lād); *Bolehul* e14[1], 1308 (from hyll 'a hill', with either bol 'a smooth, rounded hill', or bola, bolr 'a tree-trunk'); *Boughfield alias Bowe-Field alias Bullfield* 1651; *the Brainehulme*, *Brainehulme Bothom* 1677 (*v.* hulm, botm); *le Brandemedewe* 1353 ('burnt meadow', *v.* brende[2], mǣd);

le Brodemor 1315 ('broad marsh', *v.* brād, mōr[1]); *le Cornel del Bromiknol* 1349 ('the corner of the broomy hillock', *v.* corner, brōmig, cnoll); *bromilegamor* 1260–70, *le bromileg(h)mor* l13, e14[1] ('(moor at) the broomy clearing', *v.* brōmig, lēah, mōr[1]); *Broomshawes* 1647 (*v.* brōm, sceaga); *Browne-shawes* 1651 (*v.* brūn[1], sceaga); *le Byrcheles* 1280 ('the little birch-trees', *v.* bircel); *Caldewalleflatte* 1345 ('plot of ground near a cold spring', *v.* cald, wælla, flat); *Calver Croft* 1647 ('calves' croft', *v.* calf (gen.pl. calfra), croft); *Caluerheye* e14[1] ('calves enclosure', *v.* calf (gen.pl. calfra, (ge)hæg); *le Castelweye* l13, 1315, -*way* 1329, -*waie(gate)* 1349, -*wei(a)* e14[1], *le Catelleyate*, *porta del Castellone* 1329 ('way, gate-way and lane near a castle', *v.* castel(l), weg, geat, lane. The castle has not been located. It may refer to a motte at Little Moreton Hall *supra*); *le Cherchefeld* e14[1], *le Chirchefild* 1353 (*v.* cirice, feld); *le clyf* e14[1] (*v.* clif); *le Clothacre* 1345 (from æcer, with either ME *cloth* (OE *clāþ*) 'cloth' or clot(t) 'a mass, a lump, a hill'); *two Connygates* 1605 ('rabbit warren', *v.* cony-gat, cf. coni, gata); *Cowhousend* 1647 (*v.* cū, hūs, ende[1]); *Croneberehalgh* 1353 (probably 'nook where the cranberry grows', from cranberry and halh, *v. Croneberyhalvch* 145 *supra*); *Denyldescroft* 1353 ('Denehild's enclosure', from an OE fem. pers.n. *Denehild* and croft); *Dianysecroft* 1308 ('Denise's croft', from the ME fem. pers.n. *Dionysia*, *Denise* and croft); *the Dudles Moore* 1631; *Halwarte Flatte* 1345 (perhaps from the ON pers.n. *Hallvarðr*, ODan *Halwarth* and flat); *Great & Little Harratt* 1668 (*v.* here-geatu); *the Half Acre* 1666, *the Haveakers* 1677 (*v.* half, æcer); *Heath Place* 1668 (*v.* hǣð, place); *del Hokes* 1340 (p), -*Okus* 1346 (p), (*v.* āc); *Holmes bridges* 1619 (*v.* brēc, bryce); *Holt Field* 1668 (*v.* holt); *Huginesfeld* 1349 ('Hugin's field', from the ME pers.n. *Hugin*, diminutive of *Hugh*, and feld); *Hullileye* c.1260–70, *le Hullileg'yord* e14[1], *le Hullilegh* 1349 ('hilly clearing', from hulli, lēah, geard); *Holleruding* E1, *Hulle Ruding* e14[1] ('hill clearing', *v.* hyll, ryding); *Kinerbeslac* c.1370; *le Lineshalleyes* c.1291 ('(clearings at) the wood at a place where flax grows', *v.* līn, sceaga, lēah); *le Longelegh'* 1349 ('long clearing', *v.* lang, lēah); *Lumpes-, Lompesmosse* 1509, *Lump(e)s Mosse* 1583, 1651 (perhaps 'lumpy bog', *v.* lump, mos); *le lynalyusforde* e14[1] ('(ford at) the flax nook', *v.* līn, halh, ford); *Mekerleg'* 1280, *Mekerslegh* 1314[1] (p), *Meken(en)isley* c.1300, *Mekenaslegh in Rode* 1327, *Mekanesl'* 1329, *Mekenesleg(h)* c.1330, 1340, 1350, *Mekynsleg(h)* c.1300, 1327 (p), *Mekynes-* 1345, *Mekanesleg'* 1313, *Mekunsleg'* 1330 (p) (from lēah 'a clearing', probably with a pers.n., perhaps OIr *Maicín*, or the derived surname *Ó Maicín*, cf. *Rugonnyscroft infra*, Scholar Green *supra*); *le middul diche* 1349 (*v.* middel, dīc); *le midylflat* 1308 (*v.* middel, flat); *(le) middilyort(h)* 1315 ('the middle ground', *v.* middel, eorðe); *Nibb(e)field* 1649, 1658 (perhaps a pointed field, *v.* nib); *Northbrock, le Brock* 1315, *le broc* 1329, *le broch* e14 (*v.* norð, brōc); *le Oldefild(mor)* 1312[1], -*feld* 1329, 1350, -*filde* 1509, *le Holdefild* c.1360 (*v.* ald, feld, mōr[1]); *Oldelandeschawe* 1293 ('(wood at) the old land', *v.* ald, land, sceaga); *Orchard Croft* 1605 (*v.* orceard, croft); *Outerfield* 1605 (*v.* ūterra, feld); *the Paddocke* 1647 (*v.* pearroc); *manerium cum edificiis scitum infra le parck* 1315, *le Park* 1330, *le Parcehalle* 1368, *le parke hall* 1368[1], 1453 ('(the hall in) the park', *v.* park, hall); *(le) pecheneruding* e14[1], *Pechinruding* 1349 (perhaps from the ME surname *Peccin, Pechin*, diminutive of *Peche* (OFr *peche* 'sin'), *v.* ryding); *the Randalls* 1647; *le rauenusholtusmor* e14[1] ('(moor at) the raven's wood', from hræfn, perhaps as a pers.n., *v.* holt, mōr[1]); *del Rowleye* 1362 (p) ('the rough clearing', *v.* rūh, lēah); *Rugonnyscroft* 1308 (*v.* croft. The first el. may be a pers.n., perhaps a form of OFr *Rogo* or even OIr *Ruadacán* or the derived surname *Ó Ruadhagáin*, cf. *Mekerleg' supra*); *Ruykroft* e14[1] (*v.* ryge, croft); *Selsacre* 1647; *the Shitlock* 1647 ('the midden-yard', *v.* scite, loca); *le Schycciokesfeld* e14; *le Sindredflat* c.1370 ('plot of land full of cinders', *v.* flat. The first el. is ME *sindered*, ModE *cindered* (NED *scindred* 1430) pa.part.adj. 'cindered; reduced to, or having, cinders', *v.* sinder); *Skeylhornrudyng* 1315, *Skelhornes Ruding* 1330 (from ryding 'a clearing', with either the local surname *Skelhorne*, or its original p.n. 'horn of land at a hut', *v.* skáli, horn, cf. Skellorn Green 1 184); *the Slacke* 1647 (*v.* slakki); *Snellacres* 1605, 1654; *Solinhac* c.1260–70 (the name of an oak-tree in *AddCh* 37035, *v.* āc. The first el. may be solein 'lonely', cf. *Solengak* 327 *infra*, *Sulinesfeld* 186 *supra*); *Soutersfeeld* 1329 ('the cobbler's field', *v.* sūtere, feld); *Stodfoldis lache* c.1260–70 ('(boggy stream at) the studfold', *v.* stōd-fald, læc(c)); *le Sty-*, *Stifordlone* 1329 ('(lane to) the pathway ford', *v.* stīg, ford, lane, cf. Street Lane, Styphers Field *supra*); *le sych* e14[1] (*v.* sīc); *Tunstall* 1368 (p) (*v.* tūn-stall); *Turners Yate* 1605 (from geat 'a gate' and the surname *Turner*); *Twemlowes Meadow* 1647 (probably the surname from Twemlow 230 *supra*, but it may mean 'meadow at *Twemlow* (at the two mounds)', *v.* twæm, hlāw); *Tyrqueneflat* 1308 (from flat 'a flat piece of ground'. Dr von Feilitzen thinks an OE fem. pers.n. *Tīrcwēn* improbable because the pers.n. el. *Tīr-* is too archaic. He suggests for the first el. ON **tyr-hvin* 'gorse for firing', *v.* hvin, cf. tyri, ON *tyrviðr* 'firewood'); *the Wolfeth Close* 1631 ('(enclosure at) the wolf heath', *v.* wulf, hæð, clos).

10. SMALLWOOD (110–8060)

> *Smelewde* e13 Orm[2], *Smelwood* 1209 Tab
> *Smal(e)wode(e)* 1252 Ch, 1274, 1276, 1283 Ipm, 1275 Cl *et freq*
>   with variant spellings *-wood(e)*, *-wodde*; *-iuxta Astbury* 1443 Plea,
>   *-in Astburye* 1559 Pat
> *Smallwode* 1398 ChRR, *-wod* 1452 Orm[2], *-wood* 1558 (1582) *AddCh*
> *Smawode* 1460 ChRR (p)

'Narrow wood', *v.* smæl, wudu. Cf. Thurlwood 309 *supra*.

ABBEY GROVE.   BANK HO, named from Wharams Bank *infra*. BROOKHOUSE FM, GREEN & MOSS, *Brookhowse Green in Smalewoode* 1591 AD, *the Brooke* 1721 *BW* (a house), *Brookhouse Moss* 1831 Bry, 'house by a brook', *v.* brōc, hūs, grēne[2], mos.   BROOM CROFT, cf. *Broomy Croft* 1839 *TA*.   CROSS LANE, 'lane to a cross', *v.* cros. DAYHOUSE GREEN, DEERSGREEN, *le Deers* 1518 ChRR, *Deares* 1558 *AddCh*, *Dayhouse Green* 1735 *BW*, *Days field*, *Deer House Meadow* 1839 *TA*, 'green at a dairy-house', *v.* dey-hus, grēne[2], cf. Dog Lane

276 *supra*. FOURLANES END, *Four Lane Ends* 1831 Bry. GREEN-
BANK. GREENFIELD COTTAGE, cf. *Green Field* 1839 *TA*. HANG-
MAN'S LANE, *v.* hangeman. MANOR HO. MARTIN'S MOSS,
Overton Moss 1831 Bry, *Marton Moss* 1839 *TA*, *Martin Moss* 1860
White, *v.* mos 'a moss, a bog'. The earlier name is from Overton
Hall *infra*. The later is probably *marten* 'a weasel, a marten'. MILL
FM, *Chequer Houses* 1831 Bry, cf. *Chequer Field* 1839 *TA*, *v.* cheker.
MOSS FM, named from Rue Moss *infra*. MOSSBANK FM, named
from Martin's Moss *supra*, *v.* banke. MOSSEND (FM), *Moss End*
1831 Bry, named from Brookhouse Moss *supra*, *v.* ende[1]. NOAH'S
ARK. OVERTON GREEN & HALL, 1831 Bry, *Overton House* 1656
Sheaf, 'higher farm', *v.* uferra, tūn. POOLS LANE, *Brook Lane*
1831 Bry, *v.* brōc, pōl[1]. RUEMOSS, 1831 ib, 'rough moss', *v.* rūh,
mos. SCHOOL FM, 1860 White, *The Knowls or White Lion Farm*
1831 Bry, cf. *le Knolls* n.d. AD (A. 11218), *v.* cnoll 'a hillock'.
SIMFIELD HO, cf. *Sim Field* 1839 *TA*, *Sims Green* 1860 White, from
the pers.n. *Sim*, short for *Simeon* or *Simon*, *v.* grēne[2], feld. SMALL-
WOODHOUSE FM, *Bears Head Farm* 1831 Bry. SMALLWOOD MILL,
Smalwode mulne 1404 *MinAcct*, cf. *a water mill in Smalewode* 1299 Cl,
v. myln. SPARK LANE, 1842 OS, cf. *Spark(s)* 1839 *TA*, cf. Spark
Lane 277 *supra*, *v.* spearca 'brushwood'. SPEN GREEN & MOSS,
1831 Bry, *Spen Green* 1700 Sheaf, cf. *Spend bridge* 1619 ib, *v.* spenne,
brycg, grēne[2], mos. STONYFLATS, *Stoney-* 1839 *TA*, *v.* stānig,
flat. STREET LANE, *The Strete* 1604 Sheaf, cf. *Street Field* 1839
TA, *v.* strǣt, cf. 309 *supra*, I 44. WHARAMS BANK, *Wearhams Bank*
1831 Bry, *Warams Bank* 1842 OS, probably with a surname derived
from Weaverham 327 *infra*, *v.* banke 'a hill-side'. WILACRE
LANE, *v.* 277 *supra*. YEWTREE FM, 1842 OS, *Yewtree House* 1708
BW.

FIELD-NAMES

The undated forms are 1839 *TA* 357. Of the others, 1280 is P, 1402 ChRR,
1443 Plea, 1479, 1518 AD, 1727 Sheaf, 1732 *AddCh*, 1831 Bry, 1842 OS.

(a) Bar Croft; Barn Acre; Bent (*v.* beonet); Birch Hill, Knowl & Moss;
Birchen (*v.* bircen[1]); Blackwide Fd; Blake Butts (*v.* blæc, butte); Broad Oak;
Brook Shute (*v.* brōc, scēat); Buck Moss (*v.* bucca, mos); Burnt Hill & Yard
(*v.* brende[2], geard); Big Butterton, Butterton Mdw (*v.* butere, tūn); Long-,
Short- & Lower Butts (*v.* butte); Carters Fd (cf. *Carters Lane* 1831 Bry, *v.*
305 *supra*); Catterley Croft; Cock Shutes (*v.* cocc-scyte); Crookhouse Moss;
Cross Butts (*v.* cros, butte); Cutting Knife (*v.* 326 *infra*); Two-, Four-, Five-,
Six Day(s) Work (*v.* day-work); Dove; Entry Croft (*v.* entre(e)); Big-,
Long-, Square- & Gawsey Finney (cf. *Finney* 326 *infra*); Five Pennyworth

(*v.* peni(n)g-weorð); Flag Moss 1842 (*Heron Moss* 1831, 'moss where flags grow', '-haunted by herons', *v.* flagge, he(i)roun); Flatts (*v.* flat); Furnival Hall Fd; Gawsy Croft (*v.* gorstig); Gillever Acre ('gilly-flower acre'); Golden Slack, Golders Lack ('golden hollow', *v.* gylden, slakki); Hob Acre (*v.* hobbe); Iron Gate Fd; Lay Fd (*v.* lǣge); Leeches (*v.* lǣc(c)); Long Acre; Long Shutes (*v.* scēat); Looms (dial. *loom* 'a wide land or selion', cf. land); Mare Fd & Lees (*v.* mere[2], lǣs); Marl Fd, Marle Moss (*v.* marle); Old House Mdw; Orange Fd; Ottershayes ('otter woods', *v.* oter, sc(e)aga); Ox Heys; Oylershaw ('alder wood', *v.* alor, sceaga); Peavers Croft (cf. 314 *supra*); the Plump Ridding 1732 (*v.* ryding); Quarters (*v.* quarter); Red Hills; Ridding fd (*v.* ryding); Rough Acre; Roundabout (*v.* 327 *infra*); Rous Fd; Salters Fd (*v.* saltere); Sandhill Bank; Seamans Croft; Shay Croft (*v.* sc(e)aga); Sherman's Mdw 1727; Slum Mdw (cf. Slum Wood 321 *infra*, *v.* slump); Spout Mdw (*v.* spoute, cf. dial. *spout* 'a spring'); Walker Acre; Welch Croft; White Fd; White Leech (*v.* lǣc(c)).

(*b*) *Ladywode* 1479 ('lady's wood', *v.* hlǣfdige, wudu); (pasture called) *Lucas Haywode* 1489, *Lucas in Haywod* 1518 ('Lucas's part of Haywood', from the ME pers.n. *Lucas* and a p.n. 'enclosed wood', *v.* (ge)hæg, wudu); *Witheneford* 1280 (p), *Wythyford* 1402 (p), *Withiford* 1443 (p) ('ford growing with willow-trees', *v.* wiðigen, ford).

11. SOMERFORD, *olim* SOMERFORD (CUM) RADNOR (110–8264), *Somerford et Radnore* 1430 Dav, *Somerford Radnor* 1597 *ib*, 1842 *TA*, *Somerford cum Radnor* 1831 Bry, *v.* Radnor, Somerford *infra*.

SOMERFORD HALL, PARK & FM ['sumər-, 'sʌmər-]

Sumreford 1086 DB, *Sumerford* 13 Dav (p), *Summer-* 1463 ChRR (p)

Somerford 1190–1220 Chest *et freq* with variant spellings *-fordia*, *-forde*, *-fort*, *Somir-*, *-ur-*, *Sommer-*; *-iuxta Davenporte* 1297 Tab, *-Swetenham* 1377 Plea, *-in Northwich* 1442 ib, *Nether-Somer-forde* 1510 ChRR, *Somerford Hall* 1724 NotCestr

'Ford used in summer', *v.* sumor, ford. The ford was probably a crossing of R. Dane, perhaps at Radnor Bridge *infra*. It is distinguished as in Northwich Hundred and as 'nether', *v.* neoðera, from Somerford Booths in Macclesfield Hundred 1 63. It adjoins Davenport and Swettenham 301, 283 *supra*.

RADNOR BRIDGE, HALL & WOOD (110–8364), *Radenoure* 1188 Orm[2] (p), *-or(e)* 1270 Dav, l13 AddCh (p), *Radnovre* 13 Orm[2], *-or(e)* 1385 IpmR, 1398 ChRR (p) *et freq*, *Radnor House* 1593 JCJ, *Radnor Bridge* 1619 Sheaf, *-Lane*, *-Farm & Woods* 1831 Bry, *le Redenor* 1316 Tab (p), 'at the red bank', *v.* rēad (wk. dat.sg. rēadan), ōra[1].

LANE END COTTAGES. LIGHTWOOD FM, 1831 Bry, v. lēoht, wudu.
LOACHBROOK (BRIDGE & FM), v. Loach Brook 1 30. PECKLOW
COB (110–812645), 1831 Bry, *Peck Lowe Hill or Windmill Hill*
1688 *AddCh*, giving name to Pecklow 277 *supra*, 'pointed mound',
v. pēac, hlāw, cobb(e). POOL WOOD, 1842 OS. SANDY LANE.

FIELD-NAMES

The undated forms are 1842 *TA* 360 (Somerford) & 334 (Radnor). Of the
others, 1831 is Bry, 1842 OS, the rest *Dav.*

(a) Alder Bank; Bakehouse Fd; Bank Bottom & Fd (v. botm); Berry
Croft (v. berige); Brick Kiln Fd; Buckham Fd; Clatty Mdw (v. clǣte);
Clewley (*Clouelowe* l13, probably similar to Cleulow 1 165, v. hlāw);
Cockley Mdw (v. cocc², lēah); Corn Heys (v. corn¹); Two Day Math,
Demaith (v. day-math); Dole (*le Longedole* c.1300, 'the long allotment', v.
lang, dāl); Downs Loom (dial. *loom* 'a broad land or selion', cf. land); Flat;
Fox Holes (v. fox-hol); Hollins Greave (v. holegn, grǣfe); Holms Intack
(v. holmr, inntak); Hunger Hill (v. hungor); Kiln Stone (v. cyln, stān);
Landry Wharf (v. waroð); Maidins Wd (v. mægden); Marl Fd; Mill Eye
(v. ēg); The Moss; Out Loom (v. ūt, cf. Downs Loom *supra*); Paradise (v.
paradis); Pierre Point Mdw; Pool; Red Croft; Great Rough Clough (*le Cloch*
l13, 'the dell', v. clōh); Round Ridding (v. ryding); Scar 1842 (a bluff on
the south bank of R. Dane, probably the same as *Hengeclif*, -*clyf* 13, l13,
'the hanging cliff', v. hencg, clif, sker); Slade Gate ('valley gate', v. slæd,
geat); Soon Fd (v. sand); Stanley Mdw; Stop Moss; Tenter Fd (v. tentour);
Three Nooked-, -Nooks Fd (v. nōk); Walk-Mill Mdw (v. walke-milne);
Watwing Fd (perhaps analogous with Wetwang YE 128, from vǽtt-vangr 'a
field for the trial of a legal action', but more probably 'wet meadow', v.
wēt, wang); West-Heath Plantation (cf. *West Heath Mill Farm* 1831, v. myln,
West Heath 299 *supra*); Whilstone Edge (cf. Whetstonedge 288 *supra*);
Wilney Mdw ('island growing with willows', v. wiligen, ēg); Wilsey Mdw
(v. ēg).

(b) *Anacher* 13 (perhaps 'lonely ploughland', v. āna, æcer); *Briddiscroft*
l13 ('the bird's croft', v. bridd, croft); *Choucishul* l13 (the final el. is hyll 'a
hill'); *Denesciche* l13 ('watercourse in a valley', v. denu, sīc); *Egmundisey*
c.1262, *Egmundushey* l13 ('Egmund's island or enclosure', from the OE pers.
n. *Ecgmund* and ēg or (ge)hæg); *le Ewode* 13, *le Heuuode* c.1300 ('wood by a
stream or river', v. ēa, wudu); *Eycanecroft* 13 (perhaps from the OIr pers.n.
Echán, v. croft); *le Flaxcroft* 13 (v. fleax, croft); *Harewodehacrus* c.1300
('(ploughlands at) hoar-wood', v. hār² (wk. dat.sg. hāran), wudu, æcer);
Hegwallehull 1307 (perhaps 'woodpecker hill', from hyll and an early form
of *hickwall* 'the green woodpecker' (NED), but the second el. may be wælla
'a well, a spring'); *Holedich* c.1270 (p) ('ditch in a hollow', v. hol², dīc); *le
hore heystowe* l13 ('the ancient hedged place', from hege and stōw, with hār²,
cf. hege-stall); *leyhey*, *Lyhey(bothum)* l13 (a place beside R. Dane '(bottom
land at) fallow enclosure', v. lǣge, (ge)hæg, boðm); *le Lydyate* l13 ('the

swing-gate', *v.* hlid-geat); *Lyulfesbruche* 113 ('Liulf's intake', from the pers.n. discussed by Feilitzen s.n. *Ligulf* and bryce. The derivation of the ME form *Liulf* from the ODan pers.n. *Lithulf* or an ON *Liðolfr* (Feilitzen 320) is borne out by the various forms in Ch records of the Christian name *Liulph* (*Lidulphus*, etc.) borne by successive members of the house of Twemlow 230 *supra* in the twelfth and thirteenth centuries); *le Longelache* 113 ('the long bog', *v.* lang, læc(c)); *Teuerkishul* 113 (*v.* hyll. The first el. looks like an unidentified pers.n.); *le Tounmeduwe* 113 ('the common meadow', *v.* toun, mǣd); *le Waterfal* 113 (falling into R. Dane, *v.* wæter-gefall); *Westbroc* 113 (*v.* west, brōc); *Westeg* 113 (*v.* west, ēg); *Wistanishey* 113 ('Wīgstān's enclosure', from the OE pers.n. *Wīgstān* and (ge)hæg); *Woluedish* 13 ('wolf enclosure', *v.* wulf, edisc).

xiii. Church Lawton

The parish of Church Lawton comprises the one township. It was originally part of Astbury parish, and is not separately listed in 1291 Tax, *v.* Orm² III 21.

1. CHURCH LAWTON (110–8255)

    Lautune 1086 DB, *-tun* 13 *Dav* (p), 1313 *BW* (p), *-tona* 1119 (1150)
        Chest *et freq* ib to 1310 (with erroneous variant *Lantrona*), *-ton*
        e13 Dieul *et freq* to 1527 ChCert, (*-subtus Lymam*) 1258 Chest,
        (*-iuxta Lym'*) 1305 Plea, (*-iuxta Bechynton*) 1308 Pat, *Chirche-*
        1333 Plea *et freq* to 1490 ChRR, *Kirke-* 1356 Indict, *Kerke-* 1402
        BW, *Churche-* 1489 ChRR, *Chirch-* 1490 ib
    Laughton 1288 Court (p), 1434, 1437 Pat, 1454 ChRR, c.1540 Dugd,
        Church- 1331 ChRR, *Lagthton* 1289 Court (p), *Laugton* 1471
        MinAcct, *Churchelaugton* c.1540 Dugd
    Laweton 1295 Ch, CRC, 1466 ChRR, *Lawton* 1311 ib (p) *et freq*,
        Churche- 1509 AddCh, *Church-* 1684 Sheaf, (*Lawton alias-*) 1724
        NotCestr, *Lauuton* 1468 *MinAcct*
    Lautton 1304 Chamb (p)
    Lenton juxta Berthinton 1308 InqAqd
    Launton 1336 Chamb (? for *Lauu-*)

    'Farm by a mound', *v.* hlāw, tūn. The affix *Church-* (*v.* cirice, cf. *ecclesia de Lauton* 1297 CRV, 1365 *Chol*) and the relation to Betchton 325 *infra*, The Lyme 1 2, distinguish this from Buglawton 290 *supra*.

LAWTON-GATE (110–809560)

    passagium de Lauton, *-Lawton* 1302 Chamb, 1311 ChRR *et freq* to
    1365 ib

le Lyde3ate, -lideyate 1353, 1356 *Indict* (p), *Lawton Lydeyate* 1389
ChRR, (*passagium de*) *Lawton-Lyde3ate* 1406 ib *et freq* with
variant spellings as for Lawton *supra*, and *Lyd-, Lid(e)yate,*
-gate, -iate, -3ate, Ledeyate
Lawton-Gate 1621 Orm[2]

'The toll-gate, the swing-gate, at Lawton', *v.* hlid-geat, cf. MedLat
passagium 'a passage, passage-money'. This place was the entry to
Ch on the routes from Newcastle St to Warrington La, 1 43, 44.

SNAPE COTTAGE (lost), 1831 Bry, 1842 OS, SNAPE'S BRIDGE, *la-*,
le Snape 1265–72, 1269–91 Chest, *Snape* 1708 *BW*, 'the bog', *v.*
snæp.

STONE CLIFF WOOD, 1842 OS, *Stancliues cloht* 1265–72 Chest,
Stancliff(isclouh) 1265–76 ib, *le Stanclif* 1265–91 ib, '(dell at) the
stone cliff', *v.* stān, clif, clōh.

AIDENSWOOD.   BRIDGE FM.   BULL COVERT, 1839 *TA*, cf. Red
Bull *infra*.   BUTT LANE (FM), *Butt Lane* 1752 Sheaf, cf. Butt Lane
in Audley St, *v.* butte.   FLEE CROWS, 1839 *TA*, *v.* crew.   GREEN-
BANK, 1831 Bry.   GREEN FM, 1831 ib, *v.* grēne[2].   GRINDLE-
STONE, *v.* grind(el)-stān.   THE GROVE, 1831 ib.   HALL O' LEE,
the Hall of Lee 1581 ChRR, *Lee Hall alias-* 1721 *BW*, 'hall in a
clearing', *v.* hall, lēah.   HARDINGS WOOD, *Hardingewood* 1839 *TA*,
probably named after John, Philip, Richard and William *Harding*
1265–91 Chest 791, 793, 802, *v.* wudu.   HIGHER PARK, 1839 *TA*.
KNOWSLEY LANE, *Knowles Hollows* 1831 Bry, cf. *Knowsley Meadow*
1839 *TA*, 'knolls clearing', 'hollows near the knolls', *v.* cnoll, lēah,
hol[1].   LAWTON HALL, 1724 NotCestr, cf. *Hall Green* 1675 *AddCh*,
-& Hays 1839 *TA*, *v.* hall, grēne[2].   LAWTON HEATH, 1831 Bry,
bruera in Lauton 1265–91 Chest, *v.* hǣð.   LAWTON MERE, *-Meer*
1849 *TA*, *v.* mere[1].   LINLEY LANE & WOOD, 1831 Bry, probably
'linden wood', *v.* lind, lēah.   MERE COTTAGE, 1831 ib, *v.* mere[1].
MILL LANE, 1839 *TA*.   MOSS HO, *Moss Farm* 1831 Bry, *Moss*
House 1839 *TA*, cf. *Lawton Moss* 1720 *BW*, *v.* mos.   MOSS WOOD,
Gorsty Knowles 1831 Bry, *-Knowl(es)* 1839 *TA*, *v.* gorstig, cnoll.
RALPH'S WOOD, 1839 *ib*.   RED BULL (BANK & BRIDGE), *Red Bull*
(*Inn*) 1831 Bry, 1842 OS, an inn-sign name, cf. *Red Bull Wood* 1842
OS, *Bull Lane* 1839 *TA*, and Bull Covert *supra*.   RYE LOW, 1839
ib, probably 'hill where rye grows', *v.* ryge, hlāw.   SLUM WOOD,

1839 *ib*, *v.* **wudu**. The first el. is probably ModEdial. **slump** 'a boggy place', cf. Slump Fd 327 *infra*. The form *Slum* appears in (The) Slum 327 *infra*, 264, 273 *supra*, Slum Mdw 318 *supra*. Cf. Slam (Bank) 327 *infra*. WHARTONS POOL, *Waltons Pool* 1839 *TA*, *v.* pōl[1]. The first el. is probably a surname. WOODLANDS, *Floodgates* 1831 Bry, *The-* 1882 Orm[2], *v.* flōd-yate.

FIELD-NAMES

The undated forms are 1839 *TA* 115. Of the others, 1265–89, 1271, 1275, c.1280, 1708 are *BW*, 1440 *Rental*, 1831 Bry, 1842 OS, and the rest Chest.

(*a*) Alsager Mdw (*v.* Alsager 325 *infra*); The Bank; Barrowdish (*v.* 307 *supra*); Boat Fd (*v.* bōt); Bran; Chamber Banks; Church Fd (cf. *le Chircheruding* 1265–91, *v.* cirice, ryding); Crappilous Mdw (cf. Crappilow, Craplow Mdw 326, 326 *infra*. The final el. common to these is hlāw 'a mound, a hill'. The first el. is crappe as in Crap Moss 326 *infra*); Delph Mdw (*v.* (ge)delf); Dingle (*v.* dingle); The Ditches (*le Diches* 1265–91, *le Dyches* 1271, 'the ditches', *v.* dīc); Drumble Willow Bed (dial. *drumble* 'a wooded ravine', cf. dumbel); Gorsty Hay, Gorsty Knowl(es) (*v.* gorstig, (ge)hæg, cnoll); Griggy Bank (from either ModEdial. grig[1] 'a cricket', or grig[2] 'heath, heather'); Hob Ridding (*v.* hobbe, ryding); The Hollows (*v.* holh); Long Hurst (cf. *le Hurst* 1265–76, *v.* lang, hyrst); Intake (*v.* inntak); Long Ley (*v.* lang, lēah); Marl (Pit) Fd (cf. *marlera prope le Twisse cloch* 1265–91, *v.* marle, marle-pytt); New Looms (from nīwe and dial. *loom* 'a broad selion, cf. land); Odd Rode Wd (cf. Old Rode 306 *supra*); Pavement Fd & Plantation (*Lawton Pavement* 1831 Bry, 1842 OS, at 110–810560 to 820555, *v.* pavement); Pit Fd (cf. *le Puttes* 1265–76, *v.* pytt); Roundabout (*v.* 327 *infra*); Shoulder of Mutton (*v.* 327 *infra*); Slope (*v.* slope); Smethwick (*v.* smiŏ, wic, cf. Smethwick 275 *supra*); Spans (*Spanne House or Ground* 1708, cf. *le Sponne* 1265–76, 1265–91, *v.* spann[1]); Talk Hurst (*Talkhurstesford* 1265–72, 'ford at the wooded hill at Talke', named from Talke St, *v.* hyrst, ford); Toll Gate Plantation (named from a turnpike, *v.* toll-gate); Town Fd (*v.* toun); Well Stich (*v.* wella, stycce); Wheatley (cf. *Quethul* 1265–91, 'wheat hill', *v.* hwǣte, hyll, lēah); Whey Fd (*v.* hwǣg); Wood Fd (cf. *boscus de Lautona* 13).

(*b*) *Aschinehalgh* 1249–65, *Aschene-* 1269–91, *Assenehalh* 1265–72 ('nook growing with ash-trees', *v.* æscen, halh); *Badilford* 1265–72 (*v.* ford 'a ford'); *Beterbacheforde* 1265–76 (*v.* bæce[1] 'a stream, a valley', ford. The first el. may be miscopied *boter* from butere 'butter', cf. Butter Bache 325 *infra*); *Bircheleg'* 1265–91, *Birchinlegh* 1289 ('birch wood', *v.* birce, bircen[2], lēah); *le Brereleg' forde* 1265–91 ('(ford at) the briary clearing', *v.* brēr, lēah, ford); *le Brock* 1265–72 (*v.* brōc); *le Brodeleg'* 1265–91, *Prode-* 1269–91 (*v.* brād, lēah); *Brodelond* 1265–91 (*v.* brād, land); *Bromegge* 1440 (*v.* brōm, ecg); *Buthineleg'* 1265–91 (*v.* lēah); *le Cokshute lond* 1265–91 ('the cock-shoot selion', *v.* cocc-scyte, land); *le Coulone* 1265–91 (*v.* cū, lane); *Euerardis ruding*, -*yng* 13, 1265–91, c.1311 (from the ME pers.n. *Everard* (OGer

Eburhard) and **ryding**); (*le*) *Ferfeld* 13, 1265–76, 1265–91 ('the far field', *v.*
feor, feld); *Feyre Pleckes* 1265–72 ('the fair plots', *v.* fæger, plek); (*le*)
Greuelond(*es*) 1265–91 ('selions near a wood', *v.* grǣfe, land); *le Halh* 1265–
76, *le Halg*' 1265–91 (*v.* halh 'a nook, a corner'); *Hawardisruding* 13 ('Haward's clearing', from the ME pers.n. *Haward* (ON *Hávarðr*, ODan *Hawarth*)
and **ryding**); *le Heye* 1265–72 ('the enclosure', *v.* (ge)hæg); *Lawtonroue*
1265–91 (*v.* rāw 'a row (of trees, houses)'); *Leysich'hurst* 1265–76 ('(wood at)
the watercourse at fallow land', *v.* lǣge, sīc, hyrst); *Line Halfland* 1265–91
(perhaps 'half selion where flax is grown', from līn, half-land); *Litlelond*
1265–76 (*v.* lȳtel, land); *Liueresleg'euese* 1265–76, -*leghnese* 1265–91 ('(the
edge of) Lēofhere's wood or clearing', from the OE pers.n. *Lēofhere*, *v.*
lēah, efes); (*le*) *Long*(*e*)*ford*(*e*) 1265–76, 1275 (*v.* lang, ford); *le Lun* 1265–91,
Lund 1265–76 (p), *le Lundlidgate* 1265–76, *Luntlidgate* 1265–91, *le Lunte-
ruding* 13 ('(swing-gate and clearing at) the grove', *v.* lundr, hlid-geat,
ryding); *le Lym puttes* 1265–72 ('the lime pits', *v.* lim, pytt); *le Merewey*
1265–91 ('the way to a pool', *v.* mere[1], weg); *le Midilforlong* 1265–91 (*v.*
middel, furlang); *Mora* 1265–72 (*v.* mōr[1]); *Morwaldis Medue* 13 (from the
OE pers.n. *Mōrwald* and mǣd 'a meadow'); *le Newland* 1440 (*v.* nīwe, land);
Radilforde 1265–72, *Radilegforde* 1265–91 ('(ford at) the red clearing', *v.*
rēad, lēah, ford); *le Ruth* 1265–76, 1265–91, *le Rothe* 1265–89, 1265–91
(lit. *Roye*), ('the clearing', *v.* ruð, roð); *Salteres-*, *Salterisbach-* (*hurst &*
-*walle*) 1265–91 ('(wood and spring at) the salter's valley', *v.* saltere,
bæce[1], with hyrst, and wælla); *Siwardeleg*' 1265–91 ('Siward's clearing',
from the pers.n. OE *Sigeweard* or ODan *Sigwarth* and lēah); *Smaleleg*'
1265–72 ('narrow clearing', *v.* smæl, lēah); (*le*) *Stanwey*(*e*)*rud*(*ing*) 13,
1265–91 ('(clearing at) the stone road', *v.* stān, weg, ryding); *Stappe
grene* 1265–91 ('step green', *v.* stæpe, grēne[2]); *Sullunhull* 1265–76, *Sulyn*-
1265–91, *le Solmehullus* c.1280 (*v.* hyll. Professor Löfvenberg reads *Soline-*
for *Solme-* here and in *Solmegrenes* 215 *supra*, and proposes as first el. an OE
*sylen, *solen (from sol, -en[2]) 'muddy, dirty', as in *Sulinfeld* 186 *supra*.
Sullunhull is 'muddy hill', cf. Solihull Wa 67); *le Suthleg*' 1265–91 ('the
south clearing', *v.* suð, lēah); (bruera vocata) *Tr*(*h*)*e-*, *Threlowenhet*, -*lawen-*
13, 1265–91, 1311 ('(heath at) the three mounds', *v.* þrēo, hlāw (dat.pl.
hlāwum), hǣð); *le Tvertouercloh* 1265–72 ('the dell which runs across', *v.*
thwert-over (cf. þverr, ofer[3]), clōh); *le Twisse cloch* 1265–91 ('forked valley'
or 'dell with a forked stream', *v.* (ge)twis, clōh); *Werstanl*(*eg'sponne*) 1265–
76, *Werstanleg*', -*ley*, *Parua Werstanl*', *Werstonesleg'spone* 1265–91, *Westan-
leye*, -*leygersponne* c.1280, -*legh* 1440 ('Wǣrstān's clearing', from the OE
pers.n. *Wǣrstān* and lēah, with spann[1] 'a hand's breadth, a span, a strip of
land').

INDEX OF CROSS-REFERENCES

References in Part II of *The Place-Names of Cheshire*, to names and topics contained in subsequent Parts. Township- and parish-names are cited simply; other names are followed by the name of the township or parish in which they lie. The bold figure indicates the Part in which the name or subject will appear.

Acton nr. Nantwich, 42: **3**
Acton nr. Weaverham, 42, 115: **3**
Acton Bridge (Acton nr. Weaverham), 116: **3**
Agden nr. Malpas, 42, 146: **4**
Alsager, 184, 277, 322: **3**
Alvanley, 50: **3**
Amsterdam Covert, *v.* Analysis *infra*
Analysis of field-names, etc.,: **5**
  Amsterdam Covert, 87
  Bastard Fd, 22
  Bitter Nails, 55
  Buttermilk Fd, 88
  Cape of Good Hope, 91
  Crash 'em Down, 14
  Cutting Knife, 317
  Dear Bought, 70, 153, 293
  Drinkwaterfeild, 133
  France, 293
  Geneses Mdw, 72
  Genesis Wd, 93
  Half Crown Fd, 283
  Handkerchief, 22, 33
  Isle of Man, 175, 239
  Land of Goshen, 312
  Leg of Mutton, 130
  Little Grace, 312
  Make Good Hay, 49
  Matress Fd, 293
  Poverty, 19, 234
  Purgatory, 100
  Roundabout, 41, 63, 71, 240, 259, 260, 268, 273, 294, 318, 322
  Saddle Back Fd, 294
  Shoulder of Mutton, 41, 94, 106, 250, 260, 261, 273, 311, 322
  Too Lail, 294
  Turn Penny Fd, 294
  Two Penneworth, 256
  Virjuice, 26
Austerson, 127: **3**

Banners Style (Overpool), 246: **4**

Barnston, 226: **4**
Barrow's Green (Leighton nr. Nantwich), 250: **3**
le Barude (Henhull), 307: **3**
Bastard Fd, *v.* Analysis *supra*
Batherton, 107: **3**
Bebington, Lower, 198: **4**
Betchton, 184, 264, 269, 320: **3**
Birkenhead, 58: **4**
Bitter Nails, *v.* Analysis *supra*
Blakeden (Over), 222: **3**
Bradford (Whitegate), 210: **3**
Brassey Bank (Woolstanwood), 206: **3**
Brassey Green (Tiverton), 206: **3**
Brassey Hall (Willaston nr. Wybunbury), 206: **3**
Broxton, 114: **4**
Budworth, Lt., 60, 108: **3**
Butter Bache (Huntington), 322: **4**
Buttermilk Fd, *v.* Analysis *supra*

Caldy Hundred, 2: **4**
Cape of Good Hope, *v.* Analysis *supra*
Carden nr. Tilston, 131: **4**
Caryngfeld (Newton by Chester), 18: **4**
Castle Northwich, 193, 194: **3**
Catten Hall (Kingsley), 163, 194: **3**
Chester, 6, 241: **5**
Cholmondeley, 247: **4**
Chorlton nr. Wybunbury, 133: **3**
C(h)rimes (Acton nr. Weaverham), 171: **3**
  (Beeston), 171: **3**
  (Bickley), 171: **4**
  (Foulk Stapleford), 171: **4**
Christleton, 20: **4**
Church Minshull, 184, 247, 250, 261: **3**
Church Minshull Bridge (Church Minshull), 249: **3**
Churchyard Side (Nantwich), 242: **3**
Clatterdishes (Hurleston), 115: **3**
Claughton, 95: **4**
Claverton, 194: **4**

Clayhanger (Haslington), 52: **3**
Clemhunger (Over), 52: **3**
Clemley (Wistaston), 49, 52, 78, 249: **3**
Codingeheye (Coddington), 8: **4**
Cookspit (Faddiley), 289: **3**
Coppenhall, 259: **3**
Cotton nr. Christleton, 280: **4**
Craplow Mdw (Betchton), 322: **3**
Crap Moss (Oakmere), 322: **3**
Crappilow (Alsager), 322: **3**
Crash'em Down, *v.* Analysis *supra*
Crewood (Crowton nr. Weaverham), 161, 163: **3**
The Crime (Church Coppenhall), 171: **3**
Crime Fd (Hankelow), 171: **3**
Crimes Brook (Beeston), 171: **3**
Crimmer Lane (Woolstanwood), 171: **3**
Croft Mellon (Caldy), 12, 19: **4**
Crowton nr. Weaverham, 194: **3**
le Cruymbes (Clutton nr. Farndon), 171: **4**
Cutting Knife, *v.* Analysis *supra*

Dear Bought, *v.* Analysis *supra*
Dodcott, 264: **3**
Donkinson's Oak (Church Coppenhall), 262: **3**
Drinkwaterfeild, *v.* Analysis *supra*
Dunham on the Hill, 20, 293: **3**
Dunkirk (Lea by Backford), 196, 276: **4**
Duttons (Church Minshull), 112: **3**

Eaton nr. Tarporley, 205: **3**
Eddisbury Hundred, 184: **3**
Elton nr. Thornton le Moors, 258: **3**
Eton, 205: **4**

Finney (Kingsley), 70, 245, 317: **3**
Flash, Bottom & Top, (Over), 235: **3**
(Weaver), 235: **3**
Foxtwist (Over), 14: **3**
France, *v.* Analysis *supra*
Frodsham, 180, 182, 221: **3**
Fulwich (Wychough), 192: **4**

Gayton, 95: **4**
Geneses Mdw, *v.* Analysis *supra*
Genesis Wd, *v.* Analysis *supra*
George St. (Chester), 296: **5**
Grene Mening Wei (Bulkeley), 250: **4**

Half Crown Fd, *v.* Analysis *supra*
Handkerchief, *v.* Analysis *supra*
Handley, 173: **4**
Hartford, 206: **3**
Haslington, 274: **3**
Hassall, 184, 264, 270: **3**
Heronbridge (St Mary, Chester), 171, (s.n. Stubborn Oryon) 240, 278: **5**
Horton (Hartford), 207: **3**
(Horton cum Peel), 200: **3**
Hough nr. Wybunbury, 52: **3**

Iddinshall, 8: **3**
Island Fm (Acton nr. Weaverham), 113: **3**
Isle of Man, *v.* Analysis *supra*

Kelsall, 23, 261: **3**
Kingsley, 163: **3**

Land of Goshen, *v.* Analysis *supra*
Larton, 95: **4**
Leg of Mutton, *v.* Analysis *supra*
Leighton Moss (Leighton nr. Nantwich) 249: **3**
Little Grace, *v.* Analysis *supra*

Make Good Hay, *v.* Analysis *supra*
Marbury (Marbury cum Quoisley), 117: **3**
Marton nr. Whitgate, 187: **3**
Matress Fd, *v.* Analysis *supra*
Mayowse (Leighton nr. Nantwich), 250: **3**
Mediolanum (Stretton nr. Malpas), 196, 238: **4**
Melestrete (Nantwich), 296: **3**
Moslin (Betchton), 313: **3**
Mossocks Moor (Ashton nr. Tarvin), 278: **3**

Nantwich, 187, 192, 238, 241: **3**
Nantwich Hundred, 2, 184, 262: **3**
Newbridge (Over), 207: **3**
New Pale (Delamere), 28: **3**

Old Pale (Delamere), 28: **3**
Oulton (Lt. Budworth), 31, 191: **3**
Over, 214: **3**

Peck Mill (Alvanley), 84: **3**

Peel (Horton cum Peel), 218, 288, 305: **3**
Pepper St. (Chester), 7, 37, 68–9, 84, 99, 120, 150, 242, 272, 294: **5**
Pickering's Cut (Crowton), 114: **3**
Poverty, *v*. Analysis *supra*
Purgatory, *v*. Analysis *supra*

Raby, 135: **4**
Radway Green (Barthomley), 250: **3**
Rapdowl(e)s (Frodsham), 314: **3**
Rope, 314: **3**
Roundabout, *v*. Analysis *supra*

Saddle Back, *v*. Analysis *supra*
Shaghteles (Barrow), 41: **3**
Shavington (Shavington cum Gresty), 192: **3**
Shoulder of Mutton, *v*. Analysis *supra*
Siddenhall (Tattenhall), 229: **4**
Sinepool (Frodsham), 181: **3**
Slam (Bank) (Blakenhall), 322: **3**
(The) Slum (Alsager), 322: **3**
   (Barthomley), 322: **3**
   (Betchton), 322: **3**
   (Crewe), 322: **3**
Slump Fd (Weaverham), 322: **3**
Solengak (Norbury nr. Marbury), 316: **3**
Stanlow, 160: **3**
Stapleford, 144: **4**
Storeton, 95: **4**
Stromby (Thurstaston), 5: **4**

Stubborn Oryon, 240, *v*. Heronbridge *supra*
Sutton, Great, 217: **4**
Sutton, Little, 217: **4**
Swanwick (Norbury nr. Marbury), 228, 256: **3**
Sydney (Monks Coppenhall), 229, 273: **3**

Tarporley, 123: **3**
le Tolstok (Nantwich), 246: **3**
Too Lail, *v*. Analysis *supra*
Turn Penny, *v*. Analysis *supra*
Tushingham, 8: **4**
Two Penneworth, *v*. Analysis *supra*
Tyrant (Betchton), 278: **3**

Vale Royal (Whitegate), 205: **3**
Virjuice, *v*. Analysis *supra*

Wallerscote, 106, 185: **3**
Wardle, 245: **3**
Waverton, 213: **4**
Weaver, 184, 232, 247: **3**
Weaverham, 317: **3**
Welsh Lane (Over), 235: **3**
Wettenhall, 103, 284: **3**
Winnington, 92, 106, 207: **3**
Winsford (Over), 202, 214 (2x), 232: **3**
Witton chapelry (Eddisbury Hundred), 95, 184: **3**

Yeanley (Rushton), 173: **3**

INDEX OF PARISHES AND TOWNSHIPS
IN PART II

Acton Grange, 146
Agden (Bucklow Hundred), 42
Alcumlow, *v.* Moreton cum Alcumlow
Allostock, 216
Altrincham, 7
Anderton, 95
Antrobus, 127
Appleton, formerly Hull Appleton, 96
Arclid, 264
Ashley, 10
Ashton on Mersey, 3
Ashton on Mersey par., 3, 5
Astbury, *v.* Newbold Astbury
Astbury par., 285
Aston by Budworth, 101
Aston by Sutton, 160
Aston Grange, 159

Baguley, 12
Barnshaw, *v.* Goostrey cum Barnshaw
Barnton, 105
Bartington, 106
Bexton, 72
Birches, 185
Blackden, 222
Bollington (Bucklow Hundred), 43
Bostock, 202
Bowdon, 15
Bowdon par., 3, 7, 42
Bradford, *v.* Shurlach cum Bradford
Bradwall, 265
Brereton par., 274
Brereton cum Smethwick, 274
Bucklow Hundred, 1
Budworth, Great, 107
Buglawton, 290
Byley cum Yatehouse, 232

Carrington, 17
Church Hulme Chapelry, 278
Church Lawton par., 320
Clifton, 164
Clive, 234
Cogshall, 109
Comberbach, 111
Congleton, 294
Cotton nr. Cranage, 280

Cranage, 223
Crowley, 131
Croxton, 236

Daresbury, 148
Daresbury Chapelry, 137, 146
Davenham, 203
Davenham par., 202
Davenport, 301
Dunham Massey, 19
Dutton, 112

Eaton, nr. Davenham, 204
Elton nr. Warmingham, 258

Goostrey Chapelry, 222
Goostrey cum Barnshaw, 226
Grappenhall, 140
Grappenhall par., 140
Great Budworth par., 95

Hale, 23
Halton, 166
Halton Hundred, 2
Hatton, 149
High Legh, 45
Holmes Chapel, or Church Hulme, 278
Hull, v. Appleton
Hulme, *v.* Kinderton cum Hulme
Hulme, Church, or Holmes Chapel, 278
Hulme Walfield, 302
Hulse, 185

Keckwick, 151
Kermincham, 281
Kinderton cum Hulme, 236
Knutsford, Nether, 73
Knutsford, Over, 76
Knutsford par., 72

Lach Dennis, 186
Latchford, 143
Lawton, Church, 320
Leese, 229
Leftwich, 205
Little Leigh, 115
Lostock Gralam, 189

Lymm, 36
Lymm par., 36

Marbury (Bucklow Hundred), 117
Marston, 118, 119
Marthall cum Warford, 82
Mere, 51
Middlewich, 240
Middlewich par., 232
Millington, 54
Minshull Vernon, 247
Mobberley, 65
Mobberley par., 65
Moore, 153
Mooresbarrow cum Parme, 251
Moreton cum Alcumlow, 304
Moston, 259
Moulton, 207

Nether Peover Chapelry, 90, 216
Newall, 208
Newbold Astbury, 285
Newton by Daresbury, 154
Northwich, 192
Northwich Hundred, 184
Norton, 173

Occlestone, 252
Odd Rode, 306
Ollerton, 79
Over Peover Chapelry, 82

Parme, v. Mooresbarrow cum Parme
Partington, 27
Peover Inferior, 90
Peover, Nether, 220
Peover Superior, 85
Pickmere, 120
Plumley, 90
Preston on the Hill, or Preston Brook, 156

Radnor, v. Somerford (cum) Radnor
Ravenscroft, 253
Ringway, 28
Rostherne, 56
Rostherne par., 42, 45
Rudheath Lordship, 198
Runcorn, 176
Runcorn par., 145, 159

Sale, 5
Sandbach, 269
Sandbach par., 264

Seven Oaks, 133
Shipbrook, 208
Shurlach cum Bradford, 210
Smallwood, 316
Smethwick, v. Brereton cum Smethwick
Somerford (cum) Radnor, 318
Sproston, 254
Stanthorne, 211
Stockham, 179
Stockton Heath, 145
Stretton (Bucklow Hundred), 121
Stublach, 255
Sutton nr. Middlewich, 256
Sutton Weaver, or Sutton iuxta Frodsham, 180
Swettenham, 283
Swettenham par., 281

Tabley Inferior, 122
Tabley Superior, 60
Tatton, 64
Tetton, 260
Thelwall, 138
Timperley, 31
Toft, 81
Tunendun(e) Hundred, 1
Twambrook, v. Witton cum Twambrook
Twemlow, 230

Walfield, v. Hulme Walfield
Walton Inferior, 157
Walton Superior, 158
Warburton, 34
Warburton par., 34
Warford, Little, v. Marthall cum Warford
Warmingham, 262
Warmingham par., 258
Weston, nr. Runcorn, 182
Wharton, 213
Whatcroft, 215
Wheelock, 273
Whitley, Higher, 124
Whitley, Lower, 134
Whitley Lordship, 124
Wimboldsley, 257
Wincham, 136
Witton Chapelry, 184
Witton cum Twambrook, 194

Yatehouse, v. Byley cum Yatehouse